SUBJECT TO OTHERS

SUBJECT TO OTHERS

*British Women Writers and
Colonial Slavery, 1670–1834*

MOIRA FERGUSON

ROUTLEDGE   NEW YORK   LONDON

Published in 1992 by

Routledge
An imprint of Routledge, Chapman and Hall, Inc.
29 West 35th Street
New York, NY 10001

Published in Great Britain by

Routledge
11 New Fetter Lane
London EC4P 4EE

Copyright © 1992 by Routledge, Chapman and Hall, Inc.

Printed in the United States of America on acid free paper.

Library of Congress Cataloging in Publication Data

Ferguson, Moira.
    Subject to others : British women writers and colonial slavery,
    1670–1834 / Moira Ferguson.
        p.   cm.
    Includes bibliographical references and index.
    ISBN 0-415-90475-7.   ISBN 0-415-90476-5 (pbk.)
    1. English literature—Women authors—History and criticism.
2. Slavery—Great Britain—Colonies—Anti-slavery movements.
3. Feminism and literature—Great Britain—History. 4. Women and
literature—Great Britain—History. 5. Slavery and slaves in
literature. 6. Colonies in literature. 7. Blacks in literature.
I. Title.
PR408.S57F47   1992
820.9′9287—dc20   92-14984
                                                      CIP

British Library Cataloguing in Publication Data also available

For Kraz

Slaves speak "through and by virtue of the European imagination."
Edward W. Said , *Orientalism*

The Slave's Address

Natives of a Land of Glory,
　　Daughters of the good and brave!
Hear the injured Negro's story;—
　　Hear and help the kneeling Slave.

Think how nought but death can sever
　　Your lov'd children from your hold;—
Still alive—but lost for ever—
　　Ours are parted, bought, and sold!

Seize, oh! seize the favouring season—
　　Scorning censure or applause:
JUSTICE TRUTH, RELIGION, REASON,
　　Are your LEADERS in the cause!

Follow!—faithful, firm, confiding;—
　　Spread our wrongs from shore to
shore;
Mercy's God your efforts guiding,
　　Slavery shall be known no more.

Susanna Watts

Contents

Acknowledgments

Research into the origins of feminist ideas in English would be incomplete without the responses of British women writers to slavery. The 1788 poem, "On the Inhumanity of the Slave Trade," by the British milkwoman-poet Ann Yearsley is a case in point. I began this study with a one-month fellowship at the Huntington Library, groping slowly through the complex debate among past and present historians over the movements for abolition and emancipation. I thank the Huntington Library staff for their friendliness and expertise in facilitating my journey.

I would also like to thank the staff of the British Library where staff members were consistently helpful. I thank Peter Hogg and David Paisey of the British Library for several valuable conversations. I am also much indebted to the following libraries, and to the curators and librarians who generously answered my queries and opened up their collections to me: the Friends Library, Euston Road, London, most especially curator Malcolm Thomas, who made insightful suggestions and supplied me with invaluable reproductions of materials; Jill Shefrin, Librarian, the Osborne Collection of Early Children's Books, Toronto Public Library who pointed me in new directions and supplied useful information; Albert W. Fowler of the Friends Historical Library, Swarthmore College, Pennsylvania; the curators of the Friends National Library, Eustace Street, Dublin, and Haverford College Library, Pennsylvania, who answered questions about Friend Mary Birkett; Melanie Wisner of the Houghton Library, Harvard University; Laetitia Yeandle of the Folger Shakespeare Library; Miss J. V. Dansie, Local Studies Librarian, Libraries, Essex County Council; Special Collections at the Bristol Public Library; the Hunterian Library, University of Glasgow; and the Rare Books Room, University of Edinburgh.

My research on the African-Caribbean writer, Mary Prince, was particularly aided by the late Helen Rowe, archivist of the Bermudian Archives, Hamilton, Bermuda, and assistant archivist Sandra Bouja. I also thank Bridget Harris, Archivist, and Desmond V. Nicholson, Director, Museum of Antigua and Barbuda, St. Johns, Antigua. I thank, too, Nancy Cardwell who helped me track down information about Mary Prince's early life and owners, and Natalie Porter who negotiated access to this information. I am also indebted to the following: June Tomlinson, senior library assistant at the Institute of Advanced Legal Studies, London, who painstakingly ferreted out references to the court cases in which Mary Prince was involved; Dulcie Mapondera who led me to this avenue of pursuit; Anne Enscott, senior librarian, Mitchell Library, North Road, Glasgow, who capably assisted me; Miss G. A. Matheson, Keeper of the Manuscripts and the staff of the John Rylands University Library of Manchester; and Angela Whitelegge, senior assistant librarian, Goldsmiths' Library, University of London, Senate House.

I have several friends and colleagues to thank warmly for many forms of assistance that included answering queries and providing information and insights: Sergio Aiolfi, Carol Barash, Stephen Behrendt, Maureen Bell, Robert Bergstrom, Thomas Bestul, Jacqueline Bratton, Philippa Brewster, Louis Crompton, Leonore Davidoff, Deborah Dickinson, David V. Erdman, Henry Louis Gates, Jr., Barbara Hanrahan, Ned Hedges, Maureen Honey, Cora Kaplan, Greg Kuzma, Lemuel Johnson, Candida Lacey, Donna Landry, Edith Larsen, Jennifer Lehmann, Gerda Lerner, Frederick Link, Joanna Lipking, Gerald Maclean, Jay McPherson, Elizabeth Meese, Claire Midgeley, Charles Mignon, Mitzi Myers, Richard Ohmann, Marshall Olds, Ruth Perry, Ellen Pollack, Ann Schteir, Jan Sellers, Robert Stock, Amy Swerdlow, Vron Ware, and Judith Zinsser. I also thank members of the London History Workshop for an enthusiastic exchange in the summer of 1988 and Anna Davin for arranging that meeting. I owe an especial debt of thanks to Ziggi Alexander who offered valuable advice and information, Peter Fryer who furnished me with significant sources and graciously exchanged ideas, Isobel Grundy who supplied me with materials and good leads, Catherine Hall who generously shared her ideas, and Ron Ramdin for informative conversations.

Several friends and colleagues read early sections and drafts of chapters and provided me with helpful comments: Ziggi Alexander, Bettina Aptheker, Bruce Erlich, James Fultz, Oyekan Owomoyela, Linda Ray Pratt, and Martha Vicinus. For valuable readings of individual chapters in the final draft, I am grateful to Katherine Blake, Elaine

Hobby, Lee Lemon, Ross Mandel, Irma Nippert, Felicity Nussbaum, and Gayatri Chakravorty Spivak. For an incisive reading of the final draft, an ardent thank you to Catherine Hall and Gail Malmgreen. Thanks, too, for all their invaluable assistance to William Germano, my Routledge editor, and Michael J. Esposito.

I am appreciative of financial support from The American Council of Learned Societies and from fellowship programs at the University of Nebraska at Lincoln that enabled me to carry out my research.

To my home institution, the University of Nebraska at Lincoln, I owe a large debt. Without the unstinting assistance of Shirley Rockwell, Kitty McGinnis, and Brian Zillig in the Inter-Library Loan Office, Love Library, I could not have completed my research. For the thorough compilation of the bibliography, heartfelt thanks to Judy Levin, and to Wayne Hayden-Moreland for added assistance at the end. I thank Darlene Curtis and Andrew Robinson for typing and scanning the final drafts, Nicolle French, Roger Furrer, Stephen Hayes, Tammy Marshall, Patricia Mockler, and Thomas Rudder, for their fine help with the library work, and Kate Flaherty for her careful compilation of the index. Most particularly, I thank Stephen Kyle for being an excellent research assistant.

Also at my home institution I have incurred my largest debts to staff members in the English Department, LeAnn Messing and Roma Rector. In the early stages of the manuscript, LeAnn Messing typed several chapters with her customary skill and care. Roma Rector typed the final draft of the manuscript with unsurpassed expertise, grace, and good humor, going well beyond the call of duty. I thank her warmly.

Phase One

Chapter 1

Colonial Slavery and Protest:
Text and Context

PREAMBLE

In this volume I argue that anti-slavery protest in prose and poetry by Anglo-Saxon female authors contributed to the development of feminism over a two-hundred-year period. Concurrently, their texts misrepresented the very African-Caribbean slaves whose freedom they advocated. These writers, moreover, displaced anxieties about their own assumed powerlessness and inferiority onto their representations of slaves. The condition of white middle-class women's lives—their conscious or unconscious sense of themselves as inferior—set the terms of the anti-slavery debate. Let me briefly contextualize this argument.

Beginning hesitantly in the seventeenth century, women bold enough to write about slavery expressed opposition ambiguously, but still managed to inject their dissent with gender-specific concerns; they articulated a feminist version, as it were, of male frontal assaults on slavery. Then, up to the mid 1780s, protests zigzagged from senti-mental pleas for improved conditions in slaves' lives and condemnation of atrocities to moral contempt for the fracture of families induced by slavery and limited advocacy of rebellion.

After the Abolition Committee was formed in 1788, for at least a year, protests conformed to a rather sensationalized, Manichaean formula that typecast slaves and slaveowners alike. In the early and mid 1790s, bolstered by French revolutionary commitment to abolition based on arguments that assumed natural rights, radicals added overtly political arguments to those already urged. They claimed freedom as the entitlement of every individual. The political vantage

3

point of such writers helped to narrow the gap between the colonizers and colonized.

The revolutionary position, however, was short-lived. Once Britain declared war on France in 1793, championing slaves' rights became anathema—especially in the wake of the successful revolution by slaves and freed Africans in San Domingo. Although former slaves living in Britain wrote letters and memoirs that demanded emancipation while Caribbean slaves waged overt and covert rebellion, radically-inclined women writers reverted to a camouflaged language of sentiment, suicide, and patriotism that purported to attack slavery as long as docile slaves accepted European social and political control.

Once the slave trade was legally abolished in 1807, emancipationist writers did not resume agitation in earnest until the 1820s. Thousands of women from the provinces who had been mythologized as domestic angels and the nation's moral instructors took to the streets, writing and distributing political resolutions door-to-door, and using their economic power as consumers by refusing to buy slave-grown sugar, tea, and coffee.

As these author-agitators battled for emancipation, they wrote and spoke of Africans as a totalized, undifferentiated mass, denying the Continent and its people any authentic heterogeneity. Despite anti-slavery beliefs, they retained the view of slavers: they imagined slaves as essentially different from themselves. In fact, they drew on stereotypes of slaves and slavery, as well as Africans and Africa, that had become part of an orthodox perspective during one hundred and fifty years of anti-slavery protest. Slaves had become near-fixed embodiments of a Eurocentric sense of slave reality.

This homogeneous conceptualization of Africans as pious converts, moribund slaves, collaborators, and rebels was also bound up and overlapped with projections of patriarchally prescribed female roles and idealized self-images: these ranged from abused victim, orphan, and grieving mother, to altruist and loyal "servant." Women mediated their own needs and desires, their unconscious sense of social invalidation, through representations of the colonial other, who in the process became more severely objectified and marginalized—a silent or silenced individual in need of protection and pity who must always remain "under control." Thus at every point of female entry into this public debate, gender differences infused their protests. Authors frequently drew on alleged female attributes to evoke pity for male slaves and attached the same attributes to slavewomen. Toward the end of the campaign, for example, their resolutions demanded an end to the flogging of female slaves. Concurrently, they excoriated the separation of mothers and children and in doing so exemplified an unprecedented empathy with African-Caribbean slavewomen.

Moreover, the participation of thousands of provincial, middle-class, preponderantly religious women—evangelical and non-evangelical alike—in mainstream controversy was the origin of a self-directed female political vanguard. Anti-slavery agitation contributed directly to the upcoming struggle for white women's rights in Victorian England and the near-exclusion of black women from that debate.

This book, then, chronicles writings from 1670 to 1834 by Anglo-Saxon women and one African-Caribbean ex-slavewoman on abolition of the slave trade and the emancipation of slaves. Among the thirty white women on whose texts I focus are Aphra Behn and Alice Curwen from the seventeenth century; the Countess of Hertford, Charlotte Charke, Sarah Scott, Elizabeth Helme, Sophia Lee, and Lucy Peacock from the early eighteenth century to the 1780s; and Hannah More, Rachel Wilson, Elizabeth Bentley, Ann Yearsley, Mary Birkett, Mary Wollstonecraft, Helen Maria Williams, Maria Edgeworth and Anna Maria Falconbridge from 1788 to the post-revolutionary aftermath and the passage of the Abolition Bill in 1807. In the final chapters I focus on Elizabeth Heyrick and Harriet Martineau, activist authors in the emancipation campaign of the 1820s and 1830s, diverse evangelical writers, and Mary Prince, the only ex-slavewoman presently known to have written in Britain against slavery.

Stated succinctly, I am arguing that white British women and one Irish Friend, as a result of their class position, religious affiliation, and evolving conceptions of sexual difference, constructed a colonial discourse about Africans in general and slaves in particular. In historian Winthrop Jordan's words: "to be Christian was to be civilized rather than barbarous, English rather than African, white rather than black."[1] This discourse that I have called Anglo-Africanism came to be accepted by a majority of the white population as an authentic expression of slavery's "reality"; what these writers said about slaves came to be what was generally thought.[2]

But the limited and distorted view that was propounded by this Anglo-Africanist rhetoric always implied its opposite, the potential rebellion of slaves a shadowy textual presence at all times. These customarily unheard, often invisible resistances culminated in the highly varied responses to the triumphant San Domingan slave revolution in 1791. The definitive counter to the conventional abolitionist position was *The History of Mary Prince, a West Indian Slave, Related by Herself.* Mary Prince was a slave who walked away, then dictated her life experiences to an evangelical female poet at London's anti-slavery headquarters.[3] At one stroke, she proclaimed a vigorous sense of self, turned upside down the usual presentation of slavery by describing the black experience from the inside and the white experience from the outside, and exposed the process by which the black experience of slavery had been translated into a version acceptable to whites.

Lastly, I argue that the historical intersection of a feminist impulse with anti-slavery agitation helped secure white British women's political self-empowerment. Concurrently, that intersection fundamentally, though unintentionally, damaged future race relations. Eurocentric constructions of Africans and slaves that were integral to women's anti-slavery polemics meant that issues of race, gender, and class equality for freed African-Caribbean slaves did not seriously enter white British texts after emancipation. Thus, we cannot understand how by the 1850s the mythology of "lost" and "dark" Africa came to be so readily accepted as the reality of all African countries without understanding the evolution of this Anglo-Africanist way of talking and thinking. Anti-slavery colonial discourse, in other words, played a significant role in generating and consolidating nineteenth-century British imperialist and "domestic-racist" ideology.[4]

INTRODUCTION

In the texts of white British female abolitionists, the principal focus of this book, the voices of die-hard plantocrats as well as African slaves in pursuit of freedom frequently resound. Since the voices of slavers and slaves usually speak only indirectly through the voices of abolitionist author-narrators, I begin my argument with extracts from specific texts by a proslaveryite, an abolitionist, and an ex-slave. By so doing, I intend to intensify these silent dialogues throughout my study of anti-slavery texts. At the same time, I mean to undermine the facade of single-voiced utterances.

The first extract comes from the epistolary travel journal of Janet Schaw: *Journal of a Lady of Quality, Being the Narrative of a Journey from Scotland to the West Indies, North Carolina, and Portugal, in the Years 1774 to 1776*.

> The Negroes who are all in troops are sorted so as to match each other in size and strength. Every ten Negroes have a driver, who walks behind them, holding in his hand a short whip and a long

one. You will too easily guess the use of these weapons; a circumstance of all others the most horrid. They are naked, male and
female, down to the girdle, and you constantly observe where the
applications has been made. But however dreadful this must appear
to a humane European, I will do the creoles the justice to say, they
would be as averse to it as we are, could it be avoided, which has
often been tried to no purpose. When one comes to be better
acquainted with the nature of the Negroes, the horrour of it must
wear off. It is the suffering of the human mind that constitutes the
greatest misery of punishment, but with them it is merely corporeal.
As to the brutes it inflicts no wound on their mind, whose Natures
seem made to bear it, and whose sufferings are not attended with
shame or pain beyond the present moment. . . . Since I am on the
chapter of Negroes' feelings, I must tell you that I was some days
ago in town, when a number for market came from on board a ship.
They stood up to be looked at with perfect unconcern. The husband
was to be divided from the wife, the infant from the mother; but the
most perfect indifference ran thro' the whole. They were laughing
and jumping, making faces at each other, and not caring a single
farthing for their fate.[5]

Schaw starts from the premise that Africans—enslaved or not—are
subhuman. On this basis she can brush aside personal "gut-level"
repulsion at what she observes. The very sight of half-naked women,
let alone their bodies being insistently flogged, would cause a forty-
year-old Presbyterian Scotswoman, steeped in notions of female modesty and genteel proprieties, to recoil. But even though she openly
confesses that a "humane European" (like herself) might flinch automatically at cold-blooded cruelty, indoctrination by slave-owning
hosts has refashioned her understanding: "Negroes" are devoid of
feeling. She buttresses this new-found belief by tendering florid
"proof." Negroes frolic at human auctions as family members are
pawed over, then permanently separated. European agents who "arrange" slaves in evenly matched piles like floor tiles are invisible
except as they speak through her. As a "lady of quality" from an old
Scottish family, a Hanoverian, and a third cousin once removed of Sir
Walter Scott, Janet Schaw dares not break rank. She must uphold the
prejudices of her class and her hosts. Consequently, in the course of
this passage, she disperses her initial revulsion. By the end she closes
out her humanity, her conflictual gaze so contorted that she construes
misery and degradation as feckless merriment; having capitulated for
(we suspect) social though ultimately political reasons, she now sees
through the eyes of her pro-slavery host.

An inveterate plantocratic male counterpart living in London, Edward Long, writing *The History of Jamaica* in 1774, the same year that Schaw began her journal, betrayed no such genteel compunction. Indeed, his text became one of the pro-slavery lobby's guides to "scholarly" opinion on slavery. Tailoring his unbridled fantasies to an eager British readership, he argues his case forthrightly:

> In general, they are void of genius, and seem almost incapable of making any progress in civility of science. They have no plan or system of morality among them. Their barbarity to their children debases their nature even below that of brutes. They have no moral sensations; no taste but for women; gormondizing, and drinking to excess; no wish but to be idle.[6]

Against the foil of Schaw's and Long's flagrant caricatures, abolitionists proffered contrasting scenarios. The following extract is part of Hannah More's celebrated "Slavery, A Poem," written at the request of the Abolition Committee as a boost to the Abolition Bill that was about to be introduced into the House of Commons in May, 1788.

> Was it decreed, fair Freedom! at thy birth,
> That thou shou'd'st ne'er irradiate all the earth?
> While Britain basks in thy full blaze of light,
> Why lies sad Afric quench'd in total night? . . .
> Does then th' immortal principle within
> Change with the casual colour of a skin?
> Does matter govern spirit? or is mind
> Degraded by the form to which 'tis join'd?
> No: they have heads to think, and hearts to feel,
> And souls to act, with firm, tho' erring zeal; . . .
> Strong, but luxuriant virtues boldly shoot
> From the wild vigour of a savage root . . .
> See the dire victim torn from social life,
> The shrieking babe, the agonizing wife! . . .
> She, wretch forlorn! is dragg'd by hostile hands,
> To distant tyrants sold, in distant lands! . . .
> Tho' dark and savage, ignorant and blind,
> They claim the common privilege of kind;
> Let Malice strip them of each others plea,
> They still are men, and men shou'd still be free. . . .
> Not to herself [i.e., Britain] the glorious gift confin'd,
> She spreads the blessing wide as humankind;
> O may that god-like deed, that shining page,
> Redeem our fame, and consecrate our age![7]

For More, slavery is primarily a blemish on the national character that throws Britain's supposed reputation as a land of freedom and goodness into disrepute. (I elaborate on More's motivation in two later chapters.) As a secondary consideration, in contrast to Schaw who takes pains to nullify any discernible human attributes among African people, More pointedly punctuates that very humanity while similarly denying heterogeneity. Even though Africans are ugly, rationally inferior, and basically savage, Christian values dictate that they do feel.[8] By debasing Africans, by kidnapping, selling, and brutalizing them, Britons only debase themselves.

The narratives of such distinguished contemporary Africans as Olaudah Equiano, living in London at the time, redressed but could not staunch these caricatures. Abolitionists probably deemed Equiano exceptional, since even most opponents of the slave trade did not consider Africans on an even par with Europeans. Hence the overlappings between Schaw's and More's unabashed, seemingly univocal discourse that shut out the voices and ultimately denied the full humanity of the colonized other.[9] At different levels, their texts leave in place the differential status of blacks *vis à vis* whites. On the other hand, the differences between Schaw and the basically conservative More, a thinker with virtually no access to first-hand knowledge of Africa and slavery testify to the dynamic force, though limited to be sure, of evangelical Christianity.

The last extract—rare if not unique—comes from an autobiographical narrative by a former slavewoman, *The History of Mary Prince, A West Indian Slave, Related by Herself.*

> The black morning at length came; it came too soon for my poor mother and us. Whilst she was putting on us the new osnaburgs in which we were to be sold, she said in a sorrowful voice, (I shall never forget it!) "See, I am shrouding my poor children; what a task for a mother!"—She then called Miss Betsey to take leave of us. "I am going to carry my little chickens to market," (these were her very words) "take your last look of them; may be you will see them no more. . . . After this, I fell ill again with the rheumatism, and was sick a long time; but whether sick or well, I had my work to do. About this time I asked my master and mistress to let me buy my own freedom. . . . Mrs. Wood was very angry—she grew quite outrageous—she called me a black devil, and asked me who had put freedom into my head. "To be free is very sweet," I said: but she took good care to keep me a slave. I saw her change colour, and I left the room. . . . I am often much vexed, and I feel great sorrow when I hear some people in this country say, that the slaves

do not need better usage, and do not want to be free. . . . But they put a cloak about the truth. It is not so. All slaves want to be free—to be free is very sweet. I will say the truth to English people who may read this history that my good friend, Miss S——, is now writing down for me. I have been a slave myself—I know what slaves feel—I can tell by myself what other slaves feel, and by what they have told me. . . . They hire servants in England; and if they don't like them, they send them away: they can't lick them. Let them work ever so hard in England, they are far better off than slaves. If they get a bad master, they give warning and go hire to another. They have their liberty. That's just what we want. We don't mind hard work, if we had proper treatment, and proper wages like English servants, and proper time given in the week to keep us from breaking the Sabbath. But they won't give it; they will have work——work——work, night and day, sick or well, till we are quite done up; and we must not speak up nor look amiss, however much we be abused. And then when we are quite done up, who cares for us, more than for a lame horse? This is slavery. I tell it to let English people know the truth; and I hope they will never leave off to pray God, and call loud to the great King of England, till all the poor blacks be given free, and slavery done up for evermore.[10]

A silenced, gazed-upon "other" denied experience and individuality in both pro- and anti-slavery texts, Mary Prince identifies herself to the world as a thinking, feeling woman. She accomplishes this despite censorship by evangelical editors eager to promote values like Hannah More's. In this world, she stresses, mothers mourn while bullying owners call sick laboring slaves "black devils." The use of the word devil intertextually invokes Scripture's use of blackness, the result of Old Testament Cham's disobedience.[11] In defiantly constituting herself through her utterance, in speaking for herself and other slaves, Mary Prince dissolves bipartisan attempts to coalesce "Africans" into one undifferentiated multitude or, in critic Mary Louise Pratt's words, to homogenize "the people to be othered . . . into a collective they."[12] Simultaneously, she validates herself and invalidates Eurocentric myths. She will have none of this plantocratic buffoonery or abolitionist contentions about racial inferiority.

Warring over slavery, one section of the white ruling class argues for the right to its practice while another advocates wage labor, an argument that ultimately propels them to an anti-slavery analysis.[13] Both factions argue on behalf of their economic interests as competitive white capitalists in a commodity market, where the demand for commodities had gone up from 15 percent of British trade with colonies in 1700 to one-third in 1775.[14] Mary Prince inserts her own reality into the debate by insisting on her right to be treated as a waged laborer like her white British counterpart. Claiming subjectivity through speech, experience, and labor, she declines subjection to others; to shift orientation somewhat, she prefers to be subject to capital through wage labor.

Oppositional to one another, these parleying voices of the slaver and the slave inform every anti-slavery text, sometimes silently, at other times in open dissension. With these polyphonic texts in mind, I now want to look at two other contemporary phenomena that were known as "slaveries"—Barbary Coast bondage and the domination of women—and see to what extent their designation as slaveries denoted national attitudes toward colonial slavery.

HISTORICAL BACKGROUND

First, I want to contrast these responses to West African Caribbean slavery with British responses to the slavery of Britons themselves, a phenomenon known loosely as Barbary Coast slavery.[15] This practice roughly paralleled chronologically the gradual institutionalization of the West African slave trade and the scattered objections it elicited.

The roots of British colonial slavery that ultimately engaged women in the massive national campaign for slave emancipation in the 1830s harkened back to early Tudor times. In Folaris Shyllons's words, "the Portugese capture of the Moorish stronghold in Ceuta in North Africa in 1415 opened the way for European penetration of black Africa."[16] British expeditions to Africa commenced a century later. Queen Elizabeth's open letter to the Lord Mayor of London in 1596 about African slaves settling in Britain: "Her Majesty's pleasure ... ys that those kinde of people should be [expelled from] the lande" plainly reflects growing disapproval by a preponderantly white British public.[17] Between the seventeenth and nineteenth centuries, "Britain's share of the Atlantic [slave] trade amounted to about 50 percent of the total, involving the forcible transference and brutal acculturation of probably two million African blacks."[18]

By the 1680s Britain had reached a period of colonial expansion in the slave trade after earlier illegal and halting but determined efforts by mercantilist-entrepreneurs in the sixteenth and early seventeenth centuries to inaugurate a major slave-trading operation.[19] Before 1640 the British had established several sugar plantations in the Caribbean, for which slaves were considered a valuable labor force.[20] Granted a charter in 1660, the Royal African Company sold ninety thousand slaves by auction in the West Indies during the next three decades, undeterred by the fatalities on the voyage from West Africa. About one-third of the imported slaves did not survive that sailing on the notorious Middle Passage.[21] The Company's monopoly provoked considerable discussion since the rapidly growing slave traffic involved wealthy, competitive sectors of British and white Caribbean society—merchants, plantation owners, shipbuilders, shipowners, manufacturers, and bankers. Engagement in the slave trade was money in the bank for them. As the pro-slavery lobby in England debated the merits of free enterprise and monopoly among themselves, mounting negrophobic propaganda ran parallel, frequently propagated by the same people.[22]

Throughout the seventeenth century, a scant few protested, commentaries and testimonials by Quaker contemporaries and a few isolated individuals notwithstanding.[23] Such British Protestants as Richard Baxter and Morgan Godwyn in 1673 and 1680 respectively, argued that slavery and Christianity were incompatible, an idea that infuriated slaveowners.[24] But the fact was, as historian David Brion Davis states it, that "British missionaries and philanthropists regarded the Negro slave as a man possessing an immortal soul, but the institution of slavery they accepted without question. In practice, indeed, their labors were designed to impose restrictive controls over the few areas of the Negro's life which remained undisciplined."[25] A dedicatee of one of Aphra Behn's plays, Thomas Tryon, published a proto-abolitionist pamphlet entitled *Friendly Advice to the Gentlemen-Planters of the East and West Indies* in 1684, four years prior to the publication of Behn's prose fiction, *Oroonoko*. A committed vegetarian and mystic, Tryon outlined a profile of slavery from the slaves' point of view. In Tryon's text, slaves scoff at "Masters professing Christianity in the West Indian Plantations" and condemn "inconsiderate and unmerciful Overseers [who] make nothing to whip and Beat us, and the best words they can afford us, are Damn'd Doggs, Black Ugly Devils, idle Sons of Ethiopean Whores, and the Like."[26] Tryon's diatribe conjures up the very ethos that may have prompted Behn to endow Oroonoko with European features in order to staunch conditioned responses to Africans during that period.[27]

In Letter XXXIII "To a Planter of Sugar," in a work entitled *Letters, Domestick and Foreign*, Tryon encourages the planter to "stem the Current of Groans, Signs, Melancholly Lamentations, and Turmoil of your Servant, into a Pleasant, calm, serene Life, of happy Employment." He recommends that African men and women be taught to spin and weave and that women (in particular, it seems) receive humane treatment.[28] "Nothing hath more hurt and injur'd the Plantations," he continues, "than the hard Labour and unkind Usage Towards your Black women, for the whole preservation of Mankind as to encrease, Health, and Strength resides in the prudent Conduct of women." (*Letters, Domestick and Foreign,* pp. 185–86). Such solicitude for the welfare of female slaves only became a significant issue in the general population in the 1820s and 1830s after a few parliamentarians demanded an end to female flogging. Tryon's belief in the mystical harmony between nature and spirit prompts him to warn planters that the slave population will decrease if conditions do not improve:[29] [If] "There be not a due proportion between the Labour, Food and Rest, then Nature must by degrees sink and dwindle into a consumption, extraordinary. Labour calls for Extraordinary Meats, Drinks, and Rest, more especially in hot Climate." (*Letters, Domestick and Foreign,* p. 186). He appeals to self-preservation in warning planters that downtrodden people rightfully seek redress and revenge: "The groaning of him that suffereth pain is the beginning of trouble and misery to him that caused it; and it is not to be doubted, but under this black Character of Oppression and Violence, the Sugar Plantations do now lye under" (*Letters, Domestick and Foreign,* p. 187).

Tryon's views were exceptional in the 1600s. A poem by one of his contemporaries in a collection entitled *Miscellanea* sounded a more traditional note.[30] The anonymous poet celebrated the appointment on November 26, 1687, of Christopher Monck, the second Duke of Albemarle, as Governor-General of Jamaica.[31] In praising the royal couple, the poet wished them Godspeed in their voyage to Jamaica and observed how the lives of slaves would benefit from their Christian presence. Unfortunately the poet's thesis had little time to be tested since the Duke died early the following autumn:

> Your Presence still we wou'd implore
> Did not the Indies court You to their shore
> Go then, lov'd Prince, Success your Actions crown, . . .
> How shall the slaves to labour, born, and toil,
> When your kind Person shall refresh the *Isle,*
> Wonder with joy to see each other smile?
> The Spirits which, to them, you shall dispence,
> So much than once—vex't Souls will influence,
> That they shall banish all sad sorrows thence.
> What ease shall Natives, what delight possess;
> Whom from blest you derive their Happiness?
> New Kings at home have Acts of Grace bestow'd,
> And Albemarle gives jubilees abroad. ("To Their Graces" p. 59)

The poet sympathizes with the "sad sorrow" of slavery, while unques-
tioningly embracing it as an institution.

BARBARY COAST SLAVERY

Despite overall acceptance of colonial slavery throughout the Restoration and early eighteenth century, the phenomenon of slavery
along the Barbary Coast—named for "its indigenous Berber inhabitants [in North Africa, close to the Mediterranean], tribes of pastoralists
and mountain dwellers"—was roundly denounced.[32] For nearly two
centuries, but beginning seriously with the rise of the Barbary states
in the fifteenth century, corsairs from the North Coast of Africa (popularly known as the Barbary Coast) ceaselessly raided the ships and
coasts of European Christian countries, invoking the custom of *usanza
del mare*.[33] North African pirates' probable resentment of European
incursions into waters on the border of the Mediterranean and North
Africa was never an issue in the British press. Moreover, persistent
usage of the word Barbary although originally limited to the Berbers
reinforced ethnocentric usage of the word "barbarian" for "uncivilized" Africans. Originally, Phoenicians, Romans, and Byzantines—
townspeople and conquerors—had used the term to deride the alleged
lack of sophistication of the rural Berbers. The pirates stripped pas-
sengers and crew of clothes and possessions, then put their captives
to work either rowing the galleys (the most abject form of servitude
customarily reserved for Christians) or working in fields or in construction. Although slave masters on their deathbeds had been known
to grant manumission, many Europeans died in captivity in the *ba-
gnios* (jails). Rulers of the countries involved—the Regency of Tripoli
to the Empire of Morocco and the Straits of Gibralter—tried to make
their actions work two ways: primarily, they strove to convert able-
bodied men or force women who struck them as beautiful to stock
and replenish their armies and harems. Second, they sought large
ransoms. Britons considered the enslavement of alleged civilians by
what they deemed pagan pirates as a public scandal. Especially, the
public abhorred the victims' possible capitulation to apostasy after
capture. Consequently, a national hero of the Napoleonic wars, Admiral Sir Sidney Smith, was encouraged to organize a society, the mission
of which was contained in its title: The Society of Knights Liberators
of the White Slaves in Africa. The admiral solicited contributions from
European courts to the ransom funds and "drew attention to the . . .
scandal of Christian standards being continually affronted by the

practice of enslaving and selling innocent men, women and children."[34] The most egregious disgrace—as he saw it—was the subjection of white British women to these atrocities. Female captives consequently commanded ransoms, larger than the customary one of 38
pounds a head, including custom dues: in 1646 Sarah Riply of London
cost 800 pounds, Mary Riply and her two children 1,000 pounds, Alice
Hayes of Edinburgh 1,100 pounds; and Mary Bruster of Youghal, 1,329
pounds. In 1720 George I ordered an ambassador to negotiate a peace
treaty with the Sultan of Algiers that resulted in the release of 296
British captives, of whom about one-twelfth were ships' masters.

Discursive responses by Europeans to these activities—the capture
of Europeans on the high seas and the kidnapping of Africans on the
West Coast of Africa—differed dramatically. As long as Africans were
the victims, almost no one seemed to mind. But when Christians like
themselves became the victims, writers changed their tune. North
African territorial integrity was not an issue. In contrast to persistent
outrage over white slavery was the self-justifying suspicion that in the
case of West African slavery, Africans might even be better off working
for Christian owners in the Caribbean than living under "barbaric"
chiefs in Guinea. Public reactions to Barbary Coast slavery signified a
double standard: all men and women were not considered equal
and, as Janet Schaw routinely repeats in her *Journal,* alleged African
subhumanity was a popular subject of debate.

Nor could anyone claim to know about one slave economy and not
the other. Protest about alleged piracy on the West African coast grew.
Advertisements for slaves and runaways regularly appeared in the
press as growing numbers of Africans arrived in Britain to live.[35] Even
the press commented adversely on colonial slavery. David Brion Davis
reports that "as early as the 1730s an occasional essay or letter to a
periodical made the momentous observation that, because all men
were born free and equal, Negro slavery was a violation of the natural
rights of man."[36] To put the matter simply, enslavement of Europeans
by North Africans was in a sense taken personally and always categorically condemned while protests against West African enslavement, a
phenomenon that was not tied to patriotism or a sense of common
identity, took much longer to gain ground.

WRITERS ON BARBARY COAST SLAVERY: MARY BARBER, ELIZA HAYWOOD, ELIZABETH ROWE

By the time Mary Barber's poem on Mediterranean or Barbary Coast
slavery was published in 1734, every issue of *The Gentleman's Maga-*

zine was reporting on colonial affairs and opposition to colonial slavery. The *London Magazine* also published articles on the subject. In
a poem entitled "On Public Spirit" in 1737, Richard Savage warned
slaveholders that "yoke may yoke, and blood may blood repay."[37] That
same year, the popular *Tunbridge Miscellany* published a brief poem
entitled "An Essay on Humanity. Inscrib'd to the Bristol Captains,"
about the vile practices of Bristol captains and the barbarity of slavery.
The author fortified distorted views of Africans by suggesting that
cannibalism was common practice:

> Kind are the Cannibals, compar'd with you,
> For we must give to every one his Due;
> They are by Hunger prompted to destroy;
> You murder with a Countenance of Joy;
> They kill for sake of Food, and nothing more,
> You feed your Cruelty with Christian Gore;
> Then talk no more of Savages for Shame,
> All Men agree that you are most to blame,
> And as a Punishment so justly due,
> Which you deserve, henceforward each of you,
> As a Reproach, shall be nick-nam'd by all
> An unrelenting Bristol-Cannibal.[38]

Mary Barber's poem, "On Seeing the Captives lately redeem'd from
Barbary by His Majesty," addressed an actual incident that involved
the return of ransomed European captives in November of 1734. At
Saint James, captives expressing their gratitude to King George II for
their ransom were compensated with money from members of the
royal family. The poem elaborates on their horrid experiences.[39] Barber implies that she would broaden her specific condemnation into a
categorical denunciation of slavery were it not for the balance of
exports, the need for profit, and patriotic sentiment.

While abolition of the slave trade had scarcely been voiced, Barber's
poem eulogizes the king for delivering supposedly innocent captives
and recuperating Britain's reputation as a freedom-loving land. London crowds rejoice at their return:

> See, as they pass, the crowding people press,
> Joy in their Joy, and their Deliv'rer bless.

In future, she predicts, Britain citizenship will protect people from
slave traders on the North American coast:

> Now Slavery! No more thy rigid Hand
> Shall drag the Trader to thy fatal Strand:
> No more in Iron Bonds the Wretched groan;,
> Secur'd, Britannia, by thy Guardian Throne.

What empire, Barber exclaims (with no sense of irony), can "boast of Bliss . . . that equals this."

Most ironic are Barber's fulminations against conditions suffered by European ex-slaves and their severed families. As the captives are reunited with their families:

> See Arms in Grief long folded up, extend,
> To clasp a Husband, Brother, Kinsman, Friend:
> See hoary Parents, tott'ring o'er the Grave,
> A Son long-wail'd, to prop their Age, receive;
> And, Have we liv'd to see thy Face? they cry;
> O! tis enough—We now in Peace shall die: (Barber, *Poems on Several Occasions,* p. 272)

The fiercest criticism is reserved, predictably, for traders:

> Say, ye luxurious, wbo indulge your Taste,
> And, by one Riot, might a Thousand feast;,
> Do you not blush to see his Care to feed
> The Captives by your Monarch's Bounty freed? (Barber, *Poems on Several Occasions,* p. 273)

Praise for the king and Sir Charles Wager who assisted in ransoming the corsairs' captives foreshadows expressions of gratitude half a century later toward prominent abolitionists and emancipationists; in the latter case, however, it took the inauguration of a national campaign in 1788, spearheaded by Parliament, to induce widespread public support.[40] Set alongside colonialist reality and occasional protest, the concluding couplet suggests the ethnocentricity of a fashionable view of liberty and the particular kind of subjection that was humanly untenable:

> See, Albion, be it ever giv'n to thee,
> *To break the bonds, and get the Pris'ners free.*

Barber's assault on North African slavery and the phenomenon of Barbary Coast slavery in general comes under the heading of what Edward Said has termed "Orientalism," bearing in mind, too, the slippage of meaning: Barbary coast recalled barbarians and barbarity; Eurocentrically conceived, a lack of civilization was a mark and coordinate of the colonial other. For the most part, the assumption goes, corsairs are acting "naturally" and like African slaves, they too are collectively lumped together, another classic case of Europe's "othering" the "Orient." But unlike slaves, corsairs are a nasty lot, a villainous and not a victimized mass. The othering and reductivism of Asia guaranteed shock and national honor rising to the fore in a perverse, secular rerun of the crusades: Britain's ambassadors sought to release the victims of a mysterious "Orient."

While Barber frontally attacked Mediterranean slavery, other women writers, such as Eliza Haywood and Elizabeth Rowe, in *Philidore and Placentia* (1719) and *Letters Moral and Entertaining* (1731) respectively, protested somewhat less overtly.[41] They used the North African base of operations as a picturesque and convenient structure to enable protagonists to travel, come together, and be summarily separated. By the end of Haywood's tale, everyone is reconciled, the lovers marry, and Barbary Coast slavery in all its heinous, castrating, "oriental" cruelty, stands unequivocally indicted. In Rowe's *Letters,* similar perspectives obtain. On one hand, she condemns slavery as she did in a long earlier poem about Old Testament Joseph, *The History of Joseph.*[42] But in an episode that involved accepting a gift of "two Negro's to attend me," she betrays a familiar plantocratic rationalization: slaves will spiritually benefit from a Christian master. After all, as pagans cut off from spiritual truth, they require mercy. Besides, Britain stood to gain fame and fortune from the slave trade, a not inconsiderable fact, as Eric Williams and C. L. R. James have argued.[43]

Collectively, Barber, Haywood, and Rowe castigate Barbary Coast slavery as an odious, intractable institution. People assumed to have been seized illegitimately were cut off from kith and kin and subjected to unconscionable corsair (read oriental) deviousness and coerced into servitude; worse still, they might neglect or be made to neglect their Christian duty. What could be worse? Barbary Coast slavery exposes the hypocrisy of British foreign policy regarding slavery; it illumines the dual nature of othering.

The Condition of White Females in British Society: Power and Powerlessness

As I contended in the preamble, another twist in the complex evolution of slavery was white women's displacement of anxieties about themselves, a unique response substantially determined by their own sense of subjection to a cross-class patriarchal order within British society. Throughout the entire period of colonialist protest, for instance, in references to themselves as pawns of white men, denied education as well as access to law and allied deprivations, feminists of all classes were prone to refer loosely to themselves as slaves. I want to expand on these tropes and absorptions by sketching in the material context of women's lives before, during, and after they entered the abolitionist fray. First of all, textual self-inscription was one means by which women were able to wrest back a certain amount of the power and influence they had exercised during the Civil War. By the end of that near two-century period in 1834, women's involvement in emancipationist agitation, discursive and otherwise, made agitation for their own suffrage a logical next step. Female authors accrued cultural power, gained a reputation as polite nay-sayers to illegitimate authority, and aligned themselves with like-minded rebels.

Women began their commentaries on the slavery of Africans about the time they were losing some of the gains made in the Civil War. I want to back up for a moment and outline women's immediately previous history to highlight some of the changes.[44]

While commercial and banking ventures sought to expand the slave trade in the 1640s, 1650s, and 1660s, Britain was embroiled in the Civil War and the Interregnum, which fostered for the first time in British history the emergence of laboring and middle-class white women as an active political force, both visibly and collectively organized. Radical female sectaries (members of nonconformist sects) fought for greater participation in the religious, social, and political life of the country, questioning and even seeking to overturn gender-determined roles.[45] Women engaged in active military combat and commanded besieged garrisons. In 1647 they protested conditions of employment for female servants and demanded the same recreational privileges accorded male servants.[46] Some argued for the right to challenge issues of conscience. A good example was Katherine Chidley, an activist-preacher-writer in the Brownist-Congregationalist sect, who polemicized against Thomas Edwards, a major opponent of the Brownist-Congregationists, in *The Justification of the Independent Churches of Christ* (1640).[47] Chidley affirmed her belief in the right and capacity of any individual to preach from the pulpit and elsewhere, while reasoning about women's right to moral autonomy.

Concurrently, women petitioners deplored the fact that "unlimited power [had] been given to Prelates to exercise over the consciences of women as well as men."[48] They cited Scriptures as source and inspiration when they presented their several petitions, half-heartedly conceding (one suspects) that "it may be thought strange and unbeseeming in our sex to show ourselves by way of petitions."[49] Women participated in large numbers during the movement in the 1650s, for example, to free prominent radical John Lilburne from unjust imprisonment and restore his civil rights.[50] In a statement attached to their petitions on Lilburne's behalf, they berated those who pronounced women "unworthy to petition or represent our grievances to this honourable house" and defended their right to counter injustice:

> Have we not an equal interest with the men of this Nation in those liberties and securities contained in the Petition of Right and other the [sic] good Laws of the Land? . . . . Would you have us keep at home in our houses while men . . . are fetched out of their beds and forced from their houses by soldiers, to the affrighting and undoing of themselves, their wives, children and families? . . . And are we Christians, and shall we sit still and keep at home . . . and yet must we show no sense of their sufferings, no tendernesse of affections, no bowels of compassion, nor bear any testimony against so abominable cruelty and injustice?[51]

Although many women remembered the legacy of political activism, some power had began to dissipate by the Restoration. Alice Clark describes the late seventeenth century as an epoch in which women's roles were gradually being transformed:

> While women could share their husbands' trades they suffered little from these restrictions, but with the development of capitalistic organisation the numbers of women who could find no outlet for their productive activity in partnership with their husbands were increasing and their opportunities for establishing an independent industry did not keep pace; on the contrary, such industry became even more difficult.[52]

Nonetheless, there is much debate about the position of women in this period: Maxine Berg argues rather differently, for example, that "women took on a stronger position in the household during the protoindustrial period. . . . Younger generations were freed from those patriarchal constraints so dominant in a purely peasant environment."[53] The point is that women's role was fluid and changing. Struggle for multiple forms of power was afoot.

What could be agreed on by both sides in the debate, however, is that as women's power in some traditional areas somewhat diminished, a certain profile in print emerged that became inextricably tied to many women. That profile combined educational impoverishment and supposed intellectual inferiority with a matrix of values—piety, modesty, duty, gentleness, and chastity—that later in the century would come to be associated with evangelical reformers. Supposedly, women would live up to their image as responsible daughters and then as wives and mothers who would eventually produce heirs, tend home and hearth, and leave men free to administer affairs of state.[54] Such women were subjected to a patriarchal order, privately and publicly, a foregone conclusion in a society fixated on profit and male heirs.[55] Hardline misogynous discourse reinforced threats to women's power while simultaneously confirming some insecurity about power they might have or might be gaining. Clearly no socio-cultural roles were fixed and those debates and diatribes in print reflected anxieties about gender roles.[56]

Several contemporary critics and social historians have reconstructed women's roles at this time and speculated about changes wrought in their cultural lives. Ellen Pollack succinctly sums up the matter:

> Thus, in an economy where the family with the man as its head was the primary unit of productivity, women had held a subordinate but distinctly active role in the social hierarchy. Although their political status had been unequivocally inferior, their economic contribution to family maintenance was substantial and indispensable. In an economy which operated on an individualist model that placed women in direct competition with men as wage earners, however, women lost a critical measure of their former earning power. In the working classes, the direct economic contribution of women to family welfare was becoming subsidiary to that of men, while in the more affluent classes it was becoming superfluous.[57]

Elsewhere, Pollack adds that "an analysis of the literature of the age—from popular fiction to feminine conduct manuals and periodical literature—reveals the existence by the 1680s of a pervasive social mythology of passive womanhood. It upheld a rigorously defined ideal of woman as married, conjugally faithful, modest, good-natured, cheerfully tolerant of idleness, and preeminently intent on pleasing her husband. This social mythology placed a negative value on all women who strayed from these often impossible and contradictory expectations."[58]

Roy Porter perceives the alleged differences between women and men in Restoration and eighteenth-century England this way:

Men and women were indelibly different in nature and capacity and so ought to play quite distinct social roles. Anatomy determined one's destiny, and men were designed to be on top. Men were intended (said men) to excel in reason, business, action, decision; women's forte was to be passive, maternal, submissive, modest, docile, and virtuous (reality, however, was not so simple: men were terrified of "shrewishness"; husbands who capitulated to "petticoat government" were laughing-stocks). High public office, the professions, the universities, and the Church were closed to women. . . . Throughout their lives they were as far as possible to depend on men—as daughters, on their fathers, and, once wives, on the "masculine dominion" of their husbands. At the beginning of the century it was still usual amongst the landed classes for a father to arrange his daughter's marriage: she would at best have the right to veto his choice. In common law, wives had no rights over their children or to matrimonial property . . . even a woman's "very necessary apparel, by the law, is not hers, in property." A husband had the right to beat his wife, ruled a judge, so long as the stick was no thicker than a man's thumb.[59]

Porter adds salutary reminders about women still "in deep dread of the childbirth treadmill"; (Porter, *English Society*, p. 41). Elaine Hobby's research into writings by two hundred women from 1649 to 1688, moreover, indicates that many women were fully cognizant of massive alterations in post Civil War cultural life. In place of numerous wartime pamphlets appeared gentler volumes on cooking and medical remedies, as well as almanacs, poetry, and prose fiction.[60]

Since post-Restoration authors no longer collectively insisted on religious equality and civil liberties, a different politicization set in. Nonetheless, a handful of middle-class and aristocratic women argued for their rights as women.

EXTRA-COLONIAL EXPROPRIATIONS OF THE LANGUAGE OF SLAVERY

More specifically, recurring references that feminist writers make to themselves as slaves underscore this growing sense of powerlessness.

In the first place, the metaphor of slavery was nothing new for women. When the female general in the Duchess of Newcastle's closet drama *Bell in Campo* (1662) asks "shall only men be conquerors, and women slaves?" the primary referent of "slave" is (any) "conquered

people," not the misery associated with the lived experience of colonial slaves.[61] Poets Thomas Wyatt and Sir Philip Sidney tie the old
metaphor of conquest to imagery of warfare and arrows.

Frances Boothby's *Marcelia* (1670) is another case in point. When
the heroine queries whether reason and honor should be "slaves to
love" and King Sigismond accuses Fortune of making him "at once a
King and Captive fettering my heart," the referent is more strictly
related to showy motifs in heroic drama often linked to conceptions
of so-called "oriental" slavery.[62] Plays in the heroic mode like Dryden's
Aureng-Zebe (1675) frequently featured such stock characters as captive royalty, favorite slaves, and emperors who rounded up captives
in war.[63] The language of slavery was applied promiscuously to the
two great themes of this drama: love and valor.

But what was new in both prose and poetry, starting in the late
1670s and continuing through the eighteenth-century, was colonial
slavery as a specific referent applied to the circumstances of contemporary British women. This reconceptualized frame of reference displayed women's self-perceived cultural impotence alongside the primacy they accorded their own condition. It also betrayed traditional
white supremacist attitudes and a continued sense that the language
of slavery most aptly encoded white woman's oppression. In other
words, women authors used the language of slavery in a dual if not
a multiple sense and initiated a critical discursive shift, a radical
discontinuity within texts and hence within ideology.[64]

The poet Ephelia, for one, decried her lot as a scorned woman in
poems that were particularly expressive because not only did she
expropriate the language of slavery to discuss personal tribulations
in love but the source of this infatuation was a slave trader named J. G.[65]
Ephelia talks of being "fond of my soft chain," although her heart is
not "so absolute a slave." She equates slavery with pain and cruelty,
divesting the language of its hideous quotidian reality by reserving it
for the sorrows of a free woman, neglected in love. Her poems illuminate
an especially graphic example of a subservient attitude toward the
"conqueror" that undergirded most early writings on slavery:

> Being your Slave, I'm not so vain
> To hope to have one minutes Ease
> But shou'd take pleasure in my Pain,
> If my Dear Conqu'rer it wou'd please.

Too immersed in J. G., Ephelia remained heedless of the implications
of her language, a myopia common to the age.

A few feminists employed the same language in a less subjective, more political context. Bathsua Makin, Judith Drake, and Mary Astell, to name a celebrated trio, equated the limited education of females and the consequences of marriage in women's lives with forms of enslavement. Not every woman, they reminded contemporaries, relished being molded to a preconceived norm. The particular examples I cite below suggest their political connection to the anonymous poet's perspective in *Miscellanea:* they assumed the legitimacy of colonial slavery but recoiled from its violence, their posture unconditionally ameliorative.[66]

In 1673, challenging the deleterious condition of female education in *An Essay to Restore the Antient Education of Gentlewomen,* Bathsua Makin blamed these straits on cupidinous men intent on maintaining power at all costs. In a passage ridiculing any man who would deny women the right to an education, she compares women to slaves:

> It is an easie matter to quibble and droll upon a subject of this nature, to scoff at women kept ignorant, on purpose to be made slaves. This savours not at all of a Manly Spirit, to trample upon those that are down.[67]

In 1696, less than a decade after *Oroonoko* appeared and in the year of Thomas Southerne's adaptation of *Oroonoko* for the stage, Judith Drake's *An Essay in Defence of the Female Sex* similarly linked the condition of women's lives to that of slaves. Impugning male jealousy, Drake asserted that men "trained" women to a life of:

> ease and Ignorance; as Conquerors are to do to those they reduce by Force, that so they may disarm 'em . . . and consequently make them tamely give up their Liberty, and abjectly submit their necks to a slavish Yoke. . . . As the World grew more Populous, and Mens Necessities whetted their Inventions, so it increas'd their Jealousy, and sharpen'd their Tyranny over us, till by degrees, it came to that height of Severity, I may say Cruelty, it is now at in all the Eastern parts of the World, where the Women, like our Negroes in our Western Plantations, are born slaves, and live Prisoners all their Lives.[68]

In the appendix to *Some Reflections Upon Marriage* in 1700, Mary Astell vigorously configured marriage as a form of slavery:

> What though a Husband can't deprive a Wife of Life without being responsible to the Law, he may, however, do what is much more

grievous to a generous Mind, render Life miserable, for which she has no Redress, scarce Pity, which is afforded to every other Complainant, it being thought a Wife's Duty to suffer every thing without Complaint. If *all Men are born Free,* how is it that all Women are born Slaves? As they must be, if the being subjected to the *inconstant, uncertain, unknown, arbitrary* Will of Men, be the *perfect condition of Slavery*? And, if the Essence of Freedom consists, as our Masters say it does, in having a standing Rule to live by? And why is Slavery so much condemn'd and strove against in one Case, and so highly applauded, and held so necessary and so sacred in another?[69]

In all these cases—and many more could be cited in this century and the next—women either labeled themselves slaves or labeled their situation as slavery, yet failed to accompany these incriminations with an explicit condemnation of colonial slavery itself. Only rarely did such challenges occur and when they did personal experiences tended to provoke them. Of course, all these commentaries assumed that slavery was an iniquitous institution, a vicious condition from which women must escape—the power of the reference to slavery directly and indirectly depended on that assumption. But the inculpation of slavery as it related exclusively to women's problems matches the same robust indictment of slavery in another context that referred only peripherally or implicitly to enslaved Africans: Barbary Coast slavery.

In both cases, Europeans made no bones about their contempt and intolerance for slavery. In one case, European men and women on the high seas were kidnapped by North African pirates; in the other, white Christian women were abused by callous husbands or lovers or intellectually marginalized by a patriarchal social system, victims denied agency. But when the boot was on the other foot, when it came to Africans being enslaved cruelly and systematically, few objected. The epoch itself—not just European women—rubber-stamped this double standard almost, one might say, as a matter of consensus. These feminist authors were saying nothing about the institution that would cause any "true-blooded Englishman" to raise an eyebrow. Their discourse imbedded entrenched national policy, the historical moment for massive and near-consensual European protest almost a century away. This dual standard alerts readers to a discursive density, to impacted texts conveying multiple messages. When Aphra Behn started talking about an African woman being subjected to sexual advances and forced into marriage, white female readers could understandably have decoded that situation as one that "rang a bell." Many lived similar experiences.

These multivalent messages about colonial slavery notwithstanding, protests were a long time coming; the only slaveries British people cared enough to protest were ones that involved white citizenry. Meanwhile the proslavery machine, in pursuit of trade and profit, whether before 1698 when the Royal African Company lost its monopoly, or in the later free trade mode, churned out influential and damaging objectifications of Africans.[70] The Guinea Company instructed Bartholomew Haward in 1651

> "to buy and put aboard you so many negers as yo'r ship can cary, and for what shall be wanting to supply with Cattel, as also to furnish you with victualls and provisions for the said negers and Cattell."[71]

The public encoded colonial expansion as a symbol of Britain's God-given greatness and superiority.

Surprisingly, then, at least on the surface, the first major pro-emancipation speech occurs in a Restoration text, *Oroonoko; or, The Royal Slave. A True History* (1688) by Aphra Behn. Given the virtual absence of rebellious, voiced Africans in eighteenth-century texts by British women, the fact that Oroonoko rousingly delivers an emancipationist speech is extraordinary. Certainly a number of formerly enslaved African males wrote about their experiences throughout the eighteenth century but such publications were rare and no African-Caribbean slavewomen are known to have written before the publication of Mary Prince's narrative in 1831.[72] If Aphra Behn had not visited Surinam and witnessed British colonialism at first hand, been an unremunerated spy for King Charles who was consequently thrown into debtors' prison, or become a successful dramatist and prose fiction writer who needed to survive economically, this new discursive phenomenon might not have happened so early.

Chapter 2

Oroonoko: Birth of a Paradigm

INTRODUCTION

Though chronologically not the first text by an Englishwoman to address colonial slavery, *Oroonoko: or The Royal Slave. A True History* (1688) by Aphra Behn made an effective and dramatic public statement and generated a paradigm for British colonialist discourse.[1] Although elements of the paradigm inevitably shifted as historical events unfolded, the basic construction of anti-slavery discourse remained in place well beyond the passage of the emancipation act in 1834. The diverse, seemingly contradictory hermeneutics of *Oroonoko* directly bear on the paradigm that emerged.

For three centuries critics have tried to batten down the thematics of *Oroonoko* (1688). Interpretations range from pronouncing the fiction the "first literary abolitionist [text] . . . on record in the history of fiction" to calling it a political allegory about "James, Mary, and the unborn . . . prince" that argues the "absolute power of legitimate kings"; a model of "colonial realism"; an instance of "pure romanticism"; by "an incurable romantic", the "source of the English novel"; or a debate about the concept of honor.[2] The protean nature of interpretations is related to Aphra Behn's politically ambivalent views about royalty and colonial supremacy, and about the complex relationship among the white author-narrator, the slave Oroonoko, and the colonists.

First off, the difference in age between author and narrator as a factor in determining their varying perspectives on events is noteworthy. Entranced by romantic love, the youthful narrator discusses prominent contemporaries in what she certifies is a true story and whom Behn in the preface claims as herself. This narrator admires

27

Oroonoko's heroic stand against slavery and deplores his punishment and death by torture when captured. At such a level the text is a posthumous eulogy to Oroonoko. As the forty-eight-year-old author of *Oroonoko,* Behn fuses this perspective with an assault on usurpation of royal authority. Meanwhile, as a consistent advocate of slavery (evident elsewhere in her writings), she twice has the narrator abandon her hero-friend at critical junctures. Additionally, Behn constitutes West African reality Eurocentrically in a discourse that unwittingly intensified negative attitudes toward Africans in general and slaves in particular. As Winthrop Jordan puts it: "Vis à vis the Negro the concept embedded in the term *Christian* seems to have conveyed much of the idea and feeling of *we* as against *they.*"[3]

Second, although the romantic tale of Oroonoko and Imoinda absorbs the fifteen-year-old Behn for its own sake since she lived through extraordinary experiences as an adolescent in Surinam, the more worldly Behn of 1688 in three subtle textual epiphanies chafes at misogynous sway and its wounding effect on females, such as Imoinda and (herself as) the narrator denied lawful authority in the colony.

Third, in exposing colonial administrators wantonly subverting the limits of their power, Behn obliquely indicts the "upstarts" who overthrew Charles I and now threaten James II. More to a personal point, these same usurpers disempowered Behn herself in Surinam. Behn's origins remain mysterious but one plausible theory has it that she was the "natural" daughter of Lady Willoughby, wife of the Governor of Surinam. When he drowned accidentally she could no longer claim, as she does in the preface to *Oroonoko,* that "there was none above me in that country." Thus as a multilayered semi-autobiographical tale, *Oroonoko* affirms Behn's consistent royalist politics and her evolving perspective on women. Certainly, astute readers might well have decoded the tale as an act of revenge against specific contemporaries in Caribbean government whom Behn reduces to calculating sadists. This censure lasts throughout the eighteenth century in Thomas Southerne's version of *Oroonoko* and continues, even today, in the current recuperation of Behn's literary reputation.[4]

PART ONE: THE DEBATE ABOUT SLAVERY

The plot of *Oroonoko* centers on a royal prince in West Africa, Oroonoko, who is in love with and soon betrothed to a slain general's daughter named Imoinda. No dates are given, but documented historical events that are mentioned in the story occurred in the 1660s as Britain secured its foothold in the slave trade.[5] Angered by Imoinda's love for Oroonoko and not himself, Oroonoko's grandfather sells her into slavery, an act solidly condemned by the narrator. A slaver captain and Oroonoko's former friend then treacherously kidnaps the prince in West Africa and sells him in Surinam to a Mr. Trefry, overseer of a vast plantation. Once in the Caribbean, Oroonoko and Imoinda serendipitously meet, marry, and conceive a child. Fearing life-long enslavement, Imoinda inspires Oroonoko into orchestrating a slave rebellion that then fails disastrously. As part of a suicide pact, Oroonoko kills Imoinda, after which he is caught and tortured to death by command of colonial officials.

The traditional argument that *Oroonoko* marks the first anti-slavery prose fiction in the English language turns on Oroonoko's fiery exhortation to the slaves, since all other textual commentary in *Oroonoko* points in a pro-slavery direction. The passage begins when "Imoinda [Oroonoko's wife, sold by his jealous grandfather and now enslaved in Surinam] began to show she was with child, and did nothing but sigh and weep for the captivity of her lord, herself, and the infant yet unborn, and believed, if it were so hard to gain the liberty of two [note: not all the slaves] it would be more difficult to get that for three." Oroonoko, by this time renamed Caesar by Trefry, reacts to Imoinda's promptings with a stirring speech to the slaves:

> Caesar, having singled out these men from the women and children, made an harangue to them, of the miseries and ignominies of slavery, counting up all their toils and sufferings under such loads, burdens, and drudgeries, as were fitter for beasts than men, senseless brutes, than human souls. . . . They suffered not like men, who might find a glory and fortitude in oppression, but like dogs, that loved the whip and bell, and fawned the more they were beaten; that they had lost the divine quality of men, and were become insensible asses, fit only to bear, nay, worse. . . . Whether they worked or not, whether they were faulty or meriting, they, promiscuously, the innocent with the guilty, suffered the infamous whip, the sordid stripes, from their fellow slaves, till their blood trickled from all parts of their body, blood, whose every drop ought to be revenged with a life of some of those tyrants that impose it. "And why," said he, "my dear friends and fellow-sufferers, should we be slaves to an unknown people? Have they vanquished us nobly in fight? Have they won us in honourable battle? And are we by the chance of war become their slaves? . . . No, but we are bought and sold like apes or monkeys, to be the sport of women, fools and

cowards: and the support of rogues and runagades, that have abandoned their country for rapine, murders, thefts and villanies. . . .
And shall we render obedience to such a degenerate race, who
have not one human virtue left to distinguish them from the vilest
creatures? Will you, I say, suffer the lash from such hands?" They
all replied with one accord "No no no; Caesar has spoken like a
great captain, like a great king!" (Behn, *Oroonoko,* p. 56)

In inveighing so categorically against slavery, this passage connects
to and intertextualizes an earlier assault on the treatment of slaves in
Surinam, launched in the London press in 1667 by one George Warren:
slaves there, he hissed, "are sold like dogs, and no better esteem'd
but for their Work sake, which they perform all the Week with the
severest usages for the slightest fault."[6] Small wonder that the Deputy
Governor of Surinam, William Byam, testified in 1665 to the slaves'
fierce reactions to their conditions: the "insolencies of our Negroes,
killing our stock, breaking open houses, . . . and some flying into
the woods in rebellion," approximately one year after Aphra Behn's
probable arrival in Surinam.[7] This very Byam is the one whom Behn
excoriates in her text.

The passage also raises a late seventeenth-century preoccupation
of the Royal African Company who at that time held the slave trade
monopoly: that independent traders desist from kidnapping princes
and "other important personages."[8] Walter Rodney further comments
that the counterproductive turmoil generated in slave communites by
the captivity of nobles taught Europeans to leave African nobility
alone "so long as that noble had not been voluntarily given up by his
fellows."[9] Behn's text graphically illustrates the reasons for the Royal
African Company's vigilance. Moreover, since the royal monopoly on
trading was persistently challenged during these years, her text also
quietly emphasizes the economic value of the monopoly and castigates the instability caused by such "interlopers" as the captain who
kidnapped Oroonoko.[10]

But despite the obvious reasons for revolt, the architectonics of
Oroonoko's speech raises questions both about his motives and the
narrator's. In her own words, the "told-to" narrator reports more than
half the speech and upbraids dehumanization. She upholds Christian
values and invalidates African ontological beliefs about joining ancestors as free beings after death when she has Oroonoko claim that
slavery will last forever: "He told them, it was not for days, months or
years, but for eternity" (Behn, *Oroonoko,* p. 56). Voicing in the first
person, though the narrator herself is recounting or speaking Oroo-

noko's voicing, a rare occurrence in white British texts, West African Prince and slave Oroonoko addresses "underlings" in the tone of a superior, deplores his own enslavement, and (in ominous prophecy) his role as the "sport of women, fools, and cowards." His conscious self-exclusion from the majority of slaves in his use of the second person when he mentions the lash, and his temporary identification with slaves whom he may have originally sold into slavery lend irony to his exhortations. After all, he profited from and perpetuated slavery in his own country, and has just tried to bribe overseer Trefry "with gold or a vast quantity of slaves" into freeing himself and Imoinda (Behn, *Oroonoko,* p. 42). Nor is it likely that Oroonoko could be talking English to African men, even if we suppose (which is unlikely) that they were all from Coramantien. Behn assumes authorial license here in collectivizing the slaves' ethnicity, or—despite her claims in the preface about the tale's veracity—conjures up the scene in its entirety because the scenario she presents contains decided fantastic elements. Specifically Behn exemplifes what President Kwame Nkrumah of Ghana termed much later "The Balkanization of Africa."

> There are 264 Sudanic languages (those spoken by the "true Negroes"), 183 Bantu languages, and 47 Hamitic languages. A single people, such as the Wolof of Senegal, might be divided into two or three hostile kingdoms; the Yoruba of Nigeria had ten separate states. Neither these little kingdoms nor the warring tribes around them would join together against a common enemy, and hence it was easy for the slavers to set one group against another.[11]

The people from that region in question (today's Ghana) would have spoken Ashanti, Fanti, and possibly other languages such as Twi and Ga.[12] Additionally there might well have been captives present from other regions, some of whom Oroonoko is apparently attempting to resell. Or he could have been negotiating an exchange with Trefry that depended on Oroonoko's return to West Africa and his shipping of gold and slaves to Trefry. The concoctions build on one another as the narrator's reconstruction (allowing for the existence of an original zealous speech) alerts us to a certain unreality in Oroonoko's expostulations and the slaves' dramatized univocal response. A skeptical onlooker might wonder at the ready acquiescence of slaves to follow a noble prince who is privy to a seemingly labor-free and more privileged existence in Surinam than the rest of the slaves who endure, according to Oroonoko's own account, a ravaged quotidian reality. Or perhaps high rank is meant to explain resistance to slavery.

At any rate, in wake of the abortive rebellion, Oroonoko compounds his barely veiled sense of class supremacy by scorning slaves, very much depicted as soldiers in Oroonoko's instant, makeshift army, who followed their wives' advice to choose pardon and self-preservation over recapture and possible death. African marriage within the slave community, frequently forbidden as a formal institution by Europeans, is unrealistically taken for granted. Oroonoko seems insensitive to the plight and conflicts of his fellow-slaves, so drastically different in many ways from his own. Once the rebels are overcome, the prince tells Byam, the lieutenant governor of Surinam from 1662 to 1667, "he had rather die than live upon the same earth with such dogs" (Behn, *Oroonoko,* p. 61). Thus the slaves are divided among themselves, with the "racial difference" of the majority from the light-complexioned Oroonoko on down, highlighted and disparaged: the bravery of a Europeanized Oroonoko contrasts with fetishized native cowardice and vacillation; everyone is conveniently lumped into the collective "they" of the colonial other.[13] Oroonoko's contentions about the slaves, since he is more lifelike than the silenced majority, press home an old Anglo-Africanist stereotype of the "savagery" of Africans. Doubtless the slaves reneged on a verbal contract to fight to the death, but their reasons were as good as Oroonoko's when, in a later episode, he breaks his pact with Imoinda to kill both her and himself after he avenges them both. By positioning slaves and not the "degenerate [European] race" as the "other," or, more emphatically, as a deindividuated mass set apart from an articulate individual like himself with the power to speak, Oroonoko reasserts royal power and his class identification with British colonial rule. He underscores the propriety of a ruler's outlook that coincides with Behn's royalist perspective.

Neither the emotional impact of Oroonoko's speech, "perhaps the first important abolitionist statement in the history of English literature," nor his grand personal heroism are denied by these reservations.[14] A critical presence in the text, the actualization of a resistance the reader has long awaited, that speech dramatically unveils the atrocities of slavery. We could and do welcome it as an "anti-slavery" tribute, but another keenly developed dimension in the text, as Professor K. A. Sey has pointed out, fundamentally undermines the impact: "the slave trade is not evil in itself, provided the dealers are 'gentlemen' or true Christians."[15] As long as humane traffickers (not seen as a contradiction) and philanthropic plantation owners (ditto) run the institution and felicitously convert pagan Africans to Christianity and hence to "civilized" values, then slavery and the slave trade can mesh harmoniously with the aristocratic ethic. As someone who tries to

instruct Imoinda "to the knowledge of the true God" and dispel Oroonoko's disdain for the holy trinity, the narrator attempts just that
(Behn, *Oroonoko*, p. 42): to affirm that ethic and spiritually convert
the captured couple.

Besides, the twin factors of self-determination and Oroonoko's specific rebellion fit into a general pattern of attempted island slave
revolts at that time. But no authentic corroboration, historical or
otherwise, of Oroonoko's specific disapproval of the upshot is available; nor are the views of any comparable leader of fellow slaves.
Byam's official reports seems to sanction an alternative speculation—
that cross-class Africans planned an insurrection but were defeated
by unfamiliar terrain, hasty planning, indecisiveness, and ruthless
opponents. If Byam's report is true, *Oroonoko* could be Behn's construction of a collective uprising in order to argue that, in the mis-
shapen *mise-en-scène* of West Africa and the South America mainland,
only aristocratic leaders possess the competence to stage rebellions,
a notion that slaves' historical resistance pulverizes.

Class relationships, then, are a determining factor in Aphra Behn's
outlook, for many aristocrats undoubtedly benefitted from slavery.
The King himself held the Royal African Company's monopoly. But
slave traders by and large were self-serving, often arrogant entrepreneurs who did not represent traditional values cherished by aristocrats:

> Overseas mercantile expansion brought profits and adventure but
> also a sense, in some men, of disquietude. . . . Literate Englishmen
> generally . . . were concerned with the apparent disintegration of
> social and moral controls at home; they fretted endlessly over the
> "masterless men" who had once had a proper place in the social
> order but who were now wandering about, begging, robbing, raping.
> . . . They assailed what seemed a burgeoning spirit of avaricious-
> ness, a spirit which one social critic described revealingly as "a
> barbarous or slavish desire to turne the penie."[16]

Innovative and opportunistic, slave trade entrepreneurs profited from
the straightforward sale of commodities who in this case were human
beings. Buy low, sell high was a practice far removed from the aristocratic ethic supposedly based on honor, chivalry, and heredity. Put
bluntly, the slave trade attracted "low types," moneygrubbers who
didn't mind getting their hands dirty, people who flouted age-old
codes.

Aphra Behn's views that favor beneficent plantocrats dovetail with ideas expressed elsewhere in her writings. Behn's poem published in 1687 and entitled *To the Most Illustrious Prince Christopher, Duke of Albemarle, on His Voyage to His Government of Jamaica, a Pindarick* provides a mordant example.[17] The occasion of the poem is the Duke of Albemarle's departure to assume his appointment as Governor of Jamaica. The sadness that his departure causes is paralleled, according to the staunchly royalist narrator (surely an undisguised Behn), by the good fortune of the island's inhabitants, men and women of African descent, over whom he comes to rule. By stressing the inhabitants' good fortune, the narrator accentuates the Duke's distance from barbarous non-aristocratic plantocrats. His class defeated in the civil war, the Duke of Albemarle as governor or feudal overlord revives a culture in deep and reluctant decline from feudal structures. Behn appropriately draws on the language of Roman imperialism to announce the advent of the usurping colonist:

> Prepare, ye Sun-scorch'd Natives of the Shore,
> Prepare another Rising Sun t'adore,
> Such as has never blest your Horizon before.
> And you the Brave Inhabitants of the Place,
> Who have by Conquest made it all your own,
> Whose Generous and Industrious Race
> Has paid such Useful Tribute to the Crown;
> See what your Grateful King for you has done!

Despite assumptions about the happy collective response the Duke can anticipate, Behn also signals her awareness of potential peril when she describes his departure as if doting parents were allowing their "Darling" to be exposed to "Dangers." "With trembling Doubts and Fears at last they part,/ With Vows and Prayers commit Him to/ Heav'ns Care."

Behn's conspicuous omission of any explicit reference to slavery spotlights contemporary colonialist attitudes. Aside from predictable assumptions about Britain's right to economic "benefit" and "expansionism," Behn glosses over conditions she personally witnessed. More decisively, Behn allusively reinserts public loathing for the ongoing spectacle of North African pirates kidnapping and enslaving Britons on the Barbary Coast. The press, pamphlets, and published volumes clarify that Restoration society deplored slavery when the enslaved were British men and women.[18]

In its cavalier dismissal or evasion of the reality of island life, the poem can be read as an ironic comment on *Oroonoko,* published the following year. *Oroonoko* affirms the improbability of "native" gratitude and the appropriateness of Albemarle family anxieties. Put another way, *Oroonoko* does not sustain an emancipationist reading. Power is problematized because Behn intends to highlight her sympathy for illegitimate disempowerment of royalty. Oroonoko's commitment to general emancipation lasts only as long as his personal freedom depends on revolt. Take, for example, the narrator's explanation as to why the British do not enslave South American Indians:

> So that they [the Indians] being on all occasions very useful to us, we find it absolutely necessary to caress 'em as friends, and not treat 'em as slaves, nor dare we do other, their numbers so far surpassing ours in that continent. (Behn, *Oroonoko,* p. 5)

Her nonchalance toward the indigenous peoples (though some argue she speaks ironically) strongly resembles the comfort she derives from the fact that African military customs aid British merchants in acquiring slaves more easily.[19] Opposition to slavery is not the point. Rulers' rights—British and African—are at stake. Oroonoko, his grandfather, and the Coramantien ruling class are implicated in the system of colonial slavery, although we could reasonably assume that Oroonoko would have little specific knowledge of slavery's particular configuration outside of Africa: his only model of slavery is a traditional African one that he and other members of his family practiced.[20] We also learn that the impecunious and destitute palpably deserve slavery:

> Those who want slaves, make a bargain with a master, or a captain of a ship, and contract to pay him so much a-piece, a matter of twenty pounds a head, for as many as he agrees for, and to pay for 'em when they shall be deliver'd on such a plantation. . . . Coramantien, a country of blacks so called, was one of those places in which they found the most advantageous trading for these slaves, and thither most of our great traders in that merchandize traffic; for that nation is very warlike and brave; and having a continual campaign, being always in hostility with one neighbouring prince or other, they had the fortune to take a great many captives; for all they took in battle were sold as slaves, *at least those common men who could not ransom themselves* [my italics]. Of these slaves so taken, the General only has all the profit; and of these Generals our captains and masters of ships buy all their freights. (Behn, *Oroonoko,* p. 5–6)

Nonetheless, despite certain assumptions about "great traders in that merchandize" usurping the "rights" of Africans, the narrator draws the line at the enslavement of Oroonoko and Imoinda.

Her disgust plain, she describes the captain's treachery in selling Oroonoko and "an hundred of the noblest youths in the court" into slavery: "All in one instant [they] . . . were lashed fast in irons, and betrayed to slavery. . . . Some have commended this act as brave in the captain; but I will spare my sense of it" (Behn, *Oroonoko,* p. 31). The narrator (Behn) objects to this royal *class* of people being enslaved, not to the act of enslavement itself.[21] Implicitly the text indicts anyone who meddles with "legitimate" royal authority. Earlier, for example, Oroonoko's grandfather discovers that Imoinda still dotes on Oroonoko and sells her out of jealousy as if she were a "common slave," but in retrospect he regrets inflicting this "greatest revenge and the most disgraceful of any" fate on Imoinda and conceals the "affront" from Oroonoko.

The constant misrepresentation and romanticizing of African reality similarly undercuts an emancipationist reading. When Behn depicts the journey on the Middle Passage from West Africa to the Caribbean, to take an egregious example, since that voyage accounted for the deaths of approximately one-third of all slaves, she draws on the material of fantasy.[22] The captain placates Oroonoko with promises of freedom in order to secure cooperation from the other slaves who "bear their chains with . . . bravery . . . pleased with their captivity, since by it they hoped to redeem the prince." Behn here is underlining the need for obedient "subjects." Slaves are presumed to act in Oroonoko's best interests; simple-minded and easily pleased, they assent, even relish a vile captivity. The captain, moreover, unlike almost any other captain who transported Africans across a notorious source of terror—the Middle Passage—to which Olaudah Equiano in a later narrative bears testimony, pretends to negotiate in good faith with his captors.[23]

Oroonoko's appearance besides, unlike that of common slaves, more like a hero of Restoration tragedy, conforms to Western standards of beauty and wholesale racist attitudes:[24]

> His nose was rising and Roman, instead of African and flat. . . . The whole proportion and air of his face was so nobly and exactly formed, that, bating his colour, there could be nothing in nature more beautiful, agreeable and handsome (Behn, *Oroonoko,* p. 8).

Likewise, the "natives of the place . . . have all that is called beauty, except the colour" (Behn, *Oroonoko,* pp. 1, 3). Whether Behn Europe-

anizes Oroonoko to accommodate her text to her audience, or sub-
scribes to racist physiognomical standards, remains an open question.

African customs are decried as uncouth. For example, when Oroonoko and "several English gentlemen" prevail on the slaves to stop
bemoaning the captivity of Oroonoko—who is "infinitely glad to find
his grandeur confirmed by the adoration of all the slaves"—the slaves
then prepare "all their barbarous music" (Behn, *Oroonoko,* p. 38).

Scenes at the West African court also contort reality. Behn conjures
up a picture of a Middle Eastern seraglio that is arguably indebted to
Dryden's play, *Aureng-Zebe* (1676). Even the characters pair up, except that *Aureng-Zebe*'s patriarch, who tried to steal the beloved
Indamira is reincarnated as Oroonoko's grandfather and the possibly
incestuous abuser of Imoinda.[25] Imoinda herself is not sold to a lascivious sultan—variation on a common theme—but is forcibly married
to a lustful African patriarch, who deplores her "infidelity." Oroonoko's
superhuman encounter with a tiger (tigers in Africa?) is more grist for
the mill of Anglo-Africanist fantasy. A glance at contemporary histories
of warring West African tribes gives the lie to this baroque, highly
reductive charade.

The damaging view of Africa as "uncivilized" reaches a high point
of invention in the scene where Oroonoko kills Imoinda. Behn and
those from whom her inventions derive seem unacquainted with the
fact that most African cultures condemn killing for any purpose except
war or sacrifice.[26] As Winthrop Jordan pointedly argues (in a different
and later context), such extravagance signifies "a retreat from rational
engagement with the ethical problem posed by Negro slavery."[27] In
Behn's case, the clashing admixture of real-life tragedy and sentimental love emphasizes political inflections in the narrator's outlook.
Perhaps most striking of all is the narrator's behavior when Oroonoko's life hangs in the balance. First, just prior to his death, she
states to her family, "You may believe we were in no little affliction
for Caesar and his wife." But when the reconnaisance group returns
with Caesar, the narrator intones in a different vein:

> We ran all to see him. . . . When he was well enough to speak, we
> talked to him. . . . His discourse was sad, and the earthy smell about
> him so strong, that I was persuaded to leave the place for some
> time, being myself but sickly, and very apt to fall into fits of danger-
> ous illness upon an extraordinary melancholy. The servants, and
> Trefry, and the Chirurgeons, promised all to take what possible
> care they could of the life of Caesar; and I, taking boat, went with
> other company of Colonel Martin's, about three days journey down

> the river. But I was no sooner gone, than the governor, taking Trefry
> about some pretended earnest business, a day's journey up the
> river, having communicated his design to one Banister, a wild
> Irishman, and one of the council, a fellow of absolute barbarity, and
> fit to execute any villainy, but rich, he came up to Parham, and
> forcibly took Caesar, and had him carried to the same post where
> he was whipped; and causing him to be tied to it, and a great fire
> made before him, he told him he should die like a dog, as he was.
> (Behn, *Oroonoko,* p. 71)

Both times—when Oroonoko is caught after the rebellion and when
he is found after Imoinda's death—the narrator leaves and administrators act with impunity. Her absence helps to induce, even enables
these scenarios: "for I suppose I had authority and interest enough
there, had I suspected any such thing, to have prevented it." The first
time "all the females [flew] down the river," claiming to be scared of
Oroonoko whose army had no weapons to speak of; the second time
she was "fall[ing] into fits of dangerous illness upon [her] extraordinary melancholy" (Behn, *Oroonoko,* pp. 63, 71). In the narrator's
absence, he is mauled the first time and killed the second.

The question is why. Her adolescent flight parallels the moral corruption of a mercantilist usurping authority. Too fearful or too dolorous to remain, does she flee her own contradictions when Oroonoko
threatens the status quo? Or perhaps she acts consistently:[28] as long
as Oroonoko behaves as her ideal playfellow, embracing European
control as it were, she enjoys a thrilling life. She seems fascinated by
racial difference. But once he rebels against the king (symbolically),
her mask drops and she abandons him to his fate. And does the older
Behn, recapitulating old memories, condone the narrator's (her own)
youthful departure? Does she signal with no remorse the instant
othering of the prince-turned-rebel and the impermanence of her
friendship? Given these facts, it seems reasonable to speculate that
"behind the narrator's story we read a second story, the author's
story."[29] This is the person, after all, who is designated by said tyrannical administrators to "distract" Oroonoko from thinking about escape
by shunting him on exciting trips. At its core, the text exalts Oroonoko's heroism and rebellion as long as they do not threaten British
colonialism and royal authority.

Part Two: Feminist Polemic

The complex perspectives on slavery become more discernible in
relation to the question of female subjugation, a condition many

contemporary women were aware of and were loudly protesting. Behn's play concretely addresses the fact that "the marriage market was weighted against women, that there were thirteen women to every ten men in London."[30] She had lamented women's marital power-lessness from the time of *The Forced Marriage* (1670), her first play, until *The Lucky Chance,* published two years before *Oroonoko.* According to critic Robert Root, the latter play serves as "the capstone of the marriage motif in Behn's work."[31] Behn's political engagement with the lives of white British women and colonial slaves sprang from her own, albeit imperfectly known, circumstances. Although her parentage, details of her upbringing, and reasons for her sojourn in Surinam continue to be debated, certain facts are known: she was a spy for the king and loyally refused to celebrate in print the accession of William and Mary, a royalist to the last. She condemned male cultural domination and was persecuted in print (at least) for staking out a claim as a woman writer. According to poems and other biographical data, she related sexually to both men and women.

Concurring with feminist contemporaries and heirs, in *Oroonoko* with its wide geographical span from Britain to the African continent and the East Caribbean-South American mainland, Behn pronounces female lives a form of slavery and introduces a virtuous West African female as co-protagonist. The text's unique formulation of race-gender relationships enables Behn to assault at one stroke forced marriage, rape, slavery, the repudiation of women as other, and their consignment to biological beings. According to popular seventeenth- and eighteenth-century white British prescriptions of ideal womanhood, Imoinda's physical beauty and moral purity merge in a well-nigh perfect combination, her sexual objectification virtually inevitable in a society that legally buys and sells men and women.[32]

> . . . the beautiful black Venus to our young Mars [Oroonoko] . . . and of delicate virtues. . . . She was indeed too great for any but a prince of her own nation to adore. (Behn, *Oroonoko,* p. 9)

Oroonoko is so consumed with her "lovely modesty," with "that softness in her look and sighs," that he brings her a gift of "an hundred and fifty slaves in fetters . . . trophies of her father the general's military triumphs" (Behn, *Oroonoko,* p. 9–10). A tribute to Oroonoko's ardor, this gift is standard enough to warrant no comment. After West African battles, such enslavement traditionally followed, but—a critical difference—no stigma attached to these prisoners, nor was brutality a matter of course. Within these societies, slaves were customarily regarded as work apprentices and could rise to positions of power like other citizens. In Calabar, for example, slaves were known to have become princes.[33]

After agreeing to marry Oroonoko (Behn, *Oroonoko,* p. 11), Imoinda is summoned by Oroonoko's father, the "old monarch [who] saw, and burned . . . and would not delay his Happiness" (Behn, *Oroonoko,* p. 11). On penalty of death, Imoinda had to comply when he sent her the royal veil, her "sweetness and innocence of youth and modesty" compromised and degraded when he forces her "to expose her lovely person to his withered arms" (Behn, *Oroonoko,* p. 15). Given the king's extensive regal-patriarchal authority, Imoinda had virtually no choice.

This perverse alliance contrasts with Oroonoko's subtle ravishment of a sexually timid Imoinda, or perhaps an Imoinda more alive than Oroonoko to the consequences of the king's wrath toward both of them. Like the rebels' wives, she may be more realistic or prescient about punishment, since she already knows victimization. Further, although Oroonoko procures a sexual victory with the hint of a Restoration rake about him, the polyvoiced narrator compares Oroonoko's "ravishment" with interminable assaults by the "hundred and odd years old" king while insisting on the joy of mutual "romantic" love. Through nuanced paradoxes that almost amount to whispered innuendoes about Oroonoko's sexual conduct, the narrator unconsciously seems to defend her withdrawal from the site of torture following the insurrection. Female hesitation about lusty advances haunt the scene in Behn's low-profiled reenactment of a familiar form of subjection.[34]

> The Prince softly wakened Imoinda, who was not a little surprised with joy to find him there, and yet she trembled with a thousand fears. I believe he omitted saying nothing to this young maid that might persuade her to suffer him to seize his own, and take the rights of love. And I believe she was not long resisting those arms where she so longed to be; and having opportunity, night, and silence, youth, love and desire, he soon prevailed, and ravished in a moment when his old grandfather had been endeavouring for so many months. (Behn, *Oroonoko,* p. 22)

Circumstances allowing Imoinda no time to resolve her apprehension, she justifies her conduct as if she were male property, noting "that what she did with his grandfather had robbed him (Oroonoko] of her virgin honour, . . . having reserved that for him, to whom of right it belonged" (Behn, *Oroonoko,* p. 11). Denying technical virtue to Imoinda as well as robbing Oroonoko of his rightful *rite de passage,* a magnanimous Oroonoko connives "that she was wife to another" (Behn, *Oroonoko,* p. 11). Behn mockingly overturns the age's sexual politics—"a virtuous woman is a crown to her husband"—against itself.[35]

But Imoinda ends up in a no-win situation on both continents. When the king discovers her "treachery," he orders her to be "sold off" (Behn, *Oroonoko,* p. 24). Later he regrets not having put her "nobly . . . to death" rather than selling her "like a common slave, . . . [selling being] the greatest revenge, and the most disgraceful of any" punishment (Behn, *Oroonoko,* p. 25). When she arrives in Surinam, physical beauty, European-style implied, defines Imoinda once again: "the most charming black that ever was beheld on their plantation, about fifteen or sixteen years old. . . . I have [the narrator states earlier] seen a hundred white men sighing after her" (Behn, *Oroonoko,* p. 9). After overseer Trefry's confession, the narrator explains Trefry's feelings toward Imoinda and how she reacts to the community:

> For his part he had done nothing but sigh for her ever since she came; and . . . all the white beauties he had seen never charmed him so absolutely as this fine creature had done; and . . . no man of any nation ever beheld her that did not fall in love with her; and . . . she had all the slaves perpetually at her feet; and the whole country resounded with the fame of Clemene [Imoinda's slave name], "for so", said he, "we have christened her; but she denies us all with such a noble disdain, that it is a miracle to see, that she who can give such eternal desires, should herself be all ice and all unconcern. She is adorned with the most graceful modesty that ever beautified youth, the softest sigher—that, if she were capable of love, one would swear she languished for some absent, happy man, and so retired, as if she feared a rape even from the god of day, or that the breezes would steal kisses from her delicate mouth." (Behn, *Oroonoko,* p. 39)

Once again Behn's narrative soars to fanciful Anglo-Africanist heights. Is it conceivable—given plantocratic mores concerning African women—that a beautiful, powerless woman on the Middle Passage and a South American plantation, private property of British colonialists, would be allotted space to herself and remain unnoticed, let alone unviolated? In this case, Oroonoko voices more realistic colonial sentiments, notably as an African who is implicitly configured as ultimately less civilized than plantation overseer Trefry. And notably, too, the slaves act as an unindividuated corporeal body in eternal adoration.[36]

The royal prince expresses amazement at Trefry's refusal to capitalize on his command and rape Imoinda. In the same breath assuming
a different posture, he praises Trefry's dignified manner. (Perhaps,
also, Imoinda's fear of rape is being conveyed through Trefry's projection of Imoinda's feelings.) The end of the passage punctuates the
complexities of power relationships:

> "I do not wonder!" replied the prince, "that Clemene should refuse
> slaves, being, as you say, so beautiful, but wonder how she escapes
> those that can entertain her as you can do, or why, being your
> slave, you do not oblige her to yield?" "I confess," said Trefry, "when
> I have, against her will, entertained her with love so long, as to be
> transported with my passion even above decency, I have been ready
> to make use of those advantages of strength and force nature has
> given me. But Oh! she disarms me with that modesty and weeping,
> so tender and so moving, that I retire, and thank my stars she
> overcame me." The company laughed at his civility to a slave, and
> Caesar only applauded the nobleness of his passion and nature,
> since that slave might be nobler, or what was better, have true
> notions of honour and virtue in her. Thus passed they this night,
> after having received from the slaves all imaginable respect and
> obedience. (Behn, *Oroonoko*, pp. 39–40)

Through Imoinda's name-change to Clemene, a variation on *clém-
ence* or clemency (mercy and mildness), Behn also raises the issue
of "native alienation," of predators trying to expropriate their victims'
identity by renaming them. Like married women (Behn was one),
captives lost their name and identity, legally bearing their owner's
name until they died.[37] Beyond that, connections exist among superficially unrelated situations: aspects of Imoinda's plight suggest Behn's
disquiet about the treatment doled out to her as a female dramatist,
her displaced displeasure in being denied proper authority as a writer,
and the status of British women in forced marriages. Yet Imoinda's
protests on the eve of giving birth—she is doing "nothing but sigh
and weep for the captivity of her Lord, herself, and the infant"—are
represented as fitting responses for a prince's wife. Restoration society
required a wife to be the family's moral guardian. Oroonoko, by
contrast, does not recognize the rebel wives' moral trusteeship. What
contradicts social prescription unexpectedly, however, is Imoinda's
stance as the instigator-rebel who, resembling Behn in her struggle
to be recognized as a writer, fights to the bitter end. During the
rebellion, she becomes the

heroic Imoinda, who grown big as she was did nevertheless press near her lord, having a bow and a quiver full of poisoned arrows, which she managed with such dexterity, that she wounded several, and shot the Governor into the shoulder; of which wound he had like to have died, but that an Indian woman, his mistress, sucked the wound, and cleansed it from the venom. But however, he stirred not from the place till he had parlied with Caesar, who he found was resolved to die fighting, and would not be taken; no more would Tuscan or Imoinda. (Behn, *Oroonoko,* p. 60) [Subsequently, I discuss analogies between Imoinda's wounding of the Governor and Behn's use of her text to wound deputy Governor Byam.]

A sense of family and class status transforms Imoinda from victim to rebel and back to victim. Fearing that "if it were so hard to gain the liberty of two, it would be more difficult to get that for three," she then provokes Oroonoko into orchestrating a rebellion.[38] Curiously enough, the narrator consistently calls Oroonoko by his new name, Caesar, while dropping back into calling "Clemene" by her given name, Imoinda, almost immediately. Symbolically, leader Caesar with his European nomenclature placates the British bureaucracy by turning his back on the slaves and arranging the suicide pact. Behn subtly suggests links between sexual and economic (cross-race, patriarchal) rapacity. Imoinda's body is a "private family commodity for which the man could reasonably fight or go to law" or, in this case, assassinate by consent.[39] No woman's body should be, Behn protests, a site of sexual and economic exploitation. This time she excuses her personal withdrawal from the scene by suggesting that Oroonoko himself—living symbol of honor—is tainted.

Since Oroonoko must now honorably avenge his punishment, aristocratic style, he fears that Imoinda will be left "a prey, or at best a slave to the enraged multitude" (Behn, *Oroonoko,* p. 66). She will become someone else's property (Behn, *Oroonoko,* p. 66). He therefore proposes a mutual suicide pact to be undertaken after he avenges them both. Imoinda concurs, sweetly resigned in accordance with African ontological beliefs.[40] Or at least spiritual beliefs are an acceptable (and ostensible) rationale. But Behn also interrogates the injurious consequences of British ideas concerning virtuous, submissive womanhood while discursively stressing the "racial-cultural difference" of Oroonoko and Imoinda compared to the narrator:

He told her his design, first of killing her, and then his enemies, and next himself, and the impossibility of escaping; and therefore he told her of the necessity of dying. . . . While tears trickled down his

cheeks, hers were smiling with joy she should die by so noble a
hand, and be sent into her own country (for that is their notion of
the next world) by him she so tenderly loved, and so truly adored
in this; for wives have a respect for their husbands equal to what
any other people pay a deity; and when a man finds any occasion
to quit his wife, if he loves her, she dies by his hand; if not, he sells
her, or suffers some other to kill her. (Behn, *Oroonoko,* pp. 66–67)

Oroonoko's decision not to complete the pact bespeaks male-marital
power and his unquestioned right to the last word, as it were, although
compelling reasons dictate noncompletion. Imoinda is reunited with
Oroonoko after the rebellion only to be finally separated from him,
voluntary victim of the unwilling sacrificer. Their suicide pact constitutes a terminal effort to create a reintegrated (though moribund)
family unit, including the unborn prince or princess. After Oroonoko
slices Imoinda's "face" from her skull (Is Behn affirming stereotypic
notions of alleged African ferocity?), he seesaws in torment between
revenge and self-sacrifice—his sense of personal honor at stake as he
subjects Imoinda to the kind of treatment—though differently wrought
emotionally—to which he will soon be subjected himself:

All that love could say in such cases being ended, and all the
intermitting irresolutions being adjusted, the lovely, young and
adored victim lays herself down before the sacrificer, while he, with
a hand resolved, and a heart breaking within, gave the fatal stroke,
first cutting her throat, and then severing her yet smiling face from
that delicate body, pregnant as it was with the fruits of tenderest
love. . . . But when he found she was dead, and past all retrieve,
never more to bless him with her eyes, and soft language, his grief
swelled up to rage. He tore, he raved, he roared like some monster
of the wood, calling on the loved name of Imoinda. A thousand
times he turned the fatal knife that did the deed toward his own
heart, with a resolution to go immediately after her. But dire revenge, which was now a thousand times more fierce in his soul
than before, prevents him. . . . (Behn, *Oroonoko,* pp. 67–68)

Behn ends her text with a positive sentiment about Imoinda after the
final sensationalist death of Oroonoko, who avenged both of them
through awesome bravery, honorable (in his own terms) to the end:

Thus died this great man, worthy of a better fate, and a more
sublime wit than mine to write his praise. Yet, I hope, the reputation
of my pen is considerable enough to make his glorious name to

survive to all ages, with that of the brave, the beautiful, and the constant Imoinda. (Behn, *Oroonoko,* p. 73)

As an unmarried, sexually abused female, a disenfranchised slave or colonial object, a grieving, pregnant mother, a heroic rebel-warrior, and as a speaking individual within and despite a patriarchal colonial system, Imoinda cannot survive. Imbedded within Imoinda's tragic tale is Behn's explosion of the customary life-denying conceptualization of romantic love as desirable for women, albeit mishap-prone. The killing of Imoinda may be a perceptibly loving act but in portraying the scene as she portrayed the seduction and emancipation scenes—seemingly from the vantage point of Oroonoko—she invokes Imoinda's perspective and her own. Women and power may seem to be mutually exclusive terms but by enabling women (Behn's readers, the narrator, Imoinda, and Behn herself) to contemplate their own disempowerment, female readers can begin to resist the effect of patriarchal power and refuse to internalize it as a given of female life.[41]

PART THREE: INDICTMENT OR PROJECTION: EULOGY OR EXPIATION

A formerly powerless child, now a celebrated writer forced off the stage as a dramatist in 1688, Behn enables herself through the text's authority and influence to reclaim an authority denied her (or expropriated from her, or for reasons unknown, an authority that she declined to exercise) in Surinam twenty years earlier. More speculatively put, she textually travels outside her own society to explore personal and political destabilizations she had witnessed.[42] In the Epistle Dedicatory to *Oroonoko,* Behn mentions her inability to save Oroonoko, even though "I had none above me in that country."[43] She seems to refer here to the governor's death by drowning en route to Surinam that had stripped Behn of any semblance of power.[44]

Behn's incensed depiction of colonial officials who ignore her wishes and diabolically torture and kill Oroonoko permeates the text. Concurrently, that anger directed at specific entrepreneurs, by identifying individuals rather than the institution as the problem, mystifies the evil of slavery. At the opening of the tale, she equates a brash pride in profiteering with a chauvinist insensitivity toward slaves:

Those then whom we make use of to work in our plantation of
sugar, are negroes, black-slaves all together, who are transported
thither in this manner (Behn, *Oroonoko,* p. 5). . . . [Having] arrived
[in] Surinam, . . . the merchants and gentleman . . . sold them off,
as slaves, . . . not putting any two in one lot, because they would
separate them far from each other, nor daring to trust them together, lest rage and courage should put them upon contriving
some great action, to the ruin of the colony. (Behn, *Oroonoko,* p.
34)

She deplores the fact that uncivilized British bureaucrats lack the
"refinement" to make significant class distinctions among slaves. Even
reigning liberal philosopher John Locke betrayed this contemporary
prejudice when he exempted from his examination of natural rights
prisoners of war who were taken as slaves.[45]

While this classbound perspective that Anglo-Africanizes West African reality obviously informs orthodox attitudes, Behn's implied critique of family fracture further indicts the administrators. At the end
of *Oroonoko,* the systematic dismembering of Oroonoko while tied to
the stake to dissuade potential rebels, the absence of any pretense of
just law in the kangaroo court atmosphere—all unremittingly incul-
pate the savagery of slave-owners and managers, among whom were
many imported British felons accustomed to the likes of Newgate's
harsh penal environment. Unlike the Duke of Albemarle, "these people" are uncouth colonial canaille, stalwarts of the status quo no
doubt, but from a traditional royalist's perspective, "not one of us."
Moreover, since the British perpetrators were formerly persecuted
Newgate felons, they are witnessing someone who is reliving unjust
possibilities inherent in their former existences. The relationships
between Oroonoko and Byam and his cohorts not only microcosmically reenacts the British colonial but also the British penal system.
Self-projecting and self-punishing assassins perversely gaze on themselves as they torture the prince to death.

Stated plainly, Behn's opposition to the colonial status quo is distinct from her response to slavery. Thus she vindicates herself and
her role in a friend's death, as she indicts these predators—expatriate
felons-cum colonial nouveaux riches—by presenting another version
of the "facts." Allusively her praise of Albemarle intensifies Byam's
barbarism. *Oroonoko* is Behn's private victory against Byam and his
gang, a vendetta satisfactorily concluded. Behn's anger at the colonialist ruling class derived from her royalist politics. As Jerry Beasley,
Maureen Duffy, and others persuasively argue, perhaps Aphra Behn

could be using the African-Surinam narrative to denounce the recent regicide and the subsequent diminution in royal power: Oroonoko's "honorable" character, his sophisticated education by a French tutor who invokes Charles II's Francophile court, discountenances and displaces the idea of usurping and then enslaving a prince of the royal line:[46]

> Modern depravity is represented here by the invading force of colonialism, which opposes to the true aristocracy of an ancient warrior culture the irresistible corruptions of exchange value.[47]

In a society still negotiating for stability after fundamental social change, many royalist readers would embrace this interpretation and would have decoded the tale as such. With an African cover story, Behn may be subtly reaffirming her commitment to divine right and denouncing both seventeenth-century revolutionaries ("vilest creatures" who overthrew Charles I—also known as Oroonoko) and collaborator-traitors to the King's cause (the slaves—"dogs, treacherous and cowardly"—who will not resist to the bitter end). On an autobiographical, more mischievous note, a deeply imbedded act of deft revenge against Charles II who landed Behn in debtors' prison when he refused to pay her for her post-Surinam spying services in Holland might lurk between the lines.

Lack of subsequent retribution against Oroonoko's persecutors may have fortified Behn's ire, writing decades after the event. Professor K. A. Sey hazards a likely guess that the murderers were probably among the "notorious villains" who were "afterwards hanged when the Dutch took possession of the place, others sent off in chains" (Behn, *Oroonoko,* p. 65). Behn relishes flaunting the name of Byam, the chief administrator who took over her putative father's job after his death, and reducing it, almost, to a symbol of vice. The publication of living villains' names was integral to her revenge. She portrays a heroic daughter's return, but sadly stresses her silenced condition; she is neither officially nor perhaps yet appropriately recognized, and she smarts still from emotional wounds.

Moreover, she probes beyond the debate about specifically royal power to the larger question of misogynous sway and its negative effect on unmalleable females. These include the fictional heroine, Imoinda, and Behn herself as youthful observer, as symbols of lawful female authority corruptly denied.

Many oppositions and multiple subject positions coexist in *Oroonoko:* Behn upholds slavery, the status quo, and royal power in the face of a startling trio of events: the emancipationist episode; her abandonment of Oroonoko; and jabbing attacks on the domination of women and colonial malevolence. As a distinguished representative of the colonial ruling class, the friend of Oroonoko, and a royalist, the narrator's conflicts over colonialist assumptions come most into play after the rebellion.[48] Objectively and silently, she reproves the rebellion while mourning the cold-blooded torture and murder of a royal prince as well as the destabilizing of power. Despite being Oroonoko's companion who formerly diverted him from thoughts of escape, she fails twice to support him when he is *in extremis.* She withdrew and may, in her own eyes, have forsaken her friend. Thus the "most fawning fair-tongued fellow in the world"—the narrator's characterization of Byam—could be as much a hidden self-projection as it is a denunciation of her political enemy in Surinam. Part of the text's ambivalence springs from Aphra Behn's struggle or rather "her ego's struggle against [the] painful [and] unendurable idea of abandoning her friend."[49] Here we have text as rapprochement.

Behn abandoned Oroonoko when he decisively positioned himself, pioneer precursor of Toussaint L'Ouverture, against the interests of the ruling class. On the other hand, she vilifies his torturers, unsophisticated neophytes and parvenus holding the reins of power, no match in class for a nobleman like Oroonoko who calmly smokes a pipe while being dismembered and castrated. Not only that, but just as Oroonoko silences Imoinda on the hilltop, her tongue effectively cut, just as the narrator denies her protagonists' African physiognomy, so the colonists silenced the narrator and Behn herself as well as Oroonoko—or tried to. Forced into subjection like her hero, though the narrator's status as an other takes an entirely different form, she eulogizes Oroonoko, makes quiet reparation for deserting him, and softly disparages his treatment of Imoinda. The "I" also speaks Oroonoko and Imoinda in direct and indirect speech, sounding their heroism and martyrdom into the void, into the traditional Eurocentric silence about African slave insurrectionists; the "I" sounds the pair into the very world that would never have received or believed first-person accounts by Africans themselves. Read dialogically, Byam is there too, simultaneously upheld as a British bureaucrat convicted of atrocity run amuck.

Perhaps that is why, as dramatist Thomas Southerne informs us, Behn told the story of Oroonoko "more feelingly than she writ it."[50] And, Southerne might have added, she told it formidably because to assume or reclaim the speaker's voice after the fact and retell the tale allows her to claim a new power over the situation. It was as if, on the eve of her death with nothing to lose, Behn decided to reevaluate her conduct as a young woman.[51] And perhaps unwittingly she transposed quarrels with her former actions on to villains she already despised. In *Oroonoko,* then, Behn constructs a paradigm of slavery, aspects of which became constitutive elements in colonial discourse for the next century and a half until the Emancipation Bill passed in 1834. First of all, Behn affirms an abolitionist and emancipationist perspective in Oroonoko's famed speech yet ends up implicitly privileging plantocratic ideology, inflaming Eurocentric attitudes toward Africans, and bolstering the colonial status quo. Furthermore, she airs the problematic of sexual politics in Restoration society by projecting anxieties about the condition of white British women on to her discussions of class-gender relationships in West Africa and Surinam. Lastly, *Oroonoko* is Behn's life and politics in retrospect, a reclamation of her eyes and ears, her witnessing and her voice, the avenging of the fifteen-year-old silenced subject.

Chapter 3

Seventeenth-Century Quaker Women: Displacement, Colonialism, Anti-Slavery

SPIRITUAL EQUALITY, THE RETREAT FROM MILITARISM, AND THE POLITICS OF COMPENSATION

Oroonoko's polemic on freedom as a human right that anticipated future anti-slavery demands, sounded a void in the first century of white British women's commentaries on slavery. By contrast, religious equality surpassed emancipation as a more consistently discussed topic in these hundred years. Among its liveliest early proponents were women in the Society of Friends whose spiritual beliefs and refashioned political direction explain their unorthodoxy.[1] Like Behn's writings, their commentaries derived from first-hand personal experience, but they largely confined themselves to discussions of spiritual access and compensation. Demands for full-scale emancipation within the Society, early by the standards of society in general, were a hundred years away.

I referred earlier to female militancy during the Civil War. Quaker women were in the thick of it but quickly lost any power and influence they had garnered by the Restoration. By 1661 to 1662 Quaker men and women experienced severe repercussions for opposing the status quo—so much so that, as Barry Reay compellingly argues, the Society of Friends at the point of its threatened dissolution began to conceal prior militarism to avoid persecution.[2] In Reay's words,

> Before [1661] it is impossible to talk, as it is later, of the Quakers as a predominantly pacifist group. Self-preservation after the resto-

51

ration of the monarchy in 1660, disillusionment with the effective-
ness of political action, encouraged them to project their pacifism
backwards. Pacifism was not a characteristic of the early Quakers:
it was forced upon them by the hostility of the outside world.[3]

The Quaker Act of 1662 that forbade religious assemblies of over
five members incited soldiers to invade Friends' meetings, "beating
and kicking and hurling the people on heaps and pushing them with
the ends of their muskets and weapons."[4] In the face of such gratuitous
dragooning, Quakers retreated tacitly from overt activism. However,
a few among them—Dewars Moray, Dorothy White, and Hester Bid-
dle—did continue to agitate for activism.[5] Not until two years after
the Great Fire of London (1666) did such violence substantially dimin-
ish, and then only temporarily.[6] By that time moves were afoot to
reorganize and streamline the Society in accordance with their strategic and understandably self-preserving withdrawal from vanguardist
hostilities.

During these decades of policy transformation, George Fox's epistolary exhortations to Friends in the Caribbean persisted and even
escalated.[7] By 1657 in an Epistle addressed to "Friends beyond Sea,
that have Black and Indian Slaves," he was urging unconditional access
to the gospel.[8] In 1671 he entreated planters to "endeavour to train
[slaves] up in the Fear of God . . . [and] after certain years of servitude
. . . make them free."[9] Fox's language in regard to possessing and
training slaves underscores predetermined relations of power between Friends and their slaves and upholds the colonial bureaucracy
while urging the importance of spiritual practice. In 1674 he was
encouraging Friends to step up their counseling of the reluctant or
the faithless: "and all that are not Faithful, let them [women] be
admonished to Faithfulness, that so they may come into the Light,
and Life, and service of God and Christ."[10] Caribbean administrators
abhorred this concern for slaves' spiritual welfare and subsequently
accused Friends of provoking insurrection. In 1675 slaves in Barbados
were planning the first known major rebellion, a "Coromantee plot led
by Tony and Cuffee,"[11] which was exposed after an informer, Anna,
alias Fortuna, tipped off her master, Judge Gyles Hall. White governors
grossly avenged the leaders. William Edmundson, another Friend who
traveled with Fox to Barbados in the 1670s and argued before the
governor that all souls were born with an "eternal destiny," no exceptions, was accused of incitement, since the racist governor scoffed at
the idea of slaves unilaterally executing a rebellion.[12] Unlike Fox,
Edmundson openly challenged slavery and earmarked himself as a

target for the plantocracy, an upstart oppositional outsider. Anti-Quaker laws were subsequently enacted to undermine potential support for armed rebellion.[13]

To make matters more difficult, Quakers themselves were being subjected to persecution in Barbados.

> [Since] Barbados was the first island of the West Indies to come into English possession[,] Quakers had been banished to this island and to Jamaica; and Fox visited them on his missionary journey.[14]

In the 1650s, when Lieutenant-Colonel Rous, an affluent plantation-owning friend of the Governor, had joined the Society, their Barbadian membership grew rapidly; the island became a missionary headquarters.[15] But by October 1677 William Penn and Thomas Corbett examined "the laws and charter of Barbados," with a view to addressing the King and Council [of the House of Commons] on behalf of Quaker "sufferers" there.[16] Fox was well aware of such possible responses as the "savage flogging, brandings, and imprisonments that occurred in the American colonies."

In 1678 Fox bowed to pressure, pleading his case before the Barbadian Governor against an accusation that Friends were persuading slaves to resist. Far from confessing that he sided with the rebels, Fox denounced general uprising as "a thing we utterly abhor in our hearts" and counselled slaves "to love their masters and mistresses, to be faithful and diligent [so they will receive "kind and gentle" treatment] ... nor commit adultery, nor fornication nor curse, swear, nor lie."[17] Since anti-establishment activities in Britain and Friends' aid supplied earlier to Caribbean slave insurrectionaries had threatened their sectarian existence, Fox opted for the more self-preserving tactic of non-resistance. There are clear parallels here with Quakers resorting to class order and urging servants to be obedient; these orders are coming out as official Meeting positions at the same time. Just as much or perhaps more to the point, a substantial number of Friends still owned slaves, the result of "filthy covetousness," and persisted in doing so until well into the eighteenth century.[18] Nor were Friends exempt from the double standard of society at large regarding Barbary Coast slavery. Complicitous with Caribbean slavery, Friends also engineered plans to redeem any of their members:

> taken captive by the Barbary pirates. The first appeal for funds, issued in 1679, brought in more than eleven hundred pounds and at no time did the balance fall below four hundred pounds ...

> The earliest reference so far found in the Quaker records to the redemption of captives is a note of a gift of ten pounds in 1674 to help two Friends in Turkey, and the great majority of the entries occur between 1679 and 1686.[19]

Helping enslaved Europeans and upholding colonial slavery remained as an unacknowledged contradiction. Despite compromises with the plantocracy, however, elements in the Friends' community opposed slavery. In 1688 colonial America, Francis Daniel Pastorius mounted the first public anti-slavery protest in Germantown, Pennsylvania, which inaugurated an ongoing though unsystematic series of protests until emancipation became Friends' official policy in 1761.[20]

The Effect of Pacifism on Female Friends

Quietist ideology seriously circumscribed the lives of Quaker women because, unlike women in British society at large, female Friends had wielded substantial power within the Society of Friends.[21] Not to mince matters, the pacifist retreat resulted in such restrictive roles for Quaker women that the Society's view of women became virtually indistinguishable from the view held in British society as a whole.[22] Nonetheless, Quaker women fought to hold their own and at least a celebrated handful refused to be bound by the new conservative politic.

The first person to join George Fox in the Society of Friends and a single-minded, open-hearted radical by the time she met him, Elizabeth Hooton inspired men and women alike; she probably also motivated Fox's first defense of a woman preacher. In fact, the received view of the early Fox as the Society's original proponent of women's rights disregards the fact that women's sturdy activism predates Fox's support for it, although Fox certainly welcomed women's active participation. In Elaine Hobby's words:

> Women had played important parts in the development of the Familists and Anabaptists earlier in the century . . . . [and] while it is true that Fox supported a woman's right to speak in church, the initiative in the much-cited case was taken by the woman who asked the question.[23]

Edward Burrough mentions "the very first occasion of the first setting up that meeting of women, to visit the sick and to search out the necessities of the poor, weak, widows and aged."[24] At one point, Fox rejected out of hand John Bunyan's view that women were "that simple and weak sex."[25] A certain sentence from the Bible frequently quoted by Fox more aptly expressed his views: "Christ renews man and woman up into the image of God as they were in before they fell."[26] But times changed, although the association of women with benevolence and healing did not.[27]

Monthly and quarterly meetings were established in 1667 and 1668 to organize the Society more systematically. Formal meetings, including meetings of women alone, were established "in some though not all areas about a decade later," justified by the fact that, in Fox's words, "many things . . . [are] proper for the women to look into . . . which is not so proper for the men."[28] Gender-segregated meetings signified a new direction for the Society, a recognition of female influence, and (we could speculate) an attempt to suppress or dilute that power through marginalization. Before marriages between Friends could take place, women's meetings had to grant permission; as people "in the know," more specifically home-oriented than their male counterparts, women could head off domestic strife. In response, men who objected to women's meetings and felt "subjected to the power of women" formed separatist groups.[29] They ran afoul of young and old alike.[30] Some of the most powerful women in these Women's Meetings were quite elderly—Margaret Fell herself and Theophilia Townsend, for instance. They had been around and even active during the 1650s, as Civil War activists. In fact, as Elaine Hobby puts it, one of the more distressing things about policy statements from the Women's Meetings is that they include statements by older women counselling younger women on being good and dutiful wives and mothers.

The transformative Restoration vision of ideal womanhood, spelled out by the anonymous author of *The Ladies Calling* (1673), included modesty, meekness, affability, and piety. Precisely this vision had rendered the 17th-century poet, Katherine Philips, "matchless" in the eyes of many contemporaries and stamped the earthier, more seemingly libidinal Aphra Behn beyond the pale. In the preface to *The Ladies Calling,* the anonymous author cited women's intellects "below" those of men: "Yet sure in the sublimest part of humanity, they are their equals. They have souls of as divine an Original, as endless as Duration, and as capable as infinit Beautitude." The author went on to comment that women "will forget that more intrinsic part of their being, live as if they were all body, reject the Manna, and rave after the Quails, that destruction . . . they must own to spring from themselves."[31]

Becoming a female traveling missionary in the Society of Friends may not have been what the author of *The Ladies Calling* meant by raving after quails, but in that age of patriarchal mandate and restipulation of women's roles, missionary work presented an acceptable way out of the impasse in power relations, its popularity attested to by the number of females who offered their services.[32] In the 1650s, having envisioned Friends as people with a sacred "universal mission [to carry] their message beyond seas." Fox organized groups to implement that mission. The qualification for "the ministration of the Gospel was anointing or being inspired to speak at a meeting after serious self-examination."[33] According to David Brion Davis, Friends were the first English Protestant evangelizers of African-Caribbean slaves and provided an operational model. Uneasy about slavery, Morgan Godwyn had vigorously denounced Friends, but he had also witnessed the activities of George Fox in Barbados, thereby presumably softening his opinion.[34] As Joyce Irwin comments, "in accordance with the generally prominent role of women in the Society," a strikingly high percentage of missionaries were women.[35] In 1655 Mary Fisher and Anne Austin were first in the Caribbean, Fisher having determined on "a moshon to Barbadoes."[36] Many women who joined the Society, moreover, had formerly been itinerant preachers and simply continued that practice in a new guise. By the 1660s and 1670s, missionary networks radiated far afield. When Anne Whithead wrote from England to Women's Meetings in Barbados requesting money to be distributed among local sufferers, she received a reply from 187 women.[37] Ignoring orthodox rules of behavior, some Quaker women ventured abroad to ameliorate the situation of slaves, remaining silent about any conceivable contradiction between a commitment to spiritual equality and the condoned institutionalization of human bondage. Of course, any agitation on behalf of slaves would automatically place Britons on the border territory of their community. Having said that, I want to turn now to the case of Alice Curwen, who bypassed some of Fox's proslavery accommodations, subtly and discursively querying the institution's legitimacy.

ALICE CURWEN

In the 1670s Alice Curwen insisted not only on the right of slaves to inner light and spiritual salvation but, more crucially, she anticipated an emancipationist outlook in her refusal to treat Africans as commodities. Her personal circumstances explain these novel ideas and praxis.

When Alice Curwen and Thomas Curwen, Friends from Lancashire, visited Barbados about 1675, renewed persecution was driving many Quakers from the island. Long eager to evangelize despite her husband's reluctance, Alice Curwen was undeterred. Besides, she was intent on evading the severe harassment of Quakers in Britain and the specific intimidation of her own family.[38] In the opening of *A Relation of the Labour, Travail and Suffering of Alice Curwen,* she explains how she was spiritually motivated to record her experiences. She cannot ignore God's words speaking through her; this obeisance to the law of the father enunciated through herself as ambassador for the civilizing mission permits her also to question in the name of that same law. Hence a form of double-voiced discourse emerges. Alice Curwen obeys divine patriarchal mandates but her activities stamp her as spiritually headstrong. Logically this removes her from stipulated female roles both in society at large and in the Society of Friends:

> The 10th day of the 11th month, 1677. When I was retired in my Mind waiting upon the Lord, it was opened in my Heart by the invisible Power of the living God, the vertue of which I felt, and the Springs of Life being witnessed, I was moved to write of the Dealings of the Lord with me, and of my Travels and of my Testimony in writing, since I went from my outward Being; and what I had received from Friends in writing, of the good Success, and Blessing, and Presence of the invisible God, . . . And while I questioned in my Mind, Why I should write . . . it was said in the secret of my Heart, What thou hast kept, write: but I fearing said within myself, Why should it be known? and the Answer was, For the Encouragement of them that hereafter may put their Truth in the Lord; and then I was made willing to write as followeth.[39]

Curwen then deplores the "great tribulations" suffered by "servants of the Lord" in Boston, Massachusetts, mentioning "cruel whippings . . . bonds and imprisonments" (Curwen, *A Relation,* p. 2). She and her husband journeyed to several other towns on the East Coast, but, unlike her husband, Curwen remained apprehensive about visiting Barbados. Eventually, as she tells it, her obedience to patriarchal law, her faith as she might have called it, infused her with the necessary courage. In their seven-month Barbadian visit from March to October 1677, the couple inspired several "convincements"—"we had good service both amongst White and Blacks"—which they attributed to their facility for radiating "everlasting praises." They aimed to save one and all "in every nation." In this sense of mission Alice Curwen echoed the reasons for traveling of Friend Sarah Cheevers who had set off with Katherine Evans in 1658 for Alexandria and had travelled widely abroad:

> He hath chosen me, who am the least of all: but God, who is rich in mercy, for his own name's sake hath passed by mine offences, and hath counted me worthy to bear testimony to his holy name, before the mighty men of the earth. Oh the love of the Lord to my soul! My tongue cannot express, neither hath it entered into the heart of man, to conceive of the things that God hath laid up for them that fear him. . . . What profit is there, to gain the whole world, and lose your own souls? Seek first the kingdom of God and the righteousness thereof, and all other things shall be added to you.[40]

The Curwens' visit coincided with the inception of separate Friends' meetings in Britain and the concomitant diminution in women's power. Race-segregated meetings in Barbados were initiated over the next five years. Although the island had been formerly viewed by Quakers, in Friend George Rofe's phrase, as "the nursery of the truth," a place where Friends could freely discuss and propagate their beliefs, they now felt obliged to accede to government pressure and relinquish their former more liberal practices.[41]

One remarkable incident recounted in her *Relation* denotes Alice Curwen's independent mind and spirit. Her narrative concerns her chiding a widow for making spiritual decisions on behalf of the slaves: "For in love we came to visit thee."[42] This account, printed in 1680, the year following her death, pinpoints her concern for slaves' spiritual compensation or religious conversion. She tells of hearing about a widow in Barbados named Martha Tavernor, who had "Negro's to her Servants, who were convinced of God's Eternal Truth." Whether Curwen heard this from a missionary or slaves is unclear but most likely she received her information from a missionary who in turn Eurocentrically "voiced" the opinions of slaves. Curwen goes on to describe how she "was moved to go speak to the Woman for their coming to our Meetings." Curwen's reference to "their coming to our meetings" exemplifies a familiar discourse about slaves. What Mary Louise Pratt calls a "familiar, wide-spread, and stable form of othering" is spoken by a European subject or narrator in the stance of an observer. These totalized others, Pratt goes on to say, are:

distilled even further into an iconic "he" (the standardized adult male specimen). This abstracted "he"/"they" is the subject of verbs in a timeless present tense, which characterizes anything "he" is or does not as a particular historical event but as an instance of a pregiven custom or trait. . . . Through this discourse, encounters with an Other can be textualized or processed as enumerations of such traits.[43]

In a dialogical sense, the text yields other possibilities. In at least containing within her remark the possibility of the slaves' own initiative in requesting to attend prayer-meetings, Curwen indirectly gives voice to unheard but physically present speakers and alludes to earlier dialogues that restore some humanity to now faceless, speechless "Negroes." It is not simply Widow Tavernor as the "concrete listener" who enters in but slaves, too, who could be supplicating on their own spiritual behalf, though always indirectly and through the Quaker protagonist.[44]

Moreover, if Curwen unilaterally assumes that "Negroes" would welcome, benefit from, or even more to the point, that they sought membership, then she effectively discounts slaves' own spiritual practices. African religious and ontological beliefs, thought by most white Britishers to be connected with devils, superstition, fetish, idolatry, and savagery, are thus rendered invisible. They are spiritual practices probably feared in a Quaker community that is trying to hold its own against persecution. And this invisibility and denial of African reality is reconfirmed by the fact that speechless slaves do not appear to have a (thinking) consciousness. Not subjects but objects, they occupy no space in the discourse outside of the observer's indirect statements.

When Tavernor refused Curwen's request, the latter explained her spiritual purpose in a letter: she could not "pass by, but in Love write to thee, for in Love we came to visit thee, and to invite thee and thy Family [i.e., household] to the Meeting [of Friends]." Curwen extends the Friends' all-embracing spirit to Tavernor and Tavernor's household. She compares Tavernor to "him that was invited to work in the Vineyard and went not," a reference to the parable of the two sons whose father invited them to work, whereupon the first refused "but afterward he repented, and went," while the second responded affirmatively and then did not go.[45] Just as Jesus warns that scoffing chief priests and scribes will not attain the kingdom of heaven, as repentant tax collectors and prostitutes will, so Curwen suggests that Tavernor, who affects to believe but denies and turns away, similarly jeopardizes her chance of salvation. Having summarily delivered a spiritual threat, Curwen then refers to "thy servants, *whom thou callest thy slaves*" [my emphasis]. She reprimands Tavernor for trying to "reign over" the consciences of "others" in "Matters of Worship of the Living God," reminding her that "thou thyself confessedst, that they had Souls to save as well as we." Curwen's self-conscious and perhaps sarcastically rendered rejection of the word *slaves* and her deliberate substitution of the word *servants* marks a forthright and critical rupture in the text; by redefining "slaves" she inflects the word with multiple significations, altering not only the conditions of possibility of the word but, metonymically, of slaves themselves. Curwen speaks through Tavernor to her readers and simultaneously speaks in her own voice, asking them to decide between her opinion and the law's opinion, as represented by Tavernor. A few lines later, Curwen reiterates her objection to Tavernor's terminology: "For I am persuaded that if they whom thou callest thy slaves, be Upright-hearted to God, the Lord God Almighty will set them Free in a way that thou knowest not, for there is none set Free but in Christ Jesus, for all other Freedom will prove but a Bondage." Curwen's refusal to use the term "slaves" for West African peoples signifies an anomalous non-compliance for her epoch and underscores her personal strength and political conviction; she sees herself as a spiritual model. Implicitly, her moral terminology amounts to an absolute repudiation of popular ideas in conventional society about women's silence and mental inferiority. Quakers had been positioned for so long at the receiving end of superior attitudes toward "others" that Curwen equated *Quakers* and *slaves* as synonymous and interchangeable terms in that one sense. To attack Tavernor's prejudicial household rules was part and parcel of taking up cudgels outside colonial law. Even within Quaker circles, Curwen's knife-edged responses cut at the status quo. Alice Curwen disparages Tavernor's labelling of people as "slaves" because such nomenclature denies their sacred worth. On the other hand, Curwen also "fudges" an issue here. She offers "Christ Jesus" as "Freedom", seeming to ignore, refuse, and silence the real "Bondage" that the slaves must still suffer, whatever they are called. But an ambiguity lurks here. She draws such particular attention to bondage that psychologically she renders it more abhorrent. Hence it stands out as a practice to at least address, if not think about resisting. Perhaps contemporary Quaker exhortations to *servants* to be of good behavior and morality are relevant to an understanding of Curwen's radicalism.

Certain historical transitions that occurred in the 1670s explain Curwen's temerity. In the first place, she journeyed to Barbados when controversy was rife about how to describe Africans in captivity. In the 1660s the Royal African Company still used fictional terminology to comply with requirements about what constituted legal cargo: shipped Blacks were "Negro-Servants." By 1677 after considerable posturing, the Solicitor-General proclaimed that "negroes ought to be esteemed goods and commodities."[46] Curwen unequivocally rejects the Solicitor-General's twofold denial of African humanity, experientially aware of devices employed by the powerful to run aground those perceived as outsiders. The testimony of countless Friends—and they testified in peril of their lives during the Civil War—deplored all infringements of individual liberties and physical punishment of any person. The four-year sentence that Thomas Curwen served for writing a document denouncing a Friends' political enemy, the zealous jailing of Quakers in general, and even the very name Quaker, implying ecstacy and hence incurring ridicule, kept Alice Curwen close to the consequences of persecution.[47] Resolutely and frontally, she asserts a universal human right to "inner light" by actively rejecting the language of bondage as illegitimate. Taking care of slaves was taking care of Friends.

In attempting to undermine Tavernor's individual form of religious persecution, Curwen also ironically (but unconsciously?) underlined Quaker practice in maintaining slaves and tacitly condoning the institution and their commitment to spiritual equality. Curwen's demurral at the terminology of slavery that invoked Edmundson's earlier objections placed her in a very small but distinct group of Friends who never fully supported slavery's legitimacy. These early manumission-inclined Friends foreshadowed eighteenth-century abolitionists who privileged the material rather than the spiritual condition of slaves in their advocacy of abolition and emancipation.

On the other hand, Curwen's argument about the right of slaves to unconditional spiritual expression was based on a European belief that all human beings potentially constituted God's world-wide Christian family. Her text assumes that no one would *want* to be excluded, but would, instead, crave to emulate Europeans and conform to their beliefs.

And second, as a self-appointed spokeswoman for slaves, Curwen denies, both in voice and name, slaves with a "convincement." Troped as the epitome of victimization, Africa and slaves "speak through and by virtue of the European imagination. . . . Not so much a pen writing as a voice pronouncing."[48] But we cannot discount the possibility—often mentioned covertly in slave narratives—that African-Caribbean slaves in Tavernor's household realized the advantage of accommodating themselves to organized Christian proselytizers. The stigma of immorality and innate benightedness disappear at one blow. Given the temporal reality of slavery, to mimic the Quakers would be to divide the whites and be attached to a group that was theoretically committed to humane treatment. In mimicking, too, blacks make subjects of themselves, a fact quietly implied in Curwen's text.[49] That slaveowners so violently opposed conversion suggests that slaves discerned its benefits; although Curwen technically silences and promiscuously collectivizes slaves, their presence ruptures her discourse and indicates internalized political conflicts.

Alice Curwen's *Relation* denotes an early transitional phase in female anti-slavery discourse. As Friends sought to establish a working relationship with Caribbean plantocrats, Curwen exposed a fundamental fissure between Friends' religious ideas and cultural practice. She unearthed an occasionally glimpsed cleft in Friends' response to slavery that kept widening. By the 1760s, Friends no longer could reconcile or ignore contradictions between their philosophy and practice; no surprise, the London Yearly Meeting in 1761 outlawed slavery among its members.[50]

ELIZABETH HOOTON

Elizabeth Hooton preceded Alice Curwen as a missionary drawn to emancipation, her refusal to imbibe orthodox attitudes impressively evident in her encounter with Indians in colonialist America. Like Curwen, in voicing and speaking for "others" as well as herself, she depicts Indians as "barbarous savage people, which neither know God nor Christ in any profession, [who] have been willing to receive us into their wigwams, or houses, when these professors [of the Truth, a reference to anti-Quaker Christians] would murther us."[51] Hooton refutes claims of alleged Indian ferocity in her own ironic voice while indirectly denoting the indigenous peoples as warm and hospitable to another group of persecuted "others," Quakers themselves. Her experiences moved her to ally with Indians and their sufferings rather than with truth assassins: "the love I bear to the Souls of men makes me willing to undergo whatsoever can be inflicted on me.[52]

On another occasion, Hooton's commitment to a harmonious global community based on love—albeit Eurocentrically conceived—elicited empathy for the underprivileged. Unconventionally, she blames those who provoke starving men into robbery through privation rather than blaming the black robbers themselves:

There is a great Cry of the Poore being Robbed by Rich mens Negroes. . . . Now it is the Duty of Every Man to take care and see their family have sufficient food and any thing else they stand in need of.[53]

When Hooton visited Barbados with Fox in 1671 as an official Friends' missionary, she knew that Fox had proposed limiting the terms of a slave's servitude and had advocated that the master-slave relationship be "informed by love." Just before she died, she invoked this principle when, at seventy years old, she wrote to an island governor, echoing both Fox's and Curwen's language of love and salvation in her injunction: "Soe returne to the Light in thy Conscience which will not let thee doe any Wrong to any if thou be obedient to it."[54]

By assailing the cruelty of non-Quaker whites toward Friends, Elizabeth Hooton declined to accept anything at face value. In blaming British exploiters ("Rich men") for food-stealing by "Rich mens Negroes," she similarly questioned common seventeenth-century assumptions about the sacred order of things. "Rich mens Negroes" imbeds a question as well as a statement. Why should rich men "possess" any Africans? Once again, the material conditions of Friends' lives, physical punishments they endured, the constant psychological persecution and political subjection, their heightened awareness about the necessity to retaliate in some way or other, and their devotion to the right of untrammeled spiritual access made them more likely than most European groups to contest the institution of slavery.

JOAN VOKINS

Another celebrated Quaker and traveling missionary, Joan Vokins, recited similar responses when she met slaves in 1681: "I met with many Friends at Bridgtown . . . and most Days I had two or three meetings a Day, both among the Blacks, and also among the White People. And the power manifested, so that my soul was often melted therewith, even in the Meetings of the Negro's or Blacks, as well as among Friends."[55] The segregation of British people from African-Caribbeans at certain meetings, though the causes differed, paralleled the recently mandated segregation of men and women at Friends' meetings in Britain and the Caribbean.[56] Such separations depended on an unspoken view of white men as natural leaders, of slaves as lesser beings, and of white women as people who should concern themselves with domestic and family affairs. Vokins' near surprise and boasting delight at commensurate religious power being manifested "even" at Blacks' meetings rearticulates an Anglo-Africanist discourse that definitively constructs slaves as naturally inferior colonial others; her surprise emphasizes the rarity of institutionalized equality in any form.

On the island of Nevis eight months later, Vokins's report on a potential catastrophe at sea reconfirms the segregation of prayer meetings while recapitulating Hooton's feelings of love:

> I have been most of this Winter upon the roaring Seas, Two Months at a time, and saw no Land, and my Clothes were not off Two Nights all that time, so far as I can remember, and there was no conveniency for my weak Body; There were French, and Dutch, and Irish, and Barbarians, and English, and I had sore Exercises amongst them, both inwardly and outwardly; but yet I had good service also amongst them, and they did confess to the Power of my God. And although they were most of them very wicked, yet they were chained by it, and the Passengers were kind to me for the Truth's sake; and when it pleased the Lord to bring us to Land, we arrived at the Island of Antego [Antigua], in the West Indies, and there I found a precious People, and had Two Meetings a Day for a Week, with White People and Blacks; and on the 7th Day is their Childrens Meetings, and they have also Mens and Women's Meetings, and the Gospel-order is established and establishing in those remote islands, Glory to God for ever (Vokins, *God's Mighty Power Magnified*, p. 61).

The three Quakers—Curwen, Hooton, and Vokins—collectively responded to African-Caribbean slaves as men and women entitled to certain human rights. These they defined as the right to the love of God and the right to worship, early steps in the slow movement toward general emancipation. Their perspective also highlighted what white British discourse consistently lacked: any conceptualization of the diverse humanity of slaves, any notion of their status as the equals of European men and women. But Friends' circumscribed historical consciousness—understandably—is always evident too. Whereas they agitated for their own civil, social, and political as well as religious rights as female Friends, for slaves they argued for spiritual equality within the family of God. Curwen's apparently unique call for a change in nomenclature was the only exception.

Within limitations imposed by their epoch, Friends functioned as religious apostles of British-Christian values in colonized lands. Although they sincerely meant to share spiritual abundance, their ventures added to the construct of what Howard Temperley defines as cultural imperialism.[57] With Christian conversion at stake, African peoples' distinct cultures and religions scarcely counted or registered. Nor was slave membership in the Society controversial at this time (as far as I know), although a century later discussions about "negro membership" and the rejection of individual black applicants began in earnest.[58]

Nor, to expand the argument beyond Martha Tavernor's household, does any corroborating evidence exist that Africans sought convincement-"coming to our meetings" in Alice Curwen's phrase-in order to join a white Christian family unit that would substitute for their already existing communities. Rather, slaves enacted widespread physical resistance; petitioning for convincement added to oppositional activity. Michael Craton observes that:

> Few voyages [from West Africa to the Caribbean] were ever completed without the discovery or threat of slavery conspiracy. . . .
> The sheer ignorance of all whites about internal African conditions, the complexity of African cultures, and the general psychology of slave resistance compounded the problem. . . . The one growing certainty was that there was no such creature as a genuinely docile slave."[59]

These facts were borne out by numerous incidents before 1700: four plots and one revolt in Barbados, two plots in Bermuda, six incidents of revolt, resistance, and escape in Jamaica, massive escapes and "maroon activity in Antigua, and an uprising in St. Kitts."[60] Forging alliances with spiritually radical whites, who were already on society's rim and subject to persecution, helped to identify if not unify antagonism to the plantocracy. The number of slaves who converted to Christianity in the eighteenth and early nineteenth centuries permits us to speculate that such alliances might have been a form of conscious or unconscious political strategy—as well as a form of spiritual release—in response to a ruling elite who harshly suppressed all forms of self-preserving belligerence, active or passive.

Revered in their own circles, Alice Curwen, Elizabeth Hooton, and Joan Vokins exemplified a living Christian-like altruism in their own terms. In many senses they acted as role models for other women: "Joan Vokins, for example, returned home to investigate the new departure of separate meetings for men and women, even though such meetings arguably spelled the apparent downgrading of female Friends. Vokins left husband and family behind in England during her voyages. What *is* silenced among them is an explicit defense and interrogation of women's role in their work. But they do not ally themselves with the new conservative tendency either: they are simply silent on the issue and thus their recorded actions speak, as it were, on their behalf. Their near-silence in this matter and their near-silence on questions of race and slavery might be linked; certainly they constitute absent centres in their texts."[61] The Quaker authors rechannel or displace their energies, in one sense self-denyingly, into battling for others who are victims of a very different form of institutionalized persecution. But even more tellingly, working as traveling missionaries implied an act of will and of attentiveness to others that characterized a self-determining process. The fact that these philanthropic "feminine" attributes were sometimes pressed into the service of questioning slavery marks a gendering of anti-slavery discourse. In a society uneasy about female independence and authorship and radical sectarians, the adventurous global undertakings of Elizabeth Hooton, Joan Vokins, and Alice Curwen signified a widespread, oppositional female presence.[62] According to the most recent data, if a Quaker writer were officially approved by Fox, their publications would have targeted a national audience, in terms of influence, counting distributions abroad, as many as two thousand copies *could* have been printed of each account.[63] In Joan Kelly's phrase, their missionary labor was "a feminism of practice," a public and published display of female intrepidity, a displaced way of exercising the right to moral and political decision-making.[64] Eschewing prescribed separate spheres in society and within the Society of Friends, they championed the rights of outsiders. Striking at the roots of convention, Curwen emerged as a Janus (jana)-like figure, a spiritual and political daughter of Civil War foremother-activists; one of the earliest pioneers of white proto-abolitionist ideology who discountenanced the very language that accredited slavery.

As Quaker female missionaries advocated spiritual equality, they collectively empowered themselves and deplored their denied status. Self-conscious religious propagandists and avowed spiritual equals of slaves, they also assumed the right to speak for and decide what was best for enslaved African-Caribbeans; in the manner of Jesus Christ they were defending the vulnerable and unprotected. No tension existed for them between their commitment to spiritual equality and their implied denial of self-determination to Africans.

Over the next fifty years, the Quaker position on slavery changed qualitatively as they became the first unified group of British men and women to demand abolition and emancipation. In the Restoration, those female Friends who initiated a moral discourse about slavery and the marginalized status of slaves also spoke to their own desire for social reintegration. In supporting the right of slaves, albeit in historically constrained ways, they asserted their own right (consciously or not) to a discourse on and of freedom and a public-political identity. Given the mandated roles for white British females, they tested far-reachingly the theoretical and practical possibilities of those structures. Moreover, in advocating one form of spiritual equality they paved the way for others and helped to inaugurate women's right to the discourse on freedom. Importantly too, given the reluctance of most women to speak in public, they validated not only protest itself but a vocal alliance against the morally corrupt. In this process of pioneering spiritual negotiations on behalf of slaves, however, they simultaneously helped to consolidate an Anglo-Africanist discourse that was to characterize anti-slavery prose and poems well beyond the successful passage of the Emancipation Bill in 1834.

Chapter 4

Inkle and Yarico:
An Anti-Slavery Reading

It is no wonder, if the horrid Pain of such inhuman Tortures incline them to rebel.
> —Leslie Charles, *A New History of Jamaica, 1740.*

Many of us . . . are bought . . . of a treacherous Friend, a perfidious Husband or an odious Man-stealer. These are far from conferring any Right.
> *A speech made by a Black of Gardaloupe at the funeral of a Fellow-Negro, 1709.*

My chief design . . . is to give the Reader a Brief Account of the Christian captives. . . . Their work (the slaves') consists in building and providing all Materials for it. . . . Daily bread is made of such black, rotten Barley Corn as Horses loathe . . . Nakedness . . . sometimes once in two years a Gilliby (which is a course woolen coat). . . . [They are also] belied, back-beaten, and beaten by some of their own number.
> *An account of South-West Barbary containing what is most remarkable in the Territories of the King of Fey and Morocco. Written by a person who had been a Slave.* The Author's Preface, 1713.

Aphra Behn, Alice Curwen, Elizabeth Hooton, and Joan Vokins wrote about slavery because their experiences in Surinam and the Caribbean deeply affected them. In that respect these women were exceptional pioneers since no later female authors witnessed slavery at first hand; in the eighteenth and early nineteenth centuries, most white women's writings about slavery had no basis in personal experience. For the most part, they fashioned their ideas from hearsay and popular notions about slavery often promoted by the pro-slavery lobby, as well as from newspaper articles, travel narratives, Thomas Southerne's stage adaptation of *Oroonoko,* fiction and semi-fiction in prose and verse, and putative histories.[1] Rarely did they draw on the few but increasing autobiographies and memoirs written by Africans living in Britain.[2]

After Behn and the Quakers, autobiographically-based texts dried up. Sir Robert Walpole's efforts to secure domestic stability rekindled protestation as the daily reality of slavery became more publicly visible.[3] After the revolution settlement of 1688, despite rumors of corruption and the eventual scandals of Sir Robert Walpole's administration, times improved for many upper- and middle-class English men and women. Economic stability was built on vast profits for individual entrepreneurs and institutions involved in the triangular trade. Sugar was the crucial crop.[4] By 1731, Britain imported 722,445 hundredweight of sugar compared to 300,000 in 1755, while the *beau monde* luxuriated in exotica that flooded the market. Alexander Pope's detailed description of Belinda's toilet preparations in *The Rape of Lock* (1712, 1714) stunningly exemplified how upper-middle-class women enjoyed their roles as advertisements for slave trade merchandise and the overweening vanity such a role fostered.[5] In 1705, a Dutch traveler named William Bosman tried rather clumsily to preempt objections to the trade by highlighting its malignity: "I doubt not but this trade seems very barbarous to you, but since it is followed by meer necessity it must go on; but we yet take all possible care that they are not burned too hard [with branding] especially the women, who are more tender than the men."[6]

Christopher Hill explains the attraction of the slave trade to law-abiding citizens who abided by a bill of rights, beginning with the simple fact that "between 1700 and 1780 English foreign trade nearly doubled. . . . Shipping doubled too." He quotes Joshua Green's observations in 1729 that "all this great increase in our treasure proceeds chiefly from the labour of negroes in the plantations," and then comments:

> It seemed to economists an ideal trade, since slaves were bought with British exports, and transported in British ships. Moreover slave labour prevented the plantations draining England's population, a matter that was beginning to worry publicists after a century of complaint that the country was over-populated. . . . The ending of the Royal African Company's monopoly in 1698, coupled with

the increasing demands of the sugar plantations in the West Indies, led to a rapid extension of the British slave trade. The great prosperity of Liverpool and Bristol in the eighteenth century was based very largely on this trade. . . . The War of Spanish Succession won for England the coveted *Asiento,* the monopoly of supplying slaves to the Spanish American empire. . . . England replaced the Netherlands as the greatest slave-trading nation in the world. . . . The slave trade was believed to be the most profitable of all branches of English commerce. Slaves sold in the West Indies for five times what it cost to buy them on the African coast, so losses (up to twenty per cent) in the horrible conditions of transit need not trouble the slavers unduly. There was little vocal opposition to the trade between the sixteen fifties and the loss of America, except from a few Quakers. . . . West Indian planters opposed the conversion of slaves to Christianity, and their education. The Society for Propagating the Gospel allowed no Christian instruction to be given to its slaves in Barbados. . . . Colonial legislative assemblies were not allowed to prohibit or restrict the activities of the slavers.[7]

Peter Fryer expands on the economic consequences of winning the right to the *asiento:* "The privilege of supplying 4,800 African slaves a year to south central America, the Spanish West Indies, Mexico, and Florida was conferred on the newly created South Sea Company— 'those voracious robbers,' as they were dubbed in Bristol."[8] The law helpfully accommodated this boost to national economy by maintaining that enslaved Africans in Britain were not free, nor could slaves be freed through baptism, a practice permitted by the Spanish.[9] Specifically in 1729, Sir Philip Yorke, the attorney general, and Charles Talbot, the solicitor general, argued that any slave who came to Britain or Ireland with or without a master "doth not become free . . . and baptism doth not bestow freedom on him . . . the master may legally compel him to return to the plantations."[10]

By the 1740s, general acceptance of slavery was so commonplace that when Charles de Secondat, Baron de Montesquieu in *L'Esprit des Lois* used his mordant deadpan wit to condemn the institution, many read his sarcasm as serious support for slavery.[11] Other opponents argued slavery on religious or humanitarian rather than philosophical grounds, pointing out that Scriptures censured or forbade slavery.

This formidable legal scaffolding also helped sanction attitudinal shifts toward Africans. Whereas in the 1660s, the Royal African Company still used the term "Negro Servants" for kidnapped and transported Africans, by 1675 legal terminology began to reflect the "reality of the Africans' chattel status."[12] The Navigation Act was reinterpreted so that enslaved Africans could be denoted as legal cargo. By 1677, the solicitor general was asked "whether negroes ought to be esteemed goods or commodities intended by the Acts of Trade," in keeping with the Royal African Company charter of 1672 that had included Africans in an itemized list of authorized goods. The Royal African Company could "import any redwood, elephants' teeth, negroes, slaves, hides, wax, guinea, grains, *or other commodities*" [my italics]. In 1677, the solicitor general replied that indeed "negroes ought to be esteemed goods and commodities within the Acts of Trade and Navigation."[13] "Somewhere between 1600 and 1700," summarizes James Walvin, "the English view of the African had changed." By 1700 an Englishman was able to write in his will of a Negro: "I take [him] to be in the nature and quality of my goods and chattels."[14]

The barrage of advertisements for buying and selling slaves reinforced ideas about black inferiority.[15] Slaves may or may not have known that the Royal African Company was fighting to retain its monopoly and that "the most frequent comparison drawn was between the Negro and the animal kingdom, in particular the horse," but they unequivocally demonstrated their own resistance.[16] Documenting European "first impressions" of Africa, Winthrop Jordan stresses (and the point has been argued) that difference, not inferiority, first struck the English: "radically contrasting qualities of color, religion, and style of life, as well as animality and a peculiarly potent sexuality."[17] Not until economic relations made systematic control desirable and necessary did "some Englishmen [find] special reason to lay emphasis on the Negro's savagery," and then denounce it.[18] Thus "ethocentric fallacies about Blacks were reinforced."[19]

Travelers' accounts like Bosman's helped to entrench attitudes that encoded Africans as less feeling than Europeans, but punishments meted out to slaves were so heinous that even a pro-slavery observer-advocate such as Sir Hans Sloane—the prominent naturalist and, after Isaac Newton, president of the Royal Society—attempted to excuse them. His information about slavery horrified a public that cherished its moral sensitivity:

> After they are whipp'd till they are Raw, some put on their skins Pepper and Salt to make them Smart; at other times their Masters will drop melted Wax on their Skins, and use several very exquisite torments. These punishments are sometimes merited by the Blacks, who are a very perverse Generation of People, and though they appear harsh, yet are scarce equal to some of their crimes, and inferior to what Punishments other European Nationals inflict on

their Slaves in the East-Indies as may be seen by Mocquet, and other travellers. . . . For running away they put Iron Rings of Great weight on the Ankles, or pottocks about their Necks, which are Iron Rings with two long Necks rivetted to them, or a Spur in the Mouth.[20]

Despite contemporary revulsion at such reports, national prosperity successfully staunched opposition. But grotesque punishments seemed to be one thing and attitudes toward a largely known and unseen people were another. At worst, Sir Hans Sloane's prejudice permitted the white British reading public to regard Africans as a subordinate group of people, colonized others who deserved to be marginalized.

Writing poems that execrated an individual enslavement in the 1720s and 1730s, Frances Seymour (Thynne), the Countess of Hertford and an anonymous poet (whom I shall call Anon) represented a transitional phase. They refashioned an allegedly true tale about a tragic love affair that ended in the woman's enslavement and stamped spiritual conversion as a positive solution to slavery. In centerstaging an African female protagonist, the Countess and Anon also allowed themselves to air problems faced by female contemporaries; they were among the few writers to afford black females any kind of subjectivity for at least fifty years.[21]

White British women had good reason to be concerned about their cultural status. First of all, strict injunctions about behavior and self-expression abounded. In the same decade that the Countess of Hertford and Anon published their poems on Inkle and Yarico, the corrected eleventh edition of Lord Halifax's *Advice to a Daughter* instructed women in necessary responsibilities toward husband, home, family, friendships, religion, behavior, and even conversation. The first edition that had appeared the same year as *Oroonoko* underscored, in a different way from Behn's prose fiction, the kind of values that women had been encouraged to embrace and forego; he warned women about the dangers of censure, vanity, affectation, and diversions, encapsulating his popular advice in a final blessing:

I will conclude with my warmest wishes for all that is good to you; that you may live so as to be an ornament to your family, and a pattern to your sex. That you may be blessed with a husband that may value, and children that may inherit your virtue . . . may you so raise your character . . . and leave posterity in your debt for the advantage it shall receive by your example.[22]

The Spectator characterized the perfect female profile even more succinctly:

> How faint and spiritless are the charms of a coquet when compared with the real loveliness of Sophronia's innocence, piety, good humour, and truth, virtues which add a new softness to her sex, and even beautify her beauty! That agreeableness, which must otherwise have appeared no longer in the modest virgin, is now preserved in the tender mother, the prudent friend, and the faithful wife.[23]

In satire, familiar misogynous attitudes accompanied this crippling idealization of white women. Felicity Nussbaum describes its ambivalent consequences:

> The idealized woman, so noticeably absent from seventeenth-century satire, arises in the eighteenth century within the context of satires like Pope's. Women paradoxically have been metamorphosed from embodying the disorder that men fear to embodying the values men seek. But one image does not so much replace the other as coexist with it, as the myths of feminine weakness and passivity and of woman as guardian of moral values stand beside the satiric myth of the characterless woman to mock it. In addition, this chaste and obedient woman, like an angel, is also fragile and requires patriarchal protection. The suffering pathetic maidens sentimentalize woman's supposed inferiority, and as a literary type they foster the myth of the weaker sex.[24]

Second, women's productive role in society was being threatened by the gradual shift from manual labor to work undertaken away from home or by machines. Middle- and upper-class women, meanwhile, had to contend with an increasingly leisured life.[25]

A third allied reason concerned male carnality and the problematic of courtship and marriage, namely that a woman's person and property had to be legally surrendered to her spouse.[26] Lord Halifax advised women to connive at male immorality in order to preserve a domestic reputation because:

> you live in a time which hath rendered some kind of Frailties so habitual, that they lay claim to large grains of allowance. The world in this is somewhat unequal, and our Sex seemeth to play the Tyrant in distinguishing partiality for ourselves, by making that in the utmost degree Criminal in the Woman which in a Man passeth

under a much gentler Censure . . . But if in this it [your sex] lieth under any Disadvantage, you are more than recompens'd, by having the Honour of Families in your keeping. (Halifax, *Advice to a Daughter*, p. 29).

Not only that, but as F. W. Tickner boldly stated it:

This was the age also of lax marriage laws, and therefore of Fleet Prison marriage and elopements to Gretna Green. Young ladies, especially if they were heiresses, were at the mercy of dissolute gentlemen or smooth-tongued adventurers, and many of them suffered in consequence, until Lord Hardwicke's Marriage Act, 1753, did something to prevent clandestine marriages. (Tickner, *Women in English Economic History*, p. 101).

Long before Pamela and Clarissa enacted variant aspects of patriarchal entrapment, many women painfully empathized with the heroines' situations; they either recognized such abuse as integral to woman's everyday existence, or they had experienced abuse of some sort at first hand.

Several outraged women thundered against these steadfast denials of female rights and the impunity with which men interfered in their lives; in doing so they often borrowed late seventeenth-century invocations of the language of slavery. Among frequent feminist polemics on the subject, three stand out. In *The Ladies Defence* (1701), Lady Mary Chudleigh fired a salvo at a misogynous sermon on marriage by the Reverend John Sprint, reminding women of the need to educate themselves and resist male domination.[27] In a 1703 couplet on marriage addressed "To the Ladies," she encapsulated the matter: "Wife and servant are the same,/ But only differ in the name."[28] Anne Finch, Countess of Winchilsea rang changes on a similar theme in "The Unequal Fetters." Though marriage may "slightly tie men," the speaker declared, it makes "close prisoners" of women.[29]

By defining women's life from start to finish as a form of slavery, Sarah Fyge Field Egerton assaulted that concept of white British female slavery more comprehensively than most in her poem, "The Emulation."

> From the first dawn of life, unto the grave,
> Poor womankind's in every state, a slave.
> The nurse, the mistress, parent and the swain;
> For love she must, there's none escape that pain.[30]

But women refused to polemicize against limited opportunities and widespread abuse and leave it at that. Instead, they capitalized on the cult of sentiment to garner influence and affect the cultural mainstream. Sentimental literature enabled women to tap an unexpected outlet that doubled as a political platform. They went places with piety, feeling, and philanthropy.

This voguish sentimentalism, as it came to be called, burst on the public scene as early as 1690 when a nonjuring clergyman named Jeremy Collier condemned immorality on stage as a threat to public morals and social calm. In its place he advocated drama that upheld Christian values.[31] One hugely successful play under the new dispensation, *Love's Last Shift* by Colley Cibber, showed how much theatre audiences longed for a change; the middle class "wanted . . . sensitive heroes and distressed heroines."[32] From Cibber's play to Sir Richard Steele's *The Tender Husband* (1705) and multiple performances of *Oroonoko* up to and beyond the midcentury mark, audiences wept self-indulgently. Emotional drama was the rage.[33]

Important spiritual leaders backed—some might argue precipitated—this shift toward feeling. The latitudinarian Anglican divine, Archbishop Tillotson, counseled parishioners to do "good to the souls of man and endeavour . . . to promote their spiritual and eternal happiness." Another conspicuous Christian act, he added, was "the procuring of their temporal good and contributing as much as may be to their happiness in this present life."[34]

In *Characteristics* (1711) Lord Shaftesbury conjectured that emotions and ethics were linked, that goodness and virtue were natural partners: "The love of doing Good [would have to be] a good and right inclination."[35] Developing Lord Shaftesbury's ideas, the Scottish philosopher Frances Hutcheson reasoned that compassion typified humanity.[36]

Female responses to an age that prioritized feeling took diverse forms. The Countess of Hertford and Anon, for example, reinterpreted a celebrated tale, popularized in *The Spectator* by Sir Richard Steele. A romantic allegory of female subordination at one level, the poem permitted female readers to exorcise grievances through empathizing with a young woman's tragic plight. The Countess could validate Christian values and simultaneously enhance the reputation of pious women. Writing about virtue in an age of female powerlessness amounted to a form of moral compensation.[37]

The tale in question was the legend of Inkle and Yarico. In 1725 the Countess wrote two linked poems on their relationship while Anon fashioned a third in 1734. The title page of the Countess's first work acknowledged Steele's version in *Spectator No. 11* as its source. In compliance with female modesty, the title page coyly acknowledged only the author's rank and gender but not her title—the Countess of *****, it read.

Three male versions had preceded the Countess's poems. In John Mocquet's original version, vouchsafed as a true story, a youthful shipwrecked English merchant and an islander enjoy a loving relationship for several years until a ship picks up the couple and their child.[38] Neither the location of the shipwreck nor the woman's homeland is ever specified. On board, the merchant busily denies his love, painting his former beloved as a "savage" to the crew. Ironically or tragically, the woman had relentlessly scanned the seas for a rescue ship so they could live happily and luxuriously in London as her lover had promised. Realizing his *volte-face* she rips the baby in half, symbolizing his base treachery by throwing one half toward him. Narrator Mocquet cannot abide the merchant in question, who seems to have been a pilot on board the ship Mocquet was (later?) traveling on:

> The Seamen . . . asked him, why he had left this woman; but he pretended she was a Savage, and that he did not now heed her; which was an extream ingratitude and wickedness in him: Hearing this, I could not look upon him, but always with Horrour and great Detestation.[39]

While in prison, a man named Richard Ligon penned a second version of the tale, this time with a specifically Barbadian setting.[40] Yarico became "an Indian woman, a slave in the house," pregnant by a Christian servant. Indians intercepted a shipwrecked European crew "and some were kill'd."[41] The "Indian maid" saved "a young man." After they boarded the rescue ship and landed in Barbados, he "sold her for a slave, who was as free born as he: And so poor Yarico for her love, lost her liberty." Both accounts commiserate with Yarico's agony and stress Inkle's callous opportunism. Yet they also highlight received ethnocentric ideas about innate ferocity by presenting a perverted maternality.

In a third version in 1709, Steele toned down the legend for an early eighteenth-century readership that he and Joseph Addison were trying to "civilize" though the pages of *The Spectator*.[42] Steele "puts the story into the mouth of Arietta, who relates it as it dwells in her memory out of that honest traveller Ligon in the fifty-fifth page of his account of Barbados." For the first time, Steele attaches the name of Inkle to the "youth, who is," he states (half-ironically only?), "the Hero of my

Story." Late eighteenth-century audiences, not Steele's own contemporaries, reinterpreted the tale as decidedly anti-slavery in its message. Steele's own marriage to a Caribbean heiress, at the very least complicated the tale's imprecations against planters.[43]

With a flourish, Steele presents "Mr. Thomas Inkle of London, aged twenty years . . . the third Son of an eminent Citizen, who [instilled] into his Mind an early Love of Gain. . . . [With] a ruddy vigour in his Countenance, Strength in his Limbs, with Ringlets of fair Hair loosely flowing on his shoulders," he sets out for the Caribbean "to improve his fortune by Trade and Merchandize." After a shipwreck, "the greatest Number of [the Europeans]" were slain by Indians. An "Indian Maid" named Yarico saves Inkle, enamoured of the "Limbs, Features, and wild Graces of the Naked American." A "Person of Distinction" wearing elaborate garments of "Shells, Bugles, and Bredes," she in turn is enraptured by the contrasting colors of their hair. (In *The Rape of the Lock,* Belinda uses similar ornaments after they have been thoroughly processed, purchased, and reidentified. The Countess could conceivably have intended or at least recognized this contrast between the artificial European Belinda and Yarico, the "natural" African other.)[44]

After Yarico spots a vessel "bound for Barbados" and the couple board it, Inkle experiences a change of heart, betrayed by his mercantilist mentality:

> To be short, Mr. Thomas Inkle, now coming into English Territories, began seriously to reflect upon his loss of Time, and to weigh with himself how many Days Interest of his Money he had lost during his Stay with Yarico. This Thought made the Young Man very pensive, and careful what Account he should be able to give his Friends of his Voyage. Upon which Considerations the prudent and frugal young Man sold Yarico to a Barbadian Merchant; notwithstanding that the poor Girl, to incline him to commiserate her Condition, told him that she was with Child by him: But he only made use of that Information, to rise in his Demands upon the Purchaser.[45]

Steele's hero has feet of clay, indoctrinated in a colonial value system from which love can seduce him only temporarily. The feminized man of feeling, or rather the male protagonist who foreshadows an aspect of the man of feeling's profile, succumbs to the blandishments of profit. Penury engenders the masculinist entrepreneur. Steele's "civilized" version differs from the earlier ones in that the objectively rendered line, "some [Europeans] were killed," recorroborates racist fantasies:

"the greatest number of them [were slain by Indians]." Although Inkle acts despicably toward a poor "Indian maid," the villains any sensible person would want to avoid—so the text ventures—are the slaughtering islanders.

This kind of reprioritizing of colonial values seems scarcely at odds with an age that bankrolled colonizing expeditions in order to consolidate overseas expansion and "open up" Jamaica. Contemporary histories, pamphlets, government documents, letters, accounts, and sensationalist—as well as less hyperbolized—fiction testify to massive national involvement in colonialism.[46] The incident concerning the arrival in London of Madame Chimpanzee is just one bizarre example of colonial voyeurism.[47] By contrast in 1736, there appeared a publication that flagrantly spoke for the other side: *"The Speech of Mr. John Talbot Campo-Bell, a free Christian-Negro, to his countrymen in the mountains, of Jamaica,"* the author of which stated bluntly that: "Many of us . . . are bought . . . of a treacherous Friend, a perfidious Husband or an odious Man-stealer. These are far from conferring any Right."[48]

THE COUNTESS OF HERTFORD: INKLE AND YARICO

The first woman to adapt the legend of Inkle and Yarico (in two poems) and probably the first person to set it to verse, the Countess of Hertford focused on Yarico in contrast to Steele's more generalized concentration on the couple. She devotes thirty-eight lines in her first poem of 104 lines and all of the second poem's sixty-four lines to the Barbadian setting.[49] The second poem is a versified letter entitled "An Epistle from Yarico to Inkle, After he had left her in Slavery." Following their publication in 1725 in *The New Miscellany,* both poems were reissued as single items in 1738.[50] From the preface to the 1725 version we learn that the poems had been circulating in manuscript and might have been published prior to 1725. How many of the Countess's readers knew the legend is unclear, Steele's version having appeared sixteen years earlier. Nonetheless, Steele is mentioned on the title page. Elizabeth Rowe's casual collective reference to both poems as "Inkle" in a letter dated 1725 substantiates that the poems were probably circulating among friends before their 1725 publication date.

The only entertainment I pretended to give [Mrs. St. John] was your Ladyship's composures in verse and prose, and I am sure she was

sincerely pleased. I gave her *Marion's Complaint,* but I had lent
Inkle. However, she told me 'twas printed in *The Tunbridge Miscellany.*[51]

In the first poem, the Countess included by then familiar details
of the couple's meeting—but omitting Inkle's nationality—and their
subsequent relationship: "Mutually charm'd by various acts they
strove,/ To inform each other of their mutual love." Inkle promises
Yarico the "softest silks" when they return jubilantly to his "native
country." After she espies a "European vessel," he reassesses his
situation, according top priority to personal-professional concerns,
more hard-headed by far than Steele's Inkle:

> Deep melancholy all his Thoughts o'ercast,
> Was it for this, said he, I cross'd the Main
> Only a doating Virgin's heart to gain?
> I needed not for such a prize to roam,
> There are a thousand doating maids at home.

When they stop over in Barbados and he spots planters "who trade
for goods and Negro Slaves," he seizes this ready-made opportunity
to capitalize on his shipwreck and misadventure. According to tradition "By sordid int'rest sway'd/[he] Resolv'd to sell his faithful Indian
Maid."

Nothing moves Inkle, now self-transformed into a man of commerce
incarnate, neither her pregnancy, a soul-stirring appeal to his humanity ["all my life to drag a servile chain"], nor even her last-ditch request
that he stab her to death, one of the Countess's poetic inventions.
Yarico's pagan belief that she and the unborn will join their ancestors
in death both exonerates her from the "sin" of suicide and elevates
more "superior" Christian values by contrast. Moreover, the message
of Imoinda's conduct— African and/or Indian women care for their
offspring as much as European women—is reconfirmed at a critical
time when the pro-slavery lobby is persistently broadcasting the socalled nonhuman status of Africans:

> But if thou hate me, rather let me meet
> A gentler fate, and stab me at thy feet.
> Then will I bless thee with my dying breath,
> And sink contented in the shades of death.

The Countess's emphasis on maternality highlights similarities between white women and women of color that pro-slavery and even anti-slavery discourse denies. In this sense, the Countess near-silently inscribes some further anti-patriarchal sentiment into the poem. In light of women's dictated roles and their warranted worries about manipulation in courtship, a contemporary female readership might well have decoded Yarico's plight as further evidence of a recognizable form of female entrapment and corrupt male carnality; Yarico is a mother-to-be insensibly thrust into a perilous situation, her fetus killed by Inkle's greed and lack of feeling. The Countess's poem doubles as a miniature (mis)conduct book with a difference: it sculpts the dangers that lie in wait for unsuspecting women who take men at face value. The patriotic Countess, moreover, will not go as far as to pronounce Inkle English. His nationality is left as indeterminate as the island Barbados—a British colony—where he sells Yarico. To be unversed in the ways of the world, to believe promises, to think of dedicating one's future to a virtual stranger, and to forsake parents, natal home, and even rank turns out, in the end, to be life-imperilling.[52] As long as men treat women as property, the Countess warns, unconditional trust is not only unwise but dangerous. Without the security of a Christian value system, male predators will topple the moral order and dissolve harmony.[53] The patriarchal word is no bond. Yarico's unconditional trust turns out to be as hazardous as Inkle's original journey. The Countess interpreted Steele's notorious story of Yarico as a poignant portrait of female fidelity undone, a potentially happy family severed and set at naught; she offers a sentimentally rendered yet simple caution—women must beware of male chicanery in the guise of love; male agency will take unconscionable advantage of female passivity or naiveté. Without the shipwreck the legend is a classic tale of seduction in which the hero is an African and her fate is enslavement.

The second poem concerns Yarico's conversion. The Countess reconstructs Yarico as a female Christ-figure living the exemplary life. Yarico forgives, she loves, she cares for Inkle's soul despite his responsibility for their "wretched infant's death." But most importantly Yarico writes and speaks her miseries to Inkle. A literate, voiced female slave pens "An Epistle from Yarico to Inkle, after he had left her in slavery." The implied reader knows Yarico's anger and sorrow, her need to articulate the reality of her world. Though spoken "through" a European author, such a depiction in white women's texts of a black female's oral narrative was unprecedented. More profoundly constructed than ever before, Yarico's character is, nonetheless, still deeply embedded in Anglo-Africanist discourse and values. Given the plantocratic tenor of the times, an ethnocentric layering inevitably unfolds.[54]

Yarico now becomes a wholly virtuous woman—her "unwed" pregnancy silently connived at—whose basic goodness enables her to envision the efficacy of Christianity. Her doubly jeopardized existence as a woman and a "negro maid" adds to her martyred heroic status.[55] In embracing a life free of sin and full of hope, she becomes the reconstituted hero of a religious allegory about the salvation of "foreign" souls. This sometimes "negro virgin", other times "Indian maid", approaches the status of a saint, a Christian martyr; the unregenerate white male reprobate preys self-indulgently on females, a purveyor of greed and hence forever damned. According to the Countess, commerce corrupts absolutely and it is a practice thoroughly accented with (male) gender: the anti-mercantilist politic, furthermore, makes a particular kind of ideological inscription in poems penned by an anti-bourgeois aristocrat. A secondary hero surfaces in the person of the "hoary Christian Priest," a missionary-tutor who guarantees eternal bliss to Yarico, provided she does not surrender to her pagan beliefs and kill herself. His person encompasses male European values of a different sort; he represents an "authentic" moral agency, worthy proponent of Christendom and foil to a godless Inkle. He heralds the upcoming man of feeling, but in clerical dress.

Formerly an idolatrous innocent who by implication has been made sexual subject to Inkle's moral degeneracy, Yarico ascends into the moral life through speech, action, and writing. Although Inkle wields the power to transform Yarico into his property with a nod at an auction, although he can easily transform her from a sexual object into an object for monetary exchange value, Yarico is spiritually redeemed by a colonial "protector." With her voice and text, she claims her own subjectivity and rejects Inkle's definition of her as his object of desire. Yarico slips along a scale of values from innocent pagan lover, pregnant mistress, sexually abused slave to orator, author, and Anglo-Africanist saint.[56] She plays Europe's other in multiple parts.

Ultimately, Inkle is a fixed figure, irredeemable in sensual and monetary rapacity. He does not rescue her from traditionally imaged exotic primal darkness as figures like him (but without his unmitigated greed) are said and shown to do in later texts; instead the missionary, representing Christ's feminized values, does. On the other hand, Yarico rescues him, if only temporarily, from commerical corruption. To put it another way, male middle-class values, outside of a spiritual and hence feminized context are distinctly gendered. Inkle learns to un-learn and he loves for a while but rapidly reconverts to type.

In composing an idealized female slave undergoing a Christian conversion, the Countess rejects conformist readings of Yarico as a poor, abandoned victim, dolefully watching Inkle skip off into the sunset with a wad of banknotes. Instead, Yarico's individuality is sexually inflected, and although the missionary creates her spiritually in a European God's image, she herself speaks that evolution.[57] Yarico's narrative also conveys a secular message: beware male wiles, though ultimately what matters is the capacity of Christianity, conceived as absolute altruism, to dissolve or transcend the evils of slavery. A devoted member of the Church of England, the Countess recreates the Church's teachings in her poem. The Society for the Propagation of the Gospel assessed Christianity and slavery as compatible institutions. Barbados, where Yarico is sold, was an important platform of Anglican church history in the 1720s. Christopher Codrington, a wealthy West Indian, bequeathed two sugar plantations and three hundred slaves to the Society in 1710. On these grounds the Society erected a college for slaves, the intention being to convert the slaves "by example."[58] The poem functions subtextually as a sleight-of-hand tribute to the Codrington-Christian experiment.[59]

Yarico's heart-wrenching reminder to Inkle that my "suff'rings were thy wretched infant's death" also elicits reminders of a rising eighteenth-century attentiveness to abandoned and abused children. Yarico reverberates Imoinda's earlier concern about healthy family life. Five years before the Countess of Hertford's poems were published, Thomas Coram spearheaded the establishment of a Foundling Hospital, an idea that Joseph Addison had advocated in *The Guardian* as early as 1713.[60] The Countess of Hertford's father-in-law, Charles, the sixth Duke of Somerset, was named one of the governors of the Foundling Hospital in the charter signed on the 17th of October, 1739.[61]

Philanthropy and piety, besides, had long marked individual worth, Queen Anne herself was well known as the royal benefactor. In "Some Notes on Charity Schools," W. K. Lowther Clarke includes the following information about charitable female practices from the Archives of the Society for the Propagation of Christian Knowledge:

> June 14th. £8 a yr has been bequeathed by a gentlewoman at the school at Aldgate. "'Twas observ'd that all the poor children walked very solemnly before her corps and each person invited had one of Dr. Kennet's *Christian Scholars* given to him instead of a pair of

gloves." . . . September 12th. Three schools have been opened at
Bury St. Edmunds. The mistresses are paid £12 10s. each per an-
num. The boys are provided with two caps and two neckcloths
apiece, the girls with two coifs.[62]

The Countess's reputation for philanthropy and spiritual devotion
had long earned her contemporary esteem.[63] As a saintly refashioner of
the Yarico legend, she enhanced that reputation in a cultural context.

Earlier, the poet laureate, Laurence Eusden, had penned a charm-
ingly pseudo-cryptic poem, playfully entitled "On the Countess of
H-rtf-rd," that publicly eulogized her shining reputation:

> Juno had grandeur, but not easy grace,
> And Venus wanton'd in a charming face;
> Diana shew'd the prude by virtue's boast,
> And learn'd Minerva's arts in pride were lost.
> O H-rtf-rd! how transcendently divine!
> To perfect three, four goddesses combine;
> And all their glories mix'd, with their shades, are thine.[64]

Into the bargain, James Thomson had dedicated "Spring" from *The
Seasons* to "the Gentle Hertford," the Countess's sobriquet, and other
contemporaries lauded her magnanimity toward the unfortunate Richard Savage. A biographer's paragraph summarizes her contemporary
reputation:

> A sensitive, kindly spirit, a lady of taste, she was known to her time
> for her benevolence and her modesty. "A friend of Virtue, to her
> friends a friend," might have been written in her praise.[65]

Only lack of funds, the Countess herself and her biographer inform
us, prevented her from living the life of a committed almsgiver:

> The necessity of strict economy in the face of the demands of her
> social position and the prodigal habits of her easy-going husband,
> [faint but suppressed echoes of Inkle here?] soon taught the young
> wife hard lessons. "With a heart which would have delighted in
> dispensing benefits, and relief to every creature in want," she la-
> ments, "my circumstances have been always straitened so as to
> oblige me to deal out with a scanty hand what my heart would have
> diffused with plenty."[66]

One last powerful impact on the Countess's reworking of the legend surfaced in the less predictable quarter of her feminist friends. Among them she counted her great-aunt Anne Finch, the Countess of Winchilsea, who wrote "The Unequal Fetters," and Elizabeth Rowe, who constantly railed against patriarchal strictures—in her poems Rowe metaphorized such constraints as "Theron's chains."[67] The Countess of Hertford and Elizabeth Rowe remained close friends until the latter's death.[68] Her friends undoubtedly influenced the pious Countess's incursion into what nowadays would be called sexual politics: her hinting at planters' lustful intentions upon Yarico, customarily an unfitting topic for one so holy. But perhaps the spiritual, almost ethereal, cachet that surrounds the Countess is more nuanced than it seems. Aside from her "easy-going" husband's prodigality, in 1735, for example, her distress at the sexual scandal involving her friend Henrietta, who was eventually exiled, points to a consciousness not altogether unattuned to, nor even inexperienced in, certain sexual problems constantly confronted by women.[69] Admittedly, the Countess "uses" Yarico's sexual misfortunes to draw out a Christian moral, as Richardson later did in *Pamela*. But insofar as *Pamela* doubles as a sermon and a tease, the Countess's poems combine aristocratic revulsion at go-getter mercantilist values with an implicit taboo on sexual conduct in early courtship.[70] Those who heed not are warned. The Countess's disclaimer to her son that the age held "universal disregard for religion" does not adequately cover the complex distress that permeates these poems.[71] Nor does her statement to Dr. Isaac Watts that she wrote "to amuse a leisure hour and to speak the sentiments" of her heart. The Countess depicts a Yarico to pity and admire, a character whose undoing at a sexual level replicated situations endured daily by British female contemporaries. In other words, the Countess calls for identification with Yarico *and* recognition of Yarico as Europe's other. The role of white authors is to protect the victim, to exhort and warn female readers; the Countess symbolizes Christian philanthropy at work in a text, inscribing it with feelings usually attributed to females.

ANON: INKLE AND YARICO

Nine years after the publication of the Countess's poems in 1734, an anonymous female poet—"an artless dame" she calls herself, "unlearnt in schools, unblest with natal fire"—decided, as her preface states, to "save this story [of Inkle and Yarico] from devouring fate."[72]

Anon constructs her version differently from the Countess's, but with decidedly overlapping elements. The key distinction is her assault against Inkle from the word go and her ugly depiction of islanders. She leaves behind the Countess's "before" and "after" versions of conversion poems and launches into feminist polemic. Inkle enters as a dyed-in-the-wool villain out to conquer and happy to utilize the first proposition he encounters. Anon opens by proclaiming her subject as "the dire arts of faithless man;" Inkle is so consumed with "lurking avarice" that, although he seems to possess "ev'ry charm," he remains a "stranger to virtue."

The poet immediately establishes contradictions in Inkle's character. Classical mythological elements, with homoerotic undertones, rather awkwardly enter the picture. Jove dislikes the idea of Inkle with "a form so like his own" being killed, so he screens "the fair youth . . . from hostile eyes." Then a pitiable Inkle, torn by "gloomy sorrows and unmanly fears . . . [in] his sad breast," sees Yarico, a "negro virgin [of] noble birth." The next seventy-five lines—almost one half the poem—trace the growth of their mutual love in orthodox western terms. Struck by Inkle's "face like polish'd marble . . . and long curl'd flaxen hair," Yarico "thought him a god, and low obeisance paid." Prostrating himself "low at her feet, in suppliant posture laid," Inkle throws himself on her mercy with his tale of woe:

> The tender negro look'd a kind reply . . .
> With hands uplifted, did the gods implore,
> That her relentless countrymen no more
> Might strain their native land with human gore
> (Anonymous, *Weekly Amusement*, p. 367).

Following mutual declarations of love, Inkle's safety becomes Yarico's "only care." But as soon as Yarico spots the rescue ship and the couple sail safely out of reach of her "barb'rous" friends, Inkle quickly reassumes a subject position that is all greed and treachery. This time, the narrator explains, the cold climate into which he was born spawns his callousness.[73] An undeclared subtext reindicts mercantilist values, anathema to the aristocracy.

As in the past, readers' sympathies unconditionally reside with Yarico, who unveils her feelings in a long rapt speech about problems that intersect with those of white women:

O much-lov'd youth in tender pity spare
A helpless maid, my long'd try'd faith revere.
From you this worst of human ills to prove,
Must break a heart that over-flows with love.
Break not my heart, nor drive me to despair,
Lest you deface your lovely image there.
Ah! do not with consummate woe undo
A maid that father, mother, country, left for you.
What sorrows must my tender parents mourn,
By me forsaken, never to return?
Transferr'd from them to you my love I gave;
Unjust return! to sell me for a slave,
O call to mind the sacred oaths you've given.
Remember there are thunder-bolts in heaven.

Once again Inkle epitomizes dual exploitation, both sexual and commercial. Yarico's "unwed" pregnancy stems from her forgivable pagan matrix of values, but the tragedy recalls a familiar domestic scene.[74] Inkle's crass conduct devastates parents and children alike and destroys potential domestic bliss. On this occasion, Yarico takes the stage as a speaking "negro," no longer an Indian woman; male villainy is condemned root and branch.

The poem constituted a secular variant on the Countess's version, with speech once again Yarico's principal form of resistance. No missionary popped up in a sequel—no *deus ex machina* saves the day. Like the Countess and her speakers, Anon excoriated slavery but just as or more importantly assaulted are male greed and ruthlessness that ruins family life.

Traditional attitudes suffuse and intersect throughout the text, with Inkle's corruption barely a match for "natural" ferocious behavior. Following the Countess's example, the narrator assails islanders as "men who thirst for human blood . . . upon a barbarous cost," so ignorant that they do not know how to plant and, even more obscenely, so unhealthily heathen that they offer "oblations to th' infernal power" as they "quaft their [the ship-wrecked Europeans'] streaming gore."

Both the Countess and Anon use an unspecified place to portray the amorphous evil of peoples whom they never ethnically define. Moral standards are hard and fast, formulated as a binary opposition. A Christian-abiding Europe abhors an irredeemably vicious world of pagan others.[75]

Perhaps influenced by *Robinson Crusoe*, Yarico is the one good islander—like Man Friday—who lives amid unfeeling infidels (in European terms) yet spontaneously responds humanely (and, as it turns out, foolishly) to the colonial merchant. Slightly off to the side meanwhile, cannibalistic islanders act on impulse, gratuitously massacring and eating hapless travellers. The Countess and Anon rival Behn in the hideous inventiveness of their Anglo-Africanist fantasies. Yarico's willingness to abandon her own society at Inkle's instigation without tendering any farewells is only understandable to a British readership who have been indoctrinated into certain configurations of the "other." Either Yarico is without feeling or she "intuits" (due to a positive British influence?) the homogenized moral corruption of her people. The absence of a familial farewell signifies an early eighteenth-century high point of British in(ter)vention. On this showing, a lost and even in one case a *royal* daughter would cause neither commotion nor sorrow; fiendish islanders, products of a pagan society, could not possibly care. The tension between self-preserving islanders and profit-motivated adventurers is never resolved. This ethnocentric imagining fostered by the Countess of Hertford's poems derived from a contemporary *mélange* of factors that included Anglo-Africanist perspectives, Robinson Crusoe's popularized colonialist mentality, and standard plantocratic mythologies about Africans.

Nonetheless, Anon does not conflate "negro" and Indian; possibly contemporary travel accounts had helped dispel earlier confusions.[76] And she seems to grasp the sexual implications of Yarico's fate, or at least expresses them more overtly. Planters exude a menacing lasciviousness toward Yarico, softly portrayed as an African woman, metonymically signified in subtle ways at various times as a "tender negro," a "negro virgin," a "negro maid."

Slavery is condemned at an individual but not an institutional level: the kindly Yarico does not merit a cruel fate. A nominally Christian society profiteering on colonialism would readily accept this proposition. But if Yarico could live as an enslaved Christian in the hope of permanent paradise she would be much better off than living a godless life with cold- blooded cannibals. Slavery is not a matter of rights or humanity. Anon means to elicit revulsion from her readers at the very idea of subverting a decent domestic life in London where the couple are originally headed. Inkle signifies the inseminating rake seducer who "has his way" with the maiden and then gaily skips off, male entrepreneur to a tee.

Both writers display standards that appear to apply differentially to white and black women. Although some contemporaries knew that white British parents bartered daughters who at times ended up as battered wife-objects, no one believed that these daughters were more "valuable" in a "fallen" and pregnant state of being. Yet Inkle believes that a pregnant Yarico is more valuable because she is not a human being but property. Thus her child-to-be is a potential economic bonus. Whether the Countess and Anon are stressing the construction of British women as property on a marriage market or attacking Inkle's mercantilist moral nihilism is unclear. But certainly, at a broader historical level, Inkle's attitude goes some way toward explaining the panic expressed by so many protagonists when the most visibly subjugated people threaten to respond. Inkle, in other words, helps us understand some of the seeming brittleness in female abolitionists. How they would like to react to his power (angrily and probably unconsciously) is what they shy from in potentially rebellious slaves. The texts are permeated with both potentialities. On the other hand, the apparent differences in these different forms of slavery exposed how much the word slavery itself had been transvaluated. Few British women, for instance, endured the following experience of Africans in Surinam during the Restoration:

> These wretched miseries not seldome drive them to desperate attempts for the Recovery of their Liberty, endeavouring to escape ... or if the hope of Pardon bring them again alive into their Masters power, they'l manifest their fortitude, or rather obstinacy in suffering the most exquisite tortures [that] can be inflicted upon them, for a terrour and example to others without shrinking.[77]

These poems about Inkle and Yarico attack a self-interested man throwing an innocent woman to the wolves. In one case, religion "saved" the tragic heroine; in the second, no exit opened up. Institutionally, slavery survives unscathed, largely unimpugned except in one specific episode about symbolic infanticide. That aside, slavery could denote the depths to which nominally Christian men would sink. More critically, since Inkle's enslavement of Yarico was anathema to any humane concept of family or friendship, the culprit being not so much enslavement as treachery, women stood forth as inimitable moral exemplars. In the next decade, the use of slavery in sentimental novels to underline the importance of charity sharply contrasted with the downplaying of slavery as an evil institution in the legend. Though never formulated as such in the 1720s and 1730s, an abolition-tending discourse would probably have been perceived by an eighteenth-century reading public as unpatriotic. Slavery was so profitable that any opposition was an Inkle-like treachery violating national interest.

The anti-slavery paradigm still embraces seemingly passive and virtuous female slaves who endure concupiscent advances, protean white benefactors who protect and convert slaves, predacious British villains, and slaves as a fixed, univocalized group. Bloodthirsty violent behavior now attaches, if not to slaves, certainly to people who in the text's terms are potential slaves. The rebellious Oroonoko as the independent slave-agent, the individual whom colonists most fear, has vanished.

Yarico emblemizes a version of the colonial other who resembles the new emotionally susceptible woman being constructed and displayed by Joseph Addison and Sir Richard Steele in *The Tatler* and *Spectator.* In texts about slavery soon to come, however, a man of feeling as the decision-making colonial subject will rule the roost.

Chapter 5

Sentiment and Amelioration

... Before slavery there were the ancestral identities: Ibo, Yoruba, Ashanti, Efik, Ewe, Mandinka, Wolof, and so on. Sometime between Queen Anne and Queen Victoria most of the African words and the African ethnic identities that went with them were erased from the West Indian consciousness: ... "it was the whites who took our culture away from us in the first place. I an I thought Jah gave each an every race their own language so no other than that race can overstan [understand] them but it is through we were taken from our forefathers' land and taken into slavery and now in a Babylon that we speak the white tongue."
—Sis Zulekia Moore, letter in *Voice of Rasta,* no. 18, quoted in David Sutcliffe, *British Black English,* p. 32.

The true "man of feeling" was ... seen as "feminine." Sentimental writing was "feminine" too.
—Jane Spencer, *The Rise of the Woman Novelist,* p. 77.

Humanity is in fashion—it's Popular—The Furor has seized on the people.
—Matthew Grigson, pro-slavery lobbyist for Liverpool, quoted in Averil Mackenzie-Grieve, *The Last Years of the English Slave Trade: Liverpoool 1750–1807,* p. 194.

Representations of slavery began to change slowly after the 1730s, partly in response to economic factors and the increase in female fiction writers. The amelioration of slavery and non-involvement in that institution became key ethical issues in the course of which powerless women claimed more moral authority yet unwittingly enhanced historically negative attitudes toward Africans. Philanthropic

91

female authors, furthermore, displaced socio-political concerns on to slaves.

By mid-century, the slave trade substantially affected every trading and manufacturing town in England:

> From 1730 to 1775 the value of British exports to Africa increased by some 400 percent. Birmingham iron manufacturers, Liverpool gunmakers, refiners, cutlers, dyers, weavers, packers, coopers, fishers, shipwrights, ropemakers, and sailmakers felt that their interests were sufficiently identified with the slave trade to petition at various times in its favor. Before the American Revolution approximately one third of the British merchant fleet was engaged in transporting fifty thousand Negroes a year to the New World. Closely linked with the high realms of insurance and banking, the trade rested on a wide base of speculative investment involving large and petty capitalists, and the holders of annuities and mortgages.[1]

Revenue from navigation, foreign markets, and domestic manufacture, along with French control of the sugar islands became a habitual feature of tracts on trade. The amount of sugar imported into England and Wales rose from 846,500 hundredweights between 1731 and 1735 to 962,000 hundredweights between 1751 and 1755.[2] Animosities between France and Britain escalated.[3] Sugar, molasses, and rum were big business.[4] Britain had "emerged as the world's foremost slave-traders, responsible for about a quarter of the Atlantic slave trade up to 1791."[5] Profit and patriotism developed hand in hand with planto-cratic propaganda. Tracts on Jamaica were common, protest oblique or minimal.[6] Eric Williams tersely summarizes the situation: "The West Indies had become the hub of the British Empire."[7]

The primacy accorded profit blended into female identification with sentiment and moral order to produce a new secular protagonist: the seemingly unnuanced male colonialist entrepreneur imbued with "female" sentiment. In the 1740's, Richardson's fiction had popularized the novel of sentiment and offered a form of cultural autonomy and some psychological release to hundreds of female readers and authors. Antidote to the rake, an eighteenth-century matinee idol, the gentle hero who felt life on his pulse was tailor-made for women writers. At mid-century, Tom Jones's magnanimity and Clarissa Harlowe's purity whetted the public's appetite for sentimental excess laced with sexual innuendo, morbidity, and violence. Two African princes were so overcome by a performance of *Oroonoko* that they left the theatre in a state of agitation and were extensively written up in the press.[8] Sir Charles Grandison embodied the age's twin watch-words: benevolence and feeling. In fiction, slave protagonists who asserted themselves (however unsuccessfully) were replaced by mild-mannered white patriarchs. Although the "brutish mass" of slaves lived in fiction as a common stereotype, the Oroonoko rebel-hero was still too dangerously lifelike for safe textual accommodation, the colonial other dreaded by Europe. Instead, by way of oblique identification with the disconsolate, female authors featured them-selves as fictional heroes in drag. Heroes signified and became the British quest for justice, but they did not resemble Oroonoko. On the contrary, they were troped as philanthropy-in-action. The fact that the very slaves for whom justice was sought were represented but were themselves denied speech, humanity, and consciousness was an unspoken constant textual ambivalence. Ironically then, while the British male protagonist functioned as unquestioned hero, his ob-jectified conceptual quest—abstract justice—was ironically more of a "hero" than the man himself. Like the slaves, this novel hero is a cardboard cutout—partially theorized in some indeterminate, untilled ground between humanity and thought. The novel hints that Britons live in a discursive world of their own making, that their vision of slaves emerges from their own needs and insecurities. Thus the will to truth signifies only "a purely rhetorical stance" since Africa, Afri-cans, and African-Caribbean slaves, monolithically considered, con-form to the profile of what Europe thinks Europe is not and can never be. The British Caribbean is constructed as the African continent is constructed: it's a place that lacks civilization, receiving life only from the outside.[9] In the case of the Caribbean, the midcentury "civilized" interventionists are conceived as Christian activist-owners. Jane Spencer tellingly encapsulates the evolving phenomenon of the anti-slavery sensate male narrator:

> What was happening, in fact, was that the properly "feminine" and the properly "literary" were both being re-defined along the same lines. ... The unification of feeling and morality which was at the heart of sentimental philosophy was also a characteristic of femininity as the eighteenth century defined it; and the true "man of feeling" was therefore seen as "feminine." Sentimental writing was "feminine" too. The tender feeling and delicacy of expression seen as the hallmarks of feminine writing also characterized senti-mental writing in general, and so at the height of the sentimental movement, the most fashionable kind of writing coincided with the kind of writing expected of women.[10]

As aid to slaves became another signifier of morality, the new evolving male protagonist—middle-class, white, British, and prodigiously charitable—embodied an extensive range of positive and avowedly female attributes: selflessness, modesty, piety, and forbearance. Dramatizing the beatitudes, he modelled Christ on earth, slavery being a decisive component of his virtuous agenda. This hero's relationship to the social construction of "womanhood" remained an open question.[11]

CHARLOTTE CHARKE: AMELIORATIONIST HERO-VICTIM ENTERS SUBPLOT

One early novel that featured colonial slavery, *The History of Henry Dumont and Miss Charlotte Evelyn* (1755) by Charlotte Cibber Charke, foregrounded just such a hero.[12] The pendulum had swung from fascination with exoticized slave-others toward collaboration with British largesse. Yarico as victimized islander was reborn as Alexander Jennings, a wealthy white mini-paragon living in the Caribbean who recoils from slavery and shares Yarico's forgiving piety. As agents renegotiating shifts in slavery's power relationship through acknowledgement of slaves' "rights", white male protagonists defuse the possibility of resistance by reappropriating power formerly exercised by the slave-hero. Intent on improving but not abandoning slavery, sober but basically good-natured protagonists, in the text's terms, secure and enforce colonial policy. With much less control over their lives than their heroes suggest, female novelists used gender to distance themselves and speak through those male characters about their need and desire for greater control. Oroonoko's spirited rebellion had receded into the past; benevolence not resistance now became women's proper response as "separate spheres" solidified.

Why Charke chose the Caribbean as locale is anyone's guess. Perhaps the choice was personally motivated since her renegade husband, Richard Charke (who abandoned her and their daughter) had emigrated and probably died there.[13] Besides, authors had long utilized islands as handy and exciting stage sets where heroes and villains could be whisked on and off at will. But more to the point, Charke needed to survive economically and authorship served that end. Principally an actor, the estranged daughter of Colley Cibber, poet laureate, theatre manager, and dramatist, she had tried her hand at various occupations from managing a shop and a puppet theatre to waiting tables and selling sausages.[14] Her literary repertoire amounted to a couple of plays— one a melodrama—three comparatively short novels, and an autobiography. When *Henry Dumont* was published, she was down and out at the Elephant and Castle.[15] In an age that indulged feeling yet openly disavowed and condemned homosexuality, Charke included both in *Henry Dumont* to boost sales, accrue cultural power, and perhaps introduce political statements of recognition if not commendation.[16] Having lived an arduous, adventurous life, Charke could readily identify with people excluded from mainstream society. In her shocking autobiography, she regales readers with tales about how she duped people and was duped herself, enamored as much of the telling as of human complexity itself. Exuberantly rebellious, she thrives on dramatizing injustice, mentioning, for example, how much she appreciated the camaraderie of prostitutes who posted bail for her. Hidden in the seams of *Henry Dumont* and the *Autobiography,* with their display of egregious scandal, is not only a scorn for norms but an almost palpable personal alienation, largely camouflaged.

Published in 1756, *The History of Henry Dumont and Miss Charlotte Evelyn* was "originally intended to have been published last summer, but on my saying I designed in my Preface to give a short account of my life; several [people] insisted on my swelling my Narrative to a Volume."[17] As much to the point, her precarious economic situation induced Charke to hold off publishing the novel until her sensationalized memoirs made their splash. To please the public in *The History,* Charke declared that she would:

> Keep up the noble Sentiments of Virtue so entirely consistent with the true character of an honest Soul, whether dignified with Title, or only aggrandized with innate Principles of Honour, Justice, and Humanity.
>
> I shall trouble my Reader no further, than to wish my Endeavour to entertain them may succeed, and by the Sale of my Book shall be able to judge, whether I shall ever dare to make any further Attempt of this Nature. (Charke, "The Preface," *The History of Henry Dumont,* pp. iv–v.)

The story focuses on wealthy plantation owners, the French Dumont family who settle in England and the Evelyn family, whose son Henry and daughter Charlotte, purveyors of unassailed purity, eventually marry. Any proto-abolitionist discourse must be weighed against this plantocratic backdrop. Or, to put it another way, the novel treats emotional responses toward slaves as a mark of the pure heart while promoting the benefits of colonialism within an orthodox eighteenth-century, morally unquestioned understanding of British foreign policy. The tribulations of love are woven into a chain of individual actions coded as moral and sentimental that effectively strengthen the colonial presence:

> Mr. Evelyn went home and prepared Lady Generous [Charlotte Evelyn] to her inexpressible surprize and joy to receive Mr. Dumont for a husband; in a few days their nuptials were publickly solemnized at St. Paul's cathedral, and was the bless'd means of restoration of peace and fortune to this worthy pair (Charke, *The History of Henry Dumont . . .*, pp. 255–56).

A subplot introduces the immaculate Alexander Jennings, miniature model of Henry Dumont. One day, Mr. Dumont found the orphaned Jennings with "a natural propensity to virtue" in Windsor Forest (allegorically suggestive of the philanthropic Robin Hood) where he had been "secreted. . . . in this melancholy retreat" for thirty-six hours, hiding from a cruel uncle. His kindhearted schoolmaster, Mr. Williams, had already lost an eye and "the other is much endangered" in defending Jennings against this depraved relative. Because the Dumonts befriended and educated him alongside young Henry Dumont, Jennings sought employment "in some industrious calling that may do honour to my noble benefactors, who empowered me to make the laudable pursuit" (Charke, *the History of Henry Dumont . . .*, p. 41). He also longs to leave England because he loves Miss Evelyn. A mutual friend of Count Dumont and Mr. and Mrs. Evelyn, a Caribbean merchant named Mr. Bryan, agrees to hire Jennings as his clerk and receives £500 from the Count "as a little fortune for him when he had served his clerkship" (Charke, *The History of Henry Dumont . . .*, p. 42).

After happily marrying in the Caribbean, Jennings eventually inherits a fortune from appreciative Bryan. His outlook is apparently one with which Charke identifies:

> It happened that one of the richest black planters died, who leaving only a widow behind him, and she being advanced in years, resolved to sell the plantation and a numerous stock of slaves, and retire from business. Accordingly a sale was advertised, and among the rest of the gentlemen, Mr. Jennings, Mr. Leicester, and Mr. Powell, went to make purchases of the goods; as to slaves, Mr Jennings never would deal that way, being of too tender a disposition to inflict the heavy grievances and burdens he often saw his fellow

creatures undergo. However, he went into the gardens with the rest
of the company, where these unhappy wretches were employed in
dreadful tasks in the extremity of the sultry heat, frequently receiving cruel stripes from the merciless hands of their overseers.
(Charke, *The History of Henry Dumont . . .* , pp. 225–26)

Charke's novel chimes with the times, avowing mercantile delight in
slave-trading profits, with the concomitant boost to Britain's industry
and commerce. Cultural production serves that colonial end without
fanfare. In an easy mix, Charke includes contradictory reports of
British advance with the maltreatment of slaves. A black planter challenges the idea of plantation-owning as inherently corrupt in a slave
society and implicitly suggests that black owners are as cruel as white
owners. Jennings, moreover, resembles a contrite overseer who hates
part of his job but not enough to leave in protest. In other words,
abuses are condemned but treated as gratuitously evil acts of de-
formed Christians.

Quite by chance, Jennings spots his baleful uncle among "those
miserable objects. . . . Notwithstanding his [the uncle's] former barbarity, Mr. Jennings felt all the tender emotions of heart for his misfortune." He buys his relative to free him. In turn the uncle "grew penitent
[and] became the reverse of what he had been. . . . He lived two years
only, leading a life of contrition, and died a perfect convert to religious
truth and purest laws" (Charke, *The History of Henry Dumont . . .* , p.
228).

In the final paragraph Powell resurfaces, the man who had bought
slaves the same day that Jennings' compassion made him forbear
from such transactions. But Jennings can buy an uncle—and a white
man to boot—because it is cruelty, and not the denial of human rights
from which he flinches.

Several issues are left up in the air: the treatment of slaves repels
Jennings yet heroes make livings as slave-owners. Jennings's altruism
compels him to buy his uncle back because slavery cannot be toler-
ated if Britons are the slaves. The Barbary Coast principle is at work
again. Just as much to the point, the uncle's genuine repentance is
represented as a ready embrace of pro-slavery law and a Eurocentric
concept of truth that obliquely marginalizes slaves yet further.

Formerly disadvantaged, Powell inherits a fortune from the generous Leicesters, who lament inequities he previously endured. The
artificial but understandable separation between "inequities" suffered
by individual white British males and the macrocosmic inequity that
is slavery continually and silently destabilize Charke's text. Jennings'

anathema toward the institution is the heart-throb of *The History*. Even Henry Dumont, or ideologically more likely, especially Henry Dumont, cannot go that far. Thus the projected vision for Powell's sons reconfirms a powerfully informing conflict: comfortably engaged in the slave trade, the sons possess Jennings' susceptibilities but display no reservations about slave ownership; the gradations of senti-mentality toward slaves on the eve of agitation have become very finely calibrated:

> As the father had more than a sufficient competence, [the sons] were jointly concern'd in the trade the father had successfully carried on for years, each marrying two of the greatest fortunes in the colony, and lived to be the happy instruments of good to several who from their great humanity avoided many sorrows they might have been otherwise exposed to (Charke, *The History of Henry Dumont . . .* , p. 256).

The speaker's final commentary exposes the thematics of conflict; she allies herself ideologically with the moderate wing of the pro-slavery lobby, who drew the line at physical cruelty and encouraged tender-hearted male ownership that rubber-stamped the economic status quo. On the other hand, her portrayal of the formerly victimized Jennings as a man repulsed by certain aspects of slavery renders Charke one of the first female authors to sketch a sympathetic charac-ter who heralds anti-slavery sentiment. Contemporary discourse had neither sanctioned nor made room for the historical possibility of "abolition"—slavery was too profitable and its horrors were well-hidden or rationalized; publicized inhuman practices were labelled "rumor" or the evidence was deemed "insufficient." Not to put too fine a point on it, the plantocratic lobby was wealthy and well-connected. Thus, Jennings registers his offended sensibility but, in the light of current conditions, must repress his disgust; he ameliorates the situa-tion, but little more than discursively.[18] These negotiations parallel the containment of slaves as a fixed, near-abstract entity: the European colonizer has surfaced as a hero-philanthropist, transitional forerun-ner of the anti-slavery campaigner in the following decades. Charke envisions someone on the spot who abhors this institutional violence. The emergence of agitators in Britain who use the court and then the parliamentary system to terminate abuses and then slavery itself lies a decade away. A Jennings-like "female" hero further privileges women as guardians of true feeling; such named, feeling, and thinking individ-uals as Oroonoko, Imoinda, and Yarico have vanished from fiction.

Wylie Sypher's claim that Charke's novel is the first to let "the anti-slavery tear" "for its own sake" ignores the novel's specific historical moment.[19]

Almost a decade later, Sarah Robinson Scott published a novel entitled *The History of Sir George Ellison* (1776).[20] Another plutocratic plantation owner, Sir George wants to treat his slaves with (his idea of) common decency and convert them to Christianity, his actions encoded as philanthropy in its purest form. Readers are assumed to react somewhat along the lines of Phillis Wheatley's owners. As June Jordan puts it tersely: "The Wheatleys already owned several slaves. They had done this before; the transaction would not startle or confound or embarrass or appall either one of them."[21] On the other hand, even though Sarah Scott underwrites amelioration in years when protests against slavery increased, those protests in print are proportionately few in number.[22] Nonetheless, as Scott composed her novel, Granville Sharp was initiating what was to become a protracted emancipation campaign by aiding a slave named Jonathan Strong. Grandson of an Archbishop of York, an acquaintance of the learned Catherine Talbot's mother, Sharp was a familiar figure in bluestocking circles.[23] Sarah Scott's sister, Elizabeth Robinson Montagu, presided over an eminent salon, although Scott herself lived well north of London at Batheaston. In 1765 Sharp instigated a court case on behalf of the twenty-one-year-old Strong, grievously battered and discarded by his owner, David Lisle.[24] Sharp's biographer describes his motivation: "in the first moments of his action, he had no other object in view than the relief of a miserable fellow-creature, struggling with disease and extreme indigence." (31) As Sharp pressed his case to declare slavery illegal as well as morally illegitimate and fresh facts about slavery blazoned in the press, Britain's freedom-loving reputation took a pounding. As a case in point, despite free and expert medical attention, Jonathan Strong died as a result of his injuries, four years after the court case. Sharp's action in supporting Strong emboldened women to protest, but his example initially encouraged an ameliorationist approach. Around that time, too, in the 1750s and 1760s, bluestockings were welcoming a famous South Sea Islander named Emin into their midst, in terms of contemporary Anglo-Saxon thinking a model of the "noble savage" and "natural man." With his presence the implications of slavery resonated more volubly. Elizabeth Montagu worried so much about Emin's safe return that Lord Lyttelton felt obliged to assure her that [Emin] "is alive and got home to his father."[25]

Theoretically, though in a different context, the Church of England also pursued a conservative approach to slavery and the condition of slaves. Anglican Sarah Scott's novel—and perhaps Charke's novel and the Countess of Hertford's poems—fictionalized the Church of England's fusion of pro-slavery activities and Christian charity in their Caribbean enterprises. The Church used its acquisition of extensive property in the East Caribbean—the Codrington Estates—as an opportunity to convert slaves to Christianity "by their masters and [to show] that plantations worked by Christian masters could be both profitable and orderly."[26] By 1768 when Anthony Benezet petitioned to formalize emancipation as Quaker policy, a spokesman for the Society for the Propagation of the Gospel, Dr. Daniel Burton, denied that slavery and Christianity could be reconciled, arguing instead that emancipation would foster rebellion and opposition to religious instruction.[27] This combination of factors had marked amelioration as the optimum solution to slavery, the only one that could resolve gnawing contradictions about human freedom and material profit. Advocacy of a step-by-step policy toward ending slavery fired people with a sense that they were doing something—urging a humanitarian outlook—that neither challenged nor imperilled foreign policy.

At least one celebrated freed African living in London, Ignatius Sancho, seemed to lend credence to this reformist approach. Sancho commented favorably on Sarah Scott's intentions in a letter to Laurence Sterne in 1766. (Laurence Sterne had introduced a compassionate vignette of a "negro girl" in *Tristram Shandy,* 1760–67).[28]

> Of all my favorite authors, no one has drawn a tear in favour of my miserable black brethren—excepting yourself [Sterne], and the humane author of Sir George Ellison.—I think you will forgive me;—I am sure you will applaud me for beseeching you *to give one half-hour's attention to slavery* [my italics] as it is at this day practised in our West Indies.[29]

But Sancho's double-voiced, mimicking prose meticulously distinguishes between his pleasure at writers who elicit sympathy and his implied demand for emancipation as a vital component of any worthwhile political agenda. In other words, he sought emancipation unconditionally, but if compassion, wrought British-style, worked as an interim measure to bring the public to a fuller awareness of slavery, then pragmatics dictated encouragement of such a strategy.

ALWAYS CHARITY, NEVER EQUALITY

In Scott's novel, creole George Ellison's program for slaves consists of a steady diet of gradualism, some education, and elementary religious education—appeasement or compensation for slavery in short—which served a British end.[30] Scott resolves the political tension in Charke's novel between anti-slavery Jennings and pro-ameliorative Powell in favor of the latter. Slavery has become a new litmus test of Christian altruism. In the preface to an earlier companion volume entitled *Millenium Hall* (1762), Scott proclaimed her intention and used the title to state how she hoped her text would "excite in the Reader proper Sentiments of Humanity, and lead the Mind to Love of Virtue."[31]

Scott's personal life fostered this perspective. She and Lady Barbara Montagu founded a charitable establishment outside Bath after Scott left her husband summarily in the wake of her marriage—an act that usually precipitated public scandal. *Millenium Hall* (1762) semifictionalized their experiences in promoting female employment and education.[32]

The protagonist of the two volume *History of George Ellison* is the son of a younger son of an "ancient and opulent family," who received only a small proportion of his father's wealth but by his profession was enabled to live "genteely" (Scott, *The History of Sir George Ellison,* p. 1). Apprenticed to Mr. Lamont, an "eminent merchant," Ellison travels to Jamaica and marries a wealthy widow, a plantation owner. Capably amassing a fortune, Ellison still cannot enjoy its fruits to the full because "the cruelty exercised on the part of mankind . . . preyed on his mind. It was Ellison's opinion that these creatures [slaves] would be far our superiors in merit, and indeed in nature, if they could live without committing frequent faults. . . . Negroes are naturally faithful and affectionate, though on great provocation, their resentment is unbounded, and they will indulge their revenge through their own certain destruction" (Scott, *The History of Sir George Ellison,* Vol. 1, p. 41).

Sir George's speech recasts the debate on slavery. The slaves' "natural" faithfulness and affection recalls Yarico's innocent loyalty to her beloved Inkle and reinforces supine responses to oppressors as a positive British value. But in its evocation of *Oroonoko,* of resurgent, formerly docile slaves, slavery is also encoded more problematically as an institution that provokes flight and the planting of a new colony (as in Behn's text) and suicide (as Yarico contemplates). And worse still: slavery excites an easily combustible (though self-indulgent) revenge. Such an eruption would bespeak havoc on plantations. Into this visionary prophecy of the San Domingo revolution, Scott also plants the classic European nightmare during slavery. All resistance and escape are dangerous; white control is a survival kit. Africans no longer act as happy or noble natives capering in a state of nature; they nurture a "savage" or primitive inner core, a quasi-consciousness. This new status for the colonial other is a serious affair because British lives are at stake.

Scott reviles the unchristian violence attached to the unreconstructed pro-slavery lobby. To teach an "erring" slave a lesson, Sir George (after giving the slave a second chance) sells him to a "typical" plantation-owning neighbor. Of course the slave pleads to return and Sir George's gentleness induces him to buy back the slave. Sir George's wife is a plantocratic camp follower herself, sarcastically noted by the narrator as an individual who acted "as if the difference of complexion excluded [slaves] from the human race" (Scott, *The History of Sir George Ellison,* p. 33). Disagreeing and disagreeable, she scoffs when Sir George calls Africans "fellow creatures." Undaunted, he orchestrates a plan to educate "the slaves" but worries how her prejudice might affect their son, who is "making [slaves] seek to please him by the most abject means" (Scott, *The History of Sir George Ellison,* p. 75). The text never suggests why such a woman attracted Sir George in the first place. Through Sir George's concern for his son, Scott accentuates the need to educate a new generation in laudable concerns, foreshadowing the pervasive inclusion of anti-slavery thematics in children's literature, on the rise in the following decade. Certainly, as Christopher Miller asserts, the monstrosity of the tendered profile of slaves evokes "the ambivalent profile of a certain non-Western object."[33] Charlotte Charke's uneasy resolution for the sons of a plantocratic father—they own slaves but acknowledge their Christian duty to extend charity to the less fortunate—is reconfirmed with different twists in Scott's field of view.

When Sir George decides to return to Britain, partly for his son's sake, slaves implore him in pidgin English to stay. "If go, steward whip, beat, kill poor slave; no go, no go, you go we die" (Scott, *The History of Sir George Ellison,* Vol. 1, p. 82). Luckily, the virtuous Mr. Hammond, who will replace Sir George, is able to transform the slaves, "stupefied by ill-usage and oppression," into "not only sincere but rational Christians" (Scott, *The History of Sir George Ellison,* Vol. 1, p. 92). Underscoring the superiority of conversion that earlier writers favored at the expense of unstated West African religious beliefs, Scott suggests that Christian values will foster a more "rational" discourse among slaves. Implicitly she refutes pro-slavery contentions that Africans felt but could not think.

Slaves' simplified language was standard for the time, talking pidgin signifying a limited intelligence. Outside of language scholars and traders, few were aware that the complex linguistic creation known as Creole was necessitated by the need of slaves in the Caribbean who spoke different African languages, known as Pidgins, to communicate with English speakers and vice versa. Put plainly, a "Creole" (language) was a pidgin that [had] become a mother tongue, in this case in the "New World."[34]

> Unlike 'normal languages' a pidgin language usually comes into existence for a specific reason, lasts just as long as the situation that called it into being, and then goes quickly out of use. . . . A pidgin acquires a longer lease on life only by becoming the native language of a group of speakers (becoming creolized), and thereby passes over to the status of a 'normal' language. From this point of view, we can speak of pidgins as having 'life-cycles,' and of their being 'inherently weak' in that, not their linguistic structure, but their social standing is normally not hardy enough to enable them to be used outside of their original context.[35]

That colonists spoke pidgin too and helped develop it as a means of controlling the population was also little understood.[36] Lack of knowledge about slaves' speech, chauvinist ideas about language and so-called grammatical propriety continued to reinforce stereotypes about Africans as childlike people, barely participants in the symbolic order. In Quaker texts concerning slaves, spiritual subjection was an issue. The same is true at differing levels in mid-century novels. But the introduction of linguistic difference—the alleged and erroneously perceived contrast between speech in "formal" English and slaves' "scant" English—emphasizes the "stupidity" of slaves. This in turn reinforces the need for British intervention. The construction of the other as the only stunted speaker demands or necessitates a protective posture from the colonizer despite the fact that the discourse of such contemporary Africans as Equiano gives the lie to this popular mythology about language difference. For the time being, this construction of a monolithic, mentally inferior, and vulnerable other explains part of Jennings' and Ellison's stature. They bring light and knowledge to barely speaking entities.[37]

In England later, Sir George enjoys the news of his "Negroe's" continuing happiness. "Nothing," he exults, "could yield him higher satisfaction" (Scott, *The History of Sir George Ellison,* Vol. 2, p. 2). Family values revalidate themselves. A substitute father, Sir George tends to his slaves as much as he tends to his own children, "underdeveloped" people who rely on munificent protection, even *in absentia.* "Each planter in fact is a Patriarch."[38] In the community back home, Sir George aids the poor, imprisoned, and jobless, and implements a plan to educate males and females: kindness toward slaves is synonymous with charity toward poor villagers. Ownership of Africans is never gainsaid. It is always a given. In the colonial-domestic novel of manners, childlike adults—some of them white women—as well as children have no rights at all. In those few instances where white British women are degraded and rendered powerless, Scott introduces an unspoken connection in her text. Both slaves and white women are controlled by politically empowered males. Though very faint, an anti-patriarchal whisper is sounded.

Scott's seemingly categorical endorsement of the status quo, provided slave owners act benignly, reverberates elsewhere. Sir George, for instance, vocally opposes miscegenation; his authoritarian discourse denies his worst fears. Promoting marriage among his servants, he states unabashedly that "he did not wish a union between those of different complexions, the connections appearing indelicate and almost unnatural" (Scott, *The History of Sir George Ellison,* Vol. 2, p. 48). Miscegenation not only pushes philanthropy too far, it is a perversion; slaves might act as loyally as children, but beneath their good-humored surface lies an untamed barbarism, always ready to strike. Slaves must be entrusted to the civilized or they will act as unbridled as "the poor," given half a chance. Enforced subjection or subalternity guarantees and even epitomizes goodness on this moral scale.[39]

Wylie Sypher's characterization of *The History of Sir George Ellison* as a mature novel of anti-slavery more than misses the mark.[40] What counts here is altruism encapsulated in Sir George's motto: "The pleasure of serving other[s] is sufficient of itself" (Scott, *The History of Sir George Ellison,* Vol. 1, p. 72). Slavery resembles any other charity; the unstated subtextual monster is profit, cornerstone of the rising and predacious capitalist-colonialist economy.

When Sir George returns to England, he visits Millennium Hall, where several *déclassé,* formerly middle-class females oversee a number of charitable projects; self-effacing and victimized versions of Lady Bountiful, they are female versions of Sir George who spotlight the contrast between his power and their own. Although geographically unrelated, the sections politically conjoin in important ways: the actions of cruel slave owners and a female overseer's relatives (a Miss Alston) who forced her to marry are barely distinguishable.

After three years of ill-usage by her father and his mistress, Miss Alston was a "walking corpse." When she informs her father that a young man had tried to "render his daughter an infamous prostitute," her father treats her "roughly." After a servant discloses that her father plotted with a vile suitor, she escapes but not before Scott has run the gamut of pernicious "masculine" values (Scott, *The History of Sir George Ellison*, Vol. 2, pp. 98–117). Sir George's response to Miss Alston's nightmare morally contextualizes his treatment of slaves. He told her that:

> he much approved her reserve; for nothing so well became a child as to conceal the failings of her parents, but few, he trusted, had been so severely tried; for the account she had given him had chilled his blood with horror, and shewed such baseness as must appear incredible to any person who had not observed how one vice serves only as the first step towards iniquity, always leading to many others; an invincible reason for avoiding the least criminal indulgence. The first sin, he observed, is generally committed with reluctance, and followed by compunction; but by repeated wounds, conscience grows callous; and he who trembled at the first wrong step, rising by degrees to the summit of wickedness, commits at last the greatest crimes almost without remorse.

Cobbling together disapprobation of inhuman owners and paternalistic values, Scott quietly invokes her personal escape from a distressing marriage. Furthermore, as an acquaintance and friend of London bluestocking circles through her sister, Elizabeth Montagu, Scott would have been well aware of arranged and infelicitous marriages. A circle of women who hosted and frequented cultural salon gatherings in the later decades of the eighteenth century, the bluestockings formed firm and lasting friendships with one another and exemplified a form of social and intellectual self-determination for women. Several bluestockings themselves described arranged marriage as a slavery and deplored its dramatic impact on women's lives although this is not to deny that the number of forced marriages in the late eighteenth century probably declined.[41] The number did, but versions of arranged marriages still occurred. Mary Delany, later Pendarvis Granville, for one, a famous pioneer bluestocking, was forced at seventeen to marry fifty-nine year old Alexander Pendarvis. She recounts this experience to the Duchess of Portland thirty years later in a roman à clef. He was, she grimaced, "altogether a person more disgusting than engaging." In 1751 in a letter to her sister Ann Dawes, she asked bitterly: "Why must women be *driven to the necessity of marrying?* . . . Has not *this* made matrimony an irksome prison to many."[42] Hester Lynch Salisbury, later Thrale Piozzi, also a bluestocking salon member, publicized an equally negative personal tale: "Vain were all my assurances that nothing resembled love *less* than Mr. Thrale's behavior."[43] A third well-known bluestocking educationalist, Hester Chapone, drily exposes her mental resistance to objectification:

> Bishop Hall . . . would reduce me to the condition of an Indian skreen, and allow my father to item me amongst his goods and chattels, and put me up to sale for the highest bidder;—or if this pleases me not, will give me leave to call myself one of his hands (I hope it is the right hand) which is to have no direction or power of acting but what he gives it; no will, no understanding of its own; and which, if it offends him, he may *cut off and cast it from him*.[44]

Scott knew the miseries of such women, facing male-mandated dictates. In an age that generated many philanthropic projects—often initiated by women—it was hardly surprising that middle-class women persistently deplored their lack of rights. Through Sir George, who treats slaves well in the Caribbean and tends to the poor, imprisoned, and jobless in his community back home in England, Scott helps to denote slavery as a bona fide charity, rightfully part of women's "active benevolence."[45] As a fictional trope, slavery hovers at the borderline between sentimentality and political principle.[46] It was still part of what Henry Mackenzie was later to deplore as the "momentary ebullition of romantic humanity."[47] Anti-slavery had not yet become specifically identified in fiction with liberty and human rights. Maltreatment of slaves was a shame, something to protest in print, like forced or abusive marriages. In fact, marital situations were still contextualized as a form of slavery; in a 1755 poem about the Egyptian female philosopher, Hypatia, for example, the poet Elizabeth Tollett condemned the "domestic chain, . . . and asked what Happiness can servitude afford."[48] Lady Sarah Pennington, whose separation from her husband and children was an eighteenth-century gossip item, could easily have answered that vexed question. In letters to her daughters, Lady Sarah explains the reasons for her departure;

> For several years [I] cannot, upon Reflection, assure myself of any Thing, but too absolute, too unreserved an Obedience to every Injunction, even where they were plainly contrary to the Dictates of my own Reason. . . . Tired with a long series of repeated insults

of a nature almost beyond the Power of Imagination to conceive, my Temper became soured.[49]

Frequent public presentation of such views empowered women as never before. No doubt the combined power of Granville Sharp, the bluestockings, and influential female charities emboldened or inspired Scott. In abandoning old identifications with the victim, she aligned herself with the feminized hero-agent, the new feeling protagonist, who spoke a "feminine" language of nurturance. Scott also boosted provincial women's power, or rather she underscored its presence.[50] Put another way, Scott stressed women's visible lack of political clout. Few women in 1760 could have lived as Sir George did, a wealthy titled aristocrat who administered a Caribbean estate, then attended to the needs of the local communities when he returned to Britain; or perhaps more women than we know of assumed such roles, as widows most likely, or even as single and married women. Certainly the list of provincial female philanthropists was high, Elizabeth Bouverie of Kent being one celebrated instance, not to mention some of the bluestockings themselves. Sarah Scott and her friend Lady Bab, besides, had earned reputations as benefactors, but just outside London rather than beyond the seas; all the middle-class heroines in *Millenium Hall* were attractively wealthy, as if to stress that known but understated public presence.[51]

For simple historical reasons, Scott could advance Christian didacticism further than the Countess of Hertford: she wrote a decade later when the discourse of natural rights began to infiltrate public discussion. By linking conversion with promotion of education, Christian instruction, and less abusive physical treatment, Scott reconnected female sexual abuse, slavery, and religion. But the African hero had vanished; the double standard inherent in attitudes toward Barbary Coast slavery was now ideologically refashioned in light of recent events. Nonetheless, protests persisted against corsair kidnappings of Europeans. Amelioration was no threat to mercantilist values and profiteering, especially since Jamaica was "on the map," being extravagantly exploited. Rising profits kept abolition at bay; that was the point. In keeping with burgeoning sentiment and a growing colonialism, white female authors began to treat Africans as a social concern. Slavery was acceptable (with echoes here of Trefry's profile in *Oroonoko*) as long as profiteers were honorable Christian gentlemen. When Sir George decided to bankroll his son's purchase of more slaves, he was "sensible that slaves must be had to cultivate the plantation." Cold talk for (in Jane Spencer's phrase) a "paragon of benevolence."

But any reasonable Christian individual, the text insists, would have seen things that way. It was a contradiction that would inform fiction, not avowedly abolitionist, until the 1800s. But even coding slavery as an opportunity for Anglo-Africanist benevolence went a fair way toward concretizing slavery; on the other hand, those who wept over slavery had no need to act.

These novels that addressed slavery and other political issues counteracted popular images of flighty middle-class women whom Mary Wollstonecraft was later to dress down with such ire. This was a time, too, in which, as Judith Newton states, the "middle-class woman was urged to relinquish self-definition; she was urged to become identified by her services to others, in particular to men."[52] Consequently, discussions of freedom in fiction functioned as resistance to prescribed passivity. And visible opposition extended well beyond novels: "matters relating to the domestic economy and the home, food prices, enclosures, evictions and the like were deemed an appropriate area for women's concern and provoked a considerable amount of social protest well before any campaign for political rights or other aspects of female emancipation."[53] Isaac Kramnick usefully sums up one aspect of the shift in social formation that in turn bred protest: "Wives were home tending to their children, totally dependent economically on their husbands."[54] By 1783, to jump a little ahead of my story, the transformation of women's socio-political role to that of a domestic nurturer was progressing apace. Meanwhile, slavery enabled middle-class women to intensify their involvement in philanthropy. Its injustice, especially with respect to the family unit, also underwrote middle-class women's dissatisfaction, not easily expressed, with the status quo. The same people who enslaved Africans forced middle-class women into marriage.

Female authors tellingly presented feminized male characters who wielded the very power they were assuming in public as spokeswomen for virtue and were thought to be denied. While subtly displaying class, race, and gender subjection, they enhanced self-definition, restructuring their image as they argued through protagonists for more opposition to anti-christian behavior toward slaves. Put succinctly, in making subjects of themselves they effectively silenced the objects of their benevolence.

Scott's attention to Sir George Ellison carried pointed postscripts, directly related to growing anti-slavery protest, especially the court case of James Somerset in 1772 and the visit of Phillis Wheatley to Britain the following year. In the next decade, Scott redacted George Ellison into pamphlet form, using approximately the same plot. Chronologically that discussion belongs in the next chapter. However, the two Ellison texts set side by side strikingly display the effect of agitation.

Ninety-four pages long, the abbreviated version of the second volume of George Ellison, reentitled *The Man of Real Sensibility*, exercises the issue of slavery for over half the text.[55] A quotation from *Sentimental Journey* on the title page emphasizes Scott's delight in Sterne's style and humanitarian concerns.

Against a Caribbean backdrop, the text focuses on Ellison's domestic tribulations and his hiring of the Jennings-like Mr. Hammond before he departs for England. The second part concentrates on "Cupid's arrows." Once again Scott dramatized forced marriage as a form of slavery. George Ellison wants to marry a Miss Allin this time around but "she received the doctor as her intended husband at her father's command, when her heart was so little prejudiced in his favor" (Scott, *The Man of Real Sensibility*, p. 55). Eventually Ellison does marry her and they immerse themselves in good works. The language of charity and its relation to female cultural roles speak for themselves:

> His benevolent disposition scarce knew any bounds; he composed all differences in his neighbourhood, was the father of the orphan, a true friend of the distressed and helpless, a visitor of the sick and those who were in prison, and many a debtor, that had not been so out of wantonness, he delivered from the unrelenting pursuits of his creditors.
>
> These scenes were indeed the great feasts of his soul; but all his hours yielded him refined pleasures, because they were all spent in the exercise of benevolence; a desire to do good to others, was so intirely his governing principle, that, however, engaged in business or pleasure, he never lost sight of it, endeavouring to promote it by every action of his life (Scott, *The Man of Real Sensibility*, pp. 65–66).

The hero is still George Ellison, a wealthy middle-class creole-philanthropist, but the James Somerset verdict two years earlier and heightened anxiety about Britain's submersion in the slave trade temper Scott's previous ideas.

She introduces a female character—the sister of the kind overseer Mr. Hammond—whose task is to educate female slaves. Thus female mini-protagonists and female slaves reenter the discourse on slavery in a limited but foreshadowing way. Another new feature is Scott's attempt at social levelling: Sir George himself becomes plain untitled George Ellison, without the Sir. Enlightenment ideas about rank, such as those expounded by John Millar in *Origins of the Ranks and Differences,* have also modified Scott's perspective.[56]

But most revealingly, while in Scott's first version slavery virtually dropped out of sight at the end, in the shorter version a seemingly moribund Mr. Ellison looks more attentively to the future. He discharges a friend's debts, obliging his son "to leave his Jamaican estate in the hands of his steward, as long as he should live, providing for all the Negroes that should remain on the plantation at the time of his stewards' death" (Scott, *The Man of Real Sensibility,* p. 79). Legal battles in Britain have now made an issue of accountability toward slaves. The albeit mute presence of James Somerset in court fighting for his rights had made a difference. By defending Somerset, Granville Sharp underscored daily violations the man endured in slavery and drew attention to his courtroom presence through evoking slaves' conditions. James Somerset was a far cry from an unindividuated, helpless brute. Yet he was forcibly silenced in court by a suggested superior articulation and social hierarchy as well as by law. (The intricate implications of the legal situation will be discussed more fully in the next chapter.) Africans still loom hazily in the background as near-silent objects of Ellison's pity, denied the status (like Somerset) of speaking subjects, but their lives are now represented as existing in and through time, history, and specific locales. They are men and women who take up space and temporality in the material world, although in fiction they still do not talk or think. Their futures, nonetheless, deserve attention. Drastically limited though the change is, it marks some kind of nascent recognition of African humanity. On the contemporary scene, the controversy over Warren Hastings and talk about colonial "responsibility" or trusteeship, as it was known, toward the East India Company made the point even more pointed and germane.

Little else had changed from one text to the other. Amelioration remained privileged as a solution, a generous patriarch could be counted on to do right by slaves, and white superiority was assumed, underscored by the "unschooled" speech of African men and women. The heroic, feminized white father—an authorial projection privileging female rectitude—tends to his "children" who are "poor blacks," supposedly dependent and keen on this quasi-familial relationship. Paternal power fuses with maternal nurturance. Feminized fathers have entered the discourse. The fact that Scott portrays an almost coerced marriage between Miss Allin and the doctor as negatively as slavery itself lucidly indicates her (and her contemporaries') sense of priorities. George Ellison may be the Lady of the Manor in drag but one charity is as deserving as the other. Ellison's agonizing over the "painful exertion of his power" reveals the historical unlikelihood in that era of confronting such a compromising ambiguity and Scott's own unconscious denial of the multiple resistances within and between the lines of her text.

These textual conflicts comment on one another. Sir George must control the potentially threatening slave-other with a forestalling temporal strategy of selfless magnanimity while he sees to it that the injured white female protagonist recovers some socio-economic power. The great chain of being that designates social place remains intact. The discourse of repression that takes simplistic constructions of large groups of people for granted is beginning to loosen; a more authentic meaning of conditions of repression is emerging. Though Ellison and Scott may not be cognizant of the potentialities involved, Sir George's eagerness to satisfy slaves partly testifies to restless insecurities and a suppressed sense of justice on the part of authors. Even though they barely talk English, slaves must be approached (in Sir George's terms) humanely. Predations on Miss Allin and on slaves, in the most obvious interfusion of race and gender oppression since *Oroonoko,* collectively indict constructed white masculinist norms.

Across Scott's text, although the main characters hold forth and attempt to wrest control from their inferiors, cross-arching dialogues reverberate among the subalterns. Involuntary servitudes comment on one another. Talking about slavery is talking about a relation in women's lives many times removed, about arranged marriages over which women have no choice and vice versa. Scott obliquely condemns the externally imposed limits on young white women's lives by showing these limits tested most severely in the lives of slaves. The introduction of Sir George himself as narrator partly frees Scott from the necessity of "unitary language"[57] and allows the reader to read the "second" story of the author, told in this case through Miss Allin and, less directly, through the slaves. Scott can say what she wants to say through Sir George, a posited author of sorts, yet she can criticize Sir George too. He alone is cast in the not-so-dignified posture of speaking for others.[58] Moreover, in externalizing their empathy, female authors can mask and sublimate the anger they feel at women's roles and simultaneously assert themselves. Opposition to slavery is becoming further evidence of women's socially prescribed moral place and the redemptive missions they undertook in partial response.

Chapter 6

Emerging Resistances

The vulgar are influenced by names and titles. Instead of SLAVES, let the [Blacks] be called ASSISTANT-PLANTERS; and we shall not then hear such violent outcries against the slave trade by pious divines, tender-hearted poetesses and short-sighted politicians.
—Folaris O. Shyllon, *Black Slaves in Britain,* quoting *The Gentleman's Magazine,* p. 149.

... In every human Breast God has implanted a Principle, which we call the love of Freedom; it is impatient of Oppression, and pants for Deliverance; and by the Leave of our modern Egyptians I will assert that the same principle lives in us. God grant Deliverance in his own Way and Time, and get him honor upon all those whose Avarice impels them in countenance and help forward the Calamities of their fellow Creatures. This I desire not for their Hurt, but to convince them of the strange Absurdity of their Conduct whose Words and Actions are so diametrically opposite. How well the cry for Liberty, and the reverse Disposition for the exercise of oppressive Power over others agree,—I humbly think it does not require the Penetration of a Philosopher to determine. Phillis Wheatley to Samuel Occam, February 11, 1774.
—Henry Louis Gates, Jr., *Figures in Black,* p. 77.

In the provinces, engaged in somewhat unconventional activities, Charlotte Cibber Charke and Sarah Robinson Scott constructed a philanthropic hero as a new paradigmatic response to slavery, while slaves themselves remained undifferentiated and brutish. Entrepreneurs and owners were still the unadulterated villains. Insurgent slaves vanished from the scene. Through their powerful male protagonists female authors could ventriloquize moral alternatives and also make visible the limits imposed by a white patriarchal world on the lives of others. Compromises with slavery, however, were short-lived as a solution; amelioration was beginning to ring false. Too much agitation, increasing exposure of conditions, and evidence of African intellectuality rendered such compromises rapidly untenable.

Granville Sharp, Thomas Clarkson, and Anthony Benezet, for example, wrote anti-slavery pamphlets and tracts while Ukawsaw Gronniosaw (James Albert), Ignatius Sancho, and Phillis Wheatley attained national reputations, writing an autobiography, letters, and poetry respectively. Various women writers attempted individual responses to this groundswell, filling the gulf between George Ellison, benevolent plantation-owner, and illiterate slaves with narratives about assertion and escape that partly echoed their own hidden desires.

The resistance of slaves, new information, and enterprising radical propaganda in the 1760s and 1770s galvanized these changes. Feminized male heroes with acute sensibilities were replaced by similarly attuned female protagonists; women writers gained sufficient confidence to inscribe their gender more openly and imbue the effect of slavery on family life with heightened meaning. In a sentimental travel narrative and a children's didactic tract, one a new form, the other a refinement of an old, Elizabeth Bonhote and Dorothy Kilner responded directly to the *cause célèbre* of James Somerset's legal opposition to his personal enslavement in Britain. Phillis Wheatley's presence in Britain inspired Mary Scott and Mary Deverell to write poems; in a prose hymn for children, Anna Laetitia Barbauld reworked an old notion about spiritual equality. Sophia Lee's novel *The Recess* condoned slave insurrection and applauded the actions of two individual women of African descent; a short novel by publisher Lucy Peacock portrayed an individual slaveowner promoting emancipation, a first in women's anti-slavery discourse.

In 1774, eight years after Scott's two-volume novel was published, the pamphlet version of *The History of George Ellison,* strikingly retitled in response to cultural fashion, *The Man of Real Sensibility,* had heralded these changes. Its decisive concentration on slavery contrasted with the novel's more diffuse responses. Anthony Benezet and Granville Sharp bombarded the public with tracts. Between 1768 and 1807, the respective dates for his tracts entitled *A Short Account of that part of Africa inhabited by Negroes* and *The System of Colonial Law,* Sharp had published eleven separate tracts on slavery and several on seamen, Sierra Leone, linguistics, initiation of public charities, and the illegality of governmental acts.[1] But emerging opposition also stemmed from other critical interventions in British socio-cultural life. First, Africans living in Britain protested slavery as Phillis Wheatley visited Britain, a fortuitous coincidence, and second, the ideology of separate spheres systematically confined middle-class women, in spirit if not in practice, to the home. I want to return to the latter point when I discuss Barbauld's *Hymn*.

In 1770 a landmark text by Ukawsaw Gronniosaw challenged conventional constructions of African life. It was lengthily entitled *Wonderous Grace Display'd in the Life and Conversion of James Albert Ukawsaw Gronniosaw, an African Prince. Giving an Account of the Religion, Customs, Manners etc. of the Native of Zaara in Africa. As related by Himself*.[2] A native of Bournou and son of a princess, Gronniosaw dedicated his narrative to the Methodist Countess of Huntington, who also helped to arrange Phillis Wheatley's visit to England. The third edition was published simultaneously at outlets in Yorkshire, Bradford, Kighley, Halifax, and Leeds. Gronniosaw's title was somewhat misleading and probably designed for maximum sale, because the memoirs' driving message was the inhumanity of slavery and the need for its abolition. His account ranges from the time he was sold to a Dutch merchant by a Gold Coast (contemporary Ghana) ivory merchant for two yards of checked cloth to his eventual life with his wife and children in Kidderminster on the edge of survival. To this day, his fate and that of his family remain unknown. Throughout the narrative, Gronniosaw highlights his moral weaknesses, his conversion, the duplicity of captains, the grief he felt at leaving his mother, and his enslavement. Gronniosaw suspects that the public will turn a deaf ear to an authentic African speaking voice: "it is possible the circumstance I am going to relate will not gain credit with many." But he proceeds undaunted to tell his tale of exploitation and perseverance. He describes trying to track down George Whitefield and how he found himself in dire financial straits due to an agricultural-industrial dispute among weavers: "we had not yet been married a year before all these misfortunes overtook us." Having survived unemployment and near starvation, he and his wife have their dead child buried, their debt unabating. He ends on a resigned, not desperate note:

> Such is our situation at present. My wife, by hard labour at the loom, does everything that can be expected from her towards the maintenance of our family; and God is pleased to incline the hearts of his People at times to yield us their charitable assistances; being myself through age and infirmity able to contribute but little to their support. As Pilgrims, and very poor Pilgrims, we are travelling through many difficulties (Gronniosaw, *Wondrous Grace*, p. 171).

Two years after Gronniosaw's chronicle, the court case of James Somerset riveted public attention, its immediate antecedent the case of Jonathan Strong. Through publicity generated by Granville Sharp around 1768, Strong's case had articulated the reality of slavery and its attendant rationalizations by slavers and their apologists. The next year Sharp published *A Representation of the Injustice and Dangerous Tendency of Tolerating Slavery; or of Admitting the Least Claim of Private Property in the Persons of Men, in England.* As Peter Fryer puts it, *A Representation* was a "tour de force of legal and humanitarian argument."[3] The irrepressible Sharp also continued physical and legal "rescues" of kidnapped slaves, including those of John and Mary Hylas and Thomas Lewis.[4] Sir William Blackstone warned Sharp about difficulties he might experience in fighting to obtain a legal decision that would outlaw both the kidnapping of African slaves in England and their forcible transportation to the colonies. But Sharp persisted nonetheless. Six years after the Strong case, he instigated another test case to prevent Caribbean owners from coercing slaves into returning to the colonies. He meant his action as a contribution toward ongoing debates about the concept of natural law. Paul Hazard puts the terms of the debate this way:

> The Slave Trade . . . would find no justification. Nature, which con-
> fers an equal dignity on all her children; or a reason, which does
> not admit that a difference in the colour of their [slaves'] skin should
> condemn a whole race to suffering and infamy.[5]

The slave in question was James Somerset, who refused to return with his owners to Boston, escaped, and was recaptured in 1771. Pressed to define the relationship in law between master and slave, Lord Mansfield delivered his famous verdict in 1772, erroneously interpreted to mean that slaves could not exist on English soil. (Mansfield's decision simply forbade owners to force slaves to leave England.):

> The power of a master over his slave has been extremely different,
> in different countries. The state of slavery is of such a nature,
> that it is incapable of being introduced on any reasons, moral or
> political; but only [by] positive law, which preserves its force long
> after the reasons, occasion, and time itself from whence it was
> created, is erased from memory: It's so odious, that nothing car be
> suffered to support it, but positive law. Whatever inconveniences,
> therefore, may follow from a decision, I cannot say this case is

allowed or approved by the law of England; and therefore the black [i.e., James Somerset] must be discharged.[6]

Unsurprisingly, Lord Mansfield's ruling repeats standard Anglo-Africanist one-dimensional discourse—"his slave," "the black" crop up— even in this authorized legal language. But the judge's insistence on diction that denies Somerset's everyday reality also elicits an embedded resistant discourse. Somerset's own unheard voice dominates the trial. He refused to return to Jamaica, he argued with his master Stewart, and contradicted Stewart's reasoning by explaining his side of slavery. Ultimately he related these actions and conversations to Granville Sharp in an unrecorded oral narrative. That voice and these dialogues are so omnipresent at the trial and in innumerable press accounts, reinforced by Somerset's physical presence and his palpably defiant spirit, that Mansfield's ruling cannot altogether suppress them.

In response to the unheard as well as the heard, when the crowds outside the courtroom heard the judge's decision, they cheered along with representatives from the black community in court.[7] Horace Walpole's dry comment to George Hardinge further indicates extensive public engagement with the issue:

> You may guess this inquiry into villeinage took its rise from that famous question of Anglo-Aethiopian liberty which is now afoot, and *sub judice,* in the King's Bench, on the habeas corpus of a negro mutineer.[8]

But the consequences of Lord Mansfield's decision—many hoped for a storm of pro-emancipation sentiment—never materialized. In Folaris Shyllon's words: "Here at last was the confirmation and admission of all that Granville Sharp stood for and contended. And the heavens did not fall."[9]

In his *Memoirs,* Granville Sharp discusses the effect of the ruling on London's black population. Since slaves were now generally thought to be free in Britain, "having now no masters to support them," about four hundred Africans gradually became destitute, having acquired no craft, profession, or skill to fall back on: "They were alarmingly conspicuous throughout the streets as common beggars."[10] This phenomenon recalled Queen Elizabeth I's earlier response and relocation was again discussed in earnest.[11]

By 1786 a "Committee for the Relief of the Black Poor" was appealing to the public for funds. Newspapers, however, continued to advertise the sale of African slaves, a commentary in itself on the Mansfield decision. That same year Sharp wrote *Regulations for the New Settlement, Sierra Leone* and, in 1790, *Free English Territory in Africa*. This commitment to the "Black Poor" and the "solution" of relocation was and is viewed as hard evidence of eighteenth-century humanitarianism. In fact, Somerset's victory unavoidably provoked discussions about escape and emancipation, in both black and white communities. The great rush to move Africans out of Britain marked a refusal on the part of a scared administration and public to deal with the implications of the Somerset decision. The decision spoke theoretically of physical equality and opened up a wider discourse of general human rights both in the United Kingdom and the Caribbean. But in fact, this discourse about emancipation was taboo until the San Domingan revolution in 1791 forced discussion into the open.

Elizabeth Bonhote and Dorothy Kilner were two of the writers who responded to the controversy. Respectively, they wrote a travel narrative and a long children's tract, each of which projected a version of James Somerset as hero and victim.

ELIZABETH BONHOTE

Elizabeth Bonhote's episodic travel-narrative *The Rambles of Mr. Frankly* (1774) contained seemingly contradictory endorsements: it applauded emancipation in Britain but excused vile behavior by a "West Indian."[12]

Among the contemporary "characters" Mr. Frankly "bumps into on his travels" are a "Black," a "West Indian," and a merchant, each of whom expresses an aspect of plantocratic and slave-trading society. For example, when Mr. Frankly meets a slave on a London street, he asks himself: "Why did I start?" and then proceeds to describe "The Black":

> That jetty countenance perhaps never blushed for guilt—and if so, his heart is as fair as his countenance is gloomy.—"A Slave!—The heart shudders at a fellow-creature's being a slave—exposed to sale in a publick market—beat and inured to hardships— monstrous!—Yet are they often lively and happy as their masters—and even that man,' said I, 'flatters himself with the hopes of revisiting his own country when he died—many cannot be made sensible of any other change, than that of returning to the country from which

he was so disgracefully sold—and the thought affords pleasure.—
So natural is our attachment to the place where we spent the early
part of our lives—it calls to mind the pleasing days of innocence—
But the slave must surely have forgotten his parents, who only
regarded him in his days of infancy as a treasure of which they
determined to make the most.—Sigh not, then, to return to such
unhospitable shores—Would that I could explain to you all the far
happier prospect that awaits you—for I doubt not but there will
one day be as many Blacks as Whites in Paradise (Bonhote, *The
Rambles,* pp. 73–4).

James Somerset's case notwithstanding, Frankly's description derives from a traditional white cultural standpoint, complete with
slaves' alleged speech patterns, so favored by sentimental literature.[13]
Denied agency, Africans will be given the "right" to white Christian
values; this undifferentiated "they" will be "allowed" to enter paradise
if they become Christians. Bonhote's narrator knows best what slaves
want. The Somerset challenge has necessitated a shift in cultural
representation in more than one sense. A humanitarian response must
be publicized, but more to the point Africans must be fashioned in a
way that affirms British modes of thinking and living. They must be
spoken for rather than speak themselves. By suggesting that the slave
would be better off in Britain rather than living back home in Africa
and that joining the ranks of the "Black Poor" and converting to
Christianity would be preferable to living with his parents in the West
African culture he grew up in and loved, Bonhote through Frankly
allies herself with received contemporary thinking. Under the guise
of benevolence, she implicitly validates the great chain of being in
conjunction with class and colonial dominance: the "poor" African is
a destined social inferior who deserves help; Frankly is a surrogate
parent horrified at an orphan's condition. *The Rambles* also hints
unselfconsciously that African parents, not white marauders, caused
the "Black's" enslavement. The text's "understanding" of African family
life matches the orthodox aspersions cast against the "gloomy" physiognomy of the colonial other. In historical terms, too, spiritual solutions are becoming dated. Granted, when no or almost no protest
was heard, any discussion of spiritual equality within the limits of a
historically determined British consciousness had at least the potential of initiating discussion about other equalities. But after Somerset's
case, authors could no longer pretend disingenuousness about a disin-
terested religious solution.

Elsewhere, *The Rambles* expresses national insecurities that the
court case stimulated and further contradictions within the benevo-

lent "ethic." A West Indian is given the benefit of the doubt about his attitudes toward slavery; a merchant is not. Mr. Frankly excuses the former when he callously strikes a beggar. To explain why the West Indian assaults the beggar with impunity, Frankly ventures that he had just left a slave-based society. Then, when he hands the beggar five guineas, having realized that the man is genuinely penurious, instantly he attains heroic status. The speaker concludes that the Creole is a "Christian and charity will guide him to Heaven" (Bonhote, *The Rambles,* p. 34).

The Rambles affords the merchant no such leniency. Mercantilism is still rendered much more morally corrupt than being a Caribbean slave-owner. Upon the merchant's forehead, "traffick is written. . . . His thoughts are constantly employed in getting money. . . . Benevolence and love cannot animate his soul." Basic conflicts previously pervading texts about Inkle and Yarico revisit late eighteenth-century variants.

In addition to Somerset's case, Laurence Sterne's form and ideas in *Sentimental Journey* (1768) are another clear influence. In *The Parental Monitor* (1788), a collection of short essays that Bonhote wrote for her children "in case she should die before she could personally oversee their upbringing," she restates her perspective on charity:

> Benevolence and philanthropy are virtues the most generous and captivating, the most exalting to human nature; they are bright emanations of the Deity, which extend their divine influence to all around, and, like the rays of the sun, diffuse universal cheerfulness, enliven the dungeon's dreary gloom, and inspire hope in the solitary inhabitant of a prison. . . . Benevolence does not confine itself merely to the relieving the bodily wants of our fellow creatures: it goes much further; it extends to the preservation of their souls.[14]

Through exhibiting the slave's destitution, Bonhote exposed at an individual level the plight of some 15,000 Africans now assumed to be free in the United Kingdom and the formerly hidden infrastructure of plantocratic slave society. Though she echoes her immediate predecessors in fiction by mouthing ambivalent values through a sentient male narrator, eighteenth-century readers could scarcely have doubted where her sympathies lay. She and Mr. Frankly seem one and the same, "connoisseurs of feeling" in Walter Allen's phrase.[15] Yet Bonhote does not borrow Somerset's argument that freedom is a natural right; she shrinks from slavery as Mr. Jennings did because slavery is emotionally and morally abhorrent. This abhorrence, however, does not prevent the narrator from mingling passivity with spiritual promise and advising victims to make the best of a bad lot and "pass over the rubs of misfortune with fortitude and patience" (Bonhote, *The Rambles*, p. 111):

> Every situation in life has its satisfactions . . . even the slave on the burning soil of Guinea has his pleasures—for the appetite which labour creates, gives a relish to the coarsest food—and the poor slave, from the little success which even that state affords, enjoys almost an equal satisfaction with a monarch when he enlarges his dominions. In the most miserable situation this consolation arises;—the knowing we cannot be more wretched, and that we shall soon arrive at a better (Bonhote, *The Rambles*, pp. 109–10).

Bonhote's long later poem, *Feeling*, invokes the language of slavery to denounce abuses suffered by British sailors; praising the successful passage of the abolitionist bill in 1807 to urge improvements in their lot, it reinscribes traditional female values of sympathy and contempt for corruption, while concurrently radiating delight in an abolitionist solution that had become acceptable by the time *Feeling* was written:

> Come Inspiration, aiding Feelings' lay,
> And breathing eloquence, their wrongs display,
> Oh! tell the British senators, the hand
> That freed the slave, and burst Oppression's band
> With pow'r humane may heal a wound as sore
> As ever Afric's injur'd native bore.[16]

Ignatius Sancho's earlier reaction to *George Ellison*, a text that prefigured Bonhote's *The Rambles* with its pre-Somerset stereotypes, is worth recalling here. Sancho had expressed appreciation of Scott's moral-sentimental reviling of slavery. By the same token, Bonhote's representation of Africans as "fellow-creatures" and Frankly's commiseration for their plight were steps taken in good faith and in the right direction. The difference concerns unspoken dialogues in some of which Bonhote silently voices white British constructions of the other. Sancho, on the other hand, underlines and encourages one aspect of Eurocentric belief—the need to show feeling for the oppressed and summon the charitable to do likewise—as a way of transforming colonial others into speaking subjects like himself. Where sentimental discourse is Bonhote's means to elicit more charity, it aids Sancho in securing a much more political and self-determining end.

Dorothy Kilner

A second fictional analogue of Somerset cropped up in *The Rotchfords,* a didactic Christian tale for children by Dorothy Kilner written most probably in the mid 1780s.[17] According to Kilner, a good Christian home can teach the evil of slavery and reconstitute a corrupt practice. Through the transformative use of the family to dissolve slavery, Kilner also reendorses the role of middle-class women as the nation's moral elders. Mrs. Rotchford—as much a projection of Kilner as Frankly is of Elizabeth Bonhote—will instruct the nation's children about what to think. Three years before *The Rotchfords* was published, Kilner had described her aims in the popular and cheerful *The Life and Perambulations of a Mouse* (1785)—"no less to instruct and improve, than ... to amuse and divert."[18] Published the year after Sophia Lee's *The Recess,* however, *The Rotchfords* strikes a slightly different note. The story of a runaway slave affirms the supposed illegality of slavery in Britain, condemns slavery in general, and applauds family values. One contemporary critic explains this new phenomenon:

> As supply and demand grow, children's books became much more definitely self-contained pieces of fiction—a recognized semi-artistic literary form, with philanthropic purpose subordinated to the story, and moral atmosphere, rather than a particular moral axiom, the mainstay. ... Religion apart, several subjects do occur with some frequency. One is the slavery question.[19]

Exemplary parents and kind-hearted neighbors teach children to live healthy Christian lives. Folded inside the narrative is a story almost eighty pages long about the chance encounter of Charles Rotchford and his father with a slave named Pompey, "a negro boy about twelve years old, crying most pitiously ... O! masters! masters! help me! Indeed me *VERY* hungry! me *very* sick!" (Kilner, *The Rotchfords,* p. 245). Pompey informs Rotchford and his son that a Captain Midas originally brought him from Africa "to be foot-boy to my mistress," then sold him to a cruel Mr. Chromis, who called him lazy and confined him without food to a coal cellar. After a starving Pompey stole a chicken, he was bestially assaulted, became ill, and was again accused of being a "lazy *black* dog." At that point he ran away. He tells the Rotchfords that after he was caught, tied up, and severely punished, "me did so wish to die before it light" (Kilner, *The Rotchfords,* p. 246). Once again, slavery's inducement of suicidal thoughts among pagan slaves recalls Thomas Day's celebrated poem, "The Dying Negro." At this point the Christ-like Rotchfords find Pompey on the road, fleeing, famished, freezing, and very ill. They adopt him informally and assume the role of foster parents.

Mrs. Rotchford elaborates on the horrors of slavery in one of the fiercest fictional statements by a female writer before abolition; slaves might well detest their captors, she confides to the children, because Africans are as entitled as anyone to physical freedom and are equal in God's sight. Kilner endows an orthodox spiritual message with judicious support for resistance.

More concretely, since the disruption of family life contradicts Christian values, Pompey's escape is justifiable. Mrs. Rotchford's offensive against white traders also evokes another matrix of associations: the Countess of Hertford's indictment of Inkle, Elizabeth Rowe's castigation of Old Testament Joseph's brothers, and Helen Maria Williams's attack on Spanish colonists in "Peru" (1784). Just as consequentially, Kilner's text assaults plantocratic myths about black subhumanity and criminality in a passage steeped in Anglo-Africanist assumptions: regardless of the members' ethnicity, a santificed family life is synonymous with Christian living:

> Nor can it be wondered at, when they, poor wretches, are torn from every comfort, from freedom, country, relatives, and friends, bound and forced by cruel whippings on board of vessels, and carried off from every thing they hold dear and valuable in life;—when the parent is torn from his family, the father from his child, the husband from his wife, the child from its parent, and separated under the agonizing idea that it is not only for ever, but that it is also to become, to be sold, the slave of a foreign, distant, and cruel master: When every tie that god and nature has sacredly cemented is thus torn inhumanly asunder, and all by white men professing themselves Christians, can it be wondered at, that they should imbibe the strongest prejudices against the whole race of whites, [who are] . . . selling them as slaves in a distant land, to masters they know not of, exposing them, helpless and pityless, as horses and cattle, for sale in a public market (Kilner, *The Rotchfords,* pp. 259–60).

Mrs. Rotchford then decries the deficient, because pagan, upbringing of Africans and their "ugly outside."[20] Inspired by spiritual love for humanity, she informs her son George that people do have "different complections" and that he should have "more sense, and good nature than to dislike persons upon account of their personal deformities."

In defining domestic service as a suitable occupation for faithful ex-slaves, Kilner updates the great chain of being; African as well as British workers should be waged.

Rotchfordian goodness proving irresistible, Pompey ultimately converts. Charles Rotchford writes a celebratory poem that reads as an evangelical gloss on James Somerset's case and encapsulates Kilner's principles:

> But British freedom henceforth shall be thine,
> Thou with the Sons of Liberty shalt join;
> Enjoy humanity's soft rites, and know
> The blessings that from British Freedom flow.
> Nor only freedom shall thy body find,
> Whilst Ignorance's dark cloud enslaves thy mind:
> That cloud dispell'd shall thy instruction be,
> And thou the beauties of Religion see
> (Kilner, *The Rotchfords*, p. 303).

Somerset comes to stand for "all slaves" yet again. He will be a son of liberty, appreciate Britain's love of freedom, abandon pagan ways, and become a Christian. Like Frankly's slave, he will be constituted and assimilated in British terms. He will be forgiven, since he cannot help it, for his physiognomy. Such mixed messages transmitted to children following the Mansfield decision and the socially mandated configuration of the colonial other were heightening at the time of Britain's increased hegemonic control of the slave trade.[21]

In *The Holiday Present,* a later children's text, Kilner goes further. Not only does the speaker disapprobate those who link their feelings for an individual to personal appearance but she roundly indicts racist name-calling in a political recognition quite remarkable for the times. Written "for the amusement of the almost infant part of the species," the tale centers on the Jennets "and their little family" of three boys and three girls. When Charlotte Jennet gets herself and the carpet covered with ink, the maid tries unsuccessfully to clean her but "she looked exactly like a tawny moor for a great many days; so that (before their Papa and Mamma told them it was not good-natured) her brothers called her Sister Tawny, and Charlotte Blackey."[22]

To what extent these reconstructions of slaves relate to white women's lives is an open question. When feminized Mr. Frankly said of the "Black": "so natural is our attachment to the place where we spent the early part of our lives it calls to mind the pleasing days of innocence," or when Charles's panegyric extols "freedom [of] . . . the body" and the dispelling of "Ignorance's dark cloud," the words could apply in a different context to women who felt pressured to marry or women deprived of education, longing for an earlier, happier life. Talking about deprivation allows authors to project some of the limitations of the white female condition and show the effect of naiveté and victimization on so many lives. Or to put the case a little differently, because Somerset's fight implicitly threatens British foreign policy, authors graft the effeteness of a George Ellison on to a potentially rebellious black protagonist; they defuse danger. Women write another kind of courtesy manual that suggests how child-men like Pompey should act, thereby asserting a normalizing pattern and their own role as colonizers. But as gender-pinioned, middle-class white women, they add a further layer of their own selves and status. In so doing, they indirectly demonstrate linkages—however subtly imbricated they may be—between gender and race oppression. Their heart-felt, though socially prescribed, actions expand the frontiers of female, anti-patriarchal resistance even while they affirm colonial power.

Both Elizabeth Bonhote and Dorothy Kilner reconstruct the James Somerset figure as a man without recourse or smart discourse, battered ruthlessly in the United Kingdom, a helpless, simple man with a hint of emasculation about him, who, above all, does not threaten women, let alone Europeans in general. Since Somerset is involuntarily exiled and therefore an orphan of sorts who cannot be fitted into a conventional family pattern, substitute parents have to be found. Hence Frankly's paternalism toward the orphan "Black" and the Rotchfords' offer of a job and housing to Pompey. With fictional protagonists, Bonhote and Kilner created the James Somerset of their repressed fears and fantasies, a Sunday School object lesson for children. As a humbler version of the heroic Toussaint L'Ouverture, stalwartly paving the way for emancipation, a standard-bearer for future generations, Somerset refused to be "under control." Not until the revolutionary 1780s and early 1790s did fear of such intransigence openly run high.

In the summer of 1773, Phillis Wheatley's visit to London in the company of her owner's son provided a different kind of corrective to pro-slavery propaganda. The British press lauded the London publication of Phillis Wheatley's volume in early September, accompanied in some cases by sarcastic comments about the hypocrisy of those who encouraged or capitalized on a poet's talent, yet kept her enslaved.[23] Commentators seemed oblivious to contradictions closer to home. Phillis Wheatley's poems that were, according to Charles Deane, printed and published while she visited London dissolved old myths about the impoverishment or nonexistence of black culture. Her warm reception in London's proto-abolitionist circles testified to the appreciation of her talent. Among those she met were Lady Cavendish, Lady Carteret Webb, Mrs. Palmer the poet, Granville Sharp, the evangelical John Thornton, and Lord Lyttleton, a friend of Elizabeth Montagu, sister to Sarah Scott. In a private letter to her friend Obour Tanner, Phillis Wheatley described her reaction to the London trip:

> The friends I found here among the nobility and gentry, their benevolent conduct towards me, the unexpected and unmerited civility and complaisance with which I was treated by all, fills me with astonishment. I can scarcely realize it (Robinson, *Phillis Wheatley,* pp. 14–15).

Though no evidence exists, Phillis Wheatley's pleasure would surely have been enhanced by her probable knowledge of the Somerset decision that had come down the previous year. Yet reviews of her poetry often dealt more with her "authenticity" as a poet than with the poems themselves. (Remember that Gronniosaw's narrative, as well as *Oroonoko,* was "authenticated.") The reviewer for the *London Chronicle,* for instance, says nothing of the poems, dwelling instead on her circumstances, informing the reader that:

> An attestation is prefixed to these Poems, signed by the Governor and Lieutenant-Governor of Boston; also by several Gentlemen of the council, many of the clergy, &c. of the Province, that they were really written by Phillis, a young Negro girl.
>
> The following letter, from the girl's master to the publisher, is likewise prefixed to these pieces, two of which are inserted after the letter:
>
> "PHILLIS was brought from Africa to America, in the year 1761, between seven and eight years of age. Without any assistance from school education, and by only what she was taught in the family, she, in 16 months from her arrival, attained the English language, to which she was an utter stranger before, to such a degree, as to read any of the most difficult parts of the sacred writings, to the great astonishment of all who heard her.
>
> "As to her WRITING, her own curiosity led her to it; and this she learnt in so short a time, that in the year 1765, she wrote a letter to the Rev. Mr. Occam, the Indian Minister, while in England.
>
> "She has a great inclination to learn the Latin tongue, and has made some progress in it. This relation is given by her Master who brought her, and with whom she now lives."
>
> Boston, Nov. 14, 1771.[24]

The degree of intentional irony in the reviewer's inclusion of corroborative testimony is hard to assess. Gronniosaw's chronicle bore no such direct attestation, nor did *Oroonoko,* although the editor of Ignatius Sancho's *Letters* in 1782 began with an apologia, and Ottobah Cugoano's *Thoughts and Sentiments on the Evils of Slavery* in 1787 opens with a self-validating commentary and complaints about those who question Africans having any "competent degree of knowledge."[25] But although she submits to the process of being "authenticated"— what else could she do?—her letters to Obour Tanner, the Earl of Dartmouth, and Samuel Occam, betray a self-knowledge about her anomalous condition. Rendering poems acceptable to a white British audience while investing them with contradictions inherent in her situation and indirectly caused by that very audience's silent complicity, points to a subtle form of mimicry. More than likely, Phillis Wheatley's gender helped to explain the attention paid by the press and others to "authenticating devices" that were tendered on her behalf.[26] Certainly, she utilized her standing as a poet to prosecute slavery, her poem to the Earl of Dartmouth with its passage of protest an apt case in point. By claiming public subjectivity, African writers reversed colonialist depictions of "others" who might be gazed upon at will. In fact, Phillis Wheatley turns those whom she addresses into objects of praise. Her elegies commemorate a certain kind of scopic European mentality.[27] She expropriates their view of her by gazing back and commenting on what she sees. She engages with white editors in what Robert Stepto has termed "race rituals." Beyond that, one contemporary critic has provocatively argued that Phillis Wheatley's poems need recontextualization to be understood at their most imaginative limit because she may have been raised in a culture in which elegies were regarded as the cultural prerogative of females.[28] Given this possibility, the self-conscious mocking voice assumes richer meaning.

MARY SCOTT

Phillis Wheatley's impact showed up almost immediately. The year following her visit to Britain, the Unitarian poet Mary Scott extolled her talents in a long poem entitled *The Female Advocate* (1774) that celebrated historical and contemporary female "worthies."[29] Probably the first such text to irradiate a contemporary female African writer, the poem marks a milestone in female literary history.

Borrowing lines for her title page from some anonymous (woman's?) poem that expropriated the language of slavery, the polemicist (scarcely distinguished from Scott herself) emblazoned her anger at patriarchal tyranny. She deplored male contentions that female slavery was natural in lines that denoted her sense of overlappings between colonial and patriarchal slavery:

> Self prais'd, and grasping at despotic pow'r,
> Man looks on slav'ry as the female dow'r;
> To nature's boon ascribes what force has giv'n,
> And usurpation deems the gift of Heav'n.

Mary Scott's background, political sympathies, and religious orientation explain her unorthodoxy. She was born about 1752 and lived for some time at Milborne Port in Somerset, West England, where her father was a linen-merchant.[30] Her mother's obituary in *The Gentleman's Magazine* (1787) acknowledges an exemplary life. The Scotts also had a son, Russell, who was a Unitarian minister in Portsmouth from 1788 to 1833. During a long courtship, Scott's suitor John Taylor taught classics at a Dissenting Academy. Scott herself seems to have embraced Unitarianism. Ill much of the time, Scott ceased writing poetry after her marriage and died at 41 after two difficult births.

In *The Female Advocate,* Scott includes a pantheon of over sixty accomplished women from the sixteenth century to the present day. She narrates a highly condensed genealogy of female learning and culture in verse. Her illumination of repressed history and the need for female education, coupled with a pronounced impatience at the devaluation of females constitute an unprecedented plea by a woman writer for public recognition of "the abilities of our sex." Among the distinguished women of the past, she singles out Catherine Parr, Lady Jane Grey, the daughters of Sir Thomas More, Katherine Phillips, Lady Mary Chudleigh, and the Duchess of Newcastle; among contemporaries that she cites, in addition to Phillis Wheatley, are Anna Laetitia Barbauld, Elizabeth Montagu, Hannah More, Hester Chapone, and Catherine Macaulay. In the preface to *The Female Advocate,* Scott identifies the African poet specifically as one of the "Female Authors of late [who] have appeared with honour."

Scott opts not to mention Phillis Wheatley's status as a slave, perhaps because she wants her judged as a poet in her own right, perhaps because she reasons that suppressing any mention of this status illuminates it more. Instead, she characterizes the poet as "a Negro Servant to Mr. Wheatley of Boston." Her avoidance of the word slave is reminiscent of Quaker Alice Curwen's refusal in the 1670s to use the terminology of slavery.[31] By locating Phillis Wheatley within a literary lineage of women poets—cultural outsiders themselves—Scott subtly emphasizes Wheatley's outsider standing as a slave. Certainly the nine reviews of Phillis Wheatley's volume of poetry that were published in September, a month after she left London, pointedly stressed the fact of her bondage.[32]

Scott's vignette further underscores the gradual reemergence of black female protagonists. But unlike Anna Laetitia Barbauld who commiserates with a "negro woman grieving for her child" in 1781, Scott invites admiration for Wheatley. She also, quite exceptionally, draws on a more rights-oriented discourse: cultural equality, she implicitly argues, must be on a par with spiritual equality. Hence she revalidates white British female virtues while Phillis Wheatley's subversive and camouflaged responses to representations of her life are audible only to the initiated.

Mary Deverell

Eight years after Phillis Wheatley's visit to London and seven years after Scott's tribute, Mary Deverell included a poem entitled "On Reading the Poems of Phillis Wheatley" in her volume *Miscellanies* (1781), "directed towards young minds."[33]

A poet and sermonist who hailed from a Gloucestershire clothier's family, Deverell was well acquainted with the female literati:

[Deverell] seems [says Mary Anne Bendixen in prefatory apparatus] to have been accepted by London society and the literary community. Dr. Johnson, Hannah More, Mrs. Siddons, and Hester Thrale were numbered among her subscribers, ... Her collections, *Sermons* (1774), was popular among the gentry and clergy and went through several reprints. *Miscellanies in Prose and Verse* (1781), the product of a long illness, offers a variety of essays and poems "particularly calculated for the improvement of younger minds." Portions of her *Miscellanies* were later reprinted, along with other essays by Hannah More as *The Ladies' Literary Companion* (1792), a book intended for "American ladies." In "On Marriage" Mary Deverell offers advice to young women: "To the moment of your marriage it is your reign; your lover is proud to oblige you, watches your smiles, is obedient to your commands, anxious to please you, and careful to avoid every thing you disapprove; but you have no

sooner pronounced that harsh word **obey,** than you give up the
reigns, and it is his turn to rule so long as you live (Deverell,
Miscellanies, p. 102).

In *Miscellanies,* Mary Deverell applauds Elizabeth Montagu's notion
that women have souls: she eulogizes Sarah Fielding, and John Duncombe who wrote *The Feminiad;* moreover, she praises Mary Scott
(thereby invoking Scott's tribute to Wheatley), who had called Duncombe a "feminist" in *The Female Advocate.*

Undoubtedly Deverell counted among her friends those who both
welcomed Phillis Wheatley to London and despised John Wheatley
for capitalizing on "his property." Her esteem for the poet matches
that of the sympathetic reviewer for the *Monthly Review* (December
1773) who deplores the hypocrisy of the Wheatley family, but bypasses
Britain's comparable pro-slavery role in the Caribbean. Still, the critic's inclusion of the poem-extract in the review lets Phillis Wheatley
speak for herself. The critic's response amounts to an open dialogue
with the African poet, organized as if two abolitionists, one white, one
black, were deploring the present system: in her verses to the Earl of
Dartmouth on his being appointed Secretary of State for the American
department, she [Phillis Wheatley] speaks, in a rare passage of explicit
self-disclosure, of her own situation and country. After narrating his
Lordship's favourable sentiments on behalf of American liberty, she
adds:

> Should you, my Lord, while you peruse my song,
> Wonder from whence my love of Freedom sprung,
> Whence flow these wishes for the common good,
> By feeling hearts alone best understood,
> I, young in life, by seeming cruel fate,
> Was snatch'd from Afric's fancied happy seat:
> What pangs excruciating must molest,
> What sorrows labour in my parents' breast?
> Steel'd was that soul, and by no misery mov'd,
> That from a father seiz'd his babe belov'd
> Such, such my case. And can I then but pray
> Others may never feel tyrannic sway?

We are much concerned. [The reviewer then continues] to find that
this ingenious young woman is yet a slave. The people of Boston
boast themselves chiefly on their principles of liberty. One such act
as the purchase of her freedom, would, in our opinion, have done

them more honour than hanging a thousand trees with ribbons and emblems (147–48).

Earlier in 1774, Deverell had published a collection of sermons, including one on a favorite eighteenth-century subject, Old Testament Joseph, that deprecates Joseph's slavery. About a half century earlier, Elizabeth Rowe had penned a long narrative poem on Joseph, feminizing his character and expanding on the reversal of sexual roles when Potiphar tried to seduce him.[34] The popularity of narratives about Joseph circuitously confirms female antagonism to bondage and tyranny.[35] Tributes to Phillis Wheatley were similarly used: while eulogizing the poet, they snapped at bondage:

Deverell's poem, "On Reading The Poems of Phillis Wheatley," reads as follows:

> To shame the formal circle of the school,
> That chain their pupils down by pedant rules,
> Curbing the insolence of learned lore,
> There lately came from India's swarthy shore,
> In nature's sable charms, a lowly maid,
> By fortune doom'd to languish in the shade;
> Till Britain call'd the seeds of genius forth,
> Maturing, like the sun, her native worth.
> Though no high birth nor titles grace her line,
> Yet humble Phillis boasts a race divine;
> Like marble that in quarries lies conceal'd,
> Till all its veins, by polish, stand reveal'd;
> From whence such groups of images arise,
> We praise the artist, and the sculpture prize.

Like Scott, Deverell elevates the talents of marginalized men and women and implicitly allies Phillis Wheatley with such eighteenth-century "natural geniuses" as Robert Burns and Ann Yearsley, the Bristol milk-woman whose poems comprise "a natural intuitive response to inspiration . . . an essential unencumbered poetic act accessible to all."[36] With no sense of irony, the speaker argues that not even slavery can suppress the powerful combination of the "untaught mind" and the "towering soul." This panegyric to Wheatley's creative powers, like Scott's praiseworthy, egalitarian statement, demythologizes time-worn propaganda about innate black intellectual inferiority. But Deverell's patriotism also leads the speaker astray. Apart from the fact that she confuses Africa with India (a common occurrence rather like the earlier confusion of "negro" with Indian in discussions of Yarico),

she attributes Wheatley's inspiration to the power of Britain's "civilization" to unlock the poet's talent, "marble . . . by polish, stands reveal'd," quite a tall claim since the poet had completed the manuscript
before she arrived in London.

After the *causes célèbres* of James Somerset and Phillis Wheatley,
several writers freshened the issue of emancipation other ways. In
1781, Anna Laetitia Barbauld foregrounded an African mother in a
volume of hymns for children, so popular that at her death in 1825
the *Christian Reporter*'s obituary charged parents with being "deficient
in the first of duties" if they did not utilize the hymns to instruct their
children.[37] Here is the portrait Barbauld draws to elicit an ethical
response from children:

> Negro women, who sittest pining in captivity, and weepest over thy
> sick child; though no one seeth thee, God seeth thee, though no
> one pitieth thee, God pitieth thee, raise thy voice, forlorn and
> abandoned one; call upon him from amidst thy bonds, for assuredly
> he will hear thee.[38]

The near-coincidence of Wheatley's London visit with the publication
of the hymns and Wheatley's impact on women's circles undoubtedly
helped to prompt Anna Barbauld's hymn, indirectly if not directly.
The African mother of *Hymn* emblemizes loss, sorrow, severed families, love, and a sense of community; she potently stands for domestic
and spiritual values that women have come to represent. Other reso-
nances sound too. Is the "Negro" mother an amalgam of the parents
Phillis Wheatley deplores leaving behind, or a variant of the griefstricken widow in Thomas Day's "dying negro," or even the lover
or wife from whom James Somerset's owner tried (let's assume) to
separate him? Barbauld's vignette, that is, seems to capture growing
contemporary disgust with slavery.

Questions about separation raised by the hymn also sing out in *The
Rambles of Mr. Frankly, The Rotchfords,* in the lives of James Somerset,
Phillis Wheatley, and in slave communities anywhere. Female writers
recognized the havoc slavery wreaked on families around the world
in an era when "separate spheres" for men and women were treated
as a given, when women were assumed to have a "natural" affinity for
domestic life.

The hymn's narrator, a scarcely disguised Barbauld, pleads for
compassion, underscores the efficacy of family unity, and assumes
the entitlement of Africans to spiritual equality. An African madonna
and child vignette hotly condemns slavery's ravages because, in a

broad political sense, enslavement of mothers and children threatens the social fabric.

Barbauld's poignant appeal to Christian-domestic values matches similar appeals from the seventeenth-century to the evangelical refashionings of the 1780s. Alice Curwen presented spiritual bonding as viable compensation for family bonding. Imoinda urged Oroonoko to rebel; if they remained slaves, Imoinda insisted, their unity as a family would be undermined, if not destroyed. Inkle's treachery in abandoning Yarico (and even the sibling treachery Elizabeth Rowe outlined in her 1734 poem on Joseph) destroyed domestic stability. Mr. Jennings purchased his uncle to recuperate domestic harmony; in both his emanations, George Ellison functioned as the benevolent patriarch of an extended family.

Nonetheless, these Anglo-Africanized Africans are still objects of pity, colonial others who need the "protection" of kind Europeans.[39] The graphic depiction of the African mother's imposed solitude also presupposes the absence of, or at least makes invisible, caring slave communities, a standard white British textual gap. On a more positive note, by choosing an African female protagonist, Barbauld restored a gynocentrically-oriented discourse on slaves that stretched back to Aphra Behn and the Countess of Hertford. The advent of feminized male heroes and the visit of Phillis Wheatley had fostered the return of the African female heroine.

The first white woman to speak—more or less—in her own voice and engage a slave as interlocutor, Barbauld draws young readers into a crucial moral-political debate. This responsible address to children about slavery stemmed from her Dissenting background. She knew powerlessness and political prejudice at first hand. The only daughter of a distinguished nonconformist clergyman, by 1758 Anna Laetitia Aikin was living in Warrington where her father taught at the Dissenting Academy. After marrying a French Huguenot refugee in 1774, the Reverend Rochemont Barbauld, she set up house in Suffolk and taught school. During that time she wrote *Hymns In Prose for Children* (1781), inspired by Isaac Watt's *Divine Songs attempted in easy language for the Use of Children* (1715). John Locke's speculations about the origin of ideas was another source. So was the doctrine of natural theology to which Barbauld was committed. People could discern God in the beauty of nature, she believed: children could be led through good values to the divine presence.[40] This idea united evangelicals with Mary Wollstonecraft, who declared that Barbauld's *Hymns* made God "obvious to the senses."[41] Ann Shteir offers two reasons why women increasingly opted to write children's literature:

> The first is publishing and publishers. The second is women latching
> on to the enabling convention of mother as teacher. . . . Publishers
> knew their audience was eager for children's literature, that people
> were buying. . . . Priscilla Wakefield's journals from 1798 are so
> money-centered that [her reasons seem to be economic].[42]

A passage in Amelia Opie's novel, *Adeline Mowbray,* (1806), succinctly sums up the moral as well as the economic advantage to
women of writing children's literature:

> The success which she had met with in instructing children, led
> her to believe that she might succeed in writing little hymns and
> tales for their benefit; a method of getting money which she looked
> upon to be more rapid and more lucrative than working plain or
> fancy work: and, in a short time, a little volume was ready to be
> offered to a bookseller; nor was it offered in vain.[43]

Children's literature empowered women to authorize themselves in
both senses: they could be mother-teachers condemning domestic
instability and corrupt governmental policies while maintaining their
public posture as chroniclers of these conditions.

Barbauld's choice of a Caribbean locale differs from most of the
Somerset-influenced texts that centered on Britain. Authors felt less
need to talk about the mechanics of slavery in Britain now that slaves,
as they thought, were technically free. Accordingly, writers focussed
more attention on the still enslaved, with Barbauld's *Hymn* a transitional text that helped forge a path for formal agitation. The year
after Barbauld wrote, Ignatius Sancho graphically described slavery's
uprooting of African cultural life—in contrast to Barbauld's "soft"
version—in his autobiographical *Letters,* written in the third person:
"A disease of the new (Caribbean) climate put an early stop to his
mother's existence; and his father defeated the miseries of slavery by
an act of suicide" (Sancho, *Letters,* p. vi).

The year after Sancho's *Letters* were published, a national scandal
aggravated anti-slavery commentary. It involved the slave-ship *Zong*
and the actions of a certain Captain Luke Collingwood on a journey
in 1781 from West Africa to Jamaica across the Middle Passage. During
the crossing, a plague broke out among the 440 slaves and 17 whites
aboard the slave ship.[44] Concerned that insurance companies would
not recompense him for a substantial loss of "cargo" if ailing slaves
died, Captain Collingwood decided to invoke a clause in his policy
which rendered the insurance company liable if any part of a cargo

had to be jettisoned to salvage the remainder. He then ordered 132 slaves to be thrown overboard. When the case came to trial in London, the issue was not murder, but who would pay for the jettisoned cargo. Expounding on ideas equating Africans and animals that had become law earlier in the century, Lord Mansfield, the trial judge, reiterated that "no doubt, though it shocks one very much, . . . the case of slaves was the same as if horses had been thrown overboard."[45] He judged against the insurers on behalf of those who had thrown the slaves overboard. The massacre shocked the British public beyond any other eighteenth-century incident.[46] Wholesale murder on the high seas that went unpunished in the British courts was going too far. The My Lai of 1780s pre-Parliamentary agitation, *Zong* led straight to the abolition debate.

Narratives that followed on the heels of the *Zong* murders took place in the Caribbean and promoted rebellion and emancipation. European expiation was at its height. In a novel by Sophia Lee entitled *The Recess* (1783–85), the heroine was Mary Queen of Scots, time-honored icon of heroic resistance.[47] Rebellious but unsuccessful slaves who battled harsh British authority microcosmically reflected the Scottish queen's battles and her ultimate failure to regain power from her rival cousin, Queen Elizabeth I.

Sophia Lee's historical novel features heroines Matilda and Ellinor—already a gender switch from Henry Dumont and George Ellison—alleged secret daughters of Mary Queen of Scots. After the death of Matilda's husband, the Earl of Leicester, she is kidnapped by Roman Catholic Lord Mortimer, whose Spanish wife is also dead. Besotted with Matilda, he takes her to Jamaica because Philip of Spain had given him "a considerable portion of land" there.

Jamaica is described as an island "in the hands of a few settlers; power is almost their only law" (Lee, *The Recess*, p. 151). Mortimer's behavior on board ship matches the settlers' colonial practice as he doggedly tries to force himself on Matilda, "no longer deign[ing] to veil his views." When they land, slaves carry Matilda on a litter "towards his plantations." She discovers that proud "Spanish domestics" vent their frustrations "for the servile exactions of duty paid to him, by lording it equally over his slaves, who, timid by nature and subdued by cruelty, seemed to have lost the very wish of any other good than that of existence" (Lee, *The Recess*, p. 156).

Mortimer immediately demands in colonizers' language that she marry him: "submit at once to your fate." But just as the ceremony is about to take place, "a yell, wild, deep, shrill, and horrible, was succeeded by a tumult universal and tremendous." Mortimer has been overthrown "by the tide of exasperated slaves." Lee is the first female author to accentuate tenacious insurrection since Behn in *Oroonoko* a century earlier.

This advocacy of resistance as a right ends almost as quickly as it began. Matilda rapidly determines that slaves are "ferocious" people who "glared death upon me." Her language is an oblique mimicking of Edward Long's racist diatribe in *History of Jamaica* (1774), in which he charged slave communities with excessive sexuality, indolence, and general inferiority.[48] Aghast at being led "suddenly into slavery, by a wild and unknown people," as she did with Mortimer, Matilda fears for her sexual safety. The incident helps to reopen the question of slavery's relation to sexual abuse.[49] Fortunately, a male slave named Aimor takes Matilda under his wing and when the rest of the slaves discover she is a princess, they start to "soften[ed] their ferocity." As in *Oroonoko,* rank counts.

Following an ambush, enslaved wives sob as they are wrenched from their husbands, thus dissolving old pro-slavery contentions that Africans neither feel nor value their families. Yet these same, now widowed African women prostrate themselves before the captors, offering up their children "to assuage the wrath of the unsensed victors." Lee's vacillation and her assault on African ontological beliefs about family life parallel earlier Anglo-Africanist episodes:

> She prays and sighs for the poor wretches, who, seduced by European crimes to a dire imitation of them, had wanted foresight to secure the common comforts (Lee, *The Recess,* p. 163).

The text scorns the gratuitous baseness of Europeans who proceed to steal every treasure they can lay their hands on; these reprobates, moreover, it is silently implied, would do worse as they capture "the female slaves and their children, bending beneath the weight of misery, fatigue, and manacles."

Matilda's delight in the very presence of Europeans, base or benign, betrays an underpinning ethnocentric framework. Africans denote the unsophisticated colonial other:

> Restored by this extraordinary means once more to civilized society, my heart acknowledged . . . the simple, the solitary charm of liberty (Lee, *The Recess,* pp. 164–65).

Only by implication are slaves entitled to the "charm of liberty," presently denied them by contemptible Europeans. The text leaves little if any space for the entry of Africans, enslaved or freed, into "civilized" society.

The Recess contains a matrix of dizzying messages about slavery, a perfect index to mixed national responses of the 1780s. First, Matilda applauds the slave uprising, but ex-slaves are "savages"; then when black rebels die, they expiate "with life the ravages they committed." Racial difference deeply affects Matilda's interchanges with the slaves, who at times seem to embody a fixed "native savagery and evil." On the other hand, Matilda upbraids Europeans for fostering barbarism in ex-slaves, but even though she terms the Europeans themselves "savages" when they rescue her and then assault Africans, she is relieved to meet up again with "her own kind." Authorial viewpoint, it seems, indicts slavery and slavers, and endows a woman, not a feminized male hero, with humanity. But Lee's conditioned belief in historical fictions permits her to encode Britons as "civilized" colonial subjects and Africans as "savage others" in common contemporary doublethink. Perhaps she thought promoting rebellion was going far enough. The colonizer's gaze notwithstanding, she does conclude the episode by attempting to throw a positive light on African women. The first character is a slave-nurse whose "untaught soul," reared in pagan superstition, is softened by Matilda's baby. Her "instructive" maternality shines through. Once again family values fuse with moral recognition. The second is "a distinguished black woman named Anana," the vicious governor's favorite. Although Anana appears to be free, a buried message links that freedom to extorted sexual favors, to the Governor's power and desire. Anana's death from smallpox symbolizes the mandated European necessity for "beauty." She aids the ailing, incarcerated Matilda after the heroine notices Anana's delightful baby. When the governor dies, leaving her a small inheritance, she uses it to buy Matilda's freedom from the new governor. Despite elements of an Anglo-Africanist vision, the incident conveys a buried message about African women who exercise selflessness toward others, despite afflictions they suffer in their own lives.

Lee's novel departs from earlier fiction in important ways. Africans have reappeared as energetic agents and rebels, though they are still largely classified as a changeless mass. The sentient white male is replaced by a daring female protagonist who conspires with African female counterparts and, like them, suffers sexual domination. Although Lee rapidly writes slaves out of the plot once Matilda returns to England, their resistant voices haunt the text. The power of that opposition shows up in negative characteristics attributed toward slaves once they escape. Matilda's (and Lee's) fear symbolizes a cus-

tomary British recoil from any self-determined actions on the part of
the other, since others and self-determination are seen, if not as a
dreaded combination, certainly as a contradiction in terms.

Just as the Abolition Committee was forming, publisher Lucy Peacock cross-references an anti-slavery message with Anglo-Africanist
fantasies in a tale entitled *The Creole* (1787).[50] In the advertisement
to another of her works, *The Little Emigrant* (1802?), she stated her
aim:[51]

> The young reader [must be brought] to the cultivation of that
> universal spirit of philanthropy, which teaches us to embrace all
> mankind as brethren, the children of one father.

The discursive wheel had turned full circle since the 1750s as
Peacock introduces an inversion of customary white owner-black
slave relationships. Freed by an impecunious female owner, grateful
ex-slaves voluntarily support her, a ridiculous farce perhaps, but one
that counteracts the old notion, expounded in *The Recess* for example,
that slavery and profit-motivated Britons transform Africans into fierce
murderers.

The Creole is a flashback story about Harriot [sic] Sedley aiding a
moribund white woman named Zemira, who then narrates her experiences up to the time of their meeting. The sick woman is the West
Indian creole of the title, her father an English merchant. Well-educated and attracting admirers from an early age, she "beheld all
mankind with equality" and sought "rational tranquility" as her life's
goal.

At twenty years old, when Zemira's parents die, she inherits a large
fortune. Subsequently, she is manipulated into marriage by George
Sedley, then known as Groveby, who converts her estates into cash
and unceremoniously departs for North America, leaving her one
plantation. Vignettes of manipulated marriage and slavery intertwine.
Although former friends desert her, slaves remain devoted. Despite
penury, she decides to free rather than sell them, a rare act of altruism
for that epoch and a far cry from George Ellison's pro-slavery paternalism. Effectively, the narrator argues that giving freedom (and thereby
retaining at least psychological control) is preferable to having it
plucked from you. The text assumes old hierarchies but delicately
covers them over:

> From my honest negroes alone I received consolation; their af-
> fection remained unshaken, and glowed with more fervor amidst
> the clouds of sorrow and misfortune that surrounded me. I could,

indeed, have raised a considerable sum by disposing of them; but, though born in a clime which authorizes the inhuman custom of bartering our fellow-creatures for gold, I ever loathed and detested the horrid practice.

Surely, my dear Madam, we have no right to tyrannize over, and treat as brutes those who will doubtless one day be made partakers with us of an immortality! Have they not the same faculties, the same passions, and the same innate sense of good and evil? Should we then, who are enlightened by the holy precepts of Christianity, refuse to stretch forth the friendly hand,

"Let us not mislike them for their complexion,
The shadow'd livery of the burnish'd sun."
(Peacock, *The Creole,* pp. 18–19.)

In a serious discussion with slaves whom she will imminently free, Zemira both echoes popular philosophical sentiments of the day and assumes the necessity of assimilation and the internalization by slaves of Eurocentric values:

"I do not," she informs them, "consider it the least of my sorrows that fortune has not left it in my power to render your age peaceful and independent, as your youth has been faithful and industrious. But that God, whom you have been taught to adore, will befriend you, if you continue to serve him with humility, with patience, and with resignation. . . . Liberty is all your poor mistress has to bestow on you, all she has left to recompense you for your faithful services." (Peacock, *The Creole,* p. 19)

Her African audience has not one "dry eye" among them, but no one speaks until one "negro girl . . . threw herself at my feet," in a feminized reenactment of Friday's deference to Crusoe. Delighted by this overt gesture of humble appreciation, Zemira invites her to tend for her baby son, Theodore, presumably for no wages (Peacock, *The Creole,* p. 19). In a reformulation of Pompey's situation, membership in a Christian family is happiness enough for the obliging former slaves. Apparently, Zemira's status or altruism absolves her from having to work—a silent comment on the nature of a finely calibrated colonial supremacy. From the second day of her "small abode, in a distinct part of the island," until twelve years later, the freed slaves donate a third of their wages to Zemira. This adoption of their former owner as a charitable cause flags a curious role reversal. After initial reluctance, Zemira accepts: "from this day they constantly persisted in devoting to me the above portion of their wages accompanied with such evident marks of satisfaction . . . they were capable of enjoying. . . . I continued, therefore, entirely supported by the affectionate negroes, by whose assistance I was supplied, not only with the necessaries, but, I may add, even with the comforts of life. This state of dependence was, however, to an ingenuous mind, painful and humiliating; but I had, alas! no other resource" (Peacock, *The Creole,* pp. 19–20). The colonial subject deplores her reduction to the status of other. At this point, slaves disappear, their role as adjuncts to the protagonist over, and the story follows the relationship between Zemira and her son and a Captain and his daughter who arrive on the island.

Peacock's text argues that charity begets further good deeds as well as personal salvation, a position with which most evangelical abolitionists would agree. But even when they are freed, African-Caribbean men and women work and support their former mistress in a drama that verges on a white British utopia.[53] The extent to which *The Creole* locates slaves within an Anglo-Africanist spiritual economy signifies in its repression how fearfully threatening the discourse of liberation had become. *The Recess* transforms freed, rebel Africans into "savages." *The Creole* transforms (orientalizes) them into a supportive governing body who nurture an impecunious ex-slave-owner, Christian love personified. Assimilation becomes a near-imperative when African-Caribbean autonomy menaces the colonizers.

From midcentury to the eve of abolition, women's colonial discourse radiated in a number of new, seemingly unrelated directions. At first in the 1750s and 1760s, being kindhearted Christian slaveowners *in loco parentis* was morally sufficient. By the 1770s and 1780s, however, that standard of morality was being slowly but fundamentally redefined. Slaves spoke out. The voiced and unvoiced texts of the morally engaged Somerset and Wheatley urged new paradigms and responses, creating salient, unprecedented texts of freedom, with an authority that implicitly refuted all attempts to concoct an other of European making and establish a "normalizing" colonial discourse. Their texts spoke for millions. Moreover, they reappropriated being gazed at and epitomized a global presence that could not be denied.

Put another way, the louder the discourse on freedom became, the more white British female writers overlapped their condition with the colonial others'. Struggles by slaves for manumission had generated a multilayered debate that reflected back on the status of the narrator-author who attempted to represent colonized men, women and children, deemed incapable or unfit to represent themselves; authors were articulating a multivalent discourse that talked almost indistinguishably of the condition of self and the condition of others. Texts exuded unconscious paradox at every turn. Barbauld's hymn about the dolorous mother both reaffirms traditional domestic values and maintains a sizable distance from traditional concepts.

At the same time, while these authors probed alterity, they seemed to speak unilaterally. They spoke, in other words, as part of a colonial structure that was underlining the fitness of British colonial policy. The other had to be controlled, converted, and objectified; the other could not face down a Briton unless, like Lord Mortimer, the Briton has forfeited any claim to the human community. In that sense, women writers were executing the colonizing mission. The harshness of their attitudes, however, suggests some psychological stake in remaining inflexible, almost as if they had some sense of twin dominations—race and gender—but for the time being had to completely look through the connection. Hence these discourses about physical and cultural autonomy automatically pressed Britons into defensive postures. Lee exhibits what she and those for whom she speaks fear most—in an ominous foreshadowing of San Domingo—while Bonhote, Kilner, and Peacock repress anxieties about the colonized by containing them. The fragility of their own powerlessness—not seen as such—nuances these deep anxieties about rebellion by the repressed. In Peacock's transitional paradigm, domestic servitude and the ability to reverse old power relations up to a point are rewards for manumission and anodynes for alleged pagan ways. One by one, successful rebels find themselves rearranged in the Christian world. In the name of freedom, freedom itself becomes prescribed and circumscribed.

Texts and subtexts comment on and contradict one another while silently and not-so-silently responding to actions and writings by African contemporaries. The classic colonial topos—that Europeans have an unquestioned right to colonize—invisibly informs every text; so does the notion that right-minded people are divorced from corrupt colonial practice. Then the question becomes: does colonialism need to include slavery? And the answer to that question seesaws from no to yes after midcentury. The ricochet from the affirmative surfaces most graphically in Lee's depiction of homicidal, lascivious "butchers." But even within a single text such as *The Recess,* the meaning of the other dramatically shifts in direct response to the destabilization of the colonizing subject's situation.

In this period of political flux and expansionism, James Somerset and Phillis Wheatley are engaged in complex, transoceanic dialogues; their contentions assume a listener who quietly nods at meanings that cannot be voiced, or at meanings that reside in silent interstices. Whether holding up under duress, commiserating over the loss of a slave family member, or acting Christ-like, the confident colonial subject has a relatively transparent facade. Continuously, that colonizing subject (author/narrator/protagonist as surrogate) defines herself in terms of (in contrast to) an always inferior colonized other. The tangled grouping of post-midcentury authors, that is, began to exhibit signs of colonial alienation and psychological subjection even while they were apparently championing and simultaneously lording it over those whom they spiritually, socially, and economically sought—consciously or not—to subject.

Phase Two

Chapter 7

The Parliamentary Campaign:
New Debates

Africa and slaves speak through and by virtue of the European imagination. . . . Not so much a pen writing as a voice pronouncing.
—Edward W. Said, *Orientalism,* pp. 56, 125.

[Nothing in May 1789] is surely so interesting as the noble effort in asking for the abolition of the slave-trade. Nothing, I think, for centuries past, has done the nation so much honour; because it must have proceeded from the most liberal motives—the purest love of history and justice. The voice of the Negroes could not have made itself heard but by the ear of pity; they might have been oppressed for ages more with impunity, if we had so pleased.
—Anna Laetitia Barbauld, *Works,* Vol. 1, p. 81.

Earlier fictional texts that shared an anti-slavery impulse from *Oroonoko* (1688) to *The Creole* (1788) also shared certain other characteristics: protagonists were named; they variously resisted their situation; they lived in and ran away from named geographical sites. Barbauld's *Hymn* (1781), in which mother and child are unnamed and unvoiced in an unspecified geographical location is one of the few exceptions in its foreshadowing of the new narrative adapted for the campaign. Oroonoko and Imoinda were kidnapped in West Africa and transported to Surinam; Yarico lamented in a first person monologue in Barbados; George Ellison's slaves pleaded for better treatment; Bonhote's "The Black" and Pompey roamed London's streets, ag-

145

grieved and vocal about their state of destitution. Zemira's freed slaves spoke and worked, their lives lived continuously through time rather than a timeless unreality. In *The Recess,* Africans overcame a callous master and had to be subdued by a more "tempered" peer. Phillis Wheatley and James Somerset provided public models for these later textual encounters and introduced the topoi of escape, cultural sophistication, and the will to power, living proof of the paucity of fictional constructions. Other favored thematics in poems and prose were atrocities, homelessness, and the loss of innocence.[1]

Not coincidentally, once avowed abolitionists started to write verse for propaganda purposes, characteristics associated with living Africans disappeared; in order to propagandize successfully and win support, they felt they had to fashion verse according to campaign demands; it was harder to endorse escape. Over and above, the public exhibition of Wheatley's and Somerset's talents and self-assertion as a self-limiting phenomenon, one of a kind, made it hard to imagine the pair as representative of Africans in general. We, Europeans seemed to say, "extend the unreturned ethnographic gaze upon you and your prodigious achievements but we still remain detached from you."

In 1788, in the interests of attuning readers to the iniquity of slavery, Hannah More coordinates many of the accumulated motifs into a verse-narrative, "Slavery, a Poem," ushering into being a formula, a kind of abolitionist shorthand that can be copied, expanded, or abbreviated at will. The fictional and real-life Africans of earlier texts, voiced, named, resistant, and inhabiting specifically denoted islands, towns, and continents have vanished. Now slaves are constructions of a different sort, unproblematized, simple-minded victims, at the mercy of spiritually dead British cut-throats.[2] They dwell in motionless indeterminate landscapes somewhere in Africa or the Caribbean. Their existence presupposes no extant culture or history. Displayed in a series of frozen murals, the malignity of slavery was calculated to swell public protest in conjunction with Parliamentary argumentation that would jointly ensure passage of the Bill.

Assuming open-minded readers, the author-narrator turns a dominative gaze upon these powerless unfortunates in what amounts to a paradigmatic first encounter between a female author, handpicked by the Abolition Committee, and the construct of depersonalized, uniform slaves. Charitably motivated, the genealogist of these new motifs pronounces what "the slave" is, since slaves cannot speak or act on their own behalf. This distillation and visibility of the representative slave attracts supporters to a now identifiable, worthy cause. Though a sound strategy in political terms, the attitudes propagated by such a strategy reinforce traditional perspectives toward Africans. What is said about "the slave" becomes, for an indoctrinated British public, what the slave is—a non-sovereign, passive, alien individual in need of European allies.

Before examining these verse-polemics, I want to return to the historical framework that engendered such poems and the choice of Hannah More as public propagandist. By inviting More to write a didactic poem in support of the campaign, the Abolition Committee signalled the active engagement of evangelical women who were to become such a decisive force in the 1830s emancipationist movement. This public recognition of political spokeswomen resulted from several factors, beginning with the tradition of benefactresses that reached back to medieval times. In contemporary life, bluestocking Elizabeth Montagu assisted poor chimney-sweeps, her "climbing boys,"[3] while the most distinguished bluestocking intellectual, Elizabeth Carter, was "a very active as well as zealous member. . .[of] an institution [the Ladies Charitable Society] for the relief of the poor, principally reduced housekeepers. . . ." Most of Elizabeth Carter's friends belonged to it, and she was an original subscriber.[4] Lady Elizabeth Middleton, friend of James Ramsay and arguably the first person to agitate for parlimentary debate on abolition, and her friend Elizabeth Bouverie, also identified themselves as philanthropists. In *A List of the Governors of the Sunday School Society,* for example, the "Honourable Mrs. Bouverie" of Teston is mentioned.[5] She also subscribed to Magdalen Hospital, which numbered among its governors others similarly devoted to charitable causes, the Duchess of Devonshire, the Countess Dowager Huntington, Lady Middleton, Lady Powys, and Mrs. Poyntz.[6] Eighteenth-century female involvement in abolition lay on this continuum of benevolence. At least eighty-five women subscribed to the Abolition Society (1787), excluding a substantial number of "Anons" and numerous unnamed contributors from General Baptist societies. The Abolition Society itself united women of diverse denominations. Such prominent Anglican women as Elizabeth Bouverie, Elizabeth Carter, Lady Middleton, and Sarah Trimmer, as well as at least one Quaker and one Unitarian woman, Hannah Gurney (the mother of Elizabeth Fry), and Mary Scott, were all members.[7]

The popularity of female sentimental novelists, poets, and hymn-writers further explains the invitation to More. Joyce Tompkins puts an eighteenth-century perspective this way in a discussion of the popular novel from 1760 to 1820:

> There was a very real belief in the civilizing function of woman in society. . . . The world of the novel, in particular, seemed incomplete; let the women now speak of their experience. . . . The female heart, it appears, experiences "the delicate sensibilities of the tender passion, in a degree of refinement of which the rougher sex is seldom capable."[8]

On a more personal note, Hannah More's cultural reputation made the committee's choice an obvious one. Volumes of her prose and verse entitled *The Search After Happiness, Sacred Dramas,* and *Florio,* published respectively in 1773, 1782 and 1786, had gone into their 9th, 6th, and 2nd editions by 1788; poems "Bas Bleu" (1780) and "Sensibility" (1782) exemplified her strong commitment to charity. In the best-selling volume, *Thoughts on the Importance of the Manners of the Great to General Society* (1786) and "Slavery, a Poem" (1788), she argued that the high-ranking audience for whom *Thoughts* was intended as well as members of Parliament shouldered (or should shoulder) responsibility for manners and ethics.[9] "Slavery" attempted to reform society by appealing to its powerful members.

More's connection with upper-class evangelical Anglicans who were influential members of the Committee, however, was probably the primary factor:

> They have invaded the Navy, [says a riled contemporary,] they thrive at the Bank, they bear sway at the India House, they count several votes in Parliament, and they have got a footing in the Royal Palace. Their activity is incredible.[10]

By 1788 More's religious conversion inspired by John Newton and William Wilberforce, the Tory evangelical and member of Parliament for Hull, had fundamentally transformed her overall perspective. Subsequently she became the only prominent female member of the Clapham Sect, a socially and politically prominent group of affluent Evangelical Anglicans, nicknamed the Saints. A sympathetic biographer of the sect describes More as "the appointed [evangelical] agent" of Wilberforce and of Henry Thornton, an eminent banker, member of Parliament, and cousin of Wilberforce.[11] In Davidoff's and Hall's words,

> Starting from a conviction of man's sinfulness, Evangelicals stressed the importance of the conversion experience and individual spiritual life which could be transformed by an infusion of grace. They believed that the spirit could work through other means than the

trappings of the church. Individual faith was the key to moral regeneration, and the primary setting for maintaining faith was a religious family and household.[12]

These beliefs influenced the political meaning of the "slave" that was gradually infusing anti-slavery propaganda; specifically Clapham Sect evangelical tenets dictated More's stress on family unity, Christian agency, and conversion of the ungodly.

With the help of Quakers, General Baptists, North American settlers and other supportive individuals, the Abolition Committee publicized its goals in the winter months of 1787. Hundreds of letters describing the Committee's history had been distributed along with thousands of copies of an abridged version of Thomas Clarkson's expansive *History of the Abolition of the Slave Trade.*[13] William Roscoe, the Liverpudlian radical philanthropist and friend of Mary Wollstonecraft, donated the proceeds from his poem, "The Wrongs of Africa," to the Committee. Petitions flooded the House of Commons; the July–December 1788 volume of *The Gentleman's Magazine* recorded thousands [of petitions] from Bridgwater, Nottingham, Bridgeworth, Bradford, Leeds, & Sheffield [that were] . . . presented, read, and ordered to lie on the table.[14]

Women worked hard in this grand petition drive. Petitioning, as a political tactic that gave voice to the dispossessed, was nothing new for women.[15] During the seventeenth-century Civil War upheaval, women had petitioned, marched on Parliament, harangued crowds, and proselytized in the streets.[16] As the first page of the Abolition Society document states, "upward of 100 petitions have been presented to the House of Commons from various parts of the country."[17] Although no data are available, all classes of women must have petitioned, because Manchester, with a population below fifty thousand attracted 10,700 signatories and was the outstanding example of female involvement in the Abolition Society:[18]

> . . . Women's support for abolition in Manchester rose to an even higher [than pre-Abolition Society] level following the formation on December 27th 1787 of a formal Society for the Purpose of Effecting the Abolition of the Slave Trade. By the following year there were a total of sixty-eight female subscribers out of around three hundred individuals. Of the £400 raised from subscriptions £118 was sent to the Abolition Society in London, but the remainder was used for the local society's own campaigning. Rather than waiting for London to give a lead, the Manchester group organised a massive petition against the slave trade, bearing over ten thousand signa-

tures, and initiated a successful nationwide campaign based on advertisements in the provincial press to get other towns to follow suit.[19]

In the 1780s, Anna Laetitia Barbauld's comment in a letter to a friend specifies the ardent, ongoing female concern about the success of the campaign:

> I hope the exertions which we are now making for abolition of the slave-trade will not prove all in vain. They will not, if the pleadings of eloquence or the cry of duty can be heard. Many of the most respectable and truly distinguished characters are really busy about it, and the press and the pulpit are both employed; so I hope that something must be done.[20]

Hannah More began "Slavery, a Poem" in late December, 1787, writing hurriedly to coincide with the parliamentary debate, explaining, "if it does not come out at the particular moment when the discussion comes on in parliament, it will not be worth a straw."[21] Though debate was postponed, the poem denoted a decisive though atypical female intervention.[22] A second edition appeared in 1791. Two hundred and ninety-four lines long, the poem incorporated motifs already popularized in poems about slavery by such male writers as Hugh Mulligan, Samuel Jackson Pratt, William Roscoe, and William Cowper: human bondage, split families, atrocities, un-christian traders, the demeaning of Britain's "name," tributes to parliamentarians, and appeals to philanthropy or "social love."

Hannah More's poem, however, casts slaves into a mode of radical alterity not previously encased in female anti-slavery discourse. As a campaigner, More does not seem to separate herself off from the narrator but talks confidently in a polemical-abolitionist mode. She presents herself as the authorized European, intertextually discussing with other Europeans, both pro- and anti-slavery, what is to be done "with" or for Africans, how values can be transmitted and legislation effected. Her outrage at the institution's inhumanity and her representation of its victims explode in the following vignette that exemplifies the subsumption of colonized people and their complex lives into a solitary unit of identification:[23]

> See the dire victim torn from social life,
> The shrieking babe, the agonizing wife!
> She, wretch forlorn! is dragg'd by hostile hands,
> To distant tyrants sold, in distant lands! . . .
> By felon hands, by one relentless stroke,

See the fond links of feeling Nature broke!
The fibres twisting round a parent's heart,
Torn from their grasp, and bleeding as they part
(More, "Slavery," p. 7).

By illumining how slavery defies Scriptures, discountenances spiritual equality and personal capacity for feeling, More challenges plantocratic contentions about African subhumanity. Uncivilized, inferior pagans "of a darker skin" though Africans may be—she argues—they still have "heads to think, and hearts to feel, and souls to act." This assertion about African intellectuality, however, seems to shift ground throughout "Slavery," indicating a certain ambivalence on More's part:

Love strong as death, and active patriot fires;
All the rude energy, the fervid flame,
Of high-soul'd passion, and ingenuous shame:
Strong, but luxuriant virtues boldly shoot
From the wild vigour of a savage root. . . .
Plead not, in reason's palpable abuse,
Their sense of feeling callous and obtuse:
From heads to hearts lies Nature's plain appeal,
Tho' few can reason, all mankind can feel"
(More, "Slavery," pp. 5–7).

More deplores the fact that no African will desire conversion as long as traders—"white savages"—function in the name of Christianity. Hypocritical entrepreneurs deny spiritual life to Africans who bear "His sacred image" and are privy to "His mercy." Only the Christian example of men like Captain Cook and William Penn will dissipate heathen ignorance, thwart the influence of traders, and restore a violated sanctity to African life, destroyed by "the burning village and the blazing town."

More's spiritual appeal is matched by another appeal as spokeswoman for the Clapham Sect; although they include prominent ruling-class members like Wilberforce, their members are marked off by their anti-slavery stance and serious religious beliefs. Chiding unruly citizens who presumably are British male and female workers, she launches into a harsh attack on the mob, "unlicens'd monster of the crowd," and on "specious" advocates of liberty who spurn law and order and "tread on grave Authority and Pow'r." This pouncing on the mob in 1788 assumed a starker significance after the French Revolution—William Wilberforce expounded on the need for constant, finely tuned demarcations of class relationships:

No one can say into what discredit Christianity may hereby grow, at a time when the unrestrained intercourse subsisting among the several ranks and classes of society, so much favours the general diffusion of the sentiments of the higher orders. To a similar ignorance may perhaps be ascribed, in so small degree, the success with which, in a neighbouring country, Christianity has of late years been attacked.[24]

Along the same political lines, More refashions the familiar story of the slave Quashi who kills himself rather than murder his master in self-defence. (The master tries to strike Quashi for the first time.) Usually troped as the epitome of victimization because he declines physical retaliation, Quashi now doubles as an idealized member of the laboring class in the eyes of middle-class conservatives who dreaded class insurrection.

Hannah More's anti-slavery poem underscores women's right to enter the cultural mainstream of the body politic. Moreover, since white middle-class women were long acquainted with the pressure to marry, with the resulting family separation and (sometimes) abuse, they implicitly introduced a reevaluation of these already familiar thematics in male anti-slavery poems. Bluestockings themselves testified to ongoing grim practices in marriages among themselves and their friends.[25] Consequently, More's poem constitutes a counterdiscourse that challenges the lives of women like herself, of considerable personal independence, influence, and earned wealth; it also challenges the lives of less public women who nonetheless longed for wider cultural options. Her feminizations of Britain, freedom, and philanthropy become more than hackneyed apostrophes in a poem that condemns slavers who destroy family life at the same time that it praises powerful patriarchs in a male-only House of Commons.

Consciously or not, More injects the poem with the contradictions of white British gender politics while maintaining a steady focus on the heinousness of slavery. Powerlessness, bereavement, deracination, sexual degradation, and whippings are the recognized hallmarks of colonial discourse; at another level, they are central concepts in a gynocentric matrix of concerns and connections. More's endeavor empowers white female abolitionists to interlace worries about themselves as subjects with concerns about colonized others.

But because "Slavery" betokens the colonial encounter between a controlling female author and slaves in an exceptional scenario for the 1780s, the text dialogizes a register of voices from slaves to plantocrats who latently confront and even protest More's construction and vantage point. Despite the poet's commanding voice, recent cultural and legal events have affirmed that slaves are not a homogenized mass, that they emphatically articulate their personal and political concerns, and resolutely fight back against oppression and exploitation. Beyond that, More responds to the major Parliamentary foe, the pro-slaveryites, by asserting the right of Africans to a spiritual ontology; although they remain almost stationary at the finely calibrated lower end of the great chain of being where the ordering of primates begins, they are still humans on that chain. Displaying an uprooted family and a disparaged mob, the text generates important counterstatements, less audible in "Slavery" than three years later after the triumphant revolutions of citizens and slaves in France and San Domingo. But these dialogues can scarcely be heard behind the contemporary circulation of "knowledge" about Africans.

In 1788 Hannah More claimed the right to a collective political voice for women and a narrative strategy for constructing slaves that depended on a sentimental approach. An inventory of topoi, a refashioned paradigm had come into being in coherent form, accompanied by a certain female gaze born of Christian love for—and perhaps a repressed identification with—the collectivized, dominated other. The compassionate, though unitary voice that told these evildoings spoke unflinchingly to the audience.

On the surface, More's poem inaugurated a normalizing discourse. She had linked an obvious branch of philanthropy—anti-slavery— with women's sentient natures and in doing so, she discursively separated women from men. This is not to deny male commitment to anti-slavery sentiment. More's sentimental approach echoes that of William Cowper who attracted ridicule among male contemporaries for his "female" concerns.[26] But following More's poem, this approach earned a new classification; it became part of female cultural-political terrain. Male anti-slavery writings—although they certainly included poems and fiction—consisted mostly of pamphlets, parliamentary speeches, testimonies to the Privy Council, histories, reports, and scriptural treatises. Though up-to-the-minute, sentimentalism as expounded in and by males was tainted as a woman's thing.[27] Women wrote about family separation from positions of moral authority and some domestic-marital experience, inaccessible to Cowper, Thomas Day, and William Roscoe. This difference stemmed from what Leonore Davidoff and Catherine Hall have called the "centrality of the sexual division of labour within families . . . [as a result of] the development of capitalist enterprise."[28] Evangelical ideas about how to live were beginning to invest daily life. Without undue fanfare, More infused her poem with an evolving evangelical definition of femininity and women's social role.

Beyond the most visible and condoned discourse of feeling, More interwove her ideological support for rigorous class division with a pledge to end slavery. In turn, the conversion of Africans could become a reality. Free trade and the establishment of Sierra Leone are additional rich subtexts.

As the invited, female inaugurator of this updated discourse concerning slaves and slavery and as a preeminent abolitionist in her own right, More drew followers committed to the cause, although these followers did not necessarily share More's conservative views of, say, the laboring class. Without the weight of her authority and influence—and the very warm reception "Slavery" received—women less self-confident might have shied away from a public voicing.

Among them were Maria Falconar, aged seventeen, and her sister, Harriet Falconar aged fourteen, both of whom were young enough to have been reared on Anna Barbauld's *Hymn,* Bonhote's *Rambles,* and *The Rotchfords.*[29] Borrowing heavily from More's formula and earlier thematics while introducing her own variants, Harriet Falconar combines a triple appeal to parliamentarians, queen, and country; a hacking away at the macabre tree of commerce; and a denunciation of suffering among fractured African families. Once again, no distance divides the poets from the speaker since the poems are polemical contributions to the campaign. Slaves continue to be molded through slavery's linguistic shorthand: "Yet reason, justice, mercy lead in vain,/ Still the sad victim drags his galling chain" (Harriet Falconar, "Slavery," p. 16) says a sad Harriet, while her sister envisages freedom coming "with her train,/ To tear from Afric's sons the galling chain" (Maria Falconar, "Slavery," p. 11). Under the branches of the new rotting tree of slavery, moreover, "the wretched parent mourn[s] her long lost child." Africans are the victims of "unjust oppressors of an injur'd race."

To More's basic formula the sisters add an anti-superstitious, anti-Catholic element and a patriotic paeon to brave soldiers and sailors. Possibly Ottobah Cugoano's deftly allusive references in *Thoughts and Sentiments on the End of Slavery,* published the year before, inspired their equation of the atrocities of slavery with Britain's Catholic past and the horror of the Inquisition, still a code word for unrestrained violence:

. . . nothing in history [Cugoano reminds contemporaries] can equal
the barbarity and cruelty of the tortures and murders committed

under various pretences in modern slavery, except the annals of the Inquisition and the bloody edicts of Popish massacres.[30]

In a panegyric to parliamentarians, the narrator (very close in beliefs, it seems, to Harriet Falconar) echoes More in applauding: "Ye noble few . . . ye just protectors." In their hands lies the power to "let justice still prevail." Then she turns to the "bleeding" of Africa, introducing a graphic biological metaphor with female overtones that images the violent, prolonged rape of a continent. Britain glitters as the fecund mother whose plains are "rich," whose "clime" is "fruitful"; she then invokes Queen Charlotte's aid as sovereign and "Daughter of Virtue," "yet parent of this happy isle . . . [whose] heart like thine, . . . feels another's pain." The concatenation of female signifiers, not unlike More's, continues with an encomium to Britain's past glories during which the narrator refers to Newton's exposure of truth as the "unveil[ing of] the beauteous maid." The strewing of female accents throughout their poems reinforces not only the newly evident prominence of women in the campaign but their insistence on conceptualizing abolition in terms of values traditionally considered "female." It also appropriates the genealogy of slaves and slavery feminocentrically and forges tacit associations, once again in a subtle anti-patriarchal hit, between the status of white British women and colonized slaves.

The sisters, moreover, invoke a matrix of associations concerning Dissent. They dedicate their volume to the tough-minded Whiggish Duchess of Devonshire and counted radicals William Roscoe and Helen Maria Williams among their subscribers. Resembling several of the earlier abolitionists (Barbauld, Mary Scott, Mary Wollstonecraft, and Helen Maria Williams), the sisters were obviously acquainted and associated with Dissenting ideas and were perhaps connected to these circles. Their uncommon stress on reason as a guide to humanity (unlike More who treats reason as a matter of practical understanding) indicates a specific philosophical debt and direction:

> To man superior reason's light was giv'n,
> Reason, the noblest gift of bounteous heav'n;
> Unfailing beam, bright intellectual ray,
> Thou steady guide through errors devious way;
> Say, wert thou first by gracious heav'n design'd,
> To stamp injustice on the human kind;
> Forbid it truth, forbid it ev'ry breast
> That heave in pity for the wretch oppress'd;
> Yet reason, justice, mercy, plead in vain,
> Still the sad victim drags his galling chain. . . .

Concurrently, the sisters' poems strengthen the Anglo-Africanist formula and the propagation of abolitionist ideas. Besides, adolescent females who exhort the public to treat benighted lesser beings with greater dignity reenforce white women's claim to a new cultural vantage point.

The press reacted zestfully to this propaganda. Although abolitionist Dissenters and evangelical Anglicans applauded the same abstractions—liberty, truth, benevolence and patriotism—the former tended to regard slavery as the antithesis of reason while evangelicals deemed it an insurmountable impediment to conversion and free trade with Africa. But coming before the French Revolution, their shared similarities obscured these differences: Hannah More herself talked of the "palpable abuse" of reason, by which she meant logical thinking rather than rationality as a philosophical principle. The press persisted in lumping female abolitionists together—just as the abolitionists frequently totalized Africans—exhibiting a wary and incredulous reaction to the presence of females in cultural affairs. More's symbolic entry into male political discourse met with pursed-lip disapproval from a reviewer who contemptuously questioned her right to appraise the contemporary scene. The reviewer ventured that her aim, "immediate and absolute emancipation," was questionable—"scarcely to be wished or expected."[31]

To add insult to pettiness, a reviewer in *The Critical Review* (September 1788) obliquely compared the Falconars' poems to earlier ones on the topic, sniffing at their lack of originality. "The subject itself precludes any novelty of ideas." Later in the same periodical, betokening a slight change in attitude, the sisters' poems were pronounced "easy and correct . . . display[ing] the accuracy that could be expected in two such juvenile composers."[32] Relishing youthful susceptibilities and endorsing conventional norms of femininity in the "Parnassian sisters," as they were dubbed, the *Monthly* reviewer stated that:

> These poetic buds promise fair for a beautiful crop, when the full flowering season arrives; if, in the mean time, they are neither nipped by the unkind blights, nor chilled by the cold severity, of criticism. For the present, we are glad to see their growth and bloom encouraged by a very handsome subscription.[33]

In the spirit of political engagement styled as sentimental altruism, Helen Maria Williams published a fourth pro-parliamentary, anti-slavery poem in 1788 to eulogize a reformist, slavery-based bill, rather than specifically advocating the passage of the Abolition Bill as More and the Falconar sisters had done. Williams used the successful passage of Sir William Dolben's Bill regulating the size of slavery ships on the Middle Passage to pitch into slavery and point up the persecution of Dissenters. Although her concerns and narrative strategy were similar to More's, albeit more radical, Williams might not have thought herself sufficiently sanctioned to express hard-core radical opinions, divorced from the sentimental tradition, until the French Revolution ventilated the question of human rights and universal tyranny.

For well over a decade Williams commanded a formidable intellectual position within the Dissenting community; like Hannah More she was an eminent figure in London circles, but unlike More her home became a cultural and political gathering place for radical Dissenters and bluestockings alike. One of her original mentors was the celebrated Unitarian Dissenter, the Reverend Andrew Kippis. In an appendix to one of the Reverend Kippis's works, Williams published an elegy to Captain Cook in which she lauds his love of humanity while denouncing the slave trade; the genocide of Indians in colonial America; and potential genocide against Africans. Like More, Williams denounces slavery as a stain on Britain's (mythological/self-promoting) reputation as a freedom-loving land. Though history has subsequently condemned Captain Cook's callous treatment toward islanders and explained his murder within that context, when Williams was writing he personified goodness and patriotism:

> Till Cook . . . along the surges cast
> Philanthropy's connecting zone,
> And spread her loveliest blessings round.—
> Not like that murd'rous band he came,
> Who stain'd with blood the new-found West;
> Nor as, with unrelenting breast,
> From Britain's free, enlighten'd land,
> Her sons now seek Angola's strand;
> Each tie most sacred to unbind,
> To load with chains a brother's frame,
> And plunge a dagger in the mind;
> Mock the sharp anguish bleeding there
> Of Nature in her last despair!
> ——Great Cook! Ambition's lofty flame,
> So oft directed to destroy,
> Led Thee to circle with thy name,
> The smile of love, and hope, and joy![34]

Four years earlier in 1784, Williams had set upon Spanish colonialists for greed and gore in a poem entitled "Peru," the advertisement to

which deplored "the unparalleled sufferings of an innocent and amia-
ble people."[35] The more radical-minded Williams still concurs with
More and most Britons about the virtue of colonization which, unlike
slavery, is a desirable institution. At the same time, Williams spends
so much time attacking slavery and metropolitan invasion that her
text amounts to a silent anti-colonial opposition.

Despite her activism and published commentaries, Williams drew
on current formulae of abstractions and motifs that constituted the
colonized other along a chain of female signifiers: Williams' poem on
the bill that had recently passed for regulating the slave trade opens
on the panorama of the Middle Passage, "the wretch new bound in
hopeless chains . . . Women . . . too weak to bear the galling chain,"
breathing:

> . . . the tainted air;
> Of mind too feeble to sustain
> The vast, accumulated pain;
> No more, in desperation wild,
> Shall madly strain her gasping child;
> With all the mother at her soul,
> With eyes where tears have ceas'd to roll,
> Shall catch the living infant's breath;
> Then sink in agonizing death.[36]

The mother-child dyad debunks plantocratic mythology by accenting
family love, a common shorthand cue for the humanity of Africans.
The homage to a loving maternity highlights Christian values and their
absence in slaves' lives. Summoning the image of a caring African
motherhood reminds readers of rough separations and white women's
awareness and (sometimes personal) recognition of western versions
of these affairs. "The poem on the bill" reaffirms the idea of motherhood as women's special sphere, whether African or British, and
upholds the profile of a monolithic, pacific, vulnerable "African." The
speaker—Williams the polemicist—recollects for readers that slavers'
sanctions provoked slaves into "unchristian" suicides before missionaries could introduce them to Christianity. Only God's mercy
staunches spiritual death.

Williams is a radical committed to Parliamentary reform, so her
commendation of parliamentarians repays a closer look. Whig parliamentarians, she states, are the noble minds who have facilitated the
"blest decree," the "great deed"—the successful passage of Sir William
Dolben's bill. Pitt and Richmond merit special esteem as men who

eased the "mourner's aching breast" and wiped the "friendless orphan's tear." "Poor wretch! on whose despairing eyes/ His cherish'd home shall never rise!" (Williams, "A Poem on the Bill," pp. 12–13).

In the 1770s, Dissenters immersed themselves in parliamentary reform of the laws regarding Dissent. Prior to the Abolition Committee, their members had established the Society for Constitutional Information (S.C.I.) to demand the repeal of the crucial Test and Corporation Acts. One clause in the Test and Corporation Acts, dating from Charles II's reign, stipulated that any person admitted to corporate office or taking up any civil position had to take Holy Communion in the Church of England. Since 1730 Dissenters had fought for repeal.[37]

Hence Williams' text abounds with reminders of contemporary persecution of Dissenters, her text amply dialogized across its different parts and to different audiences. She suggests parallels between the twin needs for an Abolition bill and laws to end discrimination against Dissenters. As a foremost spokeswoman for non-conformist ideas, Williams mounts a sophisticated, even politically perilous argument, keenly aware that evangelical politicians like Wilberforce who were spearheading the abolitionist fight also spearheaded the suppression of Dissenters' rights. Thus her praise of Pitt is double-edged at best. But her love of justice dictates these uneasy political connections with temporary allies who were shortly to indict all English Jacobins as people with "a contempt for the British Constitution and an attachment to those false principles of liberty."[38]

Like More and the Falconars, Williams genderizes her poem by vilifying slavers' destruction of family life and refined values, men "robbed of every human grace." Their "fix'd [economic] purpose" and personal barrenness contradict the altruistic values women cherish and promote:

> [Their] untir'd aim is Self alone;
> Who think in gold the essence lies
> From which extracted bliss shall rise;
> To whose dull sense, no charm appears
> In social smiles, or social tears.

The homeless, furthermore, the deracinated "millions" in "despair," "half-expiring . . . in mute affliction," possess a feminized quality; they are encoded as meek, unthreatening individuals trapped in that final suffering of an auction, "doomed lambs" in ghastly new surroundings, fearfully trying "to read . . . [the] new possessor's eye." Slaves everywhere personify coercion.

Devoid of "social tears"—crux of a feminized sensibility—the planto-cracy is spiritually irredeemable. Slaves become so "consum'd in wasting pain" that "in pining sickness [they] yield . . . life." Rather than exist under untenable conditions, many slaves would "grasp the reeking knife" in order to return "to green hills where Freedom roves," tacit acknowledgement of African beliefs about being and the afterlife. Reiterating a female attachment to feeling, religion, and domesticity, the narrator (so closely allied with Williams' values as to be virtually indistinguishable) displays the fantasy of nostalgia; she imagines an idyllic prelapsarian Africa peopled by carefree, unchanging inhabitants. They enjoy the comforts of home while adrift from their native land, slaves no less than "poor wand'rer[s]" who sustain "unremitted pain" and know "no gleam of hope." This haunting evocation of a "stateless" condition would not have been lost on certain sections of Williams' readership involved in the effort "to remove the political disabilities of Dissenters."[39] As a somewhat less direct case in point, Wollstonecraft's *Mary, a Fiction* published the same year applauded that external place where "there would be no marriage," that is, no persecution.

At the end of the poem, Britain reemerges as a mother (or is it a father? the gender marks are ambiguous) extending a "protecting hand" who will "teach . . . [people all over the globe] to make all Nature free,/ and Shine by emulating thee." An outspoken Britain androgynously blends with a paradigmatic female-nurturing Britain, protecting the unprotected; Williams appeals to humanity, eloquence, this "lov'd Britain," and the "Senate" to overcome the "wrongs of Afric's Captive Race." If Sir William Dolben's bill were a bitter drop in slavery's cup, then Williams aches to dash the whole chalice to the ground. The "impious chain" of slavery strangled life out of "the spirit." These familiar allusions and repetitious metaphors, the same objectifying shorthand and excess of feeling employed by More to crystallize the reality of slavery urge readers to become engaged.

More's influence again comes to bear in a poem by Anna Laetitia Barbauld that indicates the flexibility of this propagandistic mode. In "Epistle to William Wilberforce, Esq. on the Rejection of the Bill for Abolishing the Slave Trade" (1791), Barbauld occupies a doubled ideological position. Not unlike Williams' but gentler, her poem decries any demotion of Wilberforce's role, even though Barbauld is a Dissenter and Wilberforce is a parliamentary opponent of Dissenters' rights.[40] But as an abolitionist friend of Hannah More, Barbauld opts to transcend party politics. The "Epistle" doubles as a general statement about constitutional liberties.

Barbauld's specific addition to More's formulae is the familiar portrait of the sadistic creole plantation wife (remember George Ellison's). This image of a cruel planter's wife was a common one. As a group, plantation mistresses were frequently alleged to be deeply jealous of black female slaves and politically powerless:

> Lo! where reclined, pale Beauty courts the breeze,
> Diffused on sofas of voluptuous ease;
> With anxious awe her menial train around
> Catch her faint whispers of half-uttered sound;
> See her, in monstrous fellowship, unite
> At once the Scythian and the Sybarite!
> Blending repugnant vices, misallied,
> Which frugal nature purposed to divide;
> See her, with indolence to fierceness joined,
> Of body delicate, infirm of mind,
> With languid tones imperious mandates urge;
> With arm recumbent wield the household scourge;
> And with unruffled mien, and placid sounds,
> Contriving torture, and inflicting wounds
> (Barbauld, *Epistle,* pp. 176–77).

Carefully the speaker unites this female villain with masculinist values, "monstrous fellowship," and reinforces the importance of challenging slavery with gentle altruism. The preposterousness of a female monster spreading the disease of slavery—women had very little to do with the execution and administration of slavery—defames the influence of profiteering males. Further, it stresses decent-minded women's attempts to stem their corruption. Race and gender oppression again temporarily coalesce. Implicitly, the reprehensible mistress is striking a child if she strikes a vulnerable slave, since they share, in European eyes, a child-like helplessness.

Although More's Clapham Sect discourse has its authority "already fused to it,"[41] resistances to evangelical ideology in these 1788 poems abounded. The Falconars, Williams, and Barbauld openly emulate More's form and thematics yet insert their own contrasting perspectives, confronting More's attack on workers between the lines. This less obvious political discourse enunciated by the Dissenters spoke eloquently to omissions. Not only were the constitutional liberties of slaves absent, their own were too. The Falconars' tributes to reason and the *élan* of Williams' and Barbauld's radical ideas informed these texts with a dual message about the need to think about liberty in domestic as well as global terms. Further, More's insistence on Africans' sensate nature responds dialogically to age-old pro-slavery denials of that fact.

Moreover, and this applies to all these texts that circulated knowledge about slaves, slaves themselves talk back—in newspapers where rebellion was noted; in London where autobiographies, poems, and letters were published; on Clapham Common where black children were being "educated" while dying from the cold.[42] Most of all, slaves talk back because lives that are reductively constituted around being kidnapped, grieving for parents, being sold, and dying demand radical surgery and responses. But this configuration based primarily on victimization was a positive strategy for evangelicals, given contemporary attitudes they shared toward Africans, enslaved or free. And to some extent their strategy worked. Josiah Wedgwood's deeply influential cameo-cipher, a sculptured modification of More's shorthand in verse, is a case in point.[43]

As for the white British women themselves, their participation inevitably challenged tradition. On the one hand, they enhanced their prescribed role as sentimentalists, yet on the other they asserted a right to power, however limited, by claiming forceful identities as public polemicists voicing themselves into the body politic.[44] But this new toughness belied the very sentimentalization in which they consciously indulged. Sugar-sweet representations of African family life—an infantilization of reality as Anna Freud might have argued— masked some female anxiety about externally imposed views of women as weak and vulnerable.[45] Wollstonecraft also reiterates that women think of themselves as child-like although the diaries and letters of the period suggest that a sense of infantilization dates to midcentury rather than the late eighteenth-century.[46] Furthermore, the representations of motherhood and family life pressed home—in a subtle anti-patriarchal opposition—roles that white and black women shared globally. Projecting "slaves" as one-dimensional characters amounted to a psychic investigation of their own partriarchally-ordained, one-dimensional roles as moral caretakers, a state of affairs best exemplified in Hannah More's strong public personage. Family was an intimately felt subject. Many women still experienced or read about or knew friends subjected to pressure about their choice of marriage partner; they had heard or knew directly about uprootings from parental homes and scarcely veiled sales to unknown husbands. This subtle criss-crossing of roles—women as self-appointed cultural spokeswomen for slaves and as charity campaigners, women as controlled people and hence marginally sited on the borders of both camps—nuanced all the 1788 texts as well as texts written before and after. When Lady Eleanor Butler comments in her diary about Thomas Clarkson that he had decided to "devote himself entirely to the relief of those unhappy beings, whose sufferings are a disgrace to human nature," she might have been talking about Hannah More.[47]

By stereotyping Africans and emphasizing their own cultural command while recognizing the denial of full constitutional rights to all and their own historical exclusion from Parliamentary debate, white female polemicists centerstaged themselves as classic doubled subjects. They were involved in "a form of power which subjugates and makes subject to"; they were split between acting as agents and identifying with victims.[48]

Phillis Wheatley, James Somerset, Ukawsaw Gronniosaw, Ottobah Cugoano, Ignatius Sancho, Olaudah Equiano, and other prominent Africans exist only as (often faint) intertextual resistances to the disembodiment and disappearance of African reality.[49] In Hannah More's text, only Anglo-Africanist characters, created from a litany of available constructions, appear in this morally and spiritually schematized framework; slavers themselves were as marginalized as slaves, sinners stealing birthrights, the Cains of foreign policy, who indulged in actions that catapulted them beyond the boundaries of the human community. Put in terms of *realpolitik,* the garnering of some cultural power for white British women was won at the expense of African material reality because the closer the country came to an abolitionist politic, the more imperative writers found it to denote racial difference. The genealogy of "the slave" functioned as a method of containment, an unconscious strategy of encirclement. At the level of discourse, though clearly not at the level of lived reality, slavery and slaves had become a construct of European invention, exhibited by Europeans as subjects of "true" knowledge. Europe spoke for Africa.

In general the press agreed with this "female" perspective that so agreeably concurred with prescribed social roles. More's poem had institutionalized this mode as an acceptable form of female abolitionist discourse. Once again the *Critical Review* (February 1789) spoke somewhat unproblematically:

> The accounts lately given to the Public respecting the slave trade, were horrid enough to call into vigorous exercise the amiable sensibility of the female breast. By the ladies this subject has been contemplated through the pure medium of virtuous pity, unmixed with those political, commercial and selfish considerations which operated in steeling the hearts of some men against the pleadings of humanity: to find them, therefore, writing on it, by no means excited wonder (*Critical Review,* (February, 1989), p. 237).

White British women had expropriated and sabotaged various discourses—of law, trade, parliamentary debate—for their own positive purposes. Coupled with early petitioning and agitation by provincial women, women's verse-polemic was establishing a precedent unrevived since the Civil War when hundreds of female radical sectaries petitioned and wrote against the government. It was no coincidence that women were capitalizing on their growing moral influence at a time when relations of production were undergoing fundamental change. Moreover, since women still described themselves as slaves in prose and verse, their accent on the dreadful circumstances of a slave's life denoted a small act of vengeance on the plantocratic lobby in particular and on a male ruling class in general.

The submerged political dissonance between the evangelicals and the Dissenters did not fool Horace Walpole. He understood only too well where the rifts lay in that apparent but superficial unity. He told his friend Hannah More that he saw Helen Maria Williams and Anna Laetitia Barbauld as Deborah and Jael from Scriptures. Although they had let their nails grow, he confided to More,

> no poissonnières were there [at the Crown and Anchor in 1791 for a celebration of the French Revolution] . . . and the prophetesses had no opportunity of exercising their talents or talons."[50]

Earlier Walpole had written to More that while "Slavery" exemplified a genuine "compassion for blacks . . . sincere from your soul", Anna Barbauld's poem was marred by a "measure of faction."[51] Walpole identifies a distinction between Hannah More's allegedly non-political, untrammeled emotional support for the Bill and Anna Barbauld's opposition to slavery—coded as opportunist by Walpole—on the basis of her Dissenting principles. He denies the possibility of an ideological intersection of their views. Had Walpole been alive to review Hannah More's *Tracts* in the 1790's, one wonders how he would have reassessed her alleged neutrality. Walpole correctly surmised that radicals writing on parliamentary bills and abolition were addressing larger enlightenment questions of rights for all. The discourse on slavery provided radicals with another way of talking about rights, although the question of abolition as an issue of human entitlement remained somewhat unspecified until the following year. At that point the French Revolution erupted and clarified submerged political divisions. In 1788, white middle-class women claimed agency for themselves and the ungranted right to speak on behalf of slaves. The poems in 1788 put a finishing touch to a long process of Anglo-Africanist othering at the hands of white British female speaking subjects who were projecting a political-personal subjection of their own.

Chapter 8

The Radical Impulse: Before the French Revolution

How can we conceive of a revolutionary struggle that does not involve a revolution in discourse.
—Julia Kristeva, *New French Feminisms,* p. 140.

Radicalism had always been, inherently, a protest movement—voicing popular resentment against the social and political consequences of an exclusive and insensitive legislature, privilege in the established church and inequality in the law. . . . They had given unequivocal and effective support to one of the earliest, and ultimately the most successful of all protest movements—the campaign for the abolition of the slave trade.
—Albert Goodwin, *The Friends of Liberty,* p. 359.

We are by no means surprised, that *verse-men,* as well as prose-men, should take up their pens to reprobate the slave trade. . . . The Muses are by nature the friends of freedom.
Monthly Review, March 1788, p. 267.

Prior to 1788, protests about slavery by white British women veered from condemnation of atrocities and insistence on amelioration and spiritual compensation to rehabilitation for ex-slaves. For the first time, writers openly supported escape attempts and efforts to gain individual manumission.

Two important additions to these unsystematic responses were a unique attack on racial prejudice in the 1740s and a forthright attack

165

on slavery by a Quaker spokeswoman twenty years later. Beyond that, in 1788 a laboring class poet named Ann Yearsley refashioned Hannah More's abstract formula of "a slave" with a named individual slave in fiction who aggressively retaliated, regardless of consequences. Following Yearsley on the radical undercurrent came Elizabeth Bentley who concretized slavery by extolling Ignatius Sancho, an African living in London; concurrently, Bentley denounced the institution.

As Sir Robert Walpole's administration drew to a close in 1742, the well-known controversial novelist, Eliza Haywood, tackled subjects that related to slavery: the humanity of Africans and prejudice itself. As early as 1680 Morgan Godwyn had pointed out derisively that slave traders benefitted from promoting the belief "that Africans were not really men."[1] Godwyn emphasized the relativity of color which, in David Brion Davis's words, "may be taken as evidence of a common prejudice toward blackness."[2] Winthrop Jordan expands on the importance of Godwyn's comments:

> What had occurred was not a change in the justification of slavery from religion to race. . . . The shift was an alteration in emphasis within a single concept of difference rather than a development of a novel conceptualization. The amorphousness and subtlety of such a change is evident, for instance, in the famous tract, *The Negro's and Indian's Advocate,* published in 1680 by the Reverend Morgan Godwyn. Baffled and frustrated by the disinterest of planters in converting their slaves, Godwyn declared at one point that "their *Complexion,* which being most obvious to the sight, by which the *Notion* of things doth seem to be most certainly conveyed to the Understanding, is apt to make no slight impressions upon rude Minds, already prepared to admit of any thing for Truth which shall make for Interest." Altering his emphasis a few pages later, Godwyn complained that "these two words, *Negro* and *Slave*" are "by custom grown Homogeneous and Convertible; even as *Negro* and *Christian, Englishman* and *Heathen,* are by the like corrupt Custom and Partiality made Opposites." Most arresting of all, throughout the colonies the terms *Christian, free, English,* and *white* were for many years employed indiscriminately as metonyms.[3]

Throughout the eighteenth-century, the debate dragged on over such matters as the "curse of Ham," the link between people and animals, species classifications, and the importance of climate.[4] Even more tangibly, the general public as well as the press went as far as to debate excitedly the possible humanity of a chimpanzee that had arrived in London.[5] In a periodical entitled *The Female Spectator* that she edited between 1742 and 1744, Eliza Haywood contributed to this debate, one of several contemporary women responding angrily to prejudice, but the only one to discuss race as an issue of cultural supremacy. Specifically, Haywood had challenged prejudice in a tale about a young woman who declines to marry an eligible man because he is a Welshman, and therefore a foreigner, an other:

> Among the various Kinds of Errors into which Human Nature is liable to fall, there are some, which People of a true Understanding are perfectly sensible of in themselves, yet . . . still persist to act in Contradiction to the Dictates of even their own Reason and Judgment.
>
> What we call Prejudice, or Prepossession, is certainly that which stands foremost in the Rank of Frailties: . . . It is the first Thing given to the Mind to feed upon: . . . It is this fatal Propensity which binds as it were, our Reason in Chains. . . . Hence are our Conceptions bounded; our Notions meanly narrow;—our ideas, for the most part, unjust; and our Judgment shamefully led astray. . . . What I would be understood to mean by the word Prejudice . . . enters chiefly through the Ears:—when our Notions of Persons and Things, which of ourselves we know nothing of, are guided, . . . A very learned author calls this unhappy impulse *the Jaundice of the mind* [my italics]. . . . National Prejudices are yet more dangerous, and indeed much more ridiculous:—What can be a greater Absurdity than for one whole People to hate another, only for being born in a different Climate.[6]

Editing a later periodical named *The Parrot,* Haywood includes a commentary that creatively links national prejudice to the shade of an individual's complexion, possibly the first anti-racist statement by an English female writer.[7] In a deliberately understated register, Haywood also records disdain for Alexander Pope who had earlier scorned her in *The Dunciad.* By protesting the fatuity of associating race with inferiority, she invokes Pope's poem and invites reassessments of his opinions. The passage occurs when the narrator talks in the voice of the protagonist, the parrot:

> The colour I brought into the world with me, and shall never change, it seems, is an Exception against me;—some People will have it that a Negro might as well set up for a Beauty, as a Green Parrot for a good speaker;—Preposterous Assertion! as if the Complection of the Body had any influence over the Faculties of the Mind; yet meerly on this score they resolve, right or wrong, to condemn all I say beforehand.[8]

The speaker then mocks those who mindlessly mimic the opinions of others and vigorously ridicules "blind Bigotry,—such a slavish dependence on the Breath of others."[9] The individual who "labours to keep those foolish Animosities alive, in my Opinion deserves little thanks from the World, either for her Wit, or Good-will to Mankind."[10] Prejudice, she concludes, derives from a suspension of rational faculties, caused by ignorance and parental indoctrination about culture and climate; subversion, in her view, is the best counteraction.

Through subtly different levels of meaning, the speaker assaults not simply prejudice but plantocratic and Popean mythologies besides. She offers female readers a chance to challenge pernicious common assumptions about African intellectuality and reminds readers implicitly of Haywood's own purported lack of talent; then they can choose from an array of subject positions.

Two decades later Rachel Wilson from the Society of Friends revived seventeenth-century remonstrations of earlier Friends. En route to an abolitionist position forty years after Alice Curwen wrote, Friends in their epistles from the Yearly Meeting of 1727 stated that "it is the sense of this meeting that the importing of negroes from their native country . . . is not a commendable nor allowed practice, and is therefore censured."[11] By 1757 Quakers established a committee to investigate the pros and cons of slavery. The labelling of Friends as unpatriotic during the Seven Years War when they refused to pay taxes caused further marginalization and underscored this new determination.[12] So did the life-endangering treatment of American Indians that Friends witnessed in colonial America. In 1758 the London Yearly Meeting of the Society of Friends passed a resolution "to avoid being in any way concerned in" slavery[13]; this was followed by the landmark decision of 1761 when the London Yearly Meeting announced that all slave owners and slave traders should be expelled from the Society."[14] Quaker Anthony Benezet pressed North American Quakers to oppose slavery openly while transatlantically challenging the views of the Archbishop of Canterbury, the Society for the Propagation of the Gospel, and John Wesley.[15]

At that Quarterly Meeting of the Society of Friends in Philadelphia, Rachel Wilson notes that she had spoken to a meeting of "Negroes" at New River.[16] She then expresses her disquiet to the assembled body. In the years preceding Wilson's visit to North America in 1768, Granville Sharp was immersed in legal matters, trying to free numerous African slaves, beginning with the owner-maimed Barbadian slave, Jonathan Strong. The year of Wilson's published diary, the ex-slave John Hylas petitioned Sharp for the release of his kidnapped wife

Mary. Less aggressive and highpitched than Sharp and Benezet, Wilson still asserts her opinion distinctively, suggestively arguing that slavery violates natural law, spiritual kinship, and deprives all slaves of a self-actualizing humanity. Regardless of any othered status, slaves are entitled to every basic right.

> I had earnestly to desire we might walk worthy of the vocation whereunto we were called in all humility and fear, and also to request them to keep their hands clear from purchasing Negroes, as believing it never was intended for us to traffick with any part of the human species, and, if there were no buyers, there would be no sellers, that, where they were numerous, religion was at a low ebb.[17]

By 1784, Quakers were widely distributing their abolitionist demands in pamphlets and letters to prominent daily newspapers in London and the provinces. Their petition to the House of Commons for abolition of the slave trade in 1784, though instantly rejected, elicited a favorable response from the press. The *Morning Chronicle* reported that it emanated "from the most humane religious sect in the Christian World."[18] Supporting Parliament's rejection of the anti-slavery petition, Lord North pronounced slavery "a trade which had in some measure become necessary to almost every nation in Europe."[19]

Despite or perhaps in response to such setbacks, protests grew. In "Peru" (1784), a long poem that directly impugned Spanish colonialism, Helen Maria Williams hints at Britain's own immersion in the trade. A standing Parliamentary Committee of six Quakers was appointed "for the relief and liberation of the Negro slaves in the West Indies and for the discouragement of the slave trade on the coast of Africa."[20] Over the next two years, Friends sent anti-slavery tracts and pamphlets to members of Parliament and circulated them in public schools.

Meanwhile freed African males wrote and agitated, supplying with their collective voice a crucial corrective to the mythologies of Anglo-Africanist discourse. Their presence and publications infantilized European notions of a lumped-together set of others. The memoirs of Ottobah Cugoano, who corresponded with Edmund Burke, were published in 1787. Two years after *Thoughts and Sentiments,* Olaudah Equiano's autobiography attained bestseller status. From the 1780s until 1797 when he died, Equiano was still ardently campaigning for abolition and recommending the economic advantage of non-slave commerce with Africa. "The inhuman traffic of slavery," he stated the year after More's campaigning poem was published in 1788, will augment "the demand for manufacturers."[21] Equiano was also responsible for initiating proceedings in the *Zong* insurance scandal in 1782 by relaying information to Granville Sharp about the mass murders of slaves on the high seas.[22] Not long after the Abolition Committee was established, the provincial laborer-turned-poet, Ann Yearsley introduced a rebellious slave protagonist named Luco into an antislavery poem, "A Poem on the Inhumanity of the Slave-Trade." Hannah More had adopted Yearsley as a protégée until they acrimoniously severed their relationship as a result of class conflict.[23] More acutely than most, Yearsley understood the consequences of denying basic rights to individuals: as a result of penury, her emaciated mother had just died from starvation in Yearsley's presence. Without a fortuitous eleventh hour intervention, the same fate awaited Yearsley and her children and husband. Hence she was well accustomed to the status of alterity, her response being to fight back. Correspondingly, she identifies with African protagonist Luco as a class ally, downplaying helpless victimization. To do so, Yearsley elaborates on familiar scenes of traumatic family splintering: death from grief of a father and a beloved; European baseness; a gentle Luco who in many ways resembles a declassed and feminized version of Behn's royal prince, Oroonoko: he "strives to please,/ Nor once complains (as) time inures the youth . . . / (to) resignation, or a calm despair" (Yearsley, "Inhumanity," p. 16). Named and voiced, his dialogue through the narrator to the reader elicits public sympathy. Then to the familiar matrix of motifs Yearsley adds a fiendish "Christian renegade" who mercilessly baits Luco and along with his cohorts slowly burns the slave to death as a punishment for usurping the authority of the colonizer. Self-defensive retaliation, attempting to reverse subject-other domination, spells death.

Abolitionist texts did not customarily acknowledge the frequent slave rebellions that contextualize Luco's adversarial posture. Yearsley may have read press commentaries on slave revolts in the Middle Passage and the Caribbean.[24] Michael Craton lists seventy-five revolts, disturbances, plots, mutinies, unrest, and wars, of which twenty took place between 1760 and 1792. During the three years of the first phase of abolitionist writings from 1787 to 1792, a mixture of unrest, armed agitation, revolts, and war variously exploded in Jamaica, the Bahamas, Dominica, Tortola. News of the Haitian revolution had generated the unsettling atmosphere in Jamaica.[25] The *Gentleman's Magazine* for January 1790 under the section *West Indies Intelligence* states that white inhabitants of Demerara escaped a "general massacre" when one thousand "negroes" organized a rebellion. The reviewer concludes by chiding the ringleaders who were tortured and killed for "not discovering the least remorse." For Yearsley to champion Luco was a form of public confrontation, an assertion of her own sovereign subjectivity in the face of opposition.

After Luco's fight to the death, Yearsley turns on two-faced pseudo-Christian traders who effectively deny slaves a spiritual life, Eurocentrically conceived. But why, she wryly asks, should victims "profess their oppressors' beliefs?" The victimized must instead avenge iniquity or be avenged. Luco's distinctly implied inner speech claiming his right to be free converses with Yearsley's versified speeches favoring individual self-determination. Here is the critical wedge that ideologically separates More from Yearsley, although both women, in different ways, are themselves gender oppressed within the prevailing patriarchal hegemonic order. More sympathetically portrays dejected Africans to attract support for the Abolition Bill; Yearsley eschews unnamed, unvoiced abstractions and represents insurgency in the person of Luco, an oppressed individual with agency, a colonized other, acting as Yearsley acted against More. She projects into Luco part of that indomitable spirit and projects yet another part of her outraged self, demeaned by More, into "the mob" whom More disapprobates as class inferiors. At the same time, Yearsley is rhetorically distanced (though not politically or emotionally) from the speaker. Where More privileges Parliamentary action, national agitation, and condemns the "mob," Yearsley exhorts Africans and all disenfranchised people to resist; her poem is both personal and paradigmatic of class antagonisms and global power struggles; it glosses not simply More's behavior toward Yearsley but the class prejudice that characterizes More's own poem. In this respect, Yearsley's didacticism resembles that of Helen Maria Williams in her subtle poem on Sir William Dolben's bill that probes the double standard of Wilberforce's Parliamentary heroism from a Dissenting and hence distanced standpoint.

Inevitably too, Yearsley's poem exemplifies received attitudes toward African men and women. As "uncivilized" as More's constructions, Yearsley's Africans also primarily feel rather than think. The description of Luco's father succinctly encapsulates these tropes: he dwells in despair, the receptacle of "horrid and dark . . . wild, unenlighten'd pow'rs," an "untamed savage" in the contemporary idiom, comforted only by "the anarchy of wounded nature" (Yearsley, "Inhumanity," pp. 12, 13). Concurrently, Africans are human beings enduring an inhuman bondage, innocents who feel pain like everyone else and are entitled to freedom even though their "primitive" culture has involuntarily and supposedly deprived them of the benefits of western civilization. Echoing abolitionist contemporaries, Yearsley dialogizes plantocratic vauntings about insensate Africans.

Critics reacted somewhat defensively to Yearsley's dramatic exposé of hypocrisy and greed; they disliked her avoidance (deliberate or not) of the emotive elements considered appropriate in poetry by women. *The Monthly Review* for March 1788 informed readers that More "pleads the cause of the enslaved negroes in strains not less persuasive, though perhaps less vigorous and energetic than those of the animated Lactilla," Yearsley's classical name.[26] Yearsley's rapt attentiveness to buying and selling females—and its veiled reference to her own tribulations as a dependant—went unsung. So did her dual references to anguished personal experiences in nursing a mother starving to death: "West Africans as souls who feel for human woe . . . / Whose heart would shudder at a father's chains . . ." (Yearsley, "Inhumanity," p. 3); a "bending parent" agonized when deprived of a "son, or *a more tender* daughter" (Yearsley, "Inhumanity," p. 6). "O'er suffering man," she cries, encompassing the personal and the slave experience, "my soul with sorrow bends" (Yearsley, "Inhumanity," p. 4). The press read Yearsley's poem without nuance, refusing to internalize or address her multiple significations. The message was too potent. Identifying the slave community as the authentic locus of armed resistance and self-determination as a right, Yearsley offered insights beyond the reach and desire of her middle-class peers.

Norwich-based Elizabeth Bentley, a Church of England daughter of "a journeyman cordwainer," similarly introduced an African protagonist. The only difference was that Bentley's protagonist, Ignatius Sancho, was one of the most famous African contemporaries living in London. Like the poems of the Falconar sisters, Bentley's volume, *Genuine Poetical Compositions on Various Subjects* (1791) validates acceptable topics for women's verse that highlight the popularity of political issues, frequently couched as moral necessities: cruelty to animals and slavery now lie on a par with peace, friendship, virtue, and the pleasures of a summer morning.[27] In a strange twist, Bentley dedicated her volume to William Drake, a member of Parliament who opposed the Abolition Bill on the ostensible grounds that compensation to planters was not included.[28] In her earliest condemnation of slavery in "On Health and Liberty" (1787) in *Genuine. . . Compositions,* Bentley denounces slavery's denial of a full creative life:

> Or view the wretch from Afric's sultry clime,
> Who's doom'd in slavery to pass his time;

Doom'd throughout life to one continu'd thrall,
With not a moment he his own can call;
Nor happiness is his, nor social joys,
The want of liberty each bliss destroys.
Detested Slavery! Thou foe to peace,
Soon may thy pow'r in ev'ry region cease!
(Bentley, "On Health and Liberty, " pp. 6–7).

Inspired by agitation sweeping through the country, Bentley more frontally assaults slavery in "On the Abolition of the African Slave Trade, July 1789." The poem singularly commends the celebrated Ignatius Sancho amid a concatenation of familiar motifs.[29] The speaker opens by praising Parliamentarians, "Albion's Council"—who pursue "a design humanely just and kind, / Worthy to share each free-born Briton's mind" (Bentley, "On the Abolition," p. 19). Breaking the "galley chains" of "inglorious Slav'ry" must be the goal of all decent-minded citizens or slaves will be denied the delights of family life:

"Too long the vile reproach has stain'd our land, . . .
[and broken] the dearest, tend'rest ties of life,
Rend from the husband's arms the much-lov'd wife!" . . .
Fond parents from their weeping babes to force,
Viewing the plaintive tear without remorse" . . .
The grief that must the father's heart o'erflow!
The mother's frantic ecstacy of woe!
Robb'd of her only hope, her darling care,
She beats her breast, and tears her woolly hair;
In bitt'rest anguish her complaints increase,
Against the fell destroyers of her peace
(Bentley, "On the Abolition," pp. 19–20).

After a protracted diatribe against traders, "worse than savage kind," and commiseration with the "snatch'd away," the speaker—Bentley—eulogizes Sancho:

Are not their species and our own the same?
In colour only differing, not in name?
By nature are they not endu'd (sic) with pow'rs,
Affections, feelings, sense, and life like ours? . . .
Witness that man of their despised race,
Whose genius claim'd him an exalted place
Amongst the sons of learning, wit, and fame,
Whose native worth deserves a deathless name;
His heart with ev'ry virtuous passion glow'd,

> Bright sense was his, by nature's hand bestow'd;
> Which proves—in their uncultur'd minds are sown;
> The seeds of knowledge equal with our own.
> (Bentley, "On the Abolition," p. 21).

Though traditionally privileging Britain as the point of reference, Bentley's outlook, albeit Eurocentric, compares favorably with that of contemporaries. In an age that denied intrinsic humanity to Africans, Bentley boldly assumed that Africans were potentially intellectual. Differences, she asserted, depended on opportunity and circumstances.

The choice of Sancho was understandable since, in Paul Edwards' words, Sancho's *Letters,* now in a third edition by 1784, were one of the "two most striking [works] . . . by Africans writing in English . . . during the last thirty years of the eighteenth century."[30] Painted by Sir Thomas Gainsborough and a friend of Laurence Sterne with whom he corresponded, servant to an aristocratic household and ultimately a shopkeeper with a large family, Sancho was both an ordinary man and a national symbol of human equality. He held the mirror up to colonialist corruption. Contemporary Member of Parliament, Joseph Jekyll, who edited Sancho's *Letters,* described him as a man whose

> writings exhibit of epistolary talent, of rapid and just conception, of wild patriotism, and of universal philanthropy, . . . two [of his pieces] were constructed for the stage;—the Theory of Music was discussed, published, and dedicated to the Princess Royal;—and Painting was so much within the circle of Ignatius Sancho's judgment and criticism, that Mortimer came often to consult him. Such was the man whose species philosophers and anatomists have endeavoured to degrade as a deterioration of the human; and such was the man whom Fuller, with a benevolence and quaintness of phrase peculiarly his own, accounted "God's Image, though cut in Ebony."
> And he who surveys the extent of intellect to which Ignatius Sancho had attained by self-education, will perhaps conclude, that the perfection of the reasoning faculties does not depend on a peculiar conformation of the skull or the colour of a common integument.[31]

By versifying his acclaimed achievements, Bentley renders him—as Phillis Wheatley was rendered—a sanctified model and a standard of judgment, his life and letters vibrant mockeries of anti-African propaganda. Despite the objectification inherent in this hagiography of Sancho, Bentley firmly advances abolition and persuasively contradicts notions of Africans as lesser human beings. Intertextually her poem impugns colonial law and practices; it narrows cultural and social distance, denies a categorically different otherness, and renegotiates the status of the marginalized. Bentley ends by paying tribute to spiritual equality and Anglo-Africanism in the same breath: "in whose [God's] esteem the swarthy Ethiop stands,/ High as the fairest sons of Europe's lands." (Bentley, "On the Abolition," p. 23) Given their historical epoch, both Bentley and Yearsley counteract received images by introducing a more realistic African protagonist, a "real-life" African resident in England.

Despite their Eurocentric shortcomings, the combined texts of Haywood, Wilson, Yearsley, and Bentley remold the metonymic use of slaves as inferior, ugly, pitiable, and black; they move European, white, and personally and publically subjugated into the equation. They present themselves as polemicists, out to convert their readership to these ideas. Although the voice in every case is a fiction, authors mean to associate themselves with that verging-on-unitary voice. As polemicists, they stand behind their narrator's viewpoints. White British writers now find overlappings or equate themselves and their situations with African enslavement and hence reduce the distance between the colonizing subject and colonized others.

Another poet like Ann Yearsley, who suffered many personal humiliations that guaranteed her sympathy for the tyrannized, was Mary Darby Robinson, born in 1758.[32] Mary Darby Robinson's family came from Bristol where her father was a merchant. Her mother was well-connected and somewhat unceremoniously abandoned by John Darby. At fifteen she married Mr. Robinson, a student at Lincoln's Inn who disguised his fecklessness. With the Duchess of Devonshire's patronage she became an actor after she gave birth, but penury set in. She ended up imprisoned for debt. For three years she acted successfully until the attentions of the Prince of Wales "obliged her, with reluctance, to quit a profession" which was helping her acquire independence, financial stability, and success. At twenty-three, she developed rheumatic fever so painful and incurable that she wrote poetry for solace. According to her biographer "the strain of plaintive tenderness which pervades her earlier productions fully exemplifed the impression of an affected mind, strong to wander from itself."[33] Like Yearsley, Robinson vehemently opposed slavery.

However, unlike several women writers who protested slavery vociferously in one text, Mary Darby Robinson regularly published attacks on the institution throughout the 1770s, 1780s, and 1790s until her death in 1800. In an early volume in 1775, she elaborated on the song of a captured linnet.[34] In "Captivity: A Poem," dedicated to the Duchess of Devonshire, she dramatized her personal experiences in debtors' prison by zeroing in on diverse forms of captivity that included slavery.[35] The "gen'rous few" must react to such horrors; "sweet freedom" must teach "thy superior joys"; slaves are integral to the human community:

> One dungeon [in the prison] holds the coward, and the brave,
> The child of Virtue, and ignoble slave. . . .
> Round the wide world, thro' all its vast domain,
> From Britain's Isle, to Afric's scorching plain. . . .
> Sweet Liberty delights the free-born mind,
> Which laws and fetters have not Power to bind;
> The wretched slave, inur'd to every pain,
> By her inspir'd, disclaims the Captive's Chain;
> Oppress'd with labour, murmuring they go,
> And curse the source when all their miseries flow;
> Fainting and sad, they bend their toilsome way
> Thro' all the burning heats of sultry days; . . .
> Taught by experienc'd Cruelty to find,
> That savage baseness taints the human mind
> (*Poems,* 1775, p. 23).

After the Prince of Wales summarily abandoned her, exposing her to public ridicule and forcing her to abandon acting, she wrote from the subject position of an insider looking out. While many women inextricably and often allusively cut personal experience or that of friends into texts on slavery, Robinson was first to denote her life as a blatant captivity and suggest overlappings between victims of forced marriage, imprisoned debtors, and Caribbean slaves. By virtue of her ability to refract personal experiences through the text, one more female writer helped close the gap between the colonizer and the colonized.

After the termination of her twelve-years-plus relationship with Banastre Tarleton, the pro-slavery Member of Parliament from Liverpool and a hero of the colonial war in North America, Robinson freely frequented radical circles, friends with Mary Wollstonecraft and William Godwin.[36] She earned a radical claim to fame by raising Richard Polwhele's ire as an "unsex'd female" in his misogynous poem.[37] In the 1790s, she responded to Robert Merry's famous poem on the French Revolution, with the popular "Ainsi Va le Monde," lauding liberty and resistance in extravagant Della Cruscan language that excoriated tyranny.[38] Like earlier poets, particularly the 1788 cluster whose formulations she had anticipated in the 1770s, she favored abstraction to express injustice:

> What is the charm, that bids mankind disdain
> The Tyrant's mandate, and th' Oppressor's chain;
> What bids exulting Liberty impact
> Ecstatic raptures to the Human Heart;
> Calls forth each hidden spark of glorious fire,
> Bids untaught minds to valiant feats aspire;
> What gives to freedom its supreme delight?
> 'Tis Emulation, Instinct, Nature, Right!
> (Robinson, "Ainsi Va le Monde" p. 26).

In *The Cavern of Woe* written at the time of her difficult breakup with Tarleton, she underlines slaves' resistance and the power of art to reassert intellectual and political autonomy. Her notorious experiences at the hands of the Prince of Wales contribute to a multivoiced text that attacks a hydra-headed injustice:

> Now through the Cavern rush'd with iron hand
> Oppression insolent! his arm he rais'd,
> Waving his spear, with absolute command,
> While ev'ry subject Fiend retir'd, amaz'd!
> At awful distance, trembling, prostrate round,
> The sons of pining slav'ry kiss'd the ground;
> Till, darting forward, o'er the abject crowd,
> With voice exulting, menacing, and loud,
> Insatiate vengeance snatch'd the up-rais'd lance,
> While bold oppression's arm fell nerveless at his glance.
> (Robinson, *Works*, vol. 1, "The Cavern of Woe," p. 54).

In another poem entitled "The Progress of Liberty" written in the same time frame, slavery is played out as an allegorical conflict between female liberty and its opposition; subtextually Robinson whispers of private circumstances and her alliance with the other. In her particular attentiveness to the lot of enslaved women coupled with a sharp denunciation of slavery's inhumanity, she emotionally outdid her previous verse. "The Progress of Liberty" fused Robinson's political ideas with revenge on Banastre Tarleton, but even more subtly on the Prince of Wales; both had reputations as philanderers. Robinson's empathy for female slaves anticipated future anti-slavery arguments about their sexually jeopardized lives:

> The day of labour, and the night of pain; . . .
> Oh! worst of mortal miseries! behold
> The darling of his soul, his sable love,
> Selected from the trembling, timid throng
> By the wan tyrant, whose licentious touch
> Seals the dark fiat of the slave's despair!
> (Robinson, *Works,* vol. 3, "The Progress of Liberty," pp. 30–31).

Robinson as polemical speaker signs off with a salute to truth, liberty and a healthy domestic life, hinting at the unchristian disposition of plantocratic entrepreneurs, not surprising since Tarleton's family owned land and held investments in the Caribbean:

> For her dark-fated children; lead them forth
> From bondage infamous! Bid reason own
> The dignities of *Man,* whate'ver his clime,
> Estate, or colour. And, 0! sacred *truth!*
> Tell the proud lords of traffic, that the breast
> Thrice ebon-tinted, bears a crimson tide,
> As pure, as clear as Europe's sons can boast.
> Then, *Liberty,* extend thy thund'ring voice
> To Afric's scorching climes, o'er seas that bound
> To bear the blissful tidings, while all earth
> Shall hail *Humanity. The Child of Heav'n!*
> (Robinson, *Works,* vol. 3, "The Progress of Liberty," p. 31).

In tune with contemporaries and predecessors, Mary Darby Robinson applies the principle of self-determination to all humanity through her poems. She paints poignant tableaux on abstract canvases, her special brand of pleading working cumulatively on a reader's sense of justice. Through a thinly disguised persona, her ideas about justice widely known, Robinson legitimates the "up-rais'd lance" as a necessary response to the illegitimate "chain" of "submission."

The economic issue that female abolitionists frequently urged in letters as early as 1788 finally made its post-revolutionary appearance in print. As Friend Rachel Wilson's statements show, sporadically for over a century individual members of the Society of Friends had agitated against slavery. In 1792, a Dublin Quaker named Mary Birkett wrote a long, somewhat analogous verse-diatribe analyzing slavery from an economic point of view, entreating women to refuse to buy slave-produced consumer goods. Politically opposed to war as a Friend and living in Ireland, Birkett promoted what in modern parlance would be called a boycott. In doing so she was reenacting in tandem an ancient female sign of resistance and a fifty-year-old tactic against slavery.

In fact, boycotting was the subject of much debate. Hannah More had urged a personal friend, "as early as 1788, to taboo the use of West Indian sugar in their tea"; a nationwide movement, however, did not catch on until stimulated by the bill's defeat in 1791.[39] When the indefatigable Thomas Clarkson toured the provinces between 1791 and 1792, he discovered that pamphlets written by William Fox and William Bell Crafton, both Quakers, had precipitated widespread abstinence from tea and sugar. Fox's *An Address to the People of Great Britain On the Propriety of Abstaining from West Indies Sugar and Rum* reached a tenth edition in 1791 alone.[40] Thomas Clarkson's biographer Earl Griggs records "that in every town which [Clarkson] visited, at least one individual had given up the use of West Indian sugar and rum. Rich and poor, churchmen and Dissenters, had adopted the measure; Clarkson estimated that no fewer than 300,000 persons had abandoned the use of sugar. He instructed Josiah Wedgwood, another member of the Society of Friends, to arrange with a bookseller to buy 1,000 copies of Fox's pamphlet. "Sugar revenue," he added in his letter to Wedgwood "has fallen off 200,000 this quarter." Wedgwood ordered 2,000 copies and suggested for the logo frontispiece a woodcut of his seal of the manacled slave.[41] The refusal of slave produce spread far afield in the provinces, almost exclusively under the governance of women.

The same year as the publication of Birkett's poem, Maria Edgeworth discussed her refusal to boycott sugar in a letter to her friend Miss Sophy Ruxton. Influenced by her father's circle in Litchfield that included Wedgwood and the anti-slavery poet Thomas Day, Maria Edgeworth concurred with abolitionist ideas:

Have you seen any of the things that have been lately published about the negroes? We have just read a very small pamphlet about ten pages, merely an account of the facts stated to the House of Commons. Twenty-five thousand people in England have absolutely left off eating West India sugar, from the hope that when there is no longer any demand for sugar the slaves will not be so cruelly treated. Children in several schools have given up sweet things, which is surely very benevolent; though whether it will at all conduce to the end proposed is perhaps wholly uncertain, and in the mean time we go on eating apple pies sweetened with sugar instead of honey. At Mr. Keier's, however, my father avers that he ate excellent custards sweetened with honey. Will it not be rather hard upon the poor bees in the end?[42]

Edgeworth belabors her non-abstention in a wryly self-mocking letter to one of her relatives in Ireland, her persistent attention to the issue indicating an inexpressible desire to be involved in consumer-refusal activities. Later writings on the subject tend to support this hypothesis when she describes the reaction of Anna Laetitia Barbauld and her husband during their visit to the Edgeworth home where Caribbean sugar was served:

> We met at Clifton Mr. and Mrs. Barbauld. He was an amiable and benevolent man, so eager against the slave-trade that when he drank tea with us he always brought some East India sugar, that he might not share our wickedness in eating that made by the negro slave.[43]

In its condemnation of slavery, however, Mary Birkett's poem goes well beyond the tactic of refusal. After a title page addressed "to her own Sex," she assails a legal system that condemns murderers but does not condemn pro-slaveryites who "snatch a thousand lives,/ No pain, no punishment on them derives."[44] Like Ann Yearsley, she questions legal precedent as well as the abstract concept of justice. And like Yearsley and like-minded poets, she makes little effort to divide herself from the speaker: "and whence do we th' infernal doctrine hold,/ To sell th' image of our God for gold?" Chastising the "giddy and the gay" who drink slave-produced tea, she charges them with forgetting that "a white or sable skin [has] a fair inhabitant within." That the only difference between people lies in the shade of complexion, is, as David Erdman argues, a familiar idea—and a singularly advanced one—to contemporary radicals such as William Blake.[45]

After conventional set pieces about Christianity's tarnished reputation and a picturesque Africa split by fractured families, the speaker praises suicidal slaves as "freed souls" who have courageously eluded the rigors of the Middle Passage. Ultimately she presses slaves to resist, self-defence in this rendition of Quaker beliefs entirely consistent with pacifism: "What son of thine, oh Albion, would bow down,/ Would tremble at the upstart planter's frown?/ What son of thine, oh Albion, thus opprest,/ Nor feel revenge inflame his haughty breast?" (Birkett, *A Poem on the African Slave Trade,* pp. 10–11).

Her final apostrophe rouses the "Hibernian fair" to plunge into consumer refusal, an unprecedented entreaty in anti-slavery annals:

Rise and burst the Negro's chain. . . .
Yes, sisters, yes, to us the talk belongs,
Tis we increase or mitigate their wrongs.
If we the produce of their toils refuse,
If we not more the blood-stained lux'ry choose;
If from our lips we push the plant away
For which the liberties of thousands pay,
Of thousands once as blest, and born as free,
And nurs'd with care, (tho' not so soft,) as we;
If in benev'lence *firm*, we this can dare,
And in our brethren's sufferings hold no share,
In no small part their long-borne pangs will cease,
And we to souls unborn may whisper peace
(Birkett, *A Poem on the African Slave Trade*, pp. 14–16).

Birkett's companion poem honors the women who inspired it, then embarks on another panegyric to colonization.[46] In the first poem that sympathized with Europeans who feared economic collapse if slavery were abolished, the speaker had stressed the benefits of bringing God, "civilization," and a non-slave-trade colonialism to Africa. Here as elsewhere in the poem, Birkett introduces into the poem several topoi popularized by More that have begun to characterize a female abolitionist canon. Ideas that assume colonialism as a good automatically reduce Africans to the status of others who benefit from colonial practices:

Let the mild rays of commerce there [in Africa] expand . . .
And make each injur'd African thy friend.
So tides of wealth by peace and justice got,
Oh, philanthropic heart! will be thy lot.
Plant there our colonies, and to their soul,
Declare the God who form'd this boundless whole;
Improve their manners—teach them how to live,
To them the useful lore of science give;
So shall with us their praise and glory rest,
And we in blessing be supremely blest;
For 'tis a duty which we surely owe,
We to the Romans were what to us Afric now.
(Birkett, *A Poem on the African Slave Trade*, pp. 13–14).

Now the pleading speaker elaborates on the dual face of commerce: "By thee—what perfidies, what frauds arise?/ By thee—the groves of

Afric echo sighs./ Still with unequal hand thy favours flow." This Anglo-Africanist vision that somewhat echoes Hannah More's encapsulates a standard post-abolitionist colonial goal. "British learning" would dispel "the chaos of the Negros heart"; richly laden ships would expand commerce between the two countries. "Arts, industry, peace, and wealth" as well as Christianity, would "abound." With the tribulations of slavery behind them, Africans could freely develop their intellects—albeit within the framework of a British value system:

> Torn from his friends, bereav'd of every joy,
> Which might his mental faculties employ,
> Degraded, and dishonour'd—where, ah! where
> Shall sense and reason's blooming flowers appear?
> Where would the eloquence of Grattan shine?
> Where Sheridan's address?—where Pitt divine?
> If o'er their heads did Slavery's mandates roll,
> And freeze the gen'rous current of their soul.
> For only those who know it—may impart,
> How grief can mar the feelings of the heart,
> Check every noble thought—and warm desire,
> And bid poor Genius' blasted hope expire
> (Birkett, *A Poem on the African Slave Trade,* p. 17).

The conclusion recapitulates earlier addresses to Irishwomen, "friends of liberty and peace," who, "when you knew the price . . . push'd it [sugar] far away." She implores women "whose bosoms feel pity's soft glow" to use their influence with:

> . . . your brothers, husbands, sons, or friends,
> Whose precepts or whose laws you erst obey'd,
> And reverence due concomitantly paid.
> (Birkett, *A Poem on the African Slave Trade,* p. 21).

Written across the Irish sea within a Quaker community in a predominantly Roman Catholic country, Mary Birkett heavily invests the poem with a recognition of the oppression and rights of the colonized other, especially the right to resist and the need for practical action.

Over a period of forty years, Haywood, Wilson, Yearsley, Bentley, Robinson, and Birkett contributed another sediment of meaning to women's abolitionist stance. Though constituted unsystematically, their loosely connected endeavors helped to dismantle the blanket objectification of Africans and African-Caribbean slaves. They accomplished this mediation of othering by being closer in spirit and everyday experience to the lot of the disadvantaged. With a personally vested interest in attacking tyranny that accompanied a sense of themselves as public spokeswomen, they tended less to view slaves within the discrete category of simple, familiar charity cases.

Their omnipresent though often muted conversations with pro-slaveryites in particular, with abolitionist compatriots as well as male tyrants, with hesitant listeners, with grocers and other consumers, produced a dialogized discourse that unilaterally undermined European authority. That is to say, though they propagated classic Anglo-Africanist assumptions and maintained, neither consciously nor maliciously, what Edward Said has called a "flexible *positional* superiority" by talking *about* slaves, they still refused to stare at a strange, concocted other.[47] Social, historical, and spiritual concerns of their own enabled them to chart a map of different but possible subject positions that could become open to all women; they created a special context that inveighed against prejudice and promoted liberation and the concept of human rights. In this process of privileging themselves as authors and speaking subjects, they endowed Africans who lived inside and outside their prose with more of a subject rather than a subjected status. Their texts amount to small anomalies within an ever-increasing "normalizing" abolitionist discourse because they identified themselves with beliefs that embraced experiences and concerns of their own. Female abolitionists were merging with female self-determinists.

Moreover, historical events advanced the possibilities of this radical impulse one step further. Although geographically removed from the impact of the French Revolution on secular radicalism in England, Mary Birkett nonetheless reframed the old ideological format yet retained 1780s formulaic verse as her medium. In London, however, closer to political events, a group of female English Jacobins made that very format itself respond to revolutionary events. In so doing, they introduced, at least temporarily, a new abolitionist rights-based discourse.

Chapter 9

The Radical Impulse:
After the French Revolution

Man has no property in man; neither has any generation a property in the generations which are to follow.
> —Thomas Paine, *The Rights of Man,* p. 278.

For these reasons the [French] NATIONAL ASSEMBLY doth recognize and declare, in the presence of the Supreme Being, and with the hope of His blessing and favor, the following **sacred** rights of men and of citizens:

I. Men are born, and always continue, free, and equal in respect of their rights. Civil distinctions, therefore, can be founded only on public utility.

II. The end of all political associations, is, the preservation of the natural and imprescriptible rights of man; and these rights are liberty, property, security, and resistance of oppression.

III. The nation is essentially the source of all sovereignty; nor can any INDIVIDUAL, or ANY BODY OF MEN, be entitled to any authority which is not expressly derived from it.

IV. Political liberty consists in the power of doing whatever does not injure another. The exercise of the natural rights of every man has no other limits than those which are necessary to secure to every **other** man the free exercise of the same rights; and these limits are determinable only by the law.
> —Thomas Paine, *The Rights of Man,* p. 350.

In redefining the bounds of egalitarian principle, Angelina was able to make the theoretical leap from the exclusively moral and religious invocations against slavery characteristic of eighteenth-century thought, to the revolutionary call for immediate abolition which animated the life of the nineteenth century.
> —Bettina Aptheker, *Woman's Legacy,* p. 23.

185

After the French Revolution, radical writers temporarily spurned formulaic prescriptions. Mostly Jacobins, they used a discourse that invoked rights and cryptically inscribed resistances to their own subjugation as well as to slaves'. This chapter examines radical anti-slavery discursive practices in the late eighteenth century that specifically treated Africans, like Europeans, as subjects in and for themselves.

As the debate on abolition opened in the Commons in May 1789, the pro-slavery lobby had constituted itself so forcefully that they were able to engineer a postponement until more evidence could be taken. This postponement coincided with the fall of the Bastille in July 1789 which radicals and Dissenters equated with the millennium and celebrated on the spot. Anthony Lincoln explains their reasons:

> Dissenters had hardened their hearts against a State that had rejected them. Deeply and firmly established in the society of England, they formed a great, permanent undercurrent of dissatisfied criticism of the State of England. Their political philosophy demanded secularization and extension. They desired that the State should speak one language and one only: pure political language, without so much as an intonation of religion or romanticism. This mission of purification they engaged in with an almost religious zeal.[1]

Several radical women closely associated with rational Dissent—Mary Wollstonecraft, Helen Maria Williams, Charlotte Smith, Mary Hays, and Mary Darby Robinson—wove an attack on the slave trade into their commentaries and analyses of the revolutionary victory. They wrote political tracts and novels as well as verse, their radical predecessors' favored mode, less confined by socially condoned notions of female genres. Denied their own constitutional rights, they synthesized demands of the disenfranchised French with the rights of slaves as equally autonomous human beings. Furthermore, though unconnected with this circle, the travel-lettrist Anna Maria Falconbridge wrote a challenging narrative about life in Sierra Leone and her dealings with evangelicals back home.

Prior to the Revolution, Wollstonecraft had included anti-slavery extracts in a moral and educational anthology for young females, *The Female Reader* (1788).[2] The passages pinpointed Wollstonecraft's resolve to inject a political dimension into female education. Long before Thomas Paine's *Rights of Man* instructed a generation, young women in North London were learning the pros and cons of abolition in a Newington Green schoolroom.

Book 1 of the six-book *Reader* contains the story of Joseph sold by his brothers into slavery and the legend of Inkle and Yarico. (The story of Joseph had been rendered into a long verse-narrative by Elizabeth Rowe in 1738.) Both were the kind of family tragedies favored by evangelical writers; tales of treachery by family and loved ones that contained a message about salvation. Yarico's story may have struck a personal chord with Wollstonecraft who was preoccupied with domestic worries: her late mother's favoritism toward her eldest brother Ned; her father's impending expropriation of her personal inheritance; and Ned's abandonment of family duty that enhanced her sense of responsibility as the eldest daughter toward four other siblings. Extracts from William Cowper's *The Task* about "the natural bond of brotherhood" alerted pupils to the Mansfield decision: "Slaves cannot breathe in England; if their lungs/ Receive our air, that moment they are free." Cowper's image of predatory power relationships "Having power/ T' enforce the wrong, for such a worthy cause/ Dooms and devotes him as his lawful prey" foretold her assault on such relationships in the two *Vindications* (1790, 1792).[3]

The recapitulation of these themes and narratives familiarized late eighteenth-century audiences with an earlier anti-slavery impulse that had accented sexual assault and spirituality: planters preyed on Yarico while Potiphar's wife tried to seduce a vulnerable, feminized Joseph.

Nor did Scriptures justify slavery, a point argued sonorously by Granville Sharp and Anthony Benezet for years. To stress the issue even more vigorously, Wollstonecraft placed the Scriptural source for Barbauld's *Hymn*— "The Lamentations of the Jews in Captivity" from *Psalms*—before the *Hymn* itself:

> By the rivers of Babylon, there we sat down, yea, we wept, when
> we remembered Zion.
> We hanged our harps upon the willows in the midst thereof.
> For there they that carried us away captive required of us a
> song; and they that wasted us required of us mirth, saying, Sing
> us one of the songs of Zion.
> How shall we sing the Lord's song in a strange land?
> If I forget thee, 0 Jerusalem, let my right hand forget her
> cunning.
> If I do not remember thee, let my tongue cleave to the roof of
> my mouth: if I prefer not Jerusalem above my chief joy.[4]

Casting *Lamentations* in gendered terms, the "Hymn" sits adjacently, with female concerns and evangelical tenets as its primary focus:

Negro woman, who sittest pining in captivity, and weepest over thy
sick child: though no one seeth thee, God seeth thee; though no
one pitieth thee, God pitieth thee: raise thy voice, forlorn and
abandoned one; call upon him amidst thy bonds, for assuredly he
will hear thee.[5]

The revolution dramatically restructured this orientation. In *A Vindication of the Rights of Men,* Wollstonecraft denounced Burke's praise
of ancient liberties and hereditary property that collectively impeded
progress and substituted natural rights and individual freedom.[6] Most
audaciously, she pronounced resistance a duty when such rights
were denied. For Europeans, her words that ominously predict San
Domingo may well have been seen to do so in retrospect:

It is necessary emphatically to repeat, that there are rights which
men inherit at their birth, as rational creatures, who were raised
above the brute creation by their improvable faculties; and that,
in receiving these, . . . prescription can never undermine natural
rights.
A father may dissipate his property without his child having any
right to complain;—but should he attempt to sell him for a slave,
or fetter him with laws contrary to reason; nature, in enabling him
to discern good from evil, teaches him to break the ignoble chain
(Wollstonecraft, *Rights of Men,* pp. 22–3).

She castigates Burke's "servile reverence for antiquity" as a coverup
or rationale for perpetuating slavery: "The whole tenor of his (Burke's)
argument settles slavery on an everlasting foundation" (Wollstonecraft, *Rights of Men,* p. 23). Like Equiano, Wollstonecraft strikes at the
root of slavery's longevity—profit—-while indicting the principle of
private property upon which slavery is built and fundamentally depends. This brief sharp blow at slavery's economic roots stamps Mary
Wollstonecraft as the first white British woman to mount a twin-
pronged philosophical and economic assault on the institution:

The slave trade ought never be abolished if Burke's ideas hold sway;
and, because our ignorant forefathers, not understanding the native
dignity of man, sanctioned a traffic that outrages every suggestion
of reason and religion, we are to submit to the inhuman custom,
and term an atrocious insult to humanity the love of our country,
and a proper submission to the laws by which our property is
secured.—Security of property! Behold, in a few words, the defini-

tion of English liberty. And to this selfish principle every nobler one is sacrificed (Wollstonecraft, *Rights of Men,* pp. 23–24).

The abolition of "this abominable traffic," she declaims, "is consonant with justice, with the common principles of humanity" (Wollstonecraft, *Rights of Men,* pp. 128, 129–30). The second *Vindication* more explicitly denies the legitimacy of male control.[7] After a traditional comparison of women to slaves, she reexamines the strategy of economic boycott:

> Is sugar always to be produced by vital blood? Is one half of the human species, like the poor African slaves, to be subject to prejudices that brutalize them, when principles would be a surer guard, only to sweeten the cup of man?
> (Wollstonecraft, *Rights of Woman,* pp. 144–145).

Wollstonecraft revitalizes this attack the following year with a salutary review of *The Negro Equalled by Few Europeans,* Joseph LaVallée's text on black superiority, abolition, and Africans; in it, she stresses an unspoken but understood presence in the *Vindication* and a familiar abolitionist topos: slavery's devastation of family life.[8] An abducted female on board a slave ship commits suicide by drowning herself and her newborn child. Translating Salzmann's educational treatise the same year, Wollstonecraft drafts her attack on slavery and tyranny: "I have here [she asserts in the preface] also inserted a little tale to lead children to consider the Indians as their brothers, because the omission of this subject appeared to me a chasm in a well-digested system."[9]

With comparable energy, Wollstonecraft's friend and political ally, Helen Maria Williams, excoriated the denial of peoples' rights. Williams' commitment to such issues was already well-publicized in "Peru" (1784) where she overtly opposed Spanish colonialism and in her tribute to Sir William Dolben in 1788 for his successful sponsorship of the slave ship regulation bill. Williams' revolutionary ardor also translated into emigration to Paris where she arrived with her sister in July 1790 on the first anniversary of the storming of the Bastille.[10]

By September of that year, Williams had returned to England and published a chronicle of her experiences, the first of eight volumes entitled *Letters from France.* She spoke glowingly of abolitionist Mirabeau's speech at the National Assembly at a time when Mirabeau was engaged in a voluminous correspondence with Thomas Clarkson who was soliciting support in France for the British campaign. Paraphrasing Mirabeau, Williams compares progressive French attitudes with recalcitrant British ones:

> Mons. Mirabeau has another very powerful claim on my partiality: he is the professed friend (and I must and will love him for being so) of the African race. He has proposed the abolition of the slave trade to the National Assembly; and, though the Assembly have delayed the consideration of this subject, . . . yet perhaps, if our senators continue to doze over this affair as they have hitherto done, the French will have the glory of setting us an example. . . . But I trust the period will never come, when England will submit to be taught by another nation the lesson of humanity. I trust an English House of Commons will never resist in thinking, that what is morally wrong, can be politically right; that the virtue and the prosperity of a people are things at variance with each other; and that a country which abounds with so many sources of wealth, cannot afford to close one polluted channel, which is stained with the blood of our fellow creatures.[11]

In the next paragraph she pleads patriotically for "the honour, the spirit, the generosity of Englishmen who will surely call for an end to the trade," stopping short of a Wollstonecraft's, an Oroonoko's, or a Yearsley's call to arms. Even if they (the English) fail to recognize their humanitarian duty, she predicts that revolutionary ideas will open people's eyes to injustice. Abandoning earlier support for amorphous social love as a solution, Williams now insists that nothing short of a hard-headed grasp of the facts will overthrow slavery and end tyranny. The advent of the French Revolution had enabled these female radical interventions:

> The Africans have not long to suffer, nor their oppressors to triumph. Europe is hastening towards a period too enlightened for the perpetuation of such monstrous abuses. The mists of ignorance and error are rolling fast away, and the benign beams of philosophy are spreading their lustre over the nations. (pp. 49–50).

Anna Laetitia Barbauld expressed similar sentiments in *Sins of Government, Sins of the Nation* (1790) where she questioned illicit control. Should Britain, she asked, be assuming "a hard and unjust control" over "some darker-colored children."[12] In the light of this remark, Barbauld's earlier comments in her "Epistle to . . . Wilberforce" on the "creole mistress" are even harsher than they at first seem. A radical triumvirate, Wollstonecraft, Williams, and Barbauld demand constitutional equality for everyone.

Partially in response to counterrevolutionary public outcry, the abolition bill was defeated the year following Wollstonecraft's first *Vindication* by a vote of 163 to 88. Agitation to reverse that vote instantly started up. But the revived optimism was shattered four months later in August 1791, when slaves and ex-slaves explosively revolted in San Domingo.[13] The revolutionary victory handed the West Indian lobby a unique opportunity to stamp abolition as a threat to national security. Jacobin ideology and rebellious slaves could ensure Britain's social and economic downfall.

> On 26 October (1791) rumors raced around London that there had been a huge and gory catastrophe in the Caribbean. . . . The great northern plain of St. Dominique, the West Indies' wealthiest colony and Europe's main source of both sugar and coffee, had been devastated. Over 100,000 slaves were in revolt. . . . As lurid tales were told and retold . . . the price of sugar shot sky high and stocks fell immediately by 1 percent."[14]

War with France was also nearing a critical stage. Foreign interference and royal machinations foredoomed a potentially constitutional monarchy. By September 21, France had declared itself a republic and offered international support against tyrannies abroad. This announcement of global aid conjoined with the imprisonment of Louis XVI, the invasion of Belgium, the instigation of the September massacres, and the declaration of war against Prussia kindled a sense of panic in Britain; many began to feel that the revolution seriously jeopardized Britain's safety. The pro-slavery opposition correctly predicted Parliamentary victory and made much of French support for abolition.

The upshot came soon enough. During the debate in 1791, the Abolition Bill was so obviously doomed that Pitt called on Sir William Dundas, a personal friend and pro-slavery advocate, to introduce the compromise motion that amply accommodated Caribbean economic interests in the House. By 230 to 85 votes a motion for gradual abolition passed; January 1, 1796 was set as the date. At the end of a letter to her friend, Jane Pollard, in May of 1792, Dorothy Wordsworth raged at the contrivance of Dundas's compromise:

> I hope you were an *immediate* abolitionist, and are angry with the House of Commons for continuing the traffic in human flesh so long

as till '96 but you will also rejoice that so much has been done. I
hate Mr. Dundas.[15]

Against this backdrop in 1792, Charlotte Smith's Jacobin novel,
Desmond was published.[16] Given Smith's personal circumstances,
such a commitment was striking, if not noble. Without much say-so on
her part, Charlotte Smith had been married to the son of a Caribbean
merchant in 1764 or 1765—she talks later of being sold to him—and
had borne ten children by 1777.[17] After his imprisonment for debt and
subsequent flight to France, she left him in 1787 and thereafter wrote
novels at a cracking pace to maintain her large family.

In volume three, the heroic Desmond reasons that any just government would pass an abolition bill. Using a conversation between
Desmond and a plantation-owning member of Parliament, Smith ridicules typical plantocratic racism. The planter reminds Desmond of
"the importance of this trade to the prosperity of the British nation."
Besides, he adds, slaves are monkeys; Africans cannot feel nor have
they sufficient understanding "to qualify them for any rank in society
above slaves." Desmond parries these remarks with a comment about
the planter's attraction for "monkey ladies." With that comment Smith
ingeniously reopens the issue of sexual abuse of female slaves, of
male ownership of the female body in multiple senses.

The Countess's poems on Yarico in the 1720s had hinted at rape by
"eavesdropping" on planters' innuendoes by the dockside. But in
general, social prescriptions outlawed such discussions for women,
nor were sentimental novels and poems appropriate substitute vehi-
cles for propaganda. Smith's decision to turn pro-slavery discourse
against itself testifies to a nation divided by revolution abroad and
reform agitation at home. Desmond's last words on the superior "physical and moral sensibility" of Africans and the need for abolition of
the "detestable Slave Trade" matches his revolutionary perspective
(Smith, *Desmond,* Vol. 3, pp. 161, 164).

The discourse on tyranny had moved from the realm of suffering
Africans who elicit pity to a political discourse about rights. Burdened
by oppositional restraints on their freedom as private and public
citizens, English Jacobins were much less distanced from slaves than
their conservative counterparts. Thus their double-angled discourse
merged into a general commentary on human rights. As subjects, none
should be deprived by individuals brandishing illegitimate privilege.

Four years later *The Memoirs of Emma Courtney* (1796) by Jacobin
Mary Hays responded to slavery in the light of a somewhat shifting
pattern of historical events.[18]

After the declaration of war against Britain in 1793 and the guillotin-
ing of the royal couple a few months later, Francophobia strangleheld
Britain. War became "the single most important fact of British life
from 1793–1815 . . . so popular . . . that a commentator in the *Analytical Review* noted in 1793 that it was treated by every hireling scribbler.
. . . The chief medium of war poetry were the magazines and newspapers."[19] At least three thousand war poems were published as reform
movements vanished or dried up. Mostly composed of Quakers who
opposed war on principle, the abolition committee met occasionally
in 1794, twice in 1795 and 1796 and not at all until 1804. Just before
his death in 1805, Pitt forbade the importation of slaves into newly
acquired colonies. Supporting Pitt's war policy and acts of reprisal
against domestic agitation, Wilberforce still urged abolitionist resolutions in the House of Commons, but Parliament and the country had
effectively terminated temporary support. The bill to prohibit slave-
trading with foreign countries passed the Commons but failed in the
Lords. So did a Bill which tried to confine the slave trade to certain
parts of the African Coast.

By 1793, only radicals and committed activists signed abolitionist
petitions. Under the strain of defeat, an overworked Thomas Clarkson
collapsed in 1794. The Commons took a mere fourteen days to exam-
ine the three years' worth of anti-slavery evidence since the successful
passage of Dundas's gradualist Bill.[20] In Elie Halévy's words, abolition
of the slave trade "was identified with total emancipation, and that in
turn with Jacobinism."[21] In 1794 several radicals were sentenced to
fourteen years' transportation. Thomas Hardy, Horne Tooke and other
radicals were arrested in May, the month Habeas Corpus was suspended; Robespierre's execution followed on the heels of the French
"Reign of Terror" that erupted in June and July. Indictments for treason
against Hardy, Tooke, and Holcroft, and nine other men were handed
down in October. The infamous trials lasted from October to December, 1794, with most of the accused eventually acquitted or discharged.[22] Stalwart supporters reneged on or raged more adamantly
in their support. Like many contemporaries, Charlotte Smith criticized
France after 1793, severely compromising her earlier anti-slavery
views in *The Wanderings of Warwick* (1794) and *Letters of a Solitary
Wanderer* (1799–1802).

Helen Maria Williams continued her agitation from France. Her Paris
salon had become the unofficial headquarters of the Girondins and
their British supporters; Williams herself was well acquainted with
prominent French abolitionists, among them Abbé Grégoire, Mirabeau, and Brissot who had helped found the French abolitionist group,

Amis des Noirs. Thomas Clarkson had tried to convert the French group to the cause of British abolition. Arrested as a "suspect" in October of that year, Williams was released on the recognizance of a future son-in-law and fled to Switzerland until Robespierre fell. In the avowedly autobiographical, "A Farewell for Two Years to England," Williams reaffirms her allegiance to the French Revolution, expresses disappointment at the failure of the Abolition Bill, and calls for its imminent passage:

> And when with wonder thrill'd, with mind elate,
> I mark the change sublime in Gallia's state!
> Where new-born Freedom treads the Banks of Seine,
> Hope in her eye, and Virtue in her train!
> Pours day upon the dungeons central gloom,
> And leads the captive from his living tomb . . .
> My thoughts shall fondly turn to that lov'd isle,
> Where Freedom long had shed her genial smile. . . .
> Thou [Britain] wert her leading star, her honour'd guide;
> That, long in slav'ry sunk, when taught by thee,
> She broke her fetters, and has dar'd be free.[23]

With apologies to "Afric's injur'd race" for the bill's failure, she wonders: "Why in thy senate did they plead in vain." Emblematic of global freedom, France must now set an ethical example. Intrepidly, Williams throws down a gallic gauntlet to British abolitionists: "May other Lands the bright example show . . ./ Yes, Gallia, haste! . . . that power is thine . . ./ Forget not that to all kind Nature gives/ Those common rights, the claims of all that lives." (Williams *A Farewell,* pp. 12–13)

Given such contestations, Mary Hays's volleys against slavery were tantamount to a self-marginalizing stance. A committed Jacobin who had been born into a family of rational Dissenters, Hays admired Wollstonecraft's second *Vindication* and Rousseau's views on sexuality. Her *Letters and Essays* allude to these interests while the propagandistic *The Memoirs of Emma Courtney* (1796) charts the adventures of a woman who tries to live a sexual and intellectual independence despite trying odds.[24]

As a thinly disguised Hays, Emma Courtney recounts an incident at a dinner party at which she and putative hero, Augustus Harley, debate pro-slavery advocates. Their main opponent is a planter, by then a code word for a ne'er-do-well. In youth, this "haughty, opulent, purse-proud planter, surrounded by ostentatious luxuries" had been "placed" by his father in a Caribbean commercial house (Hays, *Emma*

Courtney, pp. 34–35). Additionally Hays uses a dinner guest's reaction to Emma Courtney's literacy to mock contemporary cartooning of female intellectuality:

> Mr. Courtney! you will spoil all her feminine graces; knowledge and learning are insufferably masculine in a woman—born only for the soft solace of man! The mind of a young lady should be clear and unsullied, like a sheet of white paper, or her own fairer face (Hays, *Emma Courtney*, p. 35).

When a returning visitor to Jamaica labels soldiers "agreeable and charming," Courtney castigates "their trade [as] murder" (Hays, *Emma Courtney*, p. 37). After she scandalizes the company, Melmoth fantasizes aloud about wanting more of

> these murderers in the West Indies to keep the slaves in subordination, who, since absurd notions of liberty had been put into their heads, were grown very troublesome and refractory, and, in a short time, he supposed, would become as insolent as the English servants (Hays, *Emma Courtney*, vol. 2, p. 40).

Harley supports Courtney's contention that anyone stationed in the Caribbean is a murderer, although his later speech on justice indicates the powerful effect of the San Domingo revolution on English Jacobins:[25]

> [Harley] pleaded the cause of freedom and humanity with a bold and manly eloquence, expatiating warmly on the iniquity as well as impolicy of so accursed a traffic. Melmoth was awed into silence. Mr. Pemberton advanced some trite arguments in opposition, respecting the temporary mischiefs which might ensure, in case of an abolition, to the planters, landholders, traders, &c. Augustus explained, by contending only for the gradual emancipation, after their minds had been previously prepared, of the oppressed Africans (Hays, *Emma Courtney*, vol. 2, pp. 42–43).

Read one way, even born and bred Dissenters like Hays-Courtney had defected to Dundas's camp. Or does Hays expect the Bill to go through shortly as originally anticipated? On the other hand, Hays's message might be much more deft and double-edged than at first appears. Is gradualism a clue to Harley's flawed character, a warning to Courtney that he is not a man to be trusted? Since the reader already apprehends Harley's duplicity toward Emma Courtney, his support for the Dundas compromise could suggest an authorial moral judgment against his gradualist orientation. Hays, moreover, intertwines a feminist and an anti-slavery stance—a recognition of gender and race oppression—with Emma Courtney's bold retorts at the dinner table. Matilda's "sympathy" for slaves in *The Recess* has been replaced and even transcended by Emma Courtney's ire. Hays tenders the first white British abolitionist heroine since the movement began. Most importantly, the confusion between the words abolition and emancipation is important to note. On closer scrutiny, the argument for gradual emancipation that superficially *seems* to echo Dundas's, offers quite a different political solution. Gradual emancipation presupposes abolition of the slave trade, an assumption that transcends Dundas's half-stepping and moves to emancipationist solutions in a post-abolition era. Emma Courtney, that is, is arguing for general emancipation at some point in the future. The movement that urges that demand does not visibly establish itself until the early 1820s.

In 1796, Mary Hays's novel and Mary Darby Robinson's poems effectively closed English Jacobins' revolutionary opposition. As a school of political thought so closely allied with English Jacobinism, even rational Dissent itself was coming to an end:

> The Birmingham riots [against supporters of the French Revolution] were symbolic of the eclipse of rational Dissent. Its leaders were passing away and its meetings declining. Richard Price had died in April 1791 and Priestley . . . emigrated to the United States in 1794, dying there ten years later. As the leaders of rational Dissent passed away, their places were all too often left unfilled.[26]

In the half century that separated Haywood's attack on prejudice from Wollstonecraft's support for collective human rights, radicals had begun to suture the gap that distinctly severed colonizing subjects from colonial others. They had fashioned and adopted a counterdiscourse to the pro-slavery status quo and to slavery itself that was unique in abolition annals. Denouncing British renunciation of seventeenth-century revolutionary tenets, they lined themselves up alongside slaves as allied victims of a tyrannical global system. In the abstract they identified with the harshness that slaves endured. Most crucially, they assumed that slaves were initiating and would initiate their own struggle as did British Dissenters and radicals alike. Sharply separating herself from any responsibility for slaves, Mary Wollstonecraft presents herself as just another spokeswoman for oppressed people—her own group of English Jacobins, as well as slaves, Native

Americans, shanghaied sailors, or cross-class white British women. Radical women, it seems, were much more keenly aware of their commonalty with slaves and tended less than conservative women to displace anxieties unwittingly on to slaves and commodify them as objects of charity and political exchange; instead, they drew parallels based on experiential analogies between what they called white female slavery and colonial slavery. According to Wollstonecraft's analysis—and like-minded writers'—slaves commanded their own self-determination. Neither practical nor feasible, Wollstonecraft's discourse nonetheless suggests that a transformation of power to Africans was both necessary and appropriate. If she had spoken out loud she might have said: we support you but we know it's your affair and we're standing by with all the auxiliary support we can offer. Wollstonecraft was venturing the almost impossible position for a colonial subject in a colonizing society.

That said, the fact remained that both radical and conservative British abolitionists, at differing conscious levels, still subjected slaves to the status of the other. But radicals had narrowed the gap, making it a matter more of degree than kind. They informed their texts with the principle of human equality, believing in perfectibility throughout the global community; they thought in these terms. Theoretically they discountenanced the notion that any human being should be subject to others though their cultural conditioning made the leap from thought to act difficult. These new ideological formulations that intersected, and even conversed with earlier repetitive litanies had created a discourse about abolition that connected politically with a variety of hard-hitting texts: with Oroonoko's speech and Haywood's critique of prejudice as well as Paine's *Rights of Man.* These voices belonged to that branch of the campaign that based its argument on human rights, on principles of freedom and justice. Without an overt confrontation, political radicals were refuting the evangelical taxonomy that prioritized a domestic life for females. Their tenet of belief that "all are created equal" and their public stance as polemicists contradicted social mandates about how women should act and what they should think. However steeped they inevitably were in cultural prejudice, in principle they rejected the notion of alterity and advocated a universal right to self-determination.

Their writings constituted an oppositional discourse to that of the universal slave; moreover, they joined forces with politically conservative abolitionists against the pro-slavery community. Strengthening their own side, they plied other possibilities based on their experiences and their knowledge and assumptions about gender, class, and race prejudice. In fact, their lives and writings might have helped to engender the most conservative abolitionist construction of slaves to date: the *Cheap Repository Tracts* written in the 1790s by Hannah More.

ANNA MARIA FALCONBRIDGE

Algerians, traditionally represented . . . as shadowy figures, picturesquely backward at best and hostile and menacing at worst, are here treated with respect, dignified by close-ups, shown as speaking subjects rather than as manipulable objects. . . . The film exposes the oppressive logic of colonialism and consistently fosters our complicity with the Algerians. It is through Algerian eyes, for example, that we witness a condemned Algerian's walk to his execution. It is from *within* the casbah that we see and hear the French troops and helicopters. This time it is the colonised who are encircled and menaced and with whom we identify.

—Robert Stam, Louise Spence, "Colonialism, Racism, and Representation," *Screen*, 1983, p. 13.

The last writer in the political radical tradition was Anna Maria Falconbridge. The title of her publication explains its contents: *Narrative of Two Voyages to the River Sierra Leone, During the Years 1791–2–3, Performed by A. M. Falconbridge. With a Succinct account of the Distresses and Proceedings of that Settlement; a description of the Manner, Diversions, Arts, Commerce, Cultivation, Custom, Punishments, &c. And Every interesting Particular relating to the Sierra Leone Company. Also The present State of the Slave Trade in the West Indies, and the improbability of its total Abolition.*[27] Falconbridge wrote the account after accompanying her husband, Alexander Falconbridge, to Sierra Leone where Clapham Sect members and friends had hired him to establish and supervise the newly founded colony there.

Her motives for publishing such a narrative about Sierra Leone resulted from several factors, among them a commitment to abolition and a sense of pride in the association of her name with abolition. First in 1788, her surgeon-husband had testified before the Privy Council about the hideous conditions he witnessed as a doctor on the Middle Passage. He wrote a detailed account of these experiences in *An Account of the Slave Trade on the Coast of Africa* (1788).[28] Second, she needed money because Henry Thornton refused to honor his agreement to compensate her appropriately if her ailing and drunken husband died. Member of Parliament, wealthy banker, and Clapham Sect member, Henry Thornton was chairman of this new Sierra Leone Company; he was also its hiring agent and chief London correspondent. Enraged at his reneging, she decided to publicize the hypocrisy of politically powerful and affluent abolitionists; their behavior, she boldly asserts, provoked her book. According to Sierra Leone historian Christoper Fyfe, Falconbridge "besieged Thornton vainly for money she claimed still due to Falconbridge. When verbal entreaties failed she turned to print. . . . The first accounts of the Colony to appear in book form presented its promoters in unattractive guise."[29] She also connects their rather cavalier denials of her financial requests with their "conscious(ness) of a woman's insignificance" in the eyes of men in Sierra Leone.[30]

Lastly, since the publication appeared the year her husband died and shortly after the San Domingo victory, the narrative also functions as a eulogy to her husband that keeps his anti-slavery testimony and sentiments alive. Between the lines she reminds the public of conditions that slaves endured and indirectly defends San Domingo and the bankruptcy of the ensuing European outcry.

A specific set of circumstances engendered the Falconbridges' visit to Sierra Leone. Acting on the advice of a certain self-interested naturalist named Henry Smeathman, Europeans had selected that region in 1786 as the site of relocation for the black indigent poor who were trying to survive in London while increasingly being criticized by some vocal white citizens as a "sore spot."[31] The original plan was to promote trade from and to Sierra Leone and lay the groundwork for large-scale though gradual religious conversions. Motives behind the relocation plan were mixed, ranging from desire for commerce with Africa, initial enthusiasm, and then voluble antagonism by many potential African relocatees as well as the celebrated Equiano and Cugoano.[32] The first convoy left England on April 9, 1787 with 350 black settlers, 41 of whom were women, and 59 white women.[33] After four years, only sixty were still alive out of the 374 who survived the journey. About 10,000 Africans lived on in Britain. The second phase of the relocation project involved Anna Maria Falconbridge and her husband, with whom she had eloped. In 1791 he was appointed agent-general of St. George's Bay Company.

The complex historical context—its revolutionary milieu and the unique colonial project it depicts—matches the complex role Anna Maria Falconbridge assumes as author-narrator. First, she travels to Sierra Leone in a socially ambiguous status, her elopement having sparked consternation back in hometown Bristol. Second, although she means to further the British plan for colonialism by drawing up friendly treaties, she still sets out—as she states it—to meet Africans on their own terms despite Britain's expansionist policy. Moreover, she claims that all of this would have gone unrecorded had Henry Thornton not cheated her financially.

Put differently, Anna Maria Falconbridge forms part of a tiny white minority that favors black self-determination in certain circumstances—in this singular case when she finds herself in a community of indigenous or formerly exiled Africans demanding their rights.[34] Different factors dictated her support. After their arrival in Sierra Leone, her husband spends days in negotiations with the chief, King Naimbana, trying to retrieve land lost in the original settlement during which time she begins to record eye-witness observations of the new colony. Her initial discussion belongs to what Mary Louise Pratt terms "manners—and—customs" portraits that are told from a "normalizing," Eurocentric perspective.[35] She seems slightly amused, for example, at the King's incongruous dress yet she rouses readers' suspicions of the King's motives with the adjective "seeming." Perhaps "seeming" denotes her uneasiness at the Company's ethically bankrupt proposals. In documenting her husband's paltry offerings and depicting the pernicious colonial encounter uncritically, she still retains a somewhat ambiguous pose; she exposes for posterity the tawdriness of the Company's negotiations and hence of Director Thornton himself:

> After setting nigh half an hour, Naimbana made his appearance, and received us with seeming good will: he was dressed in a purple embroidered coat, white sattin waistcoat and breeches, *thread stockings,* and his left side emblazoned with a flaming star; his legs to be sure were *harliquined,* by a number of holes in the stockings, through which his black skin appeared. . . . Having prefaced his arguments with a small donation of rum, wine, cheese, and a gold laced hat, (which Naimbana seemed much pleased with) Falconbridge began, by explaining what advantages would accrue to his *Majesty,* and to all the inhabitants round about, by such an establishment as the St. George's Bay Company were desirous of making;—the good they wished to do—*their disinterestedness in point of obtaining wealth,* and concluded by expostulating on the injustice and imposition of dispossessing the late settlers of the grounds and houses they occupied, which had been honestly and honorably purchased by Captain Thompson of the Navy, in the name of our gracious Sovereign, His Britannic Majesty. That it was unusual for Englishmen to forego fulfilling any engagements they made; and they held in detestation every person so disposed (Falconbridge, *Narrative of Two Voyages,* pp. 34–37).

Later after Falconbridge's persistent complaints to Anna Maria that the chiefs were "only bamboozling him," these chiefs and Falconbridge finally

> . . . agreed to the re-establishment of the settlers and to their permanent tenure of the disputed land for £30-worth of trade goods. Naimbana offered [his son, Prince] John Frederic to the Company as pledge of his good faith, and it was agreed that when the Falconbridges returned to England the boy should accompany them, to be educated at the Company's expense.[36]

The remainder of the narrative knits these seemingly disparate elements: commentary on Sierra Leone and its inhabitants and a critical analysis of colonial behavior in which Britons blatantly take advantage of cultural difference. On the one hand, she describes how to extract oil from nuts, people's eating habits, weather, disease, musical instruments, the calculation of time, and other cultural codes and practices. She contends that slavery obliterates "natural" intelligence and talent but pointedly argues for the encouragement of suppressed intellectual capacities. She advocates the building of coastal schools to educate African children whose capacity, she declares, was inferior to none, black or white. They are "no less susceptible of improvement and cultivation than any other part of the human race."[37]

On the other hand, she constantly makes judgments by quietly playing out a prejudicial charade and letting it speak for itself—the slave circle is one example—or by assailing injustices. Her equivocal position also lands her in some suspect situations about which she smartly snipes: a case in point is her desire to have slave traders conduct her on a guided tour since she is tired of being cooped up in the ship, a practice her husband demands because to sleep on shore would mean accepting the hospitality of slave-traders. So the traders obligingly take her to Adam's Town where she identifies a social hierarchy that favors Britain:

> Adam's Town was the first place they took me to; it is so called from a native of that name, who has the management of all the grammattos, or free black servants, but under the control of the [Colonial] Agent (Falconbridge, *Narrative of Two Voyages*, p. 26).

A few pages further on she dialogizes their activities in the following observations:

> Involuntarily I strolled to one of the windows a little before dinner
> without the smallest suspicion of what I was to see;—judge then
> what my astonishment and feelings were, at the sight of between
> two and three hundred wretched victims, chained and parcelled
> out in circles, just satisfying the cravings of nature from a trough
> of rice placed in the centre of each circle. Offended modesty re-
> buked me with a blush for not hurrying my eyes from such dis-
> gusting scenes; but whether fascinated by female curiosity, or what-
> ever else, I could not withdraw myself for several minutes—while
> I remarked some whose hair was withering with age, reluctantly
> tasting their food—and others thoughtless from youth, greedily
> devouring all before them; be assured I avoided the prospects from
> this side of the house ever after (Falconbridge, *Narrative of Two
> Voyages,* pp. 32–33).

At other times she records some local history that confirms British
social and cultural arrogance even toward African chiefs. Although
she apparently avoids explicit judgments, a diplomacy commensurate
with her husband's job, the facts speak for themselves: in one instance
she narrates at length the casual murder of a son by a Captain Tittle
who treats the death as something of a prank; she underscores this
example of cultural imperialism by exposing discriminatory burial
practices:

> . . . we proceeded first to the burying ground for Europeans, and
> then to that for the blacks;—the only distinction between them was
> a few orange trees, that shaded two gravestones at the former,—
> one in memory of a Mr. Knight, one . . . on the supposed grave of
> a Captain Tittle, who was murdered by one Signior Domingo, a
> native chief, for (as Domingo asserts) being the cause of his son's
> death. . . .
> One day while the son of Domingo was employed by Captain
> Tittle, as a grammatto, or pull away boy (African term for an Oar-
> man], Tittle's hat by accident blew overboard, and he insisted that
> the boy should jump into the water and swim after it, as the only
> means of saving his hat.
> The boy obstinately refused, saying, he could not swim, and he
> should either be drowned, or the sharks would catch him; upon
> which Tittle pushed him into the water, and the poor boy was
> lost; but whether devoured by sharks, or suffocated by water, is
> immaterial, he was never heard of, or seen after.
> The father, though sorely grieved for his son's death, was willing
> to consider it as accidental, and requested Tittle would supply him
> with a small quantity of rum to make a cry or lamentation in their
> country custom.

The Captain, by promise, acquiesced to the demand, and sent him a cask; but, instead of Spirit, filled with emptyings from the *tubs* of his slaves.

As soon as Domingo discovered this insult and imposition, he informed Tittle he must either submit to the decision of a Palaver, or he would put him to death if ever an opportunity offered; but Tittle laughed at these threats, and disregarded them, vauntingly threw himself into the way of Domingo—while the trick played upon him, and the loss of his son were fresh in his memory.

The African, however, instead of being daunted at the sight of this headstrong man, soon convinced him he was serious: he had Tittle seized, and after confining him some time in irons, without food, ordered him to be broken to death, which was executed under the inspection of the injured father, and to the great joy and satisfaction of a multitude of spectators.

Not a sentence or hint of the affair is mentioned on the tombstone; the reason assigned for the omission, was a wish to obliterate the melancholy catastrophe, and a fear lest the record might be the means of kindling animosities at a future day (Falconbridge, *Narrative of Two Voyages,* pp. 26–30).

After a recapitulation in the second book of British-African relations and customs, she relays personal reactions to her London hosts. Although a colonizing subject herself, she constructs an "other" out of the absentee company director in London who controls the pursestrings of the Sierre Leone colonization project.

In the process, Falconbridge invokes her husband's earlier abolitionist text, his horror at the treatment of Africans, and her own revulsion. She treats land negotiations as analogues of intrinsically biased power relationships. Ironically her husband, not customary slave-traders, acts as the middleman between African negotiators and wealthy Britons. She sharply exculpates colonial administrators, several of whom were also Parliamentary abolitionists, a condemnation that refers indirectly to her motivation for publication.

This reproof of Thornton, and the Clapham Sect by association, Wilberforce included, magnifies her disgust at the treatment accorded repatriated Africans by the very Sierra Leone Company that encouraged and facilitated their relocation. In a 1794 report, the Directors ignored the lack of supervision and provisions:

By June [1794] 700 of the 1,200 settlers were ill. "I suppose two hundred scarce able to crawl about and not more, if as many, able to nurse the sick or attend to domestic or Colonial concerns." Anna Maria, astonished at her own immunity, kept up the flow of letters.

"Five or seven are dying daily," she continued, "and are buried with as little ceremony as dogs or cats. This is the depth of the rainy season, our inhabitants were not covered in before it commenced and the huts they have been able to make are neither wind nor water tight . . . they are obliged to lie on the wet ground without assistance . . . exposed to nauceous [sic] putrid stenches. . . .

I am surprised our boasted Philanthropists . . . [the Sierre Leone Directors in London] should have subjected themselves to the censure they must meet [for the poor conditions].[38]

After the arrival of over 1,000 previously enslaved Africans who had fought for the British in the colonial war of independence—black ex-loyalists from North America—she explodes again, this time at the inappropriate choice of officials sent by London. To the dismay of Governor John Clarkson, brother of famous abolitionist Thomas, some officials had taken to dressing up in "sword, cockade, and epaulettes" to exaggerate their authority (and unconsciously signal their alienation) in an environment that apparently threatened them:

Let the Directors shake off a parcel of hypocritical puritans they have about them, who, under the cloak of religion, are sucking the very vitals from the Company; let them employ men conversant in trade, acquainted with the coast of Africa and whose religious tenets have never been noticed; under this description they will find persons of sound morals fit to be instructed, but they will ever be subject to impositions while they employ a pack of canting parasites.[39]

After her first return home to London in 1791, when she heard that the Directors were negotiating a large expedition of people to Sierra Leone, she presciently commented:

It was surely a premature, hair-brained, and ill digested scheme, to think of sending such a number of people all at once, to a rude, barbarous and unhealthy country, before they were certain of possessing an acre of land; and I very much fear will terminate in disappointment, if not disgrace to the authors; though at the same time, I am persuaded the motives sprung from minds unsullied with evil meaning (Falconbridge, *Narrative of Two Voyages,* p. 125).

Her speech enfolds her support for black ex-loyalists whose struggle with British bureaucrats she faithfully reports. She is one of the few European eye-witnesses to give a first-hand account of the black exloyalist leader and spokesman Thomas Peters and of Prince Naimbana who was carefully packaged in Clapham Sect propaganda as a Christian-fearing African after he arrived in London. London's hand-picked administrators quarrel outright with Governor John Clarkson who refuses to renegotiate, let alone revoke his promise to grant land rights to the former loyalists:

> Mr. Clarkson promised [us, stated the ex-slave settlers, as Falconbridge reports] in Nova Scotia that no distinction should be made here between us and white men; we now claim this promise, we are free British subjects, and expect to be treated as such; we will not tamely submit to be trampled on any longer. Why are not our country allotments of land surveyed? Why are not all the Company's promises to us fulfilled (Falconbridge, *Narrative of Two Voyages*, pp. 205–206).

Following his statement, John Clarkson severely criticizes the priorities of the London group led by Henry Thornton who promoted the second relocation plan:

> The Company's first consignment made clear that its principal aim was not to establish a colony for oppressed blacks but to open profitable communication with Africa. Instead of food and building materials, the directors dispatched bulky sugar-boiling pans and cotton-cleaning machines with a surfeit of trade goods, such as penny knives and garden watering pots.[40]

The Society had encouraged many people to relocate to Sierra Leone, without providing the most basic amenities—in Anna Maria Falconbridge's own words—"before houses, materials for buildings, or other conveniences" (Falconbridge, *Narrative of Two Voyages*, p. 226); relocation, that is, served as an excuse for an upgraded slave labor camp instead of a site of liberation.

Alongside her championship of the loyalists' cause, her refusal to categorize Africans as manipulable objects, and her frustration at London abolitionists more interested in control than freedom, she juxtaposes the tale of Prince Naimbana. By the time she writes about him, she probably knows what he symbolically and politically means to the Clapham Sect, how, in harsher terms, they are using the Prince. Her text crosses the treatment meted out to Peters and his comrades with that accorded the Prince; it also records another silent dialogue with inveterate pro-slaveryites and her own refusal to regard the Prince as an extraordinary person. She scarcely even mentions him until after they arrive in Britain when she makes a point of ridiculing the attention he receives from the Clapham sectarians because of his royal status. Though conscious of the Prince as an apt, discerning student, she does not seem to like him much, perfectly at ease in her criticism and oblivious to her conventionally Eurocentric ideas of appearance and demeanour:

> I could not help secretly smiling to see the servile courtesy which those gentlemen paid this young man, merely from his being the son of a nominal King.
>
> It has slip'd my notice till now to describe him to you;—His person is rather below the ordinary, including to grossness, his skin nearly jet black, eyes keenly intelligent, nose flat, teeth unconnected, and filed sharp after the custom of his country, his legs a little bandied, and his deportment easy, manly, and confident withal. In his disposition he is surly, but has cunning enough to smother it where he thinks his interest is concerned; he is pettish and implacable, but I think grateful and attached to those he considers his friends; nature has been bountiful in giving him a sound intellect, very capable of improvement, and he also possesses a great thirst for knowledge.
>
> While with me, although it was seldom in my power, now and then I amused myself with teaching him the alphabet, which he quickly learned, and before we parted, could read any common print surprisingly well.
>
> He is not wanting in discernment, and has already discovered the weak side of his patrons, which he strives to turn to good account, and I dare say, by his natural subtility, will in time advantage himself considerably by it (Falconbridge, *Narrative of Two Voyages,* pp. 126–27).

Anna Maria Falconbridge's narrative fittingly concludes the temporary flowering of radical texts. She refuses to be isolated and identified as the "wife" of the former Alexander Falconbridge and the "new wife" of Isaac Dubois. By deciding to write her indignant narrative and have it published, she voices herself in public and represents the relocated Africans in Sierra Leone—realizing she is no more than a British representative. With Anna Falconbridge sounding their political demands and personal anger, black insurgents emerge as people who can speak only in mediated ways, through a white British "interpreter," even though, in the case of Peters, she couches his remarks in the first person. As a subject who speaks, writes, negotiates, travels, and refuses to be used, she candidly privileges herself within a stringently patriarchal community. Ultimately she exploits her text to unveil behind-the-scenes Henry Thornton and subvert his attempt to stigmatize herself and slaves as troublesome objects—though in very different ways—, people who threaten Britain's efforts to impose stability on a volatile, vulnerable region. By denying the alien status of Africans and expressing their just demands directly and indirectly, she offers the British public different vantage points from which to judge colonial activity, one that foregrounds the perspective of an independent female. At several levels, she asks readers to shift their usual location, change their position, look at things freshly. Her text exemplifies a measure of egalitarianism and human freedom; it exposes the interlocking mechanisms by which sections of the British patriachal ruling class sought to consolidate colonial power. Put in a somewhat different light, Anna Maria Falconbridge's narrative shows the suppressed connections between gender and race oppression.

Unlike the 1788 poets, Falconbridge does not manufacture Africans out of wholecloth. Despite traditional prejudice, she presents authentic speaking subjects although the majority of Africans as well as Britons remain mute. She agrees with Olaudah Equiano that the prospect of non-human trade or straightforward commerce with a colonial power would be "glorious." Nonetheless, she seems to recognize that expansion implies British control. But in that epoch, even avowed radicals such as Helen Maria Williams did not disparage non-slave trade colonialism; they rationalized that Britain would act fairly and Africans would benefit and even be compensated for past atrocities.

From a novel vantage point, Falconbridge records the colonizing invasion, herself and her husband included. Yet in its overt display of multiple resistances to events, Falconbridge's text barely legitimizes colonialism; it throws the "civilizing mission" distinctly into question. But the dire consequences in store for the Continent are still barely discernible or apprehended. For the time being she respects the contract negotiated with the Nova Scotians; allusively this assumption about the inviolability of contract reminds us that Thornton revoked his promise to her just as he did to the post-war black loyalists.

Anna Maria Falconbridge's anger scarcely parallels the incensed fury of these ex-loyalists and indigenous people who have already predicted a colonialist assault:

> Do not you know white men well enough [states the Palaver-Man to King Naimbana's possible successor], to be convinced they never give away their money without expecting it returned many fold?— Cannot you see the drift of this profuse, unlooked for, and unasked for present? Let me warn you against taking it—for be assured, however disinterested and friendly they appear at this moment,

they are aiming at some selfish purposes, and although they may
not discover what their wishes are immediately—before twelve
moons more you will know them (Falconbridge, *Narrative of Two
Voyages*, p. 199).

Within a decade of these events, a philanthropic Perronet Thompson
who sought work in Sierra Leone underwrote what Anna Maria Falconbridge discloses between the lines. He described what happened
when he arrived:

> A slave trader proposed bringing three hundred Negroes into the
> Colony. "They shall be apprenticed to me for fourteen years," he
> told the governor, "and when their time is half out I shall apprentice
> them again; and by that time I think they will have pretty well
> worked themselves out." In consequence, Perronet Thompson de-
> termined to write Wilberforce; "and [I] shall assert roundly that if
> every step which has been taken in this affair of the apprentices is
> not retraced instantly the colony will soon be little better than a
> slave factory."
> . . . The effect was to exasperate the Directors of the Company
> and, as he predicted, eventually to lose him his job.
> . . . He publicly charged the Company, the Colony, and the African
> Institution with condoning and practicing slave trading. Far from
> civilizing the territory, he wrote, the leaders of the enterprise "con-
> stantly purchased the natives, worked them themselves without
> pay, and hired them to others for pay; suffered slaves to be brought
> in and taken out of the colony; allowed them to be seized and
> delivered to their masters when they sought protection; permitted
> their storekeeper to supply the slave factories, slave ships, and to
> feed the trade in every possible way."[41]

Falconbridge's *Narrative of Two Voyages to the River Sierra Leone
during the Years 1791–1793* produces hitherto unknown knowledge
about Africans, understandably fashioned according to a Eurocentric
perspective. Nonetheless, Falconbridge reveals her own ability to see
through what the Governors were up to and to stand up to them. By
cheating her, they opened her eyes to the many faces of colonialism.
Since reactions to San Domingo were about to reshape articulations
of "the slave," in 1788 Falconbridge's text represents an invaluable
historical document, thoroughly imbricated with ambiguities, since it
dismantles earlier characterizations circulated by Europeans. Not too
surprisingly, the tracts initiated by Hannah More that reinaugurated
the "shorthand" view of Africans became, unlike Falconbridge's *Narrative,* national bestsellers.

Chapter 10

Reactions to San Domingo (1):
Cheap Repository Tracts

From liberty, spirituality and the rights of man good Lord deliver US.
—Hannah More in Samuel Pickering, Jr. *The Moral Tradition,* p. 51.

Political domination and economic exploitation needed the cosmetic cant of *mission civilisatrice* to seem fully commendatory. For the ideology of empire was hardly ever a brute jingoism; rather, it made subtle use of reason, and recruited science and history to serve its ends. The image of the European coloniser had to remain an honourable one: he did not come as exploiter, but as enlightener. He was not seeking mere profit, but was fulfilling his duty to his Maker and his sovereign, whilst aiding those less fortunate to rise toward his lofty level. This was the white man's burden, that reputable colonial *malaise,* that sanctioned the subjugating of entire continents.
—Rana Kabbani *Europe's Myths of Orient,* p. 6.

. . . Every measure will be taken for laying a foundation of happiness to the native, by the promotion of industry, the discouragement of polygamy, the setting up of schools, and the gradual introduction of religious and moral instruction among them. . . .
—Henry Thornton, Report of Sierra Leone Company Directors, 1791, pp. 49–50.

Several radical authors influenced by revolutionary tenets and personal experiences argued against slavery as a matter of principle. They foregrounded former slaves in Sierra Leone occupying strong leadership positions, demanding constitutional rights. By contrast, historical events caused more conservative abolitionists to refract slavery through an intensely spiritual lens that bolstered the country's physical security and moral regeneration. The subtle ideological split in the abolition movement had finally surfaced openly; formulaic verse became reproblematized.

In the early 1790s as thousands publicly committed themselves to the cause, campaigners anticipated a quick victory. For one thing, Parliamentary debates and Privy Council hearings between 1789 and 1791 rendered the reality of the slave trade and the plantocracy more publicly visible.[1] The decisive defeat of the Abolition Bill in 1791 by 163 votes to 88 did little more than induce a new round of agitation by still undaunted campaigners. Boycott pamphlets featuring poignant extracts from Cowper's "Negro's Complaint" flooded the nation. Consequently the compromise motion—there was to be no immediate end to the slave trade—that passed by 230 votes to 85 in April 1792, came as a blow, jolting those who had heedlessly ignored the effect on the campaign of two revolutions. That Prime Minister Sir William Pitt enlisted a pro-slavery friend, Sir William Dundas, to introduce the motion spoke for itself; Parliament was running scared after the triumphant San Domingo revolution in 1791.[2] Although Dundas's motion designated January 1st, 1796, as the deadline for termination of the slave trade, that year came and went without event.

The press churned out one blood-curdling story after another. One hundred thousand insurgents fought for power against the planters, the government, and their allies in the wealthiest French-controlled Caribbean colony. Additionally, since San Domingo was the main supplier for sugar and coffee imports, these transactions were jeopardized so sugar prizes zoomed. Britain reeled from an eighteenth-century version of post-traumatic shock syndrome.

Abolitionists and Jacobins were herded together as scapegoats, responsible for having stuffed slaves' heads full of dangerous ideas, as "everyone" knew that unschooled slaves were incapable by themselves of waging a triumphant revolution.[3] The anxieties and will-to-power of British conservatives provoked a denial of the realities of power for the African-Caribbean population, free and enslaved.

Working hard between the 1791 revolution and the abolition debate in 1792, the West Indian lobby predicted economic disaster and increased carnage. Even George III changed his tune.[4]

But vocal abolitionists in their dwindling numbers had a lot more to contend with when war between England and France was declared in April 1792. "In August–September the monarchy was overthrown, ... and the call [came] for total resistance to the invaders. The king was imprisoned, the foreign invasion halted by an undramatic artillery duel at Valmy."[5] When the king and queen were guillotined, increasingly paranoid Britishers saw themselves as the revolutionaries' next target; English Jacobins were reencoded as people who might get out of hand.

Dorothy Wordsworth remained an uncompromising abolitionist, denouncing Dundas's compromise Bill in a letter to her friend Jane Pollard.[6] True to form, Mary Wollstonecraft objected, but in a different way. She dared to censure a writer in the *Analytical Review* who had berated the French for debating slavery: "We are coldly told that it was imprudent in the moment of general fermentation, to lose so many days in metaphysical discussions."[7] But Wollstonecraft's disdain struck no common chord in a dazed nation for whom reform was rapidly becoming anathema. Even the British forces who invaded San Domingo—"welcomed as liberators by the white population,"—changed nothing. In fact, the revolution gained ground." By 1796, English power in the island was broken ... though they held on in isolated spots for two more years."[8] Worse than defeat, invasion exacerbated anxieties about the meaning of freedom. A cynical attempt to steal away a colony from the weakened French, though never stated publicly as such, had not paid off.

In return for territorial surrender, Toussaint L'Ouverture signed a secret treaty of friendship and trade with the British commander. A five-year occupation "during which, it is reported, forty thousand men perished and a sum of twenty million pounds was expended, had come to an ignominious close."[9] Ventriloquizing pro-slavery opinion, Dundas addressed the House of Commons on February 18, 1796, stressing the effect on abolition of this costly campaign.

He was speaking in opposition to a motion for the abolition of slavery and the slave trade. In principle Dundas agreed with the movers of the motion; this agreement in principle was routine, but, continues Dundas,

"With those who argued on the general principle of the slave trade—as inexpedient, impolitic and incompatible with the justice and humanity of the British constitution—he had always, and must still, agree. . . .

"He opposed it because he thought were it agreed to by the House, it would endanger the peace of the country."[10]

Dissent itself was dying.[11] The French Revolution and domestic affairs preoccupied radicals, denounced as traitors following San Domingo. Wollstonecraft's untimely death in 1797 symbolically tolled the passing of a short-lived phase of radical anti-slavery agitation based on natural rights. Pro-establishment abolitionists, by contrast, sought to reconcile their political contradictions. First off, they aimed to discredit Paine's revolutionary *Rights of Man.* A powerful member of the abolitionist wing of the ruling class reenlisted Hannah More to bail them out.

Beilby Porteus, evangelical Bishop of London and a friend of More, asked her to write "some little thing tending to open [the] eyes" of the "lower orders of people." More responded with *Village Politics* (1792) using the pseudonym of Will Chip. "The sort of writing repugnant to my nature, though indeed it is a question of peace rather than politics."[12] Will Chip was meant to be a working class Edmund Burke who saw "a divine purpose immanent in the existing order of things."

> . . . With him she held religion to be the basis of society, the source of peace and trust and comfort. . . . Good order, . . . was the foundation of all good things: to achieve it the people must be tractable and obedient. . . . The people were ignorant and childish, easily excited by wicked men for their own ends; they must be taught, she held, where truth lay in the great [revolutionary] debate of the day.[13]

Pro-French Tom Hood debates patriotic Jack Anvil who

> defines French liberty as murder, French democracy as government by a thousand tyrants, French equality as the pulling down of everyone above him, French philosophy as disbelief in God, the devil, heaven and hell, "the Rights of Man" as "battle, murder, and sudden death."[14]

His feet solidly on the ground and distrusting "organization," Anvil ridicules "fraternization and inviolability" as "hocus pocus"; he distrusts "organization."

The immensely successful *Village Politics* established itself as a prototype for the proliferation of tracts that followed. Inaugurated by Hannah More, supported by Clapham Sect members and their allies, and bankrolled by Henry Thornton, the *Cheap Repository Tracts* established "a new type of literature for the inferior classes—. . . safe and

cheap [and above all] unspeculative."[15] Control of British workers,
national security, and the moral life were at stake. In the words of
Leonore Davidoff and Catherine Hall:

> The evangelical struggle for English hearts and minds was con-
> ducted not through the political meeting, the ballot box or the
> hustings, but through the sermon, the tract, the Sunday school, the
> auxiliary society and the philanthropic visit. It was a struggle which
> engaged significant sectors of the middle class, both male and
> female, in constant labour as the ungodly were exhorted, admon-
> ished and reproved. . . . The conviction that "works," inspired by
> Christian love, could regenerate English society was shared by
> evangelicals of all denominations and made possible the alliance
> of middle-class Anglicans and non-conformists in the bid to rescue
> those otherwise condemned to eternal damnation.[16]

Revolutions were transforming abolitionist discourse. In writing
Village Politics, More had adapted and modified the format and moral
didacticism of a religious periodical edited by Sarah Trimmer, a prominent Anglican children's writer and co-founder of the Sunday School
movement. Trimmer

> was the sole author as well as editor of *The Family Magazine,* each
> number of which contained a sermon abridged from an Anglican
> divine, descriptions of foreign countries [pointing out how much
> worse off the poor were than in England], and instructive tales. . . .
> [These instructive tales for adults] grew out of her work for children.
> She wanted to help those who had left school and so wrote these
> artless stories of good and bad people in humble spheres of life.[17]

In *The Family Magazine* Trimmer had included in "Anecdotes of
Negroes" two unaltered accounts of slaves that had originally appeared as discrete sections in James Ramsay's *An Essay on the Treatment and Conversion of African Slaves* (1784).[18] The first told of Joseph
Rachel, a good Christian ex-slave; the second concerned the amicable
altruistic Babay. On March 1, 1788, Sarah Trimmer's friend, Lady
Denward, congratulated Trimmer for accenting in the first issue "some
account of the suffering of African slaves."[19]

> I rejoice that you intend to take up your pen in favour of those
> much injured Africans. Sure now those scenes of cruelty are come
> to light, they will never more be permitted to go on. To hear of so

many thousand immortal souls being annually sacrificed, that a few
individuals may abound in riches, strikes me with horror.[20]

In addition to her tales of Joseph Rachel and Babay, Sarah Trimmer
summarized Quaker abolitionist Anthony Benezet's *History of Guinea*
and reprinted some of Ignatius Sancho's *Letters* along with an extract
from Job ben Solomon's *History*. Although *The Family Magazine*
ceased publication in July 1789, Trimmer later reiterated her support
for abolition, apparently unfazed by the revolution, and gently insinuated that the Church of England's pro-slavery policy did not meet with
her approval.[21]

> I am very anxious [she states in her journal entry before the House
> vote in May 1791] for the abolition of the slave trade. I am confident
> that the continuance of it is totally repugnant to Christianity and I
> am persuaded that a blessing would fall upon the nation for prefer-
> ring piety and justice, to worldly policy.

HANNAH MORE AND THE CHEAP REPOSITORY TRACTS

In accordance with Clapham Sect ideology, Hannah More transformed Sarah Trimmer's medium into a new and more powerful
weapon during the mid 1790s. Africans were to be spiritually reborn.
Trimmer's tracts served Hannah More's purposes well since they
conveyed a dual message about the necessity of salvation while pre-
serving rigid social hierarchies.[22] In "Slavery," More had mooted her
distaste for self-determination through the tale of Quashi's suicide
and her lacerations of the "mob." Now with the *Tracts* she could
unequivocally state her perspective. Between them, with historical
events having propelled abolitionists into a defensive posture, Trimmer and More re-tailored anti-slavery discourse to suit the exigencies
of current events as well as evangelical ideology. Especially after 1793
when Britain waged war with France, abolitionists who opposed the
French and San Domingo Revolutions found themselves in a strained
public stance. Originally opposed to slavery because it impugned the
nation's reputation, they now found that victory in San Domingo
threatened religious values and middle-class security.

For conservative abolitionists, moral revulsion toward slavery did
not necessarily spell support for the logical extension of abolitionist
philosophy: the rebellion of slaves and workers in the interests of

liberty.[23] Well attuned to his difficult position as an anti-Jacobin who advocated abolition, parliamentary leader Wilberforce could not easily remain silent and took refuge in introducing and reintroducing a doomed abolition bill during the anti-reform war years. He even "took heat" for his stance:

> Wilberforce's conscience forced him to adopt a less bellicose tone than the Government ... Among Wilberforce's political friends there were many who questioned his wisdom in not leaving the [slave] Trade alone for the duration of the war.[24]

More also contributed to the dormant campaign, but in a qualitatively different way. Out of the one hundred and fourteen *Tracts* printed between 1795 and 1798, only four addressed slavery.[25] In general, the *Tracts* preached social and domestic obedience and charged waged workers and slaves alike: know your place, practice humility, endure scarcity and maltreatment, love God, and live the life of the holy family. More's authoritarian narrator assumed that neither British workers nor African slaves could speak for themselves, except very occasionally, and needed assistance from better informed, more "civilized" middle-class people. Workers and slaves were metonymically linked as hopefully loyal, inferior, slothful, immoral, uneducated, and possibly, worst of all, godless. From a superior vantage point, More decides what is right for the "underdog" since extending universal love is a Christian's primary duty.

In Volume 1 of *The Cheap Repository Tracts,* 1795, "True Stories of Two Good Negroes" and "The Sorrows of Yamba" appeared. "True Stories" consisted of two tales: "A True Account of a Pious Negro" and "Babay, the true story of a good Negro woman."[26] The fourth antislavery *Tract*—though not specifically billed as such—was "The Black Prince: A True Story, Being An Account of the Life and Death of Naimbana, an African King's Son."[27]

In "A True Account of a Pious Negro," the "Pious Negro" is a slave who is never freed. An "English Gentleman" who meets the slave in North America discusses slavery with him, only to discover that the Negro's Quaker master is so kind that this unnamed slave does not desire freedom. Reading the Bible avidly has taught him what a "very great sinner" he is. After questioning the bondsman closely, the "gentleman" finds him "perfectly" charming, a man with a "heavenly disposed mind." In the course of this intimate dialogue, they grow mutually attached, the slave weeping because of God's mercy, "so that we looked upon each other, and talked with that glow of Christian affection, that made me more than ever believe, what I have often too thoughtlessly professed to believe, the communion of saints, viz. that sympathy of heart and soul which unites and endears good people to each other. . . ." (*Cheap Repository Tracts,* p. 10). They part on the understanding they will meet and "live together, and love one another throughout . . . eternity" (*Cheap Repository Tracts,* p. 11).

Class and ethnic relationships are fixed on earth but the status of the slave in eternity remains unclear. The Englishman is an articulate gentleman, friends with the Quaker owner whose instruction has taught the slave that life is a blessing. The slave himself is a one-dimensional, cardboard character who speaks, admittedly, but who knows and does only what superiors tell him, little more than a cipher. Yet in his condition as a feeling individual who can lament and love like Jesus, he contradicts old mythologies about insensate Africans.

Considering the historical commitment of Quakers to abolition and their alliances with other Dissenters as well as evangelicals, the tract was historically anomalous and verged on the spiritually, if not politically scandalous. Not only does the Friend's bondsman consistently read the Bible and treat it as a source of revealed religion, uncharacteristic of "inner light" spiritual practices at the time, but the Quaker master keeps the man enslaved, a practice long outlawed and penalized by expulsion in the Society of Friends. Anthony Benezet had encapsulated Friends' teaching in *A Short Account of the People Called Quakers* (1780):

> . . . The fixed purpose of purchasing the African Negroes . . . hath particularly engaged the attention of this religious society, who have required all their members to avoid being, in any respect, concerned in the support of this infamous traffick; and . . . all their members, that have any . . . should . . . set them at liberty; and . . . such who refused . . . shall be considered as no longer in friendship with them and to have renounced their right of membership.[28]

"A True Account of a Pious Negro" was not reprinted.

The second jointly published tract—the story of Babay—had previously appeared in James Ramsay's *Essay on The Treatment and Conversion of African Slaves* (1784).[29] Subsequently, Sarah Trimmer had borrowed and reprinted it virtually untouched in *The Family Magazine.* Whether More or another contributor rewrote *Babay* in the *Tracts* is uncertain. Ramsay's original tale concerned a lieutenant who contracted the highly contagious disease termed yaws, after which "a poor negro woman" named Babay found, nursed, and cured him. With his first earnings, the Christ-like lieutenant purchased the bondswoman's freedom and welcomed her to his home, treating her with kindness and respect until she died. In his eulogy at Babay's funeral, the lieutenant reminds slaves of their earthly function:

> Take notice this woman was a Christian, and you will cease to wonder. This instance of generosity found in one of her condition, is a proof that noble and great actions are not, as many think, confined to advantages of birth and education, for she had nothing to direct her but God's grace working in a tractable heart and this benevolent temper shewed itself in every part of her behaviour through life, and was accompanied in her, with a true sense of religion; or to speak more truly, she was charitable because she was religious. . . . She always spoke on religious subjects, with an earnestness, seriousness, and knowledge, which I wish were more general than I have found them among her betters; here then is a shining example of goodness on your own level for your imitation. If ye know these things, happy are ye if ye do them.

Almost invisibly, the West and Africa are ideologically pitted against each other; to wit, colonial subject versus colonized other. If "tractable" hearts of simple people remain open, they too can become Christians and live a superior moral life. Consequently, Babay's altruism should not disconcert a European audience although the paradoxical fact that Babay assisted the lieutenant before conversion is left unexamined. Evangelical pro-conversion propaganda cannot mask its counter-revolutionary impact. Struggle is unnecessary because a life of passivity begets an eternal reward. At best, the tract argues that individuals, however inferior, should not be enslaved. Nursing the lieutenant, Babay epitomizes Christian motherhood and Christ's teaching of doing unto others. Likewise the lieutenant emulates Christ. The Christian family is the ideal site for salvation.

Every aspect of Babay's character endears her to a British public. The Eurocentric narrator denies her a voice but uses her altruism to inspire the less spiritually oriented slave congregation. Evangelicals, of course, set stock on seeking out individual black converts to Christianity. Both in Britain and Africa, they used individual leaders to spread the word to others like themselves.

Turned inside out, the story of Babay reglosses religious self-examination. Society expects evangelical women to register the same obedience and piety demanded of Babay, but Hannah More herself registers no attachment to passivity in either personal or political life. Her publicly displayed resistance to total female submission exudes a subterranean force that quietly surfaces in the tale's telling contradiction: Babay represents Christian standards despite the fact that her altruism precedes her conversion. This oddly ignored order injects a tension and a fudging of boundaries between Babay's (More's?) values and those of the lieutenant's. To put the case more strongly, the lieutenant copies Babay. He echoes and affirms her spontaneity and her selflessness, qualities that are generally associated with females.

In "The Comforts of Religion" that follows Babay's tract in the 1795 edition, the anonymous poet (perhaps More?) states that: "blest religion . . ./ can sweeten pain and soften care/ and make [the heathens'] darkness light."[30] Despite "feeble reason, tir'd and blind," religion can succor unenlightened others: "To brighten ev'ry gloomy hour;/ And soften ev'ry grief."

Countless nineteenth-century reprints of the *Tracts* omitted the tales of Babay and the "pious Negro." Quaker response can be guessed at and besides, the tale casts a rather unpatriotic light on the officer's unmentioned relations who never come to his aid, unattractive to a wartime- and a family-oriented public. The abolitionist lieutenant updates benevolent George Ellison.

In 1795, "The Sorrows of Yamba, or the Negro Woman's Lamentation" that More herself wrote from scratch was published as part of the series, the sole tract on slavery that enjoyed repeated reprintings. Unlike the earlier "Slavery: A Poem," More tenders no parliamentary solution while naming and voicing the African protagonist; Yamba describes her experiences on the Middle Passage in the first person. A married African, Yamba was kidnapped as she suckled her child and then was propelled into the hazards of the long journey: "Cramm'd . . . down a slave ship's hold,/ Where were hundreds stow'd like me."[31] Forced to dance on board the slaveship for exercise or risk whipping, she craves death; fed only "nauseous horse-beans" and force-fed upon refusal, many slaves including her child fall ill and die. Once in the Caribbean, Africans are sold like cattle for "filthy gold" to a representative hard "Massa" who will find himself easily acquitted under British laws of murdering slaves. Then comes the turning point. A missionary saves Yamba from suicide: [He] "told me 'twas the Christian's lot/ Much to suffer here below" (More, "The Sorrows of Yamba," p. 6). Converted, she blesses "my cruel capture"; moribund, she prays "that Afric might be free" and "the Gospel enter in." Where "the weary are to rest," she will meet both her husband and God (More, "The Sorrows of Yamba," p. 9). Thus slavery benefits Yamba because only by being enslaved was she exposed to Christianity and hence to a life of salvation.

With Yamba's tale, More tries to blend a now politically jeopardizing commitment to abolition with the primacy she accords conversion. Although Yamba remains a slave, she will ultimately return to an earlier state of freedom in the divine presence. To workers who will hopefully be instructed and to middle-class readers who will concur, the same message takes on class-differentiated meaning: be content with life's lot despite hardships, and recognize God's love and spiritual equality.

But "The Sorrows of Yamba" is even more densely packed than the surface message allows; many contemporary texts resound within its sing-song doggerel. From Alexander Falconbridge, More borrows the thematics and motif of yams and linguistically splices this symbol of African difference with half the name of Ramsay's protagonist— Babay—to baptize her protagonist, Yamba, and emblemize African womanhood. Falconbridge mentions yams several times in his *Account* as a staple food of slaves on board ship and links yams with wood and water as basic stock.[32] He also supplies details of slaves who loathe the horsebean diet so much that they "throw them overboard, or in each others' faces when they quarrel." He talks of coerced dancing, the kidnapping of women, the condition of pregnant women on board, severe floggings, the stench of the "bathroom" tubs, blood and mucous everywhere that cause a "longing" to die, constant sickness and death, the "scramble" to buy slaves after the journey, and occasional beheadings of bought slaves who turn out to be, in plantocratic terms, defective.

More's reverberations of Alexander Falconbridge's text frankly yet obliquely answer Anna Maria Falconbridge's objections to the behavior of the Clapham Sect. More decisively affirms that only spiritual not physical welfare matters, a sore point with Anna Maria Falconbridge. "The Sorrows of Yamba" ideologically complements Falconbridge's *Narrative* about Sierra Leone. Moreover, as both women intertextualize Alexander Falconbridge's text, they remind readers of the surgeon's hard evidence given before the Privy Council that helped the nation navigate cautiously toward an abolitionist course.[33]

But More's partial verse-paraphrase of Falconbridge's *Account* also isolates their political differences. His goal in Sierra Leone was to establish a colony for freed Africans.[34] More now temporarily withdraws from that solution and stresses conversion in such uncertain times. Spiritual equality is now enough and the colonized replummet to the status of political subordinates, an unchanging set of manipulated others who should adopt a Christian value system.

Beyond that, anti-slavery testimonies of African contemporaries resonate. In his *Autobiography,* Equiano railed against the abuse of African females.[35] Both he and Cugoano spelled out the obscenity of kidnapping, the sea voyage, and human sale at the other end.[36] Other contemporary texts filter into and through More's. A missionary saves Barbauld's solitary grieving Negro mother. Yamba's agony that echoes the captive Jews described in *Psalms* reminds readers that, like the Jews, Yamba cannot "sing to the Lord's song in a strange land." She is not only removed from her culture and its religious beliefs but the text, its unspoken utterances aside, denies their existence.

Compared to "Slavery: A Poem" in 1788, More's much shorter poem of 1795, "The Sorrows of Yamba," more thickly packs documented atrocities, troped as constants in a slave's life. In symbolizing the ideal mother, whose life a callous patriarchy disrupts and almost destroys, Yamba allows More to reaffirm evangelical gendered class values and their relation to racial subjugation. What matters to women is home and family, precisely the necessities that a deracinated, denatalized Yamba is denied. As a mediated speaking subject, she reminds readers of her homeland, lost and dead children, cruelty, and a former happy life. By mainstreaming gender issues, More helps to close the gap between slavewomen and British female writers and readers. At the conscious level, she wants conventional British women to sympathize with the slaves. Ironically, too, Yamba's distance from her homeland and domestic life underscores More's own distance from home and family although public philanthropy was an acceptable substitute for prescribed female roles— or even its logical extension. Additionally, Babay and Yamba both signify female spiritual helplessness before the advent of a good Christian man, a spiritual *deus ex machina.* In Hannah More's case, Wilberforce and John Newton assume the role of religious mentors. The lieutenant and the missionary reillumine a notable biographical dimension in More's own life. On the other hand, the slavewomen's subdued posture before male protectors magnified Hannah More's cultural autonomy in the almost exclusively male Clapham Sect. More asserts herself while promoting evangelical tenets that include a separate but equal status for women. Yamba operates in dual modes, approved by Hannah More for others but not herself; Yamba enacts acceptable roles for women and workers, both male and female. She is a feminine model of nurturance and maternity as well as a lowly person who willingly obeys class superiors.

Possibly written by John Newton, former captain of a slave ship and close evangelical friend of Hannah More, the fourth tract on slavery directly addresses Falconbridge's concerns: relocation, conversion, and colonization. Entitled *The Black Prince, A True Story: Being an*

Account of the Life and Death of Naimbana, an African King's Son, Who Arrived in England in the Year 1791, and set sail on his return in June 1793, the tract was constantly reprinted in periodicals and newspapers and written up in the dispatches of the governor of Sierra Leone.[37] Anna Maria Mackenzie used the story of Prince Naimbana as the basis of her racist, anti-semitic novel, *Slavery, or the Times* (1794), that caricatures the prince and his father.[38]

Prince Naimbana was one of the sons of an African chief in the Sierra Leone region. *The Black Prince* avers that the revival of Christianity in the late 1700s in England had prompted the king to send his son to be educated there, a slight obfuscation of the truth. In fine, the king had sent three sons to three different countries to help him decide which system of education would best suit his "subjects."[39]

Set beside Anna Maria Falconbridge's two-hundred-page reaction to Sierra Leone in general and to Prince Naimbana and his family in particular, at first glance the fourteen-page tractarian version is a highly simplified construction. The prince's conversion subdues his former passions so that he can respond appropriately inside St Paul's Cathedral.[40] Moreover, the tract suggests that the celebrated debate on the slave trade in the House of Commons that sullied "the African character" and provoked an outburst from the prince, served to reinforce the salubrious qualities of Christianity. "I will kill that fellow whenever I meet him for he has told lies of my country. . . . When he has once taken away their [Africans'] character, there is nothing which he may not do to Black people ever after." (*The Black Prince*, p. 8). According to the tale, when his chaperones inform him that Scriptures frown on anger and vengeance, he calms down instantly, in deference to Judaeo-Christian authority.

These fatuous reductions of Prince Naimbana's experiences are even more obvious than the fictional redactions of Yamba's and Babay's lives since the prince at least was a much publicized visitor. Granville Sharp, Charles Wadstrom, a Norwegian mineralogist, and the prince's two tutors offered much less tendentious descriptions of Prince Naimbana in addition to his own testimony. Two salient features are the prince's addiction to learning and his defense of Africa and Africans. More starkly put, he seems to be intent on erasing mythologies that constantly circulate about Africa. In his tutor's chauvinist vision:

> A desire of knowledge was the predominant feature in his character: he would continually urge his instructors to prolong the time of their reading together. He was forward in declaring his obligations

to every one who would assist him in the acquisition of useful learning: he would express regret if he had been led into any company where the time had passed away without improvement; and when it happened that he was left entirely to himself, he would employ not less than eight or ten hours of the day in reading. Though the disadvantages arising from the long neglect of his mental faculties were apparent, he showed signs of very good natural sense: he had also a faculty at distinguishing characters; and his mind, as might naturally be expected, was ready to receive impressions from those persons of whom he had conceived a good opinion. He had few advantages of person, but he was uncommonly pleasing [in] his behavior, showing much natural courtesy and even delicacy of manners: he was also of a kind and affectionate disposition. He was quick in all his feelings, and his temper was occasionally warm; some degree of jealousy also entering into his character: in particular, he was indisposed to answer questions put to him by strangers concerning the state of his own country; for he was apt to suspect that they meant to draw comparisons unfavourble to its character; and he would therefore, on such occasions, often turn the conversation, by remarking, that a country so unfavourably circumstanced as Sierra Leone had hitherto been, was not to be supposed capable of having made any attainments worthy of being the subject of conversation in Great Britain.[41]

In affirmation, Granville Sharp pronounced the prince an erudite man with a "natural good disposition, modesty, behaviour, and great diligence and application to learning";[42] Wadstrom, in turn, spoke of the Prince's self-conscious application to learning and of other biographical issues:

> *"It is that lady,"* [said the Prince in Wadstrom's account, pointing to Anna Maria Falconbridge,] *"to whom I owe this improvement; for she was kind enough to teach me in the passage from S. Leone."* . . . Talking to the distinguished member of parliament [Wadstrom continues] who proposed the gradual abolition of the slave-trade, he said "Mr.—— should have his carriage drawn by asses, for they go very gradually." His application to study was, as the Directors state, indefatigable; and so strong was his wish to understand the Scriptures thoroughly, and to be able to read them in the original languages, that, to his other acquisitions, during his short stay in England, he added, in his private hours, no inconsiderable proficiency in the Hebrew.[43]

The Black Prince raises several complicated issues as much as it disputes some facts. The tract gives the prince the age of twenty-three (which would account for some naiveté) whereas other accounts, including Sharp's, have him almost thirty. Furthermore, since the prince knew both Granville Sharp and Henry Thornton—he was baptized as Henry Granville presumably to acknowledge their dual assistance—he might also have been aware of the political conflicts generated by the colonization of Sierra Leone. He could conceivably have known that Thornton, in contrast to Clarkson and Sharp, was reluctant to give voting rights to black ex-loyalists in Sierra Leone, or that Olaudah Equiano had originally supported relocation and had then publicly withdrawn that support:

> Thornton himself had no strong views on the government of colonies, though he was a Tory in politics and distrusted the Nova Scotians as a possible electorate. Thomas Clarkson and Granville Sharp, on the other hand, wanted to preserve the radical democracy of the Province of Freedom. The result was a compromise. . . . Sharp and his friends had managed to salvage the representative forms, but little else. . . .
>
> Thornton was anxious to recover some of the stockholders' investment by the collection of rents. Sharp wanted to recreate as much as possible of his old utopia. Thomas Clarkson was anxious to use Sierra Leone as an outpost in the battle against the slave trade. He had little faith in the efficacy of "legitimate trade," or any other kind of trade, in civilizing Africa. Instead, he thought of the colony as a kind of bridgehead on the African continent, from which "civilization" could be extended by persuasion. To this end, he urged his brother to create three committees of council. One was to work at persuading African kings to give up the slave trade and shift to agricultural production. A second was to work for the abolition of African slavery by persuasion and by "ransoming" young slaves to serve on the Company's plantations. The third was to work for the eradication of "superstition."[44]

With these facts in mind, the Prince's wonder at St. Paul's and his explosion in Parliament radiate manifold meanings. In emotional desperation at bigotry, the Prince repudiates any Britons who downgrade Africans; obliquely he questions British values, especially those precipitating slavery and one of its outcomes, the ubiquitous "Black Poor."[45] His own oppositional ethical framework is transparent, as is his probable suppression of numerous objections to what was being done in the name of civilization and Christianity to the African continent.

Regardless, thus, of Hannah More's intention, the prince persistently calls attention to his alienation, his talents, his cultural background and values, and to the corruption he sees around him in a country embroiled in the slave trade. He insists that Africa as a continent must be assessed historically; by implication so should Britain and British values. His exacting comments about slavery disallow a mindless colonizing gaze toward West Africa. They call for and even insist on explanations and redefinitions of conduct and trade. Although he expresses willingness to forego having two wives and introduce aspects of British culture into Africa, it is all done and told in the spirit of "maybe." If it seems the right thing to do—holding out for the contrary possibility—then he will do it. The text insinuates that Prince Naimbana deliberately declines to show his hand. When he is taken seriously ill aboard ship on his return home, he poignantly evinces his devotion to Africa and his loathing for the slave trade. He leaves instructions for his brother that "as far as in him lay," he should "oppose the slave trade" (*The Black Prince,* p. 12). With his dying breath, almost literally, the prince, who is now the king-elect, accuses Britain of being Africa's damaging other in a reversal of the common relationship of domination. The prince's death dashed the hopes of Sierra Leone administrators who had hoped that he would anchor non-slave commerce in Sierra Leone on a firm footing. Wadstrom, who knew the situation intimately, put it this way: if Naimbana, this "amicable and enlightened African" had lived, "he would have been chosen king. . . . The Directors, therefore, consider the death . . . (of) so sincere a friend to the company as one of the instances wherein Providence has been pleased to disappoint their immediate hopes."[46]

Uncharacteristically, since slaves usually sailed from West Africa to London and the Caribbean, Prince Naimbana dies on a reverse Middle Passage voyage, not because he is being kidnapped from Africa, but because he is returning home from Britain to be a West African king.[47] But in psychological or even in mythic terms, that particular expanse of sea remains for Africans an unprotected, unsafe place, site of removal from harmony and symbolic of the orphaned state. Given Hannah More's feminization of his personal qualities—uncontrolled and impetuous but loyal and pious—and the detailed elaboration of his death at sea where he is "authenticated" as slaves are, by Britons, she obliquely reminds readers of the duality of white women and slaves—and now princes—as vulnerable objects of exchange. According to Prince Naimbana's apparent death-bed testimony, the Company will be reimbursed for his death.

Considered as a quartet, the tracts on slavery exemplify Britons acting in good faith toward Africans. Their didacticism, at any rate, points in that direction. They model a moral trusteeship guaranteeing that free trade initiated between the countries will be conducted in an appropriately humane way; there will be no commerce in human beings. Nonetheless, regardless of rank, Africans tend to be metonymically linked in British eyes as child-like and virtuous, in contrast to more culturally sophisticated Britons with an inherently distinguished taxonomy of values. One compelling cultural assumption is Africans' lack of morality. At the very most, Africans hold foolishly superstitious religious beliefs.[48] Nonetheless, the tracts do break with the traditional meaning of the great chain of being when they demand and imply that God's deliverance is open to all.[49] The post-revolutionary code of British-evangelical orthodoxy has constructed a new African genealogy that prioritizes conversion; a new form of colonizer versus colonized that privileges morality, loyalty, and religion above all. In the *Tracts,* a spiritual counterdiscourse to anti-slavery British Jacobinism arrived ready made.

Collectively, these tracts promote a proto-Victorian ideal of motherhood and women's sphere. British and African men alike are feminized and nurturing. Evangelical-domestic values challenge aggressive Jacobinism, while British plantocratic voices deny the idea of a learned prince or feeling Africans. With an unswerving acceptance of Africans as dehumanized or objectified yet living creatures, the *Tracts* contain or cannot countenance the idea of a white officer conducting a funeral eulogy over a former slavewoman who selflessly saved his life.

Readers enter African reality and intellectuality through other texts that punctuate "The Black Prince." The sheer fatuity of textual incompletions, the Prince's cardboard sameness permit new meanings to seep through. The univocal author says one thing about generally silenced Africans; Africans who quietly whisper tales about wide-ranging lives recite another story. They engage in limited dialogue with British others and African peers simultaneously. The tales constitute a transnational chorus of voices.

With their constantly erupting dialogues, protagonists close the gap between themselves and authors. By their own necessarily fictitious, patently reductive fixedness, they culturally negate British assumptions to those with an ear to hear. And this is inevitable at a time when early free trade policies render the entire continent less of an "inert element." Because of rich raw materials such as palm oil, African countries offer untold lavish markets to an exploitative British commerce. Then the question becomes how to represent Africa and its people, given their supposed incompatibility and non-connection with time and progress.[50] Tensions and contradictions textually edge up against and abrade one another.

But even though Clapham Sect members prefer to code Africans as a ready-made mass of people, they desire conversion and recognize the necessity and desirability of negotiating with African chiefs. That the chiefs are accustomed to manipulative British entrepreneurship is another missing element in this tragedy. Falconbridge's reference to King Naimbana's seeming good will frequently reverberates. Furthermore, the arrival of Nova Scotians in Sierra Leone demanding constitutional rights, votes, land, and decent living conditions negates the perpetual construction of "the slave" and "the African" being offered to the British public. Little wonder, then, that the democratic John Clarkson, first Governor of Sierra Leone, received short shrift from the Clapham Sect and that former slave-overseer turned evangelical, Zachary Macaulay, a much more politically accommodating candidate, was Clarkson's eventual long-term replacement.[51]

For many readers, too, not deceived by simplified propaganda, Naimbana's tale might and certainly could have kept telling itself another way. The prince's life and death reminded readers that within four tales addressing slavery, two protagonists are slaves and the other two die. The more contemporaries compute Prince Naimbana's obvious sensitivity and discerning qualities of mind, the more obviously distorted becomes the representation of the prince as a simple man devoid of an inner life. The prince refuses to accept his place because his public voice enables him to refuse; he can reinvent himself for and to himself. Even when British writers' represent the prince textually to their satisfaction, the prince shifts and re-shifts his subject positions, reacting both spontaneously and with deliberation to situations in which he finds himself. His free-ranging behavior disrupts the facade of a seamless apparatus of colonial power that the colonial ruling class tries to present.

Lastly, Naimbana not only answers the charges levelled against the Sierra Leone Company by Equiano and Falconbridge, he validates them by strongly hinting at the crude reality of greed and folly. He satirizes prejudice by substituting his own patriotism and ethical vision. Professing learning, morality, and resistance, he is anything but the imagined antidote to Toussaint L'Ouverture. He transforms their terms and transvaluates their ethical standards within his own context. The importance of emancipation in Africa—a qualitative political step beyond abolition—that he pays court to as he lies dying on board ship is a critical case in point.

In all, the tracts exemplify how social milieu and British power relations are always at play, even in tales and verse that seemingly reduce the division between "we" and "they" to its lowest common denominators. Race, class, and gender factors continually interfuse. The colonial subject authorizing the conversion of the colonized slave seems the last word in otherhood. Moreover, More's heavy onslaught against Thomas Paine via the *Tracts* did succeed to an astonishing extent in discrediting radical consciousness, at least in public, and thereby casting radicals like slaves in the role of the other. But precisely at that point of greatest separation, when it seems that Africans have been reduced to object-examples, textual stances start merging, opening outward, and becoming diaphanous at their boundaries. This resistance to a straightforward subject-other division that privileges the British narrator as the repository of values comes both from within and outside the text.

By 1795, African intellectuals had made their mark in British society and several had published chronicles, memoirs, and letters about their lives. And just as Paine's *Rights of Man* confirmed workers' full intellectual lives and potential and obliquely mocked More's characterization of "Patient Joe" in the *Tracts,* so Olaudah Equiano's autobiography mocked the coincident profiles of "Africanness" in Babay, Yamba, and Naimbana. Radicals and working people who knew about and even relished the French Revolutionary and San Domingan victories might have been able to see through the collective portrait of slaves as naturally subordinate simpletons—some surely did despite national hatred for the French and absorption in domestic issues—just as they saw through the objectified collective portrait of themselves as sinful, lazy, and naive.

Moreover, subtexts as well as texts frequently spoke back to authoritarian narrators. Yamba's life was a tapestry drawn from realistic accounts by Alexander Falconbridge, Charles Wadstrom, Olaudah Equiano, and Ottobah Cugoano. Similarly Naimbana's earlier life and his family were celebrated in the press, albeit through a narrow British vision of West Africa and its peoples. The Sierra Leone project had been initiated around 1786, negotiations for its actualization were underway for almost a decade before Naimbana visited Britain.[52] But real-life events could control didactic fictional representations only up to a point. Hannah More had attempted with the *Tracts* to transform a "one-liner" formula for a slave into a formulaic package with wider class-gender characterizations that promoted conversion as the ultimate solution to slavery. Through altruism, general virtue, and resignation, slaves and ex-slaves alike were linked to unceasing worldly trials.

A certain androgynous feminization of blacks bearing Christ-like qualities had started as early as 1788; the "Pious Negro," Babay, Yamba, and Prince Naimbana are outstanding examples. Virtuous slaves who regretfully and poignantly left the cradle of idyllic domesticity ended up, through no fault of their own, at the mercy of the godless—victims and quasi-martyrs sacrificed on the "altar" of profit and expansionism.

As war phobia deepened and reform became anathema, women writers created new ways to win support for abolition. In many ways the immensely popular *Tracts* vitally influenced that redirection.

Chapter 11

Reactions to San Domingo (2):
Sentiment, Suicide, and Patriotism

Always a firm adherent to the rules of civilised welfare, [Toussaint L'Ouverture] found it necessary [in 1798] to rebuke General John White for the barbarities of the troops under his command.

I feel that though I am a Negro, though I have not received as fine an education as you and the officers of His Britannic Majesty, I feel, I say, that such infamy on my part would reflect on my country and tarnish its glory.

—C. L. R. James, *The Black Jacobins,* p. 201.

Strait he pull'd me from the shore,
Bid me no self-murder do;
Talk'd of state when life is o'er,
All from Bible good and true.

—Hannah More, "Sorrows of Yamba," from
Cheap Repository Tracts.

SAN DOMINGO AND SLAVE RESISTANCE

War weariness and persistent fears about the French threat induced a politic of passivity in women's anti-slavery writings that differed from More's spiritual propaganda campaign.[1] Adding poignant and provocative twists to the familiar troping of victimization, female authors portrayed vulnerable bondswomen, despairing separated couples, and virtuous males who preferred suicide to a heartless

229

slavery. Quiescence was the keynote. Insurrectionary slaves contrasted with slaves who acted faithfully toward kindly owners. No longer More's worldly compensation for slavery's ills, benevolence reappeared as a transitional step toward gradual emancipation.

This traditional attentiveness to charity and social injustice heightened both female moral authority and the right to protest inequities at a time when radical writing was taboo. Their identification with the susceptible as well as the feisty was subtle. From a safe distance they could display patriarchal power at work and by overlapping problems faced by white and black women within the same text they insinuated that female subjugation at the hands of males was a common factor for all women. At the same time they strictly upheld class distinctions between colonizer subjects and slaves.

Britain's military strength and coffers were seriously depleted by the end of 1796. The nation was in no mood to enact abolition by 1796, the measure stipulated by Dundas's compromise gradualist bill in 1793:

> After three years of war, the country had lost in the West Indies 80,000 soldiers including 40,000 actually dead, the latter number exceeding the total losses of Wellington's army from death, discharges, desertion and all causes from the beginning to the end of the Peninsular War. The cost of San Domingo alone had been £300,000 in 1794, £800,000 in 1795, £2,600,000 in 1796, and in January 1797 alone it was more than £700,000. Early in 1797 the British Government decided to withdraw.[2]

Despite Anna Maria Falconbridge's indirect contentions with More's evangelical orientation toward slavery, reform was almost unilaterally denounced. However legitimate and whatever its form, self-determination was anathema. San Domingo itself—the word, the geographical territory, its alleged inhabitability, its progress—became synonymous with Anglo-Africanist barbarity that terrified most Britons, regardless of abolitionist commitment. Slave mutinies spelled anarchy and assassination.

Elizabeth Helme articulates a graphic instance of early public reaction to the San Domingo revolution in *The Farmer of Inglewood Forest* (1796), a novel so popular that it went into at least four editions and a French translation in 1824.[3] Part of the story centers on the character of Felix, a servant of Mrs. Palmer from Inglewood. Recounting his former experiences to the forest inhabitants, Felix explains how he was captured from the west coast of Africa and purchased in the

Caribbean by a Mr. Walters, currently married to a harsh, slave-branding creole. Due to the charity of Walters and his son Henry, Felix escapes branding and out of gratitude declines to participate in a slave revolt.

Despite the constant troping of slaves as victims of "repeated provocations," men of "bodily strength and undaunted courage . . . cruelly oppressed" (Helme, *The Farmer*, pp. 242–245), it's vengeance that gets stressed: slaves are "deluging the estates with the blood of their oppressors." Helme dramatizes San Domingo and the British nightmare at a high pitch: "Mr and Mrs. Walters, dead, naked, and disfigured, were carried and exposed to the open court, together with several overseers." After these deaths, Felix pleads for the son's life; when the impending martyr Henry bares his breast to the slaves, they repentantly clamor with one voice: "Live white man, live to conquer black man by humanity." Attitudes of the murdered beneficent Walters and loyal Felix provide the ethical framework for judging rebellion in a stage-setting that refigures pre-movement texts. By the end, in a vivid reverse-image of *Oroonoko,* Felix comfortably smokes a pipe, emblem of unthreatening manhood, enjoying the fruits of cooperation with his British employers.

The Farmer represents the assassins as a uniform mass of slaves bent on bloody revenge. Yet the sight of a white man's bared breast carried aloft halts slaves in their tracks because presumably, despite untamed pagan ways, they can still appreciate a Christ-like gesture of humble self-sacrifice. At the point of crisis, Helme contests the old plantocratic chestnut that slaves cannot feel and even more subtly pays tribute to More's *Tracts* since these slaves now might become, the text suggests, more attentive to Christian precepts.

A decade later in "The Grateful Negro," Maria Edgeworth further complicates slave revolutionaries, offering a perspective that matches her social and political affiliation with Dissenters.[4] Where *The Farmer* underscored confrontation in one episode, Edgeworth's entire tale concentrates on conflict. Not only do slave rebels urge resistance but a tenderhearted British plantation-owner promotes two distinct positions on emancipation: one, it is best prepared for slowly so that slaves have a chance to acclimatize themselves to the idea; and two, in both the short and long run, the labor of freed men is distinctly more profitable than coerced labor.[5]

The tale turns on the fortunes of Caesar, a diligent slave on Mr. Jeffries' plantation, whose beloved Clara is to be sold. To prevent this cruel separation and subversion of family values, charitable Mr. Edwards next door buys Caesar and Clara from Jeffries who "with the most perfect indifference to the happiness of those whom he considered of a different species from himself, acceded to this proposal" (Edgeworth, "The Grateful Negro," p. 205). To Edwards is given the tale's overt political agenda; he thinks slaves should be treated

> with all possible humanity and kindness. He wished that there was no such thing as slavery in the world; but he was convinced ... that the sudden emancipation of the negroes would rather increase than diminish their miseries. His benevolence, therefore, confined itself within reason (Edgeworth, "The Grateful Negro," p. 195).

Nonetheless, Edwards' avowed support for a very gradual emancipation handled by gentle owners and entrepreneurs is deeply undercut by the oxymoronic yoking of benevolence with confinement. Consciously or not, Edgeworth hints at the inherent and ultimately untenable contradiction in gradualist politics. In a subsequent discussion of natural rights, Edwards adapts Adam Smith's argument in *The Wealth of Nations* (1776) that hiring individuals is more profitable than enslaving them:

> Granting it to be physically impossible that the world should exist without rum, sugar, and indigo, why could they not be produced by freemen as well as by slaves? If we hired negroes for labourers, instead of purchasing them for slaves, do you think they would not work as well as they do now? Does any negro, under the fear of an overseer, work harder than a Birmingham journeyman, or a Newcastle collier, who toil for themselves and their families? (Edgeworth, "The Grateful Negro," p. 202)

Thus the text argues in tandem for gradual emancipation and for the logic of waged rather than slave labor.

Similarly veiled tensions obtain in descriptions of the mutineers. The leader of this conspiracy that plans "to extirpate every white man, woman, and child, in the island" is a bold Koromantyn (Coramantien) named Hector, the double of the "grateful negro" Caesar, except in one respect. They both consider revenge a virtue, but a Christ-like Caesar can always forgive his enemies. Although Hector's character is sensationalized—he delights in fantasies of whites "weltering in their blood"—he is also the voiced and named revolutionary who speaks for justice and natural rights:

I cannot, replied Hector, listen with patience to one who between the rising and the setting sun can forget all his resolution, all his promises; who by a few soft words can be so wrought upon as to forget all the insults, all the injuries he has received from this accursed race; and can even call a white man friend! (Edgeworth, "The Grateful Negro," pp. 211–212)[6]

But none of the Anglo-Africanist elaborations can negate the reality of revolt and the ultimate righteousness of the rebels' cause. Despite Hector's impulsively attempted murder of Caesar, despite the evil, obeah-practising Esther who "stimulated the revengeful temper of Hector almost to phrensy" (Edgeworth, "The Grateful Negro," p. 219), despite a footnote almost four pages long denouncing obeah that Edgeworth extracted from Bryan Edwards' negrophobic *History . . . of the British Colonies in the West Indies,* the text emphatically commends emancipation.[7] Thus while devoted Caesar is the sanctified hero, the slave-icon idealized by scared Britons, Hector represents collective self-determination, vindicated politically if not emotionally.

The text's ambivalence might have been connected to Edgeworth's role as a liberal Protestant landowner in Ireland. She knew the difficulty of resolving the "bitter racial and religious differences in the south and west of Ireland between a Protestant possessing class of predominantly British or pseudo-British origin and a mass of Catholic peasants, making up what had always constituted the lower orders of the country."[8] She believed in "good treatment of tenants, the spread of education and better agricultural methods, genuine religious toleration for Catholics and Protestants alike, the improvement of the standard of justice at all levels"[9] Perhaps she could sympathize with both sides because she discerned parallels between the respective plights of enslaved Africans and a colonized Irish peasantry.

The tale hovers in a space that condemns all rebellions and supports a revolutionary solution. Even the ending underscores this possibility. The self-exiled cruel owner rails at the "treachery of the whole race of slaves" that typifies the most intimidating consequences of San Domingo—expropriation of European profits, property, and life and, above all, of slaves taking matters into their own hands. Perhaps more to the point, "The Grateful Negro" warns plantocrats about the consequences of slavery just as "The Master and the Slave" (1780) by Anna Laetitia Barbauld and her brother had done. Edgeworth had read that text.[10]

Following the denunciation and departure of the Jeffries, the narrator coyly comments: "Our readers, we hope, will think that at least one exception may be made, in FAVOUR OF THE GRATEFUL NEGRO" (Edgeworth, "The Grateful Negro," p. 241). In fact, the ending quietly questions whether the counterblasts of abused men and women can be termed treacherous. Some of the textual riddles spring from Edgeworth's assumptions in pre-abolition England that the slave trade should be abolished and the process of emancipation set in motion. But the question of British control remains. If slaves left agitation to British supporters, the text hints, emancipation could be effected with less bloodshed and violence.

The stark, binary opposition between the allegedly barbaric and the grateful also breaks down. As a leader, Hector is subject to no one, except perhaps Esther, whose cultural practices are used to demean African philosophical beliefs. Slaves remain slaves in their physical lives only. The power that enslaves Hector and his allies is nothing more than brute force and atrocities, all categorically condemned. The social, emotional, and psychological inner life of the community, the clandestine plotting, the complex organization, the continuous political debates endow insurrectionists with energy and enhance their subjectivity as conspiratorial agents. Open-armed Edwards hearkens back to mid-century George Ellison in his attempts to educate and convert his slaves. Caesar is a named but passive subject. Despite a confusion of messages, the life of the text resides in the oppositional activities of Hector and the co-conspirators.

In "The Good Aunt," written three years before "The Grateful Negro," Edgeworth frames an oblique response to San Domingo that omits rebellion and recasts "The Creole" by Lucy Peacock in 1787.[11] As Richard Edgeworth states in the preface, Maria Edgeworth fully intended to point out the advantages of "a judicious early education," portraying the good aunt, Frances Howard, as a limited emancipationist. When the aunt sells her plantation out of an ethical uneasiness about owning slaves, she stipulates that aged slaves, at least, should be freed. One ex-slave named Cuba who travels intrepidly to London in the face of adversity to see former mistress Howard, ends up as a quasi-independent, happy seamstress. Edgeworth's young readers learn that slaves work willingly when freed in London as well as in the Caribbean.

In a nominal demographic displacement from San Domingo to the Spanish colony, Cuba represents the enslaved and recalls *The Wealth of Nations* as well as Dundas's compromise. Gradual abolition had not come to pass—the 1796 deadline was almost a decade gone and people with vision began to reconsider emancipation itself.

THE TROPING OF THE UNPROTECTED

Vulnerabilities of African men and women and, in one case, a white British woman also stand out. In "The Good Aunt," Frances Howard is temporarily swindled out of her fortune by a conspiracy of entrepreneurial white males while an unaccompanied Cuba, travelling alone to London, is seriously injured by one of their sons. In virtue and passivity, the feminized Felix and Caesar match Frances Howard and Cuba. The Christian model is invoked as morally upright ex-slaves work happily for apparently altruistic masters in a celebration of transcontinental assimilation. Unlike Frances Howard, however, the slaves and ex-slaves do not rediscover their lost fortunes. Class power relationships are firmly maintained. The aunt is only a temporary object of pity where slaves and ex-slaves are permanently coded as such. They are given voice as mediated speaking subjects only when they opt for British values.

The Farmer offers another specific example of gendered class values when the issue of sexual abuse reemerges. Before Edwin Godwin "ruined" one of the morally upright Barnard sisters, he had already sexually violated the slave Jenny and later, thwarted, he poisoned her. The tale of Jenny is narrated by a servant named Julia in the form of English reserved for slaves. Knowing Edwin has designs on gentle European-owner Anna, Julia arrives to prevent another rape:

> "And could you conjecture," replied Editha, "what had disordered the mulatto? I remember her well; she died about a year before my mother."
>
> 'Ah Missey! me know very well—your mother well know too what kill her.—Your fader tease poor mulatoo because she pretty; but Jenny love your moder, having no ting to say with your fader. One night your fader made she drink glass punch—den poor Jenny sleep,—sleep,—sleep,—no strength, no life,—den massa use ill.— Poor Jenny cry so sadly, and tell me—me tell you moder—moder try comfort poor Jenny—Jenny have no comfort—poor Jenny die— Missy not live long—so grieve!" . . . [Editha] was no sooner alone than she gave free vent to her tears; and recollected with horror some circumstances that corroborated Julia's story, such as the affection and pity her mother always expressed for the young mulatto; and the dislike her father had to hear her named (Helme, *The Farmer*, pp. 392–393).[12]

Black and white women confront comparable sexual predations, even the same predators. From a distance, authors are troping the dangers to which these women are subjected in a society ruled by men who resemble neither Felix, Caesar, nor Mr. Edwards.

Another case in point is a poem by the evangelical writer, Mary Stockdale, daughter of indicted publisher John Stockdale. The young, sexually vulnerable Fidèlle of the title sings a dirge on the Middle Passage as she journeys from West Africa to the Caribbean, an indeterminate space where potential anarchy—in the form of slave attacks and suicides—clashes with attempted order and chaotic atrocities:

> An outcast from my native home,
> A helpless maid forlorn,
> O'er dangerous seas I'm doom'd to roam,
> From friends and country torn.
> No mother's smile that soothes my grief;
> A Christian me, beguil'd;
> But ah! he scorns to give relief,
> Or ease a poor black child.
>
> My father now, unhappy man!
> Weeps for his lov'd Fidèlle,
> And wonders much that Christians can
> Poor negroes buy and sell
> O had you heard him beg and pray,
> And seen his looks be wild!
> He cried, "O let me bless this day;
> O spare my darling child!"
>
> But, O! their hearts were hearts of stone;
> They tore me from his arms;
> A Christian savage scoffs to groan
> Caus'd by a black's alarms.
> They chain'd me to this dungeon deep,
> And on my sorrows Smil'd,
> Then left, alas! to sigh, and weep,
> The Slave! the negro child![13]

The condition of the "helpless and forlorn Fidèlle," "beguil'd" by trader-owners, whose fate is bemoaned by a distraught father, hints at a potential choreography of sexual perversions that dooms every slave [woman] to roam, and try to escape. Mary Darby Robinson's "The Negro Girl" solidifies Stockdale's suggestiveness when the mentor-owner in Robinson's poem is encoded as a sexual abuser who motivates Zelma's decision to escape: "My tyrant sought my love," the protagonist states tersely.[14]

These intimations of female violation point to a growing authorial awareness of the frail status of females generally. Granted, situations of middle-class white women and enslaved black women are fundamentally different but in some areas of masculinist exploitation, abuses lap over one another. Lack of protection and rights underpin anxious texts; in their somewhat ironic status as authors with assumed authority, white writers betray the limits of their social power. By illustrating such polarities as bad and good Africans, bad and good Britons, writers expand new possibilities for self-expression while underscoring a nation-wide disquiet about the calamitous consequences of revolution.

SUICIDE

Dual representations of slaves as vengeful or vulnerable rendered them people to be feared or objects of pity or admiration. In the 1790s this latter trope of the loyal or assailable slave broadened to include the most defenseless slave of all—the one about to die—who paradoxically exercised a form of agency that could not be gainsaid.

Aside from *Oroonoko,* the obvious source for this contemporary revival was "The Dying Negro" by Thomas Day that enjoyed overnight success in 1773.[15] Within two years the poem had gone into a corrected third printing. Published the year after Lord Mansfield's misunderstood decision concerning James Somerset's freedom, Day's poem had capitalized on the enormous publicity that Somerset's case attracted. In fact, Day underscored the generally ignored limitations of Lord Mansfield's decision and its negligible effect on slave-owners by versifying a true published report in 1773 about an escaped black slave in Britain. In "The Advertisement" to the poem, Day states: "Having agreed to marry a white woman, his fellow-servant, . . . and [having] procured himself to be baptized; [he was] detected and taken.[16] Day pleaded with the public to accord a just hearing to this tragic hero by recording the slave's grief over the unjust conditions he endured:

> O God of Nature! art thou call'd in vain!
> Did'st thou for this sustain a mortal wound,
> While Heav'n, and Earth, and Hell, hung trembling
>   round?
> That these vile fetters might my body bind,
> And agony like this distract my mind?
> (Day, "The Dying Negro," pp. 172–173)

In different guise, this agonized speaker appears twenty-five years later in "The Negro Boy's Tale: A Poem Addressed to Children" (1795) by Amelia Opie that was still being reprinted in the throes of the emancipation struggle.[17] Its heroes are a young slave, Zambo and his champion, the gentle daughter of a captain who refuses her appeals to let the slave board a ship bound for England and freedom. The overseer on shore who typifies unchristian cruelties provokes Zambo's suicide.

Zambo's dying words underline his gentle love for family and homeland and the horrors of institutionalized slavery. However Eurocentrically conceptualized his language is, he still speaks for and through the experiences of the enslaved:

> It is long time since lass ve meet,
> Ven I vas take by bad Vite man,
> And moder cry, and kiss his feet,
> And shrieking after Zambo ran. . . .
> How glad me vas she did not see
> De heavy chain my body bear;
> Nor close, how close, ve crowded be;
> Nor feel how bad, how sick, de air!
> (Opie, *The Negro Boy's Tale,* p. 4)

Although slaves had spoken versions of child-like Pidgin English since midcentury, from George Ellison's slaves' "Me no wanna leave Massa" to Yamba's dirge, the choice of children's literature and the use of slave-children themselves for this kind of speech reidentified Africans with simplistic mentalities and rank powerlessness.[18] Short of a dead slave, who could be less threatening than a naive slave child pleading "ungrammatically" for help from a kindly but impotent female adolescent. Pidgin English reinforces racial difference, the separation of the other although Benita Parry persuasively argues that a different language augments political strength and the possibility of numberless viewpoints.[19]

The speaker's contention that different shades of complexions cannot occlude a common humanity echoes William Blake's argument in *Visions of Albion* and "The Little Black Boy": as Opie's protagonist puts it:

> Yon cocoa-nut no smooth as silk,
> But rough and ugly is de rind;
> Ope it, sweet meat and sweeter milk

Vidin dat ugly coat ve find.
Ah missa! smiling in your tear,
I see you know what I'd impart;
De cocoa husk de skin I vear,
De milk vidin the Zambo's heart (7).

As David Erdman explains:

> To avoid a chauvinistic interpretation Blake explained that any skin color is a cloud that cannot obscure the essential brotherhood of man in a fully enlightened society, such as Heaven. "These black bodies and this sun-burnt face," said the little black boy, are "but a cloud." If the Negro is free of his black cloud, the little English boy must be likewise free from his "white cloud," which is equally opaque. "When I from black and he from white cloud free," I will "be like him and he will then love me."[20]

Although Zambo's death is meant to garner maximum support for the movement, in economic terms the slave's personal solution defeats the plantocracy head-on. Seemingly stereotyped, the child-victim represents an ontologically self-validating agent pitted against plantocrats whom he symbolically castrates by killing himself, their private property. The dialogue between the slave and the captain's daughter establishes an ethical framework that contrasts sharply with the planters' ruthlessness. Notwithstanding, the plantocracy's economic power still incapacitates Anna's father until it is too late.

Echoing evangelical values, Opie's speaker contrasts the lack of domestic unity while positing strategies of resistance. Anna's subservience to her father parallels Zambo's self-preserving deference to the overseer. Yet both try to subvert the power that a plantocratic-patriarchal combination wields over them. Zambo's fight to the death with the waves, his political and emotional bond with empathetic Anna, signifies human, cross-race harmony, ongoing struggle, and self-consciousness in the fight for freedom and autonomy. The young African transforms himself into his own boss, an activist who refuses the other's values and subverts barbarity in accordance with African religious beliefs. Undercover, the (sub)text draws a misty picture of female suppression and sabotage. In a homiletic closing stanza, the narrator (Opie) praises Anna's "virtuous woe" and the father's "keen remorse." If enough Britons like Anna would commit themselves to the slave's cause, Zambo's death could be averted; charity reverberates as a key response to slavery. Somewhat unconventionally, however,

Anna sheds no tears for Zambo's death, treating his suicide as a legitimate means of escape.

Opie's later poem, "The Lucayan's Song" (1808), about Spanish not British trickery toward indigenous peoples, reminds readers that slaves carried out a successful revolution on Hispaniola: she recontextualizes the idea that forcible relocation and heinous conduct in the name of Christianity demand a harsh price.[21] The memory of San Domingo is a mandatory veiled text. Unapologetically she reverses the relationship of domination, a bold stance, yet muted by the displacement of revolutionary victory from San Domingo to Hispaniola. Her stout philippic against Spanish colonialism interweaves with a diatribe against males who perpetuate that system.

In the autumn of 1797, Frances (Fanny) Holcroft, the daughter of Thomas Holcroft, celebrated radical and treason trial defendant, fashioned another verse-vignette in "The Negro" about a slave whose life hangs in the balance.[22] This protagonist is another feminized but now adult male. His moribundity and mild manner cannot antagonize a panic-stricken public: "This Christian crew,/ the dying Negro can forgive." Torn from his mother and from nature, he lies "transpierc'd with many a streaming wound." His imprecations against the life of a slave shower traditional contempt on pseudo-Christians who allegedly teach "faith, hope and love." The text discreetly contrasts his humble exoneration of corrupt practices with slavers' proliferation of "hatred, woe, wild despair." The "Christian God" should "move thy people's hearts . . . to justice, gentleness, and love." In contrast to Opie's upbeat ending, Holcroft rattles a gruesome warning to planters and traders alike:

> The suffering ceas'd, death chill'd his veins:
> His mangl'd limbs grew stiff and cold;
> Yet whips nor racks inflict the pains
> Men feel who barter Man for Gold
> (Holcroft, "The Negro," p. 286).

The first-person narration endows the slave-protagonist with enhanced awareness. Another pious, sentient slave, symbolically emasculated, enunciates a dignified awareness of socio-political realities.

Not coincidentally, a third member of radical intellectual circles, Mary Darby Robinson represents slave lovers, Zelma and Draco in "The Negro Girl," speaking their woes and their dying.[23] Contemporary readers of periodicals might have spotted Robinson's crosshatching references to another shorter poem she wrote entitled "The Storm" that addresses the same theme.[24] In "The Storm," the protagonists are white sailor William, and his sweetheart Nancy who ardently deplores the slavery that "binds" her beloved to the slave ship. This ship in turn, precipitates personal catastrophe. As Privy Council testimony and Thomas Clarkson's investigations in Bristol a decade earlier bore out, the lives of British seamen seem to have troubled the public more than the lives and deaths of slaves. Robinson's dual version of the dying couple calls to mind the old double standard of Barbary Coast slavery compared to its Caribbean counterpart.

In "The Negro Girl," the couple die together by mutual consent, an eventuality foreshadowed in *Oroonoko* and worked through in Eliza Knipe's poem in 1787 about title characters, Atamboka and Omaza, a similarly resilient, self-determined pair.[25] "Love-lorn" Zelma implores the metaphoric tempest to cease, begging Nature to explain why "she" (Nature) kidnaps Africans when Africans are actually as mentally endowed as Europeans:

> Thou gav'st, in thy caprice, the Soul
> Peculiarly enshrin'd;
> Nor from the ebon Casket stole
> The Jewel of the mind!
> Then wherefore let the suff'ring Negro's breast
> Bow to his fellow MAN, in brighter colours drest (171).

To stress her point about African intellectuality, Robinson has Zelma explain how she became literate. The slavemaster instructed Zelma in human equality only to find his tutelage rebounding; he presses sexual advances after which Zelma flees. The poem stresses the difficulty of attaining formal education, especially for a female slave:

> The Tyrant WHITE MAN taught my mind
> The letter'd page to trace;
> He taught me in the Soul to find
> No tint, as in the face:
> He bade my reason blossom like the tree—
> But fond affection gave the ripen'd fruits to thee
> [Draco] (173).

The poem also reverses a common master-slave relationship because, in this version, the master becomes the giver and the slave-pupil receives the white male middle-class privilege of literacy. Zelma uses instruction and her intellect to enrich the life of her beloved and their community. Shaded in here is the land of shared cultural community to which Prince Naimbana obliquely refers. Understanding the power of literacy, Zelma, representative of all Africans and slaves, attempts to set that power in motion.

And lastly, as if to historicize suicide definitively in the light of San Domingo, a variant on the popular story of Quashi reappears. In his acclaimed anti-slavery essay, James Ramsay had highprofiled Quashi as a noble hero; Hannah More then amplified Ramsay's portrait to punctuate the notion that virtuous Quashi knew his "social place," as all workers should. In "The Slave," Elizabeth Sophia Tomlins recapitulates the tale of Quashi, a slave of the utmost honor and dignity who kills himself rather than risk a lowered self-esteem.[26] After an altercation with his Spanish master, Alvaro, Quashi declares loyalty and love for his master and his subdued passion for Alvaro's sister, "for whom this heart long heav'd with many a groan." Here, incidentally, Tomlin's narrator quietly inserts an answer to traditional ethnocentric charges against Africans of untamed lust. Preferring to die rather than be marked and maimed by his master, Quashi vindicates his imminent act of vengeance and/or self-murder by trouncing slavery:

> But why my Soul this vain recital make?
> Think on my wrongs, and to Revenge awake!
> Think on the guilt of that degen'rate race,
> On Europe's sons, mean, mercenary, base: . . .
> This arm shall strike, this heart shall cease to groan,
> And Europe's dastard Sons the great revenge shall own!
> Then "In *his own gen'rous breast* he plung'd the steel . . .
> To seek the home where happy Spirits dwell
> (Tomlin, *Tributes of Affection,* pp. 100–101).

In Tomlin's version, Quashi's confrontation with an owner who has been accommodated for decades illuminates daily atrocities, profiteering, sabotage, and double-edged conciliatory behavior. Quashi's speech cancels Alvaro's badge of illegitimate authority. But there the text stops short. To represent Quashi as a fictional Toussaint L'Ouverture would incense a 1790s audience, with treason trials fresh in their minds.[27] Instead "The Slave" romantically sanctifies its hero as an active martyr-rebel who undermines the principle of ownership by destroying Alvaro's property (that is, the slave himself). Concurrently, the text champions the slave's right to agency, whatever the cost and by whatever means the slave chooses. In an age that dreaded revolution by the tyrannized, Quashi's story provided an appropriate bromide and an adept challenge.

In these assorted and unprecedented paradigms of moribundity and sexual abuse, authors re-present Europe's other as articulate subjects and self-determining agents in the last extremity. With the abolition movement effectively dismantled, authors revert to earlier thematics of sentimentality and infantilization. White male aggressors tend to be shadowy off-stage presences. Female authors surrender visible subjectivity, index to national and personal anxieties about the welfare of reformers. The speaking "I" now lies partially hidden.

Inevitably, the revolution in San Domingo and Hannah More's *Tracts* are aptly commemorated. Beaten-down slaves have nothing left to live for, not even a heavenly reward, so they take their lives into their own hands. These actions are the flipside of Hector's ferocity. Underscoring the malevolence of slavery explicates and even vindicates San Domingo. The self-effacing, turn-the-other-cheek profile of Holcroft's adult African male epitomizes heroic status when radicals are under siege, taking refuge. Eliciting maximum empathy for a submissive, woebegone individual is Jacobin revenge at its subtlest.

A surprising number of female slaves also appear in highly jeopardized situations.[28] Unspoken wanton murder across gender lines, at the hands of the unchecked who are also the governing, stalks every text. By recoding the reality of San Domingo, authors predict a future that heralds multiple San Domingan victories. None of the slaves, indeed, reach dry land, their lives lived permanently in water at the edge of possibility.[29] Boundary points rather than fixed centers, such as plantation life, have become new sites of resistance and discourse; paths to refashioned identities lie open.

Natural rights are key. By dint of demanding a life worth living and in forfeiting life because near-categorical abjection denies that possibility, tragic heroes and their mediating authors underscore the bitter pill of such an existence. They claim the right to decide between life and death. Instead of missionaries promising objectified victims a hereafter, slaves recognize the limits of toleration, their actions bespeaking a collective denunciation of inhuman exploitation. Allusively all these writings invoke the century-old phenomenon reported by Captain Phillips, talking of Whydaw slaves. What Captain Phillips does not mention is the fact that suicide validates and underwrites fundamental cornerstones of African religious beliefs:

> They often leap'd out of the canoes, boat and ship, and kept under
> water till they were drowned to avoid being taken up and saved

by our boats, which pursued them; they having more dreadful apprehension of Barbados than we have of hell.[30]

In his memoirs, Olaudah Equiano describes his attempt to kill himself on board ship as a commonly understood phenomenon.[31] A serious intervention with bite in traditional master-slave power relationships, suicide is transformed into the final, autonomous act for laboring, remembering, myth-denouncing, suffering individuals. Slaves retain a variety of dignified and moral subject positions in the face of dehumanization. While affirming orthodox African beliefs, suicide destroys the plantocratic economic base in capital goods and machinery. British control is curbed by its own contradictions. The dying of the slaves foreshadows and—borrowing Edward Said's characterization of the copula—IS the dying of the institution.[32]

Feminized moribund African males also enable female writers to assault slavery and displace private and social insecurities about their own powerlessness and apparent relegation to society's borders. They claim moral authority by instructing contemporaries in decent attitudes and practices; in children's texts, they instruct the next generation about the necessity (and obligation) to reverse social wrongs. Since reform is prohibited, their writings subversively attack censorship. Furthermore, many white female authors know full well that they are treated as pieces of property of a different sort when they embark on the marriage market. Centering on suicide, then, enables these authors to throw a doubled focus on the white middle-class female subject. At the level of projection, killing slaves is killing subjugated white females, drawing reluctant attention to conditions that do not meet minimum requirements for a worthwhile existence. Authors are repudiating the trivialization of women that is being promoted throughout the nation, the mode of behavior toward females that the *Anti-Jacobin Review* and anti-Jacobins in general exalt in the late 1790s;[33] in *Letters on Subjects of Importance to the Happiness of Young Females,* for example, Helena Wells typically recommends the "deportment to be observed, on entering into life, in order to conciliate the esteem and affection of others, and, consequently, to facilitate the acquisition of happiness."[34]

Configuring Europe's abject slave-other as a reflection of a white middle-class unitary self speaks to a nadir in women's self-esteem and an attempt to regain some of it in an era of interdiction. Leonore Davidoff's and Catherine Hall's thesis that white middle-class women were much more aware of their own worth than is customarily thought is well supported by these speculations and by authorial displacement of slaves' ordeals.[35] That female writers cannot recontextualize their relationship to society fundamentally circumscribes their view, even at the unconscious level. They cannot historically go beyond a vision of their individuality as a fixed "selfhood," although none of this is obvious. But read against the grain, the construction of slaves is partially modelled on white male counsel to women in middle-class courtesy manuals. Righteously aggrieved slaves obsequiously forgive their oppressors. They love and long for home and family. Unself-regarding, they resign themselves to their fate, aware that sacrifice is integral to the "female condition."

Furthermore, mythologies about African sexuality and coded allusions to the troubling import of sexuality in women's lives come into play around the common vision of uniform loyalty and a coerced moribundity. Alienated suicidal orphans inured to their lot suggest virginity, a refusal to be sullied, a desire in several cases for a merging with water that also works psychologically and metaphorically as the locus of sexual union. As Fidèlle pines away (and dies?) in a "dungeon deep" (the sea), as Zambo dives to death in the receptive waves, and as Nancy joins the drowning William, so Zelma joins her beloved in an oceanic death of women writers longing for primal unity. Preoccupation with water also involves unconscious ideas about "intra-uterine life, . . . existence in the womb, and . . . the act of birth."[36] Sigmund Freud argues that diving, plunging, and sinking into water in dreams is a way of talking about birth in reverse. In that sense, suicide poems return author-slaves to the safety of the womb, a time of harmony. Water imagery fuses African ontology and repressed desire into one symbol of freedom-longing for African slaves and white British women alike; it births a new coalition.

This final array of texts that emerges before the successful passage of the Abolition Bill demonstrates the disintegration of the movement and the absence of an identifiable goal. Many contemporaries knew that abolition was a matter of time. The gendering of middle-class values significantly continued; home and family were sites of value at the heart of every text. Domestic unity was pointedly absent and always desired, family fracture structured in many different ways, and probably the most ordinary motif of all. The abolitionist formulae of describing the kidnapping first, then Middle Passage experiences, and lastly, the process of buying and selling all but departed.

Trustworthy ex-slaves as candidates for the colonial workplace began to appear. Comparable ex-slave workers had already peopled texts during the 1780s in the wake of the Somerset decision while domestic tales of assimilation punctuated the 1790s. But working and waged ex-slaves in the Caribbean suggested, of all things, a general emancipation. The international division of waged labor was making an early though hazy appearance. This concept of waged not slave labor contrasted sharply with conversion, the alternative solution propounded in More's *Tracts.* The white British worker and the ex-slave merge more closely in texts by Helme and Edgeworth, for example, that provide secular options to slavery. They are no longer separated, according to distinct oppressions, as they were in the *Tracts.*

The issue of values also becomes paramount; so does the question of who identifies with whom. Everyone but utter villains—certainly slaves, and ex-slaves—are feminized, suggesting strong though unsystematic support for a gynocentric, quasi-utopian world. At no other time is there such a collectivized matrix of traditionally female-based values. Not to put too fine a point on it, this idyllic notion seems particularly incongruous at a time when any discourse favoring miscegenation induces massive furor. Marginalizing male aggression while denoting altruism as an unchanging practice across gender and race lines blurs distinctions between subject and other, inside and outside. Morally respectable people form a community of sorts, informed by feminocentric values. Everyone is the spiritual equal of everyone else. Only the socio-political aspect of the great chain of being remains.

Slaves have become near-beatified figures, characteristically imaged as women; heroic male slaves display attributes admired in females. Felix and Caesar are dependable workers around the home and plantation, models of sanctity; they obey their owners and thwart rebellion. They are as characteristically Christ-like as humble slaves on the verge of death, unmistakably marked by selfless feelings, women's hallmark. This suggested ethical congruence between slaves and white British females demolishes ancient plantocratic lies about insensate Africans. Slaves now talk more frequently in the first person, and though authorial intervention is almost palpable, slaves assume an existence and a reality not previously seen or heard. Direct speech specifies a physical speaker, multiplies the possibilities of his or her responses, offers more subject positions from which to speak, and projects, displaces, and mediates the colonial other.[37] Male ruling-class values constituted in international and domestic violence receive a not-so-silent drubbing.

What continues unmistakably, however, are class distinctions. Mr. Edwards may be as loving as Zambo but he remains in charge. Within the undifferentiated taxonomy of virtue, there lie layers of domination.

The poems and tales of the 1790s constitute a fairy-tale world of sorts where nice white men, tender black men, and unprotected, cross-class women are subjected to a handful of villains like Alvaro, Jeffries, and Zelma's tyrant. These villains stultify happiness because they control economic power.

The question of Hector and slave revolts remain. At least emotionally, the narrator (Maria Edgeworth?) does not see entirely eye to eye with Caesar. Does she even, one wonders, wryly mock his non-collaborative leadership by naming him after an assassinated Roman emperor disappointed in love? Yet at no point does "The Grateful Negro" suggest that Hector resembles Toussaint L'Ouverture although contemporaries would inevitably have recalled the heroes of that revolution in any text thematizing revolt. The public had enthusiastically received Wordsworth's popular sonnet to L'Ouverture two years earlier. African readers, by contrast, might well have located Hector on a continuum of revolutionary leaders. Even though the narrator invites young people to condone Caesar's actions, the theoretically disparaged revolutionaries possess an energy that spills out and over the stereotyped San Domingan slave caricatures. Hector stands for slaves everywhere who vote for emancipation with their feet.

The only absolute other in raw form is Esther, the woman who practices obeah and poisons the spears, a vilified Eve-like figure who—it is half suggested—mesmerizes and controls Hector himself. This monstrous, Eurocentric depiction of villainous female subalternity, embodiment of dual British worries about women in general and slave insurrectionaries in particular, sites male radicals in a more favorable light.[38] A transcendently evil female figure mitigates customary male villainy whereas Caesar and Edwards are repositories of humility, kindness, charm, and other desirable female qualities.

Within the numerous levels of domination and signification, authorial control remains an issue. By connoting and denoting slaves as insiders and subjects with implied inner lives and active communities, female authors display themselves as self-respecting moral guardians with the right to adjudicate public morals. At one and the same time, authors contain Africans and let them speak for themselves. Mary Poovey tellingly summarizes the intricate relationship of female authors to countless voices and self-identity: "Nearly every woman who wrote was able to internalize a self-conception at least temporarily at odds with the norm." Hence the ease with which women's texts can be doubly read "as acquiescence to the norm and as departure from it." Poovey judiciously emphasizes that "the prevalence of these strategies does not always mean that women writers were conscious of the restrictions they faced or that they deliberately struggled to transcend them."[39]

These multiple vantage points of authors and characters cancel any possibility of unalloyed univocality.[40] All the whispered and unspoken dialogues and constant references to textual outsiders diffuse the unvarying language of pity, charity, and moral pronouncement. Rebel speeches oppose pious observations; dying entreaties infuse objective descriptions; oppositional accounts of slavery by Equiano and Cugoano challenge the stasis and status of Dundas's Bill and the tensions of Bryan Edwards' popular ethnocentric history.

To suggest that a slave is vibrantly audible in these texts is not to suggest that the discourse has dispensed with its traditional Anglo-Africanist assumptions. Slaves are still schematically divided up into good and bad; they are removed from or do not exist in time and place; some are irredeemably pagan. No "natural" African voice is heard. Nonetheless, the very evidence of rebellions at that time speaks more eloquently than anything to potent silences in insurgent-free texts. These silences bespeak rebellion on a global scale. As Maria Edgeworth certainly knew, Hector actively participated in a much larger context of revolts that had recently surged throughout the Caribbean, spurred by the Haitian revolution. Major sites of resistance were Guyana, Grenada, where the revolt led by Fédon involved most of the slaves, St. Vincent with its second Carib war, Dominica, St. Lucia, and especially Jamaica where Maroons waged a fierce war between July 1795 and March 1796.[41]

In subsequent decades, as a result of the evolving attacks on slavery, the largest mass movement in support of emancipation in the history of Britain burst forth, with women visibly in the vanguard.

Chapter 12

Women in the Provinces and Across the Irish Sea: Explosion of Agitation

Let us remember the utter helplessness of the objects of our sympathy,—that they cannot plead for themselves—that they have none in the land of their captivity to plead for them.
—Elizabeth Heyrick, *Apology for Ladies Anti-Slavery Associations, 1828.*

Woman is then compelled, in marriage, . . . to be the literal unequivocal slave of the man who may be styled her husband.
—William Thompson and Anna Wheeler, *Appeal of One Half of the Human Race, 1825.*

Early in the 1820s evangelical Anglican women and Nonconformists, especially Quaker women, established themselves nationally as an emancipationist moral vanguard.[1] Activities in the last fifty years had set the precedent. After a mixture of radical and conservative women had jumped headlong into the 1780s campaign, radicals added natural rights to the agenda in the early 1790s but then gradually immersed themselves in sharp contests over Dissent, the French Revolution, and British women's rights.[2] Hannah More and other evangelical women moved forward in the 1790s with a manifestly religious orientation— salvation mattered most—while more radical-minded women featured a mixture of despairing, loyal, or resistant slaves in prose and poems.[3] Promotion of conversion, education, and commerce in Africa; the infantilization and assimilation of Africans; and the social rehabilitation of the European ungodly—these Anglo-Africanist concerns appeared in adult and children's publications in the decades following the Abolition Act of 1807. As a political battle-ground emancipation lay dormant; Anna Maria Porter, for example, transformed the legendary tale of Inkle and Yarico, emblematic of mercantilist corruption, into a paean of praise for spiritual salvation.[4]

Not until colonial legislatures and Caribbean plantation owners reacted to the Abolition Act—conditions for slaves worsened rather than improved— did agitation resume in earnest. Having promised to renew French slave-trading rights, the Congress of Vienna (1815) restimulated the debate on freedom; within a month eight hundred petitions had flowed into Parliament, the final number of signatures totaling one and a half million from a population of twelve million.[5]

The Society for the Mitigation and Gradual Abolition of Slavery (popularly known as the Anti-Slavery Society) was formed in 1823. During the parliamentary debate of that year on the Emancipation Bill, Foreign Secretary George Canning argued that Christianity and slavery could coexist even though

> the spirit of the Christian religion is hostile to slavery. . . . The sense of Parliament and of the country, has been awakened to the evil, and is determined as soon as possible and expedient, to remedy it; not with *injurious and indiscreet haste, but with a temperate and well considered dispositive to remove a practical defect.*[6]

Canning's determination to manumit slaves in the long run and in the short run to end the flogging of female slaves created critical issues for the campaign and precipitated the involvement of thousands of white British women. The Christian defense of global womanhood was inaugurated in earnest.

Although Thomas Fowell Buxton, the major parliamentary spokesman for emancipation argued that slavery "ought gradually to be abolished," women around the country rejected ameliorative solutions outright.[7] In particular, a Quaker named Elizabeth Heyrick flouted all received notions of female gentility by writing pamphlets demanding immediate and unconditional emancipation.[8]

Heyrick's demand intertextualized the voices of slaves, ex-slaves, and black radicals, oppositional since slavery began. Prior to the publication of her first immediatist tract, the working-class black activists, William Davidson and Robert Wedderburn, had publicly defended African self-determination. Before being hanged for high treason, Davidson defended a people's right to rebel against tyranny:

"Would you not rather govern a country of spirited men, than cowards," he asked with his final words.[9] Robert Wedderburn, a Jamaican living in London who had joined the society of Spencean Philanthropists and opened his own meeting house, was even more explicit. At one of many lively debates in the autumn of 1819, Wedderburn had vigorously concurred when the assembled body unanimously supported a slave's right to kill a master.[10] Urging advocacy of slave resistance, he invited two black West Indian speakers

> to expose a Wesleyan scheme of sending missionaries to the West Indies. Effectively he spent two years in jail for his uncompromising attitudes [he had already denounced anti-slavery petitioning as degrading]." "Prepare for flight," he warned the Jamaican legislature in 1817, "for the fate of San Domingo awaits you."[11]

In addition to the demands of individual black activists living in Britain, the slave rebellion in Demerara that began with a group of forty slaves demanding unconditional freedom from Governor Murray provoked massive public outrage. The specific event propelling infuriated people into the anti-slavery movement was the death in a Demerara jail in February 1824 of ailing missionary John Smith, following his court-martial on the charge of inciting insurrectionary slaves. More than any other single individual at the time, Smith imaged the intransigence and cruelty of slave-owners and colonial bureaucracies. The "trauma of the Smith case," argues Eric Williams, converted ameliorationists into emancipationists.[12]

Before discussing Elizabeth Heyrick's immediatist pamphleteering, I want to sketch the historical context that sparked such outspoken propaganda. Through occasional texts such as *The History of George Ellison* (1774) by Sarah Scott, a certain kind of activism and moral influence had become recognized as middle-class women's domain. As Leonore Davidoff and Catherine Hall explain, provincial women had long wielded power that was inextricably enmeshed with the protracted growth of capitalist relations: "a preoccupation with the domestic as a necessary basis for a good Christian life . . . was integral to the new and evolving ideology. Men [Anglo-Saxon implied] were to be active in the world as citizens and entrepreneurs, women were to be dependent as wives and mothers. . . . Serious Christian men were caught between the desire for a religious life and the need for success in the commercial 'public world.' [That success depended] heavily on wives, family and friends."[13] One of many examples, Candida Cadbury provided "practical and emotional support [that] enabled them to work well." The support of female relatives and friends was "essential for the success of the business." Moreover, to look at practical finance directly, "the *aggregate* of small investments held by women was . . . an important source of capital in early commercial and industrial development."[14]

This frequently unacknowledged financial contribution of women to early capitalist development had by the late 1780s generated self-confident political engagement that was more often than not configured as moral suasion. Still active in the 1830s movement, evangelical Anglicans Hannah More and Rachel Lloyd, relative of Mary Lloyd who was a member of the Birmingham anti-slavery association in 1823, had written and agitated as far back as 1788.[15] This transgenerational presence in the campaign cannot be discounted; repressed energies finally detonated.

Nonetheless, men still "felt the need to systematically contain women and limit their potential," a fact that helped to account for female infiltration into the anti-slavery movement, one of the few extra-domestic arenas permitted them. Denied the "active generation of lasting wealth," they generated instead the wealth of an altruistic value system.[16] Hence paradoxically, as idealized women became a familiar concept, agitation fostered a distinct shift in white women's public image. "The wise true comforter" of the Reverend Charles B. Taylor's contemporary poem entitled "Women," transported women's mission, as it came to be called, outside the home. The assumed separation between women's moral superiority in the domestic arena and the mobility and aggression associated with men was synthesized in the activities and texts of female emancipationists. Women's "ideal of the right," in T. H. Reardon's phrase, had found its niche in the synchronicity of political organizing with charity work.[17] These combined factors promoted the very self-assurance that the much-touted "gentle sway" of women was supposed to be devoid of; women crusaded in the public sphere for legal justice.

Working women in large numbers had resisted the threat of unemployment and technological displacement in certain industries just prior to and during the anti-slavery campaign. Nor did "gentle sway" characterize the demeanor of many laboring-class female activists whose example more leisured evangelical women might well have found inspirational. These activists participated in crowd actions, in machine breaking, in food riots, in trade societies and strikes, especially the 1818 strike, and in female reform societies. The Blackburn Female Reform Society in 1819, for example, stated its intention to "instil into the minds of their children a deep and rooted hatred for their tyrannical rulers."[18]

Historically speaking, the time was ripe for female contestation. Permission was being tacitly granted, taboos quietly broken. Across class lines, women of all descriptions—unemployed, radical, homebound, provincial, evangelical, politically peripheral—were taking to the presses and the streets. The fight to pass the emancipation bill loomed large in their unstinting exertions.

ELIZABETH HEYRICK

Elizabeth Heyrick's boldly innovative pamphlets inspired female participation in the anti-slavery movement. Provincial women's writings, for example, started appearing after the House of Commons debate began in March 1823, two months after the Bill was introduced. Petitions flooded Parliament. By 1826, the *Anti-Slavery Monthly Report* records that

> The number of Anti-Slavery petitions which have been presented to the House of Commons in the last session amounts to 674. Several more would have been presented on the last day of the session had an opportunity been afforded. A like number was presented to the House of Peers. Many of these petitions conveyed the sentiments (almost always unanimous) of large county and other meetings, at which the whole subject of Colonial Slavery was fully and freely discussed; and all of them were numerously subscribed by persons of every class. The petition from London contained 72,000 signatures; that from Manchester 41,000; that from Glasgow 38,000; that from Edinburgh 17,000; that from the country of Norfolk 38,000; and from other places in a like proportion.[19]

In 1824, Heyrick wrote four pamphlets that advocated emancipation forthwith and a campaign to refuse the purchase of slave-grown sugar, tea, and coffee; in contemporary parlance, she proposed an economic boycott. By 1828 Heyrick had seven pamphlets to her credit.[20] In between, she called for people to support only those parliamentary candidates who backed immediacy in the general election. Shortly after the first pamphlet appeared, women in Birmingham (Heyrick was district treasurer) established the first Ladies Anti-Slavery Association, independent of the centralized London anti-slavery head-quarters.[21]

Heyrick's background as well as a changing political climate explain her audacity. Born in Leicester and growing up in the dissenting home of a wealthy hosiery manufacturer, her father an admirer of Thomas Paine, she met such outspoken luminaries as John Wesley and Joseph Priestley. After her husband's unexpected death, she became a Quaker. Hardworking and committed to social justice, she believed that slavery contravened divine law and was a "fundamental sinfulness that demanded it be crushed at once."[22] Leadership roles, in her view, were appropriate for women. Heyrick's membership in the Society of Friends with its atypical support for independent female thought and action clearly determined her nonconformist conscience and political radicalism.

As the former Elizabeth Coltman, Heyrick had addressed an inflammatory pamphlet "The Warning" to Britain in 1805 that predicted the end of the world if depravity—defined as tyranny, a love of superstition, and martial intentions—did not cease. In delivering millennial warnings, Coltman echoed seventeenth-century radical sectaries like Elizabeth Hooten in the age of the Civil War. But times and issues had changed; slavery (not lack of freedom of worship) now absorbed and, in Heyrick's language, cursed the nation. Entitled *Immediate, not Gradual Abolition; or, An Inquiry into the shortest, safest, and most effectual means of getting rid of West Indian Slavery,* Heyrick's first tract in 1824 denounced male gradualist politics as illusory and advocated immediate, unconditional emancipation. As her message rapidly spread throughout Britain that year and North America the next, eminent abolitionists were quick to adopt its argument.[23] Heyrick had touched a raw national nerve, calling on "the whole nation . . . to divide itself into the active supporters, and the active opposers of slavery; there is no longer any ground for a neutral party to stand upon" (Heyrick, *Immediate, Not Gradual Abolition,* p. 4). Only slightly below the surface, she asked the nation to side with contumacious slaves.

She attacked the "tricks and impostures practiced by the colonial assemblies, to hoodwink the people, to humbug the Government, and to bamboozle the saints as the friends of emancipation are scornfully termed." Why should the emancipation of slaves from "the gripe of a robber or an assassin—out of the jaws of a shark or a tiger, . . . be gradual? . . . Must hundreds of thousands of human beings continue to be disinherited from those inherent rights of humanity that a few noble lords and honourable gentlemen may experience no privation of expensive luxury. . . . And to what inheritance, or birthright, can any mortal have pretensions so just . . . as to liberty?. . . . The West Indian planter and the people of this country, stand in the same moral relation to each other, as the thief and the receiver of stolen goods?" (Heyrick, *Immediate, Not Gradual Abolition,* pp. 11, 15, 4). Heyrick summarized daily atrocities suffered by the slave, "compelled to labour without wages,—branded, chained, and flogged at the caprice of his owner" (Heyrick, *Immediate, Not Gradual Abolition,* p. 13). In a long postscript about the Demeraran uprising, she reminded readers of gruesome punishments meted out by colonists: a thousand lashes to individual slaves and working in chains for life.

Heyrick's choice of a postscript to document these atrocities does more than irradiate her engagement with *realpolitik.* The relegation to a postscript of subaltern history might be more than the tacked-on addition of late-breaking news and could suggest some suppressed personal-political conflict; a central tension exists, perhaps, between an ardent desire for emancipation that inevitably denies future political control to potentially freed slaves. If emancipation were left to slaves alone, Europeans would lose more territory and profits. Heyrick shies from the boundary intersection of rebellion and humanitarianism. At a conscious level, she identifies ethically and emotionally with the rebels. Indeed, by making their oppositional presence so focal, Heyrick turns the podium over to resistant slaves and lets their ringing voices speak for themselves. This discourse on anti-colonial insurgence and its reprisals sites Heyrick alongside slave rebels on a transhistorical continuum of struggle, activists executing complementary critical strategies. But the class conflict between British governmental authority and slaves' resistance to that authority—the colonial imperative in other words—persistently undercuts that message: she is still a complicitous colonizer *de facto* yet a committed radical ally.[24] Agitation that is dominated by colonizers (with slave rebels coded as a second front) ensures the maintenance of social hierarchies.

Combining traditional with untraditional elements, Heyrick also tropes gendered evangelical tenets throughout her polemic. She deplores the fracture of slave family life and the sexual molestation of female slaves. One mutineer "was sold and separated from his wife and family of ten children, after a marriage of eighteen years. . . . Another was a slave of no common intellect whose wife [was] forced to become the mistress of an overseer. . . . Such provocations, added to quotidian privation, seem beyond human endurance, and might instigate 'the very stones to mutiny'." Heyrick attempts to paint part of the community's inner life; she stresses the intellects of slaves and boldly reminds readers of sexual abuses. Collective struggle is her recommended solution: "the hydra-headed monster of slavery will never be destroyed by other means, than the united expression of individual opinion, and the invited exertion of individual resolution" (Heyrick, *Immediate, Not Gradual Abolition*, p. 23). Rioting slaves are implicitly inscribed in her call for "individual resolution."

Practical as well as philosophical, Heyrick calls on decent-minded people to refuse to buy Caribbean produce. She reminds readers that this tactic had been advanced "thirty years ago . . . [as] the [potential] death blow to West Indian slavery."[25] By citing the San Domingo revolution in 1791 and emphasizing that whites in San Domingo were killed only *during* slavery, Heyrick discredits popular conceptions that freed slaves would either massacre whites or refuse to work. She ridicules the idea that Africans, enslaved by Christians, would embrace Christianity and censures Foreign Secretary Canning for not forcibly implementing his ameliorative proposals. Forcefully she condemns his ineffectuality over the flogging of female slaves, accusing him of "having done nothing, or worse than nothing; with being satisfied . . . while a law . . . prevail[s] in every island of the West Indies, except Trinidad, which authorizes a female stripped in the presence of her father, husband or son, and flogged with a cart whip!" (Heyrick, *Immediate, Not Gradual Abolition*, p. 20). Once again, she assaults black and white women's estate and applauds revolt as a necessity. Additionally, in response to an evolving cultural climate that codes women as inviolable and causes men to recoil in Parliament at the idea of coerced female nudity, she introduces a new system of gendered signification for slaves, the troping of female flogging.

In a second pamphlet, Heyrick even more conspicuously validates female power. Addressing a white middle-class female readership, she decries men as perpetrators of slavery, abusers of women, and parliamentary opponents of emancipation. Without women, she contends, the campaign would disintegrate: "Never were better instruments thought of for the furtherance of our cause . . . [and] of great use in increasing the public interest in this momentous question." Even "noble veterans" like Thomas Clarkson who "furnished . . . volumes of well-authenticated facts are now, in the bitterness of successive disappointment looking to us for cooperation in their final report." She continues: "These devoted philanthropists have been our pioneers . . . [and have] spared us the labour of enquiry and investigation."[26]

Heyrick's rhetorically strategic reference to women as "weak instruments" with "sensitive natures" ironically highlights their very commitment to the cause and the centrality of female concerns (Heyrick,

Immediate, Not Gradual Abolition, p. 4). Her exclusive address to women underscores their determined separation from the institution. Acutely aware of the upheaval caused to family life and the coarse coercion of female slaves, women must use their "unlimited access ... to the hearts and consciences of our own sex [to] withdraw its [slavery's] resources and undermine its foundation" (Heyrick, *Immediate, Not Gradual Abolition,* p. 11). Mancunian women in the first campaign had unified black and white women on a similar political basis; multigenerational demands criss-crossed and reemerged. In retaliation, Heyrick encourages a door-to-door educational campaign and abstention from Caribbean products. With "zealous exertion" altruistically inspired, people had to champion immediatism for the sake of 800,000 "fellow subjects," instruments of God's word.

Heyrick's final address recuperates a traditional portrait of prostrate slaves wrenched from their families, almost as if she felt obliged to back off from the logical extension of her argument; instead of championing African self-determination, she dilutes the necessity for revolt and surrenders an authentic portrait of African culture and history to commonplace stereotypes. She recapitulates the safe popular argument that slaves cannot represent themselves. This momentary shift to received opinion only serves to underline Heyrick's own social construction and the extent of her challenge to convention.

Africans are no longer the maltreated insurgents of the first pamphlet but silent victims who depend on outside intervention. This complex form of Anglo-Africanization—indistinguishable at the time from ardent support—in which British women vehemently pamphleteer, drawing on irrefutable statistics and facts, is unprecedented in women's anti-slavery discourse. Commitment to emancipation transverses suppressed apprehension of an impending post-emancipation era in which the future of Britain colonialism will have to be confronted head on. Heyrick has changed the discourse and the process of objectification. The "civilizing mission" has been transvaluated into a pro-emancipation mission.

Furthermore, the dialogues of silenced slaves echo louder than ever.[27] To call for immediate emancipation in the name of human love silently validates the right to fight. Heyrick's pamphlets evoke past writings and activities of revolutionary slaves and ex-slaves as well as those of African contemporaries; the extensive debate on the Demeraran revolt also informs her text. The dialogue between Heyrick and the plantocracy, moreover, was masked. Deriding the very idea of neutrality, she launches easily into direct denunciation.

Heyrick's victory-bent voice sounded an early warning, too, that the fight for white British women's rights was not far off; female anti-slavery strategies had chalked a starting point. Her energetic philippics and demands constituted a crucial early stage in white women's imminent struggle for rights and more independence. And on a more personal note, that such energy and flouting of the "female role" took its toll is suggested by her friend Susanna Watts' grim comment on the negative reactions leveled against women who engaged in controversial activities. They needed, Watts stated, to be made of "invulnerable brass."

LADIES ANTI-SLAVERY ASSOCIATIONS

Although the precise influence of Elizabeth Heyrick's pamphlets on mushrooming Ladies Anti-Slavery Associations is hard to determine, Heyrick's radical demands ultimately appeared in their manifestoes. By contrast, however, members evaded public confrontations in their own name and opted not to denounce compensation. Certainly it seems no coincidence that on April 8, 1825, the West Bromwich Ladies' Society for the relief of Negro Slaves was the first, according to their own testimony, to issue an anti-slavery manifesto. Among its illustrious membership was Heyrick herself as district treasurer, Quaker Mary Lloyd and the evangelical Anglican Lucy Townsend as its secretaries, and Heyrick's close friend Susanna Watts an esteemed member; each woman held a distinguished reputation for good works. The fact that this original "Ladies Anti-slavery Association" did not advocate immediatism with the bold theorist of that position in its midst was understandable. In order to found that first group, Heyrick and other supporters of immediatism avoided alienating potential members. They probably thought that compromising with gradualists among their members would gain more lasting support; it would help them negotiate toward a position closer to immediatism.

On the other hand, determined associationists, white, largely middle-class, Dissenting and evangelical Anglican women, openly disregarded the opinions of male abolitionist counterparts: "No man can wish . . . for immediate emancipation; it can only be done gradually," declared William Allen, while James Cropper, reputedly embarrassed by Heyrick's pamphlets, was still searching in 1829 for a plan that freed slaves in thirty years. "The Abolitionists . . . almost universally have given up in hopeless despair the present existing race of slaves as unfit subjects for general emancipation," wrote another campaigner in 1827.[28]

Members also evinced a broader range of gendered concerns that included motherhood, education, and an end to the exploitation of female slaves. They also chose not to antagonize profiteers. The principle at stake was the same one applied by Friends to Africans: the "absolute necessity of an inward and spiritual grace for everyone" despite the difficulty of its attainment: "in the performance of these efforts of mercy, we abstain as much as possible from needlessly offending our Brothers, the West India Planters, while we use every proper exertion in aid especially of our Sisters, the Female Negro Slaves." Nevertheless the group's concessions to political orthodoxy lasted only eight months, at which point Lucy Townsend and Mary Lloyd signed an amended set of fifteen resolutions that included Heyrick's abstaining proposal. The complex debates waged during that time are not hard to imagine when "loving christianity" is coming to the rescue of slaves. Emancipationist discourse opened a new avenue to self-authorization and a way to oppose mandated sexual difference:

> This Society, convinced that abstinence from the use of Slave culti-vated Sugar, is one of the best modes to which recourse can be had to express its abhorrence of the system of Colonial Slavery ... earnestly desires, that its members will endeavour by their influence, as well as by their example, to promote the exclusive use of the productions of free labour in the neighborhoods in which they reside.

Activists extended the age-old female practice of body-denial and self-sacrifice in the cause of virtue to their families as well as themselves. By refusing Caribbean sugar, tea, and coffee and surrendering leisure time, they were subtly arguing that women around the world were entitled to a Christian way of life. As recognized guardians of home and children, they denounced the denial of this sacred role to African women and used their own role as consumers to restore families to wholeness, challenging plantocratic self-indulgence with mass asceti-cism. The attack on slavery conjoined with female self-empowerment; race and gender oppression criss-crossed yet again. Additionally, in their determined mobility, they obeyed cultural fiats to help the needy but betrayed alienation in both their actions and their language of displacement.

Urging reform represented a transcendence of former practices for women. Frank Prochaska has documented the existence of hundreds of late eighteenth-and early nineteenth-century charitable societies that boasted female subscribers. Rachel Lloyd was one of several whose life spanned fifty years of political activism and such cross-generational agitation helps to explain the immediate adoption of the boycott—urged by Lloyd as far back as 1788—and unconditional emancipation. But the extent of anti-slavery groups in the 1820s that favored a boycott still remains unclear. Certainly passionate demonstrations had stirred London and Manchester in the 1780s and provided an organizational model for the later movement. Moreover, in a well-known tour of provincial England in the 1790s, Thomas Clarkson had been astounded at the amount of pro-boycott action. More conventionally, but still with an eye to social change, women had also managed and predominantly subscribed to at least thirteen societies while substantially contributing to upward of 120 charitable societies, among them the London Missionary Society (1795), the Institution for Rendering Assistance to Shipwrecked Mariners (1808), the Peace Society (1816), and the Children's Friend Society (1830).[29] In the 1820s, besides, no revolutions catapulted on the scene—as the French and San Domingan revolutions had done—only to cause the curtailment of popular agitation.

Because of their inextricable connection to on-going parliamentary debate, associations circulated a counterdiscourse of women's resolutions around the country for the next ten years; from 1826 to 1831, the number of groups increased from four to thirty-nine per year, and in 1831 women subscribed £536 4s.3d. out of a total of £3399 17s.3d.[30] "Indeed from the mid-1820s onward the formation of Ladies Anti-Slavery Associations became a particular abolitionist goal. . . . They began to have political impact. . . . As early as 1826 the *Anti-Slavery Reporter* was struck by the proliferation of ladies anti-slavery associations."[31]

The Aberdeen anti-slavery society in March 1825, for instance, appealed to female Aberdonians for assistance:

> To the Ladies in this City, and throughout the country, the Committee appeals with confident hopes of success. The subject is worthy of their attraction. By their well-directed and persevering exertions in acquiring an accurate knowledge of the numerous hardships endured by the Slaves, and communicating the same in their domestic and social circles, it is almost impossible to calculate the happy effects that may result. In various parts of England, any amiable and highly-accomplished Females are now devoting some of their leisure hours to this object, in the most exemplary manner, and are

effecting a great change on public opinion. May their example be speedily followed here![32]

In his memoirs, Anglican emancipationist Sir George Stephen informed the world that "none of the antislavery meetings were well attended till after it was agreed to admit ladies to be present ... Their admission was long resented on the ground that their presence lowered the dignity of the subject."[33] The next year, the *Reporter's* editor noted that "Anti-Slavery Associations, and particularly of Ladies, are multiplying, one of whose objects is to discourage the use of slave-grown sugar . . . and to promote the substitution of that grown by free labor."[34] After 1828 women visibly dominated the movement.[35] Enthusiastically they collected subscriptions, distributed materials, solicited new recruits, gathered signatures for petitions (often women only), and discouraged people from buying Caribbean sugar, tea, and rum.[36] Accordingly, their actions contradicted orthodox notions of a female essentialism that encoded women as innately virtuous and self-sacrificial. The workbags of female abolitionists in Sheffield, for example, contained copies of the *Jamaican Gazette,* Clarkson's "Argument," excerpts from the *Christian Observer* about slavery and education, as well as pleas by Society members that recipients spread the word. Proceeds went to "circulating information," the relief of "neglected and deserted negroes" in Antigua, and promoting the "education of British slaves."[37] Their activities became critical enough in organizing public meetings, [East Indian] tea parties, and needlework groups to provoke a famous letter to *The Times* by a pro-slavery sympathizer:

> In this neighbourhood we have antislavery clubs, and antislavery needle parties, and antislavery tea parties and antislavery in so many shapes and ways that even if your enemies do not in the end destroy you by assault, those that side with you must give you up for the weariness of the subject and resentment of your supineness.[38]

The monthly volumes of the *Anti-Slavery Reporter* reinforced the energetic presence of these newly formed associations. Moral tracts condoned agitation in the name of the preservation of family life and the annihilation of the sin of slavery: " 'feminine modesty' would not be offended if they [the female abolitionists] advocated the cause to friends and family or met with ladies in the neighbourhood to make plans. Can a woman be reproved for stepping out of her character and becoming a political character if the cause of *innocent persons* be involved?"[39]

In 1833 Quakers Anne Knight and Marie Tothill collected 187,000 signatures on a petition so huge that it took four Members of Parliament to carry it to the House of Commons.[40] At the same time—and this factor might explain the quick decline in extra-domestic agitation after 1834—male emancipationists expressed fear about the encroaching power of women. As a case in point, when they reproduced desirable models of women's associationist resolutions, men used the Liverpudlian, not the more radical Birmingham model. Many men wanted women to confine their activities to fund-raising rather than political activism. One popular pamphlet, *A Dialogue,* dealt specifically with husbands' objections to wives' public works.

In slave-owning society, white British women had found the "perfect image of tyranny and despotism" that men exerted over all women. Just as abolitionist predecessors had projected fears about close-to-home inequities into their texts, so women of the 1820s condemned the economic and sexual exploitation of female slaves in a fusion of their spiritual and secular roles. Slavery, summed up a contemporary, "practically insults the feelings of every female on earth."[41]

And nowhere was this double-voiced discourse more evident than in the anger expressed in many provincial associationist resolutions over the flogging of female slaves. Point six of the Sheffield Association's Report of 1827 that addressed the cessation of physical torture in general and female abuse in particular illustrates the point:

> That this Society continue its exertions for the amelioration of the condition of the oppressed children of Africa, until the time may come when the lash shall no longer be permitted to scourge the unhappy Negro slave, or lacerate the persons of helpless Females; when our fellow-creatures shall no longer be advertised for Sale, or sold like beasts at a West Indian Slave Market, and when every Negro Mother, protected by British laws, shall press a free-born infant to her bosom.[42]

A comparable thirty-two page report drew on information from the *Anti-Slavery Reporter* about female flogging and the outrage directed at the Jamaican assembly for refusing to outlaw the practice and debating instead whether the whipping of women should exclude "indecent exposure" (p. 7). A four stanza poem by evangelical spokeswoman Charlotte Elizabeth Tonna on flogging inserted into that report, berates the very notion of violating "the female's modest pride" (p. 8).

The prominence devoted to female flogging terminated once and for all protracted efforts to decorporealize, and hence desexualize and disempower slaves. Sexual abuse that earlier texts only alluded to became a focal issue. In the parliamentary debate in 1823, Tory Foreign Secretary George Canning, successfully watered down abolitionists' original proposals, but eclipsed Buxton in his condemnation of flogging. (Along with Wilberforce and Zachary Macaulay, Buxton did not oppose flogging.) Invoking the patriarchal idea of protected womenhood, plantocratic member of parliament Charles Rose Ellis, Canning's close friend, decried "the indecent punishment of females with the whip"; putting an end to flogging, moreover, reaffirmed an eighteenth-century conservative compulsion with the reformation of manners.[43] Women could be slaves but absolutely no woman's body should be publicly exposed and violated.

Female abolitionists argued differently from male allies who declined to denounce flogging on the grounds that slaves, like all men and women who did not "naturally" belong in the ruling class, should confine themselves to a divinely allotted place. The genealogy of emancipationist discourse was responding to political renegotiations. Thomas Buxton, for example, disagreed with his sister-in-law, the prison reformer Elizabeth Fry, that the flogging of female prisoners should cease.[44] Proclaiming solidarity with slavewomen, white British women collectively condemned the idea that any woman should be stripped naked and beaten. The town of Cork in Southern Ireland spawned a society devoted to the same ends. This choric denunciation of misogynous abuse—against slavewomen as well as supposedly free British women—rang through women's texts for ten years and sounded fiercely discordant feminist dialogues. Most audible were the voices of white women who knew of or might have experienced marital violence and separation from child, husband, beloved; present, too, were the voices of women in years to come who would urge women's rights, women with different religious beliefs but comparable political conviction. Small wonder, then, that ladies' groups around the country read "the *Anti-Slavery Reporters* and other tracts aloud . . . in each others' homes."[45] In the name of public morality and family protection, women could project feelings of rage and disempowerment against a male-oriented dispensation. Fury at flogging and forced "immodesty" had become, or rather they had rendered it, an acceptable mode of expression. Gender had always featured in the slave paradigm but its emphasis was now much more explicit. Heyrick's pamphlets and Charlotte Tonna's mettlesome poem were undoubtedly part of at-home family readings.[46] Doing God's work was synonymous with lauding intrepid heroines. In noticeable contrast, resolutions rarely addressed the whipping of male slaves; any attention in that direction, especially if it involved nakedness, would have been pushing too far against traditional boundaries. Male, not female, slaves, moreover, were thought of as revolutionaries so their marginalization reinforced sexual difference and retained otherness as a vital presence.

Thus paradoxically, even though writers spoke insistently on behalf of and about slaves and even though slave voices were theoretically silenced, the gap between the colonizer and the colonial other narrowed in some respects. At the tensest point of separation—when writers were recognized nationally as ardent advocates and slaves reduced to a categorical alterity were subjected to Anglo-Africanist solutions—texts overflow with conflicts inherent in white female writers' cultural status.

Furthermore, in another seeming paradox that echoed Heyrick's, while female authors relegated Africans to a timeless mass of suffering humanity, as others for whom women spoke, they also wore their own mask of anonymity. Representing a certain provincial district *en masse,* without appending their names to polemics as did Heyrick, they surrendered individuality. Most likely, they were glad of a collective voice to avoid charges of personal forwardness.

These all-out reformist writings and activities by women in the provinces quickly spread. Familiar names—Amelia Opie's is one—reappeared, while new names connected through family and friendship with such earlier abolitionists as Mary Steele, friend of Mary Scott, published dauntless propaganda for the first time. Opie's and More's most popular works ("The Negro Boy's Tale" and "The Sorrows of Yamba," respectively) in all their reconfirming ethnocentric simplifications of Africans, were republished; popular contemporary poets, Laetitia Landon known as L. E. L. and Felicia Hemans underscored bondage in their verses.[47] Susanna Watts edited a periodical and wrote several poems that execrated slavery, both metaphorically and overtly. The title page of *The Anti-Slavery Album* (1828) that reissued "Yamba" featured a verse tribute to female activism that assumed a female readership. Nationwide, women had become thoroughly identified as writers and agitators.

> Natives of a land of glory!
> Daughters of the good and brave!
> Listen to the Negro story;—
> Hear, and help the suffering Slave.[48]

THE BOW IN THE CLOUD

A member of the women's association in Sheffield, Mary Anne Rawson compiled and edited a four hundred-page volume of anti-slavery verse and prose, *The Bow in The Cloud* (1834), which featured forty men and fourteen women.[49] Like Mary Lloyd, Rawson was a second generation anti-slaveryite. So the fact that their associations, Birmingham and Sheffield respectively, were among the most outspoken was probably no coincidence. Rawson's anthology, however, toned down associationist demands. But at the same time it included less orthodox issues because, first, the majority of contributors were men, some of whom, like Thomas Pringle, preferred women to raise funds rather than actively agitate. Second, since associations were political in nature, Rawson saw *The Bow* as propaganda along somewhat more spiritual lines. Her decision to omit a contribution that eulogized a slave leader underscores that direction. Third and related, since the anthology was *originally* scheduled to appear as part of the emancipation campaign, then a spiritually oriented volume might have been seen as appropriately complementing door-to-door agitation, one that was quite likely to sell well, at least among the already converted. Campaigning while men were at work was one thing; having a volume of poetry and prose on display at home that doubled as a how-to-agitate book was another thing altogether. Certainly the anthology illumined women's immersion in the movement as polemicists as well as their ecumenical diversity, but it stopped far short of championing agitation as the sole, indispensable tactic. Among its contributors were congregationalists Eliza Conder and Ann Taylor Gilbert, Agnes Bulmer of the Wesleyan Methodists, Unitarians Jane Roscoe Hornblower and Sarah Joanna Williams, Quaker Mary Howitt, and Anglican evangelicals Lucy Townsend and Charlotte Elliott. The latter, like Hannah More, was attached to the Clapham Sect.

The majority of women's poems underscore evangelical tenets, both echoing and diverging from associationist demands. The poets make no effort to separate themselves from the speakers in political terms. In "Rest," by Anglican evangelical Maria Benson, conventionally amassed slaves are promised compensation in heaven if not on earth while Sarah J. Williams' text, "A Voice from the Land of Bondage," suggests that Christians can civilize those "whose Powers have to themselves been lost . . . to give an anchor to the soul." Reconstituting the politics of domesticity, Quaker Mary Howitt sketches the agonies of a fieldworker forced to leave her sick infant to die. But the concluding ecstatic cry to her dead child in heaven—"Thou Art Here" (in itself an unorthodox Quaker position)—signals the ultimate significance of Christian afterlife.

Ann Gilbert seeks recognition for the common bond of maternality between white British and African women, in yet another instance of a subtly anti-patriarchal stance based on connections among women.[50] The former have a duty to help because an injury to one is an injury to all:

> Mothers,—the fair, the firm, the free,
> Of England's vaunted isle,
> Tell me if griefs like this shall be,
> and you be still the while?
> No!—strong in woman virtue rise!
> And heed the negro mother's cries!

Unitarian Jane Roscoe, daughter of the celebrated William Roscoe and herself a poet and member of the Brooke Farm Community, also foregrounds an African mother whose blood-curdling shriek symbolizes the grief of the mother-child fracture yet implies the possibility of fiery resistance. Entitled "The African Mother. A Fact," the sonnet depicts a trader who persistently kidnaps babies. "She would sit/ For hours, and in her arms encradle it . . . Again the Spoiler" until finally she cries out to God about the injustice:

> In thoughts of fire her childlessness she felt:
> The light of madness flashes from her eye!
> And loud to Heaven ascends her wild appealing cry!

The spiritual dimension of the Demeraran uprising surfaces in numerous cross-generic references to missionaries. Ann Gilbert's "Negro Infant" is an orthodox object of sorrow until a missionary-savior brings knowledge of Christ that joyfully transforms a potentially intolerable life. In her "real-life" tale of Pierre Sallah, Dinah Ball describes how Sallah, a benevolent Gambian "Negro-slave," became a religious instructor after a missionary visits "his afflicted brethren of the Jaloff tribe." After Sallah converted many Africans—an indirect validation of Britain's colonial installation of indigenous rulers—his owner agreed to ransom him for fifty pounds, an amount that was raised rapidly in 1830 by a Dublin missionary society.

Charlotte Elliott yoked graphic portrayals of torture and potential suicide with endorsements of slave marriages and conversion. Superscribed "Written after hearing Mr. Buxton's reply to Mr. Canning's speech March 1824," the "dying negress" of the title speaks her mind:

> Now, in vain his threats will urge me,
>   Hark, the blood-stained whip resounds!
> But the lash no more can scourge me;
>   Death is binding up my wounds.
>
> Yet, though *they* are fresh and bleeding,
>   And for me no cure remains,
> There are tortures far exceeding
>   Those the *outward* frame sustains.
> Scars deface my limbs all over;
>   Burning brands have scorched my skin;
> But, couldst thou my heart uncover,
>   Wounds more painful bleed within.

Alongside the conventional troping of conversion, motherhood, and family unity that links *The Bow* with *Cheap Repository Tracts* across generations of women is a limited attentiveness to somewhat less conventional demands urged by Elizabeth Heyrick and sister-associationists. Dinah Ball in "Hope," for instance, the superscription of which reads "Written after First hearing of the formation of Ladies Anti-Slavery Associations," calls on sister Britons to abandon their usually passive roles:

> Is there hope? Yes, if exerted,
>   One untried, resistless power,
> Modest, quiet, unasserted,
>   Patient through the darkest hour.

Implying (but only implying) support for the boycott, she ends by calling such political ferment the "bliss" that "Heaven reserves . . . for you." Just as radically, Eliza Conder's "The Birthright of Britons" argues that freedom is or should be a universal right.

Lucy Townsend, one of the secretaries of the West Bromwich Association that included Heyrick, applauds emancipation, notably in a poem that would have found no place in the original anthology, conceived as propaganda for the 1820s campaign exclusively. (Rawson's reasons for publishing it after emancipation remain unknown.) Townsend implores readers in "The Decision" to "wipe the Captive's Tear," since slaves are powerless victims to be sympathized with, loved, and protected. In another poem celebrating the Bill's successful passage in 1833, Agnes Bulmer's "The Negro is Free" congratulates Britain and patriotic activists for complementing the abolitionist victory of 1807. "The trumpet of justice sound/ O Albion! the happy, the favored, the free." Even a preponderantly religious text like *The Bow* invalidated evangelical Quaker Joseph Gurney's characterization of emancipationist women as invisible auxiliaries—"keen-minded wives and daughters had helped men draft petitions, had served as unpaid secretaries and had raised substantial funds for the cause."[51]

Yet spiritually oriented as it was, omissions to the anthology still reveal important splits over slavery among the female evangelicals. Rawson's countrywide solicitations elicited refusals from at least two popular evangelical writers, Mary Anne Sherwood and Barbara Hoole Hofland, who wrote elsewhere about slavery and conversion. In a letter dated May 17, 1826, four years after a tale about freeing slaves in Sierra Leone entitled *The Recaptured Negro,* Sherwood informed Rawson in her reply that

> perhaps the knowledge I have acquired abroad of the characters and general habits of the Africans and other half civilized persons makes me see the more danger in interfering with them than I should otherwise do and makes me more conscious than I should otherwise be, that our exteriors should at present be chiefly devoted to the promotion of their spiritual and intellectual good.[52]

Three years later she accentuated this refusal with another; she could not promote emancipation because "the matter is too high for me."

Barbara Hofland's reply to Rawson in 1826 recasts the message of an earlier tale she wrote about a recalcitrant white creole, Matilda of the title, who finally converts to Christianity because of her black servant Cato's virtuous example:

> My own opinion of the case will not allow me to unite in any plan which has a tendency to irritate the minds of the Negroes and render the difficulties under which the Planters now labour and have long laboured greater than they are.[53]

These replies by Sherwood and Hofland stress the fact that political division within the ranks of evangelical females is largely based on degrees of Anglo-Africanist beliefs and fantasies. When women publicized these ideas, they functioned unwittingly as agents of colonial domination. Concurrently, the promotion of these ideas might well be linked to the needs of these female authors to vent repressed anger at their own gender domination. Given the extent of inhibition and denial, however, the links between gender and race oppression generally stand unacknowledged. When Africans are undifferentiated as subhuman aggressors and configured as altogether separate from the authors in question, then emancipation is unthinkable, conversion the only recourse. The future consolidation of "Dark Continent" ideology haltingly advances. With some sense of linkage, however inchoate and probably based on the principle of even-handed justice despite contemporary attitudes, Heyrick wants immediate unconditional emancipation and a boycott. Many of the associationists follow suit and support these demands, but do so less vociferously and often anonymously. Few of the contributors to the *Bow* were openly in sympathy with radical demands; for the most part they stress the sinfulness of slavery and its irreligious interference with motherhood and family harmony.

Unpublished notes to Rawson's manuscript reveal further complexities and explicitly spell out the pervasive European fears of resistance by slaves themselves that silently inform many anti-slavery texts. Specifically Rawson rejected a thirty-two stanza poem by Dinah Ball that extols the revolutionary slave leader, Toussaint L'Ouverture. The following stanzas that constitute a manifesto of self-determination in fiction affirm that Rawson shied from infusing the anthology with a radical message that constituted a classic European nightmare:

> When Europe's unrelenting hand had swayed,
> With Scorpion rod, Domingo's land of slaves,
> And Negro vengeance had her deed repaid . . .
> Benignant Heaven, in mercy to the oppressed,
> Nurtured a Hero of the jetty race,
> His mighty soul with ample veins [?] possessed.
> And stamped with moral Dignity his face
> . . . . And has the Avenger heard the Hero's plaint
> From Gallic Dungeon, Wat'ry, dark, and deep?
> Yes—Heaven has burst upon the imprisoned saint
> Yes—France on fields of blood has learned to weep.
>
> When the dark story blots the record's page,
> The sons of Saul [?] will blush his foes to claim:
> Toussaint's renown shall reach the latest age,
> And marbles bear his venerated name.

In contrast to the space denied a celebration of slave victory, room for an unexpected politics of the (repressed) imagination opens up in a missionary tale by Charlotte Elizabeth Tonna whose autobiography records her obsessive evangelical zeal. In a conversion tale entitled *The System* (1827), the hero is an evangelical aristocrat named Sir William Belmont who visits the Caribbean plantation of his brother George.[54] On the outbound voyage, Sir William meets Caesar, a "mulatto" who plans and executes a slave uprising in response to plantocratic bestiality. A planter named Seldon, Caesar's father, has remarried a cruel woman. Caesar's sister, Lilias, has been seduced by Green, a vicious planter. Later in the story Sir William re-encounters the active Moravian missionary Kerffman, an old friend.

Sir Williams' disgusted accounts of atrocities, his fire and brimstone threats to Green about God's vengeance and "fearful storm of wrath," make Caesar's dignified decision to revolt a preferable alternative to a passive brutalized existence that pins hope on well-meaning Christian gentlemen who sermonize at the drop of a top hat. Wooden Sir William's exposure of plantocratic hypocrisy, while worthily condemnatory, compares unfavorably with courageous Caesar's impassioned, final-straw speech: "Go, sir," he sternly interrupts Sir William:

> set before your white brethren the error of their ways; bid them meditate on the crimes of rapine, murder, torturing murder, the murder of souls, to use your own mode of speaking. Tell them to repent, to repent of these, of their thefts, their adulteries, their revellings in the blood of their fellow men. Promise them an amnesty, a security from the vengeance of the African's arm, if they remove the fetter that binds it. Will they listen? Will they turn? No, they will mock, scoff, revile, spurn at the reprover and his reproof; and why should we be deluded? Admitting your good-will, and, on my soul I believe you to be sincere, yet where is your power? (Tonna, *The System,* p. 142)

Missionary Kerffman sympathizes with Caesar's position, but when his fulminating rhetoric almost runs away with him, Tonna whisks him back to the comfortable discourse of evangelese, suggesting an emotional tug-of-war that might have been Tonna's own:

> And thus it is, brother, that your first crime produces others, darkening in atrocity as they succeed. Slavery is the cockatrice's egg from whence you hatch a brood to your own external ruin. It is a whirlpool that, in its fatal vortex sucks down all surrounding objects. You brutify your fellow man, and goad him till he breaks away from your intolerable yoke. Conscious that you can expect no mercy where none has been shewn, you feel that his existence

becomes incompatible with your safety. . . . When he maketh inquisition for blood, will you say that you shed it in your own defense? Will not the reply be, Who brought the African hither? Who immolated his every right at the shrine of mammon, and wrung from his agonized veins the means to pamper a tyrant's luxury and pride? The day will come when you shall too deeply comprehend the force of that awful question, "What shall it profit a man if he gain the whole world, and lose his own soul?" (Tonna, *The System,* p. 203)

Theoretically, that is, Tonna prioritizes the state of "souls of sable brethren." Hence the deaths of Caesar and Lilias need be mentioned only perfunctorily. Even Lilias's endurance of sexual abuse is immaterial beside glory hereafter. Nonetheless, Caesar's heroic pride attracts riveting emotional support for slave revolt. In conclusion Tonna as speaker attempts to confine herself to the discourse of conversion, but her anger generates a soft natural rights argument:

The system exists with all its train of hideous deformities, all its combinations of sin and crime. There is a race of negroes groaning in bondage under the most arbitrary power, and daily liable to the very worst of all the outrages we have faintly delineated. . . . Do you lament that such things are? Do you wish they were thus no longer? Remember then that the public voice is formed of individual breathings, and let yours be lifted up, in the little circle, however small, where it can be heard, to protest against such an unnatural order of things, to reason, to plead, to persist in bringing forward the topic, until the sound reaches through your native land. . . . Some will refer you to Scripture, and tell you the Patriarchs possessed slaves: let them look to the declarations of the Levitical law on that subject; where the man-stealer, and the retainer of the stolen man, are alike condemned to die (Tonna, *The System,* pp. 229–231).

Despite detestation of upheaval and the primacy she accords salvation, Tonna slides to the side of Caesar as if her sense of justice emotionally threatened to edge out her spiritual commitment. Tonna's earlier perspective in a much more conservative tale, *Perseverance,* has become radically transformed.[55]

Chapter 13

Extending Discourse and Changing Definitions

PART ONE

In fulfilling their broadly defined spiritual roles within society, evangelical women transformed themselves into militant political agitators with power to influence the nation. Yet once the Emancipation Bill passed in 1833, that kind of unprecedented female power became diffused and women's collective energies at the national level—though not their moral authority—became substantially diminished.

Conversely, one of the radical women, though not an evangelical woman from that era, Harriet Martineau, continued to agitate against slavery transatlantically long after the Emancipation Bill became law in 1834. Her ongoing commitment was born of personal experience. Nonetheless, Martineau's cultural background did not preclude her adherence to nationwide Anglo-Saxon sentiment: a tale she wrote in good faith against slavery actually promoted ethnocentric attitudes and a colonization program. Not until she left Britain soon after the passage of the Bill, fatigued by her arduous two-year stint writing *Illustrations of Political Economy* (1832–1834), did she reject propagandist historian Bryan Edwards' plantocratic "truths." While travelling from New York to various Southern States, she debated slavery informally, met William Lloyd Garrison, and became a proponent of immediatism.[1] She also came to terms with the fact that relocation benefitted relocators, not freed slaves, and withdrew her support on the spot.

Harriet Martineau's intellectual upbringing explains her political evolution. Descended from French Huguenots, she grew up in a relatively prosperous home, studying with the eminent Unitarian, Lant Carpenter, until her father's textile manufacturing business failed in

273

1825–26: "We had lost our gentility! . . . So to work I went, with needle and pen."[2] Around 1827, she published a story on machine-breaking. Afterwards she came across a book entitled *Conversations on Political Economy* (1816) by Jane Haldimand Marcet (1769–1858), whose form she would adopt for *Illustrations of Political Economy,* a popular series of didactic tales she began composing in 1831.[3] "I took up the book," Martineau wrote later, "chiefly to see what Political Economy precisely was; and great was my surprise to find that I had been teaching it unawares, in my stories about Machinery and Wages. It struck me at once that the principles of the whole science might be advantageously conveyed in the same way,—not by being smothered up in a story, but by being exhibited in their natural workings in selected passages of social life."

In *Demerara,* a long, allusive tale in the second of nine books that make up *Illustrations,* she applied those economic principles. She posited a solution to slavery based on theories of economic law derived by Adam Smith, David Ricardo, and James Mill that chart the advantage to the capitalist of free waged labor over slave labor.[4] Thus she turned on its head a plantocratic argument about the benefits of slavery to Britain and argued that freed, not enslaved workers increased the nation's profits. In the process, she extended the range of anti-slavery discourse and the definition of white female self-empowerment.

The central incident in *Demerara* concerns a burst dam. Protagonist Alfred Bruce, a plantation owner's son, has just returned from England with his sister, Mary, after being educated there. To the planters, Alfred explains the workings of economic law within the free enterprise tradition: slavery and monoculture waste labor and capital, he claims, compared to a free labor system that mutually benefits planters and slaves. A burst mill dam that got repaired forty-five days earlier than expected because temporarily freed slaves voluntarily worked hard dramatizes his point. These actions illustrate the necessarian principle that "the characters of men originate in their external circumstances," the belief in necessity espoused by William Godwin in the 1790s. Given proper treatment and conditions slaves can be transformed into proficient waged workers.

A slave-owner himself, Alfred leaves his father's plantation half-way through the tale to administer his Barbadian estate, purposeful about transforming his ideas about freed slave labor into practice. Economic self-interest leads to emancipation: Alfred says: "I wish to have no slaves, Cassius: I would rather you should be my servants, if you worked for me at all" (Martineau, *Demerara,* pp. 90–91). After the fashion of James Mill's textual summations, Martineau appended a set of principles to the end of *Demerara* that served as a blueprint for the consolidation of post-slavery colonial power: emancipation will promote imperial control in a "more humane" form; capitalist free trade practices will dispense with legislative protection and the misery of slavery; modernity and technology will replace outmoded feudal structures.

As a further boost to this economic solution, Martineau sets the tale in Demerara, site of the recent slave insurrection and inhuman reprisals. She champions white missionary, John Smith, who preached spiritual equality and, more covertly, emancipation. (While in jail for his part in the rebellion, Smith, a frail man anyway, died, causing a public uproar in Britain.) Less enlightened slave-owners than Alfred, she suggests, have only themselves to blame if bloody uprisings ensue (Martineau, *Demerara,* p. 90). Martineau's futuristic *Demerara* with harmonious British employer/African employee relationships is paradigmatic of the utopian Eurocentric ideal for post-emancipation British as well as Caribbean society.

Demerara is the arena of a well-considered, pro-capitalist, anti-feudal alternative to slavery. As Martineau records in her autobiography: "I therein declared myself satisfied that slavery was indefensible, economically, socially, and morally. . . . From the spring of 1832 I was completely committed against slavery."[5] As she further explains, she had been approached during the composition of *Illustrations* by a person

> [who] presented himself as an anti-slavery agent. It was the well-known Elliott Cresson . . . [of] the American Colonization scheme, which he hoped to pass . . . upon us innocent provincial Britons as the same thing as anti-slavery. . . . Kind-hearted people, hearing from Mr. Cresson that a slave could be bought and settled blissfully in Liberia for seven pounds ten shillings, raised the ransom in their own families and among their neighbours, and thought all was right. Mr. Cresson . . . offered to furnish me with plenty of evidence of the productiveness of Liberia, and the capabilities of the scheme, with a view to my making it the scene and subject of one of my tales. I was willing, . . . and I promised, not to write a story, but to consider it when the evidence should have arrived. The papers arrived; and my conclusion was—not to write about Liberia.[6]

But references to Liberia in *Demerara* do not entirely match Martineau's avowed decision. Alfred, for example, gives the slave Cassius the price of the fare to Liberia after his family garden plot has been destroyed and his manumission money stolen. Later, Alfred outlines to his father the kind of society that relocated ex-slaves might build:

> "They will labour, and prosper and be happy. They will become farmers, planters, merchants, or tradespeople. They will make their own laws, guard their own rights, and be as we are, men and citizens."
>
> "Do you expect me to believe all this, son? Do you think I know so little what blacks are?"
>
> "Neither you nor I, father, can learn, in this place, what Africans are in a better place. I believe, and I certainly expect others to believe, what I have told you, on the strength of sound testimony" (Martineau, *Demerara*, p. 139).

While Harriet Martineau expounds the free labor theory and the need for a Caribbean society committed to a European conception of human rights and dignity, she concurrently promotes the colonization scheme and attendant tenets of a pro-slavery ideology. This impasse is not unusual. Frequently in evangelical texts, ingrained contemporary stereotypes about slaves and slavery battle an individual writer's sense of legal justice. Martineau is no exception. For the most part, ethnocentrism was part and parcel of everyday Anglo-Saxon life. Martineau's doubled vision reemerged during her first visit to the United States:

> During dinner, the conversation was chiefly on the Southern slave-holders, whose part was taken by Miss J. and myself, so far as to plead the involuntariness of their position, and the extreme perplexity of their case,—over and above the evil conditions of prejudice and ignorance in which they were brought up. Our line of argument was evidently worth little in the estimate of all present, who appeared to us, in our then half-informed state, hard and narrow.[7]

Martineau's borrowings from Bryan Edwards's negrophobic *History of the British Colonies in the West Indies* partly explain her unacknowledged conflicts. As a case in point, mouthpiece Alfred fuses information from Edwards and abolitionist James Cooper with necessarian beliefs. Martineau scrupulously pays tribute to these sources in her *Autobiography:* "The books of travel [that Martineau used as sources in *Demerara*] were . . . Edwards's *West Indies.* . . . Mr. Cropper of Liverpool heard of the Series early enough to furnish me with some statistics of Slavery for *Demerara.*[8]

In the preface of *Demerara,* she re-presents Edwards's vignettes. In the words of a twentieth-century commentator, his *History* was "unique as a guide to conditions in the West Indies in the last few years of the century. . . . it again took the reader behind the scenes into the world of the slave as viewed by his master. Edwards had a milder attitude towards the Negro than had [Edward] Long, but his portrait is nonetheless distorted. His typical slave was indolent, lying, thieving and promiscuous, without any of the talents and achievements upon which Europeans so prided themselves."[9] Martineau puts it this way in her validation of Edwards's mythologizing:

> If it be objected that the characters for which sympathy is claimed might have been made more interesting, I reply that our sympathy for slaves ought to increase in proportion to their vices and follies, if it can be proved that those vices and follies arise out of the position in which we place them, or allow them to remain. If the champions of the slave had but seen how his cause is aided by representing him as he is,—not only revengeful, but selfish and mean,—indolent, conceited, hypocritical, and sensual,—we should have had fewer narratives of slaves more virtuous than a free peasantry, and exposed to the delicate miseries of a refined love of which they are incapable, or of social sensibilities which can never be generated in such a social condition as theirs. . . .
>
> While endeavouring to preserve the characteristics of Negro minds and manners, I have not attempted to imitate the language of slaves. Their jargon would be intolerable to writer and readers, if carried through a volume. My personages, therefore, speak the English which would be natural to them, if they spoke what can be called English at all.[10]

In *Demerara* itself, two negatively-depicted African-Caribbeans, Robert and Sukey, pull wings off insects and gleefully rob Cassius, who thriftily tends his own crops while pretending to be lazy to reduce his price. Cassius's duplicity (an understandable part of a slave's treacherous and institutionally degraded nature within Martineau's present belief system) is compounded by a prayer overheard by Alfred in which the slave jointly curses master and overseer and wishes death upon them. Assuming a surrogate-missionary role, Alfred informs Cassius that the means to "blessings [i.e. freedom] should be left to Divine Wisdom." Having attempted to understand Alfred's "civilized" though mysterious explanations, Cassius is re-identified as a loyal African who has earned charity. For the time being, that is, Martineau reinforces dominant ideology and the British-Caribbean status quo; she enhances Britain's emerging "Dark Continent" doctrine of decades to come.[11]

Historical dehumanizations of African adults reach an apogee when Alfred invokes a necessarian rationale and compares slaves to a canary in captivity:

> Mary gave that Canary its seed and water for years, and she would have laughed if any one had told her that she knew nothing about Canary birds; but it would have been very true; for that tame little creature, drawing up its tiny bucket of water when it was bid, seeing the sunbeams shut out as soon as ever it hailed them with a burst of song, was not like one of the same species with the wild, winged creatures that flit about its native islands, and warble unchecked till twilight settles down upon the woods. And we, father, can never guess from looking at a negro sulking in the stocks, or tilling lands which yield him no harvest, what he may be where there is no white man to fear and hate, and where he may reap whatever he has sown. Happily there are some who have been to Liberia, and can tell us what a negro may become" (Martineau, *Demerara*, p. 141).

Endorsement of the Liberian project and Edwards's plantocratic scenario aside, when Martineau raises the issue of runaway slaves, she underscores several ambiguities, both affirming and denying prior tensions; she also challenges the boundaries of anti-slavery debate in extensive textual commentary on revenge, escape, rebellion, and gender power relationships. With former missionaries and travellers on the pro-emancipation speakers' circuit narrating gruesome, eye-witness tales, slave conditions and rebellion preoccupied public attention more than ever. Martineau's slave protagonist, Willy, refuses to face life as a "levied slave" about to be sold to offset creditors' debts. So he runs off with his sister Nell and ends up mangled to death by the dogs of slave hunters. The text upholds the couple's escape as logical and justifiable. Yet no wholesale condemnation of murder follows. Moreover, just before Willy's grim goring, he debates whether to leave his wounded sister behind and jump in the river, out of the bloodhounds' reach. This split-second self-preserving thought and oblivion to family ties stress the desperation of a not improbable situation. Almost instantly, Martineau has Willy correct for "his unfeeling savagery," encoded as "natural": "Willy hesitated a moment as his worse and better nature strove together." At the last moment—understandably for a pagan, even a hero perhaps, in Martineau's frame of reference—he seems to choose death and drowning.

Earlier, the siblings' escape is foreshadowed when planter Mitchelson was separated from his family and envisions "burning cane-fields, ... a murdered wife and insulted children" (Martineau, *Demerara*, p. 86). The thought of women left alone with slaves is more than Mitchelson's traditional vision can cope with, for every black heart and mind, so the Eurocentric consensus goes, plots murder. Willy's death is thus deplored against the backdrop of European-fantasized assassinations. In the recent Demeraran slave revolt of 1823, the demented punishments meted out to slave rebels—some individuals were sentenced to a thousand lashes and chains for life—seem implicitly contrasted with the hatred such atrocities inevitably generated.

Implicitly, too, Martineau raises the ghost of Toussaint L'Ouverture, whom she was to esteem in a novel entitled *The Hour and the Man*, published in 1841. In *Demerara*, she emotionally sides with those who resist unjust authority and retain personal dignity in the face of inhumanity. Yet Edwards's pernicious influence—a contemporary boost to Eurocentrism—prevents her from endowing Willy with full heroic status. Instead, with a noticeable lack of conviction, she argues that a "rational" form of emancipation will eliminate potential bloodbaths. And there is another option available within her current politic: British planters who own resurgent slaves like Willy can always opt for selective relocation.

An outspoken feminist unlike more conservative abolitionist counterparts, Martineau also raises the issue of gender relations when Mitchelson worries about insurrection and the brother-sister duo plot their escape. Throughout the text, she opposes the Caribbean version of the angel-in-the-house, deplores the impermanence of slave marriages, dictated by arbitrary European sales of slaves, and values explosions of self-possession and opposition by Nell and Alfred's sister, Mary, in situations that consign both women to bondage and passivity. But even that esteem for Nell is undercut by Martineau's implied recognition of national anxieties and a subtle nod to patriotism.

Handcuffed on return, Nell apprehended nothing but a desire "to throttle the man on whose shoulders she was carried." Endorsement of Nell's righteous retaliation battles fear of the consequences to Britons of slave uprisings. Martineau's projection of a woman thinking but unable to act upon a desire to take the law into her own hands contrasts with Martineau's seeming emotional condemnation of Nell, whose thoughts actualize a white British incubus. In one sense, Martineau projects her own spunkiness onto Nell and re-chronicles San Domingan heroism. In this twin insistence that white and black women can be rebels, she deftly wedges a further anti-patriarchal argument into the tale. Nell's reaction to a dire situation compares favorably with several responses by white women that range from feminist challenge to female helplessness. First, Mary wants to "introduce economy into our household arrangements"—a laudable desire in the book's terms—yet she is nervous about taking any domestic power—however minimal—into her own hands: "O, Alfred! I [with] any power—any responsibility of this kind? It makes me tremble to think of it." (By contrast, Alfred is a hard-hitting "new" plantocrat, a commercially and politically updated George Ellison.)

Second, plantation mistresses, including Mary's mother, cease listening and fall asleep when males talk over financial affairs (Martineau, *Demerara*, p. 119). Ironies abound here since Martineau's stalwart unorthodoxy in writing a text on economics—and in the process she claims any woman's right to do so—matches Nell's own frank expressions of self-determination. At some level, the text seems to suggest, Martineau felt obliged to introduce traditional depictions of women like Mary's mother with one spirited variation—somewhat undercut—in Mary herself. At the same time, however, Martineau's personal-political inclinations are more radical, so she tackles that dimension in the person of Nell, thereby highlighting a union of colonizer subject and alleged other, subtly in opposition to male hegemonic power. Furthermore, Martineau engages the topic of a slave wedding to castigate the immorality of slavery and reaffirm another common (though differently configured) subjugation: the status of black and white females in marriage. Thus the tale of the rebellious Nell opens up multiple questions about connections between black and white women. Beyond that, Martineau accentuates the substantially more jeopardized situation of black females, while clearly intertextualizing anti-flogging demands by associationists.

In a chapter entitled "No Haste to the Wedding in Demerara," Willy abominates the fundamental condition of slaves' lives:

> A black must be first a slave and then a man. A white woman has nobody to rule her but her husband, and nobody can hurt her without his leave: but a slave's wife must obey her master before her husband, and he cannot save her from being flogged. I saw my friend Hector throw himself on the ground when his wife was put in the stocks; and then I swore that I would never have a wife.

With all anti-patriarchal ironies intended, Martineau loosely links white female subjugation to the condition of slavery itself. By 1837, when she repudiated the claim that the United States functioned as a democracy, she made that bridge explicit.[12]

Harriet Martineau exercises these diverse anti-slavery statements to complicate an old assertion that women were slaves to men. Whereas feminists had for centuries centered on the enslavement of women by men as the primary referent of slavery, Martineau now emphasizes the role that colonial enslavement plays: the social subjugation of white females in this reading runs parallel but by no means supersedes institutionalized slavery. Martineau renders explicit the connection between race and gender oppression.

A famous feminist text written in 1825 epitomizes this reassessment if not reversal of political priorities. In *Appeal of One Half of the Human Race, Women, Against the pretentions of other Half, Men,* Anna Wheeler and William Thompson use slavery as their main analogy for British women's plight and powerlessness within marriage (white understood), asserting that "a domestic, a civil, a political slave, in the plain unsophisticated sense of the word—in no metaphorical sense—is every married women. . . . Under every vicissitude of MAN'S condition, he has always retained women as his slave."[13]

In the process of privileging colonial slavery, Martineau more accurately evaluates the relationships between these traditionally linked subjugations. In the past, female writers had alluded rather unsystematically to slavery, making it stand for severe control of women, frequently in courtship and marriage. Consequently, the analogy tended to downplay the reality of colonial slavery while it stressed inequities endured by at least physically free British females. Martineau turned the age-old metaphor of white women as slaves inside out and pressed home the interrelationship of race and gender dominations.

Still, black women in Britain found little opportunity to have their own oppositional discourse. One of the few exceptions was Mary Prince, who orally chronicled her experiences at the London Anti-Slavery headquarters. Given the severity of cultural constraints across not only race and class but also gender lines, her published narrative was an unusual occurrence; most of the outspoken African or African-Caribbean females in Britain were political activists rather than writers.

PART TWO: AN EX-SLAVEWOMAN NARRATES HER EXPERIENCES

I would rather go into my grave than go back a slave to Antigua, though I wish to go back to my husband very much—very much—

very much! I am much afraid my owners would separate me from
my husband, and use me very hard, or perhaps sell me for a field
negro;—and slavery is too bad. I would rather go into my grave!
        —Mary Prince, testimony to attorney George Stephen.

I cannot sell my birthright.
        —Nelson Mandela, Reply to South African regime's offer of
                                        conditional freedom, 1985.

In *The History of Mary Prince: A West Indian Slave. Related by
Herself* in 1831, Mary Prince claims herself as a speaking, acting,
thinking subject with an identity separate from Anglo-Africanist constructions of her past and present reality.[14] The text consists of a
preface, several postscripts, and a sixteen-page editorial supplement
that chronicle the fierce controversy following publication, and a
twenty-three-page, first-person account by Mary Prince that sketches
the period from her birth until 1828, concentrating on her life with
four sets of owners. The last five pages chronicle her experiences in
the two months prior to her oral testimony, during which she lived
with Mr. and Mrs. Wood and finally walked out on them.

Given the contending agendas of such a multitiered narrative, including imposed limitations on a female slave's right to authorship
and publication, several questions arise: did Mary Prince know in
advance, before she arrived at the London anti-slavery headquarters
and told her story to Thomas Pringle, its secretary, that evangelical
assumptions and dictates would have to inform her narrative if she
were to secure a public hearing? If so, how did she anticipate or set
about counteracting a popular abolitionist assumption that slaves
"cannot represent themselves; they must be represented."[15] In other
words, did Mary Prince actively resist being censored or caricatured
as a colonial "other" by supporters and slave-owners alike?[16] Was she
able to encode deliberately and discreetly, customarily unnamable
privations? To what extent did she acknowledge, in directing her
narrative, that both sides of the slavery debate vyed for control over
her? Or perhaps more likely, were her responses to abolitionists
fraught with ambivalence?

Mary Prince's insistent assertion of herself as subject show up
most clearly in jousts with her abolitionist-evangelical editor, Thomas
Pringle. After composing a title page featuring Mary Prince in the third
person, which rhetorically establishes his command, he discusses the
transcription and revisions of her narrative:

The idea of writing Mary Prince's history was first suggested by
herself. She wished it to be done, she said, that good people in

England might hear from a slave what a slave had felt and suffered.
. . . The narrative was taken down from Mary's own lips by a lady
. . . residing in my family as a visitor. It was written out fully, with
all the narrator's repetitions and prolixities, and afterwards pruned
into its present shape; retaining, as far as was practicable, Mary's
exact expressions and peculiar phraseology. No fact of importance
has been omitted, and not a single circumstance or sentiment has
been added. It is essentially her own, without any material alter-
ation farther than was requisite to exclude redundancies and gross
grammatical errors, so as to render it clearly intelligible.[17]

"I went over the whole," Pringle adds, "carefully examining her on
every fact and circumstance detailed,"[18] His use of footnotes to "explain," "decipher," and "elaborate" on Mary Prince's autobiographical
narration certifies his desire to present and produce her narrative
as emancipationist evidence in 1831 of the "civilizing mission"—to
"Europeanize" people of African descent, "for their own good." Her
testimony corroborates (is) his authority and vindicates his values—
or superficially seems to do so. Thus Pringle mediates between Mary
Prince and the public, refracting her oral narrative according to several considerations: the demands made by the emancipation campaign in its intense final stage and evangelical views of desirable
female behavior. Mary Prince does not, however, readily surrender
her narrative to editorial rule. Equivocal in her presentation to a
largely sympathetic European audience, she formulates herself as a
slave-representative, as well as an individual slave-agent. For example, after warmly acknowledging the assistance of "very good" missionaries, she simultaneously inscribes the presence of an additional
audience drawn from slave communities: "But [pro-slavery forces]
put a cloak about the truth. It is not so. All slaves want to be free. . . .
I know what slaves feel. . . . We don't mind hard work, if we had proper
treatment [but] when we are quite done up, who cares for us, more
than for a lame horse?" (Prince, *A History,* p. 84) The first-person
plural usage not only strikes a rhetorical alliance with slaves from
Caribbean and African-British communities who effectively co-relate
the narrative, but also pointedly signifies a familiar but silent dialogue
of lamentation based on shared experience.[19] The language of slaves
markedly differs from the language of their supporters.

Throughout her account Mary Prince responds with similar shrewd-
ness to abolitionist control, one of the deftest examples being her
panegyric on the penultimate page to the Reverend Mortimer, Thomas
Pringle's evangelical friend, that reads as follows:

> Nor must I forget, among my friends, the Rev. Mr. Mortimer, the
> good clergyman of the parish, under whose ministry I have now sat
> for upwards of twelve months. . . . He never keeps back the truth.
> . . . Mr. Mortimer tells me that he cannot open the eyes of my heart,
> but that I must pray to God to change my heart, and make me to
> know the truth, and the truth will make me free.[20]

Mary Prince proclaims that spiritual truth alone will free her when she knows full well and at painful cost that her life has been a protracted private battle against slave-owners for an elusive comprehensive liberty. Her scars, her imminent blindness, her memories of forty years' hard living speak other kinds of truths about the meaning of freedom. The mimicking, deadpan statements intimate not only her recognition of the need to accommodate her *History* to her allies' values, but constitute a sure-footed intervention in the civilizing mission, her sparring voice audible only to initiates. Implied in Mary Prince's words is the idea of a change not yet accomplished. By using the future tense, she points toward the continued absence of these "truths" at this post-conversion period of her life. Apparent obeisance to a future spiritual freedom as an end in itself, which the subtly oppositional narrative contradicts, is a rhetorical strategy to secure much more. Conversion aids social acceptance. In Homi Bhabha's words, her repetition of the Reverend Mortimer's discourse is a "mutation, a hybrid . . . [that strategically reverses] the process of domination through disavowal" by further fastening her own identity.[21] Yet people in the know, African-Caribbean reader-listeners who have lived through kindred experiences and realize she is restricted in what she can say (and is probably compensating for this containment), hear an altogether different voice—reserved, grave, mocking. Self-fashioned yea-saying inverts the binary set-up of colonial subject lording it over colonial other. Intent on survival, she must "continually guard against . . . being returned to the position of the object."[22]

To underscore her double-voiced discourse, however, is not to assume that her text is nothing more than a strategy, unproblematically conceived, for manumission. On the contrary, chances are high that Mary Prince somewhat demurred about religion yet shared many of Pringle's beliefs and perhaps even admired him, given that prayer, meditations, and conversion offer relief and escape from control. Mary Prince, after all, speaks within a certain discursive determination. Her text of counterinsurgency may win her access into the master discourse but she is still pinioned in the discourse of her violators. That constant ambivalence both engenders demystification of her situation and imprisons her vision. Some of Anna Freud's postulates help to clarify Mary Prince's probable conflicts: Freud contends that imitation forestalls rejection, increases the chance of access, and enables the threatened individual to transform [herself] into a more secure person.[23] Without her conversion experience Mary Prince would have been much more isolated in London and might not have ventured to the anti-slavery headquarters in the first place.

The *History,* as a whole, expatiates on these quiet, largely invisible contestations for power. A brief summary of the *History* will help to contextualize those contestations. Born about 1788 in Bermuda, Mary Prince describes her first twelve years living as a slave with her mother and siblings in the home of Captain Williams. Her father lives and works nearby. Around 1800 she is sold in the presence of her mother and other griefstricken members of the slave community to Captain I—— and his wife. In their house she endures persistent floggings, head-punchings, and gruesome daily experiences that include witnessing a protracted murder. She learns to work hard tending animals and children and doing numberless household chores; at one point she runs away and is returned by her father. Fortified by his presence, she denounces the owners' brutalities to their face. Five years later they sell her to a sadistic taskmaster, Mr. D—— of Turks Island, who works her exactingly in the salt ponds and heinously punishes her. Again she witnesses murders committed with impunity. Returning to Bermuda in 1810 with D——, she starts saving for manumission and sparingly but strikingly alludes to that concealed area of her life taken up with sexual abuse and harrassment. One persistently telling indicator is the carefully mentioned, especially harsh treatment she receives at the hands of her mistresses. By about 1814 she inveigles being sold to Mr. and Mrs. John Wood because they live in Antigua where manumission is less difficult to obtain. In this section, Mary Prince concentrates on illness, marriage, religion, and her complex, daily relationship with the Woods who persistently refuse to grant Mary Prince her freedom. After they travel to London and mercilessly work a severely arthritic Mary Prince, she walks off.

Battles over power are partly played out through a gradually evolving complex of decisions to escape: on page one the protagonist looks back on "the happiest period of my life [when] I was too young to understand rightly my condition as a slave." By specifically stressing this later reevaluation—her backward glance in the present at the past—she alerts readers from the very beginning not to take the account at face value. By page two she records running away, apparently mournful after learning that her first owner, Mrs. Williams, has died.[24] Here she quietly ushers into her narrative a thematics of escape.

When Mr. Williams sells Mary Prince and her siblings, Mrs. Prince talks forebodingly of "shrouding" the children as she dresses them for auction. This equation of slavery and death overflows into supplementary statements by Mary Prince, as the epigraph to this chapter denotes. Being severed from her mother and sold is a form of death, death of the family unit as well as of various individuals. Years later, when she is flogged mercilessly for a trivial offense by Captain and Mrs. I——, her second owners, she flees to her mother, trying to forestall the ominously predicted "shrouding."[25] In the I——'s house, she has already witnessed the systematic daily torture and eventual murder of the French slave Hetty, whose plenitude of chores Mary Prince inherits.[26] Resistance and vigilance determine life or death. An exhumation of sorts, Mary Prince's text restores such silenced voices as Hetty's. When her father returns her to Captain and Mrs. I——, she protests life-imperiling floggings before him and the owners: "I was weary of my life," she exclaims, but adds exultantly: "he did not flog me that day."[27] Here she signals a small victory that endorses a persistently oppositional consciousness.

Mary Prince displays a comparable opposition when she broaches the topic of sexuality. Since she converted years earlier in Antigua and confessed to immoralities, she is well attuned to evangelical dictates regarding that subject. Her response is to leave unstated the implications of her vignettes and intertextually invoke contemporary published statements about the insistent sexual abuse of female slaves.[28]

When owner D—— beats his daughter, Mary Prince records her bold intervention and community response: they laud her as a local hero. She then informs the reader that she refused to wash D—— naked in his bath: "at last I defended myself [against him and] after that I was hired to work at Cedar Hills, and every Saturday night I paid the money to my master." Moreover, when D—— agrees to sell Mary Prince, he warns the future owners that "I should not be sold to any one that would treat me ill."[29] His smug protectiveness expresses a perverse last bid for power and Mary Prince invites us to read between the lines of this proprietorial volte-face. Her incredulity at the calmness D—— exhibits as he has her beaten on Turks Island—he took snuff with composure, she says, as he watched her being flogged—suggests her perhaps initially naive shock at a common contradiction: slaveowners recklessly injuring a concubine as a magnification of power. On different registers, Mary Prince avenges herself.

Once sold by D—— to Mr. and Mrs. Wood, Mary Prince vows to become free and explains how she saved up to do so, her discourse imbedded with allusion and implied resistance. "I wanted, by all honest means, to earn money to buy my freedom."[30] The fact that she wanted to save money "honestly" highlights Pringle's values and her knowledge that other, less acceptable means were available, to which she may have yielded, given the primacy she accords freedom. To back up the obtrusive adjective "honest," she mentions doing laundry and selling coffee. She then adds that she sold "other provisions to the captains of ships." Since a certain friend of Mary Prince named Captain Abbott incensed the Woods by meeting her after a curfew imposed by them and later offered to buy her, and since Mary Prince and Captain Abbott were subsequently slandered by plantocrats for their relationship, she hails his presence elliptically. Additionally, she mentions several friendships with both free black men and white men that reaffirm her desired and actual position within a free community in the here and now; she validates her right to autonomous participation in community culture and flouts the Woods' use of curfew to curtail and even ridicule her social life. To mention a specific sexual relationship, however suggestively, would be in violation of Pringle's preference to play down any voluntary, pre-conversion sexual activities. The fact that the pro-slavery lobby attempted to expose her relationship with Captain Abbott, following publication, pinpoints how damaging such testimony was regarded by both sides.[31] Hence it is likely that Mary Prince attempts nuance, extemporizes, and gives play to the reader's imagination when she speaks of such relationships. Even if Pringle did not explicitly stipulate how he would like certain topics to be presented, Mary Prince would have known from her acquaintanceship with the Moravians that avowed Christian evangelicals considered extramarital sexual activity morally reprehensible. Hence she may have opted to play the matter down, hedged the controversial topic creatively when Pringle "carefully examin[ed] her on every fact and circumstance detailed," not as an intentional duplicity, but as a way of negotiating an acceptable way to present herself. She knows that her survival as a free woman partly depends on passing Pringle's tests. In her ambiguous representation of personal relationships, she may have been guessing that his fixed, univocal outlook would block out undesirable innuendo and collateral meanings. Suggestiveness contextualizes a necessarily suppressed reality.

One of her supporters, Joseph Phillips, responds to post-publication attacks on what plantocrats termed Mary Prince's "profligacy." Phillips asserts in Pringle's *Supplement* the commonplaceness, by Antiguan standards, of Mary Prince's relationships: "Such connexions are so common, I might almost say universal, in our slave colonies, that except by the missionaries and a few serious persons, they are considered, . . . very venial."[32] Even more graphically, in terms of forced sexual relations, Richard B. Sheridan quotes the Reverend John Barry, a Methodist missionary in Jamaica, whose testimony in a House of Lords Report of 1832 states that women were "subjected to Corporal Punishment for Non-compliance with the libidinous Desires of the Person in Authority on the Estate."[33]

Neither Pringle nor the Woods will brook the truth of these observations. For Pringle's purposes, Mary Prince had to renounce only highly generalized past sins after conversion—that nonetheless obliquely signal unchristian sexual practices—to prove her endorsement of a more becoming role: that of a repentant Christian.[34] Besides, any mention of female "immodesty" or of sexuality without defilement would be bait to the unctuous Woods who configure her as a pagan Jezebel, a recalcitrant Mary Magdalen. Since Mary Prince is enjoined to screen an everyday part of her life, she begins on page one to inveigle these forbidden affairs into her *History* in yet another veiled contestation of power.

As an adult recalling her childhood, she states that she commiserated with Mrs. Williams, disparaging Mr. Williams as "a very harsh, selfish man [given to] . . . reside in other female society."[35] Hence she subtly establishes the precedent for male slave-owners' sexual practices. By tracing a textual pattern of slave-owners' abusive behavior toward cross-class females, in bondage or not, Mary Prince ends up totalizing slave-owners as "generic" beings. She reverses customary linguistic and political power relationships since slaves are usually the ones perceived as synonymous and interchangeable—"they all look alike, act alike," in Abdul JanMohamed's words.[36]

Concurrently her expressive sorrow after conversion about prior sinfulness summons up a buried text about past sexual independence. Once again she acts pragmatically and speaks with two voices when circumstances dictate discretion. She overtly repudiates certain forms of sabotage and sexual-social autonomy, yet her continuous inscription of maltreatment by female owners suggests other readings. The sadism of Mrs. Wood and Mrs. I—— bespeaks a complex sexual jealousy partly directed at Mary Prince's implied efforts at a distinctive self-definition.

Mary Prince also enciphers motherhood obliquely, her strange silence an egregiously conspicuous omission in near-Victorian, family-conscious England. She links it with violence, elaborating on Hetty's death as a result of atrocities perpetrated during and after childbirth. Thus the floggings, the severe kicking and punching that the I——s and others repeatedly inflicted on Mary Prince, we infer, caused irreversible damage to her body. Explicit statements linking violence with sterilization would discount her text as suitable evangelical reading material. On the other hand, Mary Prince tries to communicate an alternate profile of her own domestic "fitness" (in all senses) in the absence of motherhood. She takes pleasure in working as a nursemaid, in visiting with her own mother, siblings, and other children. Weighty silence, as much as anything, speaks to the grim, damaging sexual coercion of female slaves and her discursive power in circumnavigating evangelical taboos.

Mary Prince goes on to consider new moral alignments that succeed conversion during her servitude with the Woods: marriage, then literacy not long after.[37] These are freedom-engendering structures that double as rhetorical strategies for gaining reader acceptance and self-validation. Mary Prince uses them to explore new directions for manumission and to acquire status not as a mute, colonized object, but as a voiced individual with a socially condoned moral, literate life; they mark her identity and her agency, validate her refusal to be constructed in someone else's terms. Agreeing with Pringle may have its equivocal dimension but agreement also spells social and physical security to a vulnerable woman. Her embrace of religion, moreover, justifies publication in Pringle's eyes. She talks about conversion, marriage, and literacy with self-respect: "The slave woman [she remarks] . . . asked me to go . . . to a Methodist meeting for prayer. . . . This meeting . . . led my spirit to the Moravian church; so that when I got back to town, I went and prayed to have *my name* [my italics] put down on the Missionaries book"; on a second occasion, she takes pride in the fact that, "whenever I carried the children their lunch at school, I ran round and went to hear the teachers. . . . [They] taught me to read . . . and I got on very fast"; and lastly, she underlines her own spiritual and moral regeneration while highlighting here and elsewhere the threat her marriage posed: "[I] would not say yes till he went to church with me and joined the Moravians. . . . We could not be married in the English Church. English marriage is not allowed to slaves; and no free man can marry a slave woman."[38]

So why, after establishing certain valuable securities, did Mary Prince not emulate what many resolute slaves did and save up for manumission? The obvious answer is that she did just that, but when the Woods doggedly refused to free her, she was obliged to adopt different tactics to emancipate herself.

Trying to leave their household as a free woman turns into a complex process, fraught with psychological ploys. Mary Prince discloses that the Woods agreed she could accompany them to England, despite incessant arguments about conditions of work and manumission. She does not explain this contradiction. Were they so confident of their owner-control that they could risk bringing her to a country where she would be (as it was then popularly thought) automatically free? Was it a self-aggrandizing gamble on their part to let her talk them into taking her?[39] Or did Mr. Wood's sexual desire prevail over Mrs. Wood's jealous reluctance in camouflaged but ongoing domestic disputes over a slavewoman?

At any rate, Mary Prince offers a pithy manifesto of personal insurrection, displaying what Thomas Pringle characterizes reprovingly as "a somewhat violent and hasty temper, and a considerable share of natural pride and self-importance."[40] Assertiveness irked the anti- and pro-slavery lobbies alike since it challenged and diffused their power:

> But their hearts were hard—too hard to consent. Mrs. Wood was very angry—she grew quite outrageous—she called me a black devil [sexual innuendo apparent], and asked me who had put freedom into my head. "To be free is very sweet," I said: but she took good care to keep me a slave. I saw her change colour, and I left the room.
>
> About this time my master and mistress were going to England to put their son to school, and bring their daughters home; and they took me with them to take care of the child. I was willing to come to England: I thought that by going there I should probably get cured of my rheumatism, and should return with my master and mistress, quite well, to my husband. My husband was willing for me to come away, for he had heard that my master would free me,—and I also hoped this might prove true; but it was all a false report.[41]

This scene entangles daily realities and weaves together an emancipationist declaration with multiple evidence of same: rumors that were rife in slave communities about freedom in Britain, condensed expressions of anger, quickwittedness, offstage dialogues, a manipulation of illness that could be linked to repressed anger and downright frustration, a tentative plan for escape, community ties, and a willful courage despite physical frailty. Beyond this compression of information, her claim to a general humanity—"to be free is very sweet"—not only denotes the future when she will be free from bondage but imbeds her self-awareness of continuous psychic freedom and the

incapacity of anyone to deny her consciousness. The specious rationale about leaving the warm Caribbean to cure rheumatism in damp
England accentuates her judiciously masked goal. (One wonders why
no one questioned her about that.) Perhaps she saw a chance to
capitalize on the Woods' long-witnessed internal discord over her
status, to usher the possibility of freedom into the space opened up
by their dissension.

On board ship, she made friends with a steward who was, she
pointedly states, "in the same class in the Moravian Church" as her
husband Daniel James.[42] This seemingly chance meeting might well
explain why she felt tough enough to leave the Woods. Religious
conversion had guaranteed Moravian aid even as far as London.
Chances are Mary Prince had already made her mind up in the Caribbean to leave the Woods since they made a point of advertising their
intransigence: they sold five slaves other than her even after free
friends made sundry efforts to buy her manumission.

Nonetheless she had to bide her time in London, "a stranger," as
she says, "[who] did not know one door in the street from another."[43]
Isolated and not eminently employable, she was, after all, a somewhat
penurious black woman separated from family and friends and accustomed to taking orders as a physical slave for nigh on forty-five years.
Between the time of leaving the Woods and coming to Pringle with,
in his words, "the idea of writing [her] history,"[44] she might have
become better acquainted with the substantial black community in
London among whom "a tradition [had grown up] of personal struggle
and resistance by black women."[45] Before that influence exerted itself,
however, she had to struggle between her desire for freedom and an
understandable reticence to take that ultimate, probably irreversible
step. Finally, after yet more quarreling with the Woods about being
forced to wash clothes with severely rheumatoid hands (the issue of
illness-feigning is relevant here), she lays out the dilemma she faced
and her decision to leave:

> [Mrs. Wood] said, she supposed I thought myself a free woman, but
> I was not; . . . I knew that I was free in England [Actually Mrs. Wood
> was technically correct. Since 1772, British law had stipulated that
> no individual could be *forcibly* removed from Britain] but I did not
> know where to go, or how to get my living; and therefore, I did not
> like to leave the house. But Mr. Wood said he would send for a
> constable to thrust me out; and at last I took courage and resolved
> that I would not be longer thus treated, but would go and trust to
> Providence.[46]

The Woods cannot bear to free her—or at least their grave ambivalence is palpable—nor can they cope with her claim to autonomy and the subsequent publication that verifies the difficulties involved in establishing that claim. They become the I——s and the D——s of the world if they fail to protest. Repudiating Mary Prince's narrative recuperates a semblance of their humanity even though she has already reversed the power relationship, exposed their barbarity, and claimed them as others for posterity.

The final pages of the *History* record her efforts to find work and stay free and the Anti-Slavery Society's strenuous negotiations for her legal manumission. These activities parallel the provincial women's agitation for emancipation and constant press reports of atrocities against male and female slaves. The last one-and-a-half pages are poignantly spoken in the present tense to concretize her immediate plight. They also ratify Mary Prince's new position as a publicly acknowledged, independent (though not legally free) subject: "I hope that God will find a way to give me my liberty and give me back to my dear husband." In the last fifty lines she ventriloquizes the aspirations and realities of other slaves. Afterwards she draws attention to the production of the narrative itself, referring to the white poet-amanuensis, Susanna Strickland, as "my good friend, Miss ——[who] is now writing down for me."[47] By way of thanking Strickland, Mary Prince affirms her own status as interlocutor, claiming her narrative before the very eyes of Pringle and the transcriber, her public mediators, as it were. In another unemphatic power reversal, the amanuensis has become an archetypal slave-other who takes orders and generates wealth (in this case textual wealth) simultaneously, an embodiment of Mary Prince's literacy.

In her concluding oration, she calls for "English people" [to] "know the truth," to pray and unceasingly petition the king "till all the poor blacks be given free, and slavery done up for evermore."[48] The saluted black compatriots who already "know the truth" remain silently present. With that audience as well as her white British audience in mind, Mary Prince seized the unique opportunity to exhibit both an individuated and a representative chronicle of a female slave's life in full view on the public stage, totemic of the nation's history and a challenge to its conscience.

No longer the silent, fictive object of colonial discourse, Mary Prince has asserted her entitlement to language and to a forum in the marketplace; the heterogeneity of slaves notwithstanding, she has transformed orality into a community act. Mindful of the men, women, and children whom she has geographically left behind, she elegizes and eulogizes other slaves, rendering her text a sacred repository of tales about the silenced living and the silent dead.[49] She accords an equal status to inveterately suppressed voices, those of her husband Daniel James, her mother, Caribbean domestic servants, and potentially freed slaves, who, Mary Prince argues, should be part of the British wage-labor system. Their dialogues lie in and through her own. And in fact the post-publication controversy enables some of those voices to be heard for the first time and makes manifest the power of insurgent texts, mediated or not. Moreover, she occasionally records conversations that stress a community presence as well as a subtle but ubiquitous community resistance. For example, when she arrives at the second owners' house, two bondwomen advise her to "keep a good heart, if you are to live here."[50] Laconically they alert her to imminent tribulation, offer emotional support, and counsel her to stand firm to facilitate survival. Their remarks site them on the never-ending transhistorical continuum of struggle. In that sense Mary Prince is also (with the same rider about the heterogeneity of slaves understood) a community historian, a recorder in her own right, regardless of editorial mediations.

After the publication of Mary Prince's *History* and the intense debate that it generated, Mary Prince spoke with her mind and her body on several important occasions but otherwise remained significantly silent. Let me back up for a moment. First of all, provincial evangelical women ordered copies of the *History* as anti-slavery propaganda against which opponents launched a predictable assault. Like Thomas Pringle, these women aimed to "authenticate" Mary Prince's facts with dispatch, especially her whipping experiences. Flogging had become a critical issue in provincial women's propaganda campaigns ever since Secretary of State for Foreign Affairs, George Canning, had introduced a bill in the House of Commons in 1823, arguing that flogging black females was unbecoming to a sense of Christian propriety.

In fact, flogging was one of the worst punishments evangelical women could imagine—especially, but not only, in the case of females—since it combined absolute control and remorseless abuse of the female body by males. (Such a preoccupying concern for female safety connotes their own, perhaps self-denied, vulnerabilities.) Abhorrence of flogging was also part of the longstanding theological criticism of extremes of physical punishment based on the idea that all men and women are the *imago dei* and must be accorded human dignity.[51] Flogging, in a word, was anti-Christian. Worst of all, it was a public act, involving an exposed nakedness and an unsolicited male gaze, sometimes even attracting spectators and enthusiasts.[52]

Mary Prince's repeated descriptions of floggings in her *History* reflect these anxieties and considerations; she was probably asked for the sake of the emancipationist cause to be as specific as possible about unspeakable, possibly repressed, traumas.[53] She responded by claiming a silent subjectivity, by presenting her body as a text of the "truth" of her history; this body could not lie. Once again she accepts her role within the dominant discourse yet manages to extend its possibilities to her own advantage. By the time she discusses her marriage, she had touched on almost every clause included in resolutions drawn up by Ladies Anti-Slavery Associations around the country. Mary Prince's text corroborates and consolidates associationist demands for conversion and family unity, for an end to flogging in general, and female flogging in particular. Just as Pringle certifies the "authenticity" of her narrative, so she in turn justifies evangelical women's nationwide political participation, not generally considered an appropriate activity unless understood as "charity."[54] In the appendix to the third edition of Mary Prince's *History,* Lucy Townsend, an officer of the pioneering Birmingham Ladies' Society for Relief of Negro Slaves and a solid evangelical leader, wrote a letter to Thomas Pringle asking "to be furnished with some description of the marks of former ill-usage of Mary Prince's person." Once again the Birmingham group who included Elizabeth Heyrick assumed the lead. White British female abolitionists took the flogging of Caribbean black females personally, as an affront to all women, their union on this issue another quiet anti-patriarchal attack. Pringle relayed the request to his wife, Margaret Pringle, who did not mince words in her reply to Lucy Townsend:

> The whole of the back part of her body, she states, is distinctly scarred, and, as it were, *chequered,* with the vestiges of severe floggings. Besides this, there are many large scars on the other parts of her person, exhibiting an appearance as if the flesh had been deeply cut, or lacerated with *gashes,* by some instrument wielded by most unmerciful hands. Mary affirms, that all these scars were occasioned by the various cruel punishments she has mentioned or referred to in her narrative. . . . I beg to add to my own testimony that of Miss Strickland (the lady who wrote down in this house the narrative . . . of Mary Prince) . . . together with the testimonies of my sister Susan and my friend Miss Martha Browne— all of whom were present and assisted me this day in a second inspection of Mary's body.[55]

Historically responsible, as independent-minded as they had been when they kept their Association politically separate from the London anti-slavery headquarters, and intent on mobilizing the best propaganda to change public opinion and gain political support, evangelical women configure Mary Prince within what could be thought of as a "scopic [masculinist] economy [that] signifies . . . her relegation to passivity: she will be the . . . object."[56] Her objectified body invokes the horror of slavery. But just as much to the point, Mary Prince's graphic memoirs that have been spoken as well as written down have already destabilized any possible casting of herself as object. Indeed since she would have operated well within her rights (as evangelicals conceived of them) to refuse their request to view her body on the grounds of modesty, Mary Prince not only permits but probably desires her body to be used in this way, as a space of inscription. Their request offers her a rare opportunity to speak her history—and the history of other slaves—corporeally to the world. She authenticates herself within a society in which she has little power to generate, in Robert Stepto's phrase, "authenticating devices" that will corroborate and fortify her text(s); such "devices" are usually initiated and written by others on a slave's behalf.[57] In that sense, female abolitionists become Mary Prince's instrument because she is challenging the meaning they attach to historical responsibility: they seek legal liberty for slaves; she insists on a much wider definition of liberty that includes the right to gainful employment, public voicing, a redress of received Eurocentric mythologies; and some redefinition of power and values. The meaning of freedom is being negotiated. Her act of self-exposure exposes illicit impositions of cruel force and de-emphasizes evangelical women's insistence on an end only to the flogging of females. She reminds gazers and readers alike that flogging recognizes no sexual difference. Her body-as-text announces that, regardless of gender, torture speaks and is spoken. She re-sounds the void on behalf of slave communities everywhere.

The pro-slavery lobby supported her testimony quite differently. Her "pretended history" is nothing more than a string of "hideous falsehoods and misrepresentations," according to the notorious plantocratic editor of the *Glasgow Herald,* James Macqueen. Vituperative accusations proselytized precisely what they sought to contain: her notable presence and authority. Understandably though unwittingly, defamers highlighted how Mary Prince's careful grooming, smart outfits, show of self-possession, and the free exercise of sexuality not only enhanced her self-definition but facilitated her access to life-affirming avenues of information and human communication.[58] In their ardor to denounce her "dissolute character" in graphic detail, they reaccentuated Pringle's reticence to allow sexuality to be discussed.

They affirmed its presence everywhere and its significance in her life. The competing descriptions of the pro- and anti-slavery lobbies underlined Mary Prince's refusal to be defined in their terms.

Thomas Pringle's *Supplement* summarizes the rancorous debate brought about by detractors' repudiations and thereby exposes the power of Mary Prince's narrative to provoke them. The *Supplement* includes correspondence from the Woods that slanders Mary Prince's moral character, Pringle's well-intended character sketch of Mary Prince in response and his point-by-point refutation of the Woods' charges, Joseph Phillips' and a Mrs. Forsyth's supportive testimonies, and Pringle's explanation of the Reverend James Curtin's antagonism toward Mary Prince. After the *History* appears, Mary Prince breaks a dignified post-publication silence by agreeing to an interview with the Reverend Curtin; she amplifies her authority by not flinching from prior aspersions he has publicly cast.[59] She admits to Thomas Pringle that she may have misunderstood the Reverend Curtin's conversion practices in Antigua. She accepts a small correction of fact—she was baptized in April not August. Thus she retracts testimony around the edges and, since these refutations are the best a minister charging inveterate profligacy can do to advance his case, she silently reconsolidates the veracity of her narrative. She displays slaves' everyday reality as it had not hitherto been shown in a century and a half of Anglo-Africanist portrayals.

A tug of war also exists between partisans and plantocrats over the principle of naming. Pringle opts for the metaphorically dense Mary Prince while Wood favors "the woman Molly," its casual nature and absent patronym underscoring the Woods's obsession with ownership. Mary Prince rarely names herself throughout the narrative though the range of names attributed to her offers another space in which her roles and desires can be "told." In the parliamentary petition of 1829, for example, "Mary Prince or James, commonly called Molly Wood" [asks to] return to the West Indies, but not as a slave."[60] The earliest title of the *History,* moreover, was *The Life of Mary, Princess of Wales, a West Indian Slave*—Princess of Wales being a name with which Mary Prince's owners tried to ridicule her sense of self-possession. Interestingly, the ultimate, official title privileges Mary Prince's personal narration—*The History of Mary Prince . . . Related by Herself*—and her life lived heterogeneously as well as in and through time. How much say she had in that final, more self-validating title remains unclear. This layering of names signifies her criss-crossing attachments, voluntary and coerced, but nomenclature cannot begin to define her ontological complexity. So she appears to stand somewhat apart; she is the "I" who recognizes her multiple subject positions but refuses definition on this basis alone. With such naming symbolism, both Pringle and Wood strive to contain and control her within their own separate economies, one avowedly based on spiritual values, the other based on material ownership of human beings.

Despite oppositional agendas that created a national political split, all three groups, the plantocratic lobby and male and female emancipationists as a whole press Mary Prince's narrative into the service of their own branch of dominant ideology—including that of "separate spheres" for men and women— that will secure a post-emancipation, European-dominated, colonial world. This is not to argue that Mary Prince consciously opposed such a world, but the world that she projected uncharacteristically recognized the everyday authentic reality and conflicts of African-Caribbean and black British men and women as well as white. The three groups hold widely diverse views on human equality that in turn differ from the view envisaged and enunciated by Mary Prince in her *History* and in her silent dialogues with slave narratees. Notwithstanding abolitionists' sincere commitment to emancipation, in their multiple objectifications of Mary Prince, the British colonizers are often more ideologically unified than they at first appear. At one level, they create isomorphic structures.

Set beside these homogenized, yet differently constructed or intended views, Mary Prince denies their "truth." If anything, she reverses roles with her supporters because, even though she knows they can pass a bill, find her employment, publish her narrative, she refuses "to internalize the other as the object of benevolence."[61] She makes their theory of emancipation responsible for what it says. She literalizes it. The former colonized other becomes the sovereign subject who reduces a group of ruling-class abolitionists to a one-dimensional role in colonialism: to end slavery. With the discursive means at her disposal, she attempts a reversal of power and instigates "new struggles against existing forms of power."[62] The *History* authorizes her, not them, in that her text and her body are "available" for all to read; she is no longer simply an abstract European construction of tropes, figures, and "authenticating devices"; she mocks, consciously or not, their always sincere efforts to invoke pity for slaves by depicting one-dimensional victims. She declines to be effaced or constituted as a "fixed" fetish that will primarily validate the evangelical ethic. Furthermore, she pushes plantocrats into a defensive posture as blusterers, forced to attack the "word" of an individual whose humanity they customarily deny. In Frantz Fanon's formulations, she breaks their "flaunting violence" and psychologically takes up residence in the "settler's" place.[63] Discursive guerilla warfare forces cultural reinscription. Insurgency is countermythology.

Mary Prince, then, claims subjectship from Europeans in written and spoken language. She sets herself apart, not only from contemporary emancipationists, but also from the protracted lineage of white female writers that began haltingly in the late seventeenth-century to question the legitimacy of slavery. Despite the fact that her *History* causes other texts to proliferate—prefaces, apologias, diatribes, reports in *The Times*—her account assimilates them, comments on them, and self-augments as a result; out of her conflicts with authorities and her grasp of their ideological limitations, she establishes an autonomous domain of her own. Mary Prince reverses the idea of devices such as supplements and newspaper articles to authenticate her personhood. Instead, the white British texts that seek to construct and contain her become borders around an inviolable textual frontier that she has created for herself, on her own behalf. Her published text—a version of experiential truth refracted through the lens of an invisibly manacled woman and a propagandistic editor and transcriber—signifies visible public victory for a self-motivated subject. She attains authorship while simultaneously conforming and subversively erupting (consciously and unconsciously) out of that conformity. Mary Prince inaugurates a black female counteroffensive to pro- and anti-slavery Anglo-Africanism and refuses a totalizing conception of black women as flogged, half-naked victims of slavery's entourage. Her text encourages a tripartite (though overlapping) view of emancipationist writers based on gender and racial difference. No African-British slavewoman prior to 1831 had written for publication. Mary Prince's narrative helped to name that hitherto untold history and at the same time problematized the customary univocal though politically differentiated accounts by abolitionists and plantocrats alike. Claiming voice and agency, Mary Prince debunks old mythologies, declines external definitions of slaves and ex-slaves, and clears a path for more open contestations of power in the future. She announces her participation not only in the emancipationist and anti-colonialist struggles but in the collective movement for black women's rights that was to be notably absent in the upcoming agitation for British white women's suffrage.

Chapter 14

Conclusion

Between 1823 and 1833, female emancipationists transformed the cultural face of England as a result of the discourse on slavery. Women throughout the provinces transcended their prescribed social role as philanthropic domestic angels to become political activists protected from any charge of excess by that very prescription. The female guardians of national morality had taken to the streets, attaining an unprecedentedly rich subjectivity. In founding associations, raising funds, and formulating principles, resolutions, reports, and pamphlets apart from men, women had established a firm autonomy as community publicists and historians. Systematically fostering an anti-slavery consciousness from town to town, they changed the everyday tenor of local communities. The ripple effect and the attack on profit touched everyone from small provincial grocers to slave-traders and slave-owners themselves. Activists had seized upon a startling way to display female power by capitalizing on their role as consumers in control of domestic purse strings.

Moreover, in decrying the status of slaves, these female writers displaced certain anxieties about the frequently masked limitations imposed on their own lives. In slave societies, British women had an image of tyranny that characterized, for them, male control over all women. Pressing the freedom of slaves enabled them to distance yet circulate negative facts about white women's experiences which they had little license to acknowledge openly, let alone propagandize in public. In that sense they provided a set of moral coordinates for articulating white female subjugation and aspects of colonial slavery by which attuned women could navigate; they constructed a paradigm of their own situation and a road map for its change. As moral crusaders, they converted a religious mandate, "turn the other cheek," into

299

a moral-radical taxonomy of "stand and fight." Christian love slipped into radical agency; self-propelled cultural intervention, what's more, usurped mandated confinement to the home.

Female writers who contributed to *The Bow in the Cloud* were active in a different way. As domestic missionaries, these writers urged conversion to Christianity as well as emancipation while lauding the sanctity of marriage, motherhood, and family life. They deplored the numberless daily outrages perpetrated against and in the name of these institutions. Universalized grieving African mothers, orphaned children, and ravaged slave-victims eclipsed slave insurrectionists as people to champion and protect. In other words, the immediatist, pro-boycott authorizing voices of Elizabeth Heyrick and women's anti-slavery group members harmonized only to a limited degree with the preponderantly pro-conversion propagandists. Varying priorites marked critical differences.

Any repressed anger inherent in their attacks could seldom be safely or openly admitted. Except for Harriet Martineau, Frances Wright, Owenite women, and additional female radicals, at no point did the covert challenge of female abolitionists to male hegemonic power become transparent or avowed, even though their public activities and manifestoes had stretched the ideology of separate spheres to its outermost borders. Moreover, their discourse about the mutual, though differently executed, sexual oppression of black and white women by slave-owners, entrepreneurs, rakes, and husbands—across class, cultural, and geographical lines—challenged patriarchal structures—however indirect—yet further.[1] Beyond that, through the application of physiocratic theory to the emancipation question, Harriet Martineau had reexamined and helped to reconstruct the definition of female self-empowerment. In 1832 she wrote in a letter to reformer Francis Place: "I wish I were in London, . . . I want to be doing something with the pen, since no other means of action in politics are in a woman's power."[2] And Martineau went on to sketch the advantages that single women held over married women in terms of political choices. Harriet Martineau's feminist assessments suggestively linked the strenuous activities of such agitators as Elizabeth Heyrick and Mary Anne Rawson, to their condition of widowhood, just as Martineau linked her own mobility and intellectual flexibility to her unmarried status:

> My strong will, combined with anxiety of conscience, makes me fit only to live alone; and my taste and liking are for living alone. The older I have grown, the more serious and irremediable have seemed

to me the evils and disadvantages of married life, as it exists among us at this time: and I am provided with what it is the bane of single life in ordinary cases to want,—substantial, laborious and serious occupation. My business in life has been to think and learn, and to speak out with absolute freedom what I have thought and learned. The freedom is itself a positive and never-failing enjoyment to me, after the bondage of my early life.[3]

Together, Harriet Martineau and other emancipationist women marked their discourse with class-, race-, and gender-stamped topoi. In heterogeneous formulations, their texts betrayed uneasy fusions of colonial attitudes with uncompromising anti-slavery demands. The enslavement of black women and attendant degradations affronted global "womanhood" and, Martineau further argued, social domination and cooptation also degraded white British women, though in sharply distinct ways. Ironically, Martineau championed the gendered rights of evangelical women, most of whom would have dissented on the need for such rights. The discourse on slavery had introduced an uneven, but vaguely discernible profile of women united across class, race, and gender lines by common, though diversely configured oppressors.

In part because of extensive female agitation, the absence of middle-class women's rights became palpably apparent and a movement to demand these rights quickened in subsequent decades. This is not in any way to argue that individuals from Anna Wheeler and Anne Wright to female working-class radicals, especially those in Owenite groups, were not already espousing and fomenting feminist views. A good handful were. In 1832, for example, "a number of articles appeared in [the Owenite newspaper] 'The Crisis,' taking up feminist and trade unionist issues and linking them to discussions of a female Messiah."[4] But with rare exceptions, evangelical women's beliefs based on sexual difference excluded them from that struggle; after emancipation, they kept up their charitable activities, visiting the poor and aiding foreign missions, as (or because?) more radical women championed women's rights.[5] Maintaining these beneficent projects helped to stamp their anti-slavery activities retroactively with a philanthropic cast that was rarely decoded as ideological. Furthermore, while many evangelical women excluded themselves from the discourse on rights—although some wrote books on women's nature and duties in the 1830s and 1840s that had at least an arguable political orientation—the rights of black women were never specifically raised. Writers imaged future communities where freed slaves lived under British control as domestic servants or waged laborers, social and political equality remaining an unrehearsed issue. Black men and women were in the main depicted as the other. In facilitating this reordering of social relations, pro-emancipation white female writers served the needs of an expanding capitalist culture by promoting its new forms, in accordance with the division of income, ownership, and production. Colonial emancipationist discourse, that is, fulfilled more than one crucial ideological function. In Benita Parry's words, "post-emancipation rhetoric . . . enabled the English to condemn slavery as unjust while enriching themselves through legitimized forms of exploitation."[6] Deeply rooted in a colonizer's perspective, anti-slavery discourse advanced British imperialism. Fractured families in bondage would be metamorphosed into sorely needed hard workers for the industrial state. Despite an early ambivalence about Liberia, Harriet Martineau was one of the few Europeans who gave serious thought to postemancipation society, though she remained uneasy about its potentially threatening consequences; she also paid earnest tribute to working-class radicals who saw the fight for emancipation as a conservative mystification of domestic problems:

> You [the abolitionists] are strengthening us [the English] for conflicts we have to enter upon. We have a population of our manufacturing towns almost as oppressed, and in our secluded rural districts also as ignorant as your negroes. These must be redeemed. We have also negroes in our dominions, who, though about to be entirely surrendered as property, will yet we fear, be long oppressed as citizens, if the vigilance which has freed them be not as active as ever. I regard the work of vindicating the civil standing of negroes as more arduous and dangerous than freeing them from the chain and the whip.[7]

Equally to the point, while white women's writings invariably identified slaves as the colonizers' other, they also resolidified familiar Anglo-Africanist attitudes; cultural mandates, however unsuccessful, still ostensibly forbade any equation of Africans with Europeans.[8] In its stylized repetitions of concepts and words like *pagan, ferocity, greegree, loyalty,* and allied ethnocentric formulations "which then [are] considered to have acquired, or more simply to be, reality,"[9] anti-slavery exposition attained, in Frantz Fanon's phrase, "maximum objectification." Any possibility of other frames of reference from which to discuss the reality of colonialism—a public forum of former slaves or wholesale republication of Robert Wedderburn's pamphlets, for instance—seemed inherently denied or foreclosed and the "fetishi-zation of stereotypical knowledge as power" was upheld.[10] On the other hand, definitions shifted: freedom was one thing, equality an-other; but freedom was always, too, a negotiable term. With or without authorial permission, slaves were always dialogically en route to a reclaimed subjectivity. Yet white writers tended to see themselves as separate from slaves by virtue of their class and gender—as well as their race—position within British society. Such attitudes strength-ened colonial power and the very domination of slaves that they politically opposed. Yet there was an exception to this Eurocentric outlook: the intermittent recognition that black and white women were gendered victims of different sorts within a male hegemonic order. And this very recognition always kept open the possibility of fissure and opposition to any across-the-board system of control. Thus the division between themselves and slaves that white women helped to consolidate sometimes reversed itself and prised open the connection between overlapping race and gender oppressions that were usually kept artificially separate. Nonetheless, writers gained authority by situating the other—distinct from themselves as sover-eign subjects—in a variety of fixed postures where the other was represented as a composite stereotype, rarely as a "genuinely felt and experienced force."[11] Further, most British activists saw emancipation as a final goal. Although a sizable number pursued the post-emancipa-tion fight to end Caribbean "Negro Apprenticeship" and slavery in the United States, few appraised the prejudice of post-colonial life that logically loomed. Accordingly, immersion in the anti-slavery battle-field foregrounded the battle for women's rights, while Anglo-Afri-canist and class assumptions largely confined it to the rights of a particular stratum of bourgeois women.[12]

Gendered emancipationist discourse served British colonialism in other ways too. Textual constructions of slaves and ex-slaves as people inferior to Europeans on the great chain of being were both a compulsory precondition as well an impetus for the mythological origin of the "Dark Continent."[13] Circulating and distributing European "knowledge" of what Africa and Africans were—these century-old caricatures and distortions—had helped to generate how Africa and Africans came to be viewed in Victorian England and helped propagate the "energizing myth" of British imperialism. Put another way, Anglo-Africanist discourse in the emancipation cause had gone some of the way toward reconciling internally inconsistent elements in emerging industrial-capitalist ideology. More than that, the apparent cohesive-ness of these elements within individual narratives further engaged the conflict. In the words of John Barrel and Harriet Guest in another context, such writings enabled "disparate discourse to be assembled into an aesthetic whole . . . performing the function of enabling contradictions to be uttered."[14] A necessarily hierarchical capitalist system could be encoded as a logical, even equity-producing system.

Yet most authors did not recognize these self-contradictory modes because they did not consider emancipation and bigoted attitudes (that were not perceived as bigoted) to be mutually exclusive terms. By legitimating diametrically opposed textual pronouncements, they legitimated the political economies they represented: "contradictory components of capitalist ideology can be enunciated, but can be prevented from coming into contact with each other [or being made to seem contradictory] by being made available to be sampled separately, as different readers and different occasions demand."[15]

Ultimately, however, the subsumption of the other's voice and the projection on to Africa of Britain's fears and needs undercut itself. By promoting literacy, slave marriages, happy families, and the abandonment of unchristian practices in texts, these writers encoded Africa as a continent to be aided through conquest and rule; beyond that, through silence and univocality, writers asserted the presence and voice of slaves who were denied. White abolitionists and emancipationists never shook off that cross-cutting, omnipresent ambivalence.

In the broadest sense of all, white women writers fashioned emancipationist discourse out of Anglo-Africanist givens and preoccupations. Over a protracted period, slavery had come to be synonymous with such catch-all generalizations as severed families and hideous punishments. Vignettes of slavery that had been abstracted from realistic portrayals of day-to-day community life now represented the institution itself. In part these depictions served a positive propagandistic function—clichés attracted sympathy and support—but no matter what authentic cast attached to them, they came to stand in the eyes of the British public for the sum total of slaves and slavery. Reductiveness bred and reinscribed condescension and control. Certain writers used some facts and discarded others; a consensual body of information and formulae from which to choose had accumulated gradually. But after Elizabeth Heyrick's pamphlets dislodged some of the old truth claims, a change took place because more open-ended formulations created new vantage points. Her uncompromising public stands combined the radical demands and polemical delivery of female Jacobins with spiritual commitment. While Heyrick's female peers read her works aloud to one another in private anti-slavery groups, they shied from her (signed) forthrightness in their own published texts. They preferred anonymity to adding/claiming their signatures. But many defended the boycott and harangued local grocers; in that respect they upheld the practices of earlier agitators from the 1780s and 1790s. Put another way, they rewrote their predecessors. Furthermore, with conversion cobbled to outright political demands, these texts collectively represented and fortified Britain's multiple constructions of the colonized other.

On this oppositional continuum, female activists of the 1820s and 1830s politically connected; they advocated emancipation, an economic boycott, and an end to female flogging. White agitators, moreover, implicitly tendered a challenge to patriarchal hegemony—as Mary Prince did—through their demands on behalf of enslaved black women. Additionally, Heyrick denounced compensation while Martineau argued that free laborers worked harder than slaves. Both Heyrick and Martineau employed forms of discourse customarily associated with male writers, notably pamphlets and economic treatises. Collectively the female associationists drew up manifestoes that formally echoed those of their male counterparts in the anti-slavery associations. This generic homogeneity was another, perhaps more subtle form of a publicly claimed female autonomy.

Attitudes as well as political perspectives varied too, though differences were often more unexamined than calculated. Martineau's temporary outlook on slavery and colonization derived from negrophobic Bryan Edwards' putative history; contributors to *The Bow* spoke Eurocentrically of lost souls and benighted humanity. An undercurrent of that Anglo-Africanist viewpoint informed the protective resolutions formulated by the Ladies Anti-Slavery Societies.

Thus across the political spectrum, colonial-emancipationist discourse by white British females evinced a fluid configuration and a precarious, necessarily temporary collectivity. The ideology of legal manumission subtly but insistently transversed and challenged the ruling male order. Public contestations over ends and means had created unorthodox and orthodox anti-slavery texts that functioned as spiritual as well as secular hallmarks.

Nonetheless, a critical component of anti-slavery discourse was always missing as long as the authentic voices of slaves remained silent, as long as autobiographical and epistolary texts by Africans and African-Caribbeans were not integral to the British anti-slavery corpus. So the textual assemblage of propaganda inflected with inevitable distortions about people in bondage and their quotidian lives did not add up to a comprehensive picture; the subject of white women's discourse, as well as its object—African slaves—could never be fixed as uniform subalterns, let alone as fighting insurrectionists. Hence the picture that ultimately represented slavery in white women's texts betrayed an inauthentic dimension, despite the timeliness and ardor of female radical demands. Slavery tended to be represented less as a real-life institution than as a set of familiar, preconceived references.[16] As white writers articulated and "assembled" slavery, as white readers read and considered their texts, so slavery came to be written and thought of. Their discourse over a hundred and fifty years—despite unconscious and sometimes expressed reservations—had helped to settle the parameters of anti-slavery ideology.

But the anti-slavery vision of white female writers was only one side of a kaleidoscopic picture. The commanding gazes of plantocrats as well as emancipationist male writers on colonial others differed considerably. Even more to the point, while white British women configured ex-slaves as people frequently denied a voiced subjectivity, members of the black community in London saw the matter in a number of different lights. A handful of writers and activists had given textual notice that many slaves and ex-slaves were challenging embedded Eurocentric assumptions. Thousands of slaves in the Caribbean displayed a multi-accented resistance. As Africa became gradually characterized as the "Dark Continent," Ira Aldridge was the most noted and written about, if not the most popular actor on the London stage. Despite racial persecution, he repeatedly proclaimed his primary motivation: "the honour of the stage and the depicting of human nature." Playing to packed houses all around the country and across Europe, Aldridge was deeply feared by the pro-slavery lobby:

> [Plantocratic] attacks on Aldridge grew more virulent as their position grew indefensible, and the appearance of a Negro playing the finest roles in all drama on the boards of Covent Garden was itself a damning negation, as Aldridge well knew, of their arguments and "theories" about the so-called inferior races. So the challenge was not that of actor *versus* actor. It was much more. Aldridge stood upon the stage ... as the lone protagonist of his oppressed and vilified people.[17]

Invalidating plantocratic contentions in public more directly, Nathaniel Paul, an African-American in Britain campaigning against the Liberian colonization scheme delivered nation-wide lectures that the provinces warmly received. He stated:

My lectures have been numerously attended by from two to three thousand people, the Hall and Chapels have been overflown, and hundreds have not been able to obtain admittance. I have not failed to give Uncle Sam due credit for his 2,000,000 slaves; nor to expose the cruel prejudices of the American to our colored race; or to fairly exhibit the hypocrisy of the Colonization Society, to the astonishment of the people here. And is this, say they, republican liberty? God deliver us from it.[18]

For most evangelical Anglican women and Nonconformists, especially Quakers, a successful emancipation campaign meant the end of slavery. Within the constraints of their own socio-political subjugation, they established the limits of what should be done, and when and why.

Mary Prince, however, who came to London from Antigua, saw the matter a little differently. Her goal—and the goal of free and enslaved black communities—was human freedom in a much wider sense. She was able to record her experience through a complex narrative that negotiates between the perspective of the colonized and the textual revisions of a white amanuensis.[19] As a representative party constituted within anti-slavery discourse who could apply the litmus test of her own reality to outsiders' constructions, Mary Prince stood in a different place from white female abolitionist contemporaries. Mary Prince, and men and women around the world whose multiple resistances she represented, redefined what they needed and wanted and intended to do quite differently. Her testimony simultaneously sounded all the silenced voices and repudiated Anglo-Africanist cultural assumptions that had taken hold for the past hundred and fifty years. This struggle among groups of cross-class, black and white men and women—a struggle that lies beyond the scope of this book—continues to this day.

Notes

Notes on Chapter 1

1. Winthrop D. Jordan, *White Over Black: American Attitudes Toward the Negro, 1500–1812* (Chapel Hill: University of North Carolina Press, 1968).

2. Edward Said, *Orientalism* (New York: Vintage, 1979). Borrowing from Said's conceptualization of orientalism, I am coining the concept Anglo-Africanism. I have found Said's analysis indispensible, especially his analysis of how cultural traditions are constructed and circulated; and his formulations of the ideological base of abstract categories of othering in multiple cultural productions. In *Blank Darkness: Africanist Discourse in French* (Chicago: University of Chicago Press, 1985), p. xi, Christopher Miller also discusses the issue of constructed terms. I have greatly benefitted from Christopher L. Miller's conceptualization of "an unresolvable tension between a pseudo-object projected onto the void and a real object that bears the same name: Africa."

3. *The History of Mary Prince: A West Indian Slave Related by Herself,* ed. Moira Ferguson, with a preface by Ziggi Alexander (London: Pandora, 1987). All references will be to this edition.

4. Patrick Brantlinger, *Rule of Darkness: British Literature and Imperalism, 1830–1914* (Ithaca: Cornell University Press, 1988). Patrick Brantlinger's discussion of the origins and transformations of the metaphor of Africa as the "Dark Continent" has been very important in my study, especially in helping me articulate and evaluate evolving colonizing attitudes.

5. Janet Schaw, *Journal of a Lady of Quality; Being a Narrative of a Journey from Scotland to the West Indies, North Carolina, and Portugal, in the years 1774 to 1776,* ed. Evangeline Walker Andrews, in collaboration with Charles McLean Andrews (New Haven: Yale University Press, 1921).

6. James Walvin, *The Black Presence: A documentary history of the Negro in England, 1555–1860* (New York: Schocken Books, 1972), p. 118; see also

309

Edward Long, *The History of Jamaica, or General Survey of the Antient and Modern State of That Island: With Reflections on its Situations, Settlements, Inhabitants, Climate, Products, Commerce, Laws and Government,* new edition with introduction by George Metcalf. Vol. 2, 1st ed. 1774; Frank Cass & Co., Ltd., 1970, p. 362.

7. Hannah More, *Slavery: A Poem* (London: T. Cadell, 1788).

8. Abdul JanMohamed, *Manichean Aesthetics: The Politics of Literature in Colonial Africa* (Amherst: University of Massachusetts Press, 1983). Mary Louise Pratt, "Scratches on the Face of the Country; or, What Mr. Barrow Saw in the Land of the Bushmen," in *"Race," Writing, and Difference,* ed. Henry Louis Gates, Jr. (Chicago: University of Chicago Press, 1985), pp. 138–162. Mary Louise Pratt's conceptualizations of the representation of the other in travel narratives invaluably aided me in considering the construction of Anglo-Saxon women's anti-slavery texts.

9. In discussions of dialogue and multiple voices here and elsewhere, I am drawing on the ideas of M. M. Bakhtin, "Discourse in the Novel," in *The Dialogic Imagination: Four Essays,* ed. Michael Holquist, trans. Caryl Emerson and Michael Holquist Austin: University of Texas, 1981), pp. 259–422. M. M. Bakhtin's conceptions of dialogism and double-voicedness have influenced this study, especially two related notions. One:

> Everything means, is understood, as a part of a greater whole—there is a constant interaction between meanings, all of which have the potential of conditioning others. Which will affect the other, how it will do so and in what degree is what is actually settled at the moment of utterance (p. 426).

And two "The mixing, within a single concrete utterance, of two or more different linguistic consciousnesses, often widely separated in time and social space (p. 429).

10. Mary Prince, *A History,* p. 84.

11. Jordan, *White Over Black,* p. 41.

12. Pratt, "Scratches on the Face," p. 139.

13. For helpful discussions of these questions of historical relationships, see Marc Bloch, *Feudal Society* (Chicago: University of Chicago Press, 1961); Lewis P. Simpson, *The Dispossessed Garden: Pastoral and History in Southern Literature* (Athens, GA: University of Georgia Press, 1975).

14. For elaboration of statistical information see B. W. Higman, *Slave Populations of the British Caribbean 1807–1834* (Baltimore: The Johns Hopkins University Press, 1984), especially Chapters 1 and 4.

15. Among several informative sources for the phenomenon of Barbary Coast slavery is K. G. Davies, *The Royal African Company* (London: Atheneum. 1957).

16. F. O. Shyllon, *Black Slaves in Britain* (London: Oxford University Press, 1974), p. 1.

17. Shyllon, *Black Slaves,* p. 2.

18. Michael Craton, *Sinews of Empire: A Short History of British Slavery* (Garden City: Anchor Books, 1974), p. xii.

19. There is a very large body of research and controversy on the history of slavery. Among representative texts by black and white historians and black slaves, ex-slaves, and their contemporaries are the following: Eric Williams, *Capitalism and Slavery* (Chapel Hill: University of North Carolina Press, 1944), especially pp. 3–107; C. L. R. James, *The Black Jacobins. Toussaint L'Ouverture and the San Domingo Revolution* (New York: Vintage, 1963); E. E. Rich, "The Slave Trade and National Rivalries," Part IV in Chapter VI, in *The Cambridge Economic History of Europe,* vol. 4 of *The Economy of Expanding Europe in the 16th and 17th Centuries,* ed. E. E. Rich and C. H. Wilson (Cambridge: Cambridge University Press, 1967), pp. 323–338; Peter Fryer, *Staying Power: The History of Black People in Britain* (London: Pluto Press, 1984); David Brion Davis, *The Problem of Slavery in Western Culture* (Ithaca: Cornell University Press, 1966), Parts I and II; and Roger Anstey, *The Atlantic Slave Trade and British Abolition 1760–1812* (Atlantic Highlands, NJ: Humanities Press, 1975). For a traditional overview of the activities of white British abolitionists, see Sir Reginald Coupland, *The British Anti-Slavery Movement* (London: Oxford University Press, 1933; London: Frank Cass & Co., Ltd., 1964); Frank F. Klingberg, *The Anti-Slavery Movement in England* (New Haven: Yale University Press, 1926), pp. 1–21. For statistical data, see Philip D. Curtin, *The Atlantic Slave Trade: A Census* (Madison: University of Wisconsin Press, 1969), pp. 95–126. For attitudes toward Africans and slaves, see Jordan, *White Over Black,* footnote 1; Anthony J. Barker, *The African Link: British Attitudes to the Negro in the Era of the Atlantic Slave Trade 1550–1807* (London: Frank Cass and Co., Ltd., 1978); Philip D. Curtin, *The Image of Africa: British Ideas and Action, 1780–1850* (Madison: University of Wisconsin Press, 1964). Escaped or manumitted slaves relate their experiences first hand in Ottobah Cugoano, *Thoughts and Sentiments on the Evil and Wicked Traffic of the Slavery and Commerce of the Human Species Humbly Submitted to the Inhabitants of Great Britain* (London, 1787; Reprint. Dawsons, 1969); Olaudah Equiano, *The Interesting Narrative of the Life of Olaudah Equiano, or Gustavus Vassa, the African. Written by Himself* (London: Printed and sold by the Author, 1789); Reprint. as *Equiano's Travels,* ed. Paul Edwards (London: Heinemann, 1967). *Letters of Ignatius Sancho, an African: to which are prefixed Memoirs of his Life by Joseph Jekyll, Esq. M.P.,* [1st ed. 1782] 5th ed. (1803; Reprint. 1968, with intro. by Paul Edwards). For particular information about Britain's initial entry into the colonial trade, see *The first voyage of the right worshipfull and valiant knight sir John Hawkins, sometimes treasurer of the Majesties navie Roial, made to the West Indies 1562,* in Richard Hakluyt, *Principall Navigations* (1589, 1598, etc.), Vol. 7 (London: J. M. Dent, 1926); *Slavery, Abolition and Emancipation: Black Slaves and the British Empire: A Thematic Documentary,* ed. Michael Craton, James Walvin and David Wright (London: Longman, 1976), p. 12. For more information about Hawkins' movement, see

E. E. Rich, p. 326. Specific documents that relate to the growing involvement can be found in Elizabeth Donnan, *Documents Illustrative of the History of the Slave Trade to America,* vol. 1, 1441–1700 (Washington, DC: Carnegie Institution, 1930).

20. E. E. Rich, "The Slave Trade," pp. 312, 341–45; Craton, *Sinews of Empire,* p. 12.

21. See Curtin, *The Atlantic Slave Trade,* footnote 19.

22. For information about the evolution of the West Indian lobby, see Fryer, *Staying Power,* p. 49. See also Craton for sources related to the plantocratic lobby.

23. See, for example, K. V. Thomas, "Women and the Civil War Sects," *Past and Present,* no. 13 (1958): 42–63; Ellen McArthur, "Women Petitioners and the Long Parliament," *English Historical Review* 24 (1909): 698–709; and E. M. Williams, "Women Preachers in the Civil War," *Journal of Modern History,* 1 (1929): 561–569.

24. Among the earliest protestors were Morgan Godwyn, *The Negro's and Indian's Advocate, Suing for their Admission into the Church* (London, 1680), and the celebrated nonconformist, Richard Baxter, *Chapters from a Christian Directory, or a Summ of Practical Theology and Cases of Conscience,* ed. Jeannette H. Tawney (London, 1673. Reprint. 1925). Baxter condemned slavehunters as "the common enemies of mankind," although he condoned slavery as long as it was well-regulated (Coupland, *The British Anti-Slavery Movement,* p. 40). For information about these writers, see Davis, *The Problem of Slavery,* pp. 204–206, pp. 338–341. In 1675, the Quaker William Edmundson argued with the Governor of the Barbados that Christ died for black and white people alike, while George Fox cautioned slave-owners to treat slaves humanely.

25. Davis, *The Problem of Slavery,* p. 218.

26. Thomas Tryon, *Friendly Advice to the Gentlemen-Planters of the East and West Indies* (London, 1684).

27. Professor Lemuel Johnson postulated this compelling idea at a panel on women writers and colonialism in San Francisco at a Modern Language Association panel, December, 1987.

28. *Letters, Domestick and Foreign, to Several Persons of Quality: Occasionally distributed in Subjects, Philosophicall, Theological; and Moral* (London: George Conyers and Elizabeth Harris, 1700), p. 183 and pp. 185–186.

29. For Tryon's hypothesis about nature and spirit, see Ginnie Smith, "Thomas Tryon's regimen for women: sectarian health in the seventeenth century," in *The Sexual Dynamics of History. Men's Power, Women's Resistance* ed. The London Feminist History Group (London: Pluto Press, 1983), pp. 47–65.

30. *Miscellanea: or The Second Part of Poetical Recreations. Compos'd by*

Several Authors (London: Benjamin Crayle, 1688), Part 1 by J. Barker, pp. 280–283.

31. The title of the poem is "To Their Graces, The Duke and Dutchess of Albemarle, Upon Their Voyage for Jamaica."

32. For further information about Barbary Coast slavery, see Stephen Clissold, *The Barbary Slaves* (London: Paul Elek, 1977), especially Chapter 1.

33. Clissold, *The Barbary Slaves,* pp. 55–56.

34. Clissold, *The Barbary Slaves,* p. 157.

35. Fryer, *Staying Power,* p. 23 and passim.

36. Davis, *The Problem of Slavery,* p. 412. The periodicals Davis cites are *London Magazine,* 7 (March 1938): 129, *Gentleman's Magazine,* 10 (July 1740):341, *Monthly Review,* 31 (July–December, 1764): 116, and *The Weekly Magazine, or Edinburgh Amusement,* 6 (November 30, 1769):258.

37. Richard M. Kain, "The Problem of Civilization in English Abolition Literature," *Philological Quarterly* 15, No. 4 (October 1936): 119.

38. Anonymous, *The Bath, Bristol, Tunbridge and Epsom Miscellany* (London: T. Dormer, 1735), pp. 15–16.

39. Mary Barber, *Poems on Several Occasions* (London: C. Rivington, 1734), pp. 271–274.

40. Sir Charles Wager was Commander of the Fleet and entertained the captives when they arrived in London, November 11, 1734.

41. Eliza Haywood, *Philidore and Placentia; or, L'Amour Trop Délicat,* in *Four before Richardson: Selected English Novels, 1720–1727,* ed. William Harlin McBurney (Lincoln: University of Nebraska Press, 1963), pp. 155–231; and Elizabeth Rowe, *The Works in Prose and Verse of Elizabeth Rowe* (London: Hett and Dodsley, 1739).

42. Elizabeth Rowe, *The History of Joseph. A Poem. In Ten Books. by the Author of Friendship in Death,* 2nd ed. (London: T. Worrall, 1737).

43. See endnote 19.

44. For helpful information on the long gradual shift from a society on which power was based preeminently on land to one based on capital, see *Manufacture in Town and Country Before the Factory,* eds. Maxine Berg, Pat Hudson and Michael Sornescher (Cambridge: Cambridge University Press, 1983), pp. 1–58; Leonore Davidoff and Catherine Hall, *Family Fortunes: Men and Women of the English Middle Class, 1780–1850* (London: Hutchinson, 1987), pp. 322–329 and passim.

45. See endnote 23.

46. McArthur, "Women Petitioners," p. 705.

47. Katherine Chidley (fl. 1641–1645), *The Justification of the Independent Churches of Christ. Being an answer to Mr. Edwards his booke, which hee hath written against the government of Christs Church, and the toleration of Christs*

publicke worship; briefly declaring that the congregations of the Saints ought not to have dependence in government upon any other, or direction in worship from any other than Christ, their head and law giver (London: William Lahrner, 1641), p. 457. Katherine Chidley is mentioned with other women preachers in Thomas, "Women and the Civil War Sects," pp. 49–52 and Williams, "Women Preachers," pp. 564–569.

48. McArthur, "Women Petitioners," p. 700.

49. McArthur, "Women Petitioners," p. 700.

50. *To the Parliament of the Commonwealth of England. The humble Petition of divers afflicted WOMEN, in behalf of M. John Lilburn Prisoner in Newgate,* June 25, 1653 and *Unto every individual Member of Parliament: The humble Representation of divers afflicted Women-Petitioners to the Parliament, on the bahalf of Mr. John Lilburn,* July 29, 1653.

51. McArthur, "Women Petitioners," p. 708.

52. Clark, Alice. *Working Life of Women in the Seventeenth Century* (London, 1919, Reprint. London: Routledge & Kegan Paul, 1982), pp. 234–235. See also "Alice Clark, "Working Life of Women in the Seventeenth Century." Reviewed by Christopher Hill, *History Workshop, A Journal of Socialist and Feminist Historians* 15 (Spring 1983): 174–175. I note for the record that Alice Clark's findings published in 1919 have generated considerable controversy.

53. See Berg, *Manufacture in Town and Country,* et al. eds., p. 30.

54. See Ruth Bloch, "Untangling the Roots of Modern Sex Roles: A Survey of Four Centuries of Change," *Signs: Journal of Women in Culture and Society* 4, no. 4 (Winter 1978): 236–52; Marlene LeGates, "The Cult of Womanhood in Eighteenth-Century Thought," *Eighteenth Century Studies* 10, no. 1 (Fall, 1976): 21–39; Barbara Welter, "The Cult of True Womanhood, 1820–1918," *American Quarterly* 18, no. 1 (Summer, 1966): 151–174.

55. Angeline Goreau, *The Whole Duty of a Woman. Female Writers in Seventeenth-Century England* (New York: Dial Press, Doubleday & Company, 1985), especially pp. 1–64. For a useful summation on the subject, see Bridget Hill, *Eighteenth-Century Women: An Anthology* (London: George Allen & Unwin, 1984). For the evangelical influence, see Chapters 9 and 11, particularly.

56. See Felicity A. Nussbaum, *The Brink of All We Hate. English Satires on Women 1660–1750* (Lexington: University of Kentucky Press, 1984) and Katharine M. Rogers, *The Troublesome Helpmate. A History of Misogyny in Literature* (Seattle: University of Washington Press, 1966).

57. Ellen Pollak, *The Poetics of Sexual Myth: Gender and Ideology in The Verse of Swift and Pope* (Chicago: University of Chicago Press, 1985).

58. Ellen Pollak, "Comment in Susan Gubar's 'The Female Monster in Augustan Satire'", in *Signs* 3, no. 3 (Spring 1978): 728.

59. Roy Porter, *English Society in the Eighteenth Century* (London: Penguin, 1982), pp. 37–38.

60. Elaine Hobby, *Virtue of Necessity: English Women's Writing 1649–1688* (London: Virago, 1988; Ann Arbor: University of Michigan Press, 1989).

61. Margaret Cavendish, Duchess of Newcastle, *Bell in Campo* in *Plays* (Loncon, 1662).

62. Frances Boothby, *Marcelia; or, The Treacherous Friend* (London: Will Cademan, 1670).

63. I thank Elaine Hobby for a valuable discussion of this point.

64. Michel Foucault, *The Archaeology of Knowledge and the Discourse on Language,* trans. A. M. Sheridan (New York: Pantheon Books, 1972), especially Chapter 1.

65. Ephelia [pseud. fl. 1679], *Female Poems on Several Occasions* (London: William Downing for James Courtney, 1679), p. 458.

66. See *Miscellanea,* Part. 1 by J. Barker and also pp. 280–283. To gain a sense of women's usage of the term slavery in any context in this period, I began to collect references in poetry and prose. I stopped when it became clear that writers as diverse as Katherine Philips, the Duchess of Newcastle, Aphra Behn, Mrs. Taylor, Lady Chudleigh, Sarah Fyge Field Egerton, Anne Finch, the Countess of Winchelsea, Elizabeth Rowe, Elizabeth Tollett, and many more frequently employed that metaphor to express the subjugation of women; marriage was far and away the front-runner situation in which women described themselves or other women as "enslaved." Education was a poor second and love third. Professor Ringler, senior researcher in sixteenth-century poetry at the Huntington Library, told me in a private conversation that "there were no references to women as slaves in sixteenth-century poetry except for one to the 'double yoke of marriage' in Sir Philip Sidney's *Arcadia."* He further noted that the pre-seventeenth-century convention regarding the term slavery referred exclusively to women enslaving men. (He thought it unusual for slave references to come in because of the slave trade.)

67. Bathsua Makin, "To the Reader," in *An Essay to revive the Antient Education of Gentlewomen, in religion, manners, arts and tongues with an Answer to the Objections against this Way of Education* (London: J. D. to be sold by Thomas Parkhurst, 1673), p. 5.

68. Judith Drake, *An Essay in Defence of the Female Sex. In which are inserted the Characters of a Pedant, a Squire, a Beau, a Vertuoso, a Poetaster, a City-critic, etc., In a letter to a Lady. Written by a Lady.* (London: A. Roper and E. Wilkinson, 1696, Reprint. New York: Source Book Press, 1970). Please note that Drake's authorship is disputed. For a summation of biographical data on Judith Drake, see *The Female Companion to Literature in English: Women Writers from the Middle Ages to the Present.* Eds. Virginia Blain, Isobel Grundy and Patricia Clements (London: B. T. Batsford; New Haven: Yale University Press, 1990), p. 308.

69. Mary Astell, *Some Reflections Upon Marriage. With Additions,* 5th ed.

(Dublin: S. Hyde, E. Dobson, R. Gunne and R. Owen, 1730), p. 66. I thank Ruth Perry for helpful discussions about Mary Astell and slavery.

70. Shyllon, *Black Slaves,* pp. 7–8.

71. Jordan, *White Over Black,* p. 28.

72. Likely too, as Ziggi Alexander suggests, there are many more African voices still to be found in so far uncovered documents. Ziggi Alexander, "Let It Lie Upon the Table: The Status of Black Women's Biography in the UK," in *Gender & History,* Vol. 2, No. 1 (Spring 1990), pp. 22–33.

Notes on Chapter 2

1. Aphra Behn, *Oroonoko, or The History of The Royal Slave,* ed. K. A. Sey (London: 1688; Reprint. Tema, Ghana; Ghana Publishing Corporation, 1977). All citations are from this edition.

2. A cross-range of these opinions on *Oroonoko* appear in Mary Anne O'Donnell, *Aphra Behn: An Annotated Bibliography* (New York: Garland, 1986) pp. 380, 392, 476, 481 and passim; Maureen Duffy, *The Passionate Shepherdess* (New York: Avon, 1977), p. 267ff.; George Guffey, *Aphra Behn's Oroonoko: Occasion and Accomplishment* in *Two English Novelists. Aphra Behn and Anthony Trollope. Papers read at a Clark Library Seminar, May 11, 1974* (Los Angeles: University of California, 1975); Angeline Goreau, *Reconstructing Aphra: A Social Biography of Aphra Behn* (New York: Dial Press, Doubleday & Company, 1980), p. 59 and passim. See Goreau, Chapter 5 footnote 23 for a refutation of Guffey; Thomas Tryon, *Friendly Advice to the Gentlemen-Planters of the East and the West Indies* (London: 1684); the influence on Aphra Behn of Tryon's perspective on slavery is discussed in Duffy, *The Passionate Shepherdess,* pp. 268–269, and David Brion Davis, *The Problem of Slavery in Western Culture,* (Ithaca: Cornell University Press, 1966), pp. 371–374. For a discussion of Tryon's empathy toward women and Behn's admiration for "Tryonism," see Ginnie Smith, "Thomas Tryon's regimen for women: sectarian health in the seventeenth century," in *The sexual dynamics of history. Men's power, women's resistance,* ed. The London Feminist History Group (London: Pluto Press, 1983), pp. 47–65.

3. Winthrop Jordan, *White Over Black: American Attitudes Toward the Negro, 1550–1812* (Chapel Hill: University of North Carolina Press, 1968), p. 94.

4. For a valuable discussion of differences that dramatist Thomas Southerne introduced into his play entitled *Oroonoko,* modelled on Behn's tale, see Thomas Southerne, *Oroonoko,* ed. David Stuart Rodes and Maximillian E. Novak (Lincoln: University of Nebraska Press, 1976), pp. xiii-xlii. See also the incisive argument in Laura Brown, "The Romance of Empire: *Oroonoko* and the Trade in Slaves," in *The New Eighteenth Century: Theory, Politics, English*

Literature, ed. Felicity Nussbaum and Laura Brown (New York: Methuen, 1987), pp. 41–61.

5. Although they disagree on some critical issues, Maureen Duffy and Angeline Goreau creatively reconstruct compelling historical scenarios of Behn's life. See also Frederick W. Link, *Aphra Behn* (New York: Twayne Publishers, 1968), for information about the biographical controversy and denials by earlier critics of Behn's visit to Surinam.

6. A valuable discussion of Tryon's account of black slaves follows Warren's commentary in Southerne, *Oroonoko,* p. xxx.

7. William Byam, *An Exact Narrative of the State of Guinea,* quoted in Goreau, *Reconstructing Aphra,* p. 301. For more historical background concerning Lord Willoughby and the settlement of Surinam, see also W. Cunningham, *The Growth of English Industry and Commerce,* in *Modern Times. The Mercantile System,* Part One. (Cambridge: Cambridge University Press, 1925), p. 198 and passim. See also Calendar of State Papers Colonial, American and West Indies, 1661–1668. Byam's subsequent whereabouts are outlined in Frances Lanaghan, *Antigua and the Antiguans: A Full Account of the Colony and its Inhabitants, From the Time of the Caribs to the Present Day, Interspersed with Anecdotes and Legends. Also, an Impartial View of Slavery and the Free Labour Systems: The Statistics of the Island, and Biographical Notices of the Principal Families,* 2 vols. (London: Saunders & Otley, 1844), p. 155ff., and passim.

8. K. G. Davies, *The Royal African Company* (London: Atheneum, 1957), p. 477.

9. Walter Rodney, *West Africa and the Atlantic Slave-Trade* (East African Publishing House: Historical Association of Tanzania Paper #2, 1967), p. 9.

10. For challenges to monopoly trading, see Davies, *The Royal African Company,* especially section 1, Chapter 3 and section 3.

11. Quoted in Daniel Mannix, in collaboration with Malcolm Cowley, *Black Cargoes* (New York: Viking Press, 1962), pp. 12–13.

12. I thank Oyekan Owomoyela for a helpful discussion of this point.

13. Behn's thinking on slavery concurs with contemporary ideas, notably Locke's position in *A Treatise on Government,* that war is one of the few justifications for slavery. See *Slavery, Abolition and Emancipation. Black Slaves and the British Empire. A Thematic Documentary,* ed. Michael A. Craton, James Walvin and David Wright (London: Longman, 1976), pp. 203–204. If royalty is a special kind of being—European or African—then in that context the silent listeners are not especially naive. Behn would expect British laborers to accord such respect to royalty. But the construction of others goes well beyond class bias; Behn helps to usher in a certain kind of Anglo-Africanist discourse on slavery though this is not to deny that negative discourse about Africans preceded Behn. Leo Africanus remarks that "no nation under Heaven [is] more prone to Venery" [than] "Negroes" in Winthrop

NOTES TO CHAPTER 2

D. Jordan, "First Impressions: Initial English Confrontations with Africans," in *"Race" in Britain: Continuity and Change*, ed. Charles Husband (London: Hutchinson, 1982), p. 53. For further elaboration, see Jordan, *White Over Black*, and P. J. Marshall and Glyndwr Williams, *The Great Map of Mankind. Perceptions in New Worlds in the Age of Enlightenment* (Cambridge: Harvard University Press, 1982). I am indebted to Homi Bhabha's analysis of fetishization, "Signs taken for Wonders: Questions of Ambivalence and Authority under a Tree Outside Delhi, May 1817," in *"Race," Writing and Difference*, ed. Henry Louis Gates, Jr., (Chicago: University of Chicago Press, 1985), pp. 163–184.

14. Goreau, *Reconstructing Aphra*, p. 289.

15. *Behn, Oroonoko. The History of the Royal Slave*, ed. K. A. Sey, intro. K. A. Sey, p. vii.

16. Jordan, *White Over Black*, p. 42.

17. *To the Most Illustrious Christopher, Duke of Albemarle, on his Voyage to his Government of Jamaica. A Pindarick*. London: John Newton, 1687. For further evidence of Behn's perspective, see "The Widow Ranter," in *The Works of Aphra Behn*, ed. Montague Summers, Vol. 4, (London: Heineman, 1925). I thank Carol Barash for mentioning this poem to me.

18. For references to the literature of Barbary Coast slavery, see *A True Relation of the Adventures of Mr. R. D. an English Merchant, taken by The Turks of Argeir in 1666 . . . sent in a letter to his Honored Friend, Mr. S. B.* (London: Philip Brooksby, 1672). See also Davies, *The Royal African Company*, and Stephen Clissold, *The Barbary Slaves* (London: Paul Elek, 1977), especially Chapter 1.

19. For discussions of how political affairs in West Africa were manipulated by European merchants see Mannix, *Black Cargoes*, pp. 69–103. See also Rodney, *West Africa*, p. 7ff.

20. Rodney, *West Africa*, pp, 8–9 and passim.

21. Several critics argue persuasively that *Oroonoko* is a political allegory, among them Jerry Beasley in "Politics and Moral Idealism," in *Fetter'd or Free*, ed. Mary Anne Schofield and Cecelia Macheski (Athens, OH: Ohio University Press, 1986), pp. 221–222. See also Southerne, *Oroonoko*, eds. Maximilian E. Novak and David Stuart Rodes (Lincoln: University of Nebraska Press, 1976), p. x and Duffy, *The Passionate Shepherdess*, p. 267. Note also that Behn's exposé of political enemies in *Oroonoko* echoes her intentionality in *Letters to a Nobleman* (1684–1687) which illuminates a contemporary sexual scandal involving Whigs and helps vindicate Behn's royalist cause.

22. Many texts supply often variable information about fatalities on the Middle Passage. Several firsthand accounts by Africans themselves exist, notably Olaudah Equiano's. See Chapter 1, endnote 19. See also Eric Williams, *Capitalism and Slavery* (New York: Capricorn Books, 1944), Chapter 1, endnote 19, and Basil Davidson, *Black Mother* (London: Victor Gollancz, 1961); Mannix, *Black Cargoes;* J. D. Fage *A History of West Africa. An Introductory*

Survey. The Fourth Edition of 'An Introduction to the History of West Africa' (Cambridge: Cambridge University Press, 1969); Herbert S. Klein, *The Middle Passage. Comparative Studies in the Atlantic Slave Trade* (Princeton: Princeton University Press, 1978), pp. 141–174.

23. Olaudah Equiano, *Equiano's Travels. His Autobiography. The Interesting Narrative of the Life of Olaudah Equiano or Gustavus Vassa the African,* ed. Paul Edwards (London: Heinemann, 1789, rpt. 1967), pp. 25–32.

24. From 1732 to 1750, Hogarth depicts Africans in his major satirical series much more authentically, suggesting that Behn westernized Oroonoko's appearance partly to appeal verbally and aesthetically to her audience. See David Dabydeen, *Hogarth's Blacks: Images of Blacks in 18th-Century English Art* (Denmark: Dangaroo Press, 1985). Perhaps differences between Behn's and Hogarth's depictions stem from fears expressed in daily newspapers and periodicals about the influx of black people to Britain in the 1720s. See the *Daily Journal,* 5 April 1723. A European-idealized appearance, moreover, would be another way of Behn suggesting why Oroonoko wields power over the other slaves, with more traditional features. She might also have drawn more from historical portraits in many seventeenth-century canvases that depict blacks than from authentic likenesses. See also Orlando Patterson, *Slavery and Social Death: A Comparative Study* (Cambridge: Harvard University Press, 1982). Patterson compellingly argues the significance of verbal alienation, including slave-owner's re-namings. Trefry's sense of a power relationship in which Oroonoko still commands is evident (though arguably ironically) in Trefry's choice of the name Caesar. Behn could also be using the name ironically to stress powerlessness but that hypothesis would not reflect Oroonoko's specialized treatment in Surinam compared to that of other slaves.

25. Ellen Pollak included a valuable discussion of multiple inscriptions of incest in *Oroonoko* at a paper delivered at the Modern Language Association convention in San Francisco, 1987.

26. For information on African culture that elucidates Behn's embellishments, see John S. Mbiti, *African Religions and Philosophy* (New York: Praeger, 1970); E. Bolaji Idowu, *African Traditional Religion: A Definition* (London: SMC Press, 1973); Philip Curtin, *The Image of Africa: British Ideas and Action, 1780–1850* (Madison: University of Wisconsin Press, 1964). Although Curtin's book deals with a later period, he frequently refers back to ideas from the seventeenth century and earlier. For a historical review, see Fage, *A History of West Africa.* For an older, anti-slavery, pro-missionary perspective, see J. Leighton Wilson, *Western Africa: Its History, Condition, and Prospects* (New York: J. J. Harper, 1856). I thank Oyeken Owomoyela for discussions of West African religious beliefs and for directing me to source materials.

27. Jordan, *White Over Black,* pp. 370–371.

28. I thank my class on the eighteenth-century novel, spring semester 1988, for an invigorating debate over why the narrator leaves. At the simplest level,

Behn's alliance with the colonial ruling class overrides her friendship with Oroonoko. Patricia Meyer Spacks' perceptive commentary on female ethical development is especially relevant here, too, in light of Behn's future career, *Hudson Review,* 15 (Spring 1977): 44.

29. M. M. Bakhtin, *The Dialogic Imagination. Four Essays,* ed. Michael Holquist, trans. Caryl Emerson and Michael Holquist (Austin: University of Texas Press, 1981), p. 314.

30. Goreau, *Reconstructing Aphra,* pp. 77–78. See also Lawrence Stone, *The Family, Sex, and Marriage in England, 1500–1800* (New York: Harper, 1977), pp. 77–78; and Alan Macfarlane, *Marriage and Love in England: Modes of Reproduction 1800–1840* (Oxford: Basil Blackwell, 1986).

31. Robert Root, "Aphra Behn, Arranged Marriage and Restoration Comedy," in *Women and Literature,* 5 (Spring 1977): 8.

32. See Angeline Goreau, *The Whole Duty of a Woman: Female Writers in Seventeenth-Century England* (New York: Dial Press, Doubleday & Company, 1985) and Hilda Smith, *Reason's Disciples. Seventeenth-Century English Feminists* (Urbana: University of Illinois Press, 1982).

33. Mannix, *Black Cargoes,* p. 44.

34. Critics have remarked on Behn's attentiveness to issues of rape and predation. See Behn's biographers already cited, as well as Elaine Hobby, *Virtue of Necessity: English Women's Writings 1649–1688* (London: Virago, 1988), especially pp. 96–110, 114–127.

35. Antonia Fraser, *The Weaker Vessel* (New York: Alfred Knopf, 1984), p. 41. See also an interesting discussion of these ideas in their early formation in Janet Todd, *Sensibility. An Introduction* (London: Methuen, 1986).

36. Edward W. Said's analysis in *Orientalism* (New York: Vintage, 1979) of the construction of orientalism and Mary Louise Pratt's discussion of homogeneity in "Scratches on the Face of the Country; or, What Mr. Barrow Saw in the Land of the Bushmen," in *"Race," Writing and Difference,* ed. Henry Louis Gates, Jr. (Chicago: University of Chicago Press, 1985) were especially helpful in this chapter's formulations.

37. For parasitism, see Patterson, endnote 24.

38. For expositions of slave rebellions, see Michael Craton, *Testing the Chains: Resistance to Slavery in the British West Indies* (Ithaca: Cornell University Press, 1982); Hilary Beckles, *Black Rebellion in Barbados: The Struggle Against Slavery 1627–1833* (St. Michael, Barbados, W.I.: Antilles Publication, 1984); Lucille Mathurin, *The Rebel Woman in the British West Indies During Slavery* (Jamaica, W.I.: Institute of Jamaica Publications, 1975).

39. Todd, *Sensibility,* p. 19.

40. Idowu, *African Traditional Religion,* p. 155 and passim.

41. For the notion of two voices harnessed in one, of the text resisting

and inscribing contrary meaning simultaneously, see Bakhtin, *The Dialogic Imagination,* p. 430ff.

42. Thomas Docherty suggests this possibility in another context in *On Modern Authority. The Theory and Condition of Writing 1500 to the Present Day* (New York: St. Martin's Press; Sussex: The Harvester Press, 1987), pp. 49–50. "People travel in search of stability . . . [to examine] the possibilities of different social organizations in an effort to recapture . . . 'natural' social organization." Behn adds a further twist to the personal breakdown of stable "units" by questioning the destabilization that slavery fosters.

43. Mrs. A. Behn, *Oroonoko: or, the Royal Slave. A True History* (London: Printed for Will Canning, 1688). Penultimate (unpaginated) page of epistle dedicatory.

44. Behn's relationship to Lord Willoughby is taken up extensively by Angeline Goreau who speculates that Behn may have been Lady Willoughby's "natural" daughter; see Goreau, *Reconstructing Aphra,* pp. 44–52.

45. For Locke on slavery, see endnote 13.

46. For arguments that Oroonoko is a royalist allegory, see endnote 21.

47. Michael McKeon, *The Origins of the English Novel 1600–1740* (Baltimore: The Johns Hopkins University Press, 1987), p. 250.

48. The idea that western norms need to be the moral order of business on a global scale is carefully discussed in Howard Temperley, "The Ideology of Antislavery," in *The Abolition of the Atlantic Slave Trade: Origins and Effects in Europe, Africa, and the Americas,* ed. David Eltis and James Walvin (London: Macmillan, 1985), p. 22.

49. Anna Freud, *The Writings of Anna Freud. The Ego and the Mechanisms of Defense* (New York: International Universities Press, 1966).

50. Southerne, *Oroonoko,* dedicatory epistle (unpaginated) p. 4, in University of Nebraska Press edition.

51. By the late 1680s, Behn was chronically ill and seriously short of money, the theatre having failed due to social upheaval around the succession.

Notes on Chapter 3

1. Among many good accounts of Quaker involvement in the anti-slavery struggle are Auguste Jorns, *The Quakers as Pioneers in Social Work,* trans. Thomas Kite Brown, Jr. (New York: Macmillan, 1931), and Richard Vann, *The Social Development of English Quakerism, 1655–1755* (Cambridge: Harvard University Press, 1969). Although William Braithwaite in *The Second Period of Quakerism* (London: Macmillan, 1919) confines himself to the seventeenth century, he mentions some aspects of early anti-slavery thought among Friends and provides for an understanding of the Society's later, more forward-

looking tendencies. See particularly, pp. 415, 436, 596, 618, and 621. George Fox's *Epistles* contain the fullest information about the developing view of slavery in the Society of Friends, *A Collection of Many Select and Christian Epistles, Letters and Testimonies, Written on Sundry Occasions by that Ancient Eminent, Faithful Friend and Minister of Christ and Jesus, George Fox,* with preface by George Whitehead, 2 vols. (London: T. Sowle, 1698). See also David Brion Davis, *The Problem of Slavery in Western Culture* (Ithaca: Cornell University Press, 1966).

2. Barry Reay, "The Quakers, 1659, and the Restoration of the Monarchy," in *History,* vol. 63, no. 208 (June 1978): 193–213.

3. Barry Reay, "Quakerism and Society," in *Radical Religion in the English Revolution,* ed. J. F. McGregor and B. Reay (Oxford: Oxford University Press, 1984), p. 153 and passim.

4. Braithwaite, *The Second Period of Quakerism,* p. 24.

5. This information comes in private correspondence from Elaine Hobby to Moira Ferguson, January 1991.

6. In 1672 the Declaration of Indulgence suspended the Penal Laws against Nonconformists, who could meet from that point on. At the Great Pardon of 1672 many Quakers were released. Over the next two years, discriminatory laws were reinstituted. Fox decreed sex-segregated meetings after this renewal of persecution.

7. Out of 420 epistles written by Fox, nineteen concern slavery, including two that focus on captives in Algiers. Several specifically address the inhabitants of Barbados.

8. Herbert Aptheker, "The Quakers and Negro Slavery," *Journal of Negro History,* 25 (1940): 331–62.

9. *The Journal of George Fox, Revised by Norman Penney* (London: J. M. Dent & Sons; New York: E. P. Dutton & Co., 1924), p. 277.

10. The epistle of 1674 is entitled "For the Mens and Womens Meetings—Barbados," epistle no. 324, vol. 1, p. 343. In epistle 315 of 1675, "To Friends in Barbados," Fox discusses intensified persecution in England and the supportive letters received from Friends abroad, vol. 1, p. 353.

11. Michael Craton, *Testing the Chains: Resistance to Slavery in the British West Indies* (Ithaca: Cornell University Press, 1982), pp. 105–14, 335.

12. Aptheker, "The Quakers," p. 333. See also *Early Quaker Writings,* ed. Hugh Barbour and Arthur O. Roberts (Grand Rapids, MI: Eerdmans, 1973), p. 591. Note, too, that protestors existed outside the Society of Friends: see chapter 1, endnote 24 for details of these protestors.

13. Aptheker, "The Quakers," p. 334.

14. Jorns, *The Quakers as Pioneers,* p. 198. See also William Braithwaite, *The Beginnings of Quakerism* (London: Macmillan, 1912), p. 403.

15. John Rous, son of the Lieutenant Governor, who was a rich planter,

married a daughter of Margaret Fell Fox by her first marriage to Judge Fell. See Braithwaite, *The Second Period,* p. 618.

16. Arnold Lloyd, *Quaker Social History 1669–1738,* intro. Herbert G. Wood (London: Longmans, Green and Co., 1950), p. 89.

17. *Memoirs of the Life of George Fox. The Friends Library: Comprising Journals, Doctrinal Treatises, and Other Writings of Members of the Religious Society of Friends,* vol. 1., ed. William Evans and Thomas Evans, (Philadelphia: Joseph Rakestraw, 1838), p. 81.

18. Eric Williams, *Capitalism and Slavery* (New York: Capricorn Books, 1944), pp. 43–44; Jorns, *The Quakers as Pioneers,* p. 207.

19. Lloyd, *Quaker Social History,* p. 38.

20. Jorns, *The Quakers as Pioneers,* pp. 202–203, 208. See also Aptheker, "The Quakers," pp. 335–336.

21. For an untraditional view of the role of Quaker women in the Society of Friends, see Elaine Hobby, *Virtue of Necessity: English Women in Print, 1649–1688* (London: Virago, 1988). This chapter, especially in its foregrounding of Elizabeth Hooton, is indebted to Elaine Hobby's research. See also Phyllis Mack's compelling article, "Women as Prophets During the English Civil War," *Feminist Studies* 8, No. 1 (Spring 1982): 19–45 and Mabel Richmond Brailsford, *Quaker Women, 1650–1690* (London: Duckworth & Co., 1915). For a more conventional view of women's role that is increasingly being challenged, see William Braithwaite, *The Beginnings,* p. 341. See also Reay, "Quakerism and Society," pp. 143–146. For the role of women in Civil War sects, consult K. V. Thomas, "Women and the Civil War Sects," in *Past and Present,* no. 13 (1958): 42–63; Ellen McArthur, "Women Petitioners and the Long Parliament," in *English Historical Review* 24 (1909): 698–709; and E. M. Williams, "Women Preachers in the Civil War," in *Journal of Modern History* 1 (1929):38, 561–569.

22. See particularly Hobby, *Virtue of Necessity,* pp. 47–49.

23. Elaine Hobby drew my attention to the fact that Elizabeth Hooton was "already an established preacher" prior to joining the Society of Friends. See Hobby, *Virtue of Necessity,* pp. 36–37 and Brailsford, *Quaker Women,* p. 17. See also Emily Manners, *Elizabeth Hooton: First Quaker Woman Preacher (1600–1672)* in *The Journal of Friends Historical Society,* ed. Norman Penney, Supp. 12 (London: Headly Brothers, 1914).

24. Hobby, *Virtue of Necessity,* p. 36. See Lloyd, *Quaker Social History,* p. 107ff. For the controversy about women, see also Vann, *Social Development,* pp. 103–104.

25. Lloyd, *Quaker Social History,* p. 109.

26. Lloyd, *Quaker Social History,* p. 107. For specific political differences between Burrough and Bunyan, see Braithwaite, *The Beginnings,* pp. 285–288.

27. Lloyd, *Quaker Social History,* p. 108.

28. Lloyd, *Quaker Social History,* p. 110.

29. Vann, *Social Development,* p. 103 and note 25.

30. I thank Elaine Hobby for this insight.

31. *The Ladies Calling. In Two Parts.* Second impression. At the Theater in Oxford 1673. Angeline Goreau in *The Whole Duty of Woman: Female Writers in Seventeenth-Century England* (New York: Dial Press, Doubleday & Company, 1985), p. 12, speculates that the author may have been Richard Allestree, and discusses contemporary women's rights.

32. The institution of the traveling missionary was apparently disintegrating during this period. Richard Vann cites this disintegration as "one of the first effects of persecution" in *Social Development,* p. 96. However, the women in question refused to abandon the hardwon freedoms of the 1640s, 1650s, and early 1660s. As Phyllis Mack argues, they may well have seen themselves as akin to Old Testament prophets. For hardships suffered by female traveling missionaries, see Joseph Besse, *Collection of the Sufferings of People Called Quakers* (London, 1753).

33. Vann, *Social Development,* pp. 99–100.

34. Davis, *The Problem of Slavery,* p. 214.

35. Joyce L. Irwin, *Womanhood in Radical Protestantism 1525–1675* (New York: Edwin Mellen, 1979), p. 235.

36. Brailsford, *Quaker Women,* p. 38.

37. Lloyd, *Quaker Social History,* p. 114. Elaine Hobby documents that some Quakers in London had been organizing women's meetings "since about 1657," *Virtue of Necessity,* pp. 47, 213.

38. Alice Curwen, *A Relation of the Labour, Travail and Suffering of That Faithful Servant of the Lord Alice Curwen. Who departed this Life the 7th Day of the 6th Month, 1679, and resteth in Peace with the Lord. Here is the Patience of the Saints, here are they that keep the Commandents of God, and the Faith of Jesus, Rev. 14.12. The Souls of the Righteous are precious in the Eyes of the Lord, and they shall be had in Everlasting Remembrance. Printed in the year 1680. Something of Alice Curwen's Testimony, which did he upon her to declare some few dayes before she departed out of the Body; she spoke for one to come and write, and there was one that did come, and did propose to write, but the Lord's Power and presence was so with her, that the Friends that were with her were so broken into Tenderness that there could be nothing to be written, but there was one Friend which was present with her at the time which did remember something of what she did speak as followeth, whose Name is Ann Martindall* (Huntington Library, San Marino, CA, Box 131, n.p., n.d.).

39. Curwen, *A Relation,* p. 2.

40. Irwin, *Womanhood,* pp. 236–237.

41. George Rofe, *The Righteousness of God to Man. Wherein he was created*

. . . *With a True Declaration how I lived before I knew the truth, and How I come to know the truth, and overcame deceit* (London, 1656), p. 244.

42. Alice Curwen, *A Relation,* p. 18.

43. Mary Louise Pratt, "Scratches on the Face," in *"Race," Writing and Difference,* ed. Henry Louis Gates, Jr., (Chicago: University of Chicago Press, 1985), pp. 138–162.

44. M. M. Bakhtin, "Discourse in the Novel," in *The Dialogic Imagination,* ed. Michael Holquist, trans. Caryl Emerson and Michael Holquist (Austin: University of Texas Press, 1981), p. 277.

45. Book of St. Matthew, Chap. 21, verse 28–31.

46. For this linguistic shift, see James Walvin, *Black and White: The Negro and English Society 1555–1945* (London: Penguin Press, 1973), pp. 37–43. For background and further details, see Peter Fryer, *Staying Power: The History of Black People in Britain* (London: Pluto Press, 1984), pp. 1–32.

47. Thomas Curwen, *This is an Answer to John Wiggans Book, Spread up and down in Lancashire, Cheshire and Wales, who is a Baptist and a Monarch-man. Where in maybe seen how he exalts Himself, against Christ the Light, that doth enlighten every Man . . . From the Prisoners at Lancaster, where he then opposed being then a Prisoner, Thomas Curwen, William Houlden, Henery Wood, William Wilson* (London: n.p., 1665). Preface "To the Reader" is dated the 2nd of the 5th Month 1664.

48. Edward W. Said, *Orientalism* (New York: Vintage, 1979), pp. 56, 125. 49. Jacques Lacan, *Ecrits. A Selection,* trans. Alan Sheridan (London: Tavistock Publications, Ltd., 1977), p. 101.

50. Davis, *The Problem of Slavery,* pp. 330–332.

51. Manners, *Elizabeth Hooton,* p. 45.

52. Brailsford, *Quaker Women,* p. 34.

53. Manners, *Elizabeth Hooton,* p. 71.

54. Manners, *Elizabeth Hooton,* p. 72. Her final end in the Caribbean reflects her life-long mission to build spiritual equality. She died in Jamaica in the early months of 1762. Fox reported tersely, "Wee buried Els. Hutton in Jamaica about a week after wee landed ther" (Brailsford, *Quaker Women,* pp. 38–39).

55. Joan Vokins, *God's Mightly Power Magnified: As Manifested and Revealed in her Faithful Handmaid Joan Vokins, who departed this life the 22d of the 5th month, 1690, Having finished her course, and kept the Faith. Also some account of her Exercises, Works of Faith, Labour, Love, and great travels in the Work of the Ministry, for the good of souls* (London: Thomas Northcott, 1691); pp. 42–43. The particular question is concluded by the statement: "Written aboard the ship coming from Barbados." Quaker women such as Jane Hoskins, made no reference in their writings to the black population in the Caribbean (*The Life of the Faithful Servant of Christians, Jane Hoskins, The Friends Library: Comprising Journals, Doctrinal Treatises, and Other*

Writings of Members of the Religious Society of Friends, vol. 1, ed. William Evans and Thomas Evans (Philadelphia: Joseph Rakestraw, 1846), pp. 469–71.

56. Vokins returned home hastily about 1680 when she thought "we were likely to have lost our Women's Meetings," quoted in Hobby, *Virtue of Necessity,* pp. 49, 214.

57. Note Howard Temperley's persuasive argument in "The Ideology of Antislavery," in *The Abolition of the Atlantic Slave Trade: Origins and Effects in Europe, Africa, and the Americas,* ed. David Eltis and James Walvin: "the attack on slavery [as well as the imposition of slavery] can be seen as an attempt by a dominant metropolitan ideology to impose its values on the societies of the economic periphery," (Madison: University of Wisconsin Press, 1981), p. 29. See also Howard Temperley, *British Antislavery: 1833–1870* (London: Longman, 1972).

58. Henry J. Cadbury, "Negro Membership in the Society of Friends," *The Journal of Negro History,* vol. 21, (1936): 151–213, especially pp. 172–176 for the case of Cynthia Myers, "a Mulatto woman."

59. Craton, *Testing the Chains,* pp. 24–25.

60. Craton, *Testing the Chains,* pp. 335–337.

61. This quotation comes in private correspondence from Elaine Hobby to Moira Ferguson.

62. Women spearheaded the missionary effort in Barbados just as they had pioneered missionary work somewhat earlier in southern England. See endnote 36.

63. This information was supplied in private correspondence to the writer from Maureen Bell whom I thank. Gail Malmgreen points out, however, that relatively few writings would have editions of this size. I am deeply indebted to Gail Malmgreen for an incisive reading of this chapter. Since Alice Curwen's text is rare compared to Hooton's and Vokin's, it may well be that its reproduction was very limited. See T. P. O'Malley, "'Defying the powers and tempering the spirit'": a review of Quaker control over their publications 1672–1689; *Journal of Ecclesiastical History,* vol. 33, no. 2 (January 1982): 72–88.

64. Joan Kelly, "Early Feminist Theory and the *Querelle des Femmes*" in *Women, History and Theory: The Essays of Joan Kelly* (Chicago: University of Chicago Press, 1984), p. 68.

Notes on Chapter 4

1. D.F. Foxon's catalogue, *English Verse 1701–1750: A Catalogue of Separately Printed Poems with Notes on Contemporary Collected Editions,* 2 vols., (Cambridge: Cambridge University Press, 1975), suggests the extremely lim-

ited extent of literary interest in slavery in the first half of the eighteenth century among both male and female authors. Mary Barber's poem on Barbary Coast captives is the only poem in the index listed under slaves or slavery. Under Negro is one poem about a chimney sweep; under Blacks, there is no entry; and under Africa or African, only Thomas Dodd's poems on "The African Prince." By way of contrast, note that following the first dramatic performance of *Oroonoko* in November 1695, there were at least 315 other performances during the Restoration and eighteenth century. See the introduction to Thomas Southerne, *Oroonoko,* edited by Maximillian Novak and David Rodes (Lincoln: University of Nebraska Press, 1976), p. xvi.

2. For example, Ayuba Suleiman Diallo, also known as Job ben Solomon, a well-educated Fulani who was the son of a Muslim holy man and a slave-trader himself, was captured and sold on the Gambia in 1731. Through a series of accidents, his illegal captivity was discovered and he ended up as a celebrity—though still a slave—in fashionable London circles. Despite the fact that he provided first-hand evidence of African economic and cultural life, he could not qualitatively alter contemporary opinion about African "illiteracy and heathenism," although his learning and sophistication spoke for themselves. After money was raised for his manumission in 1734 by philanthropists and well-wishers, he returned to Africa. As James Walvin states: "He was rare and lucky; a statistical freak who had avoided the alternate hammer blows of debasement and physical collapse"; James Walvin, *Black and White: The Negro and English Society 1555–1945* (London: Oxford University Press, 1977), pp. 80–83. See also Douglas Grant, *The Fortunate Slave: An Illustration of African Slavery in the Early Eighteenth Century* (London: Oxford University Press, 1968). Lady Mary Wortley Montagu refers to slavery several times throughout her writings. For example, in a letter from a Belgrade village on June 17th, 1717, to Lady Rich, an amused Lady Mary writes about Lady Rich's request that Lady Mary purchase a Greek slave. "The Greeks are Subjects, and not slaves," Lady Mary responds to her friend. "Those who are to be bought in that manner, are either such as are taken in war, or stolen by the tartars from Russia, Circassia, or Georgia," *The Complete Letters of Lady Mary Wortley Montagu,* ed. Robert Halsband (Oxford: Clarendon University Press, 1965), vol. 1, p. 367. "If [Patrons] they grow weary of 'em [slaves], they either present them to a freind (sic) or give them their freedoms. Thos that are expos'd to sale at the Markets are allways either guilty of some Crime or so entirely worthless that they are of no use at all. I am afraid you'l doubt the Truth of this Account, which I own is very different from our common Notions in England, but it is not less truth for all that," *Complete Letters,* vol. 1, p. 368.

3. For background about the effort to maintain domestic economic stability, see W. A. Speck, *Stability and Strife: Britain in the Age of Walpole,* ed. Jeremy Black (London: Macmillan, 1984), especially pp. 1–43, 121–69.

4. The importance of sugar in expanding the slave trade has been stressed by many economists and historians, Eric Williams, *Capitalism and Slavery* (New York: Capricorn Books, 1944), being the most noted. Although the

detailed controversy about the degree to which the industrial revolution was financed by profits from slavery is beyond the scope of this book, Williams demonstrates the key role that sugar played in the trade's early development. See particularly the entries for sugar in Williams' index. See also K. G. Davies, *Royal African Company* (New York: Atheneum, 1970), pp. 7, 14–15, 317–18. For specific statistics cited, see Tract 42, British Library shelfmark LR404a4, *West Indian Planters and Merchants . . . take the liberty of . . . an exact amount in a letter to a Member of Parliament, concerning the importance of our sugar-colonies to Great Britain. By a gentleman, who resided many years in the island of Jamaica* (London: Printed for J. Taylor, 1745).

5. Louis Landa examines the relationship between Belinda's toilet preparations in Alexander Pope's *The Rape of the Lock* and the increased imports of foreign goods in "Of Silkworms and Farthingales and the Will of God," in R. F. Brissenden, ed., *Studies in the Eighteenth Century,* vol. 2, (Toronto: University of Toronto, 1973), pp. 259–277, and "Pope's Belinda, The General Emporie of the World, and the Wondrous Worm," *South Atlantic Quarterly,* 70 (Spring 1971): 215–235.

6. William Bosman, *A New and Accurate Description of the Coast of Guinea divided into the Gold, the Slave, and the Ivory Coasts, etc. . . . ,* Written originally in the Dutch by William Bosman, chief factor for the Dutch at the Castle of St. George d'Elmina (London: Joseph Knapton, 1705), p. 364.

7. Christopher Hill, *Reformation to Industrial Revolution* (London: Penguin, 1967), pp. 227–229.

8. Peter Fryer, *Staying Power: The History of Black People in Britain* (London: Pluto Press, 1984), p. 35.

9. Isaac Dookham, *A Pre-Emancipation History of the West Indies* (London: Collins, 1971, 1985), pp. 124–135.

10. The opinion of Sir Philip Yorke and M. F. Talbot, solicitor general, is quoted in *Slavery, Abolition and Emancipation: Black Slaves and the British Empire,* ed. Michael Craton, James Walvin and David Wright (London: Longman, 1976), p. 165.

11. See Baron de Montesquieu, *L'Esprit des Lois,* first published 1748, trans. into English 1751 as *The Spirit of the Laws. With an Introduction by Franz Neumann,* trans. Thomas Nugent (New York: Hafner Publishing Company, 1966), especially pp. 238–239. For critical appraisals, see Shelby T. McCoy, *The Humanitarian Movement in Eighteenth-Century France* (Louisville: University of Kentucky, 1957), pp. 86–87; David Brion Davis, *The Problem of Slavery in Western Culture* (Ithaca: Cornell University Press, 1966), pp. 394–396, 402–408 and passim.

12. Walvin, *Black and White,* p. 38.

13. Walvin, *Black and White,* p, 39.

14. Walvin, *Black and White,* p. 42.

15. Folaris Shyllon, *Black People in Britain* (London: Oxford University Press, 1977), pp. 10–21. It was also fashionable to demean black servants; many owners, for example, forced black British servants to wear thick iron collars. How Africans responded to those practices was evident from the numerous "hue and cry" advertisements for escaped slaves. *The Journal of Negro History,* ed. Carter G. Woodson. *Documents:* "Eighteenth Century Slaves as Advertized by Their Masters," Vol. 1 (Lancaster, PA: The Association for the Study of Negro Life and History, Inc., 1916), pp. 163–216.

16. Walvin, *Black and White,* p. 42, n. 48.

17. Winthrop D. Jordan, *White over Black: American Attitudes Towards the Negro, 1550–1812* (Chapel Hill: University of North Carolina Press, 1968), p. 43.

18. Jordan, *White Over Black,* p. 27.

19. In *Sinews of Empire: A Short History of British Slavery* (New York: Anchor Books, 1974), Michael Craton discusses Williams' view that "the stereotype of black inferiority was a result, not a cause, of the nature of plantation society," p. 165.

20. Hans Sloane, *A Voyage to the Islands of Madeira, Barbadoes, Nieves, St. Christopher's, and Jamaica; with the Natural History of the Herbs and . . . Trees . . . [with] an Account of the Inhabitants . . . ,* vol. 1 (London: Printed for the Author, 1725), p. lvii. During the decade when Hans Sloane presided over the Royal Society, a black man attending the Society was rejected because of his color (Davis, *The Problem of Slavery,* p. 478).

21. I am talking here of subjectivity as Catherine Belsey, for example, uses it in *Critical Practice* (London: Methuen, 1980), pp. 56–84.

22. George Savile, the Marquis of Halifax, *The Lady's New-Year's Gift: or, Advice to a Daughter,* the 11th edition, exactly corrected (London: D. Midwinter, 1734). Between 1688 and 1765, Lord Halifax's text went through twenty-six editions, eleven editions by 1734 and fifteen editions by 1765.

23. Sir Richard Steele, *The Spectator,* vol. 1, ed. with an introduction and notes by Donald F. Bond (Oxford: Clarendon Press, 1965), p. 140. All references will be to this edition.

24. Felicity Nussbaum, *The Brink of All We Hate: English Satires on Women 1660–1750* (Lexington: University of Kentucky Press, 1984), p. 161; Katherine Rogers in *The Troublesome Helpmate: A History of Misogyny in Literature* (Seattle: University of Washington Press, 1969), similarly exposes endemic women-haters in the period.

25. F. W. Tickner, *Women in English Economic History* (London: J. M. Dent & Sons, Ltd., 1923), p. 95. Tickner discusses some exceptions.

26. The condition of marriage and women's situations within the institution is still debated. See particularly Lawrence Stone, *The Family, Sex and Marriage in England 1500–1800* (New York: Harper Colophon Books, 1977), partic-

ularly the chapters on the growth of affective individualism and companionate marriage; and Alan Macfarlane, *Marriage and Love in England. Modes of Reproduction 1300–1840* (Oxford: Basil Blackwell, 1986) especially chapter seven, "Who Controls the Marriage Decision," pp. 120–147. See also Leonore Davidoff and Catherine Hall, *Family Fortunes: Men and Women of the English Middle Class, 1780–1850,* (London: Hutchinson, 1987), pp. 219–221 and passim. See, too, Sylvia Harcstark Myers' summation in *The Bluestocking Circle. Women, Friendship, and the Life of the Mind in Eighteenth-Century England* (Oxford: Clarendon Press, 1990) p. 190, for the dilemma marriage posed for mid-eighteenth-century women who would become bluestockings:

> Should they let their families choose their husbands? And if so, on what basis were they to accept their choice? Was it simply enough to agree that one's family knew best? To what extent should feelings be consulted? How was a young woman to deal with the realities of her economic situation, as it related to the kind of person she might prefer as a spouse? . . . . After 1780 romantic love and the romantic novel grew together . . . [love] became a respectable motive for marriage.

For the contradictory role of women in the period, see also Ruth Perry, *Women, Letters and the Novel* (New York: AMS Press, Inc., 1980), especially Chapter 2, "The Economic Status of Women."

27. These prohibitions and women's resistance could be traced to the seventeenth century and earlier. The Reverend John Sprint's sermon was entitled "The Bride-Woman's Counsellor. Being a Sermon preach'd at a Wedding, May the 11th, 1699, at Sherbourn, in Dorsetshire," (London: H. Hills), "For the Benefit of the Poor," n.d. was reprinted as no. 6 in 1732 in a collection of sermons entitled *Conjugal Duty: Set forth in a Collection of Ingenious and Delightful Wedding-Sermons* (London: J. Watson, 1732). Included in *Conjugal Duty* was a sermon purporting to show "the Scarcity . . . of Virtuous Women." The entries in a contemporary text entitled *The Ladies Miscellany* (London: W. Hinton, 1731), published in 1732 (and possibly as early as 1718) by the notorious Edmund Curll, appealed primarily to men and suggested how openly a double standard was applied to women. The table of contents appeared as follows: Love Letters between a Gentleman and Lady; Basia: Or, the Pleasures of Kissing; The Happy Bride; The Rape of Helen; Unlawful Love; Spiritual Fornication, a Burlesque Poem wherein the case of Miss Cadiere and Father Girard is merrily Display'd; Miss Cadiere's Case very Handsomely Handled, and 29 other Curious Poems on Love and Gallantry. For a discussion of women's situations, see Angeline Goreau, *The Whole Duty of Woman* (New York: Dial Press, Doubleday & Company, 1985), p. 9 and passim. See also Moira Ferguson, *First Feminists: British Women Writers 1578–1799* (Bloomington: Indiana University Press, 1985), pp. 1–73. Ian Watt in *The Rise of the Novel: Studies in Defoe, Richardson, and Fielding* (Berkeley: University of California Press, 1957), argues that the treatment of women in this period was double-edged, pp. 157–162.

28. Mary, Lady Chudleigh, *The Ladies Defence: or a Dialogue Between Sir John Brute, Sir William Loveall, Melissa, and a Parson,* in Ferguson, *First Feminists,* p. 237.

29. Anne Finch, Countess of Winchelsea, "The Unequal Fetters," in Ferguson, *First Feminists,* p. 252.

30. Sarah Fyge Field Egerton, "The Emulation," in Ferguson, *First Feminists,* p. 169.

31. Jeremy Collier, *Short View of the Immorality of Profaneness of the English Stage* (London, 1698).

32. Colley Cibber, *Love's Last Shift* (London, 1696).

33. Eva Beatrice Dyke in *The Negro in English Romantic Thought: or, A Study of Sympathy for the Oppressed* (Washington, D.C.: The Associated Publishers, 1942), pp. 41–43.

34. *The Works of the most reverend Dr. John Tillotson, Late Lord Archbishop of Canterbury: containing 54 Sermons and Discourses, on several occasions. Together with the Rule of Faith, being all that were published by his Grace himself. And more collected into 1 volume,* 5th ed. (London: B. Aylmer, 1707), p. 191, Sermon 18.

35. Anthony Ashley Cooper, Earl of Shaftesbury, *Characteristicks of Men, Manners, Opinions, and Times* (London, 1711).

36. Frances Hutcheson, *An Inquiry into the Original of Our Ideas of Beauty and Virtue* (London, 1725). See also Roger Anstey, *The Atlantic Slave Trade and British Abolition 1760–1810* (Atlantic Highlands, NJ: Humanities Press, 1975), pp. 98–102. For a discussion of Hutcheson's views on slavery with respect to the classical model, see Wylie Sypher, "Hutcheson and the Classical Theory of Slavery," *Journal of Negro History,* 29 (July 1939): 263–80.

37. Jordan in *White Over Black* supplies a telling caveat to the rage for sentimentality regarding slaves, pp. 368–370.

38. John Mocquet, *Travels and Voyages into Africa, Asia, and America, the East and West Indies; Syria, Jerusalem, and the Holy-Land. Performed by Mr. John Mocquet, Keeper of the Cabinet of Rarities, to the King of France, in the Tuilleries. Divided into Six Books, and Enriched with Sculptures,* trans. from the French by Nathaniel Pullen (London: William Newton, Joseph Shelton, William Chandler, 1696), Book Two, p. 124ff. The first version of the tale appeared in *Voyages en Afrique, Asie, Indes orientales et occidentales (Travels and Voyages into Africa)* by the traveler John Mocquet (1st edition, 1612, in French). The British Library holds French editions of 1617 (Paris: chez I. de Heuqueville), two French editions of 1645 and 1665, and an English translation in 1696).

39. Mocquet, *Voyages en Afrique,* book two, p. 124 ff.

40. Richard Ligon, *A True and Exact History of the Island of Barbadoes* (London: Humphrey Mosely, 1657), Written from Upper Bench Prison, 1653.

41. Ligon, *A True and Exact History*, p. 8.

42. Sir Richard Steele, *The Spectator*, pp. 47–51. There is an off-key echo of the Inkle and Yarico legend in *Spectator*, p. 56. See endnote 23.

43. In Thomas Clarkson, *History of the Abolition of the Slave Trade . . .* (London: Longman, Hurst, Reese and Orme, 1808), vol. 1, p. 54, Clarkson states that Sir Richard Steele's "affecting story of Inkle and Yarico, holds up this trade again for our abhorrence." Whether this was a hindsight opinion or not is difficult to say. In 1705, Richard Steele's wife was Margaret Ford, a West Indian heiress and plantation owner with property in Barbados. Steele was thus well acquainted and associated with Caribbean interests and political life. He rejected the governorship of Crowe and Park and signed a non-partisan petition. His seeming attack on mercantilist values may have been influenced by his Caribbean connections. See George A. Aitken, *The Life of Richard Steele*, 2 vols. (London: Wm. Isbister, 1889), pp. 1, 137–139 and passim.

44. See endnote 5.

45. Steele, *The Spectator*, pp. 11, 49–51.

46. Among copious documentation denoting colonial "growth" are Leslie Charles, *A New History of Jamaica, from the earliest accounts to the taking of Porto Bello by Vice-Admiral Vernon. In thirteen letters from a Gentleman to his friend . . . With Two maps*, 2nd. ed. (London: Printed for J. Hodges, 1740); *Acts of Assembly, passed in the islands of Jamaica, from 1681 to 1737, inclusive* (London: John Baskett, 1740); Anon, *The Importance of Jamaica to Great Britain consider'd. With some account of that island, from its discovery in 1492 to this time: An account of their fruits, drugs, timber and dying-woods. With an account of their trade and produce; . . . In a letter to a gentleman* (London: Printed for A. Dodd [1740?]; John Cowley, *A description of the windward passage, and Gulf of Florida, with the course of the British trading-ships to, and from the island of Jamaica . . . Illustrated with a chart . . . To which are added, some proposals for the better securing of the British trade and navigation to and from the West-Indies . . . To which is now annexed, a very remarkable letter*, 2nd vol. (London: J. Applebee, C. Corbett, E. Nutt and E. Cook, and A. Dodd, 1739); *Some observations on the assiento trade, as it hath been exercised by the South-Sea Company; proving the damage, which will accrue thereby to the British commerce and plantations in America, and particularly to Jamaica . . . By a person who resided several years in Jamaica*, 2nd ed. (London: Printed for H. Whitridge, 1728); Edward Ward, *Female policy detected: or, the arts of a designing woman laid open treating I. of the allurements, . . . With a poetical description of a maid, wife, and widow by E. W. author of the London-Spy, and Trip to Jamaica to which is added, The batchelor's estimate of the expences of a married life* (London: Printed for John Willis and Joseph Boddington, [1725?]); *The Jamaica Lady: or, the life of Bavia. Containing an account of her intrigues, cheats, amours in England, Jamaica, and the Royal Navy . . . With the diverting humours of Capt. Fustian, . . .* (London: Tho. Bickerton, 1720); *The State of the island of Jamaica. Chiefly in*

relation to its commerce, and the conduct of the Spaniards of the West-Indies. Address'd to a member of parliament. By a person who resided several years at Jamaica (London: Printed for H. Whitridge, 1726); Philip Warton, *Some modern observations upon Jamaica: as to its natural history, improvement in trade, manner of living, &c. By an English merchant* (London: 1727); *The Groans of Jamaica, express'd in a letter from a gentlemen residing there, to his friend in London; containing a clear detection, and most convincing narrative of some of the crying grievances, and fraudulent oppressions which gave the first rise to the present growing discontents, divisions, and animosities, among the inhabitants of that Island: as also particular characters of the chief authors and promoters of these distractions* (London: 1714). I thank Carol Barash for a copy of her unpublished paper entitled "English Popular Narratives about Jamaica, 1713–1750."

47. G. S. Rousseau, "Madame Chimpanzee," Parts 1 and 2, in *The Clark Newsletter, Bulletin of the U.C.L.A. Center for 17th- and 18th-Century Studies*, No. 10 (Spring 1986): 1–14, No. 12 (Spring 1987): 4–7.

48. See John Talbot Campo-Bell, *The Speech of Mr. John Talbot Campo-Bell, a free Christian negro, to his countrymen in the mountains of Jamaica. In two parts* . . . (London: Printed for J. Robert, 1736); Mauritius Vale, *The Trial of Mauritius Vale, Esq.; . . . at St. Jago de la Vega, in the island of Jamaica, on Saturday, the 30th day of August, 1735 . . . for the murder of Mr. John Steevens, . . . Taken by a gentleman who attended in the said court . . . To which is annexed, a true copy of a letter wrote by Mr. Vale . . .* , (London: Printed for T. Cooper, 1736). Note that the authorship of John Talbot Campo-Bell's speech is contested.

49. The Countess of Hertford, "The Story of Inkle and Yarico," pp. 6–7 in *A New Miscellany: Being a Collection of Pieces of Poetry from Bath, Tunbridge, Oxford, Epsom, and other Places in the year 1725 . . . To which is added, Grongar Hill* (London: J. Cooper, 1738). This edition is mentioned indirectly in a letter to the Countess from Elizabeth Rowe.

50. The Countess of Hertford, "The Story of Inkle and Yarico"; both parts of this poem are reproduced in Lawrence Marsden Price, *Inkle and Yarico Album* (Berkeley: University of California Press, 1937). Versions of Inkle and Yarico continued up to the nineteenth century. Anna Maria Porter presents a poem on that subject in *Ballad, Romances and Other Poems* (London: Longman, Hurst, Rees, Orme and Brown, 1811). Price discusses many versions of Inkle and Yarico, French and German as well as English.

51. I have not yet located the volume that Rowe mentions. See Helen Sard Hughes, *The Gentle Hertford: Her Life and Letters* (New York: Macmillan, 1940), p. 419.

52. Orlando Patterson in *Slavery and Social Death. A Comparative Study* (Cambridge: Harvard University Press, 1982) discusses the three primary conditions of slavery that include natal alienation. See pp. 1–14. The Count-

ess's possible attribution to Yarico of unconscious motivation even at the very climax of pleasing (or seeming to please) Inkle most cannot be discounted.

53. The Countess's commentary on Inkle is anti-sentimental in an age of feeling dramatic heroes. She alerts readers to sham, artifice, and the preeminence of economic over sexual desire, or perhaps more accurately, the self-involvement that underpinned such desires. The fully-fledged sentimental hero in prose with a very different take on slavery surfaces after midcentury.

54. Montesquieu tried to refute the most common plantocratic propaganda, both legal, fictitious, and political in *L'Esprit des Lois* which he began after visiting England between 1729 and 1731. See also *Slavery, Abolition and Emancipation,* ed. Craton and others, pp. 205–06; Winthrop Jordan, "Racial Slavery: From Reasons to Rationale," in *White Over Black,* pp. 91–98 and passim; Fryer, *Staying Power,* especially the chapter entitled "The Rise of English Racism," pp. 133–190. See also Richard H. Popkin, "The Philosophical Basis of Eighteenth-Century Racism," in *Studies in Eighteenth-Century Culture,* vol. 3, (Cleveland: Case Western Reserve University, 1973), pp. 245–262; Davis, *The Problem of Slavery,* pp. 457–458; and Elliot H. Tokson, *The Popular Image of the Black Man in English Drama, 1550–1688* (Boston: G. K. Hall, 1982), p. 40. Caribbean prejudicial attitudes can be seen in *Caribbeana* (see endnote 57) where there are matter-of-fact statements about the importation of forty-two thousand "Negroes in the Exportation-trade" (Vol. II, March 26, 1735). For Wednesday, December 13, 1738 there is an entry about the need to curb stealing and a comment that slaves "are generally thieves" (Vol. II, p. 290).

55. The confusion over Yarico's racial identity and the equation of Indian with African is a contemporary phenomenon discussed by Wylie Sypher in *Guinea's Captive Kings: British Anti-Slavery Literature of the 18th Century* (Chapel Hill: University of North Carolina Press, 1942), pp. 105–106.

56. I am indebted here to some of Christopher Miller's argumentation on the question of the other in *Blank Darkness. Africanist Discourse in French* (Chicago: University of Chicago Press, 1985).

57. Whether the Countess was corroborating contemporary attitudes and speculations about the sexual exploitation of black women is unclear. Concrete evidence for this widely rumored phenomenon occurs in the pages of *Caribbeana. Containing letters and Dissertations, Together with Poetical Essays, on Various subjects and Occasions; Chiefly wrote by several hands in the West Indies, and some of them to Gentlemen residing there. Now collected together in Two Volumes. Wherein are also comprised, divine Papers relating to Trade, Government, and Laws in general; but more especially, in those of the British Sugar-Colonies, and of Barbados in particular: As likewise the Characters of the most eminent Men that have died of late Years in that Island. To which are added in an Appendix Some Pieces never before published,* Vol. 1 (London: T. Osborne, J. Clarke, S. Austin, G. Hawkins, R. Didsley, W. Lewis, 1740). In a letter to the *Barbados Gazette* for Saturday, October 7, 1732, the writer who signs himself "Champion" says: "We also offer it humbly to your

consideration, Ladies, whether the low Gallantries of our single Men, with our black Beauties, be justly reckoned among our Faults," (p. 61). He goes on to call black women a "cheap Convenience for this indispensable Operation . . . Who can say that we have different Beds All Night? When it is well known that we go no further than the Neighbouring Hammock" (p. 62), signed Champion, October 2, 1732.

58. See Davis, *The Problem of Slavery,* p. 219ff; Thomas Parry, *Codrington College, in the Island of Barbados* (London, 1847); see also J. Harry Bennett, Jr., *Bondsmen and Bishops: Slavery and Apprenticeship in the Codrington Plantation of Barbados, 1710–1838* (Berkeley: University of California Press, 1958).

59. See *British Humanitarianism. Essays Honoring Frank J. Klingberg,* ed. Samuel Clyde McCulloch (Philadelphia: The Church Historical Society, 1950); J. Harry Bennett, Jr., "The Society for the Propagation of the Gospel's Plantations and the Emancipation Crisis," (Austin: University of Texas Press), p. 18.

60. R. H. Nichols and F. A. Wray, *The History of the Foundling Hospital* (London: Oxford University Press, 1935), p. 13.

61. Nichols and Wray, *The History,* p. 347.

62. W. K. Lowther Clarke, *Eighteenth Century Piety* (London: Society for Promoting Christian Knowledge, 1944; New York and London: Macmillan, 1944), pp. 71–72.

63. Clarke, *Eighteenth Century Piety,* p. 64.

64. Laurence Eusden, quoted in Hughes, *The Gentle Herford,* pp. 420–421.

65. Hughes, *The Gentle Hertford,* p. 428.

66. Hughes, *The Gentle Hertford,* p. 24.

67. I have referred early in Chapter Two to contemporary analogues between female subalternity and the state of colonial slavery. Many female and male poets and fiction writers of the period drew on that connection. Note, too, that in an entirely different context, Elizabeth Rowe conflates dual slaveries—colonial and gendered—in a poem about Old Testament Joseph. See Elizabeth Rowe, *The History of Joseph. A Poem. In Ten Books. By the Author of Friendship in Death,* 2nd ed. (London: T. Worrall, 1737). The Preface introduces a strong religious message. "This history seems to display to all mankind, that in whatever circumstances they may be, still to remember that they are under the eye, kind direction, and almighty power, of a gracious Providence, who will at last make all things work together for their advantage, if they be the followers of that which is good," (p. viii). Nonetheless in the description of a "feminized" Joseph up against a scheming Potiphar, similar associations abound. Elizabeth Rowe's elaboration of the sexual elements in Joseph's narrative may have derived from versions translated into English in the 1620s by Joshuah Sylvester from the Italian Fracastorio, *The Maidens Blush: or, Joseph, Mirror of Modesty, Map of Pietie, Maze of Destinie, Or rather Divine Providence. From the Latin Fracastorius, Translated and Dedicated to the*

High-Hopefull Charles, Prince of Wales by Joshuah Sylvester (London: Printed by H.Z., 1620). In this version, Sabrina, Potiphar's wife, drinks a potion and "feels her all-a-fire." For background to Elizabeth Rowe, see Hilda Smith, *Reason's Disciples: Seventeenth-Century English Feminists* (Urbana: University of Illinois Press, 1982), pp. 169–177 and passim; and George Ballard, *Memoirs of Several Ladies of Great Britain who have been celebrated for their writings or skill in the learned languages, arts, and sciences* (Oxford, 1752, Reprint. ed. and intro. by Ruth Perry, New York: AMS Press, 1980); John Dunton, *The Athenian Mercury* (London, n.p.) 1691–1697, and *The Ladies Mercury* (London: n.p.), 1693; Hughes, *The Gentle Hertford;* Sidney Lee, "Rowe, Mrs. Elizabeth," vol. 17, *Dictionary of National Biography*, pp. 338–339; Myra Reynolds, *The Learned Lady in England, 1650–1760* (Boston: Houghton Mifflin Company, 1920); Henry F. Stetcher, *Elizabeth Singer Rowe: the Poetess of Frome: A Study in Eighteenth-Century Pietism* (Frankfurt: M. Peter Lang, Herbert Lang, 1973); and Theophilus Rowe, *An Account of the Life and Writings of Elizabeth Rowe,* prefixed to *Poems on Several Occasions* (London: D. Midwinter, 1759), p. 13. Hoxie Fairchild places the date of writing of *The History* "soon after her husband's death in 1715." The original poem with only eight books (and not ten) ended with Joseph's marriage (London: T. Worrall, 1736).

68. According to Henry F. Stetcher, Thomas Rowe was "noted for his love of liberty and for his opposition to all forms of tyranny," *Elizabeth Singer Rowe,* p. 107. See Isaac Watts, *Divine Songs attempted in easy language, for the use of children* (London, 1714), pp. 73–74; Thomas Rowe, "Ode on Liberty," in Theophilus Rowe, *Miscellaneous Works,* p. 134. Judging by an entry in Anon, *Caribbeana,* p. 112, Thomas Rowe's writings were viewed by white Caribbeans as less threatening than the slave structure of society. Published in 1737 but apparently written seventeen years earlier is a sympathetic poem by an anonymous eulogist to Elizabeth Rowe about Thomas Rowe's death. Histories of Joseph were very popular. "Joseph Reviv'd," 1714, for example, concentrates on Joseph's goodness. A very religious interpretation is offered in the same time frame, "Joseph Reviv'd: or The Heavenly Favourite. Being some Serious Meditations of the Divine-Providence, and the Behavior of that Prince," (London: R. Tookey, 1714). There was also a history in verse, published in Ipswich in 1736. These histories continued up through the nineteenth century. Sarah Trimmer used Joseph's history for scriptural explication. Rowe's version in *The History of Joseph,* first published in 1736, went through four editions, including three in Philadelphia, Hartford, and Boston in 1767, 1784, and 1897, respectively.

69. Hughes, *The Gentle Hertford,* pp. 120–126 and passim.

70. Ian Watt, *The Rise of the Novel. Studies in Defoe, Richardson and Fielding* (Berkeley: University of California Press, 1957).

71. Hughes, *The Gentle Hertford,* p. 59.

72. Anonymous, *Weekly Amusement,* June 7, 1766, p. 366. Reprinted in Price, pp. 8–11.

73. Climate had long been raised as a factor that touched on the question of slavery. John Dunton referred to the relationship of climate to "the blackness of the Negroes" in Vol. 3, *The Athenian Oracle,* (1696), p. 380. See also A. Owen Aldridge, "Feijoo and the Problem of Ethiopian Color," in *Studies in Eighteenth-Century Culture,* vol. 3, pp. 263–277.

74. William Law, *A Serious Call to a Devout and Holy Life. Adapted to the State and Condition of All Orders of Christians* (London: William Innys, 1729).

75. For a compelling discussion of the blank in *Heart of Darkness* to which this discussion is indebted, see Patrick Brantlinger, *Rule of Darkness. British Literature and Imperialism, 1830–1914* (Ithaca: Cornell University Press, 1988), especially Chapter 9, pp. 255–274 and Christopher Miller, *Blank Darkness,* pp. 169–183.

76. See endnote 56.

77. Quoted in Thomas Southerne, *Oroonoko,* ed. David Stuart Rodes and Maximilian E. Novak (Lincoln: University of Nebraska Press, 1976), p. xxx.

Notes on Chapter 5

1. David Brion Davis, *The Problem of Slavery in Western Culture* (Ithaca: Cornell University Press, 1976), p. 154.

2. For a comprehensive discussion of sugar see Richard B. Sheridan, *Sugar & Slavery: An Economic History of the British West Indies* (Baltimore: The Johns Hopkins Press, 1973).

3. Sheridan, *Sugar and Slavery,* p. 418.

4. Eric Williams, *Capitalism and Slavery* (New York: Capricorn Books, 1944), pp. 113–114.

5. Peter Fryer, *Staying Power. The History of Black People in Britain* (London: Pluto Press, 1984), p. 35.

6. See Chapter Four, endnote 48.

7. Williams, *Capitalism and Slavery,* p. 52.

8. Wylie Sypher, "The African Prince in London," in *Journal of the History of Ideas,* Vol. II, No. 1 (January 1941): 237–247. Note also certain evolving conditions that affected women's lives. Towers argues that Henry Fielding formulates his experience (if he does in fact utilize his experience) "in terms of the accepted attitudes of the day." Fielding's *Amelia,* for example, exalts the married state, A. R. Towers, "Amelia and the State of Matrimony," in *The Review of English Studies,* New Series, Vol. 5 (Oxford: Clarendon Press, 1954), p. 157; Susan Staves argues that "pathetic seduced maidens" are "not universal," but a frequently occurring type in eighteenth-century literature. The Marriage Act of 1753 "increased the power of parents of their minor children" in "British Seduced Maidens," *Eighteenth-Century Studies,* Vol. 14, 2 (Winter

1980/81): 133. As a result, the clergy had to follow stipulated procedures as marriage laws tightened; see Robert H. Hopkins, "Matrimony in the *Vicar of Wakefield* and *The Marriage Act*," *Studies in Philology*, Vol. 74 (Chapel Hill: University of North Carolina Press, 1977), p. 323. Note also that slaves' reaction is generally read as horror at the dramatic reality of slavery. Felicity Nussbaum points out, too, that the African princes may have been confused (and perhaps disgusted?) at the contradictions with which Oroonoko is portrayed—an African prince possessing European values yet being tortured. I thank Felicity Nussbaum for an invaluable reading of this chapter.

9. Christopher Miller, *Blank Darkness. Africanist Discourse in French* (Chicago: University of Chicago Press, 1985), pp. 15–18. Much of the argument in this section is dependent on ideas conceptualized in the section "Orientalism and Africa," in *Blank Darkness*.

10. Jane Spencer, *The Rise of the Woman Novelist. From Aphra Behn to Jane Austen* (Oxford: Basil Blackwell, 1986), pp. 77–78. See also Leonore Davidoff and Catherine Hall, *Family Fortunes: Men and Women of the English Middle Class, 1780–1850* (London: Hutchinson, 1987), especially pp. 102–148 for discussion of a weakened masculine identity (among evangelical men) that embraced more feminine qualities. The argument tends to the idea that a feminine identity for a male has a religious (or Christian-like) dimension, entirely appropriate to Scott's (and Ellison's) values.

11. There is much debate on this issue. Ruth Bloch argues that women's philanthropic tendencies—a mixture of piety and aggression—act as compensation for the circulating idea that women are allegedly less cognitive than men. Marilyn LeGates argues, however, that women were allotted/permitted these roles because men were unquestionably dominant. Barbara Welter explains the perfect ideal foisted on women, "the cult of true womanhood," but other forces gave women a better chance to prove themselves—the Civil War and missionary activity, for example—and raised the issue of who did what best. See Ruth Bloch, "Untangling the Roots of Modern Sex Roles: A Survey of Four Centuries of Change," in *Signs: Journal of Women in Culture and Society*, 4, no. 4 (Winter 1978): 236–52; Marlene LeGates, "The Cult of Womanhood in Eighteenth-Century Thought," in *Eighteenth-Century Studies*, 10, no. 1 (Fall 1976): 21–39; Barbara Welter, "The Cult of True Womanhood, 1820–1918," in *American Quarterly*, 18, no. 2 (Summer 1966): 151–74. See also Carol Gilligan, *In a Different Voice: Psychological Theory and Women's Development* (Cambridge: Harvard University Press, 1983); Mary Poovey, *The Proper Lady and the Woman Writer. Ideology as Style in the Works of Mary Wollstonecraft, Mary Shelley, and Jane Austen* (Chicago: University of Chicago Press, 1985), and Barbara Epstein, *The Politics of Domesticity. Women, Evangelism, and Temperance in Nineteenth-Century America* (Middletown, CT: Wesleyan University Press, 1981); and Davidoff and Hall, *Family Fortunes*, p. 114 and passim.

12. Charlotte Cibber Charke, *The History of Henry Dumont, Esq; and Miss*

Charlotte Evelyn. Consisting of a Variety of Entertaining Characters, and very Interesting Subjects. With Some Critical Remarks on Comick Actors, 2nd ed. (London: Printed for H. Slater, 1756). All quotations are from this edition.

13. See also Lewis Melville, *Stage Favourites of the Eighteenth Century* (Garden City: Doubleday, Doran and Company, 1929).

14. See *A Narrative of the Life of Mrs. Charlotte Charke, youngest daughter of Colley Cibber,* 2nd ed. (London, 1755; Reprint. ed. Leonard R. N. Ashley, Gainesville, FL: Scholars's Facsimiles and Reprint, 1969).

15. "Account of a Visit to Mrs. Charlotte Charke by Mr. Samuel Whyte of Dublin; Taken from Barker's *Biographica Dramatica,*" (1, p. 106), 1812." Reprinted as Preface to *A Narrative . . .* (London: W. Reeve, 1855).

16. In private conversation, Louis Crompton, who is writing a book tentatively entitled *Homosexuality and Christendom,* informed me that Charke's discussion of a gay male, even in negative terms, is a relatively rare occurrence in eighteenth-century British literature. I thank Lou Crompton for several valuable discussions and references. The strength of the taboo can be seen, for example, in Tobias Smollett's satirical poem, "Advice," in the irascible attitude towards homosexuality. See Louis Crompton, *Byron and Greek Love* (Berkeley: University of California Press, 1985), p. 55. Thus Charke's remarks may amount to an apologia or form of (unconscious) attention-seeking on a controversial issue that concerns her because even to refer to the subject (except or even derisively) usually requires justification.

17. Charlotte Charke, *A Narrative,* preface, p. A2.

18. As Michael Craton states in *Sinews of Empire: A Short History of British Slavery* (New York: Anchor Books, 1974): "Because these colonies were acquired piecemeal as the result of successive wars, however, their combined population increase was much more gradual, rising from a total of 12,000 blacks in 1750 and 30,000 in 1763, to 80,000 in 1783 and 160,000 in 1808," (p. 47). The statistics mentioned by Craton would not have been available to the general eighteenth-century population although the uneasiness expressed in Charke's contradictions is partly explained by white society's realization about an increasingly significant black presence in the colonies.

19. Wylie Sypher, *Guinea's Captive Kings: British Anti-slavery Literature of the 18th Century* (Chapel Hill: University of North Carolina Press, 1942), p. 266.

20. Sarah Robinson Scott, *The History of Sir George Ellison* (London: A. Millar, 1766).

21. June Jordan, *On Call: Political Essays* (Boston: South End Press, 1985), p. 88.

22. In 1760, a rare anti-slavery volume by Robert Wallace was published in Edinburgh. See "Notes and Documents. New Sidelights on Early Antislavery Radicalism," *The William and Mary Quarterly: A Magazine of Early American*

History, Vol. 28, No. 1 (Williamsburg: Institute of Early American History and Culture, 1971): 585–594.

23. The best source for information on Granville Sharp is his own memoirs, Prince Hoare, *Memoirs of Granville Sharp, Esq. Composed From His Own Manuscripts, Authentic Documents in the Possession of His Family and of the African Institution* (London: Henry Colburn and Co., 1820).

24. See Frank Joseph Klingberg, *The Anti-Slavery Movement in England. A Study in English Humanitarianism* (New Haven: Yale University Press, 1926), pp. 36–37.

25. *The Letters of Mrs. Elizabeth Montagu,* ed. Matthew Montagu, Vol. 6 (London: T. Cadell and W. Davies, 1813), p. 329.

26. Klingberg, *The Anti-Slavery Movement,* p. 18. See also J. Harry Bennett, Jr., *Bondsmen and Bishops: Slavery and Apprenticeship on the Codrington Plantation of Barbados, 1710–1738* (Berkeley: Univ. of California Press, 1958).

27. For Daniel Burton, see Winthrop D. Jordan, *White Over Black: American Attitudes Towards the Negro, 1550–1812* (Chapel Hill: University of North Carolina Press, 1968), pp. 197–198.

28. Laurence Sterne, *The Life and Opinions of Tristram Shandy, Gentleman* (New York: Signet Classic, 1960), p. 493.

29. Quoted in *The Slave's Narrative,* ed. Charles T. Davis and Henry Louis Gates, Jr., (Oxford: Oxford University Press, 1985), pp. 181–182.

30. The creole is the subject of an article by Wylie Sypher, "The West Indian as a 'Character' in the Eighteenth Century," in *Studies in Philology* 36, no. 3 (July 1939): 503–520.

31. *A Description of Millenium Hall and the Country Adjacent: Together with the Characters of the Inhabitants, and such Historical Anecdotes and Reflections, as May Excite in the Reader proper Sentiments of Humanity, and lead the Mind to the Love of Virtue. By A Gentleman on his Travels* (London: J. Newbury, 1762). The novel is also reprinted in a modern edition, *The Description of Millenium Hall by . . . Mrs. Sarah Scott* (London: Penguin Books, Virago Press, 1986). In *Sensibility: An Introduction* (New York: Columbia University Press, 1987), p. 97 and passim, Janet Todd offers a challenging view. In part she argues that the reader is learning (through mimicry, say, of Sir George) how to respond to slaves in fiction. Sentimental fiction supplies the fantasy for women's social decline and their prioritizing of feeling, amorality, and irrationality at the expense of thinking. Thus the archetypal man of feeling comes to seem effete and sexually enervated because feeling separated from conscience is a depravity.

32. Anna Freud argues that fantasy displaces an individual's fears and anxieties. In the *History of George Ellison,* a fictional version of philanthropy as fantasy since women rarely could possess Sir George's power, Sarah Scott reenacts *Millenium Hall* in a Caribbean context. She substitutes Sir George for surrogates of herself and Lady Bab, administering to the needs of the local

population. Empowered as an important and magnanimous plantation-owner, Sir George as Sarah Scott's surrogate can wield influence over many people's lives in ways that British society largely proscribes for women. See *The Writings of Anna Freud. The Ego and the Mechanisms of Defense* (New York: International Universities Press, Inc., 1966), pp. 80–82 and passim. See also an update of Anna Freud's theory in Joseph Sandler, with Anna Freud, *The Analysis of Defense: The Ego and the Mechanisms of Defense Revisited* (New York: International Universities Press, Inc., 1985).

33. Miller, *Blank Darkness,* p. xi.

34. David Sutcliffe, *British Black English* (Oxford: Basil Blackwell, 1982), p. 35.

35. Suzanne Romaine, *Pidgin and Creole Languages* (London: Longman, 1988), p. 115.

36. Sutcliffe, *British Black English,* p. 33ff; Romaine, *Pidgin,* p. 124.

37. Miller, *Blank Darkness,* pp. 16, 19 and passim.

38. William L. Andrews, *To Tell a Free Story* (Urbana: University of Illinois Press, 1986), p. 242.

39. I have found the Gramscian concept of subalternity helpful in formulating ideas about the colonized other, especially as it has been applied by Ranajit Guha and Gayatri Chakravorty Spivak to Indian historiography. See especially, *Selected Subaltern Studies,* ed. Ranajit Guha and Gayatri Chakravorty Spivak (New York: Oxford University Press, 1988), pp. 35–36; and "Can The Subaltern Speak" in *Marxism and The Interpretation of Culture.* ed. Cary Nelson and Lawrence Grosman (Urbana: Univ. of Illinois Press, 1987), pp. 271–313.

40. Sypher, *Guinea's Captive Kings,* p. 266.

41. Barbara Brandon Schnorrenberg has written a compelling volume on female domestic relationships entitled *The Female Condition: British Women and Their Society, 1750–1850,* forthcoming.

42. *The Autobiography and Correspondence of Mrs Delaney,* ed. Lady Llanover, 1st ser., 3 vols. (London: Rich and Bentley, 1861), vol. 3, p. 25.

43. Hester Lynch Salisbury Thrale, *Dr. Johnson's Mrs. Thrale. Autobiography, Letters and Literary Remains of Mrs. Piozzi, Edited by A. Hayward, Q.C., [1861] Newly Selected and Edited, with Introduction and Notes* (Edinburgh and London: T. N. Foulis, 1910), p. 15.

44. *The Posthumous Works of Mrs. Chapone. Containing Her Correspondence with Mr. Richardson, a Series of Letters to Mrs. Elizabeth Carter, and Some Fugitive Pieces, Never Before Published, Together with an Account of Her Life and Character, Drawn Up By Her Own Family* 2nd ed. (London: John Murray, 1808), p. 91.

45. F. K. Prochaska, *Women and Philanthrophy in Nineteenth-Century England* (Oxford: Clarendon Press, 1980), p. 6.

46. For a valuable discussion of the distinction between benevolent women and reformers, see Anne Boylan, "Women in Groups: An Analysis of Women's Benevolent Organizations in New York and Boston, 1797–1840," *Journal of American History* 71, no. 3 (December 1974), pp. 497–523.

47. Sypher, *Guinea's Captive Kings,* p. 270.

48. Elizabeth Tollet, "Hypatia," in *Poems on Several Occasions. With Anne Boleyn to King Henry VIII. An Epistle* (London: John Clarke, 1755).

49. Lady Sarah Pennington, *Letters to Her Daughters* (London, 1763), p. 92. Barbara Schorrenberg supplies important evidence for the diminution of forced marriage in the late eighteenth century. However, these texts suggest that forced marriage is still a live issue for men and women.

50. Davidoff and Hall, *Family Fortunes,* especially Part Two, Chapter 6.

51. For biographical data, see *The Life and Writings of Mrs. Sarah Scott, Novelist (1723–1795)* (Philadelphia: Walter Marion Crittenden, 1932). See also Edith Sedgwick Larson, "A Measure of Power: The Personal Charity of Elizabeth Montagu," in *Studies in Eighteenth-Century Culture,* ed. O. M. Brack, Jr., Vol. 16 (Madison: University of Wisconsin Press, 1986), pp. 197–210.

52. Judith Lowder Newton, *Women, Power and Subversion. Social Strategies in British Fiction, 1778–1860* (Athens, GA: University of Georgia Press, 1981), p. 4.

53. Malcolm I. Thomis and Jennifer Grimmett, *Women in Protest 1800–1850* (New York: St. Martin's Press, 1982).

54. Isaac Kramnick, "Children's Literature and Bourgeois Ideology: Observations on Culture and Industrial Capitalism in the Later Eighteenth Century," in *Studies in Eighteenth-Century Culture,* Vol. 12, ed. Harry C. Payne (Published for the American Society for Eighteenth-Century Studies by the University of Wisconsin Press, 1982), pp. 18–21.

55. *The Man of Real Sensibility: or the History of Sir George Ellison* (Philadelphia: Printed by James Humphreys, 1774).

56. In 1773 John Millar explains how slavery arose among early indigenous peoples. He also talks of the adverse effect of slavery on women. See *The Origin of the Distinction of Ranks; or, an Inquiry into the Circumstances which Give Rise to Influence and Authority in the Different Members of Society* (London, 1773).

57. Sir George's projected "infantile" morality is some kind of mirror-image of the slaves, too, and shows that "another kind of logic is at work," i.e., the logic of fear. See Miller, *Blank Darkness,* p. 28.

58. Michel Foucault, *Language, Counter-Memory, Practice, Selected Essays and Interviews,* ed. with intro. by Donald F. Bouchard, trans. from the French by Donald F. Bouchard and Sherry Simon (Ithaca: Cornell University Press, 1977), p. 209.

Notes on Chapter 6

1. E. C. P. Lascelles, *Granville Sharp and the Freedom of Slaves in England* (Oxford: Oxford University Press, 1928), pp. 139–143.

2. The memoirs of James Albert Ukawsaw Gronniosaw were more popularly known as *A narrative of the most remarkable particulars in the life of James Albert Ukawsaw Gronniosaw, an African prince, as related by himself,* ed. W. Shirley (Bath: S. Hazard, 1700).

3. Peter Fryer, *Staying Power: The History of Black People in Britain* (London: Pluto Press, 1984), p. 117.

4. Fryer, *Staying Power,* pp. 118–120.

5. Paul Hazard, *European Thought in the Eighteenth Century* (New Haven: Yale University Press, 1954).

6. *Slavery, Abolition and Emancipation: Black Slaves and the British Empire,* ed. Michael Craton, James Walvin and David Wright (London: Longman, 1976), p. 170.

7. Fryer, *Staying Power,* p. 125.

8. *Horace Walpole's Correspondence,* ed. W. S. Lewis, and others (New Haven: Yale University Press, 1973), p. 18.

9. Folaris O. Shyllon, *Black Slaves in Britain* (London: Published for the Institute of Race Relations, Oxford University Press, 1974), p. 110.

10. Prince Hoare, *Memoirs of Granville Sharp, Esq. Composed From His Own Manuscripts, Authentic Documents in the Possession of His Family and of the African Institution* Part III, (London: Printed for Henry Colburn and Co., 1820), pp. 258–260.

11. For a description and bibliography on black power, see Fryer, *Staying Power,* pp. 191–202, 538–540. For Queen Elizabeth's comment, see Shyllon, *Black Slaves,* pp. 2–3.

12. Elizabeth Bonhote, *The Rambles of Mr. Frankly,* vol. 1, (Dublin: Printed for Messrs. Sleater, Lynch, Williams, Potts, Chamberlaine, Wilson, Husband, Walker, Moncrieffe, and Flin, 1773).

13. Janet Todd, *Sensibility: An Introduction* (New York: Columbia University Press, 1987).

14. Elizabeth Bonhote, *The Parental Monitor,* 2 vols. (London: William Lane, 1787), Preface, pp. 105–106.

15. Walter Allen, *The English Novel. A Short Critical History* (New York: E. P. Dutton & Co., 1954), p. 77.

16. Elizabeth Bonhote, "Feeling," in *Poems* (London: William Lane, 1810).

17. Dorothy Kilner, *The Rotchfords or the Friendly Counsellor: Designed for the Instruction and Amusement of the Youth of Both Sexes.* Two Volumes in One. From the London Copy [of 1786] (Philadelphia: James Humphrey, 1801).

18. Jane Bingham and Grayce Scholt, *Fifteen Centuries of Children's Literature: An Annotated Chronology of British and American Works in Historical Contexts* (Greenwood, 1980), p. 126.

19. F. J. Harvey Darton, *Children's Books in England. Five Centuries of Social Life* (Cambridge: University of Cambridge Press, 1960), p. 158.

20. The Eurocentric debate about the "ugliness" of non-Europeans is treated comprehensively in several essays in *Studies in Eighteenth-Century Culture. Racism in the Eighteenth Century,* ed. Harold E. Pagliaro (Cleveland: Case Western Reserve University Press, 1973), pp. 239–386, especially Richard H. Popkin, "The Philosophical Basis of Eighteenth-Century Racism"; Phillip R. Sloan, "The Idea of Racial Degeneracy in Buffon's Historie Naturelle," and G. S. Rousseau, "Le Cat and the Physiology of Negroes." See also Winthrop Jordan, *White Over Black: American Attitudes Toward the Negro, 1550–1812* (Chapel Hill: University of North Carolina Press, 1968), chapters one, six and passim; and Shyllon, *Black Slaves,* especially pp. 3–4, 105–106, 241–243, and passim. For an important older account, see *An Essay on the Causes of the Variety of Complexion and Figure in the Human Species. To which are added, Animadversions on certain Remarks made on the first edition of this Essay, by Mr. Charles White, in a series of Discourses delivered before the Literary and Philosophical Society of Manchester in England. Also, Strictures on Lord Kaims' Discourse on the Original Diversity of Mankind. And An Appendix by Samuel Stanhope Smith, . . . President of the College of New Jersey; and Member of the American Philosophical Society. The Second Edition . . . Enlarged and Improved* (New Brunswick: J. Simpson and Co.; New York: Williams and Whiting; L. Deare, printer, 1810). Reissued as Samuel Stanhope Smith, *An Essay on the Causes of the Variety of Complexion and Figure in the Human Species,* ed. Winthrop D. Jordan (Cambridge: Belknap Press of Harvard University Press, 1965).

21. Roger Anstey, *The Atlantic Slave Trade and British Abolition 1760–1810* (Atlantic Highlands, NJ: Humanities Press, 1975), pp. 3–38 and Eric Williams, *Capitalism and Slavery* (New York: Capricorn Books, 1944), pp. 51–107 and passim.

22. *The Holiday* [Holy day] *Present, containing Anecedotes of Mr. and Mrs. Jennett* [sic] *and their little family, Master George, Master Charles, Master Thomas, Miss Maria, Miss Charlotte, and Miss Harriot. Interspersed with instructive and amusing stories and observations,* vol. 13 (London: J. Marshall, c. 1788; York, Wilson, Spence and Mawman, 1797). The Osborne Collection catalogue states that this text was first published c. 1780 with the running title of *The Holiday Present.*

23. William H. Robinson, *Phillis Wheatley and Her Writings* (New York: Garland, 1984), p. 39.

24. *London Chronicle,* 1773, pp. 16–18 quoted in "The British Reception of Wheatley's Poems on Various Subjects," Ukhtar Ali Isani, *The Journal of Negro History,* vol. 66, no. 2 (Summer 1981): 146.

25. *Letters of the Late Ignatius Sancho, an African* (J. Dodsley etc., 1982), I. p. vi; *Letters of the Late Ignatius Sancho,* ed. Paul Edwards (Dawsons, 1968), intro. p. xvi, facsimile reprint, p. A3; Ottobah Cugoano, *Thoughts and Sentiment on the Evil and Wicked Traffic of the Slavery and Commerce of the Human Species, Humbly Submitted to the Inhabitants of Great-Britain* (London, 1787), p. 5.

26. Robert B. Stepto, *From Behind the Veil* (Urbana: University of Illinois Press, 1979), pp. 26–31 and passim.

27. For a discussion of the sexual politics and prevalence of the gaze, see Luce Irigaray, "This Sex Which is Not One," in *New French Feminisms,* ed. Elaine Marks and Isabelle de Courtivron (New York: Schocken Books, 1981), p. 101.

28. Professor Harry Reed made this argument at a conference on "The Black Woman Writer and the Diaspora," 27–30 October, 1985, in a paper entitled "Phillis Wheatley and Black Cultural Nationalism," at Michigan State University, East Lansing, Michigan.

29. Mary Scott, *The Female Advocate: a poem occasioned by reading Mr. Duncombe's Feminead* (London: Joseph Johnson, 1774).

30. For biographical information about Mary Scott, see Moira Ferguson, "The Cause of My Sex: Mary Scott and the Female Literary Tradition," in *The Huntington Library Quarterly. Studies in English and American History and Literature,* vol. 50, no. 4, (Autumn 1987): 359–377.

31. See Chapter Three, pp. 58–62.

32. See endnote 24, Isani, "The British Reception," p. 145.

33. Mary Deverell, *Miscellanies in Prose and Verse, mostly written in the Epistolary Style; chiefly upon Moral Subjects; and particularly calculated for the Improvement of Younger Minds,* 2nd ed., vol. 2 (London: Printed for and sold by the Author, 1784).

34. Elizabeth Rowe, *The History of Joseph. A Poem. In Eight Books* (London, 1736).

35. Rowe's poem is a telling case in point. In her narrative, Joseph is—as he is typically depicted—a feminized character:

> No more disparag'd with a slave's attire,
> His faultless shape and features all admire.
> His hair, like palest amber, from his crown
> In floating curls, and shining waves fell down.

Carolyn Woodward compellingly argued the case of the feminization of the eighteenth-century hero, especially David Simple, in a paper read in 1986 at the American Association of Eighteenth-Century Studies: "The Limits of Retreat in Sarah Fielding's *David Simple.*"

36. *First Feminists. British Women Writers 1578–1799,* ed. and intro. Moira Ferguson (Bloomington: Indiana University Press; 1985), p. 255.

37. Samuel Pickering, Jr., *The Moral Tradition in English Fiction, 1785–1850* (Hanover, NH: University Press of New England, 1976), p. 150.

38. Anna Laetitia Barbauld, *Hymns in Prose for Children* (London: Joseph Johnson, 1781), p. 53.

39. For a variant view of philanthropy and distance, see Wayne Booth, "Control of Distance in Jane Austen's *Emma,*" in *The Rhetoric of Fiction* (Chicago: University of Chicago Press, 1968), pp. 24–26.

40. Samuel F. Pickering, Jr., *John Locke and Children's Books in Eighteenth-Century England* (Knoxville: University of Tennessee Press, 1981), p. 148.

41. Pickering, *John Locke,* p. 150.

42. Ann Shteir in a private letter to Moira Ferguson, February 27, 1987.

43. I thank Ann Shteir for this reference to Amelia Opie, *Adeline Mowbray,* 3rd ed., vol. 3 (London, 1810), p. 27.

44. Shyllon, *Black Slaves,* pp. 184–209.

45. Quoted in Sir Reginald Coupland, *The British Anti-Slavery Movement* with a new introduction by J. D. Fage (London: Frank Cass & Co., Ltd., 1964), pp. 59–60.

46. Fryer, *Staying Power,* p. 127.

47. Sophia Lee, *The Recess, or A Tale of Other Times* (London: T. Cadell, 1785).

48. Edward Long, *The History of Jamaica, or General Survey of the Antient and Modern State of That Island: With Reflections on its Situations, Settlements, Inhabitants, Climate, Products, Commerce, Laws and Government.* New edition with introduction by George Metcalf. Vol. 2, 1st ed. 1774; Frank Cass & Co., Ltd., 1970, pp. 351–383.

49. Among many sources, a contemporary woman and a courtesy manual attest to ongoing expectations about women's purity; see Bridget Hill, *Eighteenth-Century Women: An Anthology* (London: George Allen & Unwin, 1984), p. 19.

50. Lucy Peacock, "The Creole," in *The New Novelists Magazine; or, Entertaining Library of Pleasing and Instructive Histories, Tales, Adventures, Romances, and Other Agreeable and Exemplary Little Novels,* vol. II (London: Harrison and Sons, 1787).

51. Lucy Peacock, *The Little Emigrant, A Tale. Interspersed with Moral Anecdotes and Instructive Conversation Designed for the Perusal of Youth* (London: S. Low. For the Author at the Juvenile Library).

52. For a discussion of mental conditioning and cooptation of the oppressed that has some bearing on Peacock's colonizing view about the behavior of freed slaves, see Michel Foucault, *Discipline & Punish. The Birth of the Prison,* trans. Alan Sheridan (New York: Vintage, 1979), pp. 27–28, 174ff. and passim.

Notes on Chapter 7

1. For a contemporary account, see Thomas Clarkson, *The History of the Rise, Progress, and Accomplishment of the Abolition of the African Slave-Trade by the British Parliament,* 2 vols., vol. 1 (London, 1808; Reprint. Frank Cass, & Co., Ltd., 1968), pp. 220–229; see also Winthrop Jordan, *White Over Black: American Attitudes Toward the Negro, 1550–1812* (Chapel Hill: University of North Carolina Press, 1968), pp. 195–98; Frank J. Klingberg, *The Anti-Slavery Movement in England: A Study of English Humanitarianism* (London: Oxford University Press, 1926), pp. 66–67.

2. For discussions of the construction of the other, see Mary Louise Pratt, "Scratches on the Face of the Country; or, What Mr. Barrow Saw in the Land of the Bushmen," in *"Race," Writing and Difference,"* ed. Henry Louis Gates, Jr., (Chicago: University of Chicago Press, 1985), pp. 138–162; Christopher Miller, *Blank Darkness: Africanist Discourse in French* (Chicago: University of Chicago Press, 1985), especially pp. 169–183; Edward W. Said, *Orientalism* (New York: Viking Press, 1979), pp. 1–49.

3. George Phillips, "Mrs. Montagu and Her Climbing Boys," in *The Review of English Studies,* 25, no. 99 (July 1949): 243–44.

4. Elizabeth Carter, *Memoirs of the Life of Mrs. Elizabeth Carter, with a new edition of her poems . . . To which are added, some miscellaneous essays in prose, together with her notes on the Bible, and answer to objections concerning the Christian religion,* by the Rev. Montagu Pennington. . . . 2nd ed. 2 vols. (London: F. C. & J. Rivington, 1808), p. 319.

5. *A List of the Governors of the Sunday School Society,* British Library Tract 472, n.d., p. 18.

6. *A List of the Governors of the Magdalen Hospital,* British Library Tract 472, London, n.d., n.p.

7. *A List of the Society Instituted in 1787 for the Purpose of Effecting the Abolition of the Slave Trade. Printed in Year 1788,* No. 3, British Library Tract 472, p. a[3.]

8. Joyce M. S. Tompkins, *The Popular Novel in England. 1770–1800* (London: Methuen, 1922; Reprint. Lincoln, NE: University of Nebraska Press, 1969), p. 124.

9. M. G. Jones, *Hannah More* (Cambridge: University of Cambridge Press, 1952), especially pp. 104–107 and passim.

10. Quoted in Leonore Davidoff and Catherine Hall, *Family Fortunes: Men and Women in the English Middle Class, 1780–1850* (London: Hutchinson, 1987), p. 82.

11. Ernest Marshall Howse, *Saints in Politics: The "Clapham Sect" and the Growth of Freedom* (Toronto: University of Toronto Press, 1952), p. 19. For

further information on the Clapham Sect, see G. W. E. Russell, *The Household of Faith* (London: Oxford University Press, 1906).

12. Davidoff and Hall, *Family Fortunes,* p. 83.

13. Clarkson, *The History,* see endnote 1.

14. *Gentlemen's Magazine* (July–December 1788): 610.

15. James Walvin, "The Public Campaign—England Against Slavery 1787–1834," in *The Abolition of the Atlantic Slave Trade: Origins and Effect in Europe, Africa, and the Americas,* ed. David Eltis and James Walvin (Madison: Univerity of Wisconsin Press, 1981), p. 65.

16. Elaine Hobby, "Breaking the Silence: English Women in Print, 1640–1700," (Unpublished paper read at the Berkshire Conference of Women Historians, Smith College, MA, 1984), pp. 3–8; Ellen McArthur, "Women Petitioners and the Long Parliament," *English Historical Review* 24 (1909): 698–709.

17. See endnote 7.

18. Seymour Drescher, "Public Opinion on the Destruction of British Colonial Slavery," in *Slavery and British Society 1776–1846,* ed. James Walvin (London: Macmillan, 1982), p. 29. See also E. M. Hunt, "The Anti-Slave Trade Agitation in Manchester," in *Transactions of the Lancashire and Cheshire Antiquarian Society,* Vol. 79 (Manchester: Richmond Press, Ltd., 1977).

19. Claire Midgeley, *Women Anti-Slavery Campaigners in Britain, 1780–1870,* pp. 13, 17 and 18. Dissertation, University of Kent at Canterbury, August, 1989.

20. Grace A. Ellis, *A Memoir of Mrs. Anna Laetitia Barbauld, with many of her letters* (Boston: James. R. Osgood, 1874), p. 178.

21. William Roberts, *Memoirs of the Life and Correspondence of Mrs. Hannah More,* 2 vols. (New York: Harper & Brother, 1858), pp. 97, 99–108; Hannah More, "Slavery: A Poem" (London: Thomas Cadell, 1788).

22. Antonio Gramsci, *Selections from Prison Notebooks,* ed. and trans. Quintin Hoare and Geoffrey Nowell Smith (London: Lawrence and Wishart, 1971), p. 208 and passim.

23. Pratt, "Scratches on the Face," p. 139.

24. William Wilberforce, *Practical Christianity or, A Practical View of the Prevailing System of Professed Christians* (Boston: Manning and Loring, 1799), pp. 12–13.

25. See, for example, chapter four, endnote 26. See also Sylvia Harcstark Myers, *The Bluestocking Circle. Women, Friendship, and the Life of the Mind in Eighteenth-Century England* (Oxford: Clarendon Press, 1990), pp. 92–112, 117–119, 186–187.

26. Davidoff and Hall, *Family Fortunes,* pp. 162–167 and passim.

27. Janet Todd, *Sensibility. An Introduction* (London: Methuen, 1986), pp. 88–109 and passim.

28. Davidoff and Hall, *Family Fortunes,* p. 13.

29. Maria and Harriet Falconar, *Poems of Slavery* (London: Joseph Johnson, 1788).

30. Ottobah Cugoano, *Thoughts and Sentiments on the Evil of Slavery* (London: 1787; Reprint. ed. Paul Edwards, London: Dawsons, 1969), p. 3.

31. *Critical Review,* vol. 63, (1788): 226.

32. *Critical Review,* vol. 64, (1788): 313–14.

33. *Monthly Review,* (March 1788): 245.

34. Helen Maria Williams, "The Morai, An Ode," Appendix No. 2 in Andrew Kippis, *The Life of Captain James Cook* (London: Printed for G. Nichol, and G. G. J. and J. Robinson, 1788), pp. 524–525.

35. Helen Maria Williams "Peru." (London: T. Cadell, 1788); *Critical Review* (February 1789): 54.

36. Helen Maria Williams, "A poem on the bill lately passed for regulating the slave trade." (London: T. Cadell, 1788).

37. Carl B. Cone, *The English Jacobins. Reformers in Late 18th-Century England* (New York: Charles Scribner's Sons, 1968), p. 62 and passim.

38. James Walvin, *English Radicals and Reformers 1760–1848* (Lexington: University of Kentucky Press, 1982), p. 79.

39. Walvin, *English Radicals,* p. 43.

40. Anna Laetitia Barbauld, *Epistle to William Wilberforce, Esq. on the Rejection of the Bill for Abolishing the Slave Trade* (London: Joseph Johnson, 1791).

41. M. M. Bakhtin, *The Dialogic Imagination,* ed. Michael Holquist, trans. Caryl Emerson and Michael Holquist (Austin: University of Texas Press, 1981), p. 342.

42. For the failed "experiment" with African children, see Howse, *Saints in Politics,* pp. 49–50; Prince Hoare, *Memoirs of Granville Sharp, Esq. Composed From His Own Manuscripts, Authentic Documents in the Possession of His Family and of the African Institution* (London: Printed for Henry Colburn and Co., 1820), p. 296; Viscountess Knutsford, *Life and Letters of Zachary Macaulay by his Granddaughter* (London: Edward Arnold, 1900), p. 224.

43. For an analysis of the Saints' involvement and for the evangelical point of view, see Howse, *Saints in Politics,* p. 40 and passim; and Davidoff and Hall, *Family Fortunes,* pp. 76–106.

44. Said, *Orientalism,* p. 179.

45. Anna Freud, *The Ego and the Mechanisms of the Defense* (New York: International Universities Press, 1966), pp. 56–38 and passim.

46. I thank Catherine Hall for a valuable conversation on this point.

47. Elizabeth Mavor, *The Ladies of Llangollen* (London: Penguin, 1971), p. 159.

48. Jacques Lacan, *Ecrits. A Selection,* trans. Alan Sheridan (London: Tavistock Publications, 1977), p. 21.

49. For a compelling study of the impact of African contemporaries on the anti-slavery movement, see Keith A. Sandiford, *Measuring the Moment. Strategies of Protest in Eighteenth-Century Afro-English Writing* (Selinsgrove, PA: Susquehanna University Press, London: Associated University Press, 1988).

50. Grace Ellis, *Memoirs, Letters and a Selection from the Poems and Prose Writings of Mrs. Barbauld,* 2 vols., vol. 1 (Boston: J. R. Osgood, 1874), p. 193.

51. Ellis, *Memoirs,* p. 192.

Notes on Chapter 8

1. David Brion Davis, *The Problem of Slavery in Western Culture* (Ithaca, NY: Cornell University Press, 1966) p. 453.

2. Davis, *The Problem of Slavery,* p. 453.

3. Winthrop D. Jordan, *White Over Black. American Attitudes Toward the Negro, 1550–1812* (Chapel Hill: University of North Carolina Press, 1968), pp. 96–97.

4. Jordan, *White Over Black,* pp. 9–10, 17–20, 286–87. See also the debate over Samuel Stanhope Smith's essay "An Essay on the Causes of the Variety of Complexion and Figure in the Human Species. To which are added, Strictures on Lord Kaims's Discourse on the original Diversity of Mankind." Paradoxically, Dr. Smith is refuting Lord Kaims's contention that there is an "original diversity of species among mankind" based on such evidence as the alleged lack of hair on Native Americans' chin and body. In *Studies in Eighteenth-Century Culture,* vol. 3, edited by Harold E. Paglioro, *Racism in the Eighteenth Century,* several essays concretely address these controversies, *Studies in Eighteenth-Century Culture* (Cleveland, OH: Case Western Reserve University Press, 1973), especially pp. 239–386.

5. G. S. Rousseau, "Madame Chimpanzee," Parts 1 and 2, in *The Clark Newsletter, Bulletin of the U.C.L.A. Center for 17th-and 18th-Century Studies,* No. 10 (Spring 1986), pp. 1–14, No. 12 (Spring 1987), pp. 4–7.

6. Elizabeth Haywood, *First Feminists. British Women Writers 1578–1799,* ed. Moira Ferguson, (Bloomington: Indiana University Press, 1985) p. 459.

7. Elizabeth Haywood, *The Parrot. With a Compendium of the Times. By the Author of the Female Spectator* (London: T. Gardner, 1746), pp. B3–4.

8. Elizabeth Haywood, *The Parrot,* p. B3.

9. Elizabeth Haywood, *The Parrot,* p. B4.

10. Elizabeth Haywood, *The Female Spectator,* Vol. 4, 134. It is worth recalling, too, the overt prejudice avowed by David Hume that added credibility to the debate: *Essays Moral, Political, and Literary,* edited, with preliminary dissertations and notes, by T. H. Green and T. H. Grose. In two volumes, vol. 1 (London and New York: Longmans, Green & Co., 1889), p. 252. See, for example, the following citation from essay 21, on national characters:

> I am apt to suspect the negroes, and in general all the other species of men (for there are four or five different kinds) to be naturally inferior to the whites. There never was a civilized nation of any other complexion than white, nor even any individual eminent either in action or speculation. No ingenious manufacturers amongst them, no arts, no sciences.

11. Rufus M. Jones, *The Later Periods of Quakerism,* Vol. 1 (London: Macmillan, 1921) p. 320.

12. Davis, *The Problem of Slavery,* pp. 330–331.

13. Jones, *The Later Period,* Vol. 1, p. 320.

14. Auguste Jorns, *The Quakers as Pioneers in Social Work,* trans. Thomas Kite Brown, (New York: Macmillan, 1931), p. 208. See also Davis, *The Problem of Slavery,* p. 330.

15. For information on Antony Benezet's influential and protracted anti-slavery activities, see Davis, *The Problem of Slavery,* pp. 487–489; Jones, *The Later Period,* Vol. 2, pp. 317–320.

16. For biographical information about Rachel Wilson, see a typed version of "Note in 'The Journal of John Woolman,'" 1922, pp. 565–566, and other assorted materials kindly supplied by Malcolm Thomas, curator of The Friends Library, Euston Road, London.

17. John Somervell, *Isaac and Rachel Wilson, Quakers, of Kendal, 1714–1785* (London: The Swarthmore Press, Ltd., 1924), p. 57.

18. Jorns, *Quakers as Pioneers,* pp. 210–211.

19. Sir Reginald Coupland, *The British Anti-Slavery Movement,* intro. J. D. Fage (Oxford: Oxford University Press, rpt. London: Frank Cass & Co. Ltd., 1964), p. 64.

20. Coupland, *British Anti-Slavery Movement,* p. 20.

.21. Olaudah Equiano, *Equiano's Travels. His Autobiography. The Interesting Narrative of the Life of Olaudah Equiano, or Gustavus Vassa, the African,* ed, Paul Edwards (London: Heinemann, 1789, Reprint. 1967). For an analysis of Equiano's discourse, see also William L. Andrews, *To Tell a Free Story. The First Century of Afro-American Autobiography, 1760–1865* (Chicago: University of Chicago Press, 1986), pp. 56–60.

22. Folaris O. Shyllon, *Black Slaves in Britain* (London: Oxford University Press, 1974), pp. 188–189.

23. For further information about Ann Yearsley see Donna Landry, *The Muses of Resistance: Working-Class Women's Poetry in Britain 1739–1796* (Cambridge: Cambridge University Press, 1990); Moira Ferguson, "Resistance and Power in the Life and Writings of Ann Yearsley" *The Eighteenth Century: Theory and Interpretation* (vol. 27, no. 3, 1986), pp. 247–268; Mary Waldron, "Ann Yearsley and the Clifton Records" in *The Age of Johnson: A Scholarly Annual,* ed. Paul J. Korshin (New York: AMS Press, Inc., 1990), pp. 301–329. Yearsley's autobiographical narrative and "A Poem on the Inhumanity of the Slave-Trade," appear in *First Feminists. British Women Writers 1578–1799,* ed. and intro. Moira Ferguson (Bloomington: Indiana Univerity Press, 1985), pp. 382–396. Textual citations come from "A Poem on the Inhumanity of the Slave-Trade" (London: G. G. J. and J. Robinson, 1788).

24. Michael Craton mentions many of these resistances. See *Testing the Chains: Resistance to Slavery in the British West Indies* (Ithaca: Cornell University Press, 1982), pp. 335–339. See also Hilary Beckles, *Black Rebellion in Barbados: The Struggle Against Slavery 1627–1833* (St. Michael, Barbados, W.I.: Antilles Publications, 1984) and Barbara Bush, *Slave Women in Caribbean Society, 1650–1838* (Kingston: Heinemann; Bloomington: Indiana University Press, 1990).

25. Craton, *Testing the Chains,* pp. 336–337.

26. *The Monthly Review* (March 1788), pp. 246–247.

27. Elizabeth Bentley, *Genuine Poetical Compositions on Various Subjects* (Norwich: Crouse and Stevenson, 1791). The poems entitled "On Health and Happiness 1787" and "On the Abolition of the Slave Trade, 1789" are included in that volume.

28. *The Parliamentary History of England from the Earliest Period to the Year 1803,* Vol. 28, pp. 79–80.

29. Ignatius Sancho's much acclaimed *Letters* had been published in 1782. *Ignatius Sancho,* ed. J. Jeckyll (London, 1782; Reprint., ed. Paul Edwards, Dawsons, 1968).

30. *Ignatius Sancho,* ed. Paul Edwards, p. i.

31. *Ignatius Sancho,* ed. J. Jeckyll, p. vii–xviii.

32. See, for example, *Anon: Biography to The Political Works of the Late Mrs. Mary Robinson,* in 3 vols., (London: Richard Phillips, 1800); see also Robert D. Bass, *The Green Dragon. The Lives of Banastre Tarleton and Mary Robinson* (New York: Henry Holt and Company, 1957), and Mary Darby Robinson, *Memoirs,* 2 vols. (London, 1800). She chronicles her experiences in *Mrs. Mary Robinson. Written by Herself* in *Beaux and Belles of England* (London: The Grolier Society n.d.).

33. Anon, *Biography,* p. v–xvii.

34. Mary Darby Robinson, *Poems* (London: C. Parker, 1775), pp. 28–36.

35. Mary Darby Robinson, "Captivity: A Poem" (London: T. Beckett, 1777).

36. *Collected Letters of Mary Wollstonecraft,* ed. Ralph M. Wardle (Ithaca: Cornell University Press, 1979), pp. 370, 376 and passim.

37. Richard Polwhele, *The Unsex'd Females. A Poem, Addressed to the Author of The Pursuits of Literature* (London: Cadell and Davies, 1798).

38. For the Della Cruscan cult to which Mary Darby Robinson for some time was a devoted member, see W. N. Gargreaves-Mawdsley, *The English Della Cruscans and Their Time, 1783–1828* (The Hague: Martinus Nijhoff, 1967).

39. M. G. Jones, *Hannah More* (Cambridge: Cambridge University Press, 1952), p. 84; Mary Darby Robinson, "Ainsi Va le Monde" in *The Monthly Review* IV (2nd ser.). Monthly Catalogue, February 1791, article 16, p. 223.

40. William Fox, *An Address to the People of Great Britain on the Propriety of Abstaining from West Indies Sugar and Rum* (London, 1792).

41. Earl Leslie Griggs, *Thomas Clarkson* (Ann Arbor: University of Michigan Press, 1938), p. 69.

42. *The Life and Letters of Maria Edgeworth,* ed. Augustus J. C. Hare, 2 Vols., vol. 1 (Freeport, NY: Libraries Press, 1894; Reprint. 1971), p. 23.

43. Grace A. Ellis, *A Memoir of Mrs. Anna Laetitia Barbauld, with many of her letters* (Boston: James. R. Osgood, 1874), p. 222.

44. Mary Birkett, *A Poem on the African Slave Trade. Addressed to Her Own Sex.* 1st Part. 2nd ed. (Dublin: J. Jones, 1792), p. 3.

45. David V. Erdman, *Blake: Prophet Against Empire. A Poet's Interpretation of the History of His Own Times* (Garden City, NY: Anchor Books, 1954; Reprint. 1969), pp. 239–240. For other discussions of slavery, see pp. 228–230.

46. See endnote 44. Birkett, *A Poem.* Part two (Dublin: J. Jones, 1792).

47. Edward W. Said, *Orientalism* (New York: Vintage, 1979), p. 7.

Notes on Chapter 9

1. Anthony Lincoln, *Some Political and Social Ideas of English Dissent, 1763–1800* (New York: Octagon Books, 1971), p. 272.

2. Mary Wollstonecraft, *The Female Reader,* intro. Moira Ferguson (Delmar, NY: Scholars' Facsimiles & Reprints, 1980).

3. For a succinct version of Cowper's slave images see Eva Beatrice Dyke, *The Negro in English Romantic Thought, or A Study of Sympathy for the Oppressed* (Washington, D.C.: The Associated Publishers, Inc., 1942), pp. 15–18 and passim; see also David V. Erdman, *Blake: Prophet Against Empire. A Poet's Interpretation of the History of His Own Times* (Garden City, NY: Anchor Books, 1954, Reprint. 1969), p. 228.

4. Book of Psalms, Chap. 137, verses 1–6. I thank Robert Haller for finding this reference for me.

5. Anna Laetitia Baubauld, *Hymns in Prose for Children* (London: Joseph Johnson, 1781). David V. Erdman suggestively speculates on relationships between *Hymns* and Blake's songs. And it seems reasonable to deduce that Barbauld's *Hymn* about the African mother is ideologically related to Blake's ideas in "The Little Black Boy," see p. 332 and Chapter Ten, endnote 20; · Erdman, *Blake*, pp. 124–125.

6. Mary Wollstonecraft, *A Vindication of the Rights of Men,* intro. Eleanor Louise Nicholes (Gainesville, FL: Scholars' Facsimiles & Reprints, 1st ed. 1790; Reprint. 1980).

7. Mary Wollstonecraft, *A Vindication of the Rights of Woman. With Strictures on Political and Moral Subjects,* ed., and intro. Charles W. Hagelman, Jr., (New York: W. W. Norton & Company, Inc., 1st ed. 1792; Reprint. 1967).

8. Mary Wollstonecraft, Review in *Analytical Review,* ed. Joseph Johnson, (May, 1790), pp. 462–463. The book in question is Phillis Wheatley, *The Negro Equalled by Few Europeans. Translated from the French. To Which Are Added, Poems on Various Subjects, Moral and Entertaining.* Vol. 1, (Philadelphia: William W. Woodward, 1801).

9. *Elements of Morality, for the Use of Children. With an Introductory Address to Parents,* trans. Rev. C. G. Saltzmann (Baltimore: Joseph Robinson, 1811).

10. Lincoln, *Some Political and Social Ideas,* p. 255.

11. Helen Maria Williams, *Letters from France,* Vol. 1 (New York: Scholars' Facsimiles & Reprints, 1975), pp. 48–50.

12. Anna Laetitia Barbauld, "Sins of Government, Sins of the Nation; or a Discourse for the Fast, appointed on April 19, 1793," in Lucy Aikin, *The Works of Anna Laetitia Barbauld. With a Memoir,* Vol. 2 (London: Longman, Hurst, Rees, Orme, Brown, and Green, 1825), pp. 379–412.

13. C. L. R. James, *The Black Jacobins. Toussaint l'Ouverture and the San Domingo Revolution* 2nd. ed. rev. (New York: Vintage, 1963). See also Wenda Parkinson, *'This Gilded African' Toussaint L'Ouverture* (London: Quartet Books, 1980).

14. David Geggus, "British Opinion and the Emergence of Haiti, 1791–1805" in *Slavery and British Society 1776–1846* ed. James Walvin (London: Macmillan, 1982), p. 123.

15. *Journals of Dorothy Wordsworth,* ed. William Knight (Macmillan, 1897), p. 74.

16. Charlotte Smith, *Desmond. A Novel,* intro. Gina Luria. 3 vols. (New York: Garland, 1792; Reprint. 1974).

17. For biographical information about Charlotte Smith, see Florence May Anna Hilbish, *Charlotte Smith, Poet and Novelist 1749–1806* (Philadelphia: University of Pennsylvania Press, 1941) and Barbara Imig, *Shooting Folly*

As It Flies: A Dialogic Approach to Four Novels by Charlotte Smith, Ph.D. dissertation, University of Nebraska at Lincoln, 1989.

18. Mary Hays, *Memoirs of Emma Courtney*, intro. Gina Luria. 2 vols. (New York: Garland, 1796; Reprint. 1974).

19. Betty T. Bennett, *British War Poetry in the Age of Romanticism: 1793–1815* (New York: Garland, 1976).

20. Griggs, *Thomas Clarkson*, p. 72ff.

21. Elie Halévy, *A History of the English People in the Nineteenth Century*, vol. 1, *England in 1815* (New York: Barnes & Noble, 1961), p. 456.

22. *Selections from the Papers of the London Corresponding Society 1792–1799*, ed. and intro. Mary Thale (Cambridge: Cambridge University Press, 1983), pp. 101–236.

23. Helen Maria Williams, *A Farewell for Two Years to England* (London: Thomas Cadell, 1791), pp. 5–9.

24. Mary Hays, *Letters and Essays, Moral and Miscellaneous*, intro. Gina Luria (New York: Garland, 1793; Reprint. 1974).

25. Gary Kelly, *The English Jacobin Novel, 1780–1805* (Oxford: Clarendon Press, 1976), traces the influence of the French revolution on English Jacobinism, pp. 1–19ff.

26. Michael R. Watts, *The Dissenters. From the Reformation to the French Revolution* (Oxford: Clarendon Press, 1978), p. 487.

27. Anna Maria Falconbridge, *Narrative of Two Voyages to the River Sierra Leone, During the Years 1791-2-3, Performed by A. M. Falconbridge. With a Succinct account of the Distresses and Proceedings of that Settlement; a description of the Manner, Diversions, Arts, Commerce, Cultivation, Custom, Punishments, &c. And Every interesting Particular relating to the Sierra Leone Company. Also The present State of the Slave Trade in the West Indies, and the improbability of its total Abolition* 2nd ed. 1802 (London: L. I. Higham, 1794).

28. Alexander Falconbridge, *An Account of the Slave Trade on the Coast of Africa* (London: J. Phillips, 1788). For valuable insights into Falconbridge's reexamination of slavery and related materials, see Thomas Clarkson, *The History of the Rise, Progress, and Accomplishment of the Abolition of the African Slave-Trade by the British Parliament*, 2 vols., Vol. 1 (London: Frank Cass & Co. Ltd., 1968), pp. 345–367.

29. Christopher Fyfe, *A History of Sierra Leone* (Oxford: Oxford University Press, 1962), p. 50.

30. Fyfe, *A History*, p. 110.

31. For accounts of the choice of Sierra Leone as a relocation region, see Prince Hoare, *Memoirs of Granville Sharp, Esq. Composed From His Own Manuscripts, Authentic Documents in the Possession of His Family and of the African Institution* (London: Printed for Henry Colburn and Co., 1820), pp.

257–277, and James W. St. G. Walker, *The Black Loyalists. The Search for a Promised Land in Nova Scotia and Sierra Leone 1783–1870* (London: Longman & Dalhousie University Press, 1976), pp. 97–98 and passim.

32. Peter Fryer, *Staying Power: The History of Black People in Britain* (London: Pluto Press, 1984), p. 200ff. Olaudah Equiano, *Equiano's Travels. His Autobiography. The Interesting Narrative of the Life of Olaudah Equiano, or Gustavus Vassa, the African,* ed. Paul Edwards (London: Heinemann, 1789, Reprint. 1967) p. 162ff.; Seymour Drescher, *Capitalism and Antislavery. British Mobilization in Comparative Perspective* (London: Macmillan, 1986); Standish Meacham, *Henry Thornton of Clapham 1760–1815* (Cambridge, MA: Harvard University Press, 1964), pp. 107ff.

33. Peter Fryer, *Staying Power,* p. 201.

34. See Walker, *Black Loyalists,* pp. 149–152 and passim for a full appraisal of the demands of Sgt. Thomas Peters and other expatriated Blacks in Sierra Leone.

35. Mary Louise Pratt, "Scratches on the Face of the Country; or, What Mr. Barrow Saw in the Land of the Bushmen," in *"Race," Writing, and Difference,* ed. Henry Louis Gates, Jr., (Chicago: University of Chicago Press, 1985), pp. 138–162.

36. Averil Mackenzie-Grieve, *The Great Accomplishment* (London: Geoffrey Bles, 1953), p. 14.

37. Mackenzie-Grieve, *Great Accomplishment,* p. 18.

38. Mackenzie-Grieve, *Great Accomplishment,* p. 33.

39. Mackenzie-Grieve, *Great Accomplishment,* p. 48.

40. Ellen Gibson Wilson, *John Clarkson and the African Adventure* (London: Macmillan, 1980), p. 87.

41. Meacham, *Henry Thornton,* pp. 115–116.

Notes on Chapter 10

1. Roger Anstey, *The Atlantic Slave Trade and British Abolition 1760–1810* (Atlantic Highlands, NJ: Humanities Press, 1975), pp. 255–285 and *passim.*

2. Anstey, *Atlantic Slave Trade,* pp. 314–315. Frank Joseph Klingberg, *The Anti-Slavery Movement: A Study in English Humanitarianism* (New Haven: Yale University Press; London: Oxford University Press, 1926), pp. 94–95.

3. For an account of Jacobin ideas, see Gary Kelly, *The English Jacobin Novel, 1780–1805* (Oxford: The Clarendon Press, 1976), pp. 1–8.

4. Klingberg, *Anti-Slavery Movement,* p. 94.

5. Eric J. Hobsbawm, *The Pelican Economic History of Britain. From 1750*

to the Present Day. Industry and Empire, Vol. 3 (Middlesex: Penguin Books, 1968), p. 89.

6. Eva Beatrice Dyke, *The Negro in English Romantic Thought or, A Study of Sympathy for the Oppressed* (Washington, D.C.: The Associated Publishers, Inc., 1942), p. 74.

7. *Analytical Review,* vol. XII, Jan.–April 1792, Appendix, April 1792, pp. 505–509. For commentary on Jacobin support for the French Revolution, see Chapter Nine, endnote 25.

8. Earl Leslie Griggs and Clifford H. Prator, eds. *Henry Christophe and Thomas Clarkson. A Correspondence* (New York: Greenwood Press, 1968), pp. 15, 17.

9. Griggs and Prator, *Henry Christophe and Thomas Clarkson,* p. 17.

10. C. L. R. James, *The Black Jacobins. Toussaint L'Ouverture and the San Domingo Revolution* (New York: Vintage, 1963), p. 200.

11. Michael R. Watts, *The Dissenters. From the Reformation to the French Revolution* (Oxford: Clarendon Press, 1978), pp. 394–490.

12. M. G. Jones, *Hannah More* (Cambridge: Cambridge University Press, 1952), p. 134. See also Peter C. Hogg, *The African Slave Trade and Its Suppression* (London: Frank Cass & Co., Inc., 1973), p. 301. See also Elsa V. Goveia, *Slave Society in the British Leeward Islands at the End of the Eighteenth Century* (New Haven: Yale University Press, 1965), pp. 260–261.

13. Jones, *Hannah More,* p. 134.

14. Jones, *Hannah More,* p. 136.

15. Jones, *Hannah More,* p. 137.

16. Leonore Davidoff and Catherine Hall, *Family Fortunes. Men and Women of the English Middle-Class, 1780–1850* (London: Hutchinson, Ltd., 1987), p. 95.

17. W. K. Lowther Clarke, *Eighteenth Century Piety* (London: Society for Promoting Christian Knowledge, 1944; London: Macmillan, 1944), pp. 119–122.

18. Information about Sarah Trimmer and *The Family Magazine,* as well as *Cheap Repository Tracts* is available in G. H. Spinney, *Cheap Repository Tracts: Hazard and Marshall Edition* (Denton, TX: Texas State University, n.d.), pp. 295–340.

19. Sarah Trimmer, *Some Account of the Life and Writings of Mrs. Trimmer with Original Letters and Meditations and Prayers, Selected from Her Journal,* vol. 2, (London: J. Johnson and Co., 1814), p. 123.

20. Trimmer, *Some Account,* p. 209. In that letter, dated March 1, 1788, Lady Denward is speaking of Trimmer's inclusion of slavery in *The Family Magazine,* Vol. 1, pp. 128–129.

21. Trimmer, for example, would have been well aware of the Caribbean

estates administered by the Church of England that were slave plantations left to the Church by Christopher Codrington. Trimmer's journal entry comes from *Some Account*, Vol. 1, p. 298, May 9th, 1792.

22. W. K. Lowther Clarke, *Eighteenth Century Piety*, p. 125.

23. Anne Boylan, "Women in Groups: An Analysis of Women's Benevolent Organizations in New York and Boston, 1797–1840," *Journal of American History* 71, no. 3 (December 1974), pp. 497–523.

24. Sir Reginald Coupland, *The British Anti-Slavery Movement*, Introduction by J. D. Fage (Oxford University Press, 1933; London: Frank Cass & Co., Ltd., 1964), p. 101.

25. Jones, *Hannah More*, p. 138.

26. *Cheap Repository Tracts, Published During the Year 1795*, Vol. 1 (London: J. Marshall, 1795).

27. *The Black Prince. A True Story: Being An Account of the Life and Death of Naimbana, An African King's Son, Who arrived in England in the Year 1791, and set sail on his Return in June, 1793* (London: Howard & Evans, n.d.).

28. Anthony Benezet. A modern biography of Benezet that records his ardent commitment as an anti-slavery writer and activist is G. S. Brookes, *Friend Anthony Benezet* (Philadelphia: University of Pennsylvania Press, 1937). *A Short Account of That Part of Africa*, etc., was published in German in 1763. Benezet's publishing history is chronicled in D. B. Davis, "New Sidelights on Early Anti-Slavery Radicalism," *William and Mary Quarterly*, 3rd ser., 28 (1971), p. 591 n. The information about Benezet comes from C. Duncan Rice, *The Rise and Fall of Black Slavery* (New York: Harper and Row, 1975), pp. 198–199.

29. For an acute account of Ramsay's contribution to abolition, see Folaris Shyllon, *James Ramsay, The Unknown Abolitionist* (Edinburgh: Canongate, 1977).

30. I thank Claire Midgeley for bringing the ideological importance of this poem to my attention. See endnote 25. "The Comforts of Religion" appears on page 6 of *Cheap Repository Tracts*.

31. See endnote 26. "The Sorrows of Yamba," final tract, pp. 1–12. For an important reassessment of the tracts, see Mitzi Myers, "Hannah More's Tracts for the Times. Social Fiction and Female Ideology," in *Fetter'd or Free? British Women Novelists, 1670–1815*, ed. Mary Anne Schofield and Cecilia Macheski (Athens, OH: Ohio University Press, 1986), pp. 264–284.

32. Alexander Falconbridge, *An Account of the Slave Trade on the Coast of Africa* (London: J. Phillips, 1783), p. 10.

33. For a comparative and statistical study of the conduct of British proslavery entrepreneurs and captains on the Middle Passage, to which surgeon Falconbridge tellingly testified, see Herbert S. Klein, *The Middle Passage:*

Comparative Studies in the Atlantic Slave Trade (Princeton: Princeton University Press, 1978), pp. 141–174.

34. For a full account of these relocation and colonization efforts, see Christopher Fyfe, *A History of Sierra Leone* (Oxford: Oxford University Press, 1962), especially pp. 29–47 and passim. Interestingly enough, when evangelical Quaker William Howitt wrote *Colonization and Christianity: A Popular History of the Treatment of the Natives by the Europeans in All Their Colonies* (New York: Negro Universities Press, 1838), he omitted any reference to the treatment of Britain's slaves in the Caribbean. Since emancipation had occurred, he was technically entitled to, but one surmises the justification for that omission was also something of a patriotic relief.

35. *Equiano's Travels. His Autobiography. The Interesting Narrative of the Life of Olaudah Equiano or Gustavus Vassa the African,* ed. Paul Edwards (London: Heinemann, 1978, Reprint. 1967), pp. 31, 34 and passim.

36. Ottobah Cugoano, *Thoughts and Sentiments on the Evil of Slavery, 1787,* intro. Paul Edwards (London: Dawsons, 1969). The title of this text speaks for itself.

37. See endnote 27.

38. Anna Maria Mackenzie, *Slavery, or The Times* (London: T. Cadell, 1794).

39. See Prince Hoare, *The Memoirs of Granville Sharpe Esq. Composed From His Own Manuscripts, Authentic Documents in the Possession of His Family and of the African Institution. Pt. II,* (London: Printed for Henry Colburn, 1820), p. 365.

40. Zachary Macaulay very carefully explains the Prince's reactions in terms of the Prince's Christian conversion rather than his patriotism toward Africa and his political freethinking. See Viscountess Knutsford, *Life and Letters of Zachary Macaulay* (London: Edward Arnold, 1900), p. 35.

41. Hoare, *The Memoirs,* p. 368.

42. Hoare, *The Memoirs,* p. 367.

43. C. B. Wadstrom, *An Essay on Colonization. Particularly Applied to the Western Coast of Africa with Some Free Thoughts on Cultivation and Commerce [1794]* (New York: Augustus M. Kelley, 1968), pp. 267–268.

44. Philip D. Curtin, *The Image of Africa. British Ideas and Action, 1780–1850* (Madison: University of Wisconsin Press, 1964), pp. 108–09.

45. Keith A. Sandiford in his recent book, *Measuring the Moment. Strategies of Protest in Eighteenth-Century Afro-English Writing* (Selinsgrove, PA: Susquehanna University Press; London and Toronto: Associated University Presses, 1988), deftly dismantles the texts of several African contemporaries, most particularly those of Equiano, Cugoano, and Sancho. I am arguing that the written records of Prince Naimbana's social commentary can be similarly reevaluated.

46. Wadstrom, *An Essay,* pp. 40–41.

360 °° NOTES TO CHAPTER 11

47. For the physical and psychological significance to slaves of the Middle Passage journey, see not only Herbert Klein, *The Middle Passage,* but the accounts of slaves' individual and collective reactions in, for example, *Equiano's Travels.*

48. E. Bolaji Idowu, *Olodumare. God in Yoruba Belief* (New York: Praeger, 1973). Idowu chronicles in detail the complex systems of African ontological and spiritual beliefs.

49. I mean by this that the *Tracts* counteract any notion of spiritual hierarchies while implicitly and rhetorically maintaining political hierarchies. This counterinsistence is one of the *Tracts'* notable tensions.

50. Christopher L. Miller, *Blank Darkness: Africanist Discouse in French* (Chicago: University of Chicago Press, 1985), p. 170.

51. Ellen Gibson Wilson, *John Clarkson and The African Adventure* (London: Macmillan, 1980). See also James W. St. G. Walker, *The Black Loyalists. The Search for a Promised Land in Nova Scotia and Sierra Leone 1783–1870* (London: Longman and Dalhousie University Press, 1976).

52. See endnote 33, Christopher Fyfe, *A History,* pp. 29–47.

Notes on Chapter 11

1. C. L. R. James, *The Black Jacobins. Toussaint L'Ouverture and the San Domingo Revolution.* 2nd ed. (New York: Vintage, 1963). The anxiety aroused in Britain by San Domingo is also compellingly recorded in Lowell Joseph Ragatz, *The Fall of The Planter Class in the British Caribbean, 1763–1833. A Study in Social and Economic History* (New York: The Century Co., 1928), especially pp. 204–238.

2. C. L. R. James, *The Black Jacobins,* p. 200.

3. Elizabeth Helme, *The Farmer of Inglewood Forest,* 4 vols. (London: William Lane at Minerva Press, 1796). For additional information on editions of *The Farmer,* see Dorothy Blakey, *The Minerva Press, 1790–1820* (London: The Bibliographical Society, 1939 [for 1935].

4. Maria Edgeworth, "The Grateful Negro," in *Popular Tales* (London: J. Johnson, 1804). All references will be to this edition.

5. This concept of waged versus slave labor is most comprehensively developed in 1776 by Adam Smith in *An Inquiry Into the Nature and Causes of The Wealth of Nations* 5 vols., intro. Ludwig Von Mises (Chicago: Henry Regnery Company, 1776; Reprint. 1953), especially pp. 143–144. Smith's statement: "It appears, accordingly, from the experience of all ages and nations, I believe, that the work done by freemen comes cheaper in the end than that performed by slaves," is one to which Maria Edgeworth is an early cultural subscriber. In a nineteenth-century poem—as emancipation nears—she spe-

cifically returns to that subject, as do (among others) Hannah More and Harriet Martineau, the latter in *Demerara.*

6. Hector is a people's bandit—i.e., one who serves his/her community, as defined by Eric Hobsbawm in *Primitive Rebels* (London: Lawrence and Wishart, 1960), pp. 14–15. The notion of Esther as an evil woman is an ancient concept deriving from Eve. Rana Kabbani in *Europe's Myths of Orient. Devise and Rule* (London: Pandora Press, 1986) marshalls solid arguments about the manifestation of particularly intense misogyny around the time of African "explorers" like Sir Richard Burton, p. 51.

7. Bryan Edwards, *The History, Civil and Commercial of the British colonies in the West Indies,* 3 vols. (London, 1793). The textual note runs from pp. 215–218.

8. Marilyn Butler, *Maria Edgeworth: A Literary Biography* (Oxford: Oxford University Press, 1979), p. 17. In another literary context, Butler succinctly puts the matter in *A Dictionary of British and American Women Writers, 1660–1800,* ed. Janet Todd (Totowa, NJ: Rowman and Attenheld, 1975). "R. L. Edgeworth's liberal and tolerant attitudes in Irish politics are reflected in *Castle Rackrent*'s well-disposed (if arguably external) treatment of the native Irish" (p. 110). The *Dictionary of National Biography* refers to Richard L. Edgeworth as "an energetic and intelligent landlord, greatly improv[ing] the condition of his tenantry, p. 384.

9. Butler, *Maria Edgeworth,* p. 16.

10. John Aikin and Anna Laetitia Barbauld, "The Master and the Slave," in *Evenings at Home* (London: Joseph Johnson, 1780). In the text, which is basically a moral dialogue, a slave argues his master into seeing the economic common sense of freeing him, again a concept derived from Adam Smith.

11. Maria Edgeworth, "The Good Aunt," in *Tales and Novels,* vol. 1, *Moral Tales* (London: George Routledge and Sons, Ltd., 1893).

12. For a full discussion of Pidgin English and its usage as an othering device, see the textual argument in Chapter Five, endnotes 34, 35, and 36.

13. Mary Stockdale, "Fidèlle" in *Effusions of the Heart* (London: John Stockdale, 1798).

14. Mary Darby Robinson, "The Negro Child," in *The Poetical Works of the late Mrs. Mary Robinson including Many Pieces Never Before Published,* vol. 2 (London: Richard Phillips, 1806), pp. 170–175.

15. Thomas Day, "The Dying Negro," in *The Poems of Thomas Day* (London: Joseph Johnson, 1776), pp. 161–175. See also R. A. Davenport, "The Life of Thomas Day," in *The British Poets including translations,* vol. 58 (Chiswick: C. Whittingham, 1832), pp. 147–159.

16. Advertisement, Day, "The Dying Negro," p. 161.

17. Amelia Opie, *The Negro Boy's Tale: A Poem Addressed to Children* (London: Harvey and Darton, 1795; Reprint. 1824). Opie's polemical preface,

invoking Isaac Watts as moral mentor and instructing children to consider abolition positively shows the political usage of children's literature.

18. See footnote 12.

19. Benita Parry, "Problems in Current Theories of Colonial Discourse," in *The Oxford Literary Review: Colonialism and Other Essays,* vol. 9, (London: Central Books, 1987), pp. 27–58. The approach to language by (among others) Frantz Fanon and, more recently, Homi K. Bhabha, in terms of mimicking the colonial master is also worth bearing in mind. See Homi K. Bhabha, "Signs Taken for Wonders: Questions of Ambivalence and Authority Under a Tree Outside Delhi, May 1817," in *"Race," Writing and Difference,* ed. Henry Louis Gates, Jr., (Chicago: University of Chicago Press, 1985), especially p. 181ff., and Frantz Fanon, *Black Skin: White Masks,* trans. Charles Lam Markmann (New York: Grove Press, 1967), especially Chapters 1 and 4. See also Frantz Fanon, *The Wretched of the Earth* (New York: Grove Press, 1963), pp. 42–44, 52–53 and passim for the "native's" necessary internalization of the language of violence.

20. David V. Erdman, *Blake. Prophet against Empire. A Poet's Interpretation of the History of His Own Times* (Garden City, NY: Anchor Books, 1954), pp. 239–240.

21. Amelia Opie, "The Lucayan's Song," in *The Warrior's Return and Other Poems* (London: T. Cadell, 1808).

22. Frances (Fanny) Holcroft, "The Negro," *Monthly Magazine,* vol. 4, (October, 1797), p. 286.

23. See endnote 14. See Anne Boylan, "Women in Groups," Chapter Five, endnote 45.

24. Mary Darby Robinson, "The Storm," *The Ladies Magazine* (February 1, 1796), pp. 182–183. The incidence of women in stereotyped roles such as beloveds and mothers in post-colonial literature that has some bearing on anti-slavery texts is incisively discussed in Ketu H. Katrak, "African, Indian, and Caribbean Women Writers in English: Postcolonial Theory and Social Responsibility," Paper read at the Bunting Institute Colloquium, Cambridge, MA, April 5, 1989.

25. Eliza Knipe, "Atamboka and Omaza: An African Story," in *Six Narrative Poems* (London: C. Dilly, 1787), pp. 51–60.

26. Elizabeth Sophia Tomlins, *Tributes of Affection: with "The Slave"; and Other Poems. By a Lady: and Her Brother* (London: H. and C. Baldwin, 1797).

27. Albert Goodwin, *The Friends of Liberty. The English Democratic Movement in the Age of the French Revolution* (Cambridge, MA: Harvard University Press, 1979), pp. 333–366 and passim.

28. Not to put too fine a point on it, in that context Rana Kabbani's comments in *Europe's Myths* can be recontextualized: "The savage was noble if he belonged to a dying species."

29. The relationship of women to fluids and water as a female symbol has frequently been noted. Among many historical and contemporary examples, see Sigmund Freud, *The Interpretation of Dreams,* trans. James Strachey (New York: Discus Books, 1965), p. 435. See also Hélène Cixous, "The Laugh of the Medusa," and Luce Irigaray, "This Sex Which is Not One," in *New French Feminisms,* ed. Elaine Marks and Isabelle de Courtivron (New York: Schocken Books, 1981); and Ellen Moers, *Literary Women* (New York: Doubleday, 1976), pp. 243–264. Lucy Irigaray, "Sexual Difference," in *French Feminist Thought: A Reader,* ed. Toril Moi (Oxford: Basil Blackwell, 1987), makes a complementary argument. Irigaray suggests a linkage between silenced women and invisible and silenced slaves. In a discussion of male-female difference, she then goes on to discuss the idea of the angelic female body that can emit no mucous, a body that is, in a sense, water or fluid denied. On the other hand, she poses "the fluid basis of life and language" as alternatives to forced aridity. In the multiple suicide-death-brutality poems concerning women and feminized males as water-prone, an assertion could lurk that here in language at least is life and natural fluidity. Similarly, in a conversation between Julia Kristeva and Françoise van Rossum-Guyom in the same text, Kristeva addresses the issue of the female speaking subject who projects not so much an other as a network of associations. My point is that in eighteenth-century female authors' commentaries on water, some of these ideas might be subliminally at work:

> I should say that writing ignores sex or gender and displaces its difference in the discreet workings of language and signification (which are necessarily ideological and historical). Knots of desire are created as a result. This is one way, among others, of reacting to the radical split that constitutes the speaking subject. This eternally premature baby, prematurely separated from the world of the mother and the world of things, remedies the situation by using an invincible weapon: linguistic symbolization. Such a method deals with this fundamental change characterizing the speaking subject not by positing the existence of an other (another person or sex, which would give us psychological humanism), or an *Other* (the absolute signifier, God) but by constructing a network where drives, signifiers and meanings join together and split asunder in a dynamic and enigmatic process. As a result, a strange body comes into being, one that is neither man nor woman, young nor old. It made Freud dream of sublimation, and the Christians of angels, and it continues to put to modern rationality the embarrassing question of an identity that is sexual (among other things), and which is constantly remade and reborn through the impetus provided by a play of signs. The hasty attempt to contain the radical nature of this experience within a sexual identity is perhaps sometimes a means of modernizing or simply marketing an evasion of its most trenchant features (Luce Irigaray, "Sexual Differences," in Toril Moi, *French Feminist Thought* (Oxford: Basil Blackwell, 1987, p. 111).

The relationship between the sentiments of Cowper's protagonist in "The Castaway" and certain emotional lines that Cowper attributes to Alexander Selkirk while shipwrecked on Juan Fernando, suggests another kind of preoccupation with water and death.

30. Michael Craton, *Sinews of Empire. A Short History of British Slavery* (Garden City, NY: Anchor Books, 1974), p. 93.

31. Olaudah Equiano in *Equiano's Travels. His Autobiography. The Interesting Narrative of the Life of Olaudah Equiano or Gustavas Vassa, The African.* Ed. Paul Edwards (London: Heinemann, 1789; Reprint. 1967), p. 10.

32. Edward Said, *Orientalism* (New York: Vintage, 1979), p. 72.

33. See, for example, *Poetry of the Anti-Jacobin: Comprising the Celebrated Political and Satirical Poems of The Rt. Hons. G. Canning, John Hookham Frere, W. Pitt, The Marquis Wellesley, G. Ellis, W. Gifford, the Earl of Carlisle, and Others,* ed. Charles Edmonds, 3rd ed. (New York: G. P. Putnam's Sons, 1890) and *The Anti-Jacobin Review,* 1799, pp. 9–10.

34. Helena Wells, *Letters on Subjects of Importance to the Happiness of Young Females, Addressed by a Governess to Her Pupils, Chiefly while they were Under Her Immediate Tuition: to Which are Added, Some Practical Lessons on the Improprieties of Language, and Errors in Pronunciation, which frequently occur in common Conversation,* 2nd ed. (London: Sabine & Son, n.d.). Note the homiletic quotation from the title page:

> I often tell my Pupils, "Be yourselves; think your own Way." It is a melancholy Thing to employ young People for whole Years, in learning nothing but the Art of Repeating.

Regrettably, too, not only were abolitionists under attack from their opponents but some avid, erstwhile supporters were beginning to adopt Bryan Edwards' racist analysis. See, for instance, Charlotte Smith's texts, *The Wanderings of Warwick* (Dublin: P. Wogan, P. Byrne, J. Moore, W. Jones, W. Porter, H. Colbert, and J. Rice, 1794) and *The Solitary Wanderer* (London: Joseph Johnson, 1793). The controversy itself between Jacobins and anti-Jacobins is well explained in *Burke, Paine, Godwin, and the Revolution Controversy,* ed. Marilyn Butler (Cambridge: Cambridge University Press, 1984), p. 1–18 and passim.

35. Leonore Davidoff and Catherine Hall, *Family Fortunes: Men and Women of the English Middle-Class, 1780–1850* (London: Hutchinson, 1987). Section One and passim.

36. See endnote 29.

37. In *Marxism and the Interpretation of Culture,* ed. Cary Nelson and Lawrence Grossberg (Urbana: University of Illinois Press, 1985), Gayatri Chakravorty Spivak discusses the silence of the subaltern, especially the subaltern women, pp. 271–313. In Anglo-Saxon female abolitionist writings, the silencing of slaves is usually effected through such psychological and intellectual forms

as displacement, projection, and mediation. The net result is very similar because, except in the case of African women who publish or dictate, the lives of these silenced women are always seen as constructions and at several removes.

38. See Rana Kabbani's *Europe's Myths,* for a recent analysis of the mythological, exoticized evil women, pp. 6–7.

39. Mary Poovey, *The Proper Lady and the Woman Writer: Ideology as Style in the Works of Mary Wollstonecraft, Mary Shelley, and Jane Austen* (Chicago: University of Chicago Press, 1984), p. 41.

40. The analysis of multiple voiced texts is indebted to M. M. Bakhtin, especially "Discourse on the Novel," in *The Dialogic Imagination,* ed. Michael Holquist and trans. Caryl Emerson and Michael Holquist (Austin: University of Texas Press, 1981), pp. 259–422. See also Julia Kristeva, "Talking About Polylogue, in *French Feminist Thought,* pp. 110–117.

41. Michael Craton, *Testing the Chains: Resistance to Slavery in The British West Indies* (Ithaca: Cornell University Press, 1982), pp. 335–339 with pp. 52–57 on Quashi.

Notes on Chapter 12

1. The large and continually increasing participation by women was noted in almost every issue of the movement's periodical *The Anti-Slavery Reporter,* founded in 1823 and edited by ex-plantocrat emancipationist, Zachary Macaulay. Almost every issue included statements on newly formed Ladies Anti-Slavery Associations.

2. See, for example, a poem by the Clapham Sect evangelical, Hannah More, "Slavery, A Poem," (London: Thomas Cadell, 1788); and Mary Wollstonecraft's political transcendence of More's demand in *A Vindication of the Rights of Women* (London: Joseph Johnson, 1792).

3. Hannah More, *Cheap Repository Tracts 1795–1797.* A complete list of the *Cheap Repository Tracts* and the relationship between advice to slaves and advice to the working class respectively in the post-French Revolutionary era can be found in G. H. Spinney, *The Cheap Repository Tracts: Hazard Marshall Edition.* In *Transactions in the Bibliographical Society,* 1940; and in M. G. Jones, *Hannah More* (Cambridge: Cambridge University Press, 1952), pp. 125–150. See also Frances (Fanny) Holcroft, "The Negro," *Monthly Magazine* 4 (October 1797):286, for one of the many poems depicting "non-threatening" slaves.

4. Anna Maria Porter, "Inkle and Yarico," in *Ballads and Other Poems* (London: Hurst, Rees, Orme, Brown and Green, 1811).

5. The rise in agitation is very well documented in a number of places: among them James Walvin, "The Propaganda of Anti-Slavery," in *Slavery*

and British Society 1776–1846, ed. James Walvin (London: Macmillan, 1982). Walvin particularly mentions the role that many women played after the formation of Ladies Anti-Slavery Associations, pp. 61–63. Before then, because of their exclusion from Parliament and the fact that the emancipation debate was largely centered on slave census and registration, women played a much less extensive role. See also James Walvin, "The Public Campaign in England Against Slavery, 1787–1834," in *The Abolition of the Atlantic Slave Trade. Origins and Effects in Europe, Africa, and the Americas,* ed. David Eltis and James Walvin (Madison: University of Wisconsin Press, 1981), pp. 63–79. Note, too, that much of the rising agitation sprang from reactions to the population of black people in Britain and demographic literature discussed in the Appendix entitled "Negroes in Britain: 1750–1880," in Douglas A. Lorimer, *Colour, Class, and the Victorians: English Attitudes to the Negro in the Mid-Nineteenth Century* (Bristol: Leicester University Press, 1978), pp. 212–214. Lorimer concludes that the black population of London was approximately 14,000 or 2 percent. See also J. J. Hecht, "Continental and Colonial Servants in Eighteenth-Century England," in *Smith College Studies in History,* 40 (1954): 34. No separate statistics for black females seem presently available. Note also that Folaris Shyllon in *Black People in Britain 1555–1833* (London: Oxford University Press, 1977) discusses the formation in 1818 of the Society for the Suppression of Mendacity which commented in its report on "the wretched condition of many Africans." Shyllon goes on to comment that "blacks were unemployed and forced to seek public assistance . . . because of institutional racism and racial discrimination" (pp. 162–163). This complex situation inevitably attracted women whose social concern was considered innate or "natural."

6. George Canning, Quoted in *Sketches and Recollections of the West Indies by a Resident* (London: Smith, Elder & Co., 1828), p. 263. See also Peter Dixon, *Canning. Politician and Statesman* (London: Weidenfeld and Nicolson, 1976), p. 263.

7. Cecil Northcott, *Slavery's Martyr. John Smith of Demerara and The Emancipation Movement, 1817–24* (London: Epworth Press, 1976), p. 54; David Brion Davis, "The Emergence of Immediatism in British and American Anti-slavery Thought," in *The Mississippi Valley Historical Review: A Journal of American History,* 49, No. 2 (Sept. 1962), pp. 209–230. In an article entitled "Anti-Slavery," in *Pressure from Without in Early Victorian England,* ed. Patricia Hollis (London: Edward Arnold, 1974), p. 27–51, Howard Temperley details the evolving structure of abolitionist and emancipationist societies and discusses the shift from a gradualist to an immediatist position. See also Joseph Lowell Ragatz, *The Fall of the Planter Class in the British Caribbean, 1763–1833. A Study in Social and Economic History;* William Law Mathieson, *British Slavery and Its Abolition 1823–1838,* and Charles Harris Wesley, "The Neglected Period of Emancipation in Great Britain, 1807–1823," *Journal of Negro History,* 17 (1932), pp. 156–179. The religious implications of recommendations about amelioration sent to colonial legislatures by the colonial secretary, Earl Bathurst, in 1827 are discussed by Robert Worthington Smith in

"The Attempt of British Humanitarianism to Modify Chattel Slavery," in *British Humanitarianism: Essays Honoring Frank J. Klingberg*, ed. Samuel Clyde McCulloch (Philadelphia: The Church Historical Society, 1950), pp. 174–177.

8. This view of women as benevolent was all pervasive. The encapsulation of women's prescribed roles is summarized in Sarah Stickney Ellis, *The Wives of England, Their Relative Duties, Domestic Influence, and Social Obligations* (New York: Edward Walker, 1850). A male version is T. H. Reardon, "Woman's Mission," *Westminster Review*, 52 (1849–1850): 352–367. An earlier account that rails against the stereotype is William Thompson [and Anna Wheeler] *Appeal to One Half the Human Race, Woman, Against the Pretensions of the Other Half, Men, To Retain Them in Political, and Thence in Civil and Domestic, Slavery. In Reply to a Paragraph of Mr. Mill's Celebrated "Article on Government"* (London: Hurst, Rees, Orme, Brown, and Green; Wheatley and Adland, 1825; Reprint. New York: Burt Franklin, 1970). Almost all the prescriptive literature by male writers assumed sex-role distinctions that attributed modesty to women and an accompanying matrix of allied values. See, for example, Dr. James Fordyce, *Sermons to Young Women* (London: Printed L. A. Miller and T. Cadell, 1765). Women's charitable activities enhanced their depiction as the gentler sex, ably demonstrated in F. K. Prochaska, *Women and Philanthropy in Nineteenth-Century England* (Oxford: Clarendon Press, 1980). Moreover, as Nancy Cott explains, women were being continually praised from the pulpit for their moral influence and their ability to set the nation on a virtuous course. In Christian theology, women had become the guardians of a moral family life, the reformers of unregenerate husbands. Their discursive stance on abolition epitomized a partial concurrence with this role as well as a decision to manipulate that very role to the benefit of the disadvantaged in whom, unconsciously or not, they included themselves. Nancy F. Cott, *The Bonds of Womanhood: 'Woman's Sphere' in New England, 1780–1855* (New Haven: Yale University Press, 1977), pp. 128–138. See also Barbara Welter, "The Feminization of American Religion," in *Clio's Consciousness Raised: New Perspectives on the History of Women*, ed. Lois Banner and Mary S. Hartman (New York: Harper Colophon Books, 1974), pp. 137–157. Ruth H. Bloch in "Untangling the Roots of Modern Sex Roles: A Survey of Four Centuries of Change," in *Signs*, 5, No. 2 (1978): 236–252, usefully traces the development of these roles. Patricia Meyer Spacks in "Ev'ry Woman is at Heart a Rake" clearly exemplifies how "a woman has virtually no freedom of emotional expression," *Eighteenth-Century Studies*, 3, No. 2 (1980): 27–46.

9. Quoted in Peter Fryer, *Staying Power. The History of Black People in Britain* (London: Pluto Press, 1984), p. 219. See also Iain McCalman, *Robert Wedderburn: A Black Ultra-Radical in Early Nineteenth-Century London*, University of Melbourne, Paper presented to the Conference on the History of Black People in London, 27–29th November, 1984, London University, Institute of Education. I thank Peter Fryer for alerting me to this paper and supplying me with a copy.

10. Fryer, *Staying Power*, p. 224.

11. Fryer, *Staying Power,* p. 225.

12. Northcott, *Slavery's Martyr,* p. 117.

13. Leonore Davidoff and Catherine Hall, *Family Fortunes. Men and women of the English middle-class, 1780–1850* (London: Hutchinson, 1987), pp. 450–455.

14. Davidoff and Hall, *Family Fortunes,* p. 278.

15. See the obituary of Rachel Lloyd in *Twenty-Ninth Report of the Ladies' Negro's Friend Society in Birmingham, etc.* (ref. 98614), kindly supplied by N. Kingsley, Principal Archivist of the City of Birmingham, Public Libraries Department.

16. *Feminist Criticism and Social Change. Sex, Class and Race in Literature and Culture,* ed. Judith Newton and Deborah Rosenfelt (New York and London: Methuen, 1985), p. xi-xxxix. Newton and Rosenfelt carefully outline the context in which such a reversal could take place. William Wilberforce's notorious opposition to women's participation in the emancipation movement was so widely held that even anti-slavery pamphlets encouraged "sensible" husbands to remember scriptural injunctions about doing unto others: See "'What Does Your Sugar Cost?' A Cottage Conversation On the Subject of British Negro Society" (Printed for Birmingham, West-Bromwich, &c. Female Society for the Relief of British Negro Slaves by Richard Peart, Birmingham, 1828).

17. T. H. Reardon, "Woman's Mission," in *Free and Ennobled: Source Readings in the Development of Victorian Feminism,* ed. and with introductions and commentaries by Carol Bauer and Lawrence Ritt (Oxford: Pergamon Press, 1979), pp. 22–26.

18. Quoted in Malcolm I. Thomis and Jennifer Grimmett, *Women in Protest 1800–1850* (New York: St. Martin's Press, 1982), p. 92.

19. *Anti-Slavery Monthly Reporter,* No. 14 (14 July 1826): 197.

20. Elizabeth Heyrick, *Immediate not Gradual Abolition; or, an Inquiry into the shortest, safest, and most effectual means of getting rid of West Indian Slavery* (London, 1832; New York: Reprint. James V. Seaman, 1825). All future quotations will be from this edition. See also Betty Fladeland, *Men and Brothers: Anglo-American Anti-Slavery Cooperation* (Urbana: University of Illinois Press, 1972), p. 165 and passim. See also Kenneth Corfield, "Elizabeth Heyrick: Radical Quaker," *Religion in the Lives of English Women 1750–1830,* ed. Gail Malmgreen (London: Croom Helm, 1986), pp. 41–67.

21. "Ladies" Anti-Slavery Associations pamphlet, 1830, p. 9.

22. Corfield, "Elizabeth Heyrick," p. 41.

23. Sir George Stephen in *Anti-Slavery Recollections,* Reprint. Cass Library of African Studies, Slavery Series, No. 12, ed. C. Duncan Rice, American Studies Program, Yale University, n.d., pp. 196–197. Autobiographies and memoirs of other well-known abolitionists who respectfully (and with some amazement) commented that women's role was central in the potential success of the

campaign were: Charles Buxton, *Memoirs of Sir Thomas Fowell Buxton* (London: J. M. Dent, New York: E. P. Dutton, 1848), p. 152ff. David E. Swift, *Joseph John Gurney: Banker, Reformer, and Quaker* (Middletown, CT: Wesleyan University Press, 1962), pp. 187–189. The major historians who controversially prioritize the role of British humanitarians in ending the slave trade also mention the important role of women in the earlier period: Reginald Coupland, *The British Anti-Slavery Movement* (London: Frank Cass & Co., Ltd., 1933), p. 137; Frank J. Klingberg, *The Anti-Slavery Movement in England: A Study in English Humanitarianism* (New Haven: Yale University Press, 1926). For comment on the activities and success of women, see Seymour Drescher, "Public Opinion and the Destruction of British Colonial Slavery," in *Slavery and British Society*, p. 33. See also footnote 5.

24. Louis Althusser, "Ideology and Ideological State Apparatuses (Notes towards an Investigation)" in *Essays on Ideology* (London: Verso, 1984, first published by La Pensée, 1970).

25. An account of women in the "free produce" movement stressing Quaker involvement particularly in the United States can be found in Ruth Ketring Nuermberger, *The Free Produce Movement: A Quaker Protest Against Slavery* (Durham, NC: Duke University Press, 1942), pp. 5–11. It should also be noted that resolutions in Ladies Anti-Slavery Association reports frequently recorded "boycott" activities and these were frequently published in *The Anti-Slavery Reporter*. Resolution five of the Sheffield Female Anti-Slavery Society, for example, formed July 12th, 1825, read as follows: "That the members of this society will promote its great object so far as is expedient, whether it be by circulating information: by abstaining for a time from the use of West Indian produce, particularly Sugar and Coffee, the culture of which forms so great a part of the labour of slaves, and substituting East India Sugar or Sugar and coffee from any country where labourers are paid for their work and are free, or by any other means in their power." N. B. Lewis, *The Abolitionist Movement in Sheffield, 1823–1833. With Letters from Southey, Wordsworth, and Others* (Manchester, 1934), p. 381.

26. While acknowledging such noble veterans (as, say, Thomas Clarkson), women also recognized the importance of their own influence in the formation of district treasurers. See Elizabeth Heyrick, *Apology for Ladies' Anti-Slavery Associations* (London: J. Hatchard and Son, 1828), p. 4.

27. This discussion on dialogue and silenced voices is indebted to M. M. Bakhtin, "Discourse on the Novel," in *The Dialogic Imagination*, trans. Michael Holquist and Caryl Emerson, ed. Michael Holquist (Austin: University of Texas Press, 1981), p. 259.

28. Quoted in Kenneth Corfield, "Elizabeth Heyrick," in Malmgreen, *Religion in the Lives*, p. 44. Some controversy exists about the earliest established women's anti-slavery association. See Corfield, "Elizabeth Heyrick," p. 45ff and Claire Midgeley, *Women Against the Slave Trade 1787–1823*, pp. 1–83, Ph.D. dissertation, University of Canterbury at Kent, 1989.

29. See Prochaska, *Women and Philanthropy,* especially pp. 231–245.

30. Alex Tyrrell, *'Woman's Mission' and Pressure Group Politics in Britain (1825–60),* Pamphlet Reprinted from the "Bulletin of the John Rylands University Library of Manchester," Vol. 63, No. 1 (Autumn, 1980) (Manchester: John Rylands University Library), p. 211.

31. Walvin, *Slavery and British Society,* p. 62.

32. *The Anti-Slavery Reporter* (3 August 1825): 24.

33. See endnote 22.

34. *Anti-Slavery Reporter* (3 July 1826): 212.

35. Edith F. Hurwitz, *Politics and the Public Conscience: Slave Emancipation and the Abolitionist Movement in Britain* (London: George Allen & Unwin, New York: Barnes and Noble, 1973), p. 91. In light of Reardon's remarks, it is worth noting that the influence of these associations was also felt in Africa. Hannah Kilham was a Quaker missionary who travelled three times to Africa. She remarks in her "Report on A Recent Visit to the Colony of Sierra Leone" (London: Wm. Phillips, 1828), p. 10, that "A few friends at Peckham, members of the Female Antislavery Association, with some others united with them, had commissioned me to see one Village School opened . . . and had sent a donation of ten guineas for this purpose, intending to continue it annually." For further information about the link between missionaries and anti-slavery agitation (frequently conjoined by evangelical women), see Michael Craton, *Sinews of Empire: A Short History of British Slavery* (New York: Anchor Books, 1974), pp. 269–270; and C. Duncan Rice, "The Missionary Context of the British Anti-Slavery Movement" in *Slavery and British Society,* pp. 150–163. Raymond Cowherd outlines the relationship between religion and abolition in chapter four, "The Abolition of Colonial Slavery," in *The Politics of English Dissent: The Religious Aspects of Liberal and Humanitarian Reform Movements from 1815–1849* (New York: New York University Press, 1956), pp. 46–63.

36. West India-Sub-Committee minutes, 1828–1830, cited in G. R. Mellor, *British Imperial Trusteeship, 1783–1850* (London: Faber, 1951), p. 97, and in Craton, *Sinews of Empire,* p. 275.

37. Box 16, #27, Rylands Library, Manchester, Special Collections.

38. Statement by J. H. Flooks in *West Indian Sub-Committee Minutes, 1828–30,* cited by Mellor, p. 97, and in Michael Craton, *Sinews of Empire,* p. 275.

39. Hurwitz, *Politics,* p. 90.

40. In Buxton, *Memoirs,* there is a description of the scene, taken from the *Mirror of Parliament,* p. 153. See also Stephen, *Antislavery Recollections,* p. 196, and Seymour Drescher, in *Slavery,* p. 33.

41. Hurwitz, *Politics,* p. 89.

42. *Report of the Sheffield Female Anti-Slavery Society.* Established Midsummer, 1825 (Sheffield: J. Blackwell, 1827).

43. William Law Mathieson, *British Slavery and Its Abolition* (New York: Octagon Books, 1967), pp. 123–127.

44. June Rose, *Elizabeth Fry* (New York: St. Martin, 1980), pp. 79 and 84.

45. Hurwitz, *Politics,* p. 91.

46. Charlotte Elizabeth Tonna's poem is reproduced in *The Second Report of the Ladies' Association of Calne, Melksham, Devizes, and Their Respective Neighbourhoods, in Aid of the Cause of Negro Emancipation* (Calne: Printed by W. Baily, 1827), p. 8. It reads as follows:

> Bear'st thou a man's, a christian's
> name?
> If not for pity, yet for shame,
>   O fling the scourge aside!
> Her tender form may writhe and bleed,
> But deeper cuts thy barbarous deed
>   The female's modest pride.
> Sin first by woman came;—for this
> The Lord hath marr'd her earthly bliss,
>   With many a bitter throe;
> But mercy tempers wrath, and scorn
> Pursues the wretch who adds a thorn
>   To heaven-inflicted woe.
> Thine infancy was lull'd to rest
> On woman's nurt'ring bosom prest,
>   Enfolded by her arm:
> Her hand upheld thy tott'ring pace;—
> And oh! how deep the foul disgrace,
>   If thine can work her harm!
> Hush not thy nature's conscious plea,
> Weak, helpless, succourless, to thee
>   Her looks for mercy pray;
> He who records each lash, will roll
> Torrents of vengeance on thy soul:—
>   O fling that scourge away!

For a discussion of the reterritorialization of the body and its link to conservative mores and the civilizing process, see also Peter Stallybrass and Allon White, *The Politics and Poetics of Transgression* (London: Methuen, 1986).

47. Amelia Opie, "The Negro Boy's Tale: A Poem Addressed to Children," (London: Harvey & Darton, 1824). Another popular anti-slavery poem by Opie was "The Black Man's Lament," (London, 1826). This anti-slavery poem and many others directed at a young audience can be found in the Osborne Collection of Children's Literature in the Toronto Public Library. For Laetitia Landon [L.E.L.] see, for instance, *The Zenana and Minor Poems by L.E.L.* With a Memoir by Emma Roberts (London: Fisher, Son and Co.; Paris: Quai de l'Ecole, 1961). For Felicia Hemans, see *The Poetical Works of Mrs. Hemans.*

With Prefatory Memoirs, Notes, etc. (London: Frederick Warne, n.d). For accounts of the anti-slavery activities of Quaker women, see Henrietta Emma (Darwin) Litchfield, *Emma Darwin: A Century of Family Letters,* in 2 vols. (New York: D. Appleton, 1915), pp. 1, 181. Among several anonymous tracts, seemingly written by a female, see *The Negro Slave: A Tale Addressed to the Women of Great Britain* (London: Harvey and Darton, 1830), B.L. Tract 2071. Another important British female agitator with unique ideas was Frances (Fanny) Wright, whose account has been omitted from this volume since she agitated against slavery in the United States while trying to form a community for ex-slaves, but with highly questionable consequences. Illuminating accounts about the colony in Nashoba, Tennessee, can be found in A. J. G. Perkins and Theresa Wolfson, *Frances Wright: Free Enquirer. The Study of a Temperament* (New York: Harper and Row, 1939); and Celia Morris Eckhardt, *Fanny Wright. Rebel in America* (Cambridge, MA: Harvard University Press, 1984). For a contemporary indictment of Nashoba by an eye-witness, see Frances M. Trollope, *Domestic Manners of the Americans* (New York: Howard Wilford Bell, 1904), pp. 15, 27–30.

48. *The Anti-Slavery Album: Selections in Verse* (London: Howlett & Brimmer, 1828). "The Sorrows of Yamba or the Negro Woman's Lamentation" was published in so many editions that it became a prototype for pro- and anti-slavery texts. Printed pamphlets read in provincial homes, for example, referred to "Yamba" as if the poem and the character were nationally recognized cultural motifs.

49. *The Bow in the Cloud, or the Negro's Memorial,* ed. Mrs. [i.e. Mary Anne] Rawson (London: Jackson and Walford, 1834).

50. See Jean Fagan Yellin, *Women & Sisters. The Antislavery Feminists in American Culture* (New Haven and London: Yale University Press, 1989), especially pp. 25, 94, and passim.

51. David E. Swift, *Joseph John Gurney,* p. 209.

52. This information about the replies of Mary Anne Sherwood and Barbara Hofland to Mary Anne Rawson can be found in pre-publication handwritten notes to the manuscript of *The Bow in the Cloud,* available at the John Rylands Memorial Library, Manchester.

53. In addition to manuscript material, information about Rawson's process can be found in the printed introduction to *The Bow in the Cloud,* and, even more specifically, in N. B. Lewis, *The Abolitionist Movement,* pp. 377–392.

54. Charlotte Elizabeth Tonna, *The System, Or A Tale of the West Indies* (London: Westley & Davis, 1879).

55. For biographical data that helps explain Tonna's ideological shift, see Ellen Moers, *Literary Women* (New York: Doubleday, 1973), p. 25; and Elizabeth Kowaleski, "The *Personal Recollections* of Charlotte Elizabeth Tonna," in *Tulsa Studies in Women's Literature,* 1, No. 2 (Fall, 1982): 142. Joseph Kestner in *Protest and Reform: The British Social Narrative by Women 1827–1867*

(Madison: University of Wisconsin Press, 1985) discusses *The System,* pp. 39–40, and Tonna more generally throughout. See also Abel Stevens, "Charlotte Elizabeth (Tonna)," *Dictionary of National Biography* and Charlotte Elizabeth (Tonna), *Personal Reflections,* from the London edition (New York: John Taylor, 1843).

Notes on Chapter 13

1. R. K. Webb, *Harriet Martineau. A Radical Victorian* (London: Heinemann, 1960), pp. 23, 157.

2. Vera Wheatley, *The Life and Work of Harriet Martineau* (Fair Lawn, NJ: Essential Books, Inc., 1957), pp. 63, 66.

3. *Harriet Martineau on Women,* ed. Gayle Graham Yates (New Brunswick, NJ: Rutgers University Press, 1985), p. 1.

4. Harriet Martineau, *Demerara: A Tale,* vol. 2 of *Illustrations of Political Economy,* 25 vols. 2nd ed. (London: Charles Fox, 1832). See Catherine Gallagher, *The Industrial Reformation of English Fiction. Social Discourse and Narrative Form 1832–1867* (Chicago: University of Chicago Press, 1985). Offering a detailed and persuasive analysis of the debate between emancipationists and critics of industrial society, Gallagher probes the implications of the "worker-slave" metaphor in a wide variety of contexts, pp. 51–61 and passim.

5. *Harriet Martineau's Autobiography,* ed. Maria Weston Chapman (Boston: Houghton, Osgood, & Co., 1879), p. 335.

6. Martineau, *Autobiography,* vol. 1, pp. 149–150.

7. Martineau, *Autobiography,* vol. 1, p. 359.

8. Martineau, *Autobiography,* vol. 1, p. 149.

9. Some twentieth-century commentary on Edwards is to be found in James Walvin, *The Black Presence: A Documentary History of the Negro in England, 1555–1860* (New York: Schocken Books, 1972), p. 116. Martineau's assumptions before she visited the United States in the late 1830s were received opinion for the time.

10. See preface to *Demerara,* pp. xi and xii. The book in question is Bryan Edwards, *The History, Civil and Commercial of the British Colonies in the West Indies,* 2 vols. (London, 1793). Winthrop D. Jordan closely compares the historical development of attitudes in the United States and the United Kingdom in *White Over Black: American Attitudes Toward the Negro, 1550–1812* (Chapel Hill: University of North Caroline Press, 1968). Martineau's later comments on slavery in *The Martyr Age in America* that discusses, among other things, the colonization society, abolition itself, her pro-Garrison views, and the activities of Maria Weston Chapman and the Grimke sisters. She also comments on slavery in *Retrospect of Western Travel,* especially vol. 1, "First

Sight of Slavery," pp. 228–234; and vol. 2 "Restless Slaves," pp. 97–119. Gayle Graham Yates, editor of *Harriet Martineau on Women,* summarizes Martineau's views on the reception she received in the United States, pp. 41–42 and passim.

11. For a thoroughgoing conceptualization and analysis of "Dark Continent" ideology, see Patrick Brantlinger, *Rule of Darkness: British Literature and Imperialism, 1830–1914* (Ithaca: Cornell University Press, 1988), especially pp. 73–107 and 173–197; see also Brantlinger, "Victorians and Africans: The Genealogy of the Myth of the Dark Continent," in *"Race," Writing, and Difference,* ed. Henry Louis Gates, Jr. (Chicago: University of Chicago Press, 1985), pp. 185–222.

12. Yates, *Harriet Martineau on Women,* pp. 134–139.

13. William Thompson [and Anna Wheeler] *Appeal of One Half the Human Race, Women, Against the Pretensions of the Other Half, Men, to Retain them in Political, and thence in Civil and Domestic Slavery.*

14. This text was originally published in 1831 by F. Westley and A. H. David in London and Waugh and Innes in Edinburgh. It included "A Supplement to the Editor" in which Thomas Pringle, secretary of the Anti-Slavery Society, explains the circumstances of his publishing Mary Prince's narrative. The text went into a third edition that year. No copies of the second and fourth edition have so far been uncovered. A postscript to the second edition is included in the prefatory apparatus to the third edition which faithfully follows the first edition except for an appendix. Two reprintings follow the first edition. One is edited and with an introduction by Moira Ferguson and a preface by Ziggi Alexander (London and New York: Pandora), 1987. All citations are from this edition. The second, edited and with an introduction by Henry Louis Gates, Jr., appears in the volume *The Classic Slave Narratives,* along with *The Life of Olaudah Equiano, Narrative of the Life of Frederick Douglas,* and *Incidents in the Life of a Slave Girl* (New York: New American Library, 1987).

Part of the argument in this chapter about European constructions of slaves and slavery is indebted to Edward Said's thesis in *Orientalism* (New York: Vintage, 1979), especially his idea that there is little correspondence

> between the language used to depict the Orient and the Orient itself, . . . because [the aim of the language is] . . . to characterize the Orient as alien and to incorporate it schematically on a theatrical stage whose audience, manager, and actors are *for* Europe, and only for Europe. (pp. 71–72).

15. Karl Marx, *The Eighteenth Brumaire of Louis Bonaparte* (New York: International Publishers, 1963), p. 124.

16. For the discussion of colonial discourse, I am greatly indebted to the current critical debate by, for example, Homi K. Bhabha, Patrick Brantlinger, Hazel Carby, Henry Louis Gates, Jr., Abdul R. JanMohamed, Christopher Miller, Chadra Talpade Mohanty, Benita Parry, Mary Louise Pratt, Edward W. Said, Gayatri Chakravorty Spivak, and Jean Fagan Yellin.

17. Mary Prince, *The History of Mary Prince. A West Indian Slave. Related by Herself*, ed. Moira Ferguson (London: Pandora Press, 1987), p. 45. (Original editor Thomas Pringle, Edinburgh, 1831).

18. Mary Prince, *A History*, p. 45.

19. I am renegotiating Gerald Prince's concept of the "narratee" here. As recent studies in reader recognition have shown, the text is not only addressed to the person reading the book but to an auditor constructed within the narrative itself, in this case members of slave communities, or, in Gerald Prince's language, slave narratees. See Gerald Prince, "Introduction to the Study of Narratee," *Reader-Response Criticism: From Formalism to Post-Structuralism*, ed. Jane S. Tompkins (Baltimore: The Johns Hopkins University Press, 1980), pp. 7–25.

20. Mary Prince, *A History*, pp. 82–83.

21. Homi K. Bhabha, "Signs Taken for Wonders: Questions of Ambivalence and Authority Under a Tree Outside Delhi, May 1817," *"Race," Writing and Difference*, ed. Henry Louis Gates, Jr. (Chicago: University of Chicago Press, 1985), pp. 172–173.

22. Jacques Lacan analyses the gaze and the "technique of camouflage" and mimicry in *The Four Fundamental Concepts of Psycho-Analysis*, ed. Jacques-Alain Miller, trans. Alan Sheridan (New York: W. W. Norton & Company, Inc., 1981), pp. 98–99; Margaret Homans, *Bearing the Word: Language and Female Experience in Nineteenth-Century Women's Writing* (Chicago: University of Chicago Press, 1986), p. 5.

23. Anna Freud, *The Ego and the Mechanisms of Defense* (New York: International Universities Press, 1966), Part 2: 113–115. Another terse example of Mary Prince's double-voiced discourse is her statement that her "dear mistress [took] great pains to make me understand [the word of God]" (Mary Prince, *A History*, p. 82). Mary Prince's motivation, as Sigmund Freud argues in *Psychopathology of Everyday Life* (1900, Reprint. New York: Avon, 1965), is consciously or unconsciously, always purposive. Consciously she may not intend to suggest coercion or the appropriateness or inappropriateness of catechism-by-rote to someone seeking freedom, but her choice of words "gives her away."

24. Mary Prince, *A History*, p. 47. For a discussion of the politics of childhood recollections, see Frances Smith Foster, *Witnessing Slavery: The Development of AnteBellum Slave Narratives* (Westport, TN: Greenwood Press, 1979), pp. 95–96 and passim. Foster argues that many slave narratives depict childhood as "a fairly happy time punctuated by incidents which temporarily disturbed the individual and foreshadowed for the reader the disasters to come."

25. Pringle's priorities show up in the supplement to Mary Prince's narrative where he declined to print in full the names of Captain I—— and his wife (Mary Prince's third owner, and D——): they were dead when the narrative was published, Pringle argued, and would have had "to answer at a far more

376 NOTES TO CHAPTER 13

awful tribunal." "Besides," Pringle added, "it might deeply lacerate the feelings of their surviving and perhaps innocent relatives" (Mary Prince, *A History,* p. 46). In the Bermuda Archives in Hamilton, Bermuda, among file cards that refer to various church, maritime, and other records, there is evidence to suggest that Captain I—— may have been Joseph Ingham who married Mary Spencer on September 26, 1789. They lived in Spanish Point and had a son named Benjamin who was baptized on October 16, 1790. (In the text, Mary Prince states that they lived at Spanish Point and had a son Benjy, who was roughly her own age.) The identity of D—— is still a mystery. Of the possible references to Mary Prince in the Slave Registry of 1820–21 the one that appears on page 76 seems the most likely (Mary Prince was often called Molly): "Owner: Joseph Dill. Slave: Molly, female black houseservant age 28." No slaves with names similar to those in the *History* are found in the 1820–21 Slave Registry. Worth noting, too, is Thomas Pringle's background in light of his shielding of slave abusers. Thomas Pringle spent many years in South Africa after personal financial collapse in Scotland, where he espoused traditional white supremacist attitudes toward Africans, evident in his published poetry.

26. No record so far has been found of the burial of the Frenchwoman, Hetty, as the slave of Captain I——. That lack could mean she did not have an official burial due to her condition and I——'s fear of publicity. It also might indicate the Woods's insecurity about power. Tzvetan Todorov's distinction between a massacre and a sacrifice society has a suggestive bearing on ambivalence in the Woods's behavior. Hetty's unrecorded death fits roughly within Todorov's characterization of a massacre society. "The more remote and alien the victims, the better: they are exterminated without remorse, more or less identified with animals." Tzvetan Todorov, in *The Conquest of America: The Question of the Other,* trans. Richard Howard (New York: Harper and Row, 1982), p. 144. The fact that Mary Prince's presence or absence, unlike the existence of Hetty, deeply affects the Woods seems to hinge on their sense of power. To borrow loosely from Todorov: the severe floggings of Mary Prince that seem to stop short of death are more allied with his concept of sacrifice or ritual murder: "it is performed in the name of the official ideology and will be perpetrated in public places in sight of all and to everyone's knowledge. The victim's identity is determined by strict rules" (Todorov, *The Conquest,* p. 144). The more appreciated the victim is, and many witnesses testified to the confidence the Woods's placed in Mary Prince, the greater the power accruing to the perpetrator and the stronger the social fabric appears to be. Note also that the impunity with which Mary Prince's owners abused their slaves is hardly surprising on an island that introduced the treadmill in the late 1820s as a "normal corrective expedient" and a substitute for whipping.

27. Mary Prince, *A History,* p. 60.

28. Both Hilary Beckles, Barbara Bush, and Lucille Mathurin discuss the issue of sexual abuse and the courageous resistance of female slaves. Mathurin

offers compelling evidence to prove how abuse affects childbearing. See Hilary Beckles, *Black Rebellion in Barbados: The Struggle Against Slavery 1627–1833* (St. Michael, Barbados, W.I.: Antilles Publications, 1984); Barbara Bush, *Slave Women in Caribbean Society 1650–1838* (Kingston: Heinemann, Bloomington: Indiana University Press, 1990); Lucille Mathurin, *The Rebel Woman in the British West Indies During Slavery* (Jamaica, W.I.: Institute of Jamaica Publications, 1975), pp. 250ff. Sexual abuse and "systems of concubinage" are discussed at length in Elsa V. Goveia (New Haven: Yale University Press, 1965), and in Richard B. Sheridan, *Doctors and Slaves. The medical and demographic history of slavery in the British West Indies, 1680–1834* (Cambridge: Cambridge University Press, 1985). Sheridan quotes tellingly from William Taylor's testimony before the Select Committee on the Extinction of Slavery in 1832. Frances Smith Foster also discusses rape and abuse in "Adding Color and Contour to Early American Self-Portraitures: Autobiographical Writings of Afro-American Woman," in Pryse and Spillers, eds., *Conjuring: Black Woman, Fiction, and Literary Tradition* (Bloomington: Indiana University Press, 1985), p. 31, and in *Witnessing Slavery*, pp. 108–109. Whether evangelical men and women knew of the constant rebellions, particularly by female slaves, is an open question. Would they have known, for example, that the Barbados Council declared "black ladies . . . have rather a tendency to the Amazonian cast of character" (Mathurin, *The Rebel Woman*), p. 15, or that 1,782 women compared with 941 men were punished between 1824 and 1826; or that "the black female spitfire was a plague on the lives of drivers, overseers, and managers" (Mathurin, *The Rebel Woman*), p. 13? Could they have been aware of a ditty (likely of questionable morality in evangelical eyes) sung by black women in the Caribbean that suggested why they felt empowered to revolt?

> And while he palaver and preach him book
> At the negro girl he'll winkie him yeye
> "Hi! de Buckra, hi!."
> (Beckles, *Black Rebellion*, p. 16)

We do know, however, that the legal cases of such abused and exploited female slaves as Kitty Hilton, Grace, and Kate had become notorious *causes célèbres* through the propaganda of the *Anti-Slavery Reporter.* Female petitioners such as the slave Polly (mentioned in Quaker anti-slavery correspondence) also added to the composite profile of rebelling women.

29. Mary Prince, *A History*, p. 14.

30. Mary Prince, *A History*, p. 16.

31. As far as possible, Pringle wants Mary Prince to conform to an evangelical Christian model of womanhood, granting that acceptance of conversion necessitates admission as well as absolution of former sinfulness. Plantocrats, by contrast, want to sign her as a prostitute. Such pro-slaveryites as James Macqueen, a well-known editor of the *Glasgow Herald,* and the Reverend James Curtin, an Antiguan missionary and afterwards a parochial clergyman who baptized Mary Prince and then gave pro-slavery parliamentary testimony,

are two cases in point. In "The Colonial Empire of Great Britain," in *Blackwoods Magazine*, November, 1831, Macqueen vitriolically attacks Mary Prince's narrative in minute detail and offers extensive refutation by plantocrats and their supporters (pp. 744–764). *The Anti-Slavery Reporter* for February 1833 published a long report of the Reverend Curtin's testimony before a Committee of the House of Lords on the condition and treatment of slaves. "Mr. Curtin could not recollect any instances (with one or two exceptions) of cruel treatment of slaves in Antigua, during his thirty years' experience" (p. 516).

32. Mary Prince, *A History*, p. 101.

33. Sheridan, *Doctors and Slaves*, p. 243.

34. I am borrowing and renegotiating the idea of the idealized self from Erving Goffman. Goffman argues that a "performance" conforms to "officially accredited values of the society" because of the "socialization process. . . . Performers . . . offer their observers an impression that is idealized in several different ways." See Erving Goffman, *The Presentation of the Self in Everyday Life* (New York: Doubleday, 1959), p. 35. Thus I am suggesting that Mary Prince consciously offers the history of an "idealized" victim because she realizes that Thomas Pringle desires exactly such a prescribed individual. Thus she codes and fashions the abridged narrative of her life partly to conform to his construction of a slave.

35. Mary Prince, *A History*, p. 48.

36. Abdul JanMohamed, "The Economy of Manichean Allegory: The Function of Racial Difference in Colonialist Literature," *"Race," Writing, and Difference*, ed. Henry Louis Gates, Jr. (Chicago: University of Chicago Press, 1985), p. 83; and Mary Louise Pratt, "Scratches on the Face of the Country: or, What Mr. Barrow Saw in the Land of the Bushmen," Gates, *"Race," Writing and Difference*, p. 139.

37. Henry Louis Gates, Jr., *Figures in Black: Words, Signs, and the "Racial" Self* (New York: Oxford University Press, 1987), especially chapters 3, 4, and 5, tellingly foregrounds the unique importance of literacy. The sequence of Mary Prince's oral narrative parallels that of slaves' conversion narratives; possibly her evangelical editor and transcriber influenced that sequence: Mary Prince is happy, then she endures suffering, gets to Antigua, meets Moravians, marries, morally improves, is done in by unchristian owners, deserves more moral treatment, and justifiably (in God's eyes) walks away. More succinctly stated, "immorality" cannot be an issue for conversion, Q.E.D.; only after Mary Prince marries, does she convert.

38. Mary Prince, *A History*, pp. 72–74. I am not discounting other influences on Mary Prince's decision to "branch out": namely, gossip about manumission, "talk" around the Woods's house, information she heard from missionaries and other slaves about the 1807 bill, about slaves' legal status, and subsequent historical developments.

39. Mary Prince, *A History,* pp. 16–18.

40. Mary Prince, *A History,* p. 105.

41. Mary Prince, *A History,* pp. 75–76.

42. Mary Prince, *A History,* p. 76.

43. Mary Prince, *A History,* p. 77.

44. Mary Prince, *A History,* p. 45.

45. Joan Grant, "Call Loud: The History of Mary Prince," in *Trouble and Strife* 24 (Autumn 1988): 10.

46. Mary Prince, *A History,* p. 78.

47. The transcriber of Mary Prince's manuscript was Susanna Strickland (later Moodie), who wrote a volume of poems dedicated to the Moravian editor and abolitionist, James Montgomery, and later a travel narrative about her life in Canada. She was a recently converted Methodist. To date I can only speculate as to why Susannah Strickland Moodie (from the celebrated Strickland family and much biographized) seems never to have mentioned the transcription. She may simply have wanted to keep her name out of the controversy. On the other hand, it could indicate the extent to which the narrative was indeed (Pringle's disclaimers to the contrary) Mary Prince's own.

48. Mary Prince, *A History,* p. 84.

49. The discussion of multiple dialogues and voices in the text is indebted to M. M. Bakhtin's essay "Discourse in the Novel," *The Dialogic Imagination: Four Essays,* trans. Caryl Emerson and Michael Holquist (Austin: University of Texas Press, 1981), pp. 259–422.

50. Mary Prince, *A History,* p. 54.

51. Caroline Bynum, *Holy Feast and Holy Fast: The Religious Significance of Food to Medieval Women* (Berkeley: University of California Press, 1987) offers a gripping discussion of this issue. I thank Thomas Bestul for this reference.

52. The case of missionary Henry Whiteley is one example. He returned to England from Jamaica and wrote an account of the atrocities he witnessed. Two hundred thousand copies were distributed within two weeks. See C. Duncan Rice, "The Missionary Context of the British Anti-Slavery Movement," *Slavery and British Society 1776–1846,* ed. James. Walvin (London: Macmillan, 1982), p. 160.

53. Although it seems certain that religious constraints on editors and transcribers caused the censorship of many references to sexuality, it is also possible, as the cases of incest survivors suggest, that systematic brutality and male violence were not always wholly recalled or recallable. Yet, since brutality against slaves was constant, the chances of repression were not at all likely. See Sigmund Freud in *The Interpretation of Dreams,* trans. and ed.

James Strachey (New York: Avon, 1965), pp. 340–344, 626–648, on such defense mechanisms as repression, displacement, and projection.

54. Anne Boylan, "Women in Groups: An Analysis of Women's Benevolent Organizations in New York and Boston, 1797–1840," *Journal of American History* 71, no. 3 (December 1974), pp. 497–523.

55. Mary Prince, *A History,* pp. 119–120.

56. Luce Irigaray, "This Sex Which Is Not One," *New French Feminisms,* ed. Elaine Marks and Isabelle de Courtivron (New York: Schocken Books, 1981), p. 101.

57. I owe a reinterpretation of this point to a lively discussion with members of the London History Workshop, 18th July, 1988.

58. In *Slaves and Missionaries: The Disintegration of Jamaican Slave Society, 1787–1834* (Urbana: University of Illinois Press, 1982), Mary Turner discusses the importance of slaves dressing up and Anglo-Saxon recognition of the implications of that fact.

59. Mary Prince, *A History,* p. 107.

60. Mary Prince, *A History,* pp. 116–117.

61. Gayatri Chakravorty Spivak, "Post-Coloniality and the Field of Value," Plenary session talk, Conference on Cultural Value, Birkbeck College, University of London, July 16, 1988.

62. Michel Foucault, *Language, Counter-Memory, and Practice* (New York: Cornell University Press, 1977), p. 209.

63. Frantz Fanon, *The Wretched of the Earth,* (New York: Grove Press, 1963), trans. Constance Farrington, pp. 44–45.

Notes on Chapter 14

1. Jean Fagan Yellin, *Women & Sisters. The Antislavery Feminists in American Culture* (New Haven and London: Yale University Press, 1989).

2. Yates, *Harriet Martineau on Women,* p. 1.

3. Martineau, *Autobiography,* vol. 1, pp. 101–102.

4. For the evolving connections between socialism and feminism see Barbara Taylor, *Eve and the New Jerusalem. Socialism and Feminism in the Nineteenth Century* (New York: Pantheon Books, 1983). See also Kenneth Corfield, "Elizabeth Heyrick," who distinguishes Elizabeth Heyrick from a feminist (though not a class-based) tradition, pp. 57–58; Barbara Taylor, "The Woman-Power: Religious Heresy and Feminism in Early English Socialism," *Tearing the Veil. Essays on Femininity,* ed. Susan Lipshitz (London: Routledge & Kegan Paul, 1978), p. 126; and Gail Malmgreen, *Neither Bread nor Roses:*

Utopian Feminists and the English Working Class, 1800–1850 (Brighton: John Noyce, 1978).

5. For a detailed account of the wide range of these continuing activities, see F. K. Prochaska, *Women and Philanthropy in Nineteenth-Century England* (Oxford: Clarendon Press, 1980).

6. Benita Parry, "Problems in Current Theories of Colonial Discourse," in *The Oxford Literary Review,* vol. 9, *Colonialism and other essays,* p. 27.

7. Valerie Kossew Pichanick, *Harriet Martineau: The Woman and Her Work 1802–76* (Ann Arbor: University of Michigan Press, 1980), pp. 91–92

8. Frantz Fanon, *Toward the African Revolution,* trans. Haakon Chevalier (New York: Grove Press, 1967), p. 34.

9. Edward Said, *Orientalism* (New York: Vintage, 1979), p. 72; Fanon, *Toward,* p. 35.

10. Homi K. Bhabha, "Difference, Discrimination and the Discourse of Colonialism," in *The Politics of Theory. Proceedings of the Essex Conference on the Sociology of Literature, July 1982,* ed. Francis Baker, Peter Hulme, Margaret Iversen, and Diana Loxley (Colchester: University of Essex, 1983), p. 194.

11. Said, *Orientalism,* p. 208.

12. This confinement does not deny the participation of working-class (as well as aristocratic Victorian women) in the emancipation campaign. See Barbara Taylor, "The Woman-Power," endnote 4.

13. See endnote 11.

14. John Barrell and Harriet Guest, "On the Use of Contradiction: Economics and Morality in the Eighteenth-Century Long Poem," in *The New Eighteenth Century. Theory. Politics. English Literature,* ed. Felicity Nussbaum and Laura Brown (New York: Methuen, 1987), pp. 121–138.

15. Barrel and Guest, "On the Use," p. 143.

16. Said, *Orientalism,* p. 177.

17. Fryer, *Staying Power,* p. 255.

18. *The Black Abolitionist Papers. Vol. 1, The British Isles, 1830–1865,* ed. C. Peter Ripley (Chapel Hill: University of North Carolina Press, 1985), p. 38.

19. Mary Prince, *The History of Mary Prince. A West Indian Slave. Related by Herself,* ed. Moira Ferguson (London: Pandora Press, 1987).

Selected Bibliography

Printed Sources

Books, Dissertations, Long Essays, Major Pamphlets, and Primary Poems.

Abel, Annie Heloise, and Frank J. Klingberg, eds. *A Side-Light on Anglo-American Relations 1839–1858*. New York: Kelley, 1970.

Abrahams, Roger D. *The Man-of-Words in the West Indies: Performance and the Emergence of Creole Culture*. Baltimore: Johns Hopkins University Press, 1983.

Adams, M. R. *Studies in the Literary Backgrounds of English Radicalism, with Special Reference to the French Revolution*. Franklin and Marshall College Studies, no. 5. Lancaster, PA: Franklin and Marshall College, 1947.

Adams, Percy G. *Travel Literature and the Evolution of the Novel*. Lexington: University of Kentucky Press, 1983.

Adburgham, Alison. *Women in Print*. London: George Allen and Unwin, 1972.

Addison, Joseph, and Sir Richard Steele, et al. *The Spectator*. Edited by Peter Smithers, introduction by Peter Smithers. Vol. 1. New York: Dutton, Everyman's Library, 1964.

Agress, Lynne. *The Feminine Irony: Women on Women in Early-Nineteenth-Century English Literature*. London: Associated University Press, 1978.

Aikin, Lucy. *The Works of Anna Laetitia Barbauld*. Vol. 1. London: Longman, 1825.

Aitken, George. *The Life of Richard Steele*. 2 vols. London: Wm. Isbister, 1889.

Alexander, Ziggi, and Audrey Dewjee, eds. *The Wonderful Adventures of Mrs. Seacole*. Bristol: Falling Wall Press, 1984.

384 ❦ BIBLIOGRAPHY

Allen, H.C. *Great Britain and the United States: A History of Anglo-American Relations (1783–1952)*. New York: St. Martin's Press, 1955.

d'Almeras, Henri. *Paul et Virginie de Bernardin de Saint-Pierre*. Paris: Société Francaise d'Editions Littéraires et Techniques, 1937.

Altick, Richard. *The English Common Reader: A Social History of the Mass Reading Public, 1800–1900*. Chicago: University of Chicago Press, 1957.

Ames, Julius. *The Legion of Liberty and Force of Truth*. New York: Arno Press and the *New York Times*, 1969.

Andrews, William L. *To Tell a Free Story: The First Century of Afro-American Autobiography, 1760–1865*. Urbana: University of Illinois Press, 1986.

————, ed. *Black Women's Slave Narratives*. Oxford: Oxford University Press, 1987.

Anstey, Roger. *The Atlantic Slave Trade and British Abolition, 1760–1810*. Atlantic Highlands, NJ: Humanities Press, 1975.

Aptheker, Bettina. *Woman's Legacy: Essays on Race, Sex, and Class in American History*. Amherst: University of Massachusetts Press, 1982.

Armistead, Wilson. *Five Hundred Thousand Strokes for Freedom*. London: W. and F. Cash, 1853.

————. *A Tribute for the Negro: Being a Vindication of the Moral, Intellectual, and Religious Capabilities of the Colonial Portion of Mankind; with Particular Reference to the African Race*. Manchester: William Irwin, 1848. Miami: Mnemosyne Publishing, 1969.

Ashmun, Margaret. *The Singing Swan: An Account of Anna Seward*. New York: Greenwood, 1931. Reprint by Greenwood, 1968.

Ashton, Helen. *Letty Landon*. London: Collins, 1951.

Ashton, John. *Chap-Books of the Eighteenth Century*. Trowbridge: Seven Dials Press, 1969.

Ashton, T.S. *An Economic History of England: The Eighteenth Century*. London: Methuen, 1966.

————. *The Industrial Revolution 1760–1830*. London: Oxford University Press, 1966.

Asiegbu, Johnson U. J. *Slavery and the Politics of Liberation 1787–1861: A Study of Liberated African Emigration and British Anti-Slavery Policy*. London: Longman, Green, 1969.

Aspinall, Arthur. *Lord Brougham and the Whig Party*. Manchester: Manchester University Press, 1927.

Aspinwall, Bernard. "William Smith, M.P. 1756–1835, and His Importance in the Movements for Parliamentary Reform, Religious Toleration, and the Abolition of the Slave Trade." Master's Thesis, University of Manchester, England, 1962.

Astell, Mary. *Some Reflections upon Marriage*. With Additions, 5th ed. Dublin: S. Hyde, E. Dobson, R. Gunne, and R. Owen, 1730.

Augier, F. R., and Shirley C. Gordon, comps. *Sources of West Indian History*. Trinidad: Longman Caribbean, 1962.

Backsheider, Paula R. *The Plays of Elizabeth Inchbald*. 2 vols. New York: Garland, 1980.

Bacon, Margaret Hope. *Mothers of Feminism: The Story of Quaker Women in America*. San Francisco: Harper and Row, 1986.

————. *The Quiet Rebels*. New York: Basic Books, 1969.

Bahlman, Dudley W. R. *The Moral Revolution of 1688*. New Haven: Yale University Press, 1957.

Bailey, J. C. *The Poems of William Cowper*. London: Methuen, 1905.

Baillie, Joanna. *The Dramatic and Poetical Works of Joanna Baillie*. London: Longman, Brown, Green, and Longmans, 1851.

Baird, John D., and Charles Ryskamp, eds. *The Poems of William Cowper*. Vol. 1. Oxford: Clarendon Press, 1980.

Baker, Houston A. *Singers at Daybreak: Studies in Black American Literature*. Washington, D.C.: Howard University Press, 1983.

Bakhtin, Mikhail. *The Dialogic Imagination: Four Essays by M.M. Bakhtin*. Edited by Michael Holquist, translated by Caryl Emerson and Michael Holquist. Austin: University of Texas Press, 1981.

Ballard, George. *Memoirs of Several Ladies of Great Britain Who Have Been Celebrated for Their Writings or Skill in the Learned Languages, Arts and Sciences*. 1752. Edited and modernized by Ruth Perry. Detroit: Wayne State University Press, 1985.

Banks, Olive. *Biographical Dictionary of British Feminists*. Vol. 1. New York: New York University Press, 1985.

Banton, Michael. *Race Relations*. New York: Basic Books, 1967.

Barbauld, Anna Laetitia. *Hymns in Prose for Children*. London: Joseph Johnson, 1781.

Barber, Mary. *Poems on Several Occasions*. London: C. Rivington, 1734.

Barbour, Hugh, and Arthur O. Roberts, eds. *Early Quaker Writings 1650–1700*. Grand Rapids: Eerdmans, 1973.

Barker, Anthony J. *The African Link: British Attitudes to the Negro in the Era of the Atlantic Slave Trade, 1550–1807*. London: Frank Cass & Co., Inc., 1978.

Barker, Francis, Peter Hulme, Margaret Iversen, and Diana Loxley, eds. *The Politics of Theory*. Proceedings of the Essex Conference on the Sociology of Literature, July 1982. Colchester: Essex University Press, 1983.

————. *Europe and Its Others*. Proceedings of the Essex Conference on the

Sociology of Literature, July 1984. 2 vols. Colchester: Essex University Press, 1985.

————. *Literature, Politics and Theory: Papers from the Essex Conference 1976–84.* London: Methuen, 1986.

Barrow, John. *An Account of Travels into the Interior of Southern Africa, in the Years 1797 and 1798.* London: T. Cadell Jun. and W. Davies, 1801.

Barry, Florence. *A Century of Children's Books.* New York: George H. Doran, n.d. (c1920).

Barry, Kathleen, Charlotte Bunch, and Shirley Castley. *International Feminism: Networking Against Female Sexual Slavery.* Report of the Global Feminist Workshop to Organize Against Traffic in Women, Rotterdam, the Netherlands, April 6–15, 1983. New York: International Women's Tribune Center, 1984.

Barton, Bernard. *Selections from the Poems and Letters of Bernard Barton.* Edited by his daughter. London: Hall, Virtue, 1849.

Bass, Robert D. *The Green Dragoon: The Lives of Banastre Tarleton and Mary Robinson.* New York: Henry Holt and Company, 1957.

Baxter, Richard. *Chapters from a Christian Director, or a Summ of Practical Theology and Cases of Conscience,* ed. Jeanne H. Tawney. London, 1664/65; Reprint, 1925.

Bayler, Joseph. *Biographical Dictionary of Modern British Radicals.* Brighton: Harvester, 1985.

Beale, Catherine Hutton, ed. *Catherine Hutton and Her Friends.* Birmingham, Cornish Brothers, 1895.

Beckles, Hilary. *Black Rebellion in Barbados: The Struggle Against Slavery 1627–1833.* St. Michael, Barbados, W.I.: Antilles Publications, 1984.

————. *Natural Rebels. A Social History of Enslaved Black Women in Barbados* London: Zed Books Ltd., 1989.

Beers, Henry. *A History of English Romanticism in the Eighteenth Century.* New York: Henry Holt and Company, 1899.

Behn, Aphra. *The Plays, Histories, and Novels of the Ingenious Mrs. Aphra Behn, With Life and Memoirs.* 6 vols. Vol. 3, four plays. London: John Pearson, 1871.

————. *The Works of Aphra Behn,* ed. Montague Summers. Vol. 3, four plays. London: Heinemann, 1915.

————. *Oroonoko, or The History of the Royal Slave,* ed. K. A. Sey. Tema, Ghana: Ghana Publishing Corporation, 1977.

Bell, Susan Groag, and Karen M. Offen, eds. *Women, the Family, and Freedom: The Debate in Documents.* Vol. 1, 1750–1880. Stanford, Calif.: Stanford University Press, 1983.

Belsey, Catherine. *Critical Practice.* London: Methuen, 1980.

Belsham, Thomas. *Memoirs of the Late Rev. Theophilus Lindsey.* London: J. Johnson, 1812.

Benezet, Anthony. *A short account of the people called Quakers, their rise, religious principles and settlement in America, mostly collected from different authors, for the information of all serious inquiries.* Philadelphia, Joseph Cruikshank, 1780.

Bennett, Betty T. *British War Poetry in the Age of Romanticism: 1793–1815.* New York: Garland, 1976.

Bennett, J. Harry. Jr. *Bondsmen and Bishops: Slavery and Apprenticeship on the Codrington Plantation of Barbados, 1710–1838.* Berkeley, University of California Press, 1958.

Bentley, Elizabeth. *Genuine Poetical Compositions on Various Subjects.* Norwich: Crouse and Stevenson, 1791.

Berg, Maxine, Pat Hudson, Michael Sonenscher, eds. *Manufacture in Town and Country Before the Factory.* Cambridge: Cambridge University Press, 1983.

Besse, Joseph. *Collection of the Sufferings of People Called Quakers.* London, 1753.

Betham, Matilda. *A Biographical Dictionary of the Celebrated Women of Every Age and Country.* London: Crosby, 1804.

Biller, Sarah, ed. *Memoir of Hannah Kilham.* London: Darton and Harvey, 1837.

Bissell, Benjamin. *The American Indian in English Literature of the Eighteenth Century.* New Haven: Yale University Press, 1925.

Black, Jeremy. *Britain in the Age of Walpole.* Problems in Focus series. London: Macmillan, 1984.

Blake, William O. *History of Slavery and the Slave Trade: Compiled from Authentic Material.* Published and Sold Exclusively by Subscription. Columbus, OH: J. and H. Miller, 1857.

Blassingame, John W. *The Slave Community: Plantation Life in the Antebellum South.* New York: Oxford University Press, 1972.

Bloch, Marc. *Feudal Society.* Chicago: University of Chicago Press, 1961.

Bloomfield, Edward H. *The Opposition to the English Separatists, 1570–1625: A Survey of the Polemical Literature Written by the Opponents to Separatism.* Washington, D.C.: University Press of America, 1981.

Bolt, Christine. *The Anti-slavery Movement and Reconstruction: A Study in Anglo-American Co-operation, 1833–77.* London: Oxford University Press, 1969.

———. *Victorian Attitudes to Race.* Studies in Social History, edited by Harold Perkin. London: Routledge & Kegan Paul, 1971.

Bolt, Christine, and Seymour Drescher, eds. *Anti-Slavery, Religion, and Reform: Essays in Memory of Roger Anstey.* Kent, England: Dawson, 1980.

Bond, Richmond P. *Studies in the Early English Periodical.* Chapel Hill: University of North Carolina Press, 1957.

Bonhote, Elizabeth. *The Rambles of Mr. Frankly,* vol. 1. Dublin: Printed for Messrs. Sleater, Lynch, Williams, Potts, Chamberlaine, Wilson, Husband, Walker, Moncrieffe, and Flin, 1773.

Bonwick, Colin. *English Radicals and the American Revolution.* Chapel Hill: University of North Carolina Press, 1977.

Bosman, William. *A New and Accurate Description of the Coast of Guinea divided into the Gold, the Slave, and the Ivory Coasts, etc. . . .* Written originally in the Dutch by William Bosman, chief factor for the Dutch at the Castle of St. George d'Elmina. London: Joseph Knapton, 1705.

Bouce, Paul Gabriel. *Sexuality in Eighteenth-Century Britain.* Manchester: Manchester University Press. Totowa, NJ: Barnes and Noble, 1982.

Boulton, James T. *The Language of Politics in the Ages of Wilkes and Burke.* London: Routledge and Kegan Paul, 1963.

Bourne, Ruth. *Queen Anne's Navy in the West Indies.* New Haven: Yale University Press, 1939.

Brack, O. M., Jr. *Studies in Eighteenth-Century Culture.* Vol. 16. Madison: University of Wisconsin Press, 1986.

Brailsford, Mabel Richmond. *Quaker Women 1650–1690.* London: Duckworth, 1915.

Braithwaite, John. *The Life of the Rev. John Braithwaite.* London: Broadbent, 1825.

Braithwaite, Joseph Bevan. *Memoirs of Anna Braithwaite.* London: Headley Brothers, 1905.

Braithwaite, William C. *The Beginnings of Quakerism.* London: Macmillan, 1912.

———. *The Second Period of Quakerism.* London: Macmillan, 1919.

Branca, Patricia. *Silent Sisterhood: Middle-Class Women in the Victorian Home.* Pittsburgh: Carnegie-Mellon University Press, 1975.

Brantlinger, Patrick. *Rule of Darkness: British Literature and Imperialism, 1830–1914.* Ithaca: Cornell University Press, 1988.

Bready, J. Wesley. *England: Before and After Wesley.* New York: Russell and Russell, 1938.

Bredvold, Louis I. *The Natural History of Sensibility.* Detroit: Wayne State University Press, 1962.

de la Bretonne, Restif. *Monsieur Nicolas.* New York: Clarkson Potter, 1966.

Breunig, Charles. *The Age of Revolution and Reaction 1789–1850.* 2nd ed.

Norton History of Modern Europe, edited by Felix Gilbert. New York: W. W. Norton & Company, Inc., 1970.

A Brief Sketch of the life of Anna Backhouse. Burlington, NJ: John Rodgers, 1852.

Brightwell, Cecelia Lucy. *Memorials of Amelia Opie.* London: Religious Tract Society, 1855.

Brinton, Crane. *The Political Ideas of the English Romanticists.* New York: Russell and Russell, 1926. Reissued, 1962.

Brinton, Howard H., ed. *Children of Light.* New York: Macmillan, 1938.

Brissenden, R. F. *Virtue in Distress.* London: Macmillan, 1974.

Bristow, Edward J. *Vice and Vigilance.* Dublin: Gill and Macmillan, 1977.

Brougham, Henry Lord. *Critical and Miscellaneous Writings of Henry Lord Brougham.* Philadelphia: Lea and Blanchard, 1841.

Brown, Ford K. *Fathers of the Victorians.* Cambridge: Cambridge University Press, 1961.

Brownlow, John. *The History and Design of the Foundling Hospital, with a Memoir of the Founder.* London: W. and H. S. Warr, 1858.

Bruce, Henry. *Life of General Oglethorpe.* Makers of America series. New York: Dodd, Mead, 1890.

Bruner, Charlotte H. *Unwinding Threads: Writing by Women in Africa.* African Writers series, no. 256. London: Heinemann, 1983.

Buer, M.C. *Health, Wealth, and Population in the Early Days of the Industrial Revolution.* George Routledge and Sons, 1926. London: Routledge & Kegan Paul, 1968.

Burdett-Coutts, Baroness Angela, ed. *Woman's Mission: A Series of Congress Papers on the Philanthropic Work of Women.* New York: Scribner's, 1893.

Bush, Barbara. *Slave Women in Caribbean Society 1650–1838.* Kingston: Heinemann; Bloomington: Indiana University Press, 1990.

Butcher, Philip. *The Minority Presence in American Literature, 1600–1900: A Reader and Course Guide.* Vol. 1. Washington, D.C.: Howard University Press, 1977.

Butler, Frances Anne. *The Journal of Frances Anne Butler, Better Known as Fanny Kemble.* 2 vols. London: John Murray, 1835. New York: Benjamin Blom, 1970.

Butler, Marilyn. *Burke, Paine, Godwin, and the Revolution Controversy.* Cambridge: Cambridge University Press, 1984.

———. *Maria Edgeworth: A Literary Biography.* Oxford: Clarendon Press, 1972.

Butterfield, Stephen. *Black Autobiography in America.* Amherst: University of Massachusetts Press, 1974.

Butterworth, Charles C. *The Literary Lineage of the King James Bible.* Philadelphia: University of Pennsylvania Press, 1941.

Buxton, Charles. *Memoirs of Sir Thomas Fowell Buxton.* London and Toronto: J. M. Dent. New York: E. P. Dutton, 1848.

Calder, Angus. *Revolutionary Empire: The Rise of the English-Speaking Empires from the Fifteenth Century to the 1780s.* London: Jonathan Cape, 1981.

Campo-Bell, John Talbot. *The Speech of Mr. John Talbot Campo-bell, a free Christian-negro, to his countrymen in the mountains of Jamaica. In two parts* . . . London: Printed for J. Robert, 1736.

Caribbeana. Containing letters and Dissertations, Together with Poetical Essays, on Various subjects and Occasions; Chiefly wrote by several hands in the West Indies, and some of them to Gentlemen residing there. Now collected together in Two Volumes. Wherein are also comprised, diverse Papers relating to Trade, Government, and Laws in general; but more especially, to those of the British Sugar-Colonies, and of Barbados in particular: as likewise the Characters of the most eminent Men that have died of late Years in that Island. To which are added in an Appendix Some Pieces never before published, Vol. 1. London: T. Osborne, J. Clarke, S. Austin, G. Hawkins, R. Didsley, W. Lewis, 1741.

Carter, Elizabeth. *Letters from Mrs. Elizabeth Carter, to Mrs. Montagu, Between the Years 1755 and 1800. Chiefly Upon Literary and Moral Subjects.* 3 vols. London: F. C. and J. Rivington, 1817.

————. *Memoirs of the Life of Mrs. Elizabeth Carter, with a new edition of her poems* . . . *To which are added, some miscellaneous essays in prose, together with her notes on the Bible, and answers to objections concerning the Christian religion.* ed. Rev. Montagu Pennington. . . . 2nd ed. [With a portrait.] 2 vols. London: F. C. & J. Rivington, 1808.

Catterall, Helen T. *Judicial Cases Concerning American Slavery and the Negro.* Washington, D.C.: Carnegie Institution, 1926.

Cazamian, Louis. *The Social Novel in England 1830–1850.* Translated by Martin Fido. London: Routledge & Kegan Paul, 1973.

Chapone, Hester. *Letters on the Improvement of the Mind.* New York: Richard S. D. Fanshaw, 1818.

————. *The Posthumous Works of Mrs. Chapone. Containing Her Correspondence with Mr. Richardson, a Series of Letters to Mrs. Elizabeth Carter, and Some Fugitive Pieces, Never Before Published, Together with an Account of Her Life and Character, Drawn Up By Her Own Family* 2nd. ed. London: John Murray, 1808.

Charke, Charlotte Cibber. *A Narrative of the Life of Mrs. Charlotte Charke, youngest daughter of Colley Cibber,* 2nd ed. (London, 1755); Reprint. edited by Leonard R. N. Ashley. Gainesville, FL: Scholars' Facsimiles and Reprint, 1969.

Charles, Leslie. *A New History of Jamaica, from the earliest accounts of the taking of Porto Bello by Vice-Admiral Vernon. In thirteen letters from a gentleman to his friend . . . With two maps,* 2nd ed. London: printed for J. Hodges, 1740.

Charles, Lindsey and Lorna Duffin, eds. *Women and Work in Pre-Industrial England.* London: Croom Helm, 1985.

Chaytor, Miranda and Jane Lewis, ed. *Working Life of Women in the Seventeenth Century.* London, 1919; Reprint. London: Routledge & Kegan Paul, 1982.

Childe, Gordon. *What Happened in History: A Study of the Rise and Decline of Cultural and Moral Values in the Old World up to the Fall of the Roman Empire.* n.p.: Pelican, 1954.

Clark, Alice. *Working Life of Women in the Seventeenth Century.* London: 1919; Reprint. London: Routledge & Kegan Paul, 1982.

Clark, Donald. *Alexander Pope.* New York: Twayne, 1967.

Clark, Henry. *William Roscoe and His Life.* Liverpool: H. Young, 1883.

Clarke, William Kemp Lowther. *Eighteenth Century Piety.* London: Macmillan and Society for Promoting Christian Knowledge, 1944.

Clarkson, Thomas. *The history of the Rise, Progress, and Accomplishment of the Abolition of the African Slave-Trade by the British Parliament.* Vols. 1 and 2. London: Frank Cass & Co., Inc., 1968.

Clay, Edith. *Lady Blessington at Naples.* London: Hamish Hamilton, 1979.

Clayden, Peter W. *The Early Life of Samuel Rogers.* London: Smith, Elder, 1887.

Clissold, Stephen. *The Barbary Slaves.* London: Paul Elek, 1977.

Cobb, Thomas R.R. *An Historical Sketch of Slavery from the Earliest Periods.* Philadelphia: T. and J. W. Johnson, 1858. Reprint. Detroit: Negro History Press, n.d.

Cockburn, Catherine Trotter. *Agnes de Castro.* London: H. Rhodes, 1696.

Coleman, D.C. *The British Paper Industry 1495–1860.* Oxford: Clarendon Press, 1958.

Collier, Jeremy. *A Defence of the Short View of the Profaneness and Immorality of the English Stage.* New York: Garland, 1972.

Colvin, Christina. *Maria Edgeworth: Letters from England 1813–1844.* Oxford: Clarendon Press, 1971.

Conant, Martha Pike. *The Oriental Tale in England in the Eighteenth Century.* New York: Octagon Books, 1966.

Conder, Eustace R. *Josiah Conder, a Memoir.* London: John Snow, 1857.

Conder, Josiah. *Wages or the Whip: An Essay on the Comparative Cost and*

Productiveness of Free and Slave Labour. London: Hutchard and Son, 1833.

Cone, Carl B. *The English Jacobins: Reformers in Late Eighteenth-Century England.* New York: Charles Scribner's Sons, 1968.

————. *Torchbearer of Freedom: The Influence of Richard Price on Eighteenth-Century Thought.* Lexington: University of Kentucky Press, 1952.

Conybeare, Frances Anne. *Dingle Bank: The Home of the Croppers.* Cambridge: W. Heffer, 1925.

Copley, Esther. *A History of Slavery and Its Abolition.* 2d ed. London: Houlston and Stoneman, 1839. Reprint. Detroit: Negro History Press, 1962.

Cott, Nancy F. *The Bonds of Womanhood: "Woman's Sphere" in New England, 1780–1835.* New Haven: Yale University Press, 1977.

Cotton, Nancy. *Women Playwrights in England c. 1363–1750.* London: Associated University Presses, 1980.

Coupland, Sir Reginald. *The British Anti-Slavery Movement.* Oxford: Oxford University Press, 1933. London: Frank Cass & Co., Inc., 1964.

————. *Wilberforce: A Narrative.* Oxford: Clarendon Press, 1923.

Courtney, Luther Weeks. *Hannah More's Interest in Education and Government.* Waco: Baylor University Press, 1929.

Cowherd, Raymond G. *The Politics of English Dissent: The Religious Aspects of Liberal and Humanitarian Reform Movements from 1815 to 1848.* New York: New York University Press, 1956.

Cowper, William. *The Letters and Prose Writings of William Cowper.* Vols. 1–5, 1750–1799. Edited by James King and Charles Ryskamp. Oxford: Clarendon Press, 1986.

————. *The Poems of William Cowper.* Vol. 1, 1748–1782. Edited by John D. Baird and Charles Ryskamp. Oxford: Clarendon Press, 1980.

Crafton, William Bell. *A Short Sketch of the Evidence for the Abolition of the Slave Trade.* London, 1792, Reprint. Daniel Lawrence, Philadelphia, 1792.

Craton, Michael. *A History of the Bahamas.* London: Collins, 1969.

————. *Searching for the Invisible Man: Slaves and Plantation Life in Jamaica.* With the assistance of Garry Greenland. Cambridge: Harvard University Press, 1978.

————. *Sinews of Empire: A Short History of British Slavery.* Garden City: Anchor, 1974.

————. *Testing the Chains: Resistance to Slavery in the British West Indies.* Ithaca: Cornell University Press, 1982.

————, ed. *Roots and Branches: Current Directions in Slave Studies.* Toronto and New York: Pergamon Press, 1979.

Craton, Michael, and James Walvin. *A Jamaican Plantation: The History of Worthy Park 1670–1970.* Toronto: University of Toronto Press, 1970.

Craton, Michael, James Walvin, and David Wright. *Slavery, Abolition and Emancipation: Black Slaves and the British Empire.* London: Longman, 1976.

Craton, Michael, and H. W. McReedy. *The Great Liberal Revival, 1903–6.* London: Hansard Society for Parliamentary Government, 1967.

Cressy, David. *Literacy and the Social Order.* Cambridge: Cambridge University Press, 1980.

Crittenden, Walter M. *A Description of Millenium Hall by Mrs. Sarah Scott.* New York: Bookman Association, 1955.

———. *The Life and Writings of Mrs. Sarah Scott—Novelist (1723–1795).* Ph.D. diss., University of Pennsylvania, 1932.

Croft, Rev. George. *Thoughts Concerning the Methodists and the Established Clergy.* London: Rivington, 1795.

Cropper, Margaret. *Sparks Among Stubble.* London: Longmans, Green, 1955.

Crow, Duncan. *The Victorian Woman.* London: George Allen and Unwin, 1971.

Crump, M., and M. Harris, eds.. *Searching the Eighteenth Century: Papers Presented at the Symposium on the Eighteenth Century Short Title Catalogue in July 1982.* London: British Library in association with the Department of Extra-Mural Studies, University of London, 1983.

Cudjoe, Selwyn. *Resistance and Caribbean Literature.* Chicago: Ohio University Press, 1980.

Cugoano, Ottobah. *Thoughts and Sentiments on the Evil and Wicked Traffic of the Slavery and Commerce of the Human Species, Humbly Submitted to the Inhabitants of Great Britain.* London, 1787. London: Dawsons, 1969.

Cundall, Frank. *Bibliographia Jamaicensis: A List of Jamaica books and Pamphlets, Magazine Articles, Newspapers, and Maps, Most of Which are in the Library of the Institute of Jamaica.* Kingston, Jamaica: The Institute of Jamaica: Date Tree Hall, n.d..

———. *Lady Nugent's Journal.* London: Adam and Charles Block, 1907.

Cunningham, W. *The Growth of English Industry and Commerce,* in *Modern Times. The Mercantile System,* Part One. Cambridge: Cambridge University Press, 1925.

The Curious Traveller. Being a Choice Collection of Very Remarkable Histories, Voyages, Travels, etc. Digested into Familiar Letters and Conversations. London: J. Rowland, 1742.

Curtin, Philip. *Africa Remembered.* Madison: University of Wisconsin Press, 1967.

———. *The Atlantic Slave Trade: A Census.* Madison: University of Wisconsin Press, 1969.

Curwen, Alice. *A Relation of the Labour, Travail and Suffering of That Faithful Servant of the Lord Alice Curwen. Who departed this Life the 7th Day of the 6th Month, 1679, and resteth in Peace with the Lord. Here is the Patience of the Saints, here are they that keep the Commandments of God, and the Faith of Jesus, Rev. 14.12. The Souls of the Righteous are precious in the Eyes of the Lord, and they shall be had in Everlasting Remembrance. Printed in the year 1680. Some of Alice Curwen's Testimony. such did he upon her to declare some few dayes before she departed out of the Body; she spoke for one to come and write, and there was one that did come, and did propose to write, but the Lord's Power and presence was so with her, that the Friends that were with her were so broken into Tenderness that they could do nothing to be written, but there was one Friend which was present with her at the time which did remember something of what she did speak as followeth, whose Name is Ann Martindall* (Huntington Library, San Marino, CA, Box 131).

Dabydeen, David. *Hogarth's Blacks: Images of Blacks in Eighteenth-Century English Art.* Denmark: Dangaroo, 1985.

Damrosch, Leopold, Jr. *God's Plot and Man's Stories: Studies in the Fictional Imagination from Milton to Fielding.* Chicago: University of Chicago Press, 1985.

Darton, F. J. Harvey. *Children's Books in England: Five Centuries of Social Life.* 2d ed., 1958. 3rd ed., rev. Brian Alderson. Cambridge: Cambridge University Press, 1982.

————, ed. *The Life and Times of Mrs. Sherwood (1775–1851).* London: Wells Gardner, Darton and Co., 1910.

D'Arusmont, Frances Wright. *Biography and Notes of Frances D'Arusmont.* Boston: J. P. Mendum, 1848.

Darwin, Emma. *A Century of Family Letters 1792–1896.* Edited by Henrietta Litchfield. Vols. 1 and 2. New York: Appleton, 1915.

Davidoff, Leonore, and Catherine Hall. *Family Fortunes: Men and Women of the English Middle Class, 1780–1850.* London: Hutchinson, 1987.

Davidson, Basil. *The African Slave Trade.* Boston: Little, Brown, 1980.

————. *Black Mother: The Years of the African Slave Trade.* Boston: Little, Brown, 1961.

————. *The Liberation of Guine': Aspects of an African Revolution.* Baltimore: Penguin, 1969.

————. *The Story of Africa.* Based on the television series *Africa.* London: Mitchell Beazley, 1984.

Davies, K. G. *The Royal African Company.* Studies in American Negro Life, August Meier, general editor. New York: Atheneum, 1970.

Davis, Charles T. *Black is the Color of the Cosmos: Essays on Afro-American Literature and Culture, 1942–81.* New York: Garland, 1982.

Davis, Charles T., and Henry Louis Gates, Jr. *The Slave's Narrative.* Oxford: Oxford University Press, 1985.

Davis, David Brion. *The Problem of Slavery in the Age of Revolution 1770–1823.* Ithaca: Cornell University Press, 1975.

——. *The Problem of Slavery in Western Culture.* Ithaca: Cornell University Press, 1966.

Davis, H. P. *Black Democracy: The Story of Haiti.* Rev. ed. New York: Dodge Publishing Co., 1936.

Deane, Phyllis, and W. A. Cole. *British Economic Growth 1688–1959: Trends and Structure.* 2nd ed. Cambridge: Cambridge University Press, 1967.

Deerr, Noël. *The History of Sugar.* London: Chapman and Hall, 1949.

Delany, Mary Granville Pendarves. *The Autobiography and Correspondence of Mrs. Delany.* ed. Lady Llanover, 1st ser. 3 vols. London: Richard Bentley, 1861.

Deverell, Mary. *Sermons on Various Subjects.* London: Mary Deverell, 1777.

Dick, James C. *The Songs of Robert Burns.* Hatboro, PA: Folklore Associates, 1962.

Dickinson, H. T. *British Radicalism and the French Revolution 1789–1815.* Oxford: Basil Blackwell, 1985.

Dillon, Morton L. *Benjamin Lundy and the Struggle for Negro Freedom.* Urbana: University of Illinois Press, 1966.

Dixon, Peter. *Canning: Politician and Statesman.* London: Weidenfeld and Nicolson, 1976.

Docherty, Thomas. *On Modern Authority. The Theory and Condition of Writing 1500 to the Present Day.* New York: St. Martin's Press. Sussex: Harvester, 1987.

Dodds, John Wendell. *Thomas Southerne, Dramatist.* New Haven: Yale University Press. London: Humphrey Milford and Oxford University Press, 1933.

Dookham, Isaac. *A Pre-Emancipation History of the West Indies.* London: Collins, 1971, 1985.

Donnan, Elizabeth. *Documents Illustrative of the History of the Slave Trade to America.* Vols 1 and 2. Washington, D.C.: Carnegie Institution, 1930.

Doyle, John Robert, Jr. *Thomas Pringle.* New York: Twayne Publishers, 1972.

Drescher, Seymour. *Capitalism and Antislavery. British Mobilization in Comparative Perspective.* London: Macmillan, 1986.

Dryden, John. *Aureng-Zebe.* Lincoln: University of Nebraska Press, 1971.

Duberman, Martin, ed. *The Antislavery Vanguard: New Essays on the Abolitionists.* Princeton, N.J.: Princeton University Press, 1965.

Duff, William. *Letters on the Intellectual and Moral Character of Women.* New York: Garland, 1974.

Duffy, Maureen. *The Passionate Shepherdess.* New York: Avon, 1977.

Dunston, Frederick Warburton. *Roscoeana: Being Some Account of the Kinsfolk of William Roscoe of Liverpool and Jane (née Griffies) His Wife, by their Descendent Frederick Warburton Dunston.* Privately printed.

Dutton, Anne. *Divine, Moral, and Historical Miscellanies in Prose and Verse; Containing Many Valuable Originals.* London: J. Fuller and T. Luckman, 1761.

———. *Hymns Composed on Several Subjects.* London, 1734.

Dyke, Eva Beatrice. *The Negro in English Romantic Thought; Or, A Study of Sympathy for the Oppressed.* Washington: Associated Publishers, 1942.

Eagleton, Terry. *Against the Grain: Essays, 1975–1985.* London: Verso, 1986.

———. *Marxism and Literary Criticism.* Berkeley and Los Angeles: University of California Press, 1976.

Eaves, T. C. Duncan, and Ben D. Kimpel. *Samuel Richardson: A Biography.* Oxford: Clarendon Press, 1971.

Ebner, Dean. *Autobiography in Seventeenth-Century England: Theology and the Self.* The Hague: Mouton, 1971.

Eckhardt, Celia Morris. *Fanny Wright: Rebel in America.* Cambridge: Harvard University Press, 1984.

Eden, Frederick Morton. *The State of the Poor; Or, An History of the Labouring Classes from the Conquest to the Present Period.* London: J. Davis, 1797.

Edgeworth, Maria. *Belinda.* 2 vols. London: Baldwin and Cradock, Paternoster Row and Other Proprietors, 1833.

———. *Letters for Literary Ladies. To Which Is Added, an Essay on the Noble Science of Self-Justification.* London: J. Johnson, 1795.

———. *Letters from England 1813–1844.* Edited by Christina Colvin. Oxford: Clarendon Press, 1971.

———. *Tales and Novels by Maria Edgeworth.* 18 vols. London: Baldwin and Cradock, 1833–1883.

Edwards, Bryan. *The History, Civil and Commercial of the British Colonies in the West Indies.* 2 vols. London, 1793.

Edmonds, Charles, ed. *Poetry of the Anti-Jacobins.* New York: Putnam. London: Sampson Low, 1890.

Edwards, Paul, and James Walvin. *Black Personalities in the Era of the Slave Trade.* Baton Rouge: Louisiana State University Press, 1983.

Eisenstein, Hester, and Alice Jardine, eds. *The Future of Difference.* The Scholar and the Feminist, series edited by Barbara Haber, vol. 1. Papers from the Barnard College Women's Center Conference, Hester Eisenstein, general editor. Boston: G. K. Hall, 1980.

Elkins, Stanley M. *Slavery: A Problem in American Institutional and Intellectual Life.* 2d ed. Chicago: University of Chicago Press, 1968.

Elledge, Scott. Vols. 1 and 2. *Eighteenth-Century Critical Essays.* Ithaca: Cornell University Press, 1961.

Ellis, Grace. *Memoirs, Letters and a Selection from the Poems and Prose Writings of Mrs. Barbauld,* 2 vols. Boston: J. R. Osgood, 1874.

Ellis, William. *Madagascar Revisited.* London: John Murray, 1867.

———, ed. *The Missionary; Or, Christian's New Year's Gift.* London, 1833.

Eltis, David, and James Walvin, eds. *The Abolition of the Atlantic Slave Trade.* Madison: University of Wisconsin Press, 1981.

Elwin, Malcolm. *Lord Byron's Wife.* New York: Harcourt, Brace, and World, 1962.

The Enormity of the Slave-Trade; and the Duty of Seeking Moral and Spiritual Elevation of the Colored Race: Speeches of Wilberforce, and Other Documents and Records. n.d. Reprint. Freeport, NY: Books for Libraries Press, 1970.

Epstein, Barbara Leslie. *The Politics of Domesticity: Women, Evangelism, and Temperance in Nineteenth-Century America.* Middletown: Wesleyan University Press, 1981

Equiano, Olaudah. *Equiano's Travels: His Autobiography.* Abridged and edited by Paul Edwards. London: Heinemann, 1980.

Erickson, Robert A. *Mother Midnight: Birth, Sex, and Fate in Eighteenth-Century Fiction.* New York: AMS Press Inc., 1986.

Erskine, Mrs. Stuart, ed. *Anna Jameson: Letters and Friendships (1812–1860).* New York: E. P. Dutton & Co., 1916.

Escott, Paul D. *Slavery Remembered: A Record of Twentieth-Century Slave Narratives.* Chapel Hill: University of North Carolina Press, 1979.

Ettinger, Amos Aschbach. *James Edward Oglethorpe: Imperial Idealist.* Oxford: Clarendon Press, 1936.

Evans, William, and Thomas Evans, eds. *The Friends' Library.* Vol. 1. Philadelphia: Joseph Rakestraw, 1837.

———. *Memoirs of the Life of George Fox. The Friends Library: Comprising Journals, Doctrinal Treatises, and Other Writings of Members of the Religious Society of Friends.*

Fabian, Johannes. *Time and the Other: How Anthropology Meets its Object.* New York: Columbia University Press, 1983.

Faderman, Lillian. *Surpassing the Love of Men: Romantic Friendship and Love Between Women from the Renaissance to the Present.* New York: William Morrow, 1981.

Fage, J. D. *A History of West Africa: An Introductory Survey.* 4th ed. of *An*

Introduction to the History of West Africa. London: Cambridge University Press, 1969.

Fairchild, Hoxie Neale. *The Noble Savage: A Study in Romantic Naturalism.* New York: Columbia University Press, 1928. New York: Russell and Russell, 1955.

————. *Religious Trends in English Poetry.* 3 vols. New York: Columbia University Press.

Falconbridge, Alexander. *An Account of the Slave Trade on the Coast of Africa.* London: J. Phillips, 1788. New York: AMS Press, Inc., 1973.

Falconbridge, Anna Maria. *Narrative of Two Voyages to the River Sierra Leone During the Years 1791–1793.* 2d ed. London, 1802. London: Frank Cass & Co. Inc., 1967.

Falconar, Harriet and Maria. *Poems.* London: Joseph Johnson, 1788.

Fanon, Frantz. *The Wretched of the Earth.* Trans. Constance Farrington. New York: Grove Press, 1963.

————. *Black Skin, White Masks.* Trans. Charles Lam Markmann. New York: Grove Press, 1967.

Fay, Bernard. *The Revolutionary Spirit in France and America.* Translated by Ramon Guthrie. New York: Harcourt, 1927.

Felman, Shoshana, ed. *Literature and Psychoanalysis: The Question of Reading—Otherwise.* Baltimore and London: The Johns Hopkins University Press, 1982.

The Female Aegis; Or, The Duties of Women. London: J. Ginger, 1798. The Feminist Controversy in England 1788–1810, series edited by Gina Luria. New York: Garland, 1974.

Fenichel, Otto. *The Psychoanalytic Theory of Neurosis.* New York: W. W. Norton & Company, Inc., 1945.

Ferguson, Moira, ed. *First Feminists: British Women Writers 1578–1799.* Bloomington: Indiana University Press. 1985.

Figes, Eva. *Sex and Subterfuge: Women Novelists to 1850.* London: Macmillan, 1982.

Finlayson, Michael G. *Historians, Puritanism, and the English Revolution: The Religious Factor in English Politics Before and After the Interregnum.* Toronto: University of Toronto Press, 1983.

Fisher, Dexter, and Robert B. Stepto, eds. *Afro-American Literature: The Reconstruction of Instruction.* For the Commission on the Literatures and Languages of America. New York: Modern Language Association of America, 1979.

Fitzhugh, Robert T. *Robert Burns: The Man and the Poet.* Boston: Houghton Mifflin Company, 1970.

Fladeland, Betty. *Abolitionists and Working-Class Problems in the Age of Industrialization.* Baton Rouge: Louisiana State University Press, 1984.

———. *Men and Brothers: Anglo-American Antislavery Cooperation.* Urbana: University of Illinois Press, 1972.

Fletcher, Eliza Dawson. *Autobiography of Mrs. Fletcher.* Boston: Roberts Bros., 1876.

Fletcher, F. T. H. *Montesquieu and English Politics (1750–1800).* London: Edward Arnold & Co., n.d.

Flint, John E., ed. *The Cambridge History of Africa.* Vol. 5. Cambridge: Cambridge University Press, 1976.

Fogel, Robert William, and Stanley L. Engerman. *Time on the Cross: Evidence and Methods—A Supplement.* Boston: Little, Brown, 1974.

Foley, Barbara. *Telling the Truth: The Theory and Practice of Documentary Fiction.* Ithaca: Cornell University Press, 1986.

Folkenflike, Robert, ed. *The English Hero 1660–1800.* Newark: University of Delaware Press, 1982.

Foner, Laura, and Eugene D. Genovese. *Slavery in the New World.* Englewood Cliffs, NJ: Prentice-Hall, 1969.

Foner, Philip S. *The Complete Writings of Thomas Paine.* New York: Citadel, 1945.

Forbes, Margaret. *Beattie and His Friends.* Westminster: Archibald Constable, 1904.

Forster, E. M. *Marianne Thornton: A Domestic Biography, 1797–1887.* New York: Harcourt, Brace, 1956.

Foster, Frances Smith. *Witnessing Slavery: The Development of Ante-bellum Slave Narratives.* Westport: Greenwood Press, 1979.

Foster, James R. *History of the Pre-Romantic Novel in England.* New York: Modern Language Association of America, 1949.

Foster, Vere, ed. *The Two Duchesses: Family Correspondence of and Relating to Georgiana Duchess of Devonshire, Elizabeth Duchess of Devonshire, Earl of Bristol (Bishop of Derry), the Countess of Bristol, Lord and Lady Byron, the Earl of Aberdeen, Sir Augustus Foster, Bart., and Others, 1777–1854.* London: Blackie and Son, 1898.

Fothergill, John. *Chain of Friendship: Selected Letters of Dr. John Fothergill of London, 1735–1780.* Edited by Betsy C. Corner and Christopher C. Booth. Cambridge: Belknap Press of Harvard University Press, 1971.

Foucault, Michel. *Discipline and Punish: The Birth of the Prison.* Translated by Alan Sheridan. New York: Vintage, 1979.

———. *Language, Counter-Memory, Practice: Selected Essays and Interviews.* Edited by Donald F. Bouchard, translated by Donald F. Bouchard and Sherry Simon. Ithaca: Cornell University Press, 1977.

―――. *Power/Knowledge: Selected Interviews and Other Writings, 1972–1977.* Translated by Colin Gordon, Leo Marshall, John Mepham, and Kate Soper. New York: Pantheon Books, 1980.

Fox, George. *A Collection of Many Select and Christian Epistles, Letters and Testimonies, Written on Sundry Occasions by that Ancient Eminent, Faithful friend and Minister of Christ and Jesus, George Fox,* with preface by George Whitehead, 2 vols. London: T. Sowle, 1698.

―――. *The Journal of George Fox.* 1694. Revised by Norman Penney. Everyman's Library, no. 754. London: J. M. Dent, 1924.

―――. *No More But My Love: Letters of George Fox, 1624–91.* 1698. Reprint edited by Cecil W. Sharman. London: Quaker Home Service, 1980.

Fox, W. J. *Lectures Addressed Chiefly to the Working Classes.* 2 vols. London: Charles Fox, 1845.

Foxon, D. F. *English Verse 1701–1750.* Cambridge: Cambridge University Press, 1975.

Fraser, Antonia. *The Weaker Vessel.* New York: Alfred Knopf, 1984.

Fredrickson, George M. *The Black Image in the White Mind: The Debate on Afro-American Character and Destiny, 1817–1914.* New York: Harper and Row, 1971.

―――. *William Lloyd Garrison.* Englewood Cliffs, NJ: Prentice-Hall, 1968.

Freud, Anna. *The Ego and the Mechanisms of Defense.* The Writings of Anna Freud, vol. 2. Translated by Cecil Baines. New York: International Universities Press, 1966.

Freud, Sigmund. *The Interpretation of Dreams, 1900.* Translated and edited by James Strachey. New York: Avon, 1965.

Friends of the Negro. *Five Hundred Thousand Strokes for Freedom: A Series of Anti-Slavery Tracts, of Which Half a Million Are Now First Issued by the Friends of the Negro.* London: W. and F. Cash, 1853. Miami: Mnemosyne, 1969.

Fritz, Paul, and Richard Morton, eds. *Woman in the Eighteenth Century and Other Essays.* Toronto: Samuel Stevens Hakkert, 1976.

Fry, Elizabeth. *Memoir of the Life of Elizabeth Fry, with Extracts from her Journal and Letters.* 2 vols. London, 1847.

Fryer, Peter. *Staying Power: The History of Black People in Britain.* London: Pluto Press, 1984.

Fyfe, Christopher. *A History of Sierra Leone.* London: Oxford University Press, 1962.

―――. *Sierra Leone Inheritance.* London: Oxford University Press, 1964.

Gallagher, Catherine. *The Industrial Reformation of English Fiction. Social Discourse and Narrative from 1832–1867.* Chicago: University of Chicago Press, 1985.

Gates, Henry Louis, Jr., ed. *The Classic Slave Narratives.* New York: Mentor, 1987.

Gates, Henry Louis Jr., ed. *"Race," Writing and Difference.* Chicago: University of Chicago Press, 1985.

———, ed. *Black Literature and Literary Theory.* New Haven: Yale University Press, 1984.

———. *Figures in Black.* London: Oxford University Press, 1986.

Gay, Peter. *The Enlightenment: An Interpretation.* New York: Alfred Knopf, 1969.

Geertz, Clifford. *The Interpretation of Cultures.* New York: Basic Books, 1973.

Geggus, David. *Slave Resistance Studies and the Saint Domingue Slave Revolt: Some Preliminary Considerations.* Miami: Florida International University, 1983.

Genovese, Eugene D. *From Rebellion to Revolution: Afro-American Slave Revolts in the Making of the Modern World.* Baton Rouge: Louisiana State University Press, 1979.

———. *Roll, Jordan, Roll: The World the Slaves Made.* New York: Pantheon Books, 1974.

Gilbert, Anne Taylor. *Hymns for Infant Minds.* London, 1840.

Gilboy, Elizabeth W. *Wages in Eighteenth-Century England.* Harvard Economic Studies, vol. 45. Cambridge: Harvard University Press, 1934.

Gilfillan, Rev. George, ed. *The Poetical Works of William Shenstone.* Edinburgh: Nichol, 1854.

Gilligan, Carol. *In a Different Voice: Psychological Theory and Women's Development.* Cambridge: Harvard University Press, 1982.

Gilman, Sander. *Difference and Pathology: Stereotypes of Sexuality, Race, and Madness* (Ithaca: Cornell University Press, 1985).

Gisborne, Thomas. *An Enquiry into the Duties of the Female Sex.* London, 1797.

Gladwin, Thomas, and Ahmad Saidin. *Slaves of the White Myth: The Psychology of Neocolonialism.* Atlantic Highlands, NJ: Humanities Press, 1980.

Godwyn, Morgan. *The Negro's and Indian's Advocate, Suing for their Admission into the Church.* London, 1680.

Goffman, Erving. *The Presentation of the Self in Everyday Life.* New York: Doubleday, 1959.

Goodwin, Albert. *The Friends of Liberty: The English Democratic Movement in the Age of the French Revolution.* Cambridge: Harvard University Press, 1979.

Goreau, Angeline. *Reconstructing Aphra: A Social Biography of Aphra Behn.* New York: Dial Press, Doubleday & Company, 1980.

————. *The Whole Duty of a Woman. Female Writers in Seventeenth-Century England.* New York: Dial Press, Doubleday & Company, 1985.

Goveia, Elsa V. *Slave Society in the British Leeward Islands at the End of the Eighteenth Century.* New Haven: Yale University Press, 1965.

Graham, Walter J. *English Literary Periodicals.* New York: Thomas Nelson and Sons, 1930.

Gramsci, Antonio. *Selections from the Prison Notebooks of Antonio Gramsci.* Edited and translated by Quintin Hoare and Geoffrey Nowell Smith. London: Lawrence and Wishart, 1973.

Grant, Douglas, *The Fortunate Slave: An Illustration of African Slavery in the Early Eighteenth Century.* London: Oxford University Press, 1968.

Grant, Douglas, *Margaret the First: A Biography of Margaret Cavendish, Duchess of Newcastle 1623–1673.* Toronto: University of Toronto Press, 1957.

Gratus, Jack. *The Great White Lie.* London: Monthly Review Press, 1973.

Gray, B. Kirkman. *A History of English Philanthropy from the Dissolution of the Monasteries to the Taking of the First Census.* London: P. S. King and Son, 1905.

Gray, Richard, ed. *The Cambridge History of Africa.* Vol. 4, *From c. 1600 to c. 1790.* Cambridge: Cambridge University Press, 1975.

Green, T. H., and T. H. Grose, eds. *Essays Moral, Political, and Literary by David Hume.* Vol. 1. London: Longmans, 1889.

Green, William A. *British Slave Emancipation: The Sugar Colonies and the Great Experiment 1830–1865.* Oxford: Clarendon Press, 1976.

Gregory, John, Dr. *A Father's Legacy to His Daughters.* London: Strand, 1774. New York: Garland, 1974.

Griffiths, Mattie. *Autobiography of a Female Slave.* Redfield, 1857. New York: Negro University Press, 1969.

Griggs, Earl Leslie. *Thomas Clarkson: The Friend of Slaves.* Ann Arbor: University of Michigan Press, 1938.

Griggs, Earl Leslie, and Clifford H. Prator, eds. *Henry Christophe and Thomas Clarkson: A Correspondence.* New York: Greenwood Press, 1968.

Grimshawe, T.S. *Memoir of the Rev. Leigh Richmond.* New York: T. Leavitt, 1829.

Gronniosaw, James Albert Ukawsaw. *A Narrative of the most remarkable particulars in the life of James Albert Ukawsaw Gronniosaw, an African prince, as related by himself.* S. Hazard, 1700.

Guffey, George, and Andrew Wright. *Two English Novelists: Aphra Behn and Anthony Trollope.* Berkeley and Los Angeles: University of California Press, 1975.

Gummere, Amelia Mott, ed. *The Journal and Essays of John Woolman*. London: Macmillan, 1922.

Gundry, Maria. *Extracts from the Letters and Memoranda of Maria Gundry, with a Short Notice of a Beloved Elder Sister*. London: Charles Gilpin, 1851.

Gutman, Herbert G. *The Black Family in Slavery and Freedom 1750–1925*. New York: Pantheon Books, 1976.

Gwin, Minrose C. *Black and White Women of the Old South: The Peculiar Sisterhood in American Literature*. Knoxville: University of Tennessee Press, 1985.

Hack, Maria. *English Stories*. 3 vols. London: Harvey and Darton, 1820–1825.

———. *Winter Evenings, or: Tales of Travellers*. Philadelphia: Appleton, 1851.

Hair, P. E. *The Atlantic Slave Trade and Black Africa*. London: Historical Association, 1978.

Hale, Sarah J. *Woman's Record; or, Sketches of All Distinguished Women from the Creation to A.D. 1868*. New York: Harper, 1872.

Halévy, Elie. *A History of the English People in the Nineteenth Century*. Vol. 1. New York: Barnes and Noble, 1961.

Hall, Catherine and Leonore H. Davidoff. *Family Fortunes: Men and Women of the English Middle Class, 1780–1850*. London: Hutchinson, 1987.

Hall, Samuel Carter. *A Book of Memories of Great Men and Women of the Age, from Personal Acquaintance*. London: Virtue and Co., 1871.

Halsband, Robert. *The Complete Letters of Lady Mary Wortley Montagu*. 3 vols. Oxford: Clarendon Press, 1966.

Ham, Elizabeth. *Elizabeth Ham by Herself, 1783–1820*. Introduced and edited by Eric Gillett. London: Faber and Faber, 1945.

Hamalian, Leo. *Ladies on the Loose: Women Travellers of the Eighteenth and Nineteenth Centuries*. New York: Dodd, Mead, 1981.

Hamilton, Elizabeth. *Letters Addressed to the Daughter of a Nobleman on the Formation of the Religious and Moral Principle*. 2 vols. London: Cadell and Davies, 1806. New York: Garland, 1974.

———. *Translation of the Letters of a Hindoo Rajah*. London: J. Walker, 1811.

Hammond, Dorothy and Jablow Alta. *The Africa That Never Was: Four Centuries of British Writing about Africa*. New York: Twayne Publishers, 1970.

Hampson, Norman. *The Enlightenment*. Middlesex: Penguin, 1968.

Handover, P. M. *A History of the London Gazette, 1665–1965*. London: Her Majesty's Stationery Office, 1965.

Hare, August J. C. *The Life and Letters of Maria Edgeworth*. New York: Books for Libraries Press, 1971.

Hargreaves-Mawdsley, W. N. *The English Della Cruscans and Their Time, 1783–1828.* The Hague: Martinus Nijhoff, 1967.

Harlow, Vincent T. *Christopher Codrington, 1668–1710.* Oxford: Clarendon Press, 1928.

———. *Colonising Expeditions to the West Indies and Guiana, 1623–1667.* Second series, no. 56. London: Hakluyt Society, 1925.

———. *A History of Barbados, 1625–1685.* Oxford: Clarendon Press, 1926.

Harvey, A. D. *English Poetry in a Changing Society, 1780–1825.* London: Allison and Busby. New York: St. Martin's Press, 1980.

Harvey, W. W. *Sketches of Hayti.* London: L. B. Seeley and Son, 1827.

Hatch, John. *The History of Britain in Africa from the Fifteenth Century to the Present.* New York: Praeger, 1969.

Hays, Mary. *Appeal to the Men of Great Britain in Behalf of Women.* Reprint. New York: Garland, 1974.

———. *Female Biography; Or, Memoirs of Illustrious and Celebrated Women, of All Ages and Countries.* 6 vols. London: Richard Phillips, 1803.

———. *Letters and Essays, Moral and Miscellaneous.* Reprint. New York: Garland, 1974.

———. *Memoirs of Emma Courtney.* Vols. 1 and 2. Reprint. New York: Garland, 1974.

Hayward, Walter Brownell. *Bermuda Past and Present: A Descriptive and Historical Account of the Somers Islands.* New York: Dodd, Mead, 1911.

Hazard, Paul. *European Thought in the Eighteenth Century.* New Haven: Yale University Press, 1954.

Hecht, J. Jean. *The Domestic and Servant Class in Eighteenth-Century England.* London: Routledge & Kegan Paul, 1956.

Hedge, Mary Ann. *The Solace of an Invalid.* London: J. Hatchard, 1823.

Hedgeland, Isabella Kelly. *A Modern Incident in Domestic Life.* Brentford, 1803.

Heilman, Robert Bechtold. *America in English Fiction, 1760–1800.* Baton Rouge: Louisiana State University Press, 1937.

Heineman, Helen. *Restless Angels: The Friendship of Six Victorian Women.* Athens: Ohio University Press, 1983.

Helme, Elizabeth. *The Farmer of Inglewood Forest.* London: Minerva Press, 1796.

———. *Instructive Rambles in London and Adjacent Villages, Designed to Amuse the Mind and Improve the Understanding of Youth.* 2 vols. London: T. N. Longmans, 1798.

———. *Instructive Rambles Extended in London and the Adjacent Villages, Designed to Amuse the Mind and Improve the Understanding of Youth.* London: Sampson Low, 1800.

————. *Modern Times.* London: A. K. Newman, 1817.

Hemans, Felicia. *The Poetical Works of Mrs. Hemans. With Prefatory Memoirs, Notes, etc.* London: Frederick Warne & Co.

Henretta, James A. *"Salutary Neglect": Colonial Administration under the Duke of Newcastle.* Princeton: Princeton University Press, 1972.

Herford, J. H. *The Personal Life of Josiah Wedgwood the Potter.* London: Macmillan, 1915.

Hersh, Blanche Glassman. *The Slavery of Sex: Feminist-Abolitionists in America.* Urbana: University of Illinois Press, 1978.

Hibbert, Christopher. *Africa Explored: Europeans in the Dark Continent, 1769–1889.* Allen Lane, 1982. Harmondsworth: Penguin, 1984.

Higman, Barry W. *Slave Populations and Economy in Jamaica, 1807–1834.* Cambridge: Cambridge University Press, 1976.

————. *Slave Populations of the British Caribbean, 1807–1834.* Baltimore: The Johns Hopkins University Press, 1984.

————, ed. *Trade, Government, and Society in Caribbean History, 1700–1920: Essays Presented to Douglas Hall.* Kingston, Jamaica, W.I.: Heinemann, 1983.

Hilbish, Florence May Anna. *Charlotte Smith: Poet and Novelist (1749–1806).* Philadelphia: University of Pennsylvania, 1941.

Hill, Bridget. *Eighteenth-Century Women: An Anthology.* London: George Allen & Unwin, 1984.

————. *The First English Feminist.* New York: St. Martin's Press, 1986.

Hill, Christopher. *Milton and The English Revolution.* London: Faber and Faber, 1977.

————. Review of *Working Life of Women in the Seventeenth Century* by Alice Clark. *History Workshop: A Journal of Socialist and Feminist Historians* No. 15 (Spring 1983): 173–76.

————. *Reformation to Industrial Revolution.* London: Penguin, 1967.

Hill, Constance. *Maria Edgeworth and Her Circle in the Days of Buonaparte and Bourbon.* London: John Lane the Bodley Head, 1910.

Hill, George Birkbeck, and L. I. Powell. *Boswell's Life of Johnson.* Vol. 2. Oxford: Clarendon Press, 1934.

Hiro, Dilip. *Black British/White British.* Rev. ed. New York: Monthly Review Press, 1973.

Hoare, Prince. *Memoirs of Granville Sharp.* London: Henry Colburn, 1820.

Hobby, Elaine. *Virtue of Necessity: English Women's Writings 1649–1688.* London: Virago, 1988.

Hobsbawm, E.J. *The Pelican Economic History of Britain.* Vol. 3, *From 1750 to the Present Day: Industry and Empire.* Harmondsworth: Penguin, 1968.

Hofland, Barbara. *The Barbadoes Girl; a Tale for Young People.* London: A. K. Newnan and Co., n.d.

Hogg, Peter C. *The African Slave Trade and Its Suppression: A Classified and Annotated Bibliography of Books, Pamphlets and Periodical Articles.* London: Frank Cass & Co., Inc., 1973.

————. *Slavery: The Afro-American Experience.* British Library Booklets. London: British Library, 1979.

Holcroft, Frances [Fanny]. *Fortitude and Frailty.* London: W. Clowes, 1817.

————. "The Negro." *Monthly Magazine* 4 (October 1797): 286.

Hole, Charles. *Early History of the Church Mission Society for Africa and the East.* London: Church Mission Society, 1896.

Hollis, Patricia, ed. *Pressure from Without in Early Victorian England.* London: Edward Arnold, 1974.

Hollowell, Lillian, ed. *A Book of Children's Literature.* 3rd ed. New York: Holt, Rinehart and Winston, 1966.

Holt, Raymond Vincent. *The Unitarian Contribution.* London: George Allen & Unwin, 1938.

Homans, Margaret. *Bearing the Word: Language and Female Experience in Nineteenth-Century Women's Writing.* Chicago: University of Chicago Press, 1986.

Honeychurch, Lennox. *The Dominica Story: A Story of the Island.* Self-published. 1975.

Hopkins, Mary Alden. *Hannah More and Her Circle.* New York: Longman, 1947.

Hornemann, Friedrich. *Missions to the Niger.* Cambridge: Cambridge University Press, 1964.

Hotson, John Leslie. *The Commonwealth and Restoration Stage.* Cambridge: Harvard University Press, 1928.

Howard, C., ed. *West African Explorers.* The World's Classics. London: Oxford University Press, 1951.

Howard, Thomas. *Black Voyage.* Boston: Little, Brown, 1971.

Howitt, Mary. *Mary Howitt: An Autobiography.* Edited by Margaret Howitt. 2 vols. London: William Isbister, 1889.

Howitt, William. *Colonization and Christianity: A Popular History of Treatment of the Natives by the Europeans in All Their Colonies.* New York: Negro University Press, 1969.

Howse, Ernest Marshall. *Saints in Politics: The "Clapham Sect" and the Growth of Freedom.* Toronto: University of Toronto Press, 1952.

Huchon, R. *Mrs. Montagu, 1720–1800.* London: Murray, 1907.

Hughes, Helen Sard. *The Gentle Hertford: Her Life and Letters.* New York: Macmillan, 1940.

Hume, David. *Essays Moral, Political and Literary.* 2 vols. London: Longmans, Green, 1889.

Hurwitz, Edith F. *Politics and the Public Conscience: Slave Emancipation and the Abolitionist Movement in Britain.* London: George Allen & Unwin, 1973.

Husband, Charles, ed. *"Race" in Britain: Continuity and Change.* London: Hutchinson, 1982.

Hutton, Catherine. *Tour of Africa. Containing a Concise Account of All the Countries in That Quarter of the Globe, Hitherto Visited by Europeans; with the Manners and Customs of The Inhabitants. Selected From the Best Authors, and Arranged by Catherine Hutton.* Vol. 2. London: Baldwin, Cradock and Joy, Paternoster Row, 1821.

Hutton, J. E. *A History of Moravian Missions.* London: Moravian Publications Office, 1909.

Idowu, E. Bolaji. *African Traditional Religion: A Definition.* London: SCM, 1973.

———. *Olodumare: God in Yoruba Belief.* New York: Praeger, 1973.

Imlay, Gilbert. *Topographical Description of the Western Territory of North America.* 1797. New York: Johnson Reprint Corporation, 1968.

Inchbald, Elizabeth. *Nature and Art.* 2 vols. London: G. and J. Robinson, 1796.

———. *A Simple Story.* Edited by J. M. S. Tompkins. London: Oxford University Press, 1967.

Institute of Race Relations. *Book One: Roots of Racism* and *Book Two: Patterns of Racism.* London: Institute of Race Relations, 1982. *Book Three: How Racism Came to Britain.* Cartoons by Christine Smith. London: Institute of Race Relations, 1985.

Irwin, Joyce L. *Womanhood in Radical Protestantism, 1525–1675.* New York: Edwin Mellen Press, 1979.

Isichei, Elizabeth. *Victorian Quakers.* Oxford Historical Monographs, edited by N. Gibbs, et al. London: Oxford University Press, 1970.

Ives, Vernon A. *The Rich Papers: Letters from Bermuda, 1615–1646.* Toronto: University of Toronto Press, 1984.

Jahn, Janheinz. *Neo-African Literature: A History of Black Writing.* Translated by Oliver Coburn and Ursula Lehrburger. New York: Grove Press, 1968.

Jakobsson, Stiv. *Am I Not a Man and a Brother? British Missions and the Abolition of the Slave Trade and Slavery in West Africa and the West Indies, 1786–1838.* Studia Missionalia Upsaliensia 17. Uppsala, Sweden: Gleerup, 1972.

James, C. L. R. *The Black Jacobins: Toussaint L'Ouverture and the San Domingo Revolution.* New York: Vintage, 1963.

James, William. *The Naval History of Great Britain.* London: Richard Bentley, 1837.

JanMohamed, Abdul. *Manichean Aesthetics: The Politics of Literature in Colonial Africa.* Amherst: University of Massachusetts Press, 1983.

Jay, Elizabeth. *The Religion of the Heart: Anglican Evangelicalism and the Nineteenth-Century Novel.* Oxford: Clarendon Press, 1979.

Jelinek, Estelle C. *The Tradition of Women's Autobiography: From Antiquity to the Present.* Boston: Twayne Publishers, G.K. Hall, 1986.

————. *Women's Autobiography.* Bloomington: Indiana University Press, 1980.

Jerdan, William. *The Autobiography of William Jerdan.* Vol. 1. London: Arthur Hall, Virtue and Co., 1852.

Johnson, Dale A. *Women in English Religion, 1700–1925.* Studies in Women and Religion, vol. 10. New York: Edwin Mellen Press, 1983.

Johnson, Reginald Brimley, ed. *Bluestocking Letters.* London: John Lane, the Bodley Head, 1926.

————, ed. *The Letters of Hannah More.* New York: Dial Press, Doubleday & Company, 1925.

Jones, Jacqueline. *Labor of Love, Labor of Sorrow: Black Women, Work, and the Family from Slavery to the Present.* New York: Basic Books, 1985.

Jones, Mary. *Miscellanies in Prose and Verse.* Oxford: Dodsley, 1750.

Jones, M.G. *The Charity School Movement.* Cambridge: Cambridge University Press, 1938.

————. *Hannah More.* Cambridge: Cambridge University Press, 1952.

Jones, Rufus. *The Later Period of Quakerism.* 2 vols. London: Macmillan, 1921.

Jordan, Winthrop D. *White Over Black: American Attitudes Toward the Negroes, 1550–1812.* Chapel Hill: University of North Carolina Press, 1968.

Jorns, Auguste. *The Quakers as Pioneers in Social Work.* Translated by Thomas Kite Brown, Jr. New York: Macmillan, 1931.

The Journal of Negro History, ed. Carter G. Woodson. *Documents:* "Eighteenth Century Slaves as Advertized by Their Masters," Vol. 1. Lancaster, PA: The Association of the Study of Negro Life and History, Inc., 1916.

Kanner, Barbara. *The Women of England: From Anglo-Saxon Times to the Present.* Hamden, CT: Archon Books, 1979.

Kaplan, Cora. *Sea Changes: Essays on Culture and Feminism.* London: Verso, 1986.

Kelly, Gary. *The English Jacobin Novel, 1780–1805.* Oxford: Clarendon Press, 1976.

Kesteloot, Lilyan. *Black Writers in French: A Literary History of Negritude.* Translated by Ellen Conroy Kennedy. Philadelphia: Temple University Press, 1974.

Kestner, Joseph. *Protest and Reform. The British Social Narrative by Women 1827–1867.* Madison: University of Wisconsin Press, 1985.

Kilham, Hannah. *The Claims of West Africa.* London: Harvey and Darton, 1830.

———. *Memoirs of the Late H. K.* London: Harvey and Darton, 1837.

Kilner, Dorothy. *The Rotchfords; Or, the Friendly Counsellor. Designed for the Instruction and Amusement of the Youth of Both Sexes.* Two volumes in One. From the London Copy [of 1786]. Philadelphia: J. Humphreys, 1801.

Kilson, Martin L., and Robert I. Rotberg, eds. *The African Diaspora: Interpretive Essays.* Cambridge: Harvard University Press, 1976.

King, James, and Charles Ryskamp, eds. *The Letters and Prose Writings of William Cowper.* Oxford: Clarendon Press, 1982.

Klein, Herbert S. *The Middle Passage: Comparative Studies in the Atlantic Slave Trade.* Princeton: Princeton University Press, 1978.

Klingberg, Frank Joseph. *The Anti-Slavery Movement in England: A Study in English Humanitarianism.* New Haven: Yale University Press, 1926.

———. *Codrington Chronicle: An Experiment in Anglican Altruism on a Barbados Plantation, 1710–1834.* Berkeley and Los Angeles: University of California Press, 1949.

Knapp, Oswald G., ed. *The Intimate Letters of Hester Piozzi and Penelope Pennington, 1788–1821.* London: John Lane, the Bodley Head, 1914.

Knutsford, Viscountess. *Life and Letters of Zachary Macaulay.* London: Edward Arnold, 1900.

Kojève, Alexander. *Introduction to the Reading of Hegel: Lectures on the Phenomenology of Spirit.* Assembled by Raymond Queneau, edited by Allan Bloom, translated from the French by James H. Nichols, Jr. New York: Basic Books, 1969.

Koon, Helen. *Colly Cibber: A Biography.* Lexington: University Press of Kentucky, 1986.

Korshin, Paul J. *Typologies in England, 1656–1820.* Princeton: Princeton University Press, 1982.

Laing, Major Alexander Gordon. *Missions to the Niger.* Vol. 1. Cambridge: Cambridge University Press, 1964.

Landon, Laetitia [L.E.L]. *The Zenana and Minor Poems by L.E.L.* With a Memoir by Emma Roberts. London: Fisher, Son, & Co. Paris: Quai de l'Ecole, 1961.

Landry, Donna. *The Muses of Resistance: Working-Class Women's Poetry in Britain 1739–1796.* Cambridge: Cambridge University Press, 1990.

Lanternari, Vittorio. *The Religions of the Oppressed: A Study of Modern Messianic Cults.* Trans. by Lisa Sergio. London: Macgibbon & Kee, 1963.

Laqueur, Thomas Walter. *Religion and Respectability: Sunday Schools and*

Working Class Culture, 1780–1850. New Haven: Yale University Press, 1976.

Larner, Christina. *Enemies of God: The Witch-hunt in Scotland.* Baltimore: The Johns Hopkins University Press, 1981.

Lascelles, E. C. P. *Granville Sharp and The Freedom of Slaves in England.* Oxford: Oxford University Press, 1928.

Leach, Robert J. *Women Ministers: A Quaker Contribution.* Edited by Ruth Blattenberger. Pendle Hill Pamphlet 227. n.p.: Pendle Hill, 1979.

Le Breton, Anna Letitia. *Memoir of Mrs. Barbauld, Including Letters and Notices of Her Family and Friends.* London: George Bell and Sons, 1874.

Lee, Amice. *Laurels and Rosemary; Life of William and Mary Howitt.* London: Oxford, 1955.

Leishman, James Fleming. *A Son of Knox: And Other Studies Antiquarian and Biographical.* Glasgow: James Maclehose and Sons, Publishers to the University, 1909.

Leopold, Richard William. *Robert Dale Owen: A Biography.* New York: Octagon Books, 1969.

Lerner, Gerda. *The Majority Finds Its Past: Placing Women in History.* New York: Oxford University Press, 1979.

L'Estrange, Rev. A. G. *The Friendships of Mary Russell Mitford.* 2 vols. London: Hurst and Blackett, 1882.

Lewis, Gordon K. *Main Currents in Caribbean Thought: The Historical Evolution of Caribbean Society in Its Ideological Aspects, 1492–1900.* Baltimore: The Johns Hopkins University Press, 1983.

———. *Slavery, Imperialism, and Freedom: Studies in English Radical Thought.* New York: Monthly Review Press, 1978.

Lewis, N. B. *The Abolitionist Movement in Sheffield, 1823–1833. With Letters from Southey, Wordsworth, and Others.* From the Original Papers in the John Rylands Library. Manchester, 1934.

Lewis, W. S. *Horace Walpole's Correspondence.* London: Oxford University Press, and New Haven: Yale University Press, 1973.

Ligon, Richard. *A True and Exact History of the Island of Barbados.* London: Humphrey Moseley, 1657.

Lincoln, Anthony. *Some Political and Social Ideas of English Dissent, 1763–1800.* 1938. Reprint. New York: Farrar, Straus and Giroux, 1971.

Litchfield, Henrietta Emma (Darwin). *Emma Darwin: A Century of Family Letters.* 2 vols. New York: D. Appleton & Co., 1915.

Lloyd, Arnold. *Quaker Social History 1669–1738.* London: Longmans, Green, and Co., 1950.

Lloyd, Christopher. *The Navy and the Slave Trade: The Suppression of the*

African Slave Trade in the Nineteenth Century. London: Longmans, Green and Co., 1949.

Lloyd, Helen. *Amelia: The Tale of a Plain Friend.* Oxford: Oxford University Press, 1937.

Lloyd, Susette Harriet. *Sketches of Bermuda.* London: James Cochrane, 1835.

Lobban, J. H. ed. *Dr. Johnson's Mrs. Thrale. Autobiography, Letters and Literary Remains of Mrs. Piozzi, Edited by A. Hayward, Q.C., [1861] Newly Selected and Edited, with Introduction and Notes.* Edinburgh and London: T. N. Foulis, 1910.

Loewenberg, Bert James, and Ruth Bogin, eds. *Black Women in Nineteenth-Century American Life: Their Words, Their Thoughts, Their Feelings.* University Park: Pennsylvania State University Press, 1976.

Long, Edward. *The History of Jamaica, or General Survey of the Antient and Modern State of That Island: With Reflections on its Situations, Settlements, Inhabitants, Climate, Products, Commerce, Laws and Government,* new edition with introduction by George Metcalf. 3 vols., vol. 2. 1st ed. 1774; Frank Cass & Co., Ltd., 1970.

Lorimer, Douglas A. *Colour, Class, and the Victorians: English Attitudes to the Negro in the mid-nineteenth century.* London: Leicester University Press, 1978.

Luder, Hope Elizabeth. *Women and Quakerism.* Pendle Hill Pamphlet 196. n.p.: Pendle Hill, 1974.

MacCarthy, B. G. *The Female Pen: The Later Women Novelists, 1744–1818.* Cork, Ire.: Cork University Press, 1947.

————. *Women Writers and Their Contribution to the English Novel, 1621–1744.* Cork, Ire.: Cork University Press, 1944.

MacCoby, S. *The English Radical Tradition, 1763–1914.* London: Kaye, 1952.

MacDonell, Diane. *Theories of Discourse: An Introduction.* Glasgow: Dell and Bain, 1986.

Macfarlane, Alan. *Marriage and Love in England. Modes of Reproduction 1300–1840.* Oxford: Basil Blackwell, 1986.

Macherey, Pierre. *A Theory of Literary Production.* Translated by Geoffrey Wall. London: Routledge & Kegan Paul, 1978.

Mackenzie-Grieve, Averil. *The Great Accomplishment.* London: Richard Clay, 1953.

————. *The Last Years of the English Slave Trade: Liverpool 1750–1807.* London: Frank Cass & Co., 1941. Reprints of Economic Classics. New York: Augustus M. Kelley, 1968.

Madden, R. R. *The Literary Life and Correspondence of the Countess of Bessington.* Vols. 1 and 2. New York: Harper and Brothers, 1855.

Malmgreen, Gail, ed. *Religion in the Lives of English Women, 1760–1930.* Bloomington: University of Indiana Press, 1986.

Manners, Emily. *Elizabeth Hooton: First Quaker Women Preacher (1600–1672)* in *The Journal of Friends Historical Society,* ed. Norman Penney, Supp. 12. London: Headly Brothers, 1914.

Mannix, Daniel P., and Malcolm Cowley. *Black Cargoes: A History of the Atlantic Slave Trade, 1518–1865.* New York: Viking, 1962.

Mannoni, Octavio. *Prospero and Caliban: The Psychology of Colonisation.* New York, 1956.

Marshall, Madeleine Forell and Janet Todd. *English Congregational Hymns in the Eighteenth Century.* Lexington: University Press of Kentucky, 1982.

Marshall, Peter. *The Anti-Slave Trade Movement in Bristol.* Bristol: Bristol Branch of the Historical Association, 1968.

Marshall, Rosalind K. *Virgins and Viragos: A History of Women in Scotland from 1080 to 1980.* Chicago: Academy Chicago, 1983.

Martin, Eveline Christiana. *The British West African Settlements, 1750–1821.* London: Longman, 1927.

Martineau, Harriet. *Biographical Sketches.* New York: Leypoldt and Holt, 1869.

———. *Harriet Martineau's Autobiography.* 2 vols. 4th ed. Edited by Maria Weston Chapman. Boston: Houghton, 1879.

———. *Harriet Martineau's Letters to Fanny Wedgwood.* Edited by Elisabeth Sanders. Palo Alto: Stanford University Press, 1983.

———. *Harriet Martineau on Women.* Edited by Gayle Graham Yates. New Brunswick, NJ: Rutgers University Press, 1985.

———. *The Hour and the Man.* Vols. 1–3. London: Moxon, 1861.

———. *Illustrations of Political Economy.* London, Boston: Fox, 1832–34.

Mason, John Hope. *The Indispensable Rousseau.* London: Quartet Books, 1979.

Mason, Julian D., Jr., ed. *The Poems of Phillis Wheatley.* Chapel Hill: University of North Carolina Press, 1966.

Mathieson, William Law. *British Slavery and Its Abolition, 1823–1838.* New York: Octagon Books, 1967.

Mathurin, Lucille. *The Rebel Woman in the British West Indies During Slavery.* Jamaica, W.I.: Institute of Jamaica Publications, 1975.

Mbiti, John S. *African Religions and Philosophy.* New York: Praeger, 1969.

McBurney, William H. *Four Before Richardson: Selected English Novels, 1720–1727.* Lincoln: University of Nebraska Press, 1963.

McCann, Phillip, ed. *Popular Education and Socialization in the Nineteenth Century.* London: Methuen, 1977.

McCarthy, William. *Hester Thrale Piozzi.* Chapel Hill: University of North Carolina Press, 1985.

McCloy, Shelby. *The Humanitarian Movement in Eighteenth-Century France.* Lexington: University Press of Kentucky, 1957.

McCulloch, Samuel Clyde, ed. *British Humanitarianism: Essays Honoring Frank J. Klingberg.* Philadelphia: Church Historical Society, 1950.

McEwan, P. J. M., ed. *Nineteenth-Century Africa.* Readings in African History, edited by P.J.M. McEwan. London: Oxford University Press, 1968.

McGregor, J. F., and B. Reay, eds. *Radical Religion in the English Revolution.* Oxford: Oxford University Press, 1984.

McKee, William. "Elizabeth Inchbald, Novelist." Ph.D. Dissertation. Washington, D.C.: Catholic University of America, 1935.

McKeon, Michael. *The Origins of the English Novel, 1600–1740.* Baltimore: The Johns Hopkins University Press, 1988.

McLachlan, Herbert John. *The Unitarian Movement in Religious Life of England.* London: Allen and Unwin Ltd., 1934.

McLeod, Lyons. *Madagascar and Its People.* London: Longmans, Green and Co., 1865.

McPherson, James M., and William Loren Katz, advisory eds. *The Legion of Liberty and Force of Truth.* New York: Arno Press, 1969.

Meacham, Standish. *Henry Thornton of Clapham, 1760–1815.* Cambridge: Harvard University Press, 1964.

Meakin, Annette M. B. *Hannah More: A Biographical Study.* London: Smith, Elder, 1911.

Meigs, Cornelia, Anne Thaxter Eaton, Elizabeth Nesbitt, and Ruth Hill Viguers. *A Critical History of Children's Literature: A Survey of Children's Books in English.* Rev. ed. London: Macmillan, 1969.

Mellor, G. R. *British Imperial Trusteeship, 1783–1850.* London: Faber, 1951.

Memmi, Albert. *The Colonizer and the Colonized.* New York: Orion, 1965.

Menzies-Wilson, Jacobine. *Amelia: The Tale of a Plain Friend.* Oxford: Oxford University Press, 1937.

Mesick, Jane Louise. *The English Traveller in America, 1785–1835.* New York: Columbia University Press, 1922.

Messenger, Ann. *His and Hers.* Lexington: University Press of Kentucky, 1986.

Midgeley, Claire. *Women Against the Slave Trade, 1787–1823.* Ph.D. Dissertation. University of Kent at Canterbury, 1989.

Miller, Christopher L. *Blank Darkness: Africanist Discourse in French.* Chicago: University of Chicago Press, 1985.

Mineka, Francis Edward. *The Dissidence of Dissent.* Chapel Hill: University of North Carolina Press, 1944.

Mintz, Sidney. *Caribbean Transformations*. Chicago: Aldine, 1974.

———. *Sweetness and Power: The Place of Sugar in Modern History*. New York: Viking, 1985.

Mintz, Sidney W., and Sally Price, eds. *Caribbean Contours*. Johns Hopkins Studies in Atlantic History and Culture. Baltimore: The Johns Hopkins University Press, 1985.

Mitford, Mary Russell. *The Friendships of Mary Russell Mitford: As Recorded in Letters from Her Literary Correspondents*. Edited by A. G. L'Estrange. Vols. 1 and 2. London: Hurst and Blackett, 1882.

Mocquet, John. *Travels and Voyages into Africa, Asia, and America, the East and West Indies; Syria, Jerusalem, and the Holy-Land. Performed by Mr. John Mocquet, Keeper of the Cabinet of Rarities, to the King of France, in the Tuilleries. Divided into Six Books, and Enriched with Sculptures*, trans. from the French by Nathaniel Pullen. London: William Newton, Joseph Shelton, William Changler, 1696. 1st ed. *Voyages en Afrique, Asie, Indes orientales et occidentales*, Paris, 1612.

Mohanty, Chandra Talpade, Ann Russo, and Lourdes Torres, eds. *Third World Women and the Politics of Feminism*. Bloomington: Indiana University Press, 1991.

Moi, Toril. *Sexual/Textual Politics: Feminist Literary Theory*. London: Methuen, 1985.

———, ed. *French Feminist Thought: A Reader*. Oxford: Basil Blackwell, 1987.

Montagu, Elizabeth. *The Letters of Mrs. Elizabeth Montagu*, ed. Matthew Montagu. Vol. 6. London: T. Cadell and W. Davies, 1813.

Montesquieu, Baron de. *The Spirit of the Laws. With an Introduction by Franz Neumann*, trans. Thomas Nugent. New York and London: Hafner Publishing Company, 1966.

Montgomery, Henry R. *Memoirs of the Life and Writings of Sir Richard Steele*. 2 vols. 1865. Reprint. New York: Haskell House, 1971.

Montgomery, James. *Poetical Works of James Montgomery*. Boston: Phillips, Sampson, 1854.

Moorehead, Alan. *The Fatal Impact: An Account of the Invasion of the South Pacific, 1767–1840*. New York: Harper and Row, 1966.

Moorman, Mary. *William Wordsworth: The Early Years, 1770–1803*. Oxford: Clarendon Press, 1967.

More, Hannah. *Slavery: A Poem*. London: Thomas Cadell, 1788.

Muir, Percy. *English Children's Books, 1600–1900*. New York: Praeger, 1954.

Myers, Sylvia Harcstark. *The Bluestocking Circle. Women, Friendship, and the Life of the Mind in Eighteenth-Century England*. Oxford: Clarendon Press, 1990.

Nangle, Benjamin Christie. *The Monthly Review, First Series, 1749–1789: In-*

dexes of Contributors and Articles. Oxford: Clarendon Press, 1934. *Second Series, 1790–1815: Indexes of Contributors and Articles.* Oxford: Clarendon Press, 1955.

Nelson, Cary, and Lawrence Grossberg. *Marxism and the Interpretation of Culture.* Urbana: University of Illinois Press, 1988.

Newton, Judith Lowder. *Women, Power, and Subversion: Social Strategies in British Fiction, 1778–1860.* Athens: University of Georgia Press, 1981.

Newton, Judith and Deborah Rosenfelt, eds. *Feminist Criticism and Social Change. Sex, Class and Race in Literature and Culture.* New York and London: Methuen, 1985.

Nichols, Charles H. *Many Thousand Gone: The Ex-Slaves' Account of Their Bondage and Freedom.* Leiden: E. J. Brill, 1963.

Nichols, Reginald Hugh, and F. A. Wray. *The History of the Foundling Hospital.* London: Oxford University Press, 1935.

Norris, Robert. *Memoirs of the Reign of Bossa Ahadee, King of Dahomy.* 1789. Reprint. London: Frank Cass & Co., Inc., 1968.

Northcott, Cecil. *Slavery's Martyr: John Smith of Demerara and the Emancipation Movement, 1817–1824.* London: Epworth, 1976.

Nuermberger, Ruth Ketring. *The Free Produce Movement: A Quaker Protest Against Slavery.* Durham, NC: Duke University Press, 1942.

Nussbaum, Felicity A. *The Brink of All We Hate: English Satires on Women, 1660–1750.* Lexington: University Press of Kentucky, 1984.

Nussbaum, Felicity, and Laura Brown, eds. *The New Eighteenth Century: Theory, Politics, English Literature.* New York: Methuen, 1987.

Oakes, C. G. *Sir Samuel Romilly, 1757–1818.* London: George Allen & Unwin, 1935.

Odom, William. *Fifty Years of Sheffield Church Life, 1866–1916.* Sheffield: J. W. Northend, 1917.

O'Donnell, Mary Ann. *Aphra Behn: An Annotated Bibliography of Primary and Secondary Sources.* New York: Garland, 1986.

Oliver, Grace A. *The Story of the Life of Anna Laetitia Barbauld.* Boston: Cupples, 1886.

Oliver, Roland, and Anthony Atmore. *Africa Since 1800.* 2nd ed. Cambridge: Cambridge University Press, 1972.

Oliver, Roland, and J. D. Fage. *A Short History of Africa.* 2nd ed. Penguin American Library, edited by Ronald Segal. Middlesex: Penguin, 1966.

Oliver, Roland, and Caroline Oliver, eds. *Africa in the Days of Exploration.* Englewood Cliffs: Prentice-Hall, 1965.

Oliver, W. H. *Prophets and Millenialists: The Uses of Biblical Prophecy in*

England from the 1790s to the 1840s. New Zealand: Auckland University Press, 1978.

O'Malley, I. B. *Women in Subjection.* London: Duckworth, 1933.

Opie, Amelia Alderson. "The Negro Boy's Tale: A Poem Addressed to Children." London: Harvey & Darton, 1824.

———. "The Black Man's Lament." London, 1826.

———. *The Warriors Return, and Other Poems.* London: Longman, 1808.

———. *The Works of Mrs. Amelia Opie.* 3 vols. Philadelphia: James Crissey, 1843. Reprint. Women of Letters series. New York: AMS Press Inc., 1974.

Osofsky, Gilbert. *Puttin' on Ole Massa.* New York: Harper and Row, 1817.

Owen, David. *English Philanthropy, 1660–1960.* Cambridge: Belknap Press of Harvard University Press, 1964.

Packwood, Cyril. *Chained on the Rock.* New York: E. Torres, 1975.

Pagliaro, Harold E., ed. *Racism in the Eighteenth Century.* Studies of Eighteenth-Century Culture, vol. 2. Cleveland: Case Western Reserve University Press, 1973.

Park, Mungo. *Travels into the Interior of Africa.* With a New Preface by Jeremy Swift. London: J. M. Dent, 1954. Reprint. London: Eland Books, 1983.

Parkinson, Wenda. *"This Gilded African": Toussaint L'Ouverture.* London: Quartet Books, 1980.

The Parliamentary History of England from the Earliest Period to the Year 1803. Vols. 26–29. London: Longman, Hurst, Rees, Orme and Brown, with other publishers, 1816.

Patterson, Orlando. *Ethnic Chauvinism: The Reactionary Impulse.* New York: Stein and Day, 1977.

———. *Slavery and Social Death: A Comparative Study.* Cambridge: Harvard University Press, 1982.

Paulson, Ronald. *The Art of Hogarth.* London: Phaidon, 1975.

Peacock, Lucy. *The Creole* in *The New Novelists Magazine; or, Entertaining Library of Pleasing and Instructive Histories, Tales, Adventures, Romances, and Other Agreeable and Exemplary Little Novels.* Vol. 2. London: Harrison and Sons, 1787.

Pearson, Hesketh, ed. *The Swan of Litchfield (Anna Seward).* New York: Oxford University Press, 1937.

Penney, Norman. *The Journal of George Fox.* London: J. M. Dent and Sons, 1924.

Pennington, Rev. Montagu. *A Series of Letters Between Mrs. Elizabeth Carter and Miss Catherine Talbot, from the Years 1741–1770.* 4 vols. London: F. C. and J. Rivington, 1809.

Perkins, A. J. G., and Theresa Wolfson. *Frances Wright, Free Enquirer: The Study of a Temperament.* New York: Harper and Brothers, 1939.

Perkins, Erasmus, ed. *The Trial of the Rev. Robert Wedderburn (a Dissenting Minister of the Unitarian Persuasion) for Blasphemy, Before Sir Abbott, Knight, Lord Chief-Justice. . . .Containing a Verbatim Report of the Defence.* London: W. Mason, 1820.

Perry, John W. *Charles James Fox.* New York: St. Martin's, 1972.

Perry, Ruth. *The Celebrated Mary Astell: An Early English Feminist.* Women in Culture and Society series, edited by Catharine R. Stimpson. Chicago: University of Chicago Press, 1986.

————. *Women, Letters and the Novel.* New York: AMS Press, Inc., 1980.

Petersen, Kirsten Holst. *A Double Colonization: Colonial and Post-Colonial Women's Writing.* Denmark: Dangaroo, 1986.

Phillips, Catherine Payton. *Memoirs of the Life of Catherine Phillips.* London: J. Phillips, 1797.

————. *Reasons Why People Called Quakers Cannot So Fully Unite.* 22 pp. London: J. Phillips, 1792.

Pickering, Samuel F., Jr. *John Locke and Children's Books in Eighteenth-Century England.* Knoxville: University of Tennessee Press, 1981.

————. *The Moral Tradition in English Fiction, 1785–1850.* Hanover: New England University Press, 1976.

Plimmer, Charlotte, and Denis Plimmer. *Slavery: The Anglo-American Involvement.* Illustrated Sources in History series. New York: Barnes & Noble, 1973.

Plumb, J. H. *England in the Eighteenth Century.* The Pelican History of England. Baltimore: Penguin, 1950. Reprinted with rev. bibliography, 1963.

————. *The Origins of Political Stability, England 1675–1725.* Boston: Houghton Mifflin, 1967.

Podmore, Frank. *Robert Owen: A Biography.* Vol. 1. London: Hutchinson, 1906.

Pollak, Ellen. *The Poetics of Sexual Myth: Gender and Ideology in the Verse of Swift and Pope.* Women in Culture and Society series, edited by Catharine R. Stimpson. Chicago: University of Chicago Press, 1985.

Pollard, Sidney. *A History of Labour in Sheffield.* Liverpoool: Liverpool University Press, 1959.

Polwhele, Richard. *The Unsex'd Females.* Radcliffe, Mary Ann. *The Female Advocate.* 2 works in 1 vol. New York: Garland, 1974.

Poovey, Mary. *The Proper Lady and the Woman Writer: Ideology as Style in the Works of Mary Wollstonecraft, Mary Shelley, and Jane Austen.* Chicago: University of Chicago Press, 1985.

Pope-Hennessy, Una. *Agnes Strickland.* London: Chatto and Windus, 1940.

Porter, Anna Maria. *Ballads, Romances and Other Poems.* London: Longman, Hurst, Rees, Orme, and Brown, 1811.

Porter, Charles A. *Restif's Novels; Or, an Autobiography in Search of an Author.* Yale Romanic Studies, Second Series, no. 16. New Haven: Yale University Press, 1967.

Porter, Dale H. *The Abolition of the Slave Trade in England, 1784–1807.* n.p.: Archon Books, 1970.

Porter, Roy. *English Society in the Eighteenth Century.* Harmondsworth, Middlesex: Penguin, 1982.

Porteus, Beilby. *A sermon preached before the Incorporated Society for the Propagation of the Gospel in Foreign Parts, at their anniversary meeting in the parish church of St. Mary-Le-Bow, on Friday, February 21, 1783.* London, 1783.

———. *An Essay towards a plan for the more effectual civilization and conversion of the negro slaves on the trust estate in Barbados, belonging to the Society for the Propagation of the Gospel in Foreign Parts.* London, 1817.

Price, Lawrence Marsden. *Inkle and Yarico Album.* Berkeley and Los Angeles: University of California Press, 1937.

Price, Richard. *The Guiana Maroons: A Historical and Bibliographical Introduction.* Baltimore: The Johns Hopkins University Press, 1976.

———. *Maroon Societies: Rebel Slave Communities in the Americas.* Garden City, NY: Anchor Books, 1973.

Prince, Mary. *The History of Mary Prince, a West Indian Slave;* related by herself; with a supplement by the editor; to which is added The Narrative of Asa-Asa, a captured African; London: published by F. Westley and A. H. Davis, Stationer's Hall Court; and by Waugh and Innes, Edinburgh, 1831.

———. *The History of Mary Prince.* London: Pandora Press, 1986.

———. *The History of Mary Prince* in *The Classic Slave Narratives.* New York: Mentor, 1987.

Prior, Mary. *Women in English Society, 1500–1800.* London: Methuen, 1985.

Prochaska, F. K. *Women and Philanthropy in Nineteenth-Century England.* Oxford: Clarendon Press, 1980.

Pryse, Marjorie, and Hortense J. Spillers, eds. *Conjuring: Black Women, Fiction, and Literary Tradition.* Bloomington: Indiana University Press, 1985.

Quarles, Benjamin. *Black Abolitionists.* New York: Oxford University Press, 1969.

Quayle, Eric. *The Collector's Book of Children's Books.* New York: Potter, 1971.

———. *Early Children's Books.* Totowa, NJ: Barnes & Noble, 1983.

Quinault, R., and J. Stevenson. *Popular Protest and Public Order.* New York: St. Martin's, 1974.

Quinlan, Maurice J. *Victorian Prelude: A History of English Manners, 1700–1830.* New York: Columbia University Press, 1941.

Radford, Jean, ed. *The Progress of Romance: The Politics of Popular Fiction.* History Workshop series, edited by Raphael Samuel. London: Routledge & Kegan Paul, 1986.

Ragatz, Lowell Joseph. *The Fall of the Planter Class in the British Caribbean, 1763–1833.* New York: Century, 1928.

———. *A Guide for the Study of British Caribbean History, 1763–1834, including the Abolition and Emancipation Movements.* Washington, D.C.: United States Government Printing Office, 1932.

Ramchand, Kenneth, comp. *West Indian Narrative: An Introductory Anthology.* Rev. ed. Surrey: Thomas Nelson and Sons, 1980.

———. *The West Indian Novel and Its Background.* New York: Barnes & Noble, 1970.

Ramdin, Ron. *From Chattel Slave to Wage Earner: A History of Trade Unionism in Trinidad and Tobago.* London: Martin Brian and O'Keefe, 1982.

Ramsay, James. *An Inquiry into the Effects of Putting a Stop to the African Slave Trade, and of Granting Liberty to the Slaves in the British Sugar Colonies.* London: J. Phillips, 1784.

Ramsey, R. *Objections to the Abolition of the Slave Trade, with Answers.* Reprint. Miami: Mnemosyne, 1969.

Rawson, Mary Anne. *The Bow in the Cloud; Or, the Negro's Memorial.* London: Jackson and Walford, 1834.

Regal, Samuel J. *Sisters of Sacred Song.* New York: Garland, 1981.

Renfro, G. Herbert. *Life and Works of Phillis Wheatley.* Washington, D.C.: Robert L. Pendleton, 1969.

Reynolds, Edward. *Stand the Storm: A History of the Atlantic Slave Trade.* New York: Allison and Busby, 1985.

Rice, C. Duncan, ed. *The Rise and Fall of Black Slavery.* New York: Harper and Row, 1975.

———. *The Scots Abolitionists, 1833–1861.* Baton Rouge: Louisiana State University Press, 1981.

Richard, Henry. *Memoirs of Joseph Sturge.* London: S. W. Partridge, 1864.

Richardson, Marilyn, ed. *Maria Stewart: America's First Black Woman Political Writer—Essays and Speeches.* Blacks in the Diaspora series, edited by Darlene Clark Hine and John McClusky, Jr. Bloomington: Indiana University Press, 1987.

Richmond, Merle A. *Bid the Vassal Soar: Interpretive Essays on the Life and*

Poetry of Phillis Wheatley and George Moses Horton. Washington, D.C.: Howard University Press, 1974.

Ripley, C. Peter, ed. *The Black Abolitionist Papers.* Vol. 1. Chapel Hill: University of North Carolina Press, 1985.

Ritson, Joseph. *The Romance of Primitive Methodism.* London: E. Dalton, 1909.

Roach, John. *Social Reform in England, 1780–1880.* London: B. T. Batsford, 1978.

Robbins, Caroline. *The Eighteenth-Century Commonwealthman: Studies in the Transmission, Development and Circumstance of English Liberal Thought from the Restoration of Charles II until the War with the Thirteen Colonies.* Cambridge: Harvard University Press, 1961.

Roberts, Samuel. *The Negro's Friend; Or, the Sheffield Anti-Slavery Album.* Sheffield: J. Blackwell, 1826.

Roberts, William. *Memoirs of the Life and Correspondence of Mrs. Hannah More.* 2 vols. New York: Harper and Bros., 1855.

Robertson, Claire C., and Martin A. Klein, eds. *Women and Slavery in Africa.* Madison: University of Wisconsin Press, 1983.

Robinson, Henry Crabb. *Henry Crabb Robinson on Books and Their Writers.* Vols. 1–3. Edited by Edith J. Morley. London: J. M. Dent, 1938.

Robinson, Mary Darby. *Lyrical Tales.* London: T. N. Longman and O. Rees, 1800.

———. *The Political Works of the Late Mrs. Mary Robinson: including many Pieces Never Before Published in Three Volumes.* Vol. 1. London: Richard Phillips, 1806, p. 26.

———. *Poems.* 3 vols. London: T. N. Longman and O. Rees, 1810.

Robinson, William H. *Critical Essays on Phillis Wheatley.* Boston: G. K. Hall, 1982.

———. *Phillis Wheatley and Her Writings.* Critical Studies on Black Life and Culture, edited by Henry Louis Gates, Jr. New York: Garland, 1984.

———. *Phillis Wheatley in the Black American Beginnings.* Detroit: Broadside Press, 1975.

Rodgers, Betsy. *Cloak of Charity: Studies in Eighteenth-Century Philanthropy.* London: Methuen, 1949.

Rodney, Walter. *West Africa and the Atlantic Slave Trade.* Nairobi: East African Publishing House, 1967.

Rogers, Katharine M. *Feminism in Eighteenth-Century England.* Urbana: University of Illinois Press, 1982.

———. *The Troublesome Helpmate: A History of Misogyny in Literature.* Seattle: University of Washington Press, 1966.

Romaine, Suzanne. *Pidgin and Creole Languages.* Longman Linguistics Library. London: Longman, 1988.

Roscoe, William. *The Wrongs of Africa, a Poem.* Part the First. London: R. Faulder, 1787.

Rose, June. *Elizabeth Fry.* New York: St. Martin's Press, 1980.

Ross, Isabel. *Margaret Fell, Mother of Quakerism.* London: Longman, Green and Co., 1949.

Routh, Martha. *Memoir of the Life, Travels, and Religious Experience, of Martha Routh.* written by herself, or compiled from her own narrative. Second edition. New York: W. Alexander & Son, 1824.

Rowe, Elizabeth. *The Works in Prose and Verse of Elizabeth Rowe.* London: Hett and Dodsley, 1739.

Rowson, Susanna. *Charlotte Temple: A Tale of Truth. Reprinted from the Rare First American Edition (1794), over Twelve Hundred Errors in Later Editions Being Corrected, and the Preface Restored.* New York: Funk and Wagnall, 1905.

———. *The Inquisitor; or, Invisible Rambler.* Philadelphia: Matthew, Corey, 1794.

Rudé, George. *The Crowd in History: A Study of Popular Disturbances in France and England, 1730–1848.* Rev. ed. London: Lawrence and Wishart, 1981.

———. *Ideology and Popular Protest.* London: Lawrence and Wishart, 1980.

———. *Wilkes and Liberty: A Social Study.* London: Lawrence and Wishart, 1980.

Russell, George William Erskine. *The Household of Faith: Portraits and Essays.* London: Hodder and Stoughton, 1902.

Said, Edward W. *Covering Islam: How the Media and the Experts Determine How We See the Rest of the World.* New York: Pantheon Books, 1981.

———. *Orientalism.* New York: Vintage, 1979.

———. *The World, the Text, and the Critic.* Cambridge: Harvard University Press, 1983.

Sancho, Ignatius. *Letters of Ignatius Sancho, an African: to which are prefixed Memoirs of his Life by Joseph Jekyll, Esq. M. P.,* 5th ed. London, 1803; rpt. 1968, with introduction by Paul Edwards.

Sandiford, Keith. *Measuring the Moment: Strategies of Protest in Eighteenth-Century Afro-English Writing.* Selinsgrove: Susquehanna University Press. London and Toronto: Associated University Presses, 1988.

Sandler, Joseph. With Anna Freud. *The Analysis of Defence: The Ego and the Mechanisms of Defence Revisited.* New York: International Universities Press, 1985.

Schaw, Janet. *Journal of a Lady of Quality: Being the Narrative of a Journey from Scotland to the West Indies, North Carolina, and Portugal in the Years 1774 to 1776.* Edited by Evangeline Walker Andrews and Charles McLean Andrews. New Haven: Yale University Press, 1921.

Schochet, Gordon J. *Patriarchalism in Political Thought.* Oxford: Basil Blackwell, 1975.

Schofield, Mary Anne, and Cecilia Macheski, eds. *Fetter'd or Free? British Women Novelists, 1670–1815.* Athens: Ohio University Press, 1986.

Schnorrenberg, Barbara Brandon. *The Female Condition: British Women and Their Society, 1750–1850,* forthcoming.

Scott, Mary. *The Female Advocate: a poem occasioned by reading Mr. Duncombe's Feminead.* London: Joseph Johnson, 1774.

Scott, Sarah. *A Description of Millenium Hall.* Reprint. New York: Garland, 1974.

Scott, Sarah Robinson. *A Description of Millenium Hall, and the Country Adjacent: Together with the Characters of the Inhabitants, and such Historical Anecdotes and Reflections, as May Excite in the Reader proper Sentiments of Humanity and lead the Mind to the Love of Virtue. By A Gentleman on his Travels.* London: J. Newbury, 1762. The novel is also reprinted in a modern edition, *The Description of Millenium Hall by . . . Mrs. Sarah Scott.* London: Penguin, Virago, 1986.

Sedgwick, Eve Kosofsky. *Between Men: English Literature and Male Homosexual Desire.* New York: Columbia University Press, 1985.

Seeley, L. B. *Mrs. Thrale, Afterwards Mrs. Piozzi: A Sketch of Her Life and Passages from Her Diaries, Letters, and Other Writings.* London: Seeley and Co., 1891.

———. *The Rise of Free Trade Imperialism: Classical Political Economy, the Empire of Free Trade, and Imperialism, 1750–1850.* London: Cambridge University Press, 1970.

Seward, Anna. *Letters of Anna Seward.* Edinburgh: A. Constable, 1811.

———. *The Poetical Works of Anna Seward; with Extracts from Her Literary Correspondence.* Edited by Walter Scott. 3 vols. Edinburgh: James Ballantyne, 1810. Reprint, Women of Letters series. New York: AMS Press Inc., 1974.

———. *The Swan of Lichfield.* Edited by Hesketh Pearson. New York: Oxford University Press, 1937.

Sharp, Granville. *The Just Limitation of Slavery in the Laws of God.* London, 1776. Reprint. New York: Negro University Press, 1969.

———. *Tracts on Slavery and Liberty.* New York: Negro University Press, 1969.

Shenstone, William. *The Poems of William Shenstone.* Vol. 47 of *The British*

Poets. Including Translations, in One Hundred Volumes. Chiswick: C. Whittingham, College House, 1822.

Shepard, Simon. *Amazons and Warrior Women.* New York: St. Martin's Press, 1981.

Sheridan, Richard B. *Doctors and Slaves: A Medical and Demographic History of Slavery in the British West Indies, 1680–1834.* London: Cambridge University Press, 1985.

————. *Sugar and Slavery: An Economic History of the British West Indies, 1623–1775.* Baltimore: The Johns Hopkins University Press, 1973.

Sheriff, John K. *The Good-Natured Man: The Evolution of a Moral Idea, 1660–1800.* Tuscaloosa: University of Alabama Press, 1982.

Sherwood, Mary Martha. *The Re-captured Negro.* Boston: S. T. Armstrong, 1821.

Shyllon, Folaris O. *Black People in Britain, 1555–1833.* London: Oxford University Press, 1977.

————. *Black Slaves in Britain.* London: Oxford University Press, 1974.

————. *James Ramsay: The Unknown Abolitionist.* Edinburgh: Canongate, 1977.

Siebert, Fredrick Seaton. *Freedom of the Press in England, 1476–1776.* Urbana: University of Illinois Press, 1965.

Sloane, Hans. *A Voyage to the Islands of Madeira, Barbadoes, Nieves, St. Christopher's, and Jamaica; with the Natural History of the Herbs and . . . Trees . . . [with] an Account of the Inhabitants . . . .* Vol 1. London: Printed for the Author, 1725.

Smith, Charlotte Turner. *Desmond.* 3 vols. Reprint. New York: Garland, 1974.

————. *The Wanderings of Warwick.* London: J. Bell, 1794.

Smith, Hilda. *Reason's Disciples. Seventeenth-Century English Feminists.* Urbana: University of Illinois Press, 1982.

Smith, Joseph. *A Descriptive Catalogue of Friends' Books.* London: Joseph Smith, 1867.

Smith, Samuel Stanhope. *An Essay on the Causes of the Variety of Complexion and Figure in the Human Species. To which are added, Animadversions on certain Remarks made on the first edition of this Essay, by Mr. Charles White, in a series of Discourses delivered before the Literary and Philosophical Society of Manchester in England. Also, Strictures on Lord Kaims' Discourse on the Original Diversity of Mankind. And An Appendix by Samuel Stanhope Smith, D. D. L. D. President of the College of New Jersey; and Member of the American Philosophical Society. The Second Edition . . . Enlarged and Improved.* New Brunswick: Published by J. Simpson and Co. and Williams and Whiting, New York L. Deare, printer 1810. Reissued as Samuel Stanhope Smith, *An Essay on the Causes of the Variety of Complexion and Figure in the Human Species,* ed. Winthrop D. Jordan. Cambridge, MA: Belknap Press of Harvard University Press, 1965.

Smith, Sidonie. *A Poetics of Women's Autobiography: Marginality and the Fictions of Self-Representation.* Bloomington: Indiana University Press, 1987.

Simpson, Lewis P. *The Dispossessed Garden. Pastoral and History in Southern Literature.* Mercer University Lamar Memorial Lectures, No. 16. Athens: University of Georgia Press, 1975.

Soderlund, Jean R. *Quakers and Slavery: A Divided Spirit.* Princeton: Princeton University Press, 1985.

Solomon, Job Ben. *Some Memoirs of the Life of Job, the son of Solomon the Highest Priest of Boonda in Africa; who was a Slave about two years in Maryland; and afterwards brought to England, was set free and sent to his native land in the year 1734.* Ed. Thomas Bluett. London, 1734.

Somervell, John. *Isaac and Rachel Wilson, Quakers of Kendal, 1714–1785.* London: Swarthmore Press, 1924.

Sonderegger, Theo B., ed. *Psychology and Gender.* Nebraska Symposium on Motivation, 1984. Current Theory and Research in Motivation series, vol. 32. Lincoln: University of Nebraska Press, 1985.

Southerne, Thomas. *Oronooko.* Edited by Maximillian E. Novak and David Stuart Rodes. Lincoln: University of Nebraska Press, 1976.

Spacks, Patricia M. *Imagining a Self.* Cambridge: Harvard University Press, 1976.

Speck, W. A. *Stability and Strife: England, 1714–1760.* The New History of England series, edited by A. G. Dickens and Norman Gash. Cambridge: Harvard University Press, 1977.

Spencer, Jane. *The Rise of the Woman Novelist: From Aphra Behn to Jane Austen.* Oxford: Basil Blackwell, 1986.

Spengemann, William C. *The Forms of Autobiography.* New Haven: Yale University Press, 1980.

Spillers, Hortense J. and Marjorie Pryse, eds. *Conjuring: Black Women, Fiction, and Literary Tradition.* Bloomington: Indiana University Press, 1985.

Spivak, Gayatri Chakravorty. *In Other Worlds: Essays in Cultural Politics.* New York: Methuen, 1987.

Starke, Mariana. *The Sword of Peace; Or, a Voyage of Love: A Comedy, in Five Acts.* London: J. Debrett, 1789.

Starr, Edward Caryl, ed. *A Baptist Bibliography.* Philadelphia: Judson Press, 1947–76.

Staves, Susan. *Players' Scepters: Fictions of Authority in the Restoration.* Lincoln: University of Nebraska Press, 1979.

Stecher, Henry. *Elizabeth Singer Rowe, the Poetess of Frome: A Study in*

Eighteenth-Century English Pietism. European University Papers, series 14, Anglo-Saxon Language and Literature, vol. 5. Bern: Herbert Lang, 1973.

Stedman, Captain J.G. *Narrative of a Five Years Expedition Against the Revolted Negros of Surinam, in Guiana on the Wild Coast of South America from 1772 to 1777.* Holland: Imprint Society in arrangement with the Massachusetts University Press, 1971.

Steele, Anne. *The Works of Mrs. Anne Steele.* Boston: Munroe, 1808.

Steele, Mary. *The Miscellany, consisting of Extracts and Anecdotes, in Prose and Poetry, Instructive, Moral, and Religious.* London: Harvey & Darton, 1828.

Stephen, Sir George. *Anti-Slavery Recollections.* Reprint. Cass Library of African Studies, Slavery series, edited by C. Duncan Rice, no. 12. American Studies Program, Yale University, n.d.

Stephen, James. *The Slavery of the British West India Colonies.* Vol. 1, *Being a Delineation of the State in Point of Law.* London: Butterworth, 1824. Reprint. New York: Klaus Reprint Co., 1969.

Stephenson, Sarah. *Memories of the Life, and Travels, in the Service of the Gospel, of Sarah Stephenson.* London: William Phillips, 1807.

Stepto, Robert B. *Behind the Veil: A Study of Afro-American Narrative.* Urbana: Illinois University Press, 1979.

Sterndale, Mary. *The Life of a Boy.* Vol. 1. London: G. and W. B. Whittaker, 1821.

Stevenson, J., and Quinault, R. *Popular Protest and Public Order.* New York: St. Martin's Press, 1974.

St. John, Judith. *The Osborne Collection of Early Children's Books, 1566–1910: A Catalogue.* Toronto: Toronto Public Library, 1958.

Stodart, M.A. *Female Writers: Thoughts on Their Proper Sphere, and on Their Powers of Usefulness.* London: R. B. Seeley and W. Burnside, 1842.

Stone, Lawrence. *The Family, Sex, and Marriage in England, 1500–1800.* New York: Harper and Row, 1977.

Strickland, Jane M. *Life of Agnes Strickland.* Edinburgh and London: William Blackwood and Sons, 1887.

Stuart, Dorothy Margaret. *Dearest Bess: The Life and Times of Lady Elizabeth Foster, afterwards Duchess of Devonshire, from Her Unpublished Journals and Correspondence.* London: Methuen, 1955.

Suleiman, Susan Rubin. *Authoritarian Fictions: The Ideological Novel as a Literary Genre.* New York: Columbia University Press, 1983.

Sullivan, Alvin. *British Literary Magazines: The Augustan Age and the Age of Johnson, 1698–1788.* Historical Guides to the World's Periodicals and Newspapers. Westport, CT: Greenwood Press, 1983.

Sutcliffe, David. *British Black English.* Oxford: Basil Blackwell, 1982.

Swift, David E. *Joseph John Gurney: Banker, Reformer, and Quaker.* Middletown: Wesleyan University Press, 1962.

Sypher, Wylie. *Guinea's Captive Kings: British Anti-Slavery Literature of the Eighteenth Century.* Chapel Hill: University of North Carolina Press, 1942.

Taylor, Barbara. *Eve and the New Jerusalem: Socialism and Feminism in the Nineteenth Century.* New York: Pantheon, 1983.

Taylor, Clare. *British and American Abolitionists. An Episode in Transatlantic Understanding.* Edinburgh: Edinburgh University Press, 1974.

Taylor, Douglas. *Languages of the West Indies.* Baltimore: The Johns Hopkins University Press, 1977.

Taylor, Gordon Rattray. *The Angel Makers: A Study in the Psychological Origins of Historical Change, 1750–1850.* New York: E. P. Dutton, 1974.

Taylor, John. *Negro Emancipation and West Indian Independence: The True Interest of Great Britain.* Second edition. Liverpool: R. Rocklitt, 1924.

Telford, J. *A Sect that Moved the World.* London: C. H. Kelly, 1907.

Temperley, Howard. *British Antislavery, 1833–1870.* London: Longman, 1972.

Terborg-Penn, Rosalyn, Sharon Harley, and Andrea Benton Rushing, eds. *Women in Africa and the African Diaspora.* Washington, D.C.: Howard University Press, 1987.

Thale, Mary, ed. *Selections from the Papers of the London Corresponding Society, 1792–1799.* Cambridge: Cambridge University Press, 1983.

Thistlethwaite, Frank. *The Anglo-American Connection in the Early Nineteenth Century.* Philadelphia: University of Pennsylvania Press, 1959.

Thomas, Ann. *Adolphus de Biron.* Plymouth: D. Nettleton, 1795.

Thomas, Gilbert. *William Cowper and the Eighteenth Century.* 2nd ed. London: George Allen & Unwin, 1948.

Thomis, Malcolm I., and Jennifer Grimmett. *Women in Protest, 1800–1850.* New York: St. Martin's Press, 1982.

Thompson, Edward, and G. T. Garratt. *Rise and Fulfilment of British Rule in India.* London: Macmillan, 1935.

Thompson, William and Anna Wheeler. *Appeal of One Half the Human Race, Women, Against the Pretentions of the Other Half, Men, To Retain Them in Political, and Thence in Civil and Domestic Slavery. In Reply to a Paragraph of Mr. Mill's Celebrated "Article on Government."* London: Longman, Hurst, Rees, Orme, Brown, and Green; Wheatley and Adland; 1825; Reprint. New York: Burt Franklin, 1970.

Thomson, Dorothy Lampen. *Adam Smith's Daughters.* New York: Exposition Press, 1973.

Thoughts on a Future State, Occasioned by the Death of Mrs. Hester Ann

Rogers: By a Young Lady, Who Met in Her Class. Also, An Elegy on the Same Occasion, By Another Lady, Who Enjoyed the Same Privilege of Her Maternal Instructions in the Way to Glory. Birmingham: J. Belcher, 1795.

Thrale, Hester Lynch Salisbury. *Dr. Johnson's Mrs. Thrale. Autobiography, Letters and Literary Remains of Mrs. Piozzi, Edited by A. Hayward, Q.C. [1861] Newly Selected and Edited, with Introduction and Notes.* Edinburgh and London: T. N. Foulis, 1910.

Thynne, Frances, Countess of Hertford, "The Story of Inkle and Yarico," in *A New Miscellany: Being a Collection of Pieces of Poetry from Bath, Tunbridge, Oxford, Epsom, and other Places in the Year 1725 Written Chiefly by Persons of Quality, To which is added, Grongar Hill, A Poem.* London: T. Warner, 1725.

Tickner, F. Windham. *Women in English Economic History.* London: J. M. Dent and Sons, 1923.

Timpson, Thomas. *The Negroes Jubilee.* London: Ward and Co., 1834.

Tinker, Chauncey Brewster. *The Salon and English Letters: Chapters on the Interrelations of Literature and Society in the Age of Johnson.* New York: Macmillan, 1915.

Todd, Janet. *English Congregational Hymns in the Eighteenth Century.* Lexington: University Press of Kentucky, 1982.

———. *Sensibility: An Introduction.* London: Methuen, 1986.

———, ed. *A Dictionary of British and American Women Writers, 1660–1800.* Totowa, NJ: Rowman and Allanheld, 1985.

Todorov. Tzvetan. *The Conquest of America: The Question of The Other.* Trans. Richard Howard. New York: Harper and Row, 1984.

Tokson, Elliot H. *The Popular Image of the Black Man in English Drama, 1550–1688.* Boston: G. K. Hall, 1982.

Tomlins, Elizabeth and John Tomlins. *Tributes of Affection.* London: Joseph Johnson, 1797.

Tompkins, Joyce, M. S. *The Popular Novel in England, 1770–1800.* London: Methuen, 1932.

Tonna, Charlotte Elizabeth. *The System: A Tale of the West Indies.* London: F. Westley, 1827.

Trimmer, Sarah. *Instructive Tales Collected from Family Magazine.* London: J. Hatchard, 1812.

Trollope, Frances. *Domestic Manners of the Americans.* London 1832. New York: Dodd, Mead, 1901. Reprint. New York: Howard Wilford Bell, 1904.

———. *Frances Trollope: Her Life and Literary Work from George III to Victoria.* 2 vols. London: Richard Bentley and Son, 1895.

Tryon, Thomas. *Friendly Advice to the Gentleman-Planters of the East and West Indies.* London, 1684.

Tuckey, Mary. *The American Slave Ships*. Glasgow: Glasgow Ladies Society, 1838.

Turner, Mary. *Slaves and Missionaries: The Disintegration of Jamaican Slave Society, 1787–1834*. Urbana: University of Illinois Press, 1982.

Utter, Robert Palfrey, and Gwendolyn Bridges Needham. *Pamela's Daughters*. New York: Russell, 1936.

Vaux, Roberts. *Memoirs of the Life of Anthony Benezet*. New York: William Alexander, 1817.

Vale, Mauritius. *The Trial of Mauritius Vale, Esq.; . . . at St. Jago de la Vega, in the island of Jamaica, on Saturday, the 30th day of August, 1735 . . . for the murder of Mr. John Steevens, . . . Taken by a gentleman who attended in the said court. . . To which is annexed, a true copy of a letter wrote by Mr. Vale . . .* London: Printed for T. Cooper, 1736.

Van Deburg, William L. *Slavery and Race in American Popular Culture*. Madison: University of Wisconsin Press, 1984.

Vandercook, John W. *Black Majesty: The Life of Christophe, King of Haiti*. New York: Harper and Brothers, 1928.

Vann, Richard T. *The Social Development of English Quakerism, 1655–1755*. Cambridge: Harvard University Press, 1969.

Vicinus, Martha. *Independent Women: Works and Community for Single Women 1850–1920*. Chicago: University of Chicago Press, 1985.

———. *A Widening Sphere: Changing Roles of Victorian Women*. Bloomington: Indiana University Press, 1977.

Vokins, Joan. *God's Mighty Power Magnified: As Manifested and Revealed in her Faithful Handmaid Joan Vokins, who departed this life the 22d of the 5th month, 1690, Having finished her course, and kept the Faith. Also some account of her Exercises, Works of Faith, Labour, Love, and great travels in the Work of the Ministry, for the good of souls*. London: Thomas Northcott, 1961, pp. 42–43.

Vulliamy, C. E. *Aspasia: The Life and Letters of Mary Granville, Mrs. Delany*. London: Geoffrey Bles, 1935.

Wadstrom, C.B. *An Essay on Colonization, Particularly Applied to the Western Coast of Africa, with Some Free Thoughts on Cultivation and Commerce; also Brief Descriptions of the Colonies Already Formed, or Attempted, in Africa, including Those of Sierra Leone and Bulama. In Two Parts*. London: Darton and Harvey, 1794.

Wakefield, Priscilla. *Reflections on the Present Condition of the Female Sex*. New York: Garland, 1974.

———. *The Traveller in Africa*. London: James Swan, 1814.

———. *Variety; or, Selections and Essays, consisting of Anecdotes, Curious*

Facts, Interesting Narratives, with Occasional Reflections. London: Darton & Harvey, 1809.

Walker, James W. St. G. *The Black Loyalists: The Search for a Promised Land in Nova Scotia and Sierra Leone, 1783–1870.* Dalhousie African Studies series, edited by John Flint. London: Longman and Dalhousie University Press, 1976.

Wallerstein, Immanuel. *The Modern World-System.* New York: Academic Press, 1974.

Walpole, Horace. *The Letters of Horace Walpole, Fourth Earl of Oxford.* Edited by Mrs. Paget Toynbee. Vol. 15: 1791–1797. Oxford, Clarendon Press, 1905.

Walvin, James. *The Black Presence: A Documentary History of the Negro in England, 1555–1860.* New York: Schocken Books, 1972.

———. *Black and White: The Negro and English Society, 1555–1945.* London: Penguin, 1973.

———. *Slavery and British Society, 1776–1846.* Problems in Focus series. London: Macmillan, 1982.

———. *Slavery and the Slave Trade.* Jackson: University Press of Mississippi, 1983.

Warner, Oliver. *William Wilberforce and His Times.* London: Batsford, 1962.

Washington, Joseph R., Jr. *Anti-Blackness in English Religion 1500–1800.* (Texts and Studies in Religion, 19). Lewiston, NY: Edwin Mellen Press, 1985.

Waterman, William Randall. *Frances Wright.* Studies in History, Economics, and Public Law, edited by the Faculty of Political Science of Columbia University. New York: Columbia University Press, 1924.

Watts, Michael R. *The Dissenters: From the Reformation to the French Revolution.* Oxford: Clarendon Press, 1978.

Watts, Susanna. *Original Poems and Translations.* London: Nichols and Son, 1802.

Wearmouth, Robert F. *Methodism and the Common People of the Eighteenth Century.* London: Epworth, 1945.

Webb, A. F., ed. *The Fate of the Fenwicks. Letters to Mary Hays (1798–1828).* London: Methuen, 1927.

Webb, R. K. *Harriet Martineau: A Radical Victorian.* London: Heinemann, 1960.

Wedderburn, Robert. The horrors of slavery; exemplified in the life and history of the Rev. Robert Wedderburn, V.D.M. (late a prisoner in Her Majesty's gaol at Dorchester, for conscience sake), son of the late James Wedderburn, Esq., of Inveresle, by one of his slaves in the island of Jamaica; in which is included the correspondence of the Rev. Robert Wedderburn and his brother, A. Colville, Esq., alias Wedderburn, of 35 Leadenhall

Street. With remarks on, and illustrations of, the treatment of the blacks, and a view of their degraded state, and the disgusting licentiousness of the planters. London: R. Wedderburn, 1824.

Wedgwood, Barbara and Hensleigh. *The Wedgewood Circle 1730–1897: Four Generations of a Family and Their Friends.* London: Studio Vista, 1980.

Wells, Helena (later Whitford). *Constantia Neville, or The West Indian.* London: L. Whittingham, 1800.

Wesley, John. *Thoughts on Slavery.* London, 1774.

West, Jessamyn. *The Quaker Reader.* New York: Viking, 1962.

Wheatley, Vera. *The Life and Work of Harriet Martineau.* Fair Lawn: Essential Books, 1957.

Wheatley, Phillis. *Memoirs and Poems of Phillis Wheatley, A Native African and a Slave. Also, Poems by a Slave.* 3d ed. Boston, 1838. Reprint. Miami: Mnemosyne, 1969.

———. *Poems and Letters: First Collected Edition.* Edited by Chas. Fred. Heartman. Reprint. Miami: Mnemosyne, 1969.

Wheeler, Ethel Robert. *Famous Blue-Stockings.* New York: John Lane, 1910.

Whitley, William Thomas. *A Baptist Bibliography.* London: The Kingsgate Press, 1916–1922.

Whitney, Janet. *Elizabeth Fry.* London: Hazell, Watson and Viney, 1937. London: Guild, 1947.

Whitney, Lois. *Primitivism and the Idea of Progress in English Popular Literature of the Eighteenth Century.* Baltimore: The Johns Hopkins University Press, 1934.

Wilberforce, Robert Isaac, and Samuel Wilberforce. *The Life of William Wilberforce.* 5 vols. London: Murray, 1838. New ed., abridged. London: Seeley, Burnside, and Seeley, 1843.

Wilberforce, Hon. William. *The Enormity of the Slave-Trade; and the Duty of Seeking the Moral and Spiritual Elevation of the Colored Race.* Freeport: Books for Libraries Press, 1970.

———. *A Practical View of the Prevailing Religious System of Professed Christians in the Higher and Middle Classes in this Country Contrasted with Real Christianity.* Reprint. A Treasure of Christian Books, edited by Hugh Martin. London: SCM, 1958.

———. *Practical Christianity or, A Practical View of the Prevailing System of Professed Christians.* Boston: Manning and Loring, 1799.

Wilkinson, Henry C. *Bermuda from Sail to Steam: The History of the Island from 1784 to 1901.* 2 vols. London: Oxford University Press, 1973.

Williams, Eric. *British Historians and the West Indies.* New York: Charles Scribner's Sons, 1966.

———. *Capitalism and Slavery.* New York: Capricorn Books, 1944.

———. *From Columbus to Castro: The History of the Caribbean, 1492–1969.* London: Andre Deutsch, 1970.

Williams, Helen Maria. *Events in France, 1815.* Cleveland: Burrows Bros., 1895.

———. *Julia: A Novel.* 2 vols. Reprint. New York: Garland, 1974.

———. *Letters from France.* Reprint. 8 vols. in 2. Delmar, NY: Scholars' Facsimiles & Reprints, 1975.

———. *Poems.* London: Thomas Cadell, 1791.

———. *Poems on Various Subjects.* London: Whittaker, 1823.

Williams, Rev. Isaac. *Aunt Sally; Or, The Cross: The Way of Freedom.* Cincinnati: American Reform Tract and Book Society, 1858.

Williams, Raymond. *Keywords: A Vocabulary of Culture and Society.* London: Flamingo, 1976.

Wilson, Ellen Gibson. *John Clarkson and the African Adventure.* London: Macmillan, 1980.

———. *The Loyal Blacks.* New York: G. P. Putnam's Sons, 1976.

Wilson, Jacobine M. *Amelia. The Tale of a Plain Friend.* Oxford: Oxford University Press, 1937.

Winton, Calhoun. *Captain Steele: The Early Career of Richard Steele.* Baltimore: The Johns Hopkins University Press, 1964.

Wright, Frances. *Views of Society and Manners in America.* Edited by Paul R. Baker. Cambridge: Balknap Press of Harvard University Press, 1963.

Wright, Luella Margaret. *The Literary Life of the Early Friends, 1650–1725.* New York: Columbia University Press, 1932.

Yarde, D. M. *The Life and Works of Sarah Trimmer, A Lady of Brentford.* First edition. The Hounslow and District History Society, 1972.

Yates, Gayle Graham. *Harriet Martineau on Women.* New Brunswick, NJ: Rutgers University Press, 1985.

Yellin, Jean Fagan. *Women & Sisters. The Antislavery Feminists in American Culture.* New Haven and London: Yale University Press, 1989.

Zuill, William. *Bermuda Sampler 1815–1850. Being a Collection of Newspaper Items, Extracts from Books and Private Papers, together with many Explanatory Notes and a Variety of Illustrations.* Hamilton, Bermuda: Bermuda Book Stores, 1937.

Articles and Papers

Ackers, Charles W. "Our Modern Egyptians: Phyllis Wheatley and the Whig Campaign Against Slavery in Revolutionary Boston." *Journal of Negro History* (July 1975): 397–410.

Aldridge, A. Owen. "Feijoo and the Problem of Ethiopian Color." *Studies in Eighteenth-Century Culture* 3 (1973): 263–277.

Alexander, Ziggi. "Mary Seacole in Panama: Black Freedom and U.S. Influence in the 1850's." Unpublished paper.

———. "Let It Lie Upon the Table: The Status of Black Women's Biography in the UK." *Gender & History,* vol. 2, No. 1 (Spring 1990): 22–23.

Althusser, Louis. "Ideology and Ideological State Apparatuses (Notes towards an Investigation)." Pp. 127–186 in *Essays on Ideology.* London: Verso, 1984, first published by La Pensée 1970.

Aptheker, Herbert. "The Quakers and Negro Slavery." *The Journal of Negro History* 25 (1940): 331–362.

Barash, Carol. "English Popular Narratives about Jamaica, 1713–1750." Unpublished paper.

———. "The Character of Difference: The Creole Woman as Cultural Mediator in Narratives about Jamaica," *Eighteenth-Century Studies,* 23, no. 4 (Summer 1990): 407–424. A Special Issue. *The Politics of Difference,* ed. Felicity Nussbaum.

Barrell, John and Harriet Guest. "On the Use of Contradiction: Economics and Morality in the Eighteenth-Century Long Poem." Pp. 121–138 in *The New Eighteenth Century. Theory. Politics. English Literature,* edited by Felicity Nussbaum and Laura Brown. New York and London: Methuen, 1987.

Beasley, Jerry. "Politics and Moral Idealism." Pp. 221–222 in *Fetter'd or Free,* edited by Mary Anne Schofield and Cecelia Macheski. Athens, OH: Ohio University Press, 1986.

Beattie, John. "The Criminality of Women in Eighteenth-Century England." *Journal of Social History* 8 (Summer 1975): 80–116.

Bennet, J. Harry, Jr. "The Society for the Propagation of the Gospel's Plantations and the Emancipation Crisis." Pp. 15–29 in *British Humanitarianism. Essays Honoring Frank J. Klingberg,* edited by Samuel Clyde McCulloch. Philadelphia: The Church Historical Society, 1950.

Berg, Maxine. "Political Economy and the Principles of Manufacture 1700–1800." Pp. 33–58 in *Manufacture in Town and Country Before the Factory,* edited by Maxine Berg, Pat Hudson, and Michael Sonenscher. Cambridge: Cambridge University Press, 1983.

Bhabba, Homi K. "The Other Question: Difference, Discrimination and the Discourse of Colonialism." Pp. 148–172 in *The Politics of Theory. Proceedings of the Essex Conference on the Sociology of Literature, July 1982,* edited by Francis Barker, Peter Hulme, Margaret Iversen, and Diana Loxley. Colchester: University of Essex, 1983.

———. "The Other Question—The Stereotype and Colonial Discourse." *Screen* 24, No. 6 (Nov.–Dec. 1983): 18–36.

———. "Signs taken for Wonders: Questions of Ambivalence and Authority under a Tree Outside Delhi, May 1817." Pp. 163–184 in *"Race," Writing and Difference,* edited by Henry Louis Gates, Jr. Chicago: University of Chicago Press, 1985.

Bloch, Ruth H. "Untangling the Roots of Modern Sex Roles: A Survey of Four Centuries of Change." *Signs: Journal of Women in Culture and Society,* 4, no. 4 (Winter 1978): 236–252.

Booth, Wayne. "Control of Distance in Jane Austin's *Emma.*" Pp. 24–66 in *The Rhetoric of Fiction.* Chicago: University of Chicago Press, 1968.

Bourne, Jenny. "Towards an Anti-Racist Feminism." *Race and Class: A Journal for Black and Third World Liberation,* No. 25 (Summer 1983): 1–22.

Boylan, Anne. "Women in Groups: An Analysis of Women's Benevolent Organizations in New York and Boston, 1797–1840," *Journal of American History* 71, no. 3 (December 1974), 497–523.

Brantlinger, Patrick. "Victorians and Africans: The Genealogy of the Myth of the Dark Continent." Pp. 185–222 in *"Race," Writing, and Difference,* edited by Henry Louis Gates, Jr. Chicago: University of Chicago Press, 1985.

Bratton, J. S. "English Ethiopians: British Audiences and Black-Face Acts, 1835–1865." *The Yearbook of English Studies,* 11 (1981): 127–142.

Brown, Laura. "The Romance of Empire: *Oroonoko* and the Trade in Slaves." Pp. 41–61 in *The New Eighteenth Century: Theory, Politics, English Literature,* edited by Felicity Nussbaum and Laura Brown. New York: Methuen, 1987.

Brownley, Martine Watson. "The Narrator in Oroonoko." *Essays in Literature.* No. 1 (Spring 1976): 174–187.

Bush, Barbara. "White 'Ladies', Coloured 'Favourites' and Black 'Wenches'; Some Considerations on Sex, Race and Class Factors in Social Relations in White Creole Society in the British Caribbean," *Slavery and Abolition: A Journal of Comparative Studies,* vol. 2, no. 3 (December 1987) London: Frank Cass & Co., Inc., pp. 245–262.

Cadbury, Henry J. "Negro Membership in the Society of Friends." *The Journal of Negro History* (1936): 151–213.

Castle, Terry. "The Carnivalization of Eighteenth-Century English Narrative." *PMLA,* Vol. 99, No. 5 (October, 1984): 903–916.

Corfield, Kenneth. "Elizabeth Heyrick: Radical Quaker." Pp. 41–67 in *Religion in the Lives of English Women 1750–1830,* edited by Gail Malmgreen. London: Croom Helm, 1986.

Cott, Nancy F. "'Passionlessness': An Interpretation of Victorian Sexual Ideology," 1790–1850. Signs: Journal of Women in Culture and Society,* Vol. 4, No. 2, 219–233, 1978.

Crooks, J. J. "Negroes in England in Eighteenth Century." *Notes and Queries.* 154 (1928): 173–74.

Davis, David Brion. "The Emergence of Immediatism in British and American Antislavery Thought." *The Mississippi Valley Historical Review: A Journal of American History* 49, No. 2 (September 1962): 209–30.

"Debates in the Senate of Lilliput." *Gentleman's Magazine.* Anon. (September, 1741): 452–473.

Drescher, Seymour. "Public Opinion on the Destruction of British Colonial Slavery." Pp. 22–48 in *Slavery and British Society 1776–1846,* edited by James Walvin. London: Macmillan, 1982.

———. "Cart Whip and Billy Roller: Or Anti-Slavery and Reform Symbolism in Industrializing Britain." *Journal of Social History* 15, No. 1 (Fall 1981): 3–24.

Foster, Francis Smith. "Adding Color and Contour to Early American Self-Portraitures: Autobiographical Writings of Afro-American Woman." *Conjuring: Black Women, Fiction, and Literary Tradition,* edited by Hortense Spillers and Marjorie Pryse. Bloomington, IN: Indiana University Press, 1985.

Frantz, R. W. "Swift's Yahoos and the Voyagers." *Modern Philology* 29 (1931–32): 49–57.

Grant, Joan. "Call Loud: The History of Mary Prince." *Trouble and Strife* 14 (Autumn 1988): 9–12.

Greenblatt, Stephen J. "Improvisation and Power." Pp. 57–99 in *Literature and Society. Selected Papers from the English Institute, 1978,* New Series, no. 3. Baltimore: The Johns Hopkins University Press, 1980.

Hall, Catherine. "The Early Formation of Victorian Domestic Ideology." Pp. 15–32 in *Fit Work for Women,* edited by Sandra Burman. London: Croom Helm, 1979.

Halsband, Robert. " 'Condemned to Petticoats': Lady Mary Wortley Montagu as Feminist and Writer." *The Dress of Words: Essays on Restoration and Eighteenth Century Literature in Honor of Richmond P. Bond.* University of Kansas Library, 1978.

Harris, Trudier. "*On The Color Purple,* Stereotypes, and Silence." *Black American Literature Forum* 19, No. 1 (Spring 1985): 155–161.

Hecht, J. J. "Continental and Colonial Servants in Eighteenth-Century England." *Smith College Studies in History* 40 (1954): 1–61.

Higham, C. S. S. "The Negro Policy of Christopher Codrington." *Journal of Negro History* 10, No. 2 (April 1925): 150–153.

Hill, Christopher. "Robinson Crusoe." *History Workshop: A Journal of Socialist Historians* No. 10 (Autumn 1980): 6–24.

———. "Alice Clark. Working Life of Women in the Seventeenth Century." *History Workshop: A Journal of Socialist Historians* No. 15 (Spring 1983): 173–176.

Hopkins, Robert H. "Matrimony in the Vicar of Wakefield and the Marriage Act of 1753." Pp. 322–339 in *Studies in Philology*. Vol. 74. Chapel Hill: University of North Carolina Press, 1977.

Hulme, Peter. "Polytropic Man: Tropes of Sexuality and Mobility in Early Colonial Discourse." *Europe and Its Others*. Proceedings of the Essex Conference on the Sociology of Literature July 1984. Vol. 2, ed. Francis Barker, Peter Hulme, Margaret Iversen, and Diana Loxley. University of Essex, Colchester, 1985: 17–32.

Hunt, E. M. "The Anti-Slave Trade Agitation in Manchester." *Transactions of the Lancashire and Cheshire Antiquarian Society,* no. 79 (1977): 46–72.

Hunter, J. Paul. "Friday as a Convert: Defoe and the Accounts of Indian Missionaries." *Review of English Studies.* New Series 14, No. 55 (1963): 243–48.

Irvine, Dallas D. "The Abbé Raynal and British Humanitarianism." *Journal of Modern History* 3 (1931): 564–577.

Isani, Mukhtar Ali. "The British Reception of Phillis Wheatley's Poems on Various Subjects." *The Journal of Negro History* 66, No. 2 (Summer 1981): 144–149.

Jacobs, Harriet. *Linda Brent: Incidents in the Life of a Slave Girl, Written by Herself,* edited by Maria Child. Boston, 1861. Pp. 333–515 in *The Classic Slave Narratives,* ed. Henry Louis Gates, Jr. New York: New American Library, 1987.

Jameson, Frederic. "Imaginary and Symbolic in Lacan: Marxism, Psychoanalytic Criticism, and the Problem of the Subject." In *Literature and Psychoanalysis: The Question of Reading: Otherwise,* edited by Shoshana Felman. Baltimore: The Johns Hopkins University Press, 1982, pp. 338–395.

JanMohamed, Abdul. "The Economy of Manichean Allegory: The Function of Racial Difference in Colonialist Literature." Pp. 78–106 in *"Race," Writing, and Difference,* edited by Henry Louis Gates, Jr. Chicago: University of Chicago Press, 1985.

Johnson, Barbara. "Thresholds of Difference: Structures of Address in Zora Neale Hurston." Pp. 317–328 in *"Race," Writing and Difference,* ed. Henry Louis Gates, Jr. Chicago: University of Chicago Press, 1985.

Jones, Joseph. "The 'Distress'd' Negro in English Magazine Verse." University of Texas *Studies in English,* 17 (1937), 88–106.

Jordan, Winthrop D. "First Impressions: Initial English Confrontations with Africans." Pp. 42–58 in *Race in Britain: Continuity and Change,* edited by Charles Hubbard. London: Hutchinson, 1982.

Kain, Richard M. "The Problem of Civilization in English Abolition Literature." *Philological Quarterly* 15, No. 4 (October 1936): 103–125.

Kelly, Joan. "Early Feminist Theory and the *Querelle des Femmes*." Pp. 65–

109 in *Women, History and Theory: The Essays of Joan Kelly.* Chicago: The University of Chicago Press, 1984.

Kiernan, V. "Evangelicalism and the French Revolution." *Past and Present* (February 1952): 44–56.

Kirschner, Susan. "Alice Walker's Nonfictional Prose: Checklist, 1966–1984." *Black American Literature Forum* 19, No. 1 (Spring 1985): 162–163.

Kowaleski, Elizabeth. "The *Personal Recollections* of Charlotte Elizabeth Tonna." *Tulsa Studies in Women's Literature,* 1, No. 2, (Fall 1982), pp. 141–153.

Kramnick, Isaac. "Children's Literature and Bourgeois Ideology: Observations on Culture and Industrial Capitalism in the Later Eighteenth Century." Pp. 11–44 in *Studies in Eighteenth-Century Culture,* vol. 12, edited by Harry C. Payne. Society for Eighteenth-Century Studies: University of Wisconsin Press, 1983.

Landa, Louis. "Of Silkworms and Farthingales and the Will of God." Pp. 259–277 in *Studies in the Eighteenth Century,* vol. 2, edited by R. F. Brissenden. Toronto: University of Toronto Press, 1973.

———. "Pope's Belinda, the General Emporie of the World, and the Wondrous Worm." *South Atlantic Quarterly.* 70 (Spring 1971): 215–235.

Larson, Edith Sedgwick. "A Measure of Power: The Personal Charity of Elizabeth Montagu." Pp. 197–210 in *Studies in Eighteenth-Century Culture,* vol. 16, Madison: University of Wisconsin Press, 1986.

LeGates, Marlene. "The Cult of Womanhood in Eighteenth-Century Thought." *Eighteenth-Century Studies,* 10, no. 1 (Fall 1976): 21–39.

Lipking, Joanna. "Fair Originals: Women Poets in Male Commendatory Poems." *Studies in the Eighteenth Century* 7, vol. 12, n.s. 2: 58–72.

Mack, Phyllis. "Women as Prophets During the English Civil War." *Feminist Studies* 8, No. 1 (Spring 1982): 19–45.

———. "Feminine Behavior and Radical Action: Franciscans, Quakers, and the Followers of Gandhi." *Signs: Journal of Women in Culture and Society,* vol. 11, no. 3 (1986): 457–477.

Malmgreen, Gail. "Anne Knight and the Radical Subculture." *Quaker History* (Fall, 1982): 100–113.

McArthur, Ellen. "Women Petitioners and the Long Parliament." *English Historical Review* 24 (1909): 698–709.

McCalman, Ian. *Robert Wedderburn: A Black Ultra-Radical in Early Nineteenth Century London.* Paper presented to The Conference on the History of Black People in London, London University, 27–29th November, 1984.

McCulloch, Samuel Clyde and John A. Schutz. "Of the Noble and Generous Benefaction of General Christopher Codrington." Pp. 15–24 in *Codrington Chronicle: An Experiment in Anglican Altruism on a Barbados Plantation,*

1710–1834, edited by Frank J. Klingberg. Berkeley and Los Angeles: University of California Press, 1949.

Mitchell. W. J. T. "Editor's Introduction: The Politics of Interpretation." *Critical Inquiry,* 9, No. 1 (Sept. 1982): iii-viii.

Mohanty, Chandra Talpade. "Under Western Eyes: Feminist Scholarship and Colonial Discourses." *Boundary* 2, 13 (1984): 333–358.

Mtubani, Victor C. D. "The Black Voice in Eighteenth-Century Britain: African Writers Against Slavery and the Slave Trade." *Phylon* 45, no. 2 (June 1984): 85–97.

Munro, C. Lynn. Review of *In Search of Our Mothers' Gardens,* by Alice Walker. *Black American Literature* 19, No. 1 (Spring 1985): 161.

Myers, Mitzi. "Impeccable Governesses, Rational Dames, and Moral Mothers: Mary Wollstonecraft and the Female Tradition in Georgian Children's Books." Pp. 31–59 in *Children's Literature,* vol. 14, edited by Margaret Higgonet and Barbara Rosen. New Haven: Yale University Press, 1986.

O'Malley, Thomas. "'Defying the Powers and Tempering the Spirit': A Review of Quaker Control Over Their Publications 1672–1698." *Journal of Ecclesiastical History,* vol. 33, no. 2 (January 1982): 72–88.

Parry, Benita. "Problems in Current Theories of Colonial Discourse. *The Oxford Literary Review.* Vol. 9. *Colonialism and other essays,* 1986: 20–37.

Pechey, Graham. "On the Borders of Bakhtin: Dialogization, Decolonization." *Oxford Literary Review.* Vol 9. *Colonialism and other essays,* 1986: 59–84.

Pendleton, Gayle. "The Determinants of Radicalism in English Women Writers of the 1790s." Unpublished paper.

———. "The English Pamphlet Literature of the Age of the French Revolution." *Eighteenth-Century Life* 5 (1978): 29–37.

Phillips, George. "Mrs. Montagu and Her Climbing Boys." *The Review of English Studies,* 25, no. 99 (July 1949): 243–244.

Pollack, Ellen. "Comment in Susan Gubar's 'The Female Monster in Augustan Satire.'" *Signs. Journal of Women in Culture and Society,* 3, no. 3 (Spring 1978): 728–33.

Popkin, Richard H. "The Philosophical Basis of Eighteenth-Century Racism." Pp. 245–262 in *Studies in Eighteenth-Century Culture,* vol. 3. Cleveland and London: Case Western Reserve University, 1973.

Pratt, Mary Louise. "Scratches on the Face of the Country; or, What Mr. Barrow Saw in the Land of the Bushmen." Pp. 138–62 in *"Race," Writing, and Difference,* ed. by Henry Louis Gates, Jr. Chicago: University of Chicago Press, 1985.

Prince, Gerald. "Introduction to the Study of Narrative." Pp. 7–25 in *Reader-*

Response Criticism: From Formalism to Post-Structuralism, edited by Jane Tompkins. Baltimore: The Johns Hopkins University Press, 1980.

Reardon, T. H. "Woman's Mission." Pp. 22–26 in *Free and Ennobled: Source Readings in the Development of Victorian Feminism,* edited by Carol Bauer and Lawrence Ritt. Oxford: Pergamon Press, 1979.

Reay, Barry. "The Quakers, 1659, and the Restoration of the Monarchy." *History* 63, no. 208 (June 1978): 193–213.

———. "Quakerism and Society." Pp. 141–164 in *Radical Religion in the English Revolution,* edited by J. F. McGregory and B. Reay. Oxford: Oxford University Press, 1984.

Reed, Harry. "Phillis Wheatley and Black Cultural Nationalism." Paper presented at "The Black Woman Writer and the Diaspora," 27–30 October, 1985. East Lansing: University of Michigan.

Reisman, Karl. "Contrapuntal Conversation in an Antiguan Village." Pp. 110–124 in *Explorations in the Ethnography of Speaking,* edited by Richard Bauman and Joel Sherzen. Cambridge: Cambridge University Press, 1974.

Rice, Duncan C. "The Missionary Context of the British Anti-Slavery Movement." Pp. 150–163 in *Slavery and British Society, 1776–1846,* edited by James Walvin. London: Macmillan, 1982.

Rich, E. E. "The Slave Trade and National Rivalries." Pp. 323–338 in part IV in chapter VI. *The Cambridge Economic History of Europe,* vol. 4. *The Economy of Expanding Europe in the 16th and 17th Centuries,* edited by E. E. Rich and C. H. Wilson. Cambridge: Cambridge University Press, 1967.

Root, Robert. "Aphra Behn, Arranged Marriage and Restoration Comedy." *Women and Literature* 5 (Spring 1977): 5–13.

Rousseau, G. S. "Madame Chimpanzee." *The Clark Newsletter, Bulletin of the U.C.L.A. Center for 17th- and 18th-Century Studies.* Parts one and two. No. 10 (Spring 1986): 1–14, No. 12 (Spring 1987): 4–7.

Samuels, Wilfred D. "Disguised Voice in *The Interesting Narrative of Olaudah Equiano, or Gustavus Vassa, the African.*" *Black American Literature Forum* 19, No. 1 (Spring 1985): 64–69.

Seeber, Edward D. "Oroonoko and Crusoe's Man Friday." *Modern Language Quarterly* 12, No. 3 (Sept. 1951): 286–291.

Smith, Ginnie. "Thomas Tryon's regimen for women: sectarian health in the seventeenth century." Pp. 47–65 in *The sexual dynamics of history. Men's power, women's resistance* edited by London Feminist History Collective. London: Pluto Press, 1983.

Smith, Robert Worthington. "The Attempt of British Humanitarianism to Modify Chattel Slavery." Pp. 174–177 in *British Humanitarianism: Essays Honoring Frank Klingberg,* edited by Samuel Clyde McCulloch. Philadelphia: The Church Historical Society, 1950.

Spacks, Patricia Meyer. "Ev'ry Woman is at Heart a Rake." *Eighteenth-Century Studies*, 3, no. 2 (1980): 27–46.

———. "Early Fiction and the Frightened Male." *Novel* 8 (1): 5–15.

Speizman, Milton J. "A Seventeenth-Century Quaker Woman's Declaration." Transcribed with headnote by Milton Speizman and Jane C. Kronick. *Signs: Journal of Women in Culture and Society*, 1, No. 1 (Autumn 1975): 231–245.

Spivak, Gayatri Chakravorty. "Three Women's Texts and a Critique of Imperialism. *Critical Inquiry* (Autumn 1985): 243–261.

———. "The Rani of Sirmur." *Europe and Its Others*. Proceedings of the Essex Conference on the Sociology of Literature. July 1984, vol. 1, ed. Francis Barker, Peter Hulme, Margaret Iversen and Diana Loxley. University of Essex, Colchester, 1985.

Stam, Robert, and Louise Spence. "Colonialism, Racism, and Representation: An Introduction." *Screen* 24, no. 2 (March/April 1983): 2–21.

Staves, Susan. "British Seduced Maidens." *Eighteenth-Century Studies*, 14.2 (Winter 1980/81): 109–134.

Sypher, Wylie. "The West Indian as a 'Character' in the Eighteenth Century." *Studies in Philology* 36. no. 3 (July 1939): 503–520.

———. "Hutcheson and the Classical Theory of Slavery." *Journal of Negro History*, 29 (July 1939): 263–280.

———. "The African Prince in London." *Journal of the History of Ideas*, vol 2, No. 1 (January 1941): 237–227.

Temperley, Howard. "Anti-Slavery." Pp. 27–51 in *Pressure from Without in Early Victorian England*, edited by Patricia Hollis. London: Edward Arnold, 1974.

———. "The Ideology of Antislavery." Pp. 20–37 in *The Abolition of the Atlantic Slave Trade: Origins and Effects in Europe, Africa, and the Americas*, edited by David Eltis and James Walvin. London: Macmillan, 1985.

Thomas, K. V. "Women and the Civil War Sects." *Past and Present*, no. 13 (1958): 42–63.

Towers, A. R. "Amelia and the State of Matrimony." *The Review of English Studies*. New Series, vol. 5 (1954): 144–157.

Trepp, Jean. "The Liverpool Movement for the Abolition of the English Slave Trade." *Journal of Negro History* 13, no. 2 (April 1928): 265–285.

Tyrrel, Alex. "The 'Moral Radical Party' and the Anglo-Jamaican campaign for the Abolition of the Negro apprenticeship system." *The English Historical Review*, vol. 99 (July 1984): 481–502.

Waldron, Mary. "Ann Yearsley and the Clifton Records." Pp. 301–329 in *The Age of Johnson: A Scholarly Annual*, edited by Paul J. Korshin. New York: AMS Press, Inc., 1990.

Wallerstein, Immanuel. "Africa in a Capitalist World." *Issue: A Quarterly Journal of Africanist Opinion,* 3, no. 3 (Fall, 1973): 1–11.

Walvin, James. "The Public Campaign in England Against Slavery 1787–1834." Pp. 63–79 in *The Abolition of the Atlantic Slave Trade: Origins and Effects in Europe, Africa, and the Americas,* edited by David Eltis and James Walvin. Madison: University of Wisconsin Press, 1981.

———. "The Propaganda of Anti-Slavery." Pp. 49–68 in *Slavery and British Society 1776–1846,* edited by James Walvin. London: Macmillan, 1982.

Ware, Vron. "Am I not a Woman and a Sister? White Women and the Question of Slavery." Unpublished paper.

Welter, Barbara. "The Feminization of American Religion." Pp. 137–157 in *Clio's Consciousness Raised: New Perspectives on the History of Women,* edited by Lois Banner and Mary S. Hartman. New York: Harper Colophon Books, 1974.

———. "The Cult of True Womanhood, 1820–1918." *American Quarterly,* 18, no. 1 (Summer, 1966): 151–174.

Wesley, Charles Harris. "The Neglected Period of Emancipation in Great Britain, 1807–1823." *Journal of Negro History,* 17 (1932): 156–179.

Williams, E. M. "Women Preachers in the Civil War." *Journal of Modern History* 1 (1929): 561–569.

Appeals, Pamphlets, Periodicals, Secondary Poems, Reports

This section contains a selection of anonymous anti-slavery poems, regional publications, and some of the periodicals consulted.

Abstinence from Slave-Grown Produce Nothing New; Birmingham and West Bromwich Ladies' Free Labour Produce Association, 5th mo., 1849 Birmingham: printed by White and Pike.

Account of the Receipts and Disbursements of the Anti-Slavery Society, For the Years 1823–1831. With a list of Subscribers. London: Bagster and Thoms.

Account of the Receipts and Disbursements of the Anti-Slavery Society, for the Years 1823, 1824, 1825, and 1826: with a List of the Subscribers. London: Bagster and Thoms.

Account of the Receipts and Disbursements of the Anti-Slavery Society for the Years 1827 and 1828: with a List of the Subscribers. London: Bagster and Thoms.

Account of the Receipts and Disbursemens of the Anti-Slavery society, for the Years 1829 and 1830: with a List of the Subscribers. London: S. Bagster, Jun.

Account of the Receipts and Disbursements of the Anti-Slavery Society, for the Year 1831: with a List of the Subscribers. London: S. Bagster, Jun.

[Address] To the Women of Sheffield from the Members of the "Sheffield Anti-Slavery Association."

An Address to the People of Great-Britain on the Propriety of Abstaining from West-India Sugar and Rum. The ninth edition. First printed in London, Reprint. Boston: Samuel Hall, 1792.

The Adventures of Congo in Search of His Master; a Tale. Containing a True Account of a Shipwreck. Third edition. London: J. Harris, 1828.

The Anti-Slavery Reporter. London: J. Hatchard and Son, vol. 5, 1833.

An Appeal to the Christian Women of Sheffield, from the Association for the Universal Abolition of Slavery. Sheffield: R. Lader, 1837.

An Appeal to the People of England, in Behalf of the Slaves in the British Colonies; given on the authority of Mr. Knibb. Published by order of the Ladies' Anti-Slavery Association, in Sheffield, April 3, 1833.

Blasting Influence of Slavery on the Social Circle. Leeds Anti-slavery Series, No. 68.

Brief Memoir and Account of the Spiritual Labours of the Late Mrs. Stevens, By Her Sister. London, R. B. Seeley and W. Burnside, 1841.

A Brief Memorial of William Knight, of Chelmsford, Who Died at Stoke Newington, the 16th of 9th Month, 1838. London: Fry and Son, 1839.

A Brief Sketch of the Life and Labours of Mrs. Elizabeth Heyrick. Leicester: Corsley and Clarke, 1862.

Briggs, Joshua. *Vice Detected, and Virtue Recommended: Under the Influence of Sunday Schools.* Leeds: printed for the author by J. Bowling, 1783.

The British Preacher, London: Frederick Westley and H. H. Davis, vol. 1, 1831.

A Child's Evening Hymn, Leeds Anti-Slavery Juvenile Series, n.d.

Concluding Report at the Sheffield Female Anti-Slavery Society. Sheffield, 1833.

Craig, Isa. *The Essence of Slavery.* Tract No. 2. London: Victoria Press, 1863.

Dialogues Between Two Christian Ministers, on the Difference Between the Saints and the Righteous, and on Eternal Life, Righteousness, and Faith. Containing some new thoughts on these Points. New York: Wilson, Spence, and Mawman, 1799.

East India Sugar. Sheffield: J. Blackwell, n.d.

The Eclectic Review, July–December, Third Series, Vol. 12. London: Jackson and Walford, 1834.

The Eclectic Review. Sept. 1834, July–December, 1857.

Extracts from the Letters and Memoranda of Maria Gundry, with a Short Notice of a Beloved Elder Sister, 1847, printed for private circulation.

The Fifth Report of the Female Society for Birmingham, West Bromwich,

Wednesbury, Walsall and Their Respective Neighbourhoods, for the Relief of British Negro Slaves, Established in 1825. Birmingham: B. Hudson, 1830.

The First Report of the Female Society, for Birmingham, West-Bromwich, Wednesbury, Walsall, and Their Respective Neighbourhoods, for the Relief of British Negro Slaves. Birmingham: Printed at the Office of Richard Peart, 38, Bull-Street, 1826.

Friendship's Offering: A Literary Album, and Christmas and New Year's Present, for 1831. London: Smith, Elder, and Co., 65, Cornhill, 1831.

The Gentleman's Magazine. July–December 1817. London: Nichols, Son, and Bentley.

Gilbert, Ann. *Poetry: A Prayer for the Slave,* n.d.

The Glasgow Female New Association for the Abolition of Slavery. Glasgow: John MacClay and Co., Printer; Glasgow, 2nd January, 1854.

Grimke, Sarah M. *Dreadful Effects of Irresponsible Power.* Leeds Anti-Slavery Series, No. 69, n.d.

Heyrick, Elizabeth Coltman. *Immediate not Gradual Abolition of Slavery; or an Inquiry into the Shortest, Safest, and Most Effectual Means of Getting Rid of West Indian Slavery.* London, 1824.

———. *Immediate, Not Gradual Abolition; or An Inquiry into the Shortest, Safest, and Most Effectual Means of Getting Rid of West Indian Slavery;* third edition; with an appendix, containing Clarkson's *Comparison Between the State of the British Peasantry and that of the Slaves in the Colonies.* London: sold by Hatchard and Son, Piccadilly; Seeley and Son, Fleet Street; Simpkin and Marshall, Stationers' Court; Hamilton, Adams, and Co. Paternoster Row; J. and A. Arch, Cornhill; W. Darton, Holborn Hill; W. Phillips, George Yard, Lombard Street; Harvey and Darton, Gracechurch Street; 1824.

———. *An Enquiry Which of the Two Parties is Best Entitled to Freedom? The Slave or the Slave-holder?* London, 1824.

———. *An Appeal Not to the Government but to the People of England on the Subject of West Indian Slavery.* London, 1824.

———. *No British Slavery; or, an Invitation to the People to Put a Speedy End to It.* London, 1824.

———. *Letters on the Necessity of a Prompt Extinction of British Colonial Slavery.* London, 1826.

———. *Appeal to the Hearts and Consciences of British Women.* Leicester, 1828.

———. *Apology for Ladies' Anti-Slavery Associations.* London, 1828.

The Humming Bird, or Herald of Taste. All issues, 1798–1799.

Jamaica: Enslaved and Free. London: The Religious Tract Society, 1799.

The Juvenile Gleaner: or, Anecdotes and Miscellaneous Pieces, Designed for

Amusement and Instruction. By the author of *A Brief Historical Catechism of the Holy Scriptures.* York: W. Alexander and Son, 1825.

Kilham, Hannah. *Report on a Recent Visit to the Colony of Sierra Leone.* London: W. Phillips, 1828.

————. *The Claims of West Africa.* London: Harvey and Darton, 1830.

Ladies' Anti-Slavery Associations. London: Bagster and Thoms, Printers, 14, Bartholomew Close, n.d.

The Ladies' Association of Calne, Melksham and their respective Neighbourhoods, in aid of the cause of Negro Emancipation; August 11, 1825.

The Ladies' Association of Manchester and its Neighborhood, in Aid of the Cause of Negro Emancipation; November 16th, 1826.

The Ladies Choice: A Poem. London: J. How and Bragg, 1702.

The Ladies' Companion for Visiting the Poor: consisting of Familiar Addresses, Adapted to Particular Occasions; by the author of "Lucy Franklin." London: J. Hatchard, 1813.

Ladies' Petition for the Abolition of Slavery. Sheffield: Independent Office, n.d.

Ladies' Society, for the Relief of Negro Slaves; held in West-Bromwich on the 8th of April, 1825 Wednesbury: Booth, Printer, High-Street.

Ladies' Society, for the Relief of Negro Slaves; held in Walsall on the 8th of December, 1825.

Ladies Society, for the Relief of Negro Slaves, card explanatory of the contents of the Society's Work Bags, n.d.

A List of the Governors of the Sunday School Society, British Library Tract 472.

A List of the Governors of the Magdelen Hospital, British Library Tract 472.

A List of the Society Instituted in 1787 for the Purpose of Effecting the Abolition of the Slave Trade. Printed in Year 1788, No. 3, British Library Tract 472.

Little Benny, Leeds Anti-Slavery Juvenile Series, n.d.

Malmgreen, Gail. *Neither Bread nor Roses: Utopian Feminists and The English Working Class, 1800–1850.* London: John L. Noyce, 1978.

A Miscellaneous Essay Concerning the Courses Pursued by Great Britain in the Affairs of her Colonies: With Some Observations on the Great Importance of our Settlements in America, and the Trade Thereof. London: R. Baldwin, 1760.

The Monthly Review. 2 (May–August 1831). London: G. Henderson, 1831.

Murderous Treatment of a Slave Girl, Leeds Anti-Slavery Series, No. 39, n.d.

The Negro's Friend, or, The Sheffield Anti-Slavery Album. Sheffield and London: J. Blackwell and Longman, Rees, Orme, Brown, and Green, 1826.

The Negro Servant; an Authentic and Interesting Narrative of a Young Negro; in three parts. Chelsea: printed by J. Tilling, Grosvenor-row, for the Religious Tract Society, London.

Negro Slavery; No. 16; State of Religious Instruction Among the Slaves in the West Indies. London: Ellerton and Henderson, n.d.

Negro Slavery; or, A View of Some of the More Prominent Features of That State of Society, as it Exists in the United States of America and in the Colonies of the West Indies, Especially in Jamaica. London 1823.

The New Year's Gift. and Juvenile Souvenir. London: Longman, Rees, Orme, Brown, and Green, n.d.

No British Slavery; or, An Invitation to the People to Put a Speedy End to It. (London: sold by Hatchard and Son, Piccadilly; Darton and Harvey, Gracechurch Street, and T. Combe, Printer, Leicester, 1824).

No Rum!—No Sugar! or, the Voice of Blood, Being Half an Hour's Conversation, Between a Negro and an English Gentleman, Shewing the Horrible Nature of the Slave Trade, and Pointing out an Easy and Effectual Method of Terminating It. An Act of the People. London: L. Wayland, 1792.

Phillips, Joseph. *West India Questions: The Outline of a Plan for the Total, Immediate, and Safe Abolition of Slavery Throughout the British Colonies.* London: J. & A. Arch, 1833.

A Picture of Colonial Slavery, in the Year 1828, Addressed Especially to the Ladies of Great Britain. London: printed by Bagster and Thoms, 14, Bartholomew Close.

A Picture of Colonial Slavery, In the Year 1828, Addressed Especially to the Ladies of Great Britain. Tract Box No. 26. Item 1. London: Anti-Slavery Society, 1828.

Plantation Scenes, Christian Press, Leeds Anti-Slavery Series, No. 40, n.d.

The Poor Little Negro, Leeds Anti-Slavery Juvenile Series, n.d.

The Poor Little Slave, Leeds Anti-Slavery Juvenile Series, n.d.

Porteus, the Reverend Beilby. "An Essay towards a Plan for the more Effectual Civilisation and Conversion of the Negroe Slaves of the Trust Estate in Barbados, belonging to the Society for the Propagation of the Gospel in Foreign Parts," first written in 1784, and published in amended form in 1789 and in *The Works of the Right Reverend Beilby Porteus, D. D. Late Bishop of London with His Life,* by the Rev. Robert Hodgson.

Rawson, Mary Anne. *The Thompson Normal School. Jamaica.* Sheffield, 1845.

Report of the Committee of the Society for the Mitigation and Gradual Abolition of Slavery Throughout the British Dominions. London: Richard Taylor, 1824.

Report of the Sheffield Female Anti-Slavery Society, established midsummer, 1825. Sheffield, 1827.

Report of the Sheffield Female Anti-Slavery Society. Sheffield, 1826, 1827, 1832.

Rules of the Colchester Ladies' Anti-Slavery Association; July 1, 1825.

Rules and Resolutions of the Dublin Ladies' Anti-Slavery Society, with Lists of the District Treasurers, Committee and Secretaries; and of the Subscribers. Dublin, 1828.

Sale of a Negro Child. London: Howlett and Brimmer, n.d.

Scripture Evidence of the Sinfulness of Injustice and Oppression; respectfully submitted to Professing Christians, in order to call forth their sympathy and exertions, on behalf of the much-injured Africans. London: Harvey and Darton, 1828.

Serle, Ambrose. *The Happy Negro: Being a True Account of a Very Extraordinary Negro in North America, and of an Interesting Conversation he had with a Gentleman from England.* London: J. Tilling, n.d.

Silvester, James. *Hannah More. Christian Philanthropist. A Centenary Biography.* With some of her unpublished letters and an appendix containing a vindication of her character. London: Thynne & Co., Ltd., and Daily Prayer Union, 1934.

Sixth Annual Report of the Glasgow Emancipation Society: with an Appendix, List of Subscribers. Glasgow, 1840.

Slavery Illustrated in its Effects Upon Woman and Domestic Society. Boston: Isasc Knapp, 1837.

Slaves Set Free. Leeds Anti-Slavery Juvenile Series, n.d.

Society for the Relief of Negro Slaves, at a Meeting Held at Sheffield, on the 21st of June, 1825. J. Blackwell, Printer, Iris Office, Sheffield.

Suggestions occasioned by the Clause of the Act of 3 and 4 William IV. Chap. 58. Respecting the Apprenticeship of Negro Children. London: S. Bagster, Jun., 14, Bartholomew Close.

Tonna, Charlotte Elizabeth. "Slavery." *The Second Report of the Ladies' Association for Calne, Melksham, Devizes, and Their Respective Neighbourhoods, in Aid of the Cause of Negro Emancipation.* Calne: Printed by W. Baily, 1827.

To the Women of Great Britain, on the Disuse of Slave Produce, Birmingham and West Bromwich Ladies' Anti-Slavery Society, March, 1849.

The Tourist: A Literary and Anti-Slavery Journal. London: John Cross, 1833.

Trimmer, Sarah. *The Family Magazine; or, A Repository of Religious Instruction, and Rational Amusement.* London: John Marshall and Co., 1788–1789.

Tyrell, Alex. " 'Woman's Mission' and Pressure Group Politics in Britain (1825–60)." Pamphlet reprinted from *Bulletin of the John Rylands University Library of Manchester* 63 (Autumn 198): 194–230.

The Universal Magazine of Knowledge and Pleasure; Vol. 86. London, 1790.

The Warning; Recommended to the Serious Attention of All Christians, and Lovers of Their Country. London, Reprint, Philadelphia, 1807.

West India Societies for the Conversion, and Religious Instruction and Christian Education, of the Negro Slaves. Bristol, n.d.

"What Does Your Sugar Cost?" A Cottage Conversation on the Subject of British Negro Slavery, printed for the Birmingham, West-Bromwich and Female Society for the Relief of British Negro Slaves by Richard Peart. Birmingham, 1828.

A Word for the Slave, by The Ladies of the Sheffield Anti-Slavery Association: and *A Cry From Africa,* by James Montgomery. Sheffield: printed for the Benefit of the Rotherham Anti-Slavery Bazaar, by J. Blackwell, at the Iris Office, 1830.

Manuscript Sources

The Friends Library, Euston Rd., London
Friends' original materials

The House of Lords Library
Mary Prince's Parliamentary Petition.

The John Rylands Memorial Library, Manchester.
Mary Anne Rawson's collection of letters, published and unpublished materials for *The Bow and the Cloud.*

Leicester Public Library, Central Reference Division
The Scrapbook of Susanna Watts

Index

447

Old Testament, Joseph, 123, 131, 133, 187
O'Malley, T. P., 326n
Omaza (char.), 241
Opie, Amelia, 238–240, 264, 346n, 361n, 362n, 371n; *Adeline Mowbray,* 134; "The Lucayan's Song", 240
oppression, 23, 102, 113, 121, 125, 153, 161, 177, 182, 185, 196, 207, 246, 259, 269, 281, 300, 303
Orient, 18
Orientalism, 17, 145, 309n
Oroonoko (char.), 28–33, 35–51, 90, 93, 94, 98, 133, 145, 170, 190, 197
Owenites, 300, 301
Owomoyela, Oyekan, 317n, 319n

pacifism, 52, 54, 180
Paine, Thomas, 254; *The Rights of Man,* 185, 186, 197, 212, 227
Palmer, Mrs. (poet), 126
Palmer, Mrs. (char.), 230
Parham, 38
Paris, 189
Parkinson, Wanda, 354n
Parliament, 17, 148–150, 169, 172, 174, 176, 193, 199, 210, 223, 250, 253, 256, 262
The Parrot, 167
Parry, Benita, 238, 302, 362n, 381n
Parry, Thomas, 334n
Pastorius, Francis Daniel, 54
patriarchs, 37, 93, 104, 110, 133, 152, 271
patriarchal colonial system, 45
patriarchal law, 57
patriarchal order, 19, 21
patriarchal slavery, 128
patriarchal social system, 25
patriotism, 4, 15, 92, 131, 156, 157, 174, 226, 229, 279
Patterson, Orlando, 319n, 333n
Paul, Nathaniel, 306
Payne, Harry C., 342n
Peace Society, 260
Peacock, Lucy, 5, 114, 139–141, 234, 346n; *The Little Emigrant,* 138
Pendarvis, Alexander, 105
Peninsular War, 230
Penn, William, 53, 151
Penningtor, Lady Sarah, 106, 342n
Penney, Norman, 323n
periodical literature, 21
Perkins, A. G., 372n
Perry, Ruth, 316n, 330n, 336n
Peters, Thomas, 205, 206

petitions, 20, 149, 250, 253, 261
petitioning, 149
Philadelphia, 168
philanderers, 177
Philip of Spain, 135
Phillips, Captain, 243
Phillips, George, 347n
Phillips, Joseph, 287, 296
Phillips, Katherine, 55, 315n
Phoenicians, 14
physical equality, 118
physical freedom, 123
Pichanick, Valerie Kossew, 381n
Pickering, Samuel F. Jr., 209, 346n
pidgin, 103
pidgin English, 102, 238
Pidgins, 103
Piozzi, Hester Lynch Salisbury Thrale, 106, 341n
Pitt, William, 158, 159, 191, 193, 210
Place, Francis, 300
plantation owners, 32, 53, 95, 101, 114, 231, 250, 274
plantations, 13, 24, 29, 35, 41, 46, 70, 71, 96, 100, 101, 107, 110, 135, 138, 223, 234, 246, 270, 274
planters, 13, 52, 78, 85, 88, 96, 97, 104, 166, 172, 187, 194, 210, 239, 268, 270, 274, 276, 279
plantocracy, 53, 54, 65, 160, 210, 239, 257
plantocrats, 33, 34, 62, 152, 233, 239, 280, 287, 296, 297, 306
poetry, 22, 23
political rights, 108
Pollack, Ellen, 21, 314n, 319n
Pollard, Jane, 191, 211
Polly (a slave), 377n
Polwhele, Richard, 176, 353n
polygamy, 209
Pompey (char.), 122–125, 139, 145
Poovey, Mary, 247, 338n, 365n
Pope, Alexander, 328n; *The Dunciad,* 167; *The Rape of the Lock,* 70, 78
Popkin, Richard H., 334n, 344n
popular fiction, 21
Porter, Anna Maria, 250, 333n, 365n
Porter, Roy, 21, 22, 314n
Porteus, Bishop Beilby, 212
Portland, Duchess of, 105
Portsmouth, 128
post-Restoration, 22
Potiphar, 131
Powell, Mr. (char.), 96–98, 101
Powys, Lady, 147
Poyntz, Mrs., 147